IN PURSUIT OF AWARENESS

> *But I do not propose it as a variety and stock
> of knowledge, but as a variety and freedom
> of thinking; as an increase of the powers and
> activities of the mind, not as an enlargement
> of its possessions.*
>
> John Locke
> ON THE CONDUCT OF THE UNDERSTANDING

IN PURSUIT OF AWARENESS

THE COLLEGE STUDENT IN THE MODERN WORLD

Edited by Esther Kronovet
Associate Dean of University College
and Evelyn Shirk
Professor of Philosophy
both of Hofstra University

New York
Appleton-Century-Crofts
Division of Meredith Publishing Company

PREFACE

After World War II, a revolution occurred on the quiet campus of the American college and university. The American ideal of equality and hunger for personal opportunity combined to bring a flood of students clamoring for "all the rights and privileges thereof." Most of these young were, and are, first-generation college students whose parents are as unprepared to help them survive the demanding pace and sharp competition as they are ready to use every emotional strategem to push them toward the degree. Nor is the student himself prepared either intellectually or emotionally to withstand these assorted stresses.

The demand for higher education, not as a privilege but as a human right, represented a tremendous social achievement. But it also disordered the entire academic scene, throwing institutions across the country into building programs, fund-raising drives and meetings of planning committees, nonplussed regarding what and how to plan. It was not only the overtaxed physical facilities that were a cause for concern. The curriculum itself and the methods used to pursue it were forced under scrutiny. Overcrowded classrooms and a shortage of competent teachers brought faculty and administration alike to the conviction that if the goals of education were not to be lost, ways had to be found to preserve them.

The academic community mobilized both to preserve the meaning of a college education and to help the student, amid these demanding conditions, to gain his objective. All over the country grants were offered by both private and government agencies to facilitate research into new ways of going about the difficult business of meaningful education. New courses were devised and new methods constructed. Among these were courses designed to prepare freshmen for an effective experience with higher education. Some way had to be found to orient these young adults to the intellectual life and to help them responsibly accept their new adult status. Some sort of briefing, some sort of orientation, some sort of initial encounter had to be devised which would begin the student on the road to becoming not just a fact-filled automaton but a liberally educated person.

Apparently this conviction was widespread. The world of the future demanded nothing less than a responsibly educated population. Courses, programs, and presentations were devised to fill this pressing need. Hofstra University was no exception. Situated in one of the fastest growing counties in the United States, we felt the push as severely as any institution. For thirteen years we had worked, even pioneered, in a course for freshmen, and each year we worried it with continuous shaping and reshaping. We eventually reached a working consensus that, for us, the preferable method was small group discussion, the dual aim of which was to interest the student in inquiry and to cause him to reflect on his own attitudes, goals, and weaknesses. But we were unable to easily assemble appropriate materials which would implement this task. There were no collections of readings available which had the depth, span, quality, and compelling interest which we envisioned.

Last year we conducted a survey in order to ascertain how other institutions were handling the various facets of this problem. We sent a substantial questionnaire to every institution listed in *Education Directory*, 1964-1965. (The National Council on Education refers to this study as # QR 4248.) Apparently our concern was shared by educators elsewhere, because we received an exceptionally large response (64% or 1,378) to our inquiry.

Almost all of the responding institutions had developed some sort of program for freshmen, typically but not invariably under the leadership of the Dean of Students' Office and usually conducted by faculty drawn from many departments. While the approaches were diverse, they fell into three categories. First, there were assorted efforts aimed at providing some equipment for the student's intellectual journey through college. Second, there were programs aimed at providing psychological sustenance. Finally, there were a few programs which limited their scope to giving directions aimed, for example, at how to use the library and how to register without delay.

Taking the first two approaches most seriously, we set about providing a readily available book of readings attempting a fresh approach to the first course for freshmen.

Each fall, on every campus in the country, freshmen with catalogues in hand are forced to mill about, line up in queues, and go through the prescribed paces in order to be "processed" into the halls of academe. The machinery of the contemporary university tests them for flaws, sorts them, counts them, and programs them into the experience of higher learning. Our future citizens, in turn, set on their way to accumulate credits and acquire a degree, with or without understanding. They "take" courses. They "elect" subjects which happen to be "open" (i.e., able to "seat" a few more). They "choose" a major which is marketable. They "pursue" a course of studies, often with neither inclination nor commitment. They aim at status, not fulfillment. And in any case, they can expect to be buffeted by time pressures and gruelling competition, diverted by new-found maturity, and dazzled by the possibilities of "experimentation."

If this state of affairs is left unchallenged, the few precious years which might have sensitized the human spirit will have been lost. Students caught in the maze are aware that they are being cheated. Many try valiantly to retrieve their losses and to construct the values which are their due. Faculty formulate curricula and devise teaching methods designed to counteract the effects of mass education and to elicit from the student the best of which he is capable.

But though faculty and administration mourn, too many do "pass through" their college education, emerging on the other side unmoved by wonder and untouched by dedication. They are prepared, but prepared for what? They have pass-card in hand, but to what will they pass? They are certified as being "trained." But they may never have reflected on what was happening to them nor attended to the experience at hand. They may never have been clear regarding what was happening to them or why.

The student needs to stop, to sit still, and to reflect on what is and might be taking place before he is tossed headlong among the disciplines. He needs to contemplate the process itself in which he is involved. He needs to be shoved into inquiry regarding himself, his goals, his interests, his attitudes, and his future.

It is to such a first course that this book is addressed. Whether it be called "Orientation," "Freshman Seminar," "Introduction to College," "Reflective Thinking," "Man in Society," "Contemporary Issues" or any of the names used to designate this endeavor on various campuses, the goals seem much the same. Although there is wide difference of opinion regarding the method of accomplishment, each such course tries to catch and hold the freshman long enough to assure that his education will take. Each seeks a kind of rite of passage into the intellectual community.

This book is divided into seven sections or topics, each of which draws from many disciplines to illuminate what might be called an "area of concern" or involvement. The student has been immersed, however inarticulately, in these areas before he came to college and he will continue to be immersed in them long after he leaves the campus, regardless of what courses he chooses, what major he pursues, or what career he ultimately selects. In one sense, although he dimly perceives it, he submits to education for the very reason that he seeks enlightenment on these matters—matters at once so simple and so complex. Our experience with students confirms the centrality of such areas of concern in their lives. They lug books and are exhorted to use the library; they are harried by assorted stresses; they struggle with issues of conforming, belonging, rebelling, expressing sexuality, attaining identity, asserting independence, and "succeeding" in college. What could be a more appropriate time to provide them with eminently readable and exciting material illuminating just these particular matters and drawn from the very disciplines they are or soon will be studying? The realization that the stylized entity called the "curriculum" ultimately relates to the very issues that actually concern the student's life is the first and perhaps the central goal of education. It can shatter his routinized apathy. The mark of the uneducated man is his segregation of "book learning" from interest and its consequent stifling of intellectual vigor. Our educational efforts are fruitless if the student's course of study makes only peripheral or weak contact with the things which interest and distract him. But if such contact can be made early, vividly, and unencumbered by goals other than those of exploring the issues central to the student's awareness, genuine education could easily begin. This book attempts to do just that.

Each section or area of concern is divided into interpenetrating subsections which suggest some ramifications of the topic at hand. No claim is made for completeness of any kind. Nor are these subtopics to be considered a sampling of a discipline. One could hardly take an effort of that sort seriously. Only in the simple sense that each reading is drawn from a discipline does it represent that discipline. Disciplines are represented in both their sober and exuberant moods; in their prosaic currents and poetic flights. But we can never hope to do more than suggest their expanse, their richness, and their diversity. We have illuminated but a few inches of the megalopolis of the intellect and can but hint of the expanse lying beyond. Yet, should what the student sees entice him, such interest might well lead him into identifying himself with a discipline—and for affirmative, intelligible reasons.

A word must be said regarding our choice of readings in "The Arts Speak for Themselves" and "Science in Action." We have selected generic types of each enterprise rather than any particular art or any special science. We are more interested in having the student feel the indomitable spirit of man as he tries to control his world than we are in teaching him science. We are more eager in having him identify with the temper of the artist than we are in teaching him art. We prefer to galvanize the student into thinking and feeling rather than to provide him with information. We aim at tantalizing the student into readiness for the disciplines.

Each section is preceded by an Introduction setting the stage for encounter with the readings. Here, issues are raised and ramifications are noted which go beyond the readings. These may be used to suggest further directions for investigation and discussion.*

Every section and every reading is ideationally complete; each can be

---

* In order to point to the interrelation of the readings, we have frequently been obliged to provide our own titles for them. The title of each reading is that of the editors unless attributed to the author in the credit line. All footnotes in the body of the book, except where otherwise noted, are those of the original authors or translators.

read independently and in any combination. Yet each benefits by arrangement with the others. Each raises questions; each requires introspection and interpretation. Each invites comparison and contrast with the others and with the student's reaction. Each encourages the student to assert his own originality. It is only out of individual perspective and personal difference that interests form and abilities grow. And out of these the student may be able to foreshadow his own intellectual future.

The readings, in aggregate, benefit by being used as a set of building blocks of varying shapes, sizes, and textures—foundational blocks, framing members, floor boards, crosspieces, arches, and turrets which can suggest many intricate and diverse structures. A creative eye may detect many possible combinations and arrangements. To urge construction is to encourage intellectual free-association, the beginning of serious inquiry.

Having several aims, this book is not directed simply at stimulating discussion, yet it is designed to be discussed. Each reading invites it, each arrangement provokes it. Insofar as any student takes a moment to reflect on his experience as a student in a college, as a self with more or less resonant human relations and aspirations, as a member of a society, and as a citizen of a world, this book belongs to him and is dedicated to him.

———

Many persons have helped both directly and indirectly in the preparation of this volume. Were it not for the students to whom this book is dedicated, we would never have been moved to prepare it. Among them, Diane Hanken gave unstintingly of her time and energy. Leon Schor and Mary Jo Neyland assisted in reading the proof. The Hofstra Library staff have contributed their services. We want to thank those of our colleagues who took time to suggest materials for possible inclusion, and especially Frank Wekerle, Chairman of the Philosophy Department at Hofstra. His understanding of our task encouraged us, and his wisdom enriched the result. We are grateful to Helene Pescod for her tirelessness, her efficiency, and her devotion in the physical preparation of the manuscript.

Adolph Anderson, Dean of the New College at Hofstra and Professor of Chemistry, graciously consented to write the Introduction to Part VI, "The Sciences." Meyer Barash, Professor of Sociology, has helped identify the materials in Part VII, "Success." He generously wrote, as well, the Introduction to that section.

We wish to thank Hofstra University for granting a leave of absence to Evelyn Shirk and released time to Esther Kronovet for the purpose of completing this work.

E.K.
E.S.

CONTENTS

PART FIVE—THE ARTS

PART SIX—THE SCIENCES

PART SEVEN—THE IDEA OF SUCCESS

IN PURSUIT OF AWARENESS

Part one

BOOKS AND LEARNING

> *We are of the ruminating kind and it is not enough that we cram ourselves with a great load of collections; unless we chew them over again they will not give us strength and nourishment.*
>
> John Locke
> ON THE CONDUCT OF THE UNDERSTANDING

INTRODUCTION

Central to your higher education is the fact that you are now obliged to "become something," to align yourself with some kind of work, to make yourself a new identity. To choose a career is a particularly dramatic event because what you select will determine what kind of a person you will be. A "career" originally meant a racecourse. It suggests a process, a history, a type of development. As you prepare yourself for a career, it, in turn, prepares you. A program of study shapes the mind to see and feel certain things in certain ways and to express itself in a special fashion. Each determines, orders, and gives rationale to the things that you value. To select a career or job is to agree to construct a special type of self. It is no accident that the general public stereotypes the occupations, picturing them in costume and clutching their particular impedimenta. The medical man carries a bag and looks introspective. The businessman, briefcase in hand, rushes from place to place. The chemist is young; in a white coat he juggles test tubes. This type of shorthand is an oversimplified expression of the important fact that when one is educated to be a "something," he is indeed that kind of thing with all of its special traits.

Yet each person plays these roles in his own unique and induplicable way; each expresses his knowledge and skill with his own personal flair. There is a sense in which creativity is generated out of the very fact that a profession provides disciplining limits within which experimentation must be confined. To choose a career is to select a perspective through which one may be creative. And each career contributes in its own special way to the social enterprise.

A "job" is a kind of role one plays on the world's stage. Each requires a certain temperament, a particular skill, and special knowledge. You have probably tried out various roles in imagination in order to determine whether you could become just that sort of person with those relations and responsibilities. And any important decision is a risk. You may have misjudged your capabilities and liabilities; you may have been deceived regarding your interests and affinities. College is the place to view and review this deeply significant matter of who and what you might become.

The primary means for accomplishing your transformation from student to graduate is books. Have you ever noticed that the mark of the student, young or old, child or professor, is the inevitable presence of books—in bags, cases, pockets, or just by the armful? Books mark the life of the student so long as that life remains vigorous. Why?

Some would answer that books contain facts, announce truth, and are used to fill the student's emptiness; books "contain knowledge" and knowledge must be transferred from the printed page to the student's head. Others, however, would answer that books are a catalytic agent designed to contact the viscera, to arouse, to stimulate, and to entice; that the function of books is to open vistas, ramify insight, and goad to experiment.

Every book is a crystallization of another's experience, whether that experience be direct or indirect, social or personal, immediate or abstract, general or special. Some experience can only be expressed in poetry, some is modified by a disciplined knowledge of a subject matter; some is sensory and physical, some is intellectual and formal. Every author transmits his experience—experience with mathematical forms, with medical phenomena, with the behavior of rats, with social fact, with poetic or dramatic insight—to others. A book articulates a person's glimpse into some corner of the world. Writing a book requires a pause to re-encounter experience, to wrestle with it, to order and structure it, and to give it meaning. A book is an invitation to see as another saw, to make his experience our own.

Of course, not every book is written for everyone. A literary democracy does not prevail. Some books are for children, some for adults; some embrace common experience, some specialized awareness. Some books describe, some present, some probe. Some books are orderly and methodical, others are suggestive and germinal. Some are to be tasted, some to be savored, some to be swallowed, and some to be digested. But every book invites us to a repast and every author takes us into his confidence. In the aggregate, books represent our culture and fund our heritage.

And in the aggregate, they form a library. A library is a repository of human experience organized to be immediately available, accumulating the understanding of mankind, gathering it in one spot to permit a kind of dialogue between generations. A library can be the scene of a colloquy where one may speak with Herodotus, question Socrates, ponder with Aquinas, probe with Lavoisier. It puts the world of ideas at our fingertips. Imagine the facts to be unearthed, the concepts to be explored, the fantasies to be enjoyed! And consider the elaborate reference works so painstakingly compiled that, like the fairy-tale genie, they promise to answer almost every question of fact one can frame. Yet all of this is at our command by means of intricate combinations of letters, numbers, and decimal signs.

Has it ever occurred to you what an intricate task it is to arrange a world of books in such a way that they can be found with very little trouble once one masters the simple technique? Perhaps you have not thought about the fine art of classifying books or considered what a feat it is to specify exactly where each best belongs in a library. A card catalogue attempts nothing less than to harness knowledge so that it may work for us. Is it any wonder that the library is the nerve center of a campus? Nor is it surprising that grief attends the loss of books. The censor repudiates human experience; the book-burner cremates it.

You may not have known that even the ancient world had the acumen to collect and classify books although they were hand-written papyri and more than one copy was a rarity. The name "manuscript" has this early origin. Just such an early library, containing the learning of the ancient world, existed at Alexandria. After it burned, many centuries were required to retrieve the lost material. The name sometimes given to those centuries during which ancient learning was lost is, significantly enough, the "dark" ages. Even the works of Plato and Aristotle are on our shelves only because, after many centuries, texts were reconstructed in various parts of the world.

It is by means of books that your education will proceed, whether it be liberal or special, general or technical. Such varied types of education are themselves due to the proliferation of books. The growth of knowledge in all fields has been accelerating in this century at a tremendous rate. The small corners of each discipline have developed so fully and intricately that, at the highest levels of education, it is no longer possible to have a "command" of a subject matter. No one can ever hope to know a lot except about a very little. Unless one knows the brain to which the eye is so inextricably bound or the country against which the city is outlined or the economic structure in which a depression takes place, it is impossible to "know" about the eye, the city, or the depression effectively or fruitfully. Only an aerial view can reveal the place our small corner has in the scheme of things.

Therefore, the growth of knowledge requires specialization; the need for understanding demands generalization. This dilemma forces the issue regarding what constitutes a good education in our day. Our culture requires technicians but it also is sorely in need of theoreticians. By what means, by what methods can we be both liberally and specially educated? How can we be trained and yet wise? How can we expose ourselves to drill and routine and yet fan the spark of creativity? And throughout, how can we keep ourselves mindful that knowledge is empty unless used to provide understanding and vision? *That is a good question!!*

The distinction between liberal and technical education is not the only one to be profitably made. The ancient Greeks delineated at least four types of knowing which may serve to reveal the range of issues which you face. One variety embraced knowledge of what might be called "the facts" (*epistēmē*) and is exemplified in an unsystematic way by our contemporary quiz programs, namely, knowledge of such things as names, dates, places, and formulas. This kind of knowing, while indispensable to man, serves as a foundation for the other varieties. A second kind of knowing encompassed knowing how to make (*technē*) or knowing how to act, what to do (*phronēsis*); how to use the facts to construct something. Were one able to name the parts of a watch, one would exhibit *epistēmē*; were one to have the skill to put these parts into working order, he would demonstrate *technē*. A third variety of knowing, the Greeks regarded with the deepest respect. This type (*theōria*), expressed knowledge of why things worked as they did; why and because of what principles the various parts serve the function of the watch. *Theōria* is the source of invention and discovery. It makes it possible for the principles of watchmaking to be organized in a new way, to create, for instance, the metronome.

But this is yet not enough to account for all the facets of knowing. Nor is it enough for the citizen of the modern world. Knowing the principles which govern nature, we need yet know how to use these with *sophia*—the kind of wisdom which consists of understanding and dispassionateness. We need yet gain this culmination of knowledge which is and must ultimately be the goal of education at any time or place. Without wisdom, skill is but a feat and knowledge but a game. Without it, nothing disposes us to use our education constructively for the society which made it possible.

Why do we owe anything to that seemingly abstract entity, "society"? In a real sense, each of us is educated by everyone else who, in turn, was educated by everyone else. This infinitely regressing responsibility is not whimsical. You, for example, are eligible to be a college student because you have some command over spoken and written language. And language is a socially acquired gift. You have already been initiated into many of the languages devised by man to help control his world. You can work with the language of mathematics, you have had some experience with the diverse languages of the arts, you know something of the especially exact languages of the sciences. By means of these you express what you sometimes call "your" ideas. But no ideas are ever exclusively yours or mine. Ideas belong to *genus homo*. Even new ideas are formulated as revisions of earlier ones. Ideas are shared possessions. They are social as well as individual products transmitted by means of the common coin of discourse and exchangeable throughout society as a whole. In this sense, the function of college is to distribute among you our social wealth. A college aims to familiarize you with our common storehouse of the mind. It arranges for you guided tours; it utilizes your instructor's experience with his discipline, with the world, with people, with his previous teachers, to enliven and fructify your journey. From your own responsive, critical efforts will come a degree. But what will it be a degree of? A degree measures something. What will it measure in this case? What could it measure except whether the memory and skill of the past have been infused into the present for the sake of the future.

THE BOOK, THE SCHOOL, AND THE TEACHER

Books   1

Ralph Waldo Emerson

I. The first in time and the first in importance of the influences upon the mind is that of nature. Every day, the sun; and, after sunset, Night and her stars. Ever the winds blow; ever the grass grows. Every day, men and women, conversing—beholding and beholden. The scholar is he of all men whom this spectacle most engages. He must settle its value in his mind. What is nature to him? There is never a beginning, there is never an end, to the inexplicable continuity of this web of God, but always circular power return-ing into itself. Therein it resembles his own spirit, whose beginning, whose ending, he never can find—so entire, so boundless. Far too as her splendors shine, system on system shooting like rays, upward, downward, without center, without circumference—in the mass and in the particle, Nature hastens to render account of herself to the mind. Classification begins. To the young mind every thing is individual, stands by itself. By and by, it finds how to join two things and see in them one nature; then three, then three thousand; and so, tyrannized over by its own unifying instinct, it goes on tying things together, diminishing anomalies, discovering roots running under ground whereby contrary and remote things cohere and flower out from one stem. It presently learns that since the dawn of history there has been a constant accumulation and classifying of facts. But what is classifica-tion but the perceiving that these objects are not chaotic, and are not foreign, but have a law which is also a law of the human mind? The astronomer dis-covers that geometry, a pure abstraction of the human mind, is the measure of planetary motion. The chemist finds proportions and intelligible method throughout matter; and science is nothing but the finding of analogy, identity, in the most remote parts. The ambitious soul sits down before each refractory fact; one after another reduces all strange constitutions, all new powers, to

From "The American Scholar," in *Emerson's Works*, Vol. 1, by Ralph Waldo Emerson, Boston, Houghton Mifflin, 1855. An oration delivered before the Phi Beta Kappa Society at Cambridge, August 31, 1837.

their class and their law, and goes on forever to animate the last fiber of organization, the outskirts of nature, by insight.

Thus to him, to this schoolboy under the bending dome of day, is suggested that he and it proceed from one root; one is leaf and one is flower; relation, sympathy, stirring in every vein. And what is that root? Is not that the soul of his soul? A thought too bold; a dream too wild. Yet when this spiritual light shall have revealed the law of more earthly natures—when he has learned to worship the soul, and to see that the natural philosophy that now is, is only the first gropings of its gigantic hand, he shall look forward to an ever expanding knowledge as to a becoming creator. He shall see that nature is the opposite of the soul, answering to it part for part. One is seal and one is print. Its beauty is the beauty of his own mind. Its laws are the laws of his own mind. Nature then becomes to him the measure of his attainments. So much of nature as he is ignorant of, so much of his own mind does he not yet possess. And, in fine, the ancient precept, "Know thyself," and the modern precept, "Study nature," become at last one maxim.

II. The next great influence into the spirit of the scholar is the mind of the Past—in whatever form, whether of literature, of art, of institutions, that mind is inscribed. Books are the best type of the influence of the past, and perhaps we shall get at the truth—learn the amount of this influence more conveniently—by considering their value alone.

The theory of books is noble. The scholar of the first age received into him the world around; brooded thereon; gave it the new arrangement of his own mind, and uttered it again. It came into him life; it went out from him truth. It came to him short-lived actions; it went out from him immortal thoughts. It came to him business; it went from him poetry. It was dead fact; now, it is quick thought. It can stand, and it can go. It now endures, it now flies, it now inspires. Precisely in proportion to the depth of mind from which it issued, so high does it soar, so long does it sing.

Or, I might say, it depends on how far the process had gone, of transmuting life into truth. In proportion to the completeness of the distillation, so will the purity and imperishableness of the product be. But none is quite perfect. As no air-pump can by any means make a perfect vacuum, so neither can any artist entirely exclude the conventional, the local, the perishable from his book, or write a book of pure thought, that shall be as efficient, in all respects, to a remote posterity, as to contemporaries, or rather to the second age. Each age, it is found, must write its own books; or rather, each generation for the next succeeding. The books of an older period will not fit this.

Yet hence arises a grave mischief. The sacredness which attaches to the act of creation, the act of thought, is transferred to the record. The poet chanting was felt to be a divine man: henceforth the chant is divine also. The writer was a just and wise spirit: henceforward it is settled the book is perfect; as love of the hero corrupts into worship of his statue. Instantly the book becomes noxious: the guide is a tyrant. The sluggish and perverted mind of the multitude, slow to open to the incursions of Reason, having once so opened, having once received this book, stands upon it, and makes an outcry if it is disparaged. Colleges are built on it. Books are written on it by thinkers, not by Man Thinking; by men of talent, that is, who start wrong, who set out from accepted dogmas, not from their own sight of principles. Meek young men grow up in libraries, believing it their duty to accept the views which Cicero, which Locke, which Bacon, have given; forgetful that Cicero, Locke, and Bacon were only young men in libraries when they wrote these books.

Hence, instead of Man Thinking, we have the bookworm. Hence the book-learned class, who value books, as such; not as related to nature and the human constitution, but as making a sort of Third Estate with the world and the soul. Hence the restorers of readings, the emendators, the bibliomaniacs of all degrees.

Books are the best of things, well used; abused, among the worst. What is the right use? What is the one end which all means go to effect? They are for nothing but to inspire. I had better never see a book than to be warped by its attraction clean out of my own orbit, and made a satellite instead of a system. The one thing in the world, of value, is the active soul. This every man is entitled to; this every man contains within him, although in almost all men obstructed and as yet unborn. The soul active sees absolute truth and utters truth, or creates. In this action it is genius; not the privilege of here and there a favorite, but the sound estate of every man. In its essence it is progressive. The book, the college, the school of art, the institution of any kind, stop with some past utterance of genius. This is good, say they—let us hold by this. They pin me down. They look backward and not forward. But genius looks forward: the eyes of man are set in his forehead, not in his hind-head: man hopes: genius creates. Whatever talents may be, if the man create not, the pure efflux of the Deity is not his;—cinders and smoke there may be, but not yet flame. There are creative manners, there are creative actions, and creative words; manners, actions, words, that is, indicative of no custom or authority, but springing spontaneous from the mind's own sense of good and fair.

On the other part, instead of being its own seer, let it receive from another mind its truth, though it were in torrents of light, without periods of solitude, inquest, and self-recovery, and a fatal disservice is done. Genius is always sufficiently the enemy of genius by over-influence. The literature of every nation bears me witness. The English dramatic poets have Shak-spearized now for two hundred years.

Undoubtedly there is a right way of reading, so it be sternly subordinated. Man Thinking must not be subdued by his instruments. Books are for the scholar's idle times. When he can read God directly, the hour is too precious to be wasted in other men's transcripts of their readings. But when the intervals of darkness come, as come they must—when the sun is hid and the stars withdraw their shining—we repair to the lamps which were kindled by their way, to guide our steps to the East again, where the dawn is. We hear, that we may speak. The Arabian proverb says, "A fig tree, looking on a fig tree, becometh fruitful."

It is remarkable, the character of the pleasure we derive from the best books. They impress us with the conviction that one nature wrote and the same reads. We read the verses of one of the great English poets, of Chaucer, of Marvell, of Dryden, with the most modern joy—with a pleasure, I mean, which is in great part caused by the abstraction of all *time* from their verses. There is some awe mixed with the joy of our surprise, when this poet, who lived in some past world, two or three hundred years ago, says that which lies close to my own soul, that which I also had well-nigh thought and said. But for the evidence thence afforded to the philosophical doctrine of the identity of all minds, we should suppose some pre-established harmony, some foresight of souls that were to be, and some preparation of stores for their future wants, like the fact observed in insects, who lay up food before death for the young grub they shall never see.

I would not be hurried by any love of system, by any exaggeration of instincts, to underrate the Book. We all know, that as the human body can be nourished on any food, though it were boiled grass and the broth of shoes, so the human mind can be fed by any knowledge. And great and heroic men have existed who had almost no other information than by the printed page. I only would say that it needs a strong head to bear that diet. One must be an inventor to read well. As the proverb says, "He that would bring home the wealth of the Indies, must carry out the wealth of the Indies." There is then creative reading as well as creative writing. When the mind is braced by labor and invention, the page of whatever book we read becomes luminous with manifold allusion. Every sentence is doubly significant, and the sense of our author is as broad as the world. We then see, what is always true, that as the seer's hour of vision is short and rare among heavy days and months, so is its record, perchance, the least part of his volume. The discerning will read, in his Plato or Shakspeare, only that least part—only the authentic utterances of the oracle;—all the rest he rejects, were it never so many times Plato's and Shakspeare's.

Of course there is a portion of reading quite indispensable to a wise man. History and exact science he must learn by laborious reading. Colleges, in like manner, have their indispensable office—to teach elements. But they can only highly serve us when they aim not to drill, but to create; when they gather from far every ray of various genius to their hospitable halls, and by the concentrated fires, set the hearts of their youth on flame. Thought and knowledge are natures in which apparatus and pretension avail nothing.

Gowns and pecuniary foundations, though of towns of gold, can never countervail the least sentence or syllable of wit. Forget this, and our American colleges will recede in their public importance, whilst they grow richer every year.

The Meaning of a University   2
Howard Mumford Jones

The Americans have never quite understood the theory of a university. The first source of ambiguity is that since the seventeenth century we have seldom or never used the word "university" in any consistent sense. Thus Harvard College, oldest of all American academic institutions, was through the Colonial period and into the nineteenth century referred to as Harvard College or as the university in Cambridge. Ambitious makers of state constitutions in new commonwealths or of new pieces of legislation designed to bring a state swiftly into cultural maturity bestowed the word "university" upon a paper organization or upon actual institutions that were often no more than indifferent high schools or academies. The term is still so loosely employed that I have heard of a university of cosmetology.

One might think that with the maturing of the nation, the creation of the Johns Hopkins University in 1876 and the University of Chicago in 1893, the word would have been clearly understood. Not at all. The semantic confusion is now worse than ever. A common verbal syndrome follows this pattern: a normal school sheds that name and becomes a teachers college; the teachers college sheds that name and becomes a state college; the state college sheds that name and becomes a state university without making any perceptible attempt to discover what the proper function and necessary equipment of a university should be. A parallel case is the present tendency to turn honest agricultural schools or some agricultural and mechanical colleges, titles that indicate honorable functions, into state universities. Thus there are both the University of Kansas and Kansas State University, both the University of Colorado and Colorado State University. Or a complex of colleges, as in the state of New York, is transformed without any clear central purpose into a "university" supported by the state, and the four city colleges in New York City sprout an indeterminate something called the University of the City of New York. Confusion is increased by the existence of New York University, a privately endowed institution, and the Regents of the University of the

State of New York, which is simply the state board of education. Transformation in most cases has been dictated by a desire for status to impress the legislature, the alumni, donors, and the community. The great schools of technology are among the few institutions that have resisted this facile renaming.

A second source of confusion is historical. American universities, however defined, differ from Old World universities in being the creation of the state, not of the church or of a guild of learned men. This has been true since the Great and General Court of Massachusetts Bay granted a charter creating Harvard College. Creation may be by charter or by organic law. The charter, without which no college or university can grant degrees, is (or was) a grant of power by the sovereignty of the colony, the state, or the federal government. Charters were necessary for private institutions. State colleges or universities were created by the state constitution or by public law. In any case, the legislature also created a small body of men charged with the duty of bringing a university into being.

In the first case, this body is commonly called the board of trustees; in the second, the board of regents; in almost every case, it is either self-perpetuating or appointed by the governor or constituted of members *ex officiis*, together with appointed or (more rarely) elected members. In Europe, universities often preceded the state, at least in modern terms; in America, the state precedes the university. In point of law, therefore, the trustees or the regents *are* the university. Seldom chosen for learning, these boards usually begin by securing real estate. Then they hire as their agent a president, whose duty it is to devise a curriculum and find a faculty to teach it.

In other cultures universities are self-governing bodies with a minimum of state supervision except in fascist or Communist countries. If by a university one means primarily a group of scholarly experts, no American university is self-governing. The faculty are employees. Few boards of trustees or regents admit a representative or representatives of the faculty regularly as members of the board, and many do not admit a representative of the faculty to be present at their meetings except in unusual circumstances. Few include the president as a member. The president is usually the agent of the board as well as the only agent of lawful communication between the body of scholars and the nonacademic board. The situation is further complicated by the fact that nowadays the American university president is usually chosen either for his name value or his presumed managerial potentiality. If he has been a scholar, he gives up that profession.

No American university faculty is empowered either to choose a president or to depose him; and though faculty members may be formally or informally consulted by members of the board when a new president is to be chosen, the board is under no obligation to accept the recommendation of the faculty or a committee thereof, these recommendations being in fact often ignored or overruled. Most of the nineteenth century and much of the twentieth has been spent in working out a proper *modus vivendi* between a nonprofessional board, members of which incline to look upon the university as an odd sort of baffling business enterprise, and the body of professional scholars, who, unlike their European counterparts, have little or no responsibility for the financing of the university.

In older American institutions, public or private, a long record of trial and error has resulted in rough definitions and limitations of responsibility. In such universities the board is now commonly content to leave the courses, the modes of teaching, the direction to be taken by research, and the granting of degrees to the president, his academic aides (the deans of the several faculties or colleges making up the university), and the faculty. The vexed question of university finance, which necessarily determines academic policies, lies in a sort of undistributed middle that involves investments, appropriations, salaries, government contracts, fees, fellowships, promotions, and so on. Obviously the financial situation profoundly affects the nature of any university. Obviously the faculty has, at best, only an indirect, sometimes only a remote, relation to financial policy. A board may be so negligent as to permit a university president to bankrupt his institution; or it may be so fussily intrusive as to enforce standards and values that have more relation to popular trends than to the pursuit of truth and excellence.

Since all legal authority rests in the board, its members may abolish or alter parts of a university or invent new ones with or without the knowledge or consent of the faculty. With or without the advice of the faculty the board may also promulgate rules governing the lives of students and of faculty members that may or may not be consonant with the real purpose of the institution. Of course, with experience, boards tend to leave this sort of thing more and more to the "administration," but the recent turmoil at Berkeley illustrates the confusion that results when the distribution of responsibility among the board, the administration, the faculty, and the students is not clear.

The American university is further distinguished from its Old World counterpart by a confusion of aims and responsibility between undergraduate (and vocational) and graduate (and professional) education. The American college of arts and sciences is unique in the world. American graduate schools developed out of existing colleges of arts and sciences in this country late in our educational history. The graduate school of arts and sciences therefore did not, like a law school or a medical school, come into being for a unitary purpose. Indeed, in one sense there is no graduate school of arts and sciences but only departments that offer graduate work. The common denominator that makes the concept of a graduate school of arts and sciences possible is a mild uniformity in entrance requirements for graduate work (the entrant must have a bachelor's degree) and an equally mild uniformity about the mode of granting advanced degrees—the M.A. and Ph.D. A dean of a law school heads a professional body devoted to teaching law; a dean of a graduate school of arts and sciences heads ten, twenty, thirty, forty separate professional units, part of whose time is devoted to teaching students not in the graduate school and part of whose time is devoted to teaching graduate courses. Without a graduate school there can be no university, but the graduate school of arts and sciences rests upon the unstable foundation of shifting departmental interests as the school of medicine does not.

In creating Cornell University, the founder said he wanted to establish an institution in which anybody could study anything. This dictum has been widely accepted as a sound definition of university work. Consequently, television programs sending out news broadcasts, information, and domestic science courses for future housewives, the teaching of advertising layouts and the training of future football coaches, "short course" institution in agriculture, and adult education classes for retired businessmen are offered by the "university" along with advanced research in atomic physics, abstruse work in higher mathematics, chemical studies of the sun's corona, metaphysical speculation about the nature of metaphysical speculation, and a seminar in the economic background of the First Crusade. This need not obscure, but in most cases it certainly straitens, the pure idea of a university as a house of intellect. Goodwill is one of the obscuring forces in academic life.

The American university is also expected to assume responsibility for the housing, feeding, medical and psychiatric care, amusement, and in some cases religious instruction of youngsters just out of the secondary school, and has permitted itself to be surrounded by an amiable jungle of fraternity and sorority houses, religious institutions especially directed to keeping student faith alive, student journalism, intercollegiate athletics, intercollegiate debating, student dramatics, ROTC units, musical enterprises ranging from jazz to Beethoven, cooperative housing, bookstores, alumni offices and organizations, responsibility for extension courses, responsibility for nonacademic conferences on business, social, sociological, political, or international problems, alumni reunions at commencement, and so on, until the original aim of the university has disappeared.

One of the latest, most praised, and in some ways most disastrous new functions assumed by the university is the encouragement of "creativity." Creativity is not scholarship and not science, but a surrogate for them. Creativity is not research, which is an act of the controlled intellect, but as practiced on most American campuses, an emotional outlet. Courses in creative writing, creative dancing, creative painting, creative music, creative playmaking, and creative folk singing abound. In the nature of the case, these activities cannot be judged by the severe intellectual standards basic to research, nor can they be judged by the harsh, if differing, standards of professional excellence. They lie in a kind of no-man's-land more distinguished for sentiment than for severity, and the existence of this no-man's-land is one of the principal reasons for our current confusion between the "creative" arts and humane learning. If these activities are proper to college instruction, they should remain collegiate. If the intent is to be professional, they should be referred to such professional institutions as a conservatory of music. As universities are lauded for supporting a quartet in residence, a tame painter, a writers' conference, a school of the theater, or a studio for dancing or painting or sculpture, the original concept of the university becomes more and more blurred, and the public comes more and more to believe that a university fails of its true purpose (the frayed phrase about an "ivory tower" commonly appears at this point) if it does not nourish the arts.

What, then, is a university? In the Continental sense it is a collection of professional faculties—the faculty of the humanities, the faculty of science, the faculty of law, the faculty of medicine, the faculty of theology, for examples—empowered to offer mature instruction in their several professions and to grant "advanced" degrees when the student has demonstrated his ability to go it alone. In the British sense a traditional university is a collection of colleges that, taken separately, house and teach students, and taken collectively, offer general advanced instruction (the lectures) and grant degrees. In the American sense, at least as defined by the Office of Education, a university is an institution of higher learning comprising a college of arts and sciences or its equivalent, a graduate school of arts and sciences, and one or more professional schools—for example, law, medicine, or theology. A college of liberal arts and sciences may grant a bachelor's or a master's degree. Only a university can grant a Ph.D. degree, though in certain cases (again the confusion of American nomenclature!) established colleges grant the doctor's degree and so-called universities do not, the reason being that they do not have either the proper faculty or the proper facilities for advanced professional work.

I trust I shall not be considered mystical if I put the matter another way. A college is, or should be, concerned with the elements of knowledge, a university with bringing these elements into professional fruition. In this sense, therefore, a university is more especially an act or product of intellect. It is an institution created for the critical examination by professional minds of tenets, principles, laws, dogmas, and ideas that make up the ever varying body of truth. It preserves truth by perpetually subjecting conventional assumptions to critical analysis, discarding fallacies, and retaining as valid only the information or the general statements that pass severe, impersonal, and professional testing; and it extends truth by pushing forward, into the unknown, task forces of professionally trained persons who are skilled in distinguishing fact from assumption. The university climate of opinion is therefore critical. When a given group of professionally competent scholars approve of something they have thoroughly examined, be it a biblical text or a new discovery about the chemistry of meteorites, their findings circulate freely among other professional men all over the world.

The faculty of a university, however organized into schools or colleges, is a group of men and women dedicated to the assumption that there is an intellectual order in life, that they participate, however imperfectly, in that order, and that they can make this intellectual order clear, whether it be in literary history or non-Euclidean geometry, to younger scholars who can carry on learning and research in a particular field. The faculty of a university is the only body competent to determine what general knowledge and what specialized education are necessary for a continuation of professional knowledge and professional skill.

The university may develop other functions, many of them laudable in themselves, and in America they have done so, but if these other functions are not kept subordinate to the central idea of university education and university work, they can overwhelm the university idea by their very multitudinousness. The university then disappears in a smog of sentimentality, "school spirit," vocationalism, pseudo-parental responsibility, experiments in living, and fallacious political activity.

Three observations seem to me pertinent. The first is that the present amiable tendency to confuse college with university, "creativity" with scholarship, vocational training with professional education, and extension courses for high school teachers with a mature philosophy of education must somehow be subdued or clarified. We need universities as universities. The necessity for a clear definition of university work is evident in the fact that whereas fifty years ago a Ph.D. was the mark of professional education, those in charge of research in many fields are now, in despair, talking about the need of postdoctoral education to accomplish what the university was originally established to do. There is nothing shameful about being an excellent teachers college or a good agricultural school, but the highest needs of the nation are in a sense betrayed when the teachers college or the agricultural school becomes a pseudo-university granting a third-rate Ph.D.

The second is our need for a stern insistence upon the truth that university education is a privilege for the competent, not a right to be claimed by the many. American parents seem to feel that some "university" somewhere somehow should be required to accept their children upon demand. Legislatures sometimes pass laws requiring a state university to admit virtually any high school graduate. The result is general confusion, waste of funds, futile teaching, and the creation of special undergraduate "colleges" for the mentally indigent. Why do mediocre high school graduates have to go to universities? Our need, as John Gardner has said, is for excellence, not for mediocrity. If universities are overcrowded, this is only in part a result of population pressures. A more disturbing reason is the incapacity of boards and presidents to insist that a university is, precisely, *not* an institution in which anybody can study anything, but an institution for mature professional education.

Finally, the student being admitted to the high privilege of a university must be taught, if he does not know them (commonly he does not), his rights, duties, and responsibilities as a member of the great traditional republic of learning. Much has been talked about the indifference of one student generation to political issues and about the rebellion of another student generation against university regulations. No one questions the idealism of young men and women who go to Selma or Bogalusa or join the Peace Corps. No one wants to deny the student the right to express his political opinion. But the student, by becoming a student, has lost something and gained something. He has lost the opportunity of embracing anarchy, and he has gained the more durable possibility of becoming a mature citizen in both the political republic and the republic of learning. If more and more students spend more and more time in public demonstrations against this and that, they inevitably spend less and less time in scholarly pursuits, their avowed purpose in asking to be admitted to the university. In other countries the university function of an institution of higher learning was destroyed when the campus became an arena for political action as the principal manifestation of intellectual life. The American problem has not yet been thought carefully through.

The Arts of Teaching and Being Taught   3

Mark Van Doren

The liberal arts have been said by Mortimer Adler to be "nothing but the arts of teaching and being taught." If teaching and studying are imagined on their highest level, and if it is understood that great books as well as men may qualify as teachers, the definition is not oversimplified. The great books are necessary. So, however, are the men; and it is always important that men should think it honorable to be teachers. When the profession is apologetic, society is not sound. "Whom the gods hate they make schoolmasters," said Lucian. But that is true only if the gods hate men. For the gods know, even if we do not, that man is in a special sense the teachable animal. When dogs and monkeys are taught, the aim is to make them resemble another species, usually man. But men must be taught to resemble themselves. Only by education can they be said to become the kind of animal they are.

The responsibility of the teacher is so great that a full vision of it can be crushing. He has persons in his charge. The fact should sober him; but he hears in addition that he is responsible for the entire society which these

Chap. 7, "The Arts of Teaching and Being Taught" in *Liberal Education*, by Mark Van Doren, New York, Beacon Press, 1959. Copyright © 1959 by Mark Van Doren. Reprinted by permission of Mark Van Doren through Nannine Joseph.

persons represent. The size of the assignment suggests that only madmen would dare to accept it, and that such is the meaning of Lucian's sentence. But it is not as serious as all that. The teacher needs only to remember that he is neither deity nor engine; he is a man, and in proportion as he succeeds at his calling he will be surrounded by more men. He and they are society.

The liberal education that has been described in the foregoing pages, and not only described but recommended for all, needs more good teachers than now exist. The requisite number must exist, even if it takes a thousand years to produce them—that is, to educate them. They will need to have better habits than most teachers today even pretend to have. But that will never be unless some teachers in our time consent to change their own habits; the race to come must have its ancestors.

The first habit to be changed is that of assuming that all one needs to know is one's own subject. In any college a given teacher will be biased toward some form of knowledge that agrees with his nature; indeed, unless he loves particular truths he cannot make his students love truth at all. But in a good college he will unite this love with a sense of what every student is there for: the common understanding which men need. He will try to know his colleagues as well as himself; and he will believe as they do in the single, central task of the institution. This is to produce a world whose citizens know the same things, and the indispensable things; and this without the regimentation which the anarchy of our present system threatens.

Good teachers have always been and will always be, and there are good teachers now. The necessity henceforth is that fewer of them be accidents. The area of accident is reduced when there is a design which includes the education of teachers. Not the training—a contemporary term that suggests lubricating oil and precision parts, not to say reflexes and responses. The design is less for institutions that turn out teachers than for a whole view of education that sees them as being naturally made when they teach themselves, with the help of one another and their students.

"It makes no difference to me," said Comenius, "whether I teach or am taught." If Socrates was the perfect teacher, the reason is that he was the perfect student. His suspicion of the Sophists was based upon the fact that their primary desire was not to learn. They preferred to lecture, and their capital was catchwords which they used over and over again, with no warning to the listener that the meanings had shifted. The teacher learns by teaching, which is the highest form of study. The more wisdom he shares, the more he keeps; for wisdom is shared when we ask real questions, and when we want answers no matter what the source, be it ourselves or others, be it old or young, be it one in authority or the most insignificant subordinate.

Such a teacher creates in a sense his own school. "Happy the natural college," says Emerson, "thus self-instituted around every natural teacher." There is no substitute for the natural teacher, and no formula whereby he may be made. But his kind is more numerous in certain situations than in others, and the best hope for education is a landscape of learning in which he will belong. When men seriously want to be educated, says Newman, "when they aim at something precise, something refined, something really luminous, something really large, something choice, they avail themselves, in some shape or other, of the ancient method of oral instruction, of present communication between man and man, of teachers instead of teaching, of the personal influence of a master, and the humble initiation of a disciple. . . . If we wish to become exact and fully furnished in any subject of teaching which is diversified and complicated, we must consult the living man and listen to his living voice. . . . The general principles of any study you may learn by books at home; but the detail, the color, the tone, the air, the life which makes it live in us, you must catch all these from those in whom it lives already."

This is the right doctrine, despite the fact that indolent and eccentric men have taken advantage of it. Unique individual charm is not the final virtue of a teacher. The charm should be personal, meaning that the thought behind it should be better than other thought, not merely different. The most personal thing about Socrates was not his nose or his voice but his love of wisdom. "He who thinks," the friend of Phaedrus said under the plane tree, "that only in principles of justice and goodness and nobility taught and communicated orally for the sake of instruction and graven in the soul is there clearness and perfection and seriousness—this is the right sort of man." The desire of the true teacher is not to triumph but to teach, and in teaching to learn. The teacher without charm is negligible, but the teacher without anything else is contemptible; and he is most contemptible when he courts applause. The good college is the natural college in so far as it is a place where the personal wisdom of older men, grounded deeply enough in the great tradition to be free wisdom, modifies younger men. But the art of education can assist nature here, as art always assists nature, by providing more opportunity than exists for colleges to be what they can.

The good teacher is a man whose conversation is never finished, partly because it is about real things and so cannot be finished, but partly because there is always a new audience, which itself takes part. The student in learning teaches himself and his teacher. How he learns remains something of a mystery, for there is an artist in him, the teachable man, who has his own devices and proceeds to his own conclusions. The art of being taught is the art of letting the nature of learning take its course. It is a course which the teacher can free from many obstacles, and to which he can give formal aid; but he does not invent it any more than the student does. The student does not decide to have the mind with which he educates himself. He uses the one he has, both for the things that can be taught him and for those he must possess through his own effort, or according to his own desire; for just as the good teacher loves some particular knowledge more than any other, so the good student will range beyond the prescriptions of the curriculum, reading what his genius pleases in addition to what his nature requires.

The teacher will encourage these excursions. "Who is so stupidly curious as to send his son to school in order that he may learn what the teacher thinks?" This question of St. Augustine's will be remembered by a good teacher whenever he is tempted to suppress some novelty in a student's thought. It may or may not lead to knowledge, but if it is the student's own discovery it has a present importance which had better not be doubted. There is a skill in instruction, but St. Thomas Aquinas has pointed out that there is also a skill in discovery, and it is our own discoveries that best persuade us. The art of being taught is the art of discovery, as the art of teaching is the art of assisting discovery to take place.

Discovery can take place only if the relation between the teacher and the student is one of mutual respect. It is especially important that the teacher should respect the student, and it will be easy for him to do so if he assumes that the student is someone from whom he may learn. Then it will be the discovery that is mutual, though courtesy in the teacher will exaggerate this. The teacher is courteous because he is respectful, and because that is the way in which courtesy is taught. But his respect is for the subject too, which means that although he loves the student he is sometimes obligated to be severe. The teacher is kind, but to someone he is training to forget him. "My son is coming to do without me," wrote Emerson in his Journal. "And I am coming to do without Plato." The good teacher disappears out of the student's life as Virgil and Beatrice disappear out of *The Divine Comedy*. They are remembered as persons, and so is every good teacher remembered; but when the student has found his own way in the world he cannot recall how much of his wisdom he owes to another. It is his now, and that is what his teacher had intended.

The teacher who desires evidence that his students are interested should also ask for evidence that they are disinterested—that they understand what he is saying. For if they understand him they are sharing with him the experience of thought, which is not an individual experience. The true teacher is singularly innocent of ambition to be praised, loved, or remembered. He is, in fact, the best secular image of the innocent man. And the student respects no other man, least of all one who is crafty or worldly. He will see plenty of worldly men in his time, and their craft will surpass that of any mistaken teacher. It is only in the long run that the innocent man turns out to have been right. The last things learned will agree with him, and then perhaps he will be remembered. But across the "labyrinth of the world," as Comenius puts it, the student and the teacher will share in silence that "paradise of the heart" where agreement is more than a matter of debit and credit.

The teacher, of course, must have authority over the student before he can be respected in the way the student wants to respect him. But authority comes naturally with knowledge that is lucid as the liberal arts make knowledge lucid. The teacher who is not a liberal artist may indoctrinate or charm, but he will not teach. Indoctrination makes the teacher's thought prevail, but teaching is less a matter of what either the teacher or the student thinks than of what the mind itself, the third person, decides and says. The teacher will conceal none of his authority, for he is democrat enough to know that its purpose is to strengthen the student against the time when he will have to choose between accepting and rejecting it. Authority exists only to be denied by better authority; its best act is to destroy itself. The teacher is successful at the moment when his student becomes original. He must be "a kind of fate to his pupil," says Lane Cooper, "and at the same time must bestow upon him the supreme good gift of free will. . . . The original sin of the individual must be scourged and purged away; his original goodness must be cherished and encouraged." If this imputes a kind of divinity to the teacher, that is precisely what some students do. They are wrong, and every teacher knows it; but the good teacher is able to interpret and forgive the blasphemy, meanwhile letting the shadow it casts upon him measure the depth of his duty.

The education of teachers is an education in the liberal arts. When this education is good, and falls on the right ground, it produces persons with usable intellects and imaginations who know both what and why they are teaching. A teacher who can answer neither of those questions is no teacher, for thus he proves himself incapable of the one pleasure reserved for him among the pleasures possible to man: the pleasure of being intelligible. Human communication, so difficult and so rare, is his professed assignment, and at the moment in his students' lives when such success as is achieved will count forever. It will count in their understanding, and so in their happiness. It will also count, by making them more communicative themselves, in the happiness of mankind.

One kind of contemporary teacher lacks the courage of his authority, which he misconceives as authority is commonly misconceived. He thinks it is power. But power has no authority in the region of intellect and morals. Authority there is excellence in knowledge and art; and excellence in such things has indeed a special power which only the initiated know. The special power of the teacher is revealed in the competence of his search for the fundamental questions to be asked—questions fundamental enough to engage all men, so that argument can be reventilated and revived.

The search for such questions, when it goes on today, is often mistaken for its opposite. The search is itself an argument, but it is accused of a desire to stop argument forever. Curiosity about initial questions is confused with propaganda for final answers. The tolerance we practice in matters of opinion is the tolerance not of hope but of despair, as a recent distinction has it. We do not trust argument unless it is aimless—without, in other words, the background of an agreement that the purpose of it is the discovery of truth. We do not trust truth, which we identify only with those who have told lies in its name. Truth is remote, but not to care how remote it is puts one in

Dante's dark circle of those who lived without blame and without praise, but were for themselves; who from cowardice made the great refusal; who lost the good of the intellect, and so were never alive.

"To be indifferent which of two opinions is true," says John Locke in language very different from Dante's, "is the right temper of the mind that preserves it from being imposed on, and disposes it to examine with that indifferency till it has done its best to find the truth. But to be indifferent whether we embrace falsehood or truth is the great road to error." All opinions are to be tolerated for what they are worth, but the person today who endeavors to compare opinions by applying a scale of worth is seldom tolerated. His scale may be wrong, but that is not why he is criticized. There is no common search for a right scale that would make such criticism possible. The open mind is one which has begun to think, but we act as if it were one which had stopped doing so because thought can be serious and dangerous, and because it is hard work. We do not doubt well. The good doubter doubts something; we dismiss everything. One sign of this is that we think it beneath our dignity to agree—the typical professor takes no position, either his own or any other's. He calls this tolerance, and does not seem to mind that it is tolerance of bad thinking as well as good. The thing not to be tolerated is bad thinking. Perhaps Locke has explained why there is so much of it today. Cynicism paralyzes argument.

The last generation of students may never forgive its teachers who taught contempt and fear of truth. The distinction they made was the one between fact and opinion, not the one between opinion and truth. The difference itself is a fact, to be ignorant of which is neither to be armed against opinion nor to have one's own. The immediate danger is that we shall have a riot of ill-considered slogans. "Respect for the truth is an acquired taste," and the recovery of it may take a long time, for it involves an understanding that freedom has its own compulsions, and it requires a discipline in the adjustment of thought to thought which only the liberal arts can teach. To say that truth is better than falsehood is not to speak vaguely. It is more powerful, it is more interesting, and it is less lonely. "There is but one world in common for those who are awake," said Heraclitus, "but when men are asleep each turns away into a world of his own." It is the love of truth that makes men free in the common light of day.

THE STUDENT

Of Practice and Habits 4

John Locke

4. *Of Practice and Habits.* We are born with faculties and powers capable almost of anything, such at least as would carry us further than can easily be imagined: but it is only the exercise of those powers which gives us ability and skill in anything, and leads us towards perfection.

A middle-aged ploughman will scarce ever be brought to the carriage and language of a gentleman, though his body be as well-proportioned, and his joints as supple, and his natural parts not any way inferior. The legs of a dancing-master and the fingers of a musician fall as it were naturally, without thought or pains, into regular and admirable motions. Bid them change their parts, and they will in vain endeavour to produce like motions in the members not used to them, and it will require length of time and long practice to attain but some degrees of a like ability. What incredible and astonishing actions do we find rope-dancers and tumblers bring their bodies to! Not but that sundry in almost all manual arts are as wonderful; but I name those which the world takes notice of for such, because on that very account they give money to see them. All these admired motions, beyond the reach and almost conception of unpractised spectators, are nothing but the mere effects of use and industry in men whose bodies have nothing peculiar in them from those of the amazed lookers-on.

As it is in the body, so it is in the mind: practice makes it what it is; and most even of those excellencies which are looked on as natural endowments, will be found, when examined into more narrowly, to be the product of exercise, and to be raised to that pitch only by repeated actions. Some men are remarked for pleasantness in raillery; others for apologues and apposite diverting stories. This is apt to be taken for the effect of pure nature, and that the rather because it is not got by rules, and those who excel in either of them

From sec. 4, and sec. 25, in *Of the Conduct of the Understanding*, with deletions, in *The Philosophical Works of John Locke*, J. A. St. John, ed., London, G. Bell, 1898. This work was first published posthumously in 1706.

never purposely set themselves to the study of it as an art to be learnt. But yet it is true, that at first some lucky hit, which took with somebody and gained him commendation, encouraged him to try again, inclined his thoughts and endeavours that way, till at last he insensibly got a facility in it, without perceiving how; and that is attributed wholly to nature which was much more the effect of use and practice. I do not deny that natural disposition may often give the first rise to it, but that never carries a man far without use and exercise, and it is practice alone that brings the power of the mind, as well as those of the body, to their perfection. Many a good poetic vein is buried under a trade, and never produces anything for want of improvement. We see the ways of discourse and reasoning are very different, even concerning the same matter, at court and in the university. And he that will go but from Westminster-hall to the Exchange will find a different genius and turn in their ways of talking; and yet one cannot think that all whose lot fell in the city were born with different parts from those who were bred at the university or inns of court.

To what purpose all this but to show that the difference so observable in men's understandings and parts does not arise so much from their natural faculties as acquired habits. He would be laughed at that should go about to make a fine dancer out of a country hedger at past fifty. And he will not have much better success who shall endeavor at that age to make a man reason well, or speak handsomely, who has never been used to it, though you should lay before him a collection of all the best precepts of logic or oratory. Nobody is made anything by hearing of rules or laying them up in his memory; practice must settle the habit of doing without reflecting on the rule; and you may as well hope to make a good painter or musician extempore, by a lecture and instruction in the arts of music and painting, as a coherent thinker or a strict reasoner by a set of rules showing him wherein right reasoning consists.

This being so that defects and weakness in men's understanding, as well as other faculties, come from want of a right use of their own minds, I am apt to think the fault is generally mislaid upon nature, and there is often a complaint of want of parts when the fault lies in want of a due improvement of them.

.   .   .

25. *Haste.* The eagerness and strong bent of the mind after knowledge, if not warily regulated, is often a hindrance to it. It still presses into further discoveries and new objects, and catches at the variety of knowledge, and therefore often stays not long enough on what is before it to look into it as it should, for haste to pursue what is yet out of sight. He that rides post through a country may be able from the transient view to tell how in general the parts lie, and may be able to give some loose description of here a mountain and there a plain, here a morass and there a river, woodland in one part

and savannahs in another. Such superficial ideas and observations as these he may collect in galloping over it; but the more useful observations of the soil, plants, animals, and inhabitants, with their several sorts and properties, must necessarily escape him; and it is seldom men ever discover the rich mines without some digging. Nature commonly lodges her treasure and jewels in rocky ground. If the matter be knotty and the sense lies deep, the mind must stop and buckle to it, and stick upon it with labour and thought and close contemplation, and not leave it till it has mastered the difficulty and got possession of truth. But here care must be taken to avoid the other extreme; a man must not stick at every useless nicety, and expect mysteries of science in every trivial question or scruple that he may raise. He that will stand to pick up and examine every pebble that comes in his way, is as unlikely to return enriched and laden with jewels, as the other that traveled full speed. Truths are not the better nor the worse for their obviousness or difficulty, but their value is to be measured by their usefulness and tendency. Insignificant observations should not take up any of our minutes, and those that enlarge our view and give light towards further and useful discoveries should not be neglected, though they stop our course and spend some of our time in a fixed attention.

There is another haste that does often and will mislead the mind if it be left to iself and its own conduct. The understanding is naturally forward, not only to learn its knowledge by variety (which makes it skip over one to get speedily to another part of knowledge), but also eager to enlarge its views by running too fast into general observations and conclusions without a due examination of particulars enough whereon to found those general axioms. This seems to enlarge their stock, but it is of fancies, not realities; such theories, built upon narrow foundations, stand but weakly, and if they fall not of themselves, are at least very hardly to be supported against the assaults of opposition. And thus men being too hasty to erect to themselves general notions and ill-grounded theories, find themselves deceived in their stock of knowledge when they come to examine their hastily assumed maxims themselves or to have them attacked by others. General observations drawn from particulars are the jewels of knowledge, comprehending great store in a little room; but they are therefore to be made with the greater care and caution, lest if we take counterfeit for true our loss and shame be the greater when our stock comes to a severe scrutiny. One or two particulars may suggest hints of inquiry, and they do well to take those hints; but if they turn them into conclusions, and make them presently general rules, they are forward indeed, but it is only to impose on themselves by propositions assumed for truths without sufficient warrant. To make such observations is, as has been already remarked, to make the head a magazine of materials which can hardly be called knowledge, or at least it is but like a collection of lumber not reduced to use or order; and he that makes everything an observation has the same useless plenty and much more falsehood mixed with it. The extremes on both sides are to be avoided, and he will be able to give the best account of his studies who keeps his understanding in the right mean between them.

5   The Power to Think

John Dewey

We have just discussed the values to be obtained by educating the mind in habits of thought and some of the obstacles that lie in the way of its development. But nothing can grow except from germs, from potentialities that tend to some development of themselves. There must be a native stock, or capital, of resources; we cannot force the power to think upon any creature that does not first think spontaneously, "naturally," as we say. But while we cannot learn or be taught to think, we do have to learn *how* to think well, especially *how* to acquire the general *habit* of reflecting. Since this habit grows out of original native tendencies, the teacher needs to know something about the nature of the primary capital stock that constitutes the germs out of which alone the habit is to be developed. Unless we know what there is to be laid hold of and used, we work in the dark and waste time and energy. We shall probably do something even worse, striving to impose some unnatural habit from without instead of directing native tendencies toward their own best fruition.

Teaching may be compared to selling commodities. No one can sell unless someone buys. We should ridicule a merchant who said that he had sold a great many goods although no one had bought any. But perhaps there are teachers who think that they have done a good day's teaching irrespective of what pupils have learned. There is the same exact equation between teaching and learning that there is between selling and buying. The only way to increase the learning of pupils is to augment the quantity and quality of real teaching. Since learning is something that the pupil has to do himself and for himself, the initiative lies with the learner. The teacher is a guide and director; he steers the boat, but the energy that propels it must come from those who are learning. The more a teacher is aware of the past experiences of students, of their hopes, desires, chief interests, the better will he understand the forces at work that need to be directed and utilized for the formation of reflective habits. The number and quality of these factors vary from person to person. They cannot therefore be categorically enumerated in a book. But there are some tendencies and forces that operate in every normal individual, forces that must be appealed to and utilized if the best methods for the development of good habits of thought are to be employed.

From Ch. 3, "Native Resources in Training Thought": From John Dewey, *How We Think*, © 1933. Reprinted by permission of D. C. Heath and Company.

I. CURIOSITY

Every living creature, while it is awake, is in constant interaction with its surroundings. It is engaged in a process of give and take, of doing something to objects around it and receiving back something from them—impressions, stimuli. This process of interacting constitutes the framework of experience. We are fitted out with devices that help us ward off destructive influences, devices that intercept harmful influences and protect us from them. But we also have tendencies that are forward-reaching and out-reaching, that go out to make new contacts, that seek new objects, that strive to vary old objects, that revel, as it were, in experiences for their own sake and so are ceaselessly active in enlarging the range of experience. These various tendencies are summed up in curiosity. Wordsworth's saying applies particularly to childhood:

> The eye—it cannot choose but see;
> We cannot bid the ear be still;
> Our bodies feel, where'er they be,
> Against or with our will.

All our sense and motor organs are, when we are awake, acting and being acted upon by something in the environment. With adults many of these contacts have been made; grown-ups permit themselves to become stale; they fall into ruts of experience and are contented with what happens in these ruts. To children the whole world is new; there is something thrilling to the healthy being in every new contact and it is eagerly sought for, not merely passively awaited and endured. There is no single faculty called "curiosity"; every normal organ of sense and of motor activity is on the *qui vive*. It wants a chance to be active, and it needs some object in order to act. The sum total of these outgoing tendencies constitutes curiosity. It is the basic factor in enlargement of experience and therefore a prime ingredient in the germs that are to be developed into reflective thinking.

Three Stages, or Levels, of Curiosity

1. In the first manifestations, curiosity is far removed from thinking. It is a vital overflow, an expression of an abundant organic energy. A physiological uneasiness leads a child to get "into everything,"—to be reaching, poking, pounding, prying. Observers of animals have noted what one author calls "their inveterate tendency to fool." "Rats run about, smell, dig, or gnaw, without real reference to the business in hand. In the same way Jack [a dog] scrambles and jumps, the kitten wanders and picks, the otter slips about everywhere like ground lightning, the elephant fumbles ceaselessly, the monkey pulls things about." [1] The most casual observation of the activities of a young

---

[1] Hobhouse, *Mind in Evolution*, p. 195.

child reveals a ceaseless display of exploring and testing activity. Objects are sucked, fingered, and thumped; drawn and pushed; handled and thrown; in short, they are experimented with until they cease to yield new qualities. Such activities are hardly intellectual, and yet without them intellectual activity would be feeble and intermittent through lack of stuff for its operations.

2. A higher stage of curiosity develops under the influence of social stimuli. When the child learns that he can appeal to others to eke out his store of experiences, so that, if objects fail to respond interestingly to his experiments, he may call upon persons to provide interesting material, a new epoch sets in. "What is that?" "Why?" become the unfailing signs of a child's presence. At first this questioning is hardly more than a projection into social relations of the physical overflow that earlier kept the child pushing and pulling, opening and shutting. He asks in succession what holds up the house, what holds up the soil that holds the house, what holds up the earth that holds the soil; but his questions are not evidence of any genuine consciousness of rational connections. His *why* is not a demand for scientific explanation; the motive behind it is simply eagerness for a larger acquaintance with the mysterious world in which he is placed. The search is not for a law or principle, but only for another, a bigger fact. Yet there is more than a desire to accumulate just information or heap up disconnected items—although sometimes the interrogating habit threatens to degenerate into a mere disease of language. In the feeling, however dim, that the facts which directly meet the senses are not the whole story, that there is more behind them and more to come from them, lies the germ of *intellectual* curiosity.

3. Curiosity rises above the organic and the social level and becomes intellectual in the degree in which it is transformed into interest in finding out for oneself the answers to questions that are aroused by contact with persons and things. In what was just called the "social" stage, children are often more interested in the mere process of asking a question than they are in giving heed to the answer. At all events no particular question is attended to for very long; one asking succeeds another so fast that none is developed into a train of thought. Immediate asking and answering discharges curiosity. The crucial problem for the educator, whether parent or school teacher, is to utilize for *intellectual* purposes the organic curiosity of physical exploration and linguistic interrogation. This can be accomplished by attaching them to ends that are more remote, that require finding and inserting intermediate acts, objects, and ideas. To the degree that a distant end controls a sequence of inquiries and observations and binds them together as means to an end, just to that degree does curiosity assume a definitely intellectual character.

How Curiosity Is Lost

Unless transition to an intellectual plane is effected, curiosity degenerates or evaporates. Bacon's saying that we must become as little children in order to enter the kingdom of science is at once a reminder of the open-minded and flexible wonder of childhood and of the ease with which this endowment is lost. Some lose it in indifference or carelessness; others in a frivolous flippancy; many escape these evils only to become incased in a hard dogmatism that is equally fatal to the spirit of wonder. Some are so taken up with routine as to be inaccessible to new facts and problems. Others retain curiosity only with reference to what concerns their personal advantage in their chosen career. With many, curiosity is arrested on the plane of interest in local gossip and in the fortunes of their neighbors; indeed, so usual is this result that very often the first association with the word *curiosity* is a prying inquisitiveness into other people's business. With respect, then, to curiosity, the teacher has usually more to learn than to teach. Rarely can he aspire to the office of kindling or even of increasing it; his province is rather to provide the materials and the conditions by which organic curiosity will be directed into investigations that have an aim and that produce results in the way of increase of knowledge, and by which social inquisitiveness will be converted into ability to find out things known to others, an ability to ask questions of books as well as of persons. The teacher has to protect the growing person from those conditions which occasion a mere succession of excitements which have no cumulative effect, and which, therefore, make an individual either a lover of sensations and sensationalism or leave him blasé and uninterested. He has to avoid all dogmatism in instruction, for such a course gradually but surely creates the impression that everything important is already settled and nothing remains to be found out. He has to know how to give information when curiosity has created an appetite that seeks to be fed, and how to abstain from giving information when, because of lack of a questioning attitude, it would be a burden and would dull the sharp edge of the inquiring spirit.

The Well-Educated Mind   6
Theodore Meyer Greene

A searching reconsideration of liberal education must concern itself with at least three major issues. What is its proper goal? What educational process will most effectively enable it progressively to realize this goal? In what kind of an academic community can this process best be initiated and sustained? These questions can be answered in a very general way in terms of the basic presuppositions which we enumerated earlier in this lecture. We can say that the goal of education is to prepare each individual, so far as his native endowment permits, to live well in his society and in the universe in which he

Reprinted by permission of the publishers from Theodore Meyer Greene, [sec. 4, in] *Liberal Education Reconsidered,* Cambridge, Mass.: Harvard University Press, Copyright, 1953, by the President and Fellows of Harvard College.

finds himself; that that educational process is best which advances us most efficiently towards this goal; and that that academic community is best which best initiates and sustains this educational process. No one, I fancy, will quarrel with these generalizations. They fail, however, to answer such pressing questions as: What does it mean to "live well" in our society and our universe? How might education promote this good life? How should a school be constituted to assure this kind of education? Our basic concepts of structure, texture, and vitality will, I think, help us to answer these more specific questions.

Let us start with our goal—the fullest development of each individual in the context of his society and his total cosmic environment. Whatever else such development may entail, it must certainly include the development of man's mind. And our minds are well developed in proportion as they are well disciplined or well structured, individualized or well textured, and, above all, active and lively. Let us see what this might mean in more concrete academic terms.

A well-disciplined mind is one which is well equipped with the basic tools of thought and communication. These tools are, in part, "linguistic" in the broadest sense. We can think, express ourselves, and communicate with others effectively only with the aid of one or more of the languages—verbal and mathematical, symbolic and artistic—which mankind has devised for this very purpose. Most important for each of us is his mother tongue, but there are other languages which are also essential: foreign languages, for a true appreciation of the nuances of other nations and cultures; the languages of mathematics, for participation in man's most abstract and most precise thinking; the languages of the several arts, for the understanding and enjoyment of art in the various media; and, last but not least, the many specialized languages of science and history, philosophy and theology, for the comprehension of mankind's profoundest reflections about nature, man, and God.

Mastery of these "linguistic" tools, however, will not suffice. For the mind must also be trained to function powerfully and precisely with their aid—to observe and remember accurately and discriminatingly, to think clearly, to criticize judiciously. Only as we cultivate our native mental capacities do we become able to make effective uses of the complex "linguistic" apparatus available to us.

But linguistic and mental equipment are not enough. A well-developed mind is not only well equipped and well trained but also well informed. If we are to live well we must learn a great many facts about ourselves and about the physical, social, and spiritual actualities which daily confront us. And since we keep encountering new situations and new problems we must learn the techniques of fact-finding and fact-testing. Above all, we must acquire a lifelong passionate respect for fact and a deep hatred of illusion and error.

But a mind however well equipped and trained and however well stocked with factual knowledge and skilled in discovering new facts can, as we well know, easily run amuck. If our minds are to serve us well in our society and our world we must also learn how to evaluate sensitively and judiciously. We must learn how to respond generously and wisely to every type of beauty in nature and in art, to truth in every area of human concern, to goodness wherever it appears or should appear, and to all holiness worthy of our reverence. It is this cultivated capacity for evaluation—this sensitivity to all the values which enrich human life and this ability to assess them judiciously whenever they compete for our loyalty—that distinguishes wisdom from mere knowledge and maturity from adolescent irresponsibility.

These, then, are some of the attributes of a well-structured mind. But why call it well-structured? Because these attributes are equally valuable for all men, because they are our cultural heritage, and because they can all be taught. They constitute, in sum, the so-called academic "disciplines," and it is these "disciplines," in turn, which constitute the basic structure of the educational process. Traditional education has excelled in precisely this area —it has concerned itself primarily with these (or at least some of these) basic "disciplines." Why, then, has "progressive" education so violently protested and rebelled against them? Because traditional education has tended to ignore the second essential component of a well-developed mind, namely, the component of texture.

Texture, we have said, signifies the factor of uniqueness and originality. A well-textured mind is a mind that has learned how to realize and express its own individuality, to be itself and not merely a stereotype. The only educational goal worthy of man's precious uniqueness is a mind which, in becoming well equipped and trained, well informed, sensitive, and mature, achieves the richest and fullest self-realization. Our pedagogical task must therefore be to help each of our students to be himself as completely as possible, to think and explore, learn and evaluate, as effectively as he is able in his own distinctive way.

That the components of structure and texture do indeed complement one another in the field of education is clearly demonstrated by the fact that a one-sided emphasis on either component produces grave mental frustrations and unbalance. The "progressivists" in education were quite right in insisting that mere discipline, for its own sake, stifles initiative, interest, and originality. The traditionalists have been equally right in pointing out that an undisciplined mind is not free but enslaved to every passing whim and impulse, incapable of significant originality and doomed to idiosyncratic triviality. Worthwhile originality, whether it be the masterpiece or world-shaking discovery of genius, or the ingenious inventiveness of a lesser talent, or even the run-of-the-mill freshness of personality and outlook of a person of average ability who is completely himself, is always the product of discipline *and* spontaneity, mental structure *and* texture. What education should aim at, therefore, is a mind able to put the disciplines to its own uses—to express correctly and felicitously its own ideas, to gather and interpret facts in its own way, to encounter and judge values on its own matured responsibility.

But we have still not completed our account of the well-educated mind. For what we value above all else in ourselves and others is a lively mind, a mind in ferment—insatiably curious and critical, imaginative and creative. A mind that is passive rather than active, regurgitative rather than fresh and critical, lacks the vital spark, however well disciplined it may be. So is, para-doxically, an undisciplined mind, however free from social restraints, since, without discipline, it lacks the tools and stamina, the knowledge and the mature perspective, requisite for significant originality. Our ultimate educa-tional objective is a self-starting, self-criticizing, and self-nourishing mind— a mind that can function powerfully, creatively, and wisely under its own steam.

Such intellectual vitality cannot, however, be engendered by a frontal pedagogical attack, even by the most inspiring teacher. All that the inspira-tion of a teacher can do is to awaken in his students a temporary excitement which quickly dies away. We can promote the mental vitality of our students only by teaching them the disciplines in a spirit of profound respect for the individuality of each student. Here, as elsewhere, vitality is a function or by-product of structure and texture in happy combination. But it is also a pre-requisite to the acquisition of mental structure and texture. What teacher has not failed in his attempt to help his student to learn the basic disciplines and to make them serve his own interests and needs because the student has lacked the requisite initial mental vitality? And what teacher has not experi-enced the profound satisfaction of watching a lively but untutored youth gradually become able, with the help of acquired disciplines, to take charge of his own education and thus progressively to realize his own individual capabilities? Once again, the factor of vitality manifests itself simultaneously as the product of structure and texture and as a directive and vitalizing force.

It is appropriate that the goal of education be defined with major emphasis on the development of the mind, since this is the very special re-sponsibility of the school. Our task as teachers is not to condition animals but to educate human beings, and the only education worthy of man must be focused primarily on that which so signally distinguishes him from all other living beings. We must beware, however, of an intellectualism which tries to divorce the mind from the total personality and which values mental achievement for its own sake. Mental development is valued in our Western culture precisely because the unfolding of our entire personality depends so greatly upon the proper education of the mind. We will do well, then, to restate the goal of education in the more inclusive terms of personality de-velopment. What kind of person should we seek to develop in our schools?

Once again our three basic concepts will stand us in good stead. The personality we would cultivate in ourselves and in others is, first of all, a well-disciplined and well-integrated one, with useful habits well coördinated and with mind and body, reason and emotion, instinct and will in harmonious structural relation. Lack of discipline can only result in loss of integration, and an unintegrated person is a person at war with himself, frustrated and miserable. Mere discipline, however, creates not persons but human robots, as totalitarian regimentation has so tragically demonstrated in recent years. Our Western ideal of a developed personality reflects our profound respect for each man's conscience and each man's inalienable right to freedom of thought, worship, and action. Yet the freedom which we cherish is not mere license or freakishness, nor is the spontaneity we wish to encourage an individual initiative harmful to others. Our hope is rather that all men may, so far as possible, learn how to be self-creative rather than self-destructive, and how to promote human welfare rather than human misery. Only such a personality will possess, we believe, the creative vitality worthy of man's highest capacities.

Our concern for each individual's total personality dictates a corresponding concern for the humane community. For personality and community are correlative concepts; each implies the other. Only in a genuine community can personality ripen into maturity, and only through the coöperative efforts of mature persons can a community come into being and maintain itself. If its individual members lack this maturity the social group will tend either to dissolve into a state of anarchy or to rigidify into a regimented human hive. Neither an anarchistic nor a monolithic society is propitious to the development of integrated, interesting, and creative personalities.

We must therefore redefine the goal of education once again to take into account man's social necessities and obligations. The social purpose of education must be to prepare young men and women for responsible and coöperative participation in all the overlapping social groups which constitute the structure of our complex society—in the family, in a business or profession, in the local community, in the nation, and in what is now hopefully called the family of nations. All men's generic rights and duties are the same in each of these institutional groupings—all men crave family affection and all can and should help to make the family a haven of tenderness and love; all men have civil rights and civic duties; all men need economic security and all save the incapacitated can contribute something to our corporate economic welfare. A well-rounded education should therefore include the study of our complex social structure and should prepare our youth so far as possible for a lifetime of informed and enthusiastic social activity. If such activity is to be worthy of free men in a free society, moreover, each individual must learn how, within the framework of common rights and duties, to make his own unique contributions to each social group to which he belongs. For only thus can he hope to realize his special capacities to the full, and only thus can he make his richest contribution to the social texture of his community. The more successfully education assists the men and women of our nation to participate in these various social activities in this spirit, the more will it contribute to the vitality not only of the individual but of the several social groups which claim his allegiance.

Our trilogy of concepts has, I believe, helped us to define our educational goal. This goal is, first and foremost, the cultivation of the well-disciplined, highly individualized, and lively mind—of a mind strong in structure, rich in texture, dynamic and creative. But our goal is also the nurture of man's total personality through structural integration and textural individuation, the development of persons able and eager to enjoy life to the full. And it is also, and no less urgently, a preparation for life in a community, a life of conformity to social order and of responsible deviation and revolt, a life of joyful coöperation with others in common enterprises for the common good.

LIBERAL EDUCATION

Intelligence and Intellect   7
Richard Hofstadter

Before attempting to estimate the qualities in our society that make intellect unpopular, it seems necessary to say something about what intellect is usually understood to be. When one hopes to understand a common prejudice, common usage provides a good place to begin. Anyone who scans popular American writing with this interest in mind will be struck by the manifest difference between the idea of intellect and the idea of intelligence. The first is frequently used as a kind of epithet, the second never. No one questions the value of intelligence; as an abstract quality it is universally esteemed, and individuals who seem to have it in exceptional degree are highly regarded. The man of intelligence is always praised; the man of intellect is sometimes also praised, especially when it is believed that intellect involves intelligence, but he is also often looked upon with resentment or suspicion. It is he, and not the intelligent man, who may be called unreliable, superfluous, immoral, or subversive; sometimes he is even said to be, for all his intellect, unintelligent.

Although the difference between the qualities of intelligence and intellect is more often assumed than defined, the context of popular usage makes it possible to extract the nub of the distinction, which seems to be almost universally understood: intelligence is an excellence of mind that is employed within a fairly narrow, immediate, and predictable range; it is a manipulative, adjustive, unfailingly practical quality—one of the most eminent and endearing of the animal virtues. Intelligence works within the framework of limited but clearly stated goals, and may be quick to shear away questions of thought that do not seem to help in reaching them. Finally, it is of such universal use that it can daily be seen at work and admired alike by simple or complex minds.

Intellect, on the other hand, is the critical, creative, and contemplative side of mind. Whereas intelligence seeks to grasp, manipulate, re-order, adjust, intellect examines, ponders, wonders, theorizes, criticizes, imagines. Intelligence will seize the immediate meaning in a situation and evaluate it. Intellect evaluates evaluations, and looks for the meanings of situations as a whole. Intelligence can be praised as a quality in animals; intellect, being a unique manifestation of human dignity, is both praised and assailed as a quality in men. When the difference is so defined, it becomes easier to understand why we sometimes say that a mind of admittedly penetrating intelligence is relatively unintellectual; and why, by the same token, we see among minds that are unmistakably intellectual a considerable range of intelligence.

This distinction may seem excessively abstract, but it is frequently illustrated in American culture. In our education, for example, it has never been doubted that the selection and development of intelligence is a goal of central importance; but the extent to which education should foster intellect has been a matter of the most heated controversy, and the opponents of intellect in most spheres of public education have exercised preponderant power. But perhaps the most impressive illustration arises from a comparison of the American regard for inventive skill as opposed to skill in pure science. Our greatest inventive genius, Thomas A. Edison, was all but canonized by the American public, and a legend has been built around him. One cannot, I suppose, expect that achievements in pure science would receive the same public applause that came to inventions as spectacular and as directly influential on ordinary life as Edison's. But one might have expected that our greatest genius in pure science, Josiah Willard Gibbs, who laid the theoretical foundations for modern physical chemistry, would have been a figure of some comparable acclaim among the educated public. Yet Gibbs, whose work was celebrated in Europe, lived out his life in public and even professional obscurity at Yale, where he taught for thirty-two years. Yale, which led American universities in its scientific achievements during the nineteenth century, was unable in those thirty-two years to provide him with more than a half dozen or so graduate students who could understand his work, and never took the trouble to award him an honorary degree.

A special difficulty arises when we speak of the fate of intellect in society; this difficulty stems from the fact that we are compelled to speak of intellect in vocational terms, though we may recognize that intellect is not simply a matter of vocation. Intellect is considered in general usage to be an attribute of certain professions and vocations; we speak of the intellectual as being a writer or a critic, a professor or a scientist, an editor, journalist, lawyer, clergyman, or the like. As Jacques Barzun has said, the intellectual is a man who carries a brief case. It is hardly possible to dispense with this convenience; the status and the role of intellectuals are bound up with the aggregate of the brief-case-carrying professions. But few of us believe that a member of a profession, even a learned profession, is necessarily an intellectual in any discriminating or demanding sense of the word. In most professions intellect may help, but intelligence will serve well enough without it. We know, for instance, that all academic men are not intellectuals; we often lament this fact. We know that there is something about intellect, as opposed to professionally trained intelligence, which does not adhere to whole vocations but only to persons. And when we are troubled about the position of intellect and the intellectual class in our society, it is not only the status of certain vocational groups which we have in mind, but the value attached to a certain mental quality.

A great deal of what might be called the journeyman's work of our culture—the work of lawyers, editors, engineers, doctors, indeed of some writers and of most professors—though vitally dependent upon ideas, is not distinctively intellectual. A man in any of the learned or quasi-learned professions must have command of a substantial store of frozen ideas to do his work; he must, if he does it well, use them intelligently; but in his professional capacity he uses them mainly as instruments. The heart of the matter —to borrow a distinction made by Max Weber about politics—is that the professional man lives *off* ideas, not *for* them. His professional role, his professional skills, do not make him an intellectual. He is a mental worker, a technician. He may *happen* to be an intellectual as well, but if he is, it is because he brings to his profession a distinctive feeling about ideas which is not required by his job. As a professional, he has acquired a stock of mental skills that are for sale. The skills are highly developed, but we do not think of him as being an intellectual if certain qualities are missing from his work —disinterested intelligence, generalizing power, free speculation, fresh observation, creative novelty, radical criticism. At home he may happen to be an intellectual, but at his job he is a hired mental technician who uses his mind for the pursuit of externally determined ends. It is this element—the fact that ends are set from some interest or vantage point outside the intellectual process itself—which characterizes both the zealot, who lives obsessively for a single idea, and the mental technician, whose mind is used not for free speculation but for a salable end. The goal here is external and not self-determined, whereas the intellectual life has a certain spontaneous character and inner determination. It has also a peculiar poise of its own, which I believe is established by a balance between two basic qualities in the intellectual's attitude toward ideas—qualities that may be designated as playfulness and piety.

To define what is distinctively intellectual it is necessary to be able to determine what differentiates, say, a professor or a lawyer who is an intellectual from one who is not; or perhaps more properly, what enables us to say that at one moment a professor or a lawyer is acting in a purely routine professional fashion and at another moment as an intellectual. The difference is not in the character of the ideas with which he works but in his attitude toward them. I have suggested that in some sense he lives for ideas—which means that he has a sense of dedication to the life of the mind which is very much like a religious commitment. This is not surprising, for in a very important way the role of the intellectual is inherited from the office of the cleric: it implies a special sense of the ultimate value in existence of the act of comprehension. Socrates, when he said that the unexamined life is not worth living, struck the essence of it. We can hear the voices of various intellectuals in history repeating their awareness of this feeling, in accents suitable to time, place, and culture. "The proper function of the human race, taken in the aggregate," wrote Dante in *De Monarchid*, "is to actualize continually the entire capacity possible to the intellect, primarily in speculation, then through its extension and for its sake, secondarily in action." The noblest thing, and the closest possible to divinity, is thus the act of knowing. It is only a somewhat more secular and activist version of the same commitment which we hear in the first sentence of Locke's *Essay Concerning Human Understanding:* "It is the *understanding* that sets man above the rest of sensible beings, and gives him all the advantage and dominion which he has over them." Hawthorne, in a passage near the end of *The Blithedale Romance,* observes that Nature's highest purpose for man is "that of conscious intellectual life and sensibility." Finally, in our own time André Malraux puts the question in one of his novels: "How can one make the best of one's life?" and answers: "By converting as wide a range of experience as possible into conscious thought."

Intellectualism, though by no means confined to doubters, is often the sole piety of the skeptic. Some years ago a colleague asked me to read a brief essay he had written for students going on to do advanced work in his field. Its ostensible purpose was to show how the life of the mind could be cultivated within the framework of his own discipline, but its effect was to give an intensely personal expression to his dedication to intellectual work. Although it was written by a corrosively skeptical mind, I felt that I was reading a piece of devotional literature in some ways comparable to Richard Steele's *The Tradesman's Calling* or Cotton Mather's *Essays to Do Good,* for in it the intellectual task had been conceived as a *calling,* much in the fashion of the old Protestant writers. His work was undertaken as a kind of devotional exercise, a personal discipline, and to think of it in this fashion was possible because it was more than merely workmanlike and professional: it was work at thinking, work done supposedly in the service of truth. The intellectual life has here taken on a kind of primary moral significance. It is this aspect of the intellectual's feeling about ideas that I call his piety. The intellectual is *engagé*—he is pledged, committed, enlisted. What everyone else is willing to admit, namely that ideas and abstractions are of signal importance in human life, he imperatively feels.

Of course what is involved is more than a purely personal discipline and more than the life of contemplation and understanding itself. For the life of thought, even though it may be regarded as the highest form of human activity, is also a medium through which other values are refined, reasserted, and realized in the human community. Collectively, intellectuals have often tried to serve as the moral antennae of the race, anticipating and if possible clarifying fundamental moral issues before these have forced themselves upon the public consciousness. The thinker feels that he ought to be the special custodian of values like reason and justice which are related to his own search for truth, and at times he strikes out passionately as a public figure because his very identity seems to be threatened by some gross abuse. One thinks here of Voltaire defending the Calas family, of Zola speaking out for Dreyfus, of the American intellectuals outraged at the trial of Sacco and Vanzetti.

It would be unfortunate if intellectuals were alone in their concern for these values, and it is true that their enthusiasm has at times miscarried. But it is also true that intellectuals are properly more responsive to such values than others; and it is the historic glory of the intellectual class of the West in modern times that, of all the classes which could be called in any sense privileged, it has shown the largest and most consistent concern for the well-being of the classes which lie below it in the social scale. Behind the intellectual's feeling of commitment is the belief that in some measure the world should be made responsive to his capacity for rationality, his passion for justice and order: out of this conviction arises much of his value to mankind and, equally, much of his ability to do mischief.

The Social Value   8
of the College Bred
William James

Of what use is a college training? We who have had it seldom hear the question raised; we might be a little nonplussed to answer it offhand. A certain amount of meditation has brought me to this as the pithiest reply which I myself can give: The best claim that a college education can possibly make on your respect, the best thing it can aspire to accomplish for you, is this: that it should *help you to know a good man when you see him*. This is as true of women's as of men's colleges; but that it is neither a joke nor a one-sided abstraction I shall now endeavor to show.

What talk do we commonly hear about the contrast between college education and the education which business or technical or professional schools confer? The college education is called higher because it is supposed to be so general and so disinterested. At the "schools" you get a relatively

Essay 13, "Social Value of the College-Bred," with footnote omitted, in *Memories and Studies*, by William James, London, Longmans, 1911.

narrow practical skill, you are told, whereas the "colleges" give you the more liberal culture, the broader outlook, the historical perspective, the philosophic atmosphere, or something which phrases of that sort try to express. You are made into an efficient instrument for doing a definite thing, you hear, at the schools; but, apart from that, you may remain a crude and smoky kind of petroleum, incapable of spreading light. The universities and colleges, on the other hand, although they may leave you less efficient for this or that practical task, suffuse your whole mentality with something more important than skill. They redeem you, make you well-bred; they make "good company" of you mentally. If they find you with a naturally boorish or caddish mind, they cannot leave you so, as a technical school may leave you. This, at least, is pretended; this is what we hear among college-trained people when they compare their education with every other sort. Now, exactly how much does this signify?

It is certain, to begin with, that the narrowest trade or professional training does something more for a man than to make a skillful practical tool of him—it makes him also a judge of other men's skill. Whether his trade be pleading at the bar or surgery or plastering or plumbing, it develops a critical sense in him for that sort of occupation. He understands the difference between second-rate and first-rate work in his whole branch of industry; he gets to know a good job in his own line as soon as he sees it; and getting to know this in his own line, he gets a faint sense of what good work may mean anyhow, that may, if circumstances favor, spread into his judgments elsewhere. Sound work, clean work, finished work: feeble work, slack work, sham work—these words express an identical contrast in many different departments of activity. In so far forth, then, even the humblest manual trade may beget in one a certain small degree of power to judge of good work generally.

Now, what is supposed to be the line of us who have the higher college training? Is there any broader line—since our education claims primarily not to be "narrow"—in which we also are made good judges between what is first-rate and what is second-rate only? What is especially taught in the colleges has long been known by the name of the "humanities," and these are often identified with Greek and Latin. But it is only as literature, not as languages, that Greek and Latin have any general humanity-value; so that in a broad sense the humanities mean literature primarily, and in a still broader sense the study of masterpieces in almost any field of human endeavor. Literature keeps the primacy; for it not only *consists* of masterpieces, but is largely *about* masterpieces, being little more than an appreciative chronicle of human master-strokes, so far as it takes the form of criticism and history. You can give humanistic value to almost anything by teaching it historically. Geology, economics, mechanics, are humanities when taught with reference to the successive achievements of the geniuses to which these sciences owe their being. Not taught thus literature remains grammar, art a catalogue, history a list of dates, and natural science a sheet of formulas and weights and measures.

The sifting of human creations!—nothing less than this is what we ought to mean by the humanities. Essentially this means biography; what our colleges should teach is, therefore, biographical history, that not of politics merely, but of anything and everything so far as human efforts and conquests are factors that have played their part. Studying in this way, we learn what types of activity have stood the test of time; we acquire standards of the excellent and durable. All our arts and sciences and institutions are but so many quests of perfection on the part of men; and when we see how diverse the types of excellence may be, how various the tests, how flexible the adaptations, we gain a richer sense of what the terms "better" and "worse" may signify in general. Our critical sensibilities grow both more acute and less fanatical. We sympathize with men's mistakes even in the act of penetrating them; we feel the pathos of lost causes and misguided epochs even while we applaud what overcame them.

Such words are vague and such ideas are inadequate, but their meaning is unmistakable. What the colleges—teaching humanities by examples which may be special, but which must be typical and pregnant—should at least try to give us, is a general sense of what, under various disguises, *superiority* has always signified and may still signify. The feeling for a good human job anywhere, the admiration of the really admirable, the disesteem of what is cheap and trashy and impermanent—this is what we call the critical sense, the sense for ideal values. It is the better part of what men know as wisdom. Some of us are wise in this way naturally and by genius; some of us never become so. But to have spent one's youth at college, in contact with the choice and rare and precious, and yet still to be a blind prig or vulgarian, unable to scent out human excellence or to divine it amid its accidents, to know it only when ticketed and labelled and forced on us by others, this indeed should be accounted the very calamity and shipwreck of a higher education.

The sense for human superiority ought, then, to be considered our line, as boring subways is the engineer's line and the surgeon's is appendicitis. Our colleges ought to have lit up in us a lasting relish for the better kind of man, a loss of appetite for mediocrities, and a disgust for cheapjacks. We ought to smell, as it were, the difference of quality in men and their proposals when we enter the world of affairs about us. Expertness in this might well atone for some of our awkwardness at accounts, for some of our ignorance of dynamos. The best claim we can make for the higher education, the best single phrase in which we can tell what it ought to do for us, is, then, exactly what I said: it should enable us to *know a good man when we see him.*

That the phrase is anything but an empty epigram follows from the fact that if you ask in what line it is most important that a democracy like ours should have its sons and daughters skillful, you see that it is this line more than any other. "The people in their wisdom"—this is the kind of wisdom most needed by the people. Democracy is on its trial, and no one knows how it will stand the ordeal. Abounding about us are pessimistic prophets. Fickleness and violence used to be, but are no longer, the vices which they charge to democracy. What its critics now affirm is that its preferences are inveterately for the inferior. So it was in the beginning, they say, and so it will be world without end. Vulgarity enthroned and institutionalized, elbowing everything superior from the highway, this, they tell us, is our irremediable destiny; and the picture-papers of the European continent are already drawing Uncle Sam with the hog instead of the eagle for his heraldic emblem. The privileged aristocracies of the foretime, with all their iniquities, did at least preserve some taste for higher human quality, and honor certain forms of refinement by their enduring traditions. But when democracy is sovereign its doubters say, nobility will form a sort of invisible church, and sincerity and refinement, stripped of honor, precedence, and favor, will have to vegetate on sufferance in private corners. They will have no general influence. They will be harmless eccentricities.

Now, who can be absolutely certain that this may not be the career of democracy? Nothing future is quite secure; states enough have inwardly rotted; and democracy as a whole may undergo self-poisoning. But, on the other hand, democracy is a kind of religion, and we are bound not to admit its failure. Faiths and utopias are the noblest exercise of human reason, and no one with a spark of reason in him will sit down fatalistically before the croaker's picture. The best of us are filled with the contrary vision of a democracy stumbling through every error till its institutions glow with justice and its customs shine with beauty. Our better men *shall* show the way and we *shall* follow them; so we are brought round again to the mission of the higher education in helping us to know the better kind of man whenever we see him.

The notion that a people can run itself and its affairs anonymously is now well known to be the silliest of absurdities. Mankind does nothing save through initiatives on the part of inventors, great or small, and imitation by the rest of us—these are the sole factors active in human progress. Individuals of genius show the way, and set the patterns, which common people then adopt and follow. *The rivalry of the patterns is the history of the world.* Our democratic problem thus is statable in ultra-simple terms: Who are the kind of men from whom our majorities shall take their cue? Whom shall they treat as rightful leaders? We and our leaders are the x and the y of the equation here; all other historic circumstances, be they economical, political, or intellectual, are only the background of occasion on which the living drama works itself out between us.

In this very simple way does the value of our educated class define itself: we more than others should be able to divine the worthier and better leaders. The terms here are monstrously simplified, of course, but such a bird's-eye view lets us immediately take our bearings. In our democracy, where everything else is so shifting, we alumni and alumnae of the colleges are the only permanent presence that corresponds to the aristocracy in older countries. We have continuous traditions, as they have; our motto, too, is *noblesse oblige*; and, unlike them, we stand for ideal interests solely, for we have no corporate selfishness and wield no powers of corruption. We ought to have our own class-consciousness. "*Les Intellectuels!*" What prouder club-name could there be than this one, used ironically by the party of "redblood," the party of every stupid prejudice and passion, during the anti-Dreyfus craze, to satirize the men in France who still retained some critical sense and judgment! Critical sense, it has to be confessed, is not an exciting term, hardly a banner to carry in processions. Affections for old habit, currents of self-interest, and gales of passion are the forces that keep the human ship moving: and the pressure of the judicious pilot's hand upon the tiller is a relatively insignificant energy. But the affections, passions, and interests are shifting, successive, and distraught; they blow in alternation while the pilot's hand is steadfast. He knows the compass, and, with all the leeways he is obliged to tack toward, he always makes some headway. A small force, if it never lets up, will accumulate effects more considerable than those of much greater forces if these work inconsistently. The ceaseless whisper of the more permanent ideals, the steady tug of truth and justice, give them but time, *must* warp the world in their direction.

This bird's-eye view of the general steering function of the college-bred amid the driftings of democracy ought to help us to a wider vision of what our colleges themselves should aim at. If we are to be the yeast-cake for democracy's dough, if we are to make it rise with culture's preferences, we must see to it that culture spreads broad sails. We must shake the old double reefs out of the canvas into the wind and sunshine, and let in every modern subject, sure that any subject will prove humanistic, if its setting be kept only wide enough.

Stevenson says somewhere to his readers: "You think you are just making this bargain, but you are really laying down a link in the policy of mankind." Well, your technical school should enable you to make your bargain splendidly; but your college should show you just the place of that kind of bargain —a pretty poor place, possibly—in the whole policy of mankind. That is the kind of liberal outlook, of perspective, of atmosphere, which should surround every subject as a college deals with it.

We of the colleges must eradicate a curious notion which numbers of good people have about such ancient seats of learning as Harvard. To many ignorant outsiders, that name suggests little more than a kind of sterilized conceit and incapacity for being pleased. In Edith Wyatt's exquisite book of Chicago sketches called *Every One his Own Way* there is a couple who stand for culture in the sense of exclusiveness, Richard Elliot and his feminine counterpart—feeble caricatures of mankind, unable to know any good thing when they see it, incapable of enjoyment unless a printed label gives them leave. Possibly this type of culture may exist near Cambridge and Boston. There may be specimens there, for priggishness is just like painter's colic or any other trade-disease. But every good college makes its students immune against this malady, of which the microbe haunts the neighborhood of printed pages. It does so by its general tone being too hearty for the microbe's life. Real culture lives by sympathies and admirations, not by dislikes and disdains; under all misleading wrappings it pounces unerringly upon the human core. If a college, through the inferior human influences that have grown pregnant there, fails to catch the robuster tone, its failure is colossal, for its social function stops; democracy gives it a wide berth, turns toward it a deaf ear.

"Tone," to be sure, is a terribly vague word to use, but there is no other, and this whole meditation is over questions of tone. By their tone are all things human either lost or saved. If democracy is to be saved it must catch the higher, healthier tone. If we are to impress it with our preferences, we ourselves must use the proper tone, which we, in turn, must have caught from our own teachers. It all reverts in the end to the action of innumerable imitative individuals upon each other and to the question of whose tone has the highest spreading power. As a class, we college graduates should look to it that *ours* has spreading power. It ought to have the highest spreading power.

In our essential function of indicating the better men, we now have formidable competitors outside. *McClure's Magazine*, the *American Magazine*, *Collier's Weekly*, and in its fashion, the *World's Work*, constitute together a real popular university along this very line. It would be a pity if any future historian were to have to write words like these: "By the middle of the twentieth century the higher institutions of learning had lost all influence over public opinion in the United States. But the mission of raising the tone of democracy, which they had proved themselves so lamentably unfitted to exert, was assumed with rare enthusiasm and prosecuted with extraordinary skill and success by a new educational power; and for the clarification of their human sympathies and elevation of their human preferences, the people at large acquired the habit of resorting exclusively to the guidance of certain private literary adventures, commonly designated in the market by the affectionate name of ten cent magazines."

Must not we of the colleges see to it that no historian shall ever say anything like this? Vague as the phrase of knowing a good man when you see him may be, diffuse and indefinite as one must leave its application, is there any other formula that describes so well the result at which our institutions *ought* to aim? If they do that, they do the best thing conceivable. If they fail to do it, they fail in very deed. It surely is a fine synthetic formula. If our faculties and graduates could once collectively come to realize it as the great underlying purpose toward which they have always been more or less obscurely groping, a great clearness would be shed over many of their problems; and, as for their influence in the midst of our social system, it would embark upon a new career of strength.

College and the Alternatives   9
John W. Gardner

WHO SHOULD GO TO COLLEGE

All of the conflicting and confusing notions which Americans have concerning equality, excellence and the encouragement of talent may be observed with crystal clarity in the current discussions of "who should go to college." In the years ahead these discussions will become more heated. Pressure of enrollments will make it far harder to get into the better colleges, and there will be lively debate over who has a "right" to a college education.

A good deal of this debate will center around issues of quality versus quantity in education. Douglas Bush eloquently enunciated one extreme position in the phrase, "Education for all is education for none."

Arguments about quality in higher education tend to be heated and rather pointless. There are many reasons why such conversations become muddled, the foremost being that they so often degenerate into arguments over "elite" versus "mass" education. People who engage in these arguments are like the two washerwomen Sydney Smith observed leaning out of their back windows and quarreling with each other across the alley: "They could never agree," Smith said, "because they were arguing from different premises." In the case of arguments over "elite" versus "mass" education, I am convinced that both premises should be vacated, because behind the arguments is the assumption that a society must decide whether it wishes to educate a few people exceedingly well *or* to educate a great number of people rather badly.

This is an imaginary dilemma. It is possible to have excellence in education and at the same time to seek to educate everyone to the limit of his ability. A society such as ours has no choice but to seek the development of human potentialities at all levels. It takes more than an educated elite to run a complex, technological society. Every modern, industrialized society is learning that hard lesson.

The notion that so-called quality education and so-called mass education are mutually exclusive is woefully out of date. It would not have survived at all were there not a few remarkably archaic characters in our midst. We all know that some of the people calling most noisily for quality in education are those who were *never* reconciled to the widespread extension of educational opportunity. To such individuals there is something inherently vulgar about large numbers of people. At the other extreme are the fanatics who believe that the chief goal for higher education should be to get as many youngsters as possible—regardless of ability—into college classrooms. Such individuals regard quality as a concept smacking faintly of Louis XIV.

But neither extreme speaks for the American people, and neither expresses the true issues that pose themselves today. It would be fatal to allow ourselves to be tempted into an anachronistic debate. *We must seek excellence in a context of concern for all.* A democracy, no less than any other form of society, must foster excellence if it is to survive; and it should not allow the emotional scars of old battles to confuse it on this point.

Educating everyone up to the limit of his ability does not mean sending everyone to college. Part of any final answer to the college problem must be some revision of an altogether false emphasis which the American people are coming to place on college education. This false emphasis is the source of great difficulties for us. In Virginia they tell the story of the kindly Episcopal minister who was asked whether the Episcopal Church was the only path to salvation. The minister shook his head—a bit sadly, perhaps. "No, there are other paths," he said, and then added, "but no gentleman would choose them." Some of our attitudes toward college education verge dangerously on the same position.

There are some people who seem to favor almost limitless expansion of college attendance. One hears the phrase "everyone has a right to go to college." It is easy to dispose of this position in its extreme form. There are some youngsters whose mental deficiency is so severe that they cannot enter the first grade. There are a number of youngsters out of every hundred whose mental limitations make it impossible for them to get as far as junior high school. There are many more who can progress through high school only if they are placed in special programs which take into account their academic limitations. These "slow learners" could not complete high school if they were required to enroll in a college-preparatory curriculum.

It is true that some who fall in this group would not be there if it were not for social and economic handicaps. But for most of them, there is no convincing evidence that social handicaps are a major factor in their academic limitations. Children with severe or moderate intellectual limitations appear not infrequently in families which are able to give them every advantage, and in which the possibilities of treatment have been exhaustively explored. Such children can be helped by intelligent attention, but the hope that any major change can be accomplished in their academic limitations is usually doomed to disappointment.

With each higher grade an increasing number of youngsters find it difficult or impossible to keep up with the work. Some drop out. Some transfer to vocational or industrial arts programs. A great many never complete high school.

Presumably, college students should only be drawn from the group which is able to get through high school. So the question becomes: "Should all high school graduates go to college?" The answer most frequently heard is that "all should go to college who are qualified for it"—but what do we mean by *qualified?* Probably less than 1 per cent of the college-age population is qualified to attend the California Institute of Technology. There are other colleges where 10, 20, 40 or 60 per cent of college-age population is qualified to attend.

It would be possible to create institutions with standards so low that 90 per cent of the college-age population could qualify. In order to do so it would be necessary only to water down the curriculum and provide simpler subjects. Pushed to its extreme, the logic of this position would lead us to the establishment of institutions at about the intellectual level of summer camps. We could then include almost all of the population in these make-believe colleges.

Let us pursue this depressing thought. If it were certain that almost all of the eighteen- to twenty-two-year-old population could benefit greatly by full-time attendance at "colleges" of this sort, no one could reasonably object. But one must look with extreme skepticism upon the notion that all high school graduates can profit by continued formal schooling. There is no question that they can profit by continued *education.* But the character of this education will vary from one youngster to the next. Some will profit by continued book learning; others by some kind of vocational training; still others by learning on the job. Others may require other kinds of growth experiences.

Because college has gained extraordinary prestige, we are tempted to assume that the only useful learning and growth comes from attending such an institution, listening to professors talk from platforms, and reproducing required information on occasions called examinations. This is an extremely constricting notion. Even in the case of intellectually gifted individuals, it is a mistake to assume that the only kind of learning they can accomplish is in school. Many gifted individuals might be better off if they could be exposed to alternative growth experiences.

In the case of the youngster who is not very talented academically, forced continuance of education may simply prolong a situation in which he is doomed to failure. Many a youngster of low ability has been kept on pointlessly in a school which taught him no vocation, exposed him to continuous failure and then sent him out into the world with a record which convinced employers that he must forever afterward be limited to unskilled or semi-skilled work. This is not a sensible way to conserve human resources.

Properly understood, the college or university is the instrument of *one kind of further education of those whose capacities fit them for that kind of education.* It should not be regarded as the sole means of establishing one's human worth. It should not be seen as the unique key to happiness, self-respect and inner confidence.

We have all done our bit to foster these misconceptions. And the root of the difficulty is our bad habit of assuming that the only meaningful life is the "successful" life, defining success in terms of high personal attainment in the world's eyes. Today attendance at college has become virtually a prerequisite of high attainment in the world's eyes, so that it becomes, in the false value framework we have created, the only passport to a meaningful life. No wonder our colleges are crowded.

The crowding in our colleges is less regrettable than the confusion in our values. *Human dignity and worth should be assessed only in terms of those qualities of mind and spirit that are within the reach of every human being.*

This is not to say that we should not value achievement. We should value it exceedingly. It is simply to say that achievement should not be confused with human worth. Our recognition of the dignity and worth of the individual is based upon moral imperatives and should be of universal application. In other words, everyone has a "right" to that recognition. Being a college graduate involves qualities of mind which can never be universally possessed. Everyone does not have a right to be a college graduate, any more than everyone has a right to run a four-minute mile.

What we are really seeking is what James Conant had in mind when he said that the American people are concerned not only for equality of opportunity but for equality of respect. Every human being wishes to be respected regardless of his ability, and in moral terms we are bound to grant him that right. The more we allow the impression to get abroad that only the college man or woman is worthy of respect in our society, the more we contribute to a fatal confusion which works to the injury of all concerned. If we make the confusing assumption that college is the sole cradle of human dignity, need we be surprised that every citizen demands to be rocked in that cradle?

THE NEED FOR INSTITUTIONAL DIVERSITY

But a scaling down of our emphasis on college education is only part of the answer. Another important part of the answer must be a greatly increased emphasis upon individual differences, upon many kinds of talent, upon the immensely varied ways in which individual potentialities may be realized.

If we develop such an indomitable concern for individual differences, we will learn to laugh at the assumption that a college education is the only avenue to human dignity and social worth. We would educate some young-sters by sending them on to college. We would educate others in other ways. We would develop an enormous variety of patterns to fit the enormous variety of individuals. And no pattern would be regarded as socially superior or involving greater human dignity than any other pattern.

But the plain fact is that college education is firmly associated in the public mind with personal advancement, upward social mobility, market value and self-esteem. And if enough of the American people believe that one must attend college in order to be accorded respect and confidence, then the very unanimity of opinion makes the generalization true.

It is particularly true, unfortunately, in the crude categories of the employment file. A cynical friend of mine said recently, "Everyone has two personalities these days—the one under his hat and the one in his employment file. The latter is the most important—and it is made up of primitive categories. Have you held too many jobs? (Never mind why.) Did you go to a good college? (Never mind if you were the campus beachcomber.) Does your job record show a steady rise in responsibilities? (Never mind if you played politics every inch of the way.)"

If we are to do justice to individual differences, if we are to provide suitable education for each of the young men and women who crowd into our colleges and universities, then we must cultivate diversity in our higher educational system to correspond to the diversity of the clientele. There is no other way to handle within one system the enormously disparate human capacities, levels of preparedness and motivations which flow into our colleges and universities.

But we cannot hope to create or to maintain such diversity unless we honor the various aspects of that diversity. Each of the different kinds of institutions has a significant part to play in creating the total pattern, and each should be allowed to play its role with honor and recognition.

We do not want all institutions to be alike. We want institutions to develop their individualities and to keep those individualities. None must be ashamed of its distinctive features so long as it is doing something that contributes importantly to the total pattern, and so long as it is striving for excellence in performance. The highly selective, small liberal arts college should not be afraid to remain small. The large urban institution should not be ashamed that it is large. The technical institute should not be apologetic about being a technical institute. Each institution should pride itself on the role that it has chosen to play and on the special contribution which it brings to the total pattern of American higher education.

Such diversity is the only possible answer to the fact of individual differences in ability and aspirations. And furthermore, it is the only means of achieving *quality* within a framework of quantity. For we must not forget the primacy of our concern for excellence. We must have diversity, but we must also expect that every institution which makes up that diversity will be striving, in its own way, for excellence. This may require a new way of thinking about excellence in higher education—a conception that would be applicable in terms of the objectives of the institution. As things now stand, the word *excellence* is all too often reserved for the dozen or two dozen institutions which stand at the very zenith of our higher education in terms of faculty distinction, selectivity of students and difficulty of curriculum. In these terms it is simply impossible to speak of a junior college, for example, as excellent. Yet sensible men can easily conceive of excellence in a junior college.

The traditionalist might say, "Of course! Let Princeton create a junior college and one would have an institution of unquestionable excellence!" That may be correct, but it may also lead us down precisely the wrong path. If Princeton Junior College were excellent, it might not be excellent in the most important way that a community college can be excellent. It might simply be a truncated version of Princeton. A comparably meaningless result would be achieved if General Motors tried to add to its line of low-priced cars by marketing the front half of a Cadillac.

We shall have to be more flexible than that in our conception of excellence. We must develop a point of view that permits each kind of institution to achieve excellence *in terms of its own objectives.*

In higher education as in everything else there is no excellent performance without high morale. No morale, no excellence! And in a great many of our colleges and universities the most stubborn enemy of high morale has been a kind of hopelessness on the part of both administration and faculty—hopelessness about ever achieving distinction as an institution. Not only are such attitudes a corrosive influence on morale, they make it virtually certain that the institution will never achieve even that kind of excellence which is within its reach. For there *is* a kind of excellence within the reach of every institution.

In short, we reject the notion that excellence is something that can only be experienced in the most rarefied strata of higher education. It may be experienced at every level and in every serious kind of higher education. And not only may it be experienced everywhere, but we must *demand* it everywhere. We must ask for excellence in every form which higher education takes. We should not ask it lightly or amiably or good naturedly; we should demand it vigorously and insistently. We should assert that a stubborn striving for excellence is the price of admission to reputable educational circles, and that those institutions not characterized by this striving are the slatterns of higher education.

We must make the same challenging demands of students. We must never make the insolent and degrading assumption that young people unfitted for the most demanding fields of intellectual endeavor are incapable of rigorous attention to *some sort of standards*. It is an appalling error to assume —as some of our institutions seem to have assumed—that young men and women incapable of the highest standards of intellectual excellence are incapable of any standards whatsoever, and can properly be subjected to shoddy, slovenly and trashy educational fare. College should be a demanding as well as an enriching experience—demanding for the brilliant youngster at a high level of expectation and for the less brilliant at a more modest level.

It is no sin to let average as well as brilliant youngsters into college. It *is* a sin to let any substantial portion of them—average or brilliant—drift through college without effort, without growth and without a goal. That is the real scandal in many of our institutions.

Though we must make enormous concessions to individual differences in aptitude, we may properly expect that every form of education be such as to stretch the individual to the utmost of his potentialities. And we must expect each student to strive for excellence in terms of the kind of excellence that is within his reach. Here again we must recognize that there may be excellence or shoddiness in every line of human endeavor. We must learn to honor excellence (indeed to *demand* it) in every socially accepted human activity, however humble the activity, and to scorn shoddiness, however exalted the activity. As I said in another connection: "An excellent plumber is infinitely more admirable than an incompetent philosopher. The society which scorns excellence in plumbing because plumbing is a humble activity and tolerates shoddiness in philosophy because it is an exalted activity will have neither good plumbing nor good philosophy. Neither its pipes nor its theories will hold water."

OPPORTUNITIES OTHER THAN COLLEGE

Not long ago the mother of two teen-age boys came to me for advice. "Roger made a fine record in high school," she explained, "and when he was a senior we had exciting discussions of all the colleges he was interested in. Now Bobby comes along with terrible grades, and when the question of his future arises a silence descends on the dinner table. It breaks my heart!"

I knew something about Bobby's scholastic limitations, which were notable, and I asked warily what I might do to help.

"The high school principal says that with his record no college will take him," she said, "and that if one did take him he wouldn't last. I can't reconcile myself to that!"

"Have you discussed any possibilities other than college?" I asked.

She shook her head. "His father says he can get him a job driving a delivery truck. But I think he just says that to jar Bobby."

It took some time for me to explain all that I thought was deplorable in her attitude and that of her husband. Parents of academically limited children should not act as though any outcome other than college is a fate worse than death. By doing so they rule out of discussion a world of significant possibilities; and the failure to think constructively about those possibilities is a disfavor to the young person.

The great prestige which college education has achieved in our society leads us to assume—quite incorrectly—that it is the only form of continued learning after high school. The assumption is that the young person either goes to college and continues to learn, or goes to work and stops learning. Most parents, deans, counselors—indeed the young people themselves—have given little or no thought to the many ways of learning and growing which do not involve college. The result is that the path to college appears to be the only exciting possibility, the only path to self-development. No wonder many who lack the qualifications for college insist on having a try at it.

The young person who does not go to college should look forward to just as active a period of growth and learning in the post-high school years as does the college youngster.

The nature of this continued learning will depend on the young person's interests and capacities. The bright youngster who has stayed out of college for financial reasons will require a different kind of program from that of the youngster who stayed out for lack of ability.

The majority of young people—at least, of boys—who terminate their education short of college do so because they lack academic ability. Most have had unrewarding experiences in the classroom and have a negative attitude toward anything labeled "learning" or "education." Even if they are not bitter about their school experiences, they are likely to feel that, having tried that path and failed, their salvation lies elsewhere. *What they must recognize is that there are many kinds of further learning outside formal high school and college programs. The fact that they have not succeeded in high school simply means that they must continue their learning in other kinds of situations.*

The opportunities for further education of boys and girls who leave the formal educational system are numerous and varied.

Training programs within industrial corporations have expanded enormously and constitute a respectable proportion of all education today. Apprenticeship systems are not as universal as they used to be in the skilled crafts or trades, but they are still in operation in every major industry, and offer wide opportunities for the ambitious youngster. (He must be warned, however, that in some of the older crafts and trades entry is jealously guarded; indeed in some it is held within family lines as a hereditary right.)

A few labor unions have impressive educational programs. The International Ladies Garment Workers Union, for example, conducts European tours, sponsors lecture series and offers a wide variety of courses.

Various branches of government offer jobs to high school graduates which involve an opportunity to learn while working. The Armed Services offer training in a great many occupational specialties.

Night classes in the public schools are breaking all attendance records; and more than one quarter of present attendance is in trade courses for semi-skilled or unskilled workers. These courses offer a surprising range of interesting opportunities for the young person who wishes to test his aptitudes and to develop various skills.

There also exist, in the amazingly variegated pattern of American education, many special schools—art schools, music schools, nursing schools and the like—which should be considered by the young person not going on to college. The boy who wishes to become an X-ray technician and the girl who wishes to be a practical nurse, for example, will find a great many schools throughout the country at which they may receive training.

Correspondence study offers the most flexible opportunities for study beyond high school, but the young people who do not go on to college usually have little enthusiasm for paper-and-pencil work, and that is what correspondence amounts to. For those who can overcome this handicap, there is an open door to almost any conceivable subject. One can study accountancy or blueprint reading, creative writing or diesel mechanics, watch repairing or dressmaking, fingerprinting or foreign languages, music or petroleum technology. Almost the only limits are one's own interest and ability.

Educational opportunities on radio and television continue to expand. In certain parts of the country the high school graduate can study a considerable range of subjects through this medium—e.g., salesmanship, typing, composition, reading improvement and foreign languages.

Finally, jobs themselves are a form of education. Today most young people have a wide choice of jobs. They should look at the array of jobs available not simply from the standpoint of money and convenience but from the standpoint of their own further growth. If the young man is willing to think hard about his own abilities and interests, and then to look at available jobs as opportunities for self-development, he can look forward to years of learning and growth at least as rewarding as anything a college student might experience.

The possibilities reviewed here are by no means exhaustive, but they suggest the diverse paths open to the noncollege student. Some youngsters will want to get as far away as possible from "book learning" and some will not. Some will want vocational education and others may wish to continue their general education. Some will shun anything labeled a "school" or "course." But all should somehow continue learning.

In order to help young people in this direction, the following steps are essential:

1. We must make available to young people far more information than they now have on post-high school opportunities other than college.

2. Parents, teachers and high school counselors must recognize that if the youngster who is not going to college is to continue his growth and learning he must receive as much sagacious help and counsel as a college-bound student.

3. We must do what we can to alter the negative attitude toward education held by many youngsters who fail to go on to college. They must understand that they have been exposed to only one kind of learning experi-

ence and that the failures and frustrations encountered in school are not necessarily predictive of failure in every other kind of learning.

4. We must enable the young person to understand that his stature as an individual and his value as a member of society depend upon continued learning—not just for four years or a decade, but throughout life.

MISEDUCATION

Questionable Approaches to the Humanities

10

Joseph A. Mazzeo

Traditionally, humanists have maintained that their learning ultimately led to dominion over the self, however remote some of their pursuits might seem to be from this purpose. And it is doubtless a diffuse sense of this intention that has prompted educators, legislators, and even businessmen and generals to make sympathetic statements about the importance of humanistic education. Such support is welcome, of course. Nevertheless, even at the risk of discouraging some of our well-wishers, would it not be well to look at the major defects in humanistic learning in our time before leaping to its support? Like Francis Bacon, we might think of these defects as illnesses; some, serious and acute "diseases of learning," and others, "peccant humours," milder if equally difficult to cure. Before diagnosing the diseases of learning I will turn first to the "peccant humours," of which I discover about five.

The first is the purveying of some obscure form of cultural salvation in packages of one hundred or so "great books," read in chronological sequence, with or without a "syntopicon," and from a vantage point unencumbered by the results of scholarship. This is in essence no different from the educational principles governing Bible colleges, only the number of books is larger. The so-called "great conversation" these books are supposed to be having with one another takes place in a timeless vacuum, an unhistorical void, with no sense of the specific time and place in which the books were written. The classics, in this view, are really transcendental books and, paradoxically, the attempt to read them as if they were completely timeless leads often enough to reading them in much the same way as a fundamentalist reads the Bible.

Another "peccant humour" much in evidence is the assumption that the cultural tradition of Western civilization is really a seamless garment. I have been struck by the impression so many students carry away from the humani-

From "In Defense of Discontent, or, the Unfitting of the Student," by Joseph A. Mazzeo, *The Columbia University Forum*, Fall 1965, pp. 38–41. Reprinted by permission of *The Columbia University Forum* and Joseph A. Mazzeo.

ties course at Columbia that the "great conversation" is finally an amicable one. They can grow enthusiastic indifferently over Lucretius or St. Augustine, Dante or Spinoza, admire Christ or Socrates with little sense that certain ideas and values exclude each other, that utterly different acts of thought and imagination are required to understand Voltaire on the one hand and Shakespeare on the other; that, in short, they should make choices. Such catholicity of taste is so thoughtless that one is relieved to turn to Dr. Johnson's absurd attack on Milton's *Lycidas,* if only to find a man who did not like everything even if other people thought it was great.

There is a related assumption perhaps more common among nonhumanists than among humanists: that the reading and study of classics of literature and thought is really incremental, at least in some simple sense of the word. Humanistic subjects are indeed graduated, but not entirely in the sense that new information, presupposing previous knowledge, is introduced at each step. The true distinction between an elementary and an advanced course in Shakespeare is that broader experience, taste, judgment and erudition are (or should be) brought to bear on many of the same texts in a *qualitatively* different way.

A third "peccant humour" has beset humanists for a long time, and that is the assumption that the function of the study of the humanities is to make "good citizens." (To be sure, this notion has a distinguished historical precedent; the Renaissance humanist, in fact, wished to make men of the world, able citizens, and he was the first in modern times to voice the concept of a humanistic training as something distinct from, almost antithetical to, a scientific or professional one. But this distinction, however well-intentioned and plausible, has not turned out to be an unmixed blessing. It has fostered the notion that humane studies are somehow "useless" or that scientific and professional subjects are necessarily illiberal.) As A. J. P. Taylor, the English historian, recently pointed out, the assumption of "good citizenship" has validity only as it rests on the honest conviction that our society is either perfect or well on the road to perfection. Who are the good citizens among our students? The freedom rider who engages in civil disobedience? The Quaker who wants to join the Peace Corps and works to ban the bomb? I think of some of my students, and the more I think the less meaning the phrase "good citizen" has.

The notion of humanistic study fostering something vaguely called good citizenship is closely related to a fourth current ailment: the notion of the University simply as serving the community. A recent annual report written by the president of one of the most important universities in America defined his university in effect as a massive replacement depot: when doctors, lawyers, teachers and experts of one kind or another die in the front lines of their expertise, it sends out new replacements! There is a further development to this theme. If good citizenship is a "good thing," then we should make good citizens faster and serve more and more community needs. Therefore let us teach more and more subjects to more and more people faster and faster. This is "progressive" education with a vengeance. But if we place social utility above the concern for truth, we are in danger of destroying the very possibility of developing the concern for truth in our classrooms by a process of acceleration that inevitably substitutes information for knowledge, and something called "research" for inquiry. In trying to accelerate what cannot be accelerated we are going to destroy the "seed time" the young require to grow and the leisure the scholar needs to work. And I don't mean "free time" when I refer to leisure. I mean what the Romans called *otium*, an atmosphere in which there is time to generate unforced insight and in which fresh thought distills itself from reflection upon experience and from unhurried study. As long as our universities will have to expand, and as long as degrees remain licenses for jobs, the preservation of *otium* will become even more of a problem than it is now. At present we seem willing to turn our universities into processing plants for experts and good citizens, institutions in which the rhythms of the machine replace those of life.

The fifth "peccant humour" is the latest in the sub-intellectual versions of the purpose of humanistic study: the psychotherapeutic vision of the humanities. An interesting history of education could be written in terms of the different kinds of groups that have tried to diminish intellectual rigor and nullify intellectual failure. Among them we might well find clergymen armed with sermons and parents armed with tears (I leave out of consideration the fanatically ignorant and the envious), all pleading against Minerva in the interests of some higher god. We now confront the votaries of Aesculapius who suggest that the humanities should be the vehicle of psychic health. As I understand this point of view, the humanities should be "kinder" than other subjects, say physics or medicine, or "wiser"; they should somehow "enrich our lives" and make us "creative."

Now I will not for one moment deny that the study of a great subject may enhance a student's life. Nor that intellectual engagement with a great teacher and other students may not confer a lasting benefit on the personality. But so can a happy love affair, a successful marriage, an interesting job or good friends, and any of these might well perform a much greater therapeutic function than intellectual effort. It is now the time, I think, for us to argue that humanistic learning and the study of the classics should make you unhappy and discontented. Perhaps it should even make you maladjusted enough to unfit you for accepting some of the respectable options of our time. . . .

11   The Miseducated

Herbert Gold

What better career for a boy who seeks to unravel the meaning of our brief span on earth than that of philosopher? We all wonder darkly, in the forbidden hours of the night, punishing our parents and building a better world, with undefined terms. Soon, however, most of us learn to sleep soundly; or we take to pills or love-making; or we call ourselves insomniacs, not philosophers. A few attempt to define the terms.

There is no code number for the career of philosophy in school, the Army, or out beyond in real life. The man with a peculiar combination of melancholic, nostalgic, and reforming instincts stands at three possibilities early in his youth. He can choose to be a hero, an artist, or a philosopher. In olden times, war, say, or the need to clean out the old West, might make up his mind for him. The old West had been pretty well cleaned up by the time I reached a man's estate, and Gary Cooper could finish the job. Heroism was an untimely option. With much bureaucratic confusion I tried a bit of heroic war, got stuck in the machine, and returned to the hectic, Quonset campus of the GI Bill, burning to Know, Understand, and Convert. After a season of ferocious burrowing in books, I was ready to be a Teacher, which seemed a stern neighbor thing to Artist and Philosopher. I took on degrees, a Fulbright fellowship, a wife, a child, a head crammed with foolish questions and dogmatic answers despite the English school of linguistic analysis. I learned to smile, pardner, when I asked questions of philosophers trained at Oxford or Cambridge, but I asked them nonetheless. I signed petitions against McCarthy, wrote a novel, went on a treasure hunt, returned to my roots in the Middle West and stood rooted there, discussed the menace of the mass media, and had another child.

By stages not important here, I found myself teaching the Humanities at Wayne University in Detroit. I am now going to report a succession of classroom events which, retrospectively, seems to have determined my abandonment of formal dealing with this subject. The evidence does not, however, render any conclusion about education in the "Humanities" logically impregnable. It stands for a state of mind and is no substitute for formal argument. However, states of mind are important in this area of experience and metaexperience. However and however: it happens that most of the misty exalta-

"A Dog in Brooklyn, a Girl in Detroit: A Life Among the Humanities." Reprinted from *The Age of Happy Problems* by Herbert Gold. Copyright © 1952, 1954, 1957, 1958, 1959, 1960, 1961, 1962 by Herbert Gold and used with the permission of the publisher, The Dial Press, Inc.

tion of the blessed vocation of the teacher issues from the offices of deans, editors, and college presidents. The encounter with classroom reality has caused many teachers, like Abelard meeting the relatives of Eloise, to lose their bearings. Nevertheless this is a memoir, not a campaign, about a specific life in and out of the Humanities. Though I am not a great loss to the History of Everything in Culture, my own eagerness to teach is a loss to me.

1

News item of a few years ago. A young girl and her date are walking along a street in Brooklyn, New York. The girl notices that they are being followed by an enormous Great Dane. The dog is behaving peculiarly, showing its teeth and making restless movements. A moment later, sure enough, the dog, apparently maddened, leaps slavering upon the girl, who is borne to earth beneath its weight. With only an instant's hesitation, the boy jumps on the dog. Its fangs sunk first in one, then in the other, the dog causes the three of them to roll like beasts across the sidewalk.

A crowd gathers at a safe distance to watch. No one interferes. The becalmed curiosity of teevee viewers.

A few moments later a truckdriver, attracted by the crowd, pulls his vehicle over to the curb. This brave man is the only human being stirred personally enough to leave the role of passive spectator. Instantaneously analyzing the situation, he leaps into the struggle—*attacking and beating the boy.* He has naturally assumed that the dog must be protecting an innocent young lady from the unseemly actions of a juvenile delinquent.

I recounted this anecdote in the classroom in order to introduce a course which attempted a summary experience of Humanities 610 for a monumental nine credits. There were a number of points to be made about the passivity of the crowd ("don't get involved," "not my business") and the stereotypical reaction of the truck driver who had been raised to think of man's best friend as not another human being but a dog. In both cases, addicted to entertainment and clichés, the crowd and the trucker could not recognize what was actually happening before their eyes; they responded irrelevantly to the suffering of strangers; they were not a part of the maine. This led us to discussion of the notion of "community." In a closely knit society, the people on the street would have known the couple involved and felt a responsibility toward them. In a large city, everyone is a stranger. (Great art can give a sense of the brotherhood of men. Religion used to do this, too.) "Any questions?" I asked, expecting the authority of religion to be defended.

An eager hand shot up. Another. Another. Meditative bodies sprawled in their chairs. "Are all New Yorkers like that?" "Well, what can you do if there's a mad dog and you're not expecting it?" "Where does it say in what great book how you got to act in Brooklyn?"

I took note of humor in order to project humorousness. I found myself composing my face in the book of thought which teevee panelists use in order to project thinking. I discovered a serious point to elaborate—several. I mentioned consciousness and relevance and the undefined moral suggestion implied by the labor which produces any work or art or mind. A girl named Clotilda Adams asked me: "Why don't people try to get along better in this world?"

Somewhat digressively, we then discussed the nature of heroism, comparing the behavior of the boy and the truck driver. Both took extraordinary risks; why? We broke for cigarettes in the autumn air outside. Then, for fifty minutes more, we raised these interesting questions, referring forward to Plato, Aristotle, St. Thomas, Dostoevski, Tolstoi, William James, and De Gaulle; and then boy, dog, girl, truck driver, and crowd were left with me and the crowned ghosts of history in the deserted room while my students went on to Phys Ed, Music Appreciation, Sosh, and their other concerns. Having been the chief speaker, both dramatist and analyst, I was exalted by the lofty ideas floated up into the air around me. I was a little let down to return to our real life in which dog-eat-dog is man's closest pal. Fact. Neither glory nor pleasure nor power, and certainly not wisdom, provided the goal of my students. Not even wealth was the aim of most of them. They sought to make out, to do all right, more prideful than amorous in love, more security-hungry than covetous in status. I saw my duty as a teacher: Through the Humanities, to awaken them to the dream of mastery over the facts of our lives; I saw my duty plain: Through the Humanities, to lead them toward the exaltation of knowledge and the calm of control. I had a whole year in which to fulfill this obligation. It was a two-semester course.

Before she left the room, Clotilda Adams said, "You didn't answer my question." Fact.

Outside the university enclave of glass and grass, brick and trees, Detroit was agonizing in its last big year with the big cars. Automation, dispersion of factories, and imported automobiles were eroding a precarious confidence. Fear was spreading; soon the landlords would offer to decorate apartments and suffer the pain. Detroit remembered the war years with nostalgia. Brave days, endless hours, a three-shift clock, insufficient housing, men sleeping in the all-night, triple-feature movies on Woodward and Grand River. Though the area around the Greyhound and Trailways stations was still clotted with the hopeful out of the hill country of the midsouth and the driven from the deep South—they strolled diagonally across the boulevards, entire families holding hands—some people suspected what was already on its way down the road: twenty per cent unemployment in Detroit.

The semester continued. We churned through the great books. One could classify my students in three general groups, intelligent, mediocre, and stupid, allowing for the confusions of three general factors—background, capacity, and interest. This was how we classified the Humanities, too:

ancient, medieval, and modern. It made a lot of sense, and it made me itch, scratch, and tickle. Series of three-form nice distinctions. According to Jung and other authorities, they have certain mythic significances. The course was for nine credits. All the arts were touched upon. We obeyed Protagoras; man, just man, was our study. When I cited him—"Man is the measure of all things"—Clotilda Adams stirred uneasily in her seat: "By which Protagoras no doubt meant Woman, too," I assured her. She rested.

Now imagine the winter coming and enduring, with explosions of storm and exfoliations of gray slush, an engorged industrial sky overhead and sinus trouble all around. The air was full of acid and a purplish, spleeny winter mist. Most of Detroit, in Indian times before the first French trappers arrived, had been a swamp and below sea level. The swamp was still present, but invisible; city stretched out in all directions, crawling along the highways. Though Detroit was choked by a dense undergrowth of streets and buildings, irrigated only by superhighways, its work was done with frantic speed. The Rouge plant roared, deafened. The assembly lines clanked to the limit allowed by the UAW. The old Hudson factory lay empty, denuded, waiting to become a parking lot. Then the new models were being introduced! Buick! Pontiac! Dodge! Ford and Chevrolet! Ford impudently purchased a huge billboard faced toward the General Motors Building on Grand Boulevard. General Motors retaliated by offering free ginger ale to all comers, and a whole bottle of Vernor's to take home if you would only consent to test-drive the new Oldsmobile, the car with the. . . . I've forgotten what it had that year. All over town the automobile companies were holding revival meetings; hieratic salesmen preached to the converted and the hangers-back alike; lines at the loan companies stretched through the revolving doors and out onto the winter pavements. But many in those lines were trying to get additional financing on their last year's cars. The new models were an indifferent success despite all the uproar of display and Detroit's patriotic attention to it. Searchlights sliced up the heavens while the city lay under flu.

Teachers at Wayne University soon learn not to tease the American Automobile. Lèse Chrysler was a moral offense, an attack on the livelihood and the sanctity of the American garage. Detroit was a town in which men looked at hubcaps as men elsewhere have sometimes looked at ankles. The small foreign car found itself treated with a violent Halloween kidding-on-the-square, scratched, battered, and smeared (another Jungian series of three!). A passionate and sullen town, Detroit had no doubts about its proper business. All it doubted was everything else.

I often failed at inspiring my students to do the assigned reading. Many of them had part-time jobs in the automobile industry or its annexes. Even a Philosopher found it difficult to top the argument, "I couldn't read the book this week, I have to *work*," with its implied reproach for a scholar's leisure. But alas, many of these stricken proletarians drove freshly minted automobiles. They worked in order to keep up the payments, racing like laboratory mice around the cage of depreciation. Certain faculty deep thinkers, addicted to broad understanding of the problems of others, argued that these students were so poor they *had* to buy new cars in order to restore their confidence. The finance companies seemed to hear their most creative expressions, not me. Deep in that long Detroit winter, I had the task of going from the pre-Socratic mystics all the way to Sartre, for nine credits. Like an audio-visual monkey, I leaped from movie projector to records to slides, with concurrent deep labor in book and tablet. We read *The Brothers Karamazov*, but knowing the movie did not give credit. We studied "The Waste Land," and reading the footnotes did not suffice. We listened to Wanda Landowska play the harpsichord on records. We sat in the dark before a slide of Seurat's "La Grande Jatte" while I explained the importance of the measles of pointillisme to students who only wanted to see life clear and true, see it comfortably. Clotilda Adams said that this kind of painting hurt her eyes. She said that there was too much reading for one course—"piling it on. This isn't the only course we take." She said that she liked music, though. All Moses had to do was to bring the Law down the mountain to the children of Israel; I had to bring it pleasingly.

We made exegeses. I flatly turned down the request of a dean that I take attendance. As a statesmanlike compromise, I tested regularly for content and understanding.

Then, on a certain morning, I handed back some quiz papers at the beginning of class. Out on the street, a main thoroughfare through town, it was snowing; this was one of those magical days of late winter snowfall— pale, cold, clean, and the entire city momentarily muffled by the silence of snow. The room hissed with steam heat; a smell of galoshes and mackinaws arose from the class. "Let us not discuss the test—let us rise above grades. Let us try to consider nihilism as a byproduct of the Romantic revival—" I had just begun my lecture when an odd clashing, lumping noise occurred on Cass Avenue. "Eliot's later work, including 'The Four Quartets,' which we will not discuss here. . . ."

But I was interrupted by a deep sigh from the class. A product of nihilism and the romantic revival? No. It was the strange tragic sigh of horror and satisfaction. Out in the street, beyond the window against which I stood, a skidding truck had sideswiped a taxi. The truckdriver had parked and gone into a drugstore. The cab was mashed like a cruller. From the door, the driver had emerged, stumbling drunkenly on the icy road, holding his head. There was blood on his head. There was blood on his hands. He clutched his temples. The lines of two-way traffic, moving very slowly in the snow and ice, carefully avoided hitting him. There were streaks of perforated and patterned snow, frothed up by tires. He was like an island around which the sea of traffic undulated in slow waves; but he was an island that moved in the sea and held hands to head. He slid and stumbled back and forth, around and about his cab in the middle of the wide street. He was in confusion, in shock. Even at this distance I could see blood on the new-fallen snow. Drivers turned their heads upon him like angry Halloween masks, but did not get involved. Snow spit at his feet.

No one in the class moved. The large window through which we gazed was like a screen, with the volume turned down by habit, by snow, by a faulty tube. As the teacher, my authority took precedence. I ran out to lead the cab driver into the building. An elderly couple sat huddled in the car, staring at the smashed door, afraid to come out the other. They said they were unhurt.

I laid the man down on the floor. He was bleeding from the head and his face was a peculiar purplish color, with a stubble of beard like that of a dead man. There was a neat prick in his forehead where the union button in his cap had been driven into the skin. I sent a student to call for an ambulance. The cab driver's color was like that of the bruised industrial sky. "You be okay till the ambulance——?"

Foolish question. No alternative. No answer.

We waited. The class was restless. When they weren't listening to me, or talking themselves, or smudging blue books in an exam, they did not know what to do in this room devoted to the specialized absorption of ideas. Silence. Scraping of feet, crisping of paper. We watched the slow-motion traffic on the street outside.

The cab driver moved once in a rush, turning over face down against the floor, with such force that I thought he might break his nose. Then slowly, painfully, as if in a dream, he turned back and lay staring at the ceiling. His woolen lumberjacket soaked up the blood trickling from one ear; the blood traveled up separated cilia of wool, which drew it in with a will of their own. There was a swaying, osmotic movement like love-making in the eager little wisps of wool. An astounded ring of Humanities 610 students watched, some still holding their returned quiz papers. One girl in particular, Clotilda Adams, watched him and me with her eyes brilliant, wet, and bulging, and her fist crumpling the paper. I tried by imagining it to force the ambulance through the chilled and snowfallen city. I saw it weaving around the injured who strutted with shock over ice and drift, its single red Cyclops' eye turning, the orderlies hunched over on benches, chewing gum and cursing the driver. The ambulance did not arrive. Clotilda Adams' eye had a thick, impenetrable sheen over it. She watched from the cab driver to me as if we were in some way linked. When would the authorities get there? When the medics? There must have been many accidents in town, and heart attacks, and fires with cases of smoke inhalation.

Before the ambulance arrived, the police were there. They came strolling into the classroom with their legs apart, as if they remembered ancestors who rode the plains. Their mouths were heavy in thought. They had noses like salamis, red and mottled with fat. They were angry at the weather, at the school, at the crowd, at me, and especially at the prostrate man at our feet. He gave them a means to the creative expression of pique. (Everyone needs an outlet.)

Now Clotilda Adams took a step backward, and I recall thinking this odd. She had been treading hard near the pool of blood about the cab driver, but when the cops strolled up, she drifted toward the outer edge of the group of students, with a sly look of caution in her downcast, sideways-cast eyes. Her hand still crisped at the returned exam paper. This sly, lid-fallen look did not do her justice. She was a hard little girl of the sort often thought to be passionate—skinny but well-breasted, a high hard rump with a narrow curve, a nervous mouth.

The two policemen stood over the body of the cab driver. They stared at him in the classic pose—one cop with a hand resting lightly on the butt of his gun and the other on his butt, the younger cop with lips so pouted that his breath made a snuffling sound in his nose. They both had head colds. Their Ford was pulled up on the snow-covered lawn outside, with raw mud-dled marks of tread in the soft dirt. When the snow melted, there would be wounded streaks in the grass. The cab driver closed his eyes under the finick-ing, distasteful examination. At last one spoke: "See your driver's license."

The cab driver made a clumsy gesture toward his pocket. The cop bent and went into the pocket. He flipped open the wallet, glanced briefly at the photographs and cash, glanced at me, and then began lipreading the license.

The cab driver was in a state of shock. There was a mixture of thin and thick blood on his clothes and messing the floor. "This man is badly hurt," I said. "Can't we get him to the hospital first?"

"This is only your *driver* license," the cop said slowly, having carefully read through Color of Hair: Brn, Color of Eyes: Brn, and checked each item with a stare at the man on the floor. "Let me see your chauffeur license."

"He's badly hurt," I said. "Get an ambulance."

"Teach," said the old cop, "you know your business? We know ours."

"It's on the way," said the other. "Didn't you call it yourself?"

"No, one of the students . . ." I said.

He grinned with his great victory. "So—don't you trust your pupils neither?"

Shame. I felt shame at this ridicule of my authority in the classroom. A professor is not a judge, a priest, or a sea captain; he does not have the right to perform marriages on the high seas of audio-visual aids and close reasoning. But he is more than an intercom between student and fact; he can be a stranger to love for his students, but not to a passion for his subject; he is a student himself; his pride is lively. The role partakes of a certain heft and control. There is power to make decisions, power to abstain, power to bewilder, promote, hold back, adjust, and give mercy; power, an investment of pride, a risk of shame.

Clotilda Adams, still clutching her exam, stared at me with loathing.

She watched me bested by the police. She barely glanced, and only contemptuously, at the man bleeding from the head on the floor. She moved slightly forward again in order to participate fully in an action which apparently had some important meaning for her. She had lost her fear of the police when she saw how we all stood with them. The limits were established.

The police were going through the cab driver's pockets. They took out a folding pocket knife and cast significant looks at it and at each other. It had a marbled plastic hilt, like a resort souvenir. It was attached to a key ring.

"Hey!" one said to the half-conscious man. "What's this knife for?"

"Where'd you get them keys?" the other demanded, prodding the cabbie with his toe.

"A *skeleton* key. These cab companies," one of the cops decided to explain to Clotilda Adams, who was standing nearby, "they get the dregs. Hillbillies, you know?"

I said nothing, found nothing to say. I now think of Lord Acton's famous law, which is accepted as true the way it was uttered. The opposite is also true—the commoner's way: Having no power corrupts; having absolutely no power corrupts absolutely.

The bleeding seemed to have stopped. The cab driver sat up, looking no better, with his bluish, greenish, drained head hanging between his knees. His legs were crumpled stiffly. He propped himself on his hands. The police shot questions at him. He mumbled, mumbled, explained, explained.

"How long you been in Detroit? How come you come out of the mountains?"

"Why you pick up this fare?"

"What makes you think Cass is a one-way street?"

Mumbling and mumbling, explaining and explaining, the cab driver tried to satisfy them. He also said: "Hurt. Maybe you get me to the hospital, huh? Hurt real bad."

"Maybe," said one of the cops, "maybe we take you to the station house first. That boy you hit says reckless driving. I think personally you'd flunk the drunk test—what you think, Teach?"

I sent one of the students to call for an ambulance again. In the infinitesimal pause between my suggestion and his action, an attentive reluctant expectant caesura, I put a dime in his hand for the call. One of the cops gave me that long look described by silent movie critics as the slow burn. "They drive careful," he finally said. "It's snowing. They got all that expensive equipment."

The snow had started again outside the window. The skid marks on the lawn were covered. Though the sky was low and gray, the white sifting down gave a peaceful village glow to this industrial Detroit. Little gusts barely rattled the windows. With the class, the cops, and the driver, we were living deep within a snowy paperweight. I felt myself moving very slowly, swimming within thick glass, like the loosened plastic figure in a paperweight. The snow came down in large torn flakes, all over the buildings of Wayne University, grass, trees, and the pale radiance of a network of slow-motion superhighways beyond. Across the street, a modern building—glass and aluminum strips—lay unfinished in this weather. Six months ago there had been a student boarding house on that spot, filled with the artists and the beat, the guitar-wielders and the modern dancers, with a tradition going all the way back to the Korean War. Now there were wheelbarrows full of frozen cement; there were intentions to build a Japanese garden, with Japanse proportions and imported goldfish.

My student returned from the telephone. He had reached a hospital.

The cab driver was fading away. Rootlets of shock hooded his eyes: the lid was closing shut. A cop asked him another question—what the button on his cap stood for—it was a union button—and then the man just went reclining on his elbow, he slipped slowly down, he lay in the little swamp of crusted blood on the floor. You know what happens when milk is boiled? The crust broke like the crust of boiled milk when a spoon goes into coffee. The cop stood with a delicate, disgusted grimace on his face. What a business to be in, he seemed to be thinking. In approximately ten years, at age forty-two, he could retire and sit comfortable in an undershirt, with a non-returnable can of beer, before the color teevee. He could relax. He could *start* to relax. But in the meantime—nag, nag, nag. Drunk cabbies, goddamn hillbillies. The reckless driver on the floor seemed to sleep. His lips moved. He was alive.

Then a puffing intern rushed into the room. I had not heard the ambulance. The policeman gave room and the intern kneeled. He undid his bag. The orderlies glanced at the floor and went back out for their stretcher.

I stood on one side of the body, the kneeling intern with his necklace stethescope, and the two meditative cops. On the other side was the group of students, and at their head, like a leader filled with wrath, risen in time of crisis, stood Clotilda Adams, still clutching her exam paper. There were tears in her eyes. She was in a fury. She had been thinking all this time, and now her thinking had issue: *rage.* Over the body she handed me a paper, crying out, "I don't think I deserved a D on that quiz. I answered all the questions. I can't get my credit for Philo of Ed without I get a B off you."

I must have looked at her with pure stupidity on my face. There is a Haitian proverb: *Stupidity won't kill you, but it'll make you sweat a lot.* She took the opportunity to make me sweat, took my silence for guilt, took my open-mouthed gaze for weakness. She said: "If I was a white girl, you'd grade me easier."

Guilt, a hundred years, a thousand years of it; pity for the disaster of ignorance and fear, pity for ambition rising out of ignorance; adoration of desire; trancelike response to passion—passion which justifies itself because passionate. . . . I looked at her with mixed feelings. I could not simply put her down. In order to *put down*, your own mind must be made up, put down. She had beauty and dignity, stretched tall and wrathful, with teeth for biting and eyes for striking dead.

"But I know my rights," she said, "*Mister*. My mother told me about your kind—lent my father money on his car and then hounded him out of town. He been gone since fifty-three. But you can't keep us down forever, no sir, you can't *always* keep us down—"

She was talking and I was yelling. She was talking and yelling about injustice and I, under clamps, under ice, was yelling in a whisper about the sick man. She was blaming me for all her troubles, all the troubles she had seen, and I was blaming her for not seeing what lay before her, and we were making an appointment to meet in my office and discuss this thing more calmly, Miss Adams. Okay. All right. Later.

The police, the doctor, the orderlies, and the injured cab driver were gone. The police car out front was gone and the snow was covering its traces. The janitor came in and swept up the bloodstains with green disinfectant powder. The frightened couple in the cab were released. They all disappeared silently into the great city, into the routine of disaster and recovery of a great city. I dismissed the class until tomorrow.

The next day I tried to explain to Miss Adams what I meant about her failing to respond adequately to the facts of our life together. Her mouth quivered. Yesterday rage; today a threat of tears. What did I mean she wasn't *adequate*? What did I know about adequate anyhow? Nothing. Just a word. Agreed, Miss Adams. I was trying to say that there were two questions at issue between us—her exam grade and her choice of occasion to dispute it. I would like to discuss each matter separately. I tried to explain why putting the two events together had disturbed me. I tried to explain the notions of empirical evidence and metaphor. I recalled, without successful communication, the story of the young couple and the dog in Brooklyn.

She did not see why she shouldn't have at least a B on her quiz. Her back was strong, her head was high, she didn't need to be compared to no black dog in Brooklyn.

Finally I urged her to have her exam looked at by the head of the department, but she refused because she knew in advance that he would support me. "White is Right," she said.

"Do you want to drop out of the class?"

"No. I'll stay," she said with a sudden patient, weary acceptance of her fate. "I'll do what I can."

"I'll do what I can too," I said.

She smiled hopefully at me. She was tuckered out by the continual alert for combat everywhere. She was willing to forgive and go easy. When she left my office, this smile, shy, pretty, and conventional, tried to tell me that she could be generous—a friend.

We had come to Thomas Hobbes and John Locke in our tour through time and the river of humanities. I pointed out that the English philosophers were noted for clarity and eloquence of style. I answered this question: The French? Isn't French noted for clarity? Yes, they too, but they are more abstract. On the whole. In general.

The class took notes on the truths we unfolded together. Spring came and the snow melted. There was that brief Detroit flowering of the new season—jasmine and dogwood—which, something like it, must have captivated the Frenchman, Antoine de la Mothe Cadillac, when he paused on the straits of Detroit in 1701. University gardeners planted grass seed where the patrol car had parked on the lawn. The new models, all except the Cadillac, were going at mean discounts.

"The 'Humanities,'" wrote Clotilda Adams in her final essay, "are a necessary additive to any teacher's development worth her 'salt' in the perilous times of today. The West and the 'Free World' must stand up to the war of ideas against the 'Iron' Curtain." This was in answer to a question about Beethoven, Goethe, and German romanticism. She did not pass the course, but she was nevertheless admitted on probation to the student-teacher program because of the teacher shortage and the great need to educate our children in these perilous times. Of today.

3

Humanities 610 provided ballast for the ship of culture as it pitched and reeled in the heavy seas of real life; I lashed myself to the mast, but after hearing the siren song of grand course outlines, I cut myself free and leaned over the rail with the inside of my lip showing.

It would be oversimplifying to say that I left off teaching Humanities merely because of an experience. Such an argument is fit to be published under the title "I Was a Teen-Age Humanities Professor." I also left for fitter jobs, more money, a different life. Still, what I remember of the formal study of Truth and Beauty, for advanced credit in education, is a great confusion of generalities, committees, conferences, audio-visual importunities, and poor contact. "Contact!" cried the desperate deans and chairmen, like radio operators in ancient war movies. And much, much discussion of how to get through to the students. How to get through? Miss Adams and Mr. Gold, cab driver and Thomas Hobbes, policeman and the faceless student who paused an instant for a dime for the telephone—we all have to discover how relevant we are to each other. Or do we *have* to? No, we can merely perish, shot down like mad dogs or diminished into time with no more than a glimpse of the light.

Words fade; our experience does not touch; we make do with babble and time-serving. We need to learn the meaning of words, the meaning of the reality those words refer to; we must clasp reality close. We cannot flirt forever, brown-nosing or brow-beating. We must act and build out of our own spirits. How? How? We continually need a new politics, new cities, new marriages and families, new ways of work and leisure. We also need the fine old ways. For me, the primitive appeal to pleasure and pain of writing stories is a possible action, is the way in and out again, as teaching was not. As a teacher, I caught my students too late and only at the top of their heads, at the raw point of pride and ambition, and I had not enough love and pressure as a teacher to open the way through their intentions to the common humanity which remains locked within. As a writer, I could hope to hit them in their bodies and needs, where lusts and ideals were murkily nurtured together, calling to the prime fears and joys directly, rising with them from the truths of innocence into the truths of experience.

The peculiar combination of ignorance and jadedness built into most institutions is a desperate parody of personal innocence, personal experience. Nevertheless, education, which means a drawing out—even formal education, a formal drawing out—is a variety of experience, and experience is the only evidence we have. After evidence comes our thinking upon it. Do the scientists, secreting their honey in distant hives, hear the barking of the black dog which follows them? Will the politicians accept the lead of life, or will they insist on a grade of B in Power and Dominion over a doomed race? We need to give proper answers to the proper questions. I would like for myself and everyone else to have more experience of the humanities.

Particular life is still the best map to truth. When we search our hearts and strip our pretenses, we all know this. Particular life—we know only what we *know*. Therefore the policemen stay with me: I have learned to despise most authority. The cab driver remains in his sick bleeding: pity for the fallen and helpless. And I think of Clotilda Adams in her power and weakness; like the cops, she has an authority of stupidity; like the victim of an accident, she is fallen and helpless. But someplace, since we persist in our cold joke against the ideal of democracy, the cops still have the right to push people around, Clotilda is leading children in the Pledge of Allegiance. We must find a way to teach better and to learn.

Part two

THE SELF

The greatest thing in the world is to know how to belong to ourselves.

Montaigne
Essays

No friends today—Oh, let me meet no friends Until my leave for blossom–viewing ends.

Kyorai
A Net of Fireflies

INTRODUCTION

In every language in the world there is probably no idea more frequently taken for granted than "I" and its objective form, "me." What is this self to which we make so much reference? To ask "Who am I?" sounds more like a child's riddle than a serious question. Yet any answer is elusive and far from simple.

At the root of all our activities lies the animal self that we share with dogs, monkeys, and turtles. This is the self that is driven by hunger and pain, that jumps in reflex action, that is pushed by fear to protect and defend itself. This is the self that responds to the lure of pleasure with which nature baits living organisms, prompting them to do those things which preserve their life and contribute to the preservation of their species. This self pours even the most elevated sentiments into a physical mold. It dictates, for instance, that joy should be expressed by feasting and sorrow by fasting; that love should be expressed by a kiss and hate by a blow. This is the self that huddles for warmth; the self that lies motionless in illness and writhes in pain. This is the self of the hiccup and the shiver. This is the beast that lurks behind our most civilized occupations and peers through our most cultivated activities.

The animal self reverberates with what William James calls a "blooming, buzzing confusion" which is the disquietude of sensation. Our quintet of senses (with a few unnamed ones playing an obligato), intermix and fuse to inform of events immediately impinging on us. But the human self is not only perceptive and sensate, it is also aware. Self-perception is perhaps the most curious trait of the human animal. Many far from satisfactory efforts have been made to account for its presence. Yet were the self merely sensate, the human self and animal self would be indistinguishable.

Out of awareness and self-consciousness emerge that set of functions which separates *genus homo* from all other animals. Any attempt to enumerate the types of activities which come under the heading of "thinking" must inevitably be inadequate. Man names and classifies, infers and deduces, predicts and remembers, calculates, plans, samples, projects, recognizes similarities and differences, and engages in a host of other activities which have been termed "cognitive." Perhaps the most foundational of these is the ability to name. The human animal utilizes its capacity to make sounds by shaping them and

73

arranging them in language. Language permits us to classify events and connect them with other events. It makes thinking possible. To "know" a world is to articulate it and to articulate it is to give it meaning.

Sensing, feeling, and thinking all center in a particular entity which forms a unity. I experience, I think, I feel. We say "I was born," or "I will go to France," or "I am studying Chemistry." All things I do or encounter happen to me; I possess them and they are part of me. An "I" is, in part, its history; it extends into the past, reaches into the future and is in the present. In a simple sense our history unifies our experience precisely because we remember it. But have we not complicated the problem? What is memory? On the one hand it is connected with habit and in this respect has a physical locus. In this sense even cells are said to be imprinted with a "memory" which causes them to behave as they do. In this sense, "memory" means being "programmed" to habitually perform in a certain way to a particular stimulus. A happens to B and B acts to do C. Our memory is this, but it is so much more.

Human memory does not consist merely of the mechanical imprint of habit. It does not merely retain experience but elaborates, embroiders, and structures it. The self's memory does not merely reproduce the past, but orders it, arranges it, and invests it with significance. Human memory funds the past and utilizes it to construct the future. The novelist Proust has said that we only understand in retrospect; that only in memory can we reconstruct what has happened and give it meaning. Memory reinforces our unity; it threads our experience on a continuum.

Memory distinguishes each self from every other. The anthropologist Clyde Kluckhohn has said that each man is like all others in some respects, is like some others in some respects, and is like no others in some respects. Each is a member of the human race and is an illustration of human nature. All men eat, see color, and remember. You may wish to object, thinking of the conditions which disturb these functions. But the fact that we name anorexia, colorblindness, and amnesia as ailments testifies to the fact that the states for which these are aberrations exist as a norm for all men. In some very significant senses, all men are brothers.

But each man is like some others in some respects. Each man shares some experience with groups of men. Some men are fair-skinned and are easily burned by the sun, some are members of that melancholy fraternity whose stomachs are ulcerated; some have visual memories, some belong to the tribe of "God's Angry Men," some belong to the group with IQ's over 150. Each man is typically and habitually a type of person and he shares his traits with others of the same type. We could, of course, elucidate an infinite number of such types. Men can be classified according to physical characteristics, emotional propensities, intellectual capabilities. They can be typed in terms of what is sometimes called their "character" structure or those ingrained habits of evaluation in terms of which they act toward themselves and others.

Finally, each self is unique and induplicable. Each is born at just this time and at that place. Each inherits his own particular genetic fall-out which shapes him in special ways. Each has his own history, his own experience, his own vantage point in terms of which to view his world and which no one else can ever fully share. Except in a derivative or metaphysical sense no one else can see for us, digest for us, or die for us. No one else can feel the particular quality for our pain. Each is the site of certain peculiarities and idiosyncrasies of physical structure, temperament, taste, and intellect. Each has his own brand of curiosity and creativity. Each makes a unique appropriation of and a unique contribution to the world we all share.

But each self not only "is," it "becomes." Each self is defined by a ceaseless unfolding of inner potentiality for either better or worse. At conception each was committed to an ongoing career—to a process which ceases only in death. We are set in certain directions by what we have been and yet, at any point, we can change course be it ever so slightly. And at no point in our history are we exactly as we are at any other point. As a temporal process with a beginning, a middle, and an end, each is in flux. Each is capable of a culmination and a degradation. Each may realize his potentialities or inhibit them. The self is an opportunity—an opportunity to become human or to become brutalized.

Up to now we have been speaking of "the" self. But have you ever considered how many selves you really are? On one hand there is the self that is habit-bound and routinized—body, feelings, and mind, all of which can become habituated. We tend to become hungry at the same time each day, to react continually with anger at certain affronts, and to use the same type of reasoning to verify an idea. This side of self has much in common with a machine; it is the self of the conditioned reflex and the predictable reaction.

On the other hand there is the spontaneous self, the self of whim and fancy that can unexpectedly and unaccountably depart from well-trodden paths. It has been said that all forms of creativity owe some if not all of their origin to this self. This self can be wayward and whimsical, but it can be constructive and reforming. It can bring chaos, but it can bring visionary awareness.

Then there are the many selves that are social and outgoing and that reach toward others. These are the selves we permit others to see and share. Our public selves are the roles we play and the appearances we present to others. But they are neither disguises nor frauds. To be a parent, a salesman, a committeeman or a resident of a town are not only genuine selves but they partially define a particular self. They can enhance sensitivity and broaden experience for anyone who plays them.

Important as our social selves are, they are counterbalanced by our private selves which we do not and frequently cannot display. The private self knows nuances of feeling, random thoughts, isolated sensations, and snatches of disconnected experience which are frequently difficult to communicate, except possibly through the intuitive language of art. As against the open self, the closed self may be unknown even to itself. This is the self that emerges in dreams, that causes slips of the tongue, and "accidents" which accomplish obscure goals. This is the self of which Freud speaks; the one that hides and is difficult to entice into view. When other parts of the self are under serious stress, the disguised self sometimes emerges with vigor. It can generate impulsive but meaningful actions; it can concoct compulsions, phobias, and other seemingly inexplicable phenomena. This self can surprise and shock; it can entrance and dismay. Though a clown, it has deeply serious purposes.

But the many-faceted self is hardly delineated by these few dichotomies. There is the self that thinks, plans, calculates, and proposes and there is the self that feels, desires, expresses sentiment and inclination. There is the vegetative self that takes life with adjustive equanimity and there is the critical self, never satisfied with things as they are. There is the random self which moves with the breeze and the goal-directed self that pursues an end with the persistence and precision of a bullet. There is the hedonic self that plunges headlong into pleasure, and there is the ascetic self that withdraws, withholds, and denies to itself even those things necessary for its well-being. There is the exploratory and the cautious self, the cooperative and the hostile self, the courageous and the cowardly self. Such is the complexity of the "I," the parts of which must be perpetually juggled into a working harmony. To manage one's "self" is every bit as formidable as the Socratic injunction to "Know thyself"!

THE HUMAN ANIMAL

The Self As Animal 12
Charles Darwin

The main conclusion here arrived at, and now held by many naturalists who are well competent to form a sound judgment, is that man is descended from some less highly organized form. The grounds upon which this conclusion rests will never be shaken, for the close similarity between man and the lower animals in embryonic development, as well as in innumerable points of structure and constitution, both of high and of the most trifling importance—the rudiments which he retains, and the abnormal reversions to which he is occasionally liable—are facts which cannot be disputed. They have long been known, but until recently they told us nothing with respect to the origin of man. Now when viewed by the light of our knowledge of the whole organic world, their meaning is unmistakable. The great principle of evolution stands up clear and firm, when these groups of facts are considered in connection with others, such as the mutual affinities of the members of the same group, their geographical distribution in past and present times, and their geological succession. It is incredible that all these facts should speak falsely. He who is not content to look, like a savage, at the phenomena of nature as disconnected, cannot any longer believe that man is the work of a separate act of creation. He will be forced to admit that the close resemblance of the embryo of man to that, for instance, of a dog—the construction of his skull, limbs, and whole frame on the same plan with that of other mammals, independently of the uses to which the parts may be put—the occasional reappearance of various structures, for instance of several muscles, which man does not normally possess, but which are common to the Quadrumana—and a crowd of analogous facts—all point in the plainest manner to the conclusion that man is the co-descendant with other mammals of a common progenitor.

We have seen that man incessantly presents individual differences in all

From Ch. 21, "General Summary and Conclusion," with deletions, in *The Descent of Man,* by Charles Darwin, New York, Hurst & Co., n.d. This work was first published in 1871.

parts of his body and in his mental faculties. These differences or variations seem to be induced by the same general causes, and to obey the same laws as with the lower animals. In both cases similar laws of inheritance prevail. Man tends to increase at a greater rate than his means of subsistence; consequently he is occasionally subjected to a severe struggle for existence, and natural selection will have effected whatever lies within its scope. A succession of strongly marked variations of a similar nature is by no means requisite; slight fluctuating differences in the individual suffice for the work of natural selection; not that we have any reason to suppose that, in the same species, all parts of the organization tend to vary to the same degree. We may feel assured that the inherited effects of the long-continued use or disuse of parts will have done much in the same direction with natural selection. Modifications formerly of importance, though no longer of any special use, are long inherited. When one part is modified, other parts change through the principle of correlation, of which we have instances in many curious cases of correlated monstrosities. Something may be attributed to the direct and definite action of the surrounding conditions of life, such as abundant food, heat, or moisture; and lastly, many characters of slight physiological importance, some indeed of considerable importance, have been gained through sexual selection.

No doubt man, as well as every other animal, presents structures which seem to our limited knowledge not to be now of any service to him, nor to have been so formerly, either for the general conditions of life or in the relations of one sex to the other. Such structures cannot be accounted for by any form of selection, or by the inherited effects of the use and disuse of parts. We know, however, that many strange and strongly marked peculiarities of structure occasionally appear in our domesticated productions, and if their unknown causes were to act more uniformly, they would probably become common to all the individuals of the species. We may hope hereafter to understand something about the causes of such occasional modifications, especially through the study of monstrosities; hence the labors of experimentalists, such as those of M. Camille Dareste, are full of promise for the future. In general we can only say that the cause of each slight variation and of each monstrosity lies much more in the constitution of the organism than in the nature of the surrounding conditions; though new and changed conditions certainly play an important part in exciting organic changes of many kinds.

Through the means just specified, aided perhaps by others as yet undiscovered, man has been raised to his present state. But since he attained to the rank of manhood, he has diverged into distinct races, or, as they may be more fitly called, sub-species. Some of these, such as the Negro and European, are so distinct that, if specimens had been brought to a naturalist wthout any further information, they would undoubtedly have been considered by him as good and true species. Nevertheless all the races agree in so many unimportant details of structure and in so many mental peculiarities, that these can be accounted for only by inheritance from a common progenitor; and a progenitor thus characterized would probably deserve to rank as man.

It must not be supposed that the divergence of each race from the other races, and of all from a common stock, can be traced back to any one pair of progenitors. On the contrary, at every stage in the process of modification, all the individuals which were in any way better fitted for their conditions of life, though in different degrees, would have survived in greater numbers than the less well fitted. The process would have been like that followed by man, when he does not intentionally select particular individuals, but breeds from all the superior individuals, and neglects the inferior. He thus slowly but surely modifies his stock, and unconsciously forms a new strain. So with respect to modifications acquired independently of selection, and due to variations arising from the nature of the organism and the action of the surrounding conditions, or from changed habits of life, no single pair will have been modified much more than the other pairs inhabiting the same country, for all will have been continually blended through free intercrossing.

By considering the embryological structure of man—the homologies which he presents with the lower animals—the rudiments which he retains—and the reversions to which he is liable, we can partly recall in imagination the former condition of our early progenitors; and can approximately place them in their proper place in the zoological series. We thus learn that man is descended from a hairy, tailed quadruped, probably arboreal in its habits, and an inhabitant of the Old World. This creature, if its whole structure had been examined by a naturalist, would have been classed among the Quadrumana, as surely as the still more ancient progenitor of the Old and New World monkeys. The Quadrumana and all the higher mammals are probably derived from an ancient marsupial animal, and this through a long line of diversified forms, from some amphibian-like creature, and this again from some fish-like animal. In the dim obscurity of the past we can see that the early progenitor of all the Vertebrata must have been an aquatic animal, provided with branchiæ, with the two sexes united in the same individual, and with the most important organs of the body (such as the brain and heart) imperfectly or not at all developed. This animal seems to have been more like the larvæ of the existing marine Ascidians than any other known form.

The high standard of our intellectual powers and moral disposition is the greatest difficulty which presents itself, after we have been driven to this conclusion on the origin of man. But everyone who admits the principle of evolution must see that the mental powers of the higher animals, which are the same in kind with those of man, though so different in degree, are capable of advancement. Thus the interval between the mental powers of one of the higher apes and of a fish, or between those of an ant and scale-insect, is immense; yet their development does not offer any special difficulty; for, with our domesticated animals, the mental faculties are certainly variable, and the variations are inherited. No one doubts that they are of the utmost importance to animals in a state of nature. Therefore the conditions are favorable for their development through natural selection. The same conclusion may be extended to man; the intellect must have been all-important to him, even at a very remote period, as enabling him to invent and use language, to make weapons, tools, traps, etc., whereby, with the aid of his social habits, he long ago became the most dominant of all living creatures.

A great stride in the development of the intellect will have followed, as soon as the half-art and half-instinct of language came into use; for the continued use of language will have reacted on the brain and produced an inherited effect; and this again will have reacted on the improvement of language. As Mr. Chauncey Wright[1] has well remarked, the largeness of the brain in man, relatively to his body, compared with the lower animals, may be attributed in chief part to the early use of some simple form of language— that wonderful engine which affixes signs to all sorts of objects and qualities, and excites trains of thought which would never arise from the mere impression of the senses, or if they did arise could not be followed out. The higher intellectual powers of man, such as those of ratiocination, abstraction, self-consciousness, etc., probably follow from the continued improvement and exercise of the other mental faculties.

The development of the moral qualities is a more interesting problem. The foundation lies in the social instincts, including under this term the family ties. These instincts are highly complex, and in the case of the lower animals give special tendencies toward certain definite actions; but the more important elements are love, and the distinct emotion of sympathy. Animals endowed with the social instincts take pleasure in one another's company, warn one another of danger, defend and aid one another in many ways. These instincts do not extend to all the individuals of the species, but only to those of the same community. As they are highly beneficial to the species, they have in all probability been acquired through natural selection.

A moral being is one who is capable of reflecting on his past actions and their motives—of approving of some and disapproving of others; and the fact that man is the one being who certainly deserves this designation, is the greatest of all distinctions between him and the lower animals. But in the fourth chapter I have endeavored to show that the moral sense follows, firstly, from the enduring and ever-present nature of the social instincts; secondly, from man's appreciation of the approbation and disapprobation of his fellows; and thirdly, from the high activity of his mental faculties, with past impressions extremely vivid; and in these latter respects he differs from the lower animals. Owing to this condition of mind, man cannot avoid looking both

[1] "On the Limits of Natural Selection," in the "North American Review," Oct. 1876, p. 295.

backward and forward, and comparing past impressions. Hence after some temporary desire or passion has mastered his social instincts, he reflects and compares the now weakened impression of such past impulses with the ever-present social instincts; and he then feels that sense of dissatisfaction which all unsatisfied instincts leave behind them, he therefore resolves to act differently for the future—and this is conscience. Any instinct permanently stronger or more enduring than another gives rise to a feeling which we express by saying that it ought to be obeyed. A pointer dog, if able to reflect on his past conduct, would say to himself, I ought (as indeed we say of him) to have pointed at that hare and not have yielded to the passing temptation of hunting it.

Social animals are impelled partly by a wish to aid the members of their community in a general manner, but more commonly to perform certain definite actions. Man is impelled by the same general wish to aid his fellows; but has few or no special instincts. He differs also from the lower animals in the power of expressing his desires by words, which thus become a guide to the aid required and bestowed. The motive to give aid is likewise much modified in man: it no longer consists solely of a blind instinctive impulse, but is much influenced by the praise or blame of his fellows. The appreciation and the bestowal of praise and blame both rest on sympathy; and this emotion, as we have seen, is one of the most important elements of the social instincts. Sympathy, though gained as an instinct, is also much strengthened by exercise or habit. As all men desire their own happiness, praise or blame is bestowed on actions and motives, according as they lead to this end; and as happiness is an essential part of the general good, the greatest-happiness principle indirectly serves as a nearly safe standard of right and wrong. As the reasoning powers advance and experience is gained, the remoter effects of certain lines of conduct on the character of the individual, and on the general good, are perceived; and then the self-regarding virtues come within the scope of public opinion, and receive praise, and their opposites blame. But with the less civilized nations reason often errs, and many bad customs and base superstitions come within the same scope, and are then esteemed as high virtues, and their breach as heavy crimes.

The moral faculties are generally and justly esteemed as of higher value than the intellectual powers. But we should bear in mind that the activity of the mind in vividly recalling past impressions is one of the fundamental, though secondary, bases of conscience. This affords the strongest argument for educating and stimulating in all possible ways the intellectual faculties of every human being. No doubt a man with a torpid mind, if his social affections and sympathies are well developed, will be led to good actions, and may have a fairly sensitive conscience. But whatever renders the imagination more vivid, and strengthens the habit of recalling and comparing past impressions, will make the conscience more sensitive, and may even somewhat compensate for weak social affections and sympathies.

The moral nature of man has reached its present standard partly through the advancement of his reasoning powers, and consequently of a just public opinion, but especially from his sympathies having been rendered more tender and widely diffused through the effects of habit, example, instruction, and reflection. It is not improbable that after long practice virtuous tendencies may be inherited. With the more civilized races, the conviction of the existence of an all-seeing Deity has had a potent influence on the advance of morality. Ultimately man does not accept the praise or blame of his fellows as his sole guide, though few escape this influence, but his habitual convictions, controlled by reason, afford him the safest rule. His conscience then becomes the supreme judge and monitor. Nevertheless the first foundation or origin of the moral sense lies in the social instincts, including sympathy; and these instincts no doubt were primarily gained, as in the case of the lower animals, through natural selection.

.   .   .

The main conclusion arrived at in this work, namely, that man is descended from some lowly organized form, will, I regret to think, be highly distasteful to many. But there can hardly be a doubt that we are descended from barbarians. The astonishment which I felt on first seeing a party of Fuegians on a wild and broken shore will never be forgotten by me, for the reflection at once rushed into my mind—such were our ancestors. These men were absolutely naked and bedaubed with paint, their long hair was tangled, their mouths frothed with excitement, and their expression was wild, startled, and distrustful. They possessed hardly any arts, and, like wild animals, lived on what they could catch; they had no government, and were merciless to everyone not of their own small tribe. He who has seen a savage in his native land will not feel much shame if forced to acknowledge that the blood of some more humble creature flows in his veins. For my own part, I would as soon be descended from that heroic little monkey who braved his dreaded enemy in order to save the life of his keeper, or from that old baboon, who, descending from the mountains, carried away in triumph his young comrade from a crowd of astonished dogs—as from a savage who delights to torture his enemies, offers up bloody sacrifices, practises infanticide without remorse, treats his wives like slaves, knows no decency, and is haunted by the grossest superstitions.

Man may be excused for feeling some pride at having risen, though not through his own exertions, to the very summit of the organic scale; and the fact of his having thus risen, instead of having been aboriginally placed there, may give him hope for a still higher destiny in the distant future. But we are not here concerned with hopes or fears, only with the truth as far as our reason permits us to discover it; and I have given the evidence to the best of my ability. We must, however, acknowledge, as it seems to me, that man, with all his noble qualities, with sympathy which feels for the most debased, with benevolence which extends not only to other men but to the humblest living creature, with his god-like intellect which has penetrated into the movements and constitution of the solar system—with all these exalted powers—Man still bears in his bodily frame the indelible stamp of his lowly origin.

The Self As Machine 13
Norbert Weiner

It is the thesis of this book that society can only be understood through a study of the messages and the communication facilities which belong to it; and that in the future development of these messages and communication facilities, messages between man and machines, between machines and man, and between machine and machine, are destined to play an ever-increasing part.

When I give an order to a machine, the situation is not essentially different from that which arises when I give an order to a person. In other words, as far as my consciousness goes I am aware of the order that has gone out and of the signal of compliance that has come back. To me, personally, the fact that the signal in its intermediate stages has gone through a machine rather than through a person is irrelevant and does not in any case greatly change my relation to the signal. Thus the theory of control in engineering, whether human or animal or mechanical, is a chapter in the theory of messages.

Naturally there are detailed differences in messages and in problems of control, not only between a living organism and a machine, but within each narrower class of beings. It is the purpose of Cybernetics to develop a language and techniques that will enable us indeed to attack the problem of control and communication in general, but also to find the proper repertory of ideas and techniques to classify their particular manifestations under certain concepts.

The commands through which we exercise our control over our environment are a kind of information which we impart to it. Like any form of information, these commands are subject to disorganization in transit. They generally come through in less coherent fashion and certainly not more coherently than they were sent. In control and communication we are always fighting nature's tendency to degrade the organized and to destroy the meaningful; the tendency, as Gibbs has shown us, for entropy to increase.

Much of this book concerns the limits of communication within and among individuals. Man is immersed in a world which he perceives through his sense organs. Information that he receives is coordinated through his brain and nervous system until, after the proper process of storage, collation,

From Ch. 1, "Cybernetics in History," with deletions, in *The Human Use of Human Beings,* by Norbert Wiener, Boston, Houghton Mifflin Company, 1950. Reprinted by permission of Houghton Mifflin Company.

and selection, it emerges through effector organs, generally his muscles. These in turn act on the external world, and also react on the central nervous system through receptor organs such as the end organs of kinaesthesia; and the information received by the kinaesthetic organs is combined with his already accumulated store of information to influence future action.

Information is a name for the content of what is exchanged with the outer world as we adjust to it, and make our adjustment felt upon it. The process of receiving and of using information is the process of our adjusting to the contingencies of the outer environment, and of our living effectively within that environment. The needs and the complexity of modern life make greater demands on this process of information than ever before, and our press, our museums, our scientific laboratories, our universities, our libraries and textbooks, are obliged to meet the needs of this process or fail in their purpose. To live effectively is to live with adequate information. Thus, communication and control belong to the essence of man's inner life, even as they belong to his life in society.

Messages are themselves a form of pattern and organization. Indeed, it is possible to treat sets of messages as having an entropy like sets of states of the external world. Just as entropy is a measure of disorganization, the information carried by a set of messages is a measure of organization. In fact, it is possible to interpret the information carried by a message as essentially the negative of its entropy, and the negative logarithm of its probability. That is, the more probable the message, the less information it gives. Clichés, for example, are less illuminating than great poems.

I have already referred to Leibnitz's interest in automata, an interest incidentally shared by his contemporary, Pascal, who made real contributions to the development of what we now know as the desk adding-machine. Leibnitz saw in the concordance of the time given by clocks set at the same time, the model for the pre-established harmony of his monads. For the technique embodied in the automata of his time was that of the clockmaker. Let us consider the activity of the little figures which dance on the top of a music box. They move in accordance with a pattern, but it is a pattern which is set in advance, and in which the past activity of the figures has practically nothing to do with the pattern of their future activity. The probability that they will diverge from this pattern is nil. There is a message, indeed; but it goes from the machinery of the music box to the figures, and stops there. The figures themselves have no trace of communication with the outer world, except this one-way stage of communication with the pre-established mechanism of the music box. They are blind, deaf and dumb, and cannot vary their activity in the least from the conventionalized pattern.

Contrast with them the behavior of man, or indeed of any moderately intelligent animal such as a kitten. I call to the kitten and it looks up. I have sent it a message which it has received by its sensory organs, and which it registers in action. The kitten is hungry and lets out a pitiful wail. This time it is the sender of a message. The kitten bats at a swinging spool. The spool swings to its left, and the kitten catches it with its left paw. This time messages of a very complicated nature are both sent and received within the kitten's own nervous system through certain nerve end-bodies in its joints, muscles, and tendons; and by means of nervous messages sent by these organs, the animal is aware of the actual position and tensions of its tissues. It is only through these organs that anything like a manual skill is possible.

I have contrasted the prearranged behavior of the little figures on the music box on the one hand, and the contingent behavior of human beings and animals on the other. But we must not suppose that the music box is typical of all machine behavior.

The older machines, and in particular the older attempts to produce automata, did in fact function on a closed clockwork basis. But modern automatic machines such as the controlled missile, the proximity fuse, the automatic door opener, the control apparatus for a chemical factory, and the rest of the modern armory of automatic machines which perform military or industrial functions, possess sense organs; that is, receptors for messages coming from the outside. These may be as simple as photoelectric cells which change electrically when a light falls on them, and which can tell light from dark, or as complicated as a television set. They may measure a tension by the change it produces in the conductivity of a wire exposed to it, or they may measure temperature by means of a thermocouple, which is an instrument consisting of two distinct metals in contact with one another through which a current flows when one of the points of contact is heated. Every instrument in the repertory of the scientific-instrument maker is a possible sense organ, and may be made to record its reading remotely through the intervention of appropriate electrical apparatus. Thus the machine which is conditioned by its relation to the external world, and by the things happening in the external world, is with us and has been with us for some time.

The machine which acts on the external world by means of messages is also familiar. The automatic photoelectric door opener is known to every person who has passed through the Pennsylvania Station in New York, and is used in many other buildings as well. When a message consisting of the interception of a beam of light is sent to the apparatus, this message actuates the door, and opens it so that the passenger may go through.

The steps between the actuation of a machine of this type by sense organs and its performance of a task may be as simple as in the case of the electric door; or it may be in fact of any desired degree of complexity within the limits of our engineering techniques. A complex action is one in which the data introduced, which we call the *input*, to obtain an effect on the outer world, which we call the *output*, may involve a large number of combinations. These are combinations, both of the data put in at the moment and of the records taken from the past stored data which we call the *memory*. These are recorded in the machine. The most complicated machines yet made which transform input data into output data are the high-speed electrical computing machines, of which I shall speak later in more detail. The determination of the mode of conduct of these machines is given through a special sort of input, which frequently consists of punched cards or tapes or of magnetized wires, and which determines the way in which the machine is going to act in one operation, as distinct from the way in which it might have acted in another. Because of the frequent use of punched or magnetic tape in the control, the data which are fed in, and which indicate the mode of operation of one of these machines for combining information, are called the *taping*.

I have said that man and the animal have a kinaesthetic sense, by which they keep a record of the position and tensions of their muscles. For any machine subject to a varied external environment to act effectively it is necessary that information concerning the results of its own action be furnished to it as part of the information on which it must continue to act. For example, if we are running an elevator, it is not enough to open the outside door because the orders we have given should make the elevator be at that door at the time we open it. It is important that the release for opening the door be dependent on the fact that the elevator is actually at the door; otherwise something might have detained it, and the passenger might step into the empty shaft. This control of a machine on the basis of its *actual* performance rather than its *expected* performance is known as *feedback,* and involves sensory members which are actuated by motor members and perform the function of *tell-tales* or *monitors*—that is, of elements which indicate a performance. It is the function of these mechanisms to control the mechanical tendency toward disorganization; in other words, to produce a temporary and local reversal of the normal direction of entropy.

I have just mentioned the elevator as an example of feedback. There are other cases where the importance of feedback is even more apparent. For example, a gun-pointer takes information from his instruments of observation, and conveys it to the gun, so that the latter will point in such a direction that the missile will pass through the moving target at a certain time. Now, the gun itself must be used under all conditions of weather. In some of these the grease is warm, and the gun swings easily and rapidly. Under other conditions the grease is frozen or mixed with sand, and the gun is slow to answer the orders given to it. If these orders are reinforced by an extra push given when the gun fails to respond easily to the orders and lags behind them, then the error of the gun-pointer will be decreased. To obtain a performance as uniform as possible, it is customary to put into the gun a control feedback element which reads the lag of the gun behind the position it should have according to the orders given it, and which uses this difference to give the gun an extra push.

It is true that precautions must be taken so that the push is not too hard, for if it is, the gun will swing past its proper position, and will have to be pulled back in a series of oscillations, which may well become wider and wider, and lead to a disastrous instability. If the feedback system is itself controlled—if, in other words, its own entropic tendencies are checked by still other controlling mechanisms—and kept within limits sufficiently stringent, this will not occur, and the existence of the feedback will increase the stability of performance of the gun. In other words, the performance will become less dependent on the frictional load; or what is the same thing, on the drag created by the stiffness of the grease.

Something very similar to this occurs in human action. If I pick up my cigar, I do not will to move any specific muscles. Indeed in many cases, I do not know what those muscles are. What I do is turn into action a certain feedback mechanism; namely a reflex in which the amount by which I have yet failed to pick up the cigar is turned into a new and increased order to the lagging muscles, whichever they may be. In this way, a fairly uniform voluntary command will enable the same task to be performed from widely varying initial positions, and irrespective of the decrease of contraction due to fatigue of the muscles. Similarly, when I drive a car, I do not follow out a series of commands dependent simply on a mental image of the road and the task I am doing. If I find the car swerving too much to the right, that causes me to pull it to the left. This depends on the actual performance of the car, and not simply on the road; and it allows me to drive with nearly equal efficiency a light Austin or a heavy truck, without having formed separate habits for the driving of the two. I shall have more to say about this in the chapter in this book on special machines, where we shall discuss the service that can be done to neuropathology by the study of machines with defects in performance similar to those occurring in the human mechanism.

It is my thesis that the physical functioning of the living individual and the operation of some of the newer communication machines are precisely parallel in their analogous attempts to control entropy through feedback. Both of them have sensory receptors as one stage in their cycle of operation: that is, in both of them there exists a special apparatus for collecting information from the outer world at low energy levels, and for making it available in the operation of the individual or of the machine. In both cases these external messages are not taken *neat*, but through the internal transforming powers of the apparatus, whether it be alive or dead. The information is then turned into a new form available for the further stages of performance. In both the animal and the machine this performance is made to be effective on the outer world. In both of them, their *performed* action on the outer world, and not merely their *intended* action, is reported back to the central regulatory apparatus. This complex of behavior is ignored by the average man, and in particular does not play the role that it should in our habitual analysis of society; for just as individual physical responses may be seen from this point of view, so may the organic responses of society itself. I do not mean that the sociologist is unaware of the existence and complex nature of communications in society, but until recently he has tended to overlook the extent to which they are the cement which binds its fabric together.

14   The Self As Human
Evelyn Shirk

To possess and to be possessed by ideals, to live and die for them, has sometimes been considered the culmination of ethical experience. What are ideals? Ideals are envisioned ends of improvement, of the better, of the excellent, of the perfect, against which we measure actual achivement. They guide performance toward its fulfillment. They are measuring rods by which we envision desirable ends worthy of allegiance. For example, love, friendship, loyalty, toleration, and beauty are some of the ideals against which we measure the achievements and failures of interpersonal conduct; efficiency, liberty, and equality are some of the ideals against which we measure the actual social relations in a civil state. Ideals are hopes and aspirations for the better which are projected into the future. They are goals of excellence and perfection.

When we ask "excellence and perfection of *what?*" it becomes clear that ideals live and have their being within human experience. They represent the goodness or excellence which any individual idea, thing, or event expresses. The very fact of being able to speak of *better* bears testimony to the presence of ideals and guarantees them a vigorous role in any kind of experience. All things are subject to improvement; all are capable of excellence. In this sense it is possible to see that some things are closer to the ideal than others; some exhibit greater degrees of excellence or goodness than others which have been encountered or imagined. We may speak, for example, of a good political choice, or a better one or an excellent one. Or we may speak of a good painting, a better one or a great one.

The idea, thing, or act concomitant with the excellence or ideal of which we are concerned may be more or less general in nature. Hence, ideals themselves will have greater or less generality. For example, in describing our ideal we may speak of *a* good political choice, we may speak of good political choice or, we may generalize to a still greater degree and speak of good government in general. We may speak of *a* beautiful painting, beautiful art, or beauty in general.

From Ch. 2, "Good, Better, and Best," in *The Ethical Dimension,* by Evelyn Shirk, New York, Appleton-Century-Crofts, 1965. Reprinted with permission of Appleton-Century-Crofts.

Men have held ideals in two very different ways which might be called genuinely as against spuriously. Ideals held genuinely are granted habitation in this world. They are goals of improvement to which any situation lends itself. They spring from the actual workings of a situation and represent an imaginative projection of the possibilities for better and more effective functioning. They are seen to arise from an imaginative envisagement of the possibilities within what is. An ideal, then, in the sense of the excellence to which anything may lend itself, is both within a specific situation and beyond it. It is the largest, most complete expression of a good which men have experienced. It is that which we would want if all things were equal and if unfavorable conditions could be eliminated.

As recognitions of the possibilities (if not actualities) of experience, ideals relate to the future. Although they arise from what is, they represent a foreshadowing of what is latent in it. Moving within the limits of a context, yet projecting hope beyond it, genuine ideals imply not just the better, but the best that can be imagined. Even though ideals are more general perfections than any situation can provide, they spring from and serve a context by directing performance. They can make any situation more meaningful and less parochial or local by relating its uniqueness to more general human aspirations. They connect its limited existence in space and time to more pervasive human goods. Context-rooted ideals originate in, develop through, and are certified by experience. Yet they represent aspiration and hope which is sometimes of the subtlest and most imaginative kind and which survives the vicissitudes of daily life.

The consideration that ideals are, in a sense, beyond the present must not obscure the fact that they are present in a less large and less complete expression within any situation of good. It must not obfuscate the point that they spring from human life. It is a property of all things to be amenable to improvement and to be good or desirable to some extent under some circumstances.

The persistence of ideals beyond practice is justified by the meaning and resonance they bring. Perhaps the stimulus to envisage ideals lie precisely in the existence of inept, unsatisfactory activity, in human disappointment and frustration. While this does not justify disappointment and failure as a means to ideals as ends, nor support whatever is as being right, good and necessary, it is nonetheless true that the disappointments of experience stimulate and motivate the human being to renew his efforts.

Genuine or realizable ideals are relevant to particular cases. They, like the cases they guide, have a history. Ideals have altered as the situations men face alter; they develop as both men and situations develop. Ideals, in short, are like any other conception—products of a time and a place. Our hopes for life, liberty, and the pursuit of happiness in the twentieth century take the form of demands for protection from war, for economic, political, and personal security, and for methods of governing a closely interrelated and conflict-ridden world. They are hardly the ideals which the eighteenth century envisioned by the use of these same terms. Far from representing the eternal and immortal, the history of human ideals shows that what has been held dear has varied in meaning, has changed in practice, and has altered with a changing world.

Ideals, however, may be held spuriously. We may wrest the goodness from things and understand it as an entity—which has its own separate existence. We may tear fulfillments from their intimate connection with what is and understand them as some total or complete perfection which has either lost contact with what is or has never reflected such contact. When we speak of ideals as perfections, we are in danger of assigning them to an existence beyond any particular expression—to life outside of the events and acts to which they give hue and color. The motivation to conceive of ideals in this way is strong. We yearn to protect our excellences from being sullied by contact with defect.

It is when we both divorce excellences from their connections with the world of the actual and generalize them to the greatest degree that ideals become spurious. Ideals understood to exist apart from any situation become products of wishful thinking. Isolated from the changes of time and the limitations of space, they are felt to be especially sacred because of their remoteness from the facts of life. The "idealist," in these terms, becomes the hero serving the unobtainable.

Unattainable ideals must not be confused with those which are especially complex and difficult to achieve or the fulfillment of which is exceedingly far-reaching and even remote. Comprehensive goals have often challenged human courage and led men to fulfillments far beyond their expectations. History abounds with examples where extravagant hopes for the extension of knowledge have been realized. What makes an ideal unattainable or spurious is not just that we assert in advance that it cannot be achieved. It is spurious because the very statement of its goal fails to connect it with problems, to root it in a situation, to make contact with the knowledge and techniques we have. It is spurious because it evades any context within which it might be realized.

Spurious idealism severs the relationship between the valuer and the valued. Its hopes exist in vacuo; its wishes may exist apart from possibilities and characteristics of the context. The spurious idealist disregards the present in the service of the forever unreachable perfection. Spurious ideals are artful dodges of reality set apart from the conditions of life. False idealism is a kind of ethical distraction, a sentimental yearning for the world of "as if." The spurious idealist wishes to move toward heaven without benefit of transportation.

Adherents of static and frozen ideals usually understand them to be timeless. Such ideals have been said to live a peculiar kind of life of their own. Since they do not exist in any typical sense, they have been held to "subsist," that is, to exist in some way which is more or less unexaminable and perhaps inscrutable. Perfect love, perfect peace, perfect well-being, for example, have been believed to exist in this way. Considerable energy has been devoted to defining their status. In fact, proponents of this view hold it to be especially significant that ideals are unattainable. The very fact that they are rootless and apart from all specific situations is felt to make them, like the mistletoe, creatures of some special domain the fact that they are unrealizable makes them seem particularly noble.

Adherence to spurious ideals has had fascination for all those with the Faustian urge or the Quixotic temperament. Pursuit of the unattainable has had a special appeal for many men. Impossible causes have never lacked adherents. Perhaps the world has gained from these efforts, heroic and sacrificial as they indeed are. But it is at least questionable whether their appeal lies as much in their unattainability as in the fact that they offer an enduringness which the individual person cannot hope to gain for himself. Perhaps it lies as much in their unrealizability as in the satisfaction that can come from personal identification with goals that are less transient and mortal than any human being.

Spurious ideals subject the valuer to many pitfalls. First, one's eye on the sun often tends to blind one to what is under foot. It can cause one to be contemptuous of present problems, the choice regarding which does indeed change future events. In the light of the shimmer of perfection, common though urgent problems seem mundane. As we saw in our account of perspectival error, overly-long, overly-wide, and overly-deep goals distort the nature of the actual situation.

Since counterfeit ideals are noncontextual and muddled, they can sanction activities which have most imperfect outcomes and which, when viewed with sobriety, are most undesirable. Even such ideals as piety and holiness, when spuriously held, have sanctioned murderous crusades, vengeful witch hunts, and persecutions of all kinds. Men have held the ideal of peace so abstractly that they have engaged in bloody wars to achieve it. In behalf of the ideal of love they have committed atrocious violence on others. As Santayana puts it, "Fanaticism consists in redoubling your effort when you have forgotten your aim."

Whether ideals are spurious or genuine, there is a sense in which the very fact that man can so envision improvement and so imaginatively construct excellence is remarkable. That men can perform such an operation on their experience is, in itself, a most important fact about that experience. Why do men, unlike other animals, create, nourish, and cherish ideals to which they give allegiance? The intense quality of human eagerness for excellence is arresting and problematical. It manifests a special kind of love and longing, desire and yearning.

THE TRAITS OF SELF

15   The Self As Cooperative and Constructive

Andras Angyal

The over-all pattern of personality function can be described from two different vantage points. Viewed from one of these vantage points, the human being seems to be striving basically to assert and to expand his self-determination. He is an autonomous being, a self-governing entity that asserts itself actively instead of reacting passively like a physical body to the impacts of the surrounding world. This fundamental tendency expresses itself in a striving of the person to consolidate and increase his self-government, in other words to exercise his freedom and to organize the relevant items of his world out of the autonomous center of government that is his self. This tendency—which I have termed "the trend toward increased autonomy"—expresses itself in spontaneity, self-assertiveness, striving for freedom and for mastery. In an objective fashion this tendency can be described as follows: the human being is an autonomous unity that, acting upon the surrounding world, molds and modifies it. His life is a resultant of self-determination on the one hand and the impacts of the surrounding world, the situation, on the other. This basic tendency, the trend toward increased autonomy, expresses the person's striving from a state of lesser self-determination (and greater situational influence) to a state of greater self-determination (and lesser situational influence).

Seen from another vantage point, human life reveals a very different basic pattern from the one described above. From this point of view the person appears to seek a place for himself in a larger unit of which he strives to become a part. In the first tendency we see him struggling for centrality in his world, trying to mold, to organize, the objects and the events of his world, to bring them under his own jurisdiction and government. In the second tendency he seems rather to strive to surrender himself willingly to seek a home for himself in and *to become an organic part of something that*

From "A Theoretical Model for Personality Studies," by Andras Angyal, *Journal of Personality*, September, 1951. Reprinted by permission of Duke University Press.

he conceives as greater than himself. The superindividual unit of which one feels oneself a part, or wishes to become a part, may be variously formulated according to one's cultural background and personal understanding. The superordinate whole may be represented for a person by a social unit—family, clan, nation—by a cause, by an ideology, or by a meaningfully ordered universe. In the realm of aesthetic, social, and moral attitudes this basic human tendency has a central significance. Its clearest manifestation, however, is in the religious attitude and religious experience.

I wish to state with emphasis that I am not speaking here about a tendency which is an exclusive prerogative of some people only, e.g., of those with a particular religious bent or aesthetic sensitivity, but of a tendency that I conceive as a universal and basic characteristic in all human beings.

These two tendencies of the human being, the tendency to increase his self-determination in his expanding personal world, and the tendency to surrender himself willingly to a superordinate whole, can be summed up by saying that the human being comports himself *as if he were a whole of an intermediate order.* By this I mean a "part-Gestalt" like, for example, the cardiovascular system, or the central nervous system, each of which is a *whole,* an organization of many parts, but at the same time a *part* with regard to its superordinate whole, the body. The human being is both a *unifier,* an organizer of his immediate personal world, and a *participant* in what he conceives as the superordinate whole to which he belongs.

The basic human attitude that makes man behave as a part of a larger whole reflects itself also in his "horizontal relationships," that is in his relationship to the other "parts," to other persons. Were man's behavior determined exclusively by his urge for mastery, his attitude toward others could be only as toward means to his ends. Experiencing others as coparticipants in a larger whole brings, however, another facet of his nature into manifestation. To avoid the coining of some outlandish term, we call this basic relation "love." In common usage this word has been badly misused to denote not only cheap sentimentality but even relationships that are actually founded on exploitation, possessiveness, helplessness, and similar destructive attitudes. The basic nature of love consists in a recognition of the *value* and acceptance of the *otherness* of the loved "object" while at the same time one experiences an essential *sameness* that exists between oneself and what one loves.

16 The Self As Hostile and Destructive

Leon Saul

All words signifying emotion present difficulties of definition. They require not merely intellectual comprehension but emotional realization; that is, they have to be felt as well as understood. We have all had the experience of reading something easily, simply, and then years later understanding what it really was all about, what it really meant. And anyone who has had some psychoanalysis knows the dramatic differences between the first intellectual awareness of some psychological force and the later, emotional impact of true insight into and appreciation of it.

As to hostility, happy is he who has suffered so little from his own hates and angers and from the attacks of his fellow men that he requires a "feeling" definition. What we mean by hostility in this book is the tendency of an organism to do something harmful to another organism or to itself. It is not just aggression: aggression (from the Latin, meaning moving actively) may have a constructive meaning (as in getting a good job done); it need not be hostile, and, conversely, hostility need not be aggressive; it may be passively expressed.

Nor is hostility anger, necessarily, for anger reflects a transient feeling which can be compatible with love. One can fully, without interruption and alteration, love someone despite periods of anger, as every husband, wife, child, parent and friend knows.

Hostility can be hate; hate expresses hostility and something deeper than anger. Hate, like hostility, implies hurt to others, expresses enmity and seeks directly no socially constructive end. There can be hostility without hate. Hate is one kind of hostility.

Hostility can take almost limitless forms, can be used for every sort of purpose, and can range in intensity from a glance or a breath of gossip to vindictiveness, violence, brutality and murder.

For hostility is the essential evil in people. Wrongness in personal and social behavior might well be judged by this touchstone: Is it *for* life, for the development, adjustment, happiness and fulfillment of society and its individuals, or is it against it?

As a technical definition one might hazard the following: Hostility is a motivating force—an impulse, urge, tendency, intent, motivation or reaction

—toward injury or destruction of some kind or degree, toward an object which can be animate (including oneself) or inanimate, usually accompanied in humans by the feeling or emotion of anger; the hostility can be conscious or unconscious. As we shall see, even a single-celled animal, like the ameba, can have hostility in the sense of a reaction of destructiveness against threats and irritants to it.

It has always been important to understand the motives by which we live, love, reproduce—and hate. But today, with the finding of new, unlimitable forces of energy, it is particularly important. For today we stand at an historic crossroads; in one discovery—the discovery of nuclear energy—we have found the means by which we can, on the one hand, destroy ourselves as a species, or, on the other, literally create a land of milk and honey, of health and happiness, a veritable heaven on earth the like of which man has never seen before.

Which choice we make depends on each of us. Human behavior has become the key to survival or to total destruction. Each individual in our society is activated by strong asocial and antisocial motivations, as well as by social ones. Only by understanding these two sets of motives, the one against life, and the other for it, can we implement those that are prohuman and reduce those that are antihuman; only in this way can we avoid the terror, tyranny, war and want that threaten us all.

All this seems clear enough on the surface, but there will be those who will resist understanding it none the less. For as well as the difficulty of understanding emotional terms in general, there is a special controversial difficulty about hostility that makes it hard to consider it calmly. Just as discussions of sex, dependency, prestige and like motivations arouse passionate feelings in most people, so does hostility, and true detachment in dealing with it is rare indeed.

Some of this stems from prejudice and rationalization. Many people like to believe that hostility is inherited, and therefore should be dismissed as something about which nothing, for the present at least, can be done. Others believe, falsely, that hostility is a strength, that without it men and women would be left defenseless in a world all too ready to attack and exploit the weak. And some will resist the study of hostility just from the tendency of mankind to resist any new idea. The great physician William Harvey feared to make known what is now accepted as a commonplace fact—the circulation of the blood. "I not only fear injury to myself from the envy of a few, but I tremble lest I have mankind at large for my enemies, so much does wont and custom become second nature," he said. "Doctrine once sown strikes deeply at its root and respect for antiquity influences all men. Still the die is cast and my trust is in the love of truth and the candor of cultivated minds."

Besides such general reasons for shunning the problem of hostility, there are others more individual and deep-seated. Some people balk at accepting hostility as a psychological force because of hostile reactions within themselves. A friend of mine, hearing of this study, reacted quite unsympathetically. Because he was basically a man of good will, his reaction aroused my interest. He was one of those people whose hostilities were overinhibited when he was a child and as a result he felt that his wings were clipped, that he lacked the capacity of self-defense even for proper purposes. In shunning this unpleasant conflict within himself, he reacted like an ostrich, put his head in the sand and maintained that the less said about hostility the better.

Guilt for one's own known hostile reactions and deeds may also impair objective understanding, for the feeling of guilt brings conscience reactions and a need for punishment. Some people may even prefer punishment to cure and suffering to happiness. Indeed, in psychoanalytical practice it is not uncommon to see patients who truly feel that they do not deserve to be cured. This masochism, this need for suffering, is so widespread that it often extends to society in general, with a resulting feeling, usually unconscious, that mankind deserves its miseries and should not be helped toward a better life.

Freud himself started his study of the neuroses by focusing on the sexual drives and did not face squarely the vital importance of hostility until late in life, when he was unable to give it the detailed clinical attention which he gave to the libidinal impulses. However, he expanded his instinct theory into a broad dualistic view of life as fundamentally an interplay between the forces of destruction and death (Thanatos) and of creativity (Eros).

"I know that we have always had before our eyes manifestations of the destruction instinct fused with erotism, directed outwards and inwards in sadism and masochism, but I can no longer understand how we could have overlooked the universality of non-erotic aggression and destruction and could have omitted to give it its due significance in our interpretation of life," he wrote in Civilization and Its Discontents, published in 1931, some eight years before his death at 83.

"I can remember my own defensive attitude," he went on, "when the idea of an instinct of destruction first made its appearance in psychoanalytical literature and how long it took until I accepted it. That others should have shown the same resistance, and still show it, surprises me less. Those who love fairy tales do not like it when people speak of the innate tendencies in mankind toward aggression, destruction and, in addition, cruelty."

He discusses this further and then forthrightly declares:

"In all that follows I take up the standpoint that the tendency toward aggression is an innate, independent, instinctual disposition in man and that it constitutes the most powerful obstacle to culture."

What can we do about this "tendency toward aggression," this *hostility* (to label it more accurately)?

Each of us can focus attention upon the problem and then discern what his contribution is—and try to make it.

I believe man's hostility to man is the central problem in human affairs. I also believe it is recognizable in its various forms, that it is a disease to be cured and prevented like cancer, tuberculosis or smallpox, and that its cure will result in healthier, better living—not only for society in general but for each individual in particular.

The Self As Hidden   17
Sigmund Freud

We shall now begin, not with postulates, but with an investigation. For this purpose we shall select certain phenomena which are very frequent, very familiar, and much overlooked, and which have nothing to do with illness, since they may be observed in every healthy person. I refer to the errors that everyone commits: as when anyone wishes to say a certain thing but uses the wrong word ('slip of the tongue'); [1] or when the same sort of mistake is made in writing ('slip of the pen'),[2] in which case one may or may not notice it; or when anyone reads in print or writing something other than what is actually before him ('misreading'); [3] or when anyone mis-hears [4] what is said to him, naturally when there is no question of any disease of the auditory sense-organ. Another series of such phenomena are those based on forgetting [5] something temporarily, though not permanently; as, for instance, when anyone cannot think of a name which he knows quite well and is always able to recognize whenever he sees it; or when anyone forgets to carry out some intention, which he afterwards remembers, and has therefore forgotten only for a certain time. This element of transitoriness is lacking in a third class, of which mislaying [6] things so that they cannot be found is an example. This is a kind of forgetfulness which we regard differently from the usual kind; one is amazed or annoyed at it, instead of finding it comprehensible. Allied to this are certain *mistakes,* in which the temporary element is again noticeable, as when one believes something for a time which both before and afterwards one knows to be untrue, and a number of similar manifestations which we know under various names.

Some inner relation between all these kinds of occurrences is indicated

From Second, Third, and Fourth Lectures of "The Psychology of Errors," with deletions, trans. by Joan Riviere, New York, Perma Giants, 1949. From: *A General Introduction to Psychoanalysis* by Sigmund Freud. By permission of Liveright, Publishers, N.Y. Copyright © Renewed, 1963 by Joan Riviere. Also by permission of George Allen & Unwin,Ltd.

1 In German—*Versprechen.*   2 *Verschreiben.*
3 *Verlesen.*   4 *Verhören.*
5 *Vergessen.*   6 *Verlegen.*

in German, by the use of the prefix "*ver*" which is common to all the words designating them.* These words almost all refer to acts of an unimportant kind, generally temporary and without much significance in life. It is only rarely that anything of the kind, such as the loss of some object, attains any practical importance. For this reason little attention is paid to such happenings and they arouse little feeling.

I am now going to ask you to consider these phenomena.

.   .   .

Let us select slips of the tongue, as the type of error best suited to our purpose. We might equally well choose slips of the pen or of reading. Now we must first remind ourselves that, so far, we have only enquired when and under what conditions the wrong word is said, and have received an answer on that point only. Interest may be directed elsewhere, though, and the question raised why just this particular slip is made and no other: one can consider the nature of the mistake. You will see that so long as this question remains unanswered, and the *effect* of the mistake is not explained, the phenomenon remains a pure accident on the psychological side, even if a physiological explanation has been found for it. When it happens that I make a mistake in a word I could obviously do this in an infinite number of ways, in place of the right word substitute any one of a thousand others, or make innumerable distortions of the right word. Now, is there anything which forces upon me in a specific instance just this one special slip, out of all those which are possible, or does that remain accidental and arbitrary, and can nothing rational be found in answer to this question?

Two authors, Meringer and Mayer (a philologist and a psychiatrist) did indeed in 1895 make an attempt to approach the problem of slips of the tongue from this side. They collected examples and first treated them from a purely descriptive standpoint. This of course does not yet furnish any explanation, but it may lead the way to one. They differentiated the distortions which the intended phrase suffered through the slip into: interchanges (in the positions of words, syllables or letters), anticipations, perseverations, compoundings (contaminations), and substitutions. I will give you examples of these authors' main categories. As an instance of an interchange (in the position of words) someone might say "The Milo of Venus" instead of "The Venus of Milo." The well-known slip of the hotel-boy who, knocking at the bishop's door, nervously replied to the question "Who is it?" "The Lord, my boy!" is another example of such an interchange in the position of words. In the typical Spoonerism the position of certain letters is interchanged, as when the preacher said: "How often do we feel a halfwarmed fish within us!"† It is a case of anticipation if any one says: "The thought lies heartily . . ." instead of: "The thought lies heavily on my heart." A perseveration is illustrated by the well-known ill-fated toast, "Gentlemen, I call upon (*auf*) you to

* [The equivalent English prefix is "mis-," but is not so widely employed.—Tr.]
† [English examples.—Tr.]

> *hiccough* (= *auf*zustossen)
> (*auf*)   to the health of our Chief."
> (drink) (= *an*zustossen)

And when a member of the House of Commons referred to another as the "honourable member for Central *Hell*," instead of "Hull," it was a case of perseveration; as also when a soldier said to a friend "I wish there were a thousand of our men *mortified* on that hill, Bill," instead of "fortified." In one case the *ell* sound has perseverated from the previous words "member for Central," and in the other the *m* sound in "*men*" has perseverated to form "mortified." * These three types of slip are not very common. You will find those cases much more frequent in which the slip happens by a compounding or contraction, as for example when a gentleman asks a lady if he may *insort* her on her way (*begleit-digen*); this contraction is made up of *begleiten* = to escort, and *beleidigen* = to insult. (And by the way, a young man addressing a lady in this way will not have much success with her.) A substitution takes place when a poor woman says she has an "incurable *infernal* disease,"* or in Mrs. Malaprop's mind when she says, for instance, "few gentlemen know how to value the *ineffectual* qualities in a woman." *

The explanation which the two authors attempt to formulate as the basis of their collection of examples is peculiarly inadequate. They hold that the sounds and syllables of a word have different values and that the innervation of the sounds of higher value can interfere with those of lower value. They obviously base this conclusion on the cases of anticipation and perseveration which are not at all frequent; in other forms of slips of the tongue the question of such sound priorities, even if they exist, does not enter at all; for the most frequent type of slip is that in which instead of a certain word one says another which resembles it, and this resemblance is considered by many people sufficient explanation of it. For instance, a professor may say in his opening lecture, "I am not inclined (*geneigt* instead of *geeignet* = fitted) to estimate the merits of my predecessor." Or another professor says, "In the case of the female genital, in spite of the *tempting* . . . I mean, the *attempted* . . ." (*Versuchungen* instead of *Versuche*).

The commonest and also the most noticeable form of slip of the tongue, however, is that of saying the exact opposite of what one meant to say. These cases are quite outside the effect of any relations between sounds or confusion due to similarity, and in default one may therefore turn to the fact that opposites have a strong conceptual connection with one another and are psychologically very closely associated. There are well-known examples of this sort. For instance, the President of our Parliament once opened the session with the words "Gentlemen, I declare a quorum present and herewith declare the session *closed*."

.   .   .

In other cases, where the form of the slip is not exactly the opposite of what is intended, a contradictory sense may still often come to expression. "I

---

* [English examples.—Tr.]

am not *inclined* (*geneigt*) to appreciate my predecessor's merits." "Inclined"
is not the opposite of "in a position to" (*geeignet*), but it is an open confession of a thought in sharpest contradiction to the speaker's duty to meet the
situation gracefully.

In still other cases the slip simply adds a second meaning to the intended. The sentence then sounds like a contraction, an abbreviation, a
condensation of several sentences into one. Thus the determined lady who
said: "He may eat and drink whatever I choose." That is as if she had said:
"He can eat and drink what he chooses, but what does it matter what he
chooses? It is for me to do the choosing!" Slips of the tongue often give this
impression of abbreviation; for instance, when a professor of anatomy at the
end of his lecture on the nasal cavities asks whether his class has thoroughly
understood it and, after a general reply in the affirmative, goes on to say: "I
can hardly believe that that is so, since persons who can thoroughly understand the nasal cavities can be counted, even in a city of millions, on *one
finger* . . . I mean, on the fingers of one hand." The abbreviated sentence has
its own meaning: it says that there is only one person who understands the
subject.

.   .   .

We believe that we have now discovered the secret of a large number
of slips of the tongue. If we keep this clear in mind we shall be able to
comprehend still further groups hitherto entirely mysterious. Although, for
instance, in a case of distortion of a name we cannot suppose that it is always a matter of a contest between two similar but different names, yet the
second intention is easily perceived. Distortions of names are common enough
apart from slips of the tongue; they are attempts to liken the name to something derogatory or degrading, a common form of abuse, which educated
persons soon learn to avoid but nevertheless do not willingly give up. It may
be dressed up as a joke, although one of a very low order. To quote one
gross and ugly example of such a distortion of a name, the name of the
President of the French Republic, *Poincaré*, has lately been transformed into
"*Schweinskarré*." It is not going much further to assume that some such
abusive intention may also be behind distortions of names produced by a slip
of the tongue. In pursuing our idea, similar explanations suggest themselves
for cases of slips where the effect is comic or absurd. In the case of the
member of parliament who referred to the "honourable member for Central
Hell," the sober atmosphere of the House is unexpectedly disturbed by the
intrusion of a word that calls up a ludicrous and unflattering image; we are
bound to conclude from the analogy with certain offensive and abusive expressions that an impulse has interposed here, to this effect: "You needn't be
taken in. I don't mean a word of this. To hell with the fellow!" The same
applies to slips of the tongue which transform quite harmless words into
obscene and indecent ones.*

---

* [Two untranslatable examples are given in the text, *apopos* for *à propos* and
Eischeissweibchen for *Eiweisscheibchen*. (Meringer and Mayer.)—Tr.]

We are familiar with this tendency in certain people intentionally to convert harmless words into indecent ones for the sake of the amusement obtained; it passes for wit, and in fact when one hears of a case one at once asks whether it was intended as a joke or occurred unintentionally as a slip of the tongue.

Well, we seem to have solved the riddle of errors with comparatively little trouble! They are not accidents; they are serious mental acts; they have their meaning; they arise through the concurrence—perhaps better, the mutual interference—of two different intentions.

.   .   .

Accumulated and combined errors are certainly the finest flowers of the species. If we were only concerned to prove that errors had a meaning, we should have limited ourselves to them at the outset, for the meaning in them is unmistakable, even to the dullest intelligence, and strong enough to impress the most critical judgment. The repetition of the occurrences betrays a persistence which is hardly ever an attribute of chance, but which fits well with the idea of design. Further, the exchanging of one kind of mistake for another shows us what is the most important and essential element in the error; and that is, not its form, or the means of which it makes use, but the *tendency* which makes use of it and can achieve its end in the most various ways. Thus I will give you a case of repeated forgetting: Ernest Jones relates that he once allowed a letter to lie on his writing desk for several days for some unknown reason. At last he decided to post it, but received it back from the dead-letter office, for he had forgotten to address it. After he had addressed it he took it to post but this time without a stamp. At this point he finally had to admit to himself his objection to sending the letter at all.

In another case, taking up a thing by mistake is combined with mislaying it. A lady travelled to Rome with her brother-in-law, a famous artist. The visitor was much fêted by the Germans living in Rome and received, among other things, a present of an antique gold medal. The lady was vexed because her brother-in-law did not appreciate the fine specimen highly enough. After her sister had arrived she returned home and discovered, upon unpacking, that she had brought the medal with her—how, she did not know. She wrote at once to her brother-in-law telling him that she would send the stolen property back to him the next day. But the next day the medal was so cleverly mislaid that it could not be discovered and could not be returned, and then it began to dawn upon the lady what her "absent-mindedness" had meant, namely, that she wanted to keep the work of art for herself.*

I have already given you an example of a combination of forgetfulness with an error, in the case in which someone forgets an appointment, and a second time, with the firm intention of not forgetting it again, appears at an hour which is not the appointed one. A quite analogous case was told me from his own experience by a friend who pursues literary as well as scientific

* From R. Reitler.

interests. He said: "Some years ago I accepted election to the Council of a certain literary society because I hoped that the society might at some time be useful to me in getting a play of mine produced; and, although not much interested, I attended the meetings regularly every Friday. A few months ago I received an assurance that my play would be produced at a theatre in F. and since then it has invariably happened that I *forget* to attend the meetings of the society. When I read your writings on this subject, I reproached myself with my meanness in staying away now that these people can no longer be of use to me and determined on no account to forget on the following Friday. I kept reminding myself of my resolution until I carried it out and stood at the door of the meeting-room. To my amazement it was closed and the meeting was already over! I had made a mistake in the day of the week and it was then Saturday!"

It would be tempting to collect more of these examples, but I will pass on and, instead, let you glance at those cases in which interpretation has to wait for confirmation in the future.

The main condition in these cases is, as we might expect, that the mental situation at the time is unknown or cannot be ascertained. At the moment, therefore, our interpretation is no more than a supposition to which we ourselves would not ascribe too much weight. Later, however, something happens which shows us how well justified our previous interpretation was. I was once the guest of a young married couple and heard the young wife laughingly describe her latest experience, how the day after the return from the honeymoon she had called for her sister and gone shopping with her as in former times, while her husband went to his business. Suddenly she noticed a man on the other side of the street and, nudging her sister, said, "Look, there goes Mr. K." She had forgotten that this man had been her husband for some weeks. A shudder went over me as I heard the story, but I dared not draw the inference. Several years later the little incident came back to my mind after this marriage had come to a most unhappy end.

Maeder tells a story of a lady who had forgotten to try on her wedding-dress the day before the wedding, to the despair of the dressmaker, and remembered it only late in the evening. He connects it with the fact that soon after the marriage she was divorced by her husband. I know a woman now divorced from her husband who, in managing her money-affairs, frequently signed documents with her maiden name, many years before she really resumed it. I know of other women who lost their wedding-rings on the honeymoon and know, too, that the course of the marriage lent meaning to this accident. And now one striking example more, with a better ending. It is told of a famous German chemist that his marriage never took place because he forgot the hour of the ceremony and went to the laboratory instead of to the church. He was wise enough to let the matter rest with one attempt, and died unmarried at a ripe age.

Perhaps the idea has also come to you that in these examples mistakes seem to have replaced the omens or portents of the ancients. And indeed, certain kinds of portents were nothing but errors, for instance, when anyone stumbled or fell down. It is true that another group of omens bore the character of objective events rather than of subjective acts. But you would not believe how difficult it is sometimes to decide whether a specific instance belongs to the first category or to the second. The act knows so often how to disguise itself as a passive experience.

Every one of us who can look back over a fairly long experience of life would probably say that he might have spared himself many disappointments and painful surprises, if he had had the courage and resolution to interpret as omens the little mistakes which he noticed in his intercourse with others, and to regard them as signs of tendencies still in the background. For the most part one does not dare to do this; one has an impression that one would become superstitious again by a circuitous scientific path. And then, not all omens come true, and our theories will show you how it is that they need not all come true.

.   .   .

Cases of forgetting to carry out resolutions are usually so uniform and transparent, that they are of no interest for our researches. There are two points, nevertheless, at which something new can be learnt by studying this type of error. We have said that forgetting and not executing a resolution indicate an antagonistic tendency in opposition to it. This is certainly true, but our own investigations show that this "counter-will" may be of two kinds, either immediate or mediate. What is meant by the latter is best explained by one or two examples. When the patron forgets to say a good word for his protégé to some third person, it may happen because he is actually not much interested in the protégé and therefore has no great inclination to do it. This, in any case, will be the protégé's view of the patron's omission. But the matter may be more complicted. The antipathy against executing the resolution may come from some other source in the patron and be directed to some other point. It need have nothing at all to do with the protégé, but is perhaps directed against the third person to whom the recommendation was to be made. Here again, you see, what objections there are against applying our interpretations practically. In spite of having correctly interpreted the error, the protégé is in danger of becoming too suspicious and of doing his patron a grave injustice. Again, if someone forgets an appointment which he had promised and was resolved to attend, the commonest cause is certainly a direct disinclination to meet the other person. But analysis might produce evidence that the interfering tendency was concerned, not with the person, but with the place of meeting, which was avoided on account of some painful memory associated with it. Or if one forgets to post a letter the opposing tendency may be concerned with the contents of the letter; but this does not exclude the possibility that the letter in itself is harmless and becomes the subject of a counter-tendency only because something in it reminds the writer of another letter, written previously, which did in fact afford a direct basis for antipathy. It may then be said that the antipathy has been *transferred* from the earlier letter, where it was justified, to the present one where it actually has no object. So you see that restraint and caution must be exercised in applying our quite well-founded interpretations; that which is psychologically equivalent may in actuality have many meanings.

That such things should be must seem very strange to you. Perhaps you will be inclined to assume that the "indirect" counter-will is enough to characterize the incident as pathological. But I can assure you that it is also found within the boundaries of health and normality. And further, do not misunderstand me; this is in no sense a confession on my part that our analytic interpretations are not to be relied on. I have said that forgetting to execute a plan may bear many meanings, but this is so only in those cases where no analysis is undertaken and which we have to interpret according to our general principles. If an analysis of the person in the case is carried out it can always be established with sufficient certainty whether the antipathy is a direct one, or what its source is otherwise.

The following is a second point: when we find proof in a large majority of cases that the forgetting of an intention proceeds from a counter-will, we gain courage to extend this solution to another group of cases in which the person analysed does not confirm, but denies, the presence of the counter-will inferred by us. Take as an example of this such exceedingly frequent occurrences as forgetting to return borrowed books or to pay bills or debts. We will be so bold as to suggest, to the person in question, that there is an intention in his mind of keeping the books and not paying the debts, whereupon he will deny this intention but will not be able to give us any other explanation of his conduct. We then insist that he has this intention but is not aware of it; it is enough for us, though, that it betrays itself by the effect of the forgetting. He may then repeat that he had merely forgotten about it. You will recognize the situation as one in which we have already been placed once before. If we intend to carry through, to their logical conclusions, the interpretations of errors which have been proved justified in so many cases, we shall be unavoidably impelled to the assumption that tendencies exist in human beings which can effect results without their knowing of them. With this, however, we place ourselves in opposition to all views prevailing in life and in psychology.

Forgetting proper names, and foreign names and words, can be traced in the same way to a counter-tendency aiming either directly or indirectly against the name in question. I have already given you several examples of such direct antipathy. Indirect causation is particularly frequent here and careful analysis is generally required to elucidate it. Thus, for instance, in the present time of war which forces us to forego so many of our former pleasures, our ability to recall proper names suffers severely by connections of the most farfetched kind. It happened to me lately to be unable to remember the name of the harmless Moravian town of Bisenz; and analysis showed that I was guilty of no direct antagonism in the matter, but that the resemblance to the name of the Palazzo Bisenzi in Orvieto, where I had spent many happy times in the past, was responsible. As a motive of the tendency opposing the recollection of this name, we here for the first time encounter a principle which will later on reveal itself to be of quite prodigious importance in the causation of neurotic symptoms: namely, the aversion on the part of memory against recalling anything connected with painful feelings that would revive the pain if it were recalled. In this tendency towards *avoidance of pain* from recollection or other mental processes, this flight of the mind from that which is unpleasant, we may perceive the ultimate purpose at work behind not merely the forgetting of names, but also many other errors, omissions, and mistakes.

The forgetting of names seems, however, to be especially facilitated psycho-physiologically, and therefore does occur on occasions where the intervention of an unpleasantness-motive cannot be established. When anyone has a tendency to forget names, it can be confirmed by analytic investigation that names escape, not merely because he does not like them or because they remind him of something disagreeable, but also because the particular name belongs to some other chain of associations of a more intimate nature. The name is anchored there, as it were, and is refused to the other associations activated at the moment. If you recall the devices of memory systems you will realize with some surprise that the same associations which are there artificially introduced, in order to save names from being forgotten, are also responsible for their being forgotten. The most conspicuous example of this is afforded by proper names of persons, which naturally possess quite different values for different people. For instance, take a first name, such as Theodore. For some of you it will have no particular significance; for others it will be the name of father, brother, friend, or your own name. Analytic experience will show you that the former among you will be in no danger of forgetting that some stranger bears this name; whereas the latter will be continually inclined to grudge to strangers a name which to them seems reserved for an intimate relationship. Now let us assume that this inhibition due to associations may coincide with the operation of the "pain"-principle, and in addition with an indirect mechanism; you will then be able to form a commensurate idea of the complexity, in causation, of such temporary forgetting of names. An adequate analysis that does justice to the facts will, however, completely disclose all these complications.

The forgetting of impressions and experiences shows the working of the tendency to ward off from memory that which is unpleasant much more clearly and invariably than the forgetting of names. It does not of course belong in its entirety to the category of errors, but only in so far as it appears to us remarkable and unjustified, judged by the standard of general experience; as, for instance, where recent or important impressions are forgotten, or where one memory is forgotten out of an otherwise well-remembered sequence. How and why we have the capacity of forgetting in general, particularly how we are able to forget experiences which have certainly left the deepest impression on us, such as the events of our childhood, is quite a different problem, in which the defence against painful associations plays a certain part but is far from explaining everything. That unwelcome impressions are easily forgotten is an indubitable fact. Various psychologists have remarked it; and the great Darwin was so well aware of it that he made a golden rule for himself of writing down with particular care observations which seemed unfavourable to his theory, having become convinced that just these would be inclined to slip out of recollection.

Those who hear for the first time of this principle of defence against unpleasant memory by forgetfulness seldom fail to raise the objection that, on the contrary, in their experience it is just that which is painful which it is hard to forget, since it always comes back to mind to torture the person against his will—as, for example, the recollection of grievances or humiliations. This fact is quite correct, but the objection is not sound. It is important to begin early to reckon with the fact that the mind is an arena, a sort of tumbling-ground, for the struggles of antagonistic impulses; or, to express it in non-dynamic terms, that the mind is made up of contradictions and pairs of opposites. Evidence of one particular tendency does not in the least preclude its opposite; there is room for both of them. The material questions are: How do these opposites stand to one another and what effects proceed from one of them and what from the other?

Losing and mislaying objects is of especial interest on account of the numerous meanings it may have, and the multiplicity of the tendencies in the service of which these errors may be employed. What is common to all the cases is the wish to lose something; what varies in them is the reason for the wish and the aim of it. One loses something if it has become damaged; if one has an impulse to replace it with a better; if one has ceased to care for it; if it came from someone with whom unpleasantness has arisen; or if it was acquired in circumstances that one no longer wishes to think of. Letting things fall, spoiling, or breaking things, serves the same tendency. In social life it is said that unwelcome and illegitimate children are found to be far more often weakly than those conceived in happier circumstances. This result does not imply that the crude methods of the so-called baby-farmers have been employed; some degree of carelessness in the supervision of the child should be quite enough. The preservation, or otherwise, of objects may well follow the same lines as that of children.

Then too it may happen that a thing will become destined to be lost without its having shed any of its value—that is, when there is an impulse to sacrifice something to fate in order to avert some other dreaded loss. According to the findings of analysis, such conjurings of fate are still very common among us, so that our losses are often voluntary sacrifices. Losing may equally well serve the impulses of spite or of self-punishment; in short, the more remote forms of motivation behind the impulse to do away with something by losing cannot easily be exhausted.

Mistaking of objects, or erroneous performance of actions, like other errors, is often made use of to fulfil a wish which should be denied; the intention masquerades as a lucky chance. Thus, as once happened to a friend, one has to take a train, most unwillingly, in order to pay a visit in the suburbs and then, in changing trains at a connection, gets by mistake into one which is returning to town; or, on a journey someone might greatly like to make a halt at some stopping-place, which cannot be done owing to fixed engagements elsewhere, whereupon he mistakes or misses the connection, so that the desired delay is forced upon him. Or, as happened to one of my patients whom I had forbidden to telephone to the lady he was in love with, he "by mistake" and "thoughtlessly" gave the wrong number when he meant to telephone to me, so that he was suddenly connected with her. The following account by an engineer is a pretty example of the conditions under which damage to material objects may be done, and also demonstrates the practical significance of directly faulty actions.

"Some time ago I worked with several colleagues in the laboratory of a High School on a series of complicated experiments in elasticity, a piece of work we had undertaken voluntarily; it was beginning to take up more time, however, than we had anticipated. One day, as I went into the laboratory with my friend F., he remarked how annoying it was to him to lose so much time to-day as he had so much to do at home; I could not help agreeing with him and said half-jokingly, referring to an occasion the week before: 'Let us hope the machine will break down again so that we can stop work and go home early.' In arranging the work it happened that F. was given the regulation of the valve of the press; that is to say, he was, by cautiously opening the valve, to let the liquid pressure out of the accumulator slowly into the cylinder of the hydraulic press. The man who was conducting the experiment stood by the pressure gauge, and, when the right pressure was reached, called out loudly, 'Stop.' At this command F. seized the valve and turned with all his might—to the left! (All valves without exception close to the right.) Thereby the whole pressure in the accumulator suddenly came into the press, a strain for which the connecting-pipes are not designed, so that one of them instantly burst—quite a harmless accident, but one which forced us, nevertheless, to cease work for the day and go home. It is characteristic, by the way, that not long after, when we were discussing the affair, my friend F. had no recollection whatever of my remark, which I recalled with certainty."

So with this in mind you may begin to suspect that it is not always a mere chance which makes the hands of your servants such dangerous enemies to your household effects. And you may also raise the question whether it is always an accident when one injures one self or exposes oneself to danger— ideas which you may put to the test by analysis when you have an opportunity.

THE SELF AND CULTURE

18   The Self As Mirror

Charles Horton Cooley

The distinctive thing in the idea for which the pronouns of the first person are names is apparently a characteristic kind of feeling which may be called the my-feeling or sense of appropriation. Almost any sort of ideas may be associated with this feeling, and so come to be named "I" or "mine," but the feeling, and that alone it would seem, is the determining factor in the matter. As Professor James says in his admirable discussion of the self, the words "me" and "self" designate "all the things which have the power to produce in a stream of consciousness excitement of a certain peculiar sort." [1] This view is very fully set forth by Professor Hiram M. Stanley, whose work, "The Evolutionary Psychology of Feeling," has an extremely suggestive chapter on self-feeling.

I do not mean that the feeling aspect of the self is necessarily more important than any other, but that it is the immediate and decisive sign and proof of what "I" is; there is no appeal from it; if we go behind it it must be to study its history and conditions, not to question its authority. But, of course, this study of history and conditions may be quite as profitable as the direct contemplation of self-feeling. What I would wish to do is to present each aspect in its proper light.

The emotion or feeling of self may be regarded as instinctive, and was doubtless evolved in connection with its important function in· stimulating and unifying the special activities of individuals. It is thus very profoundly

From Ch. 5, "The Social Self—1. The Meaning of 'I'," with deletions and some footnotes omitted, in *Human Nature and the Social Order*, by Charles Horton Cooley, New York, Scribner, 1902.

[1] "*The words* ME, *then, and* SELF, *so far as they arouse feeling and connote emotional worth, are* OBJECTIVE *designations meaning* ALL THE THINGS *which have the power to produce in a stream of consciousness excitement of a certain peculiar sort.*" Psychology, i., p. 319. A little earlier he says: "*In its widest possible sense, however, a man's self is the sum total of all he* CAN *call his, not only his body and his psychic powers, but his clothes and his house, his wife and children, his ancestors and friends, his reputation and works, his lands and horses and yacht and bank-account. All these things give him the same emotions.*" *Idem,* p. 291.

So Wundt says of "Ich": "Es ist ein *Gefühl,* nicht eine Vorstellung, wie es häufig genannt wird." Grundriss der Psychologie, 4 Auflage, S. 265.

rooted in the history of the human race and apparently indispensable to any plan of life at all similar to ours. It seems to exist in a vague though vigorous form at the birth of each individual, and, like other instinctive ideas or germs of ideas, to be defined and developed by experience, becoming associated, or rather incorporated, with muscular, visual, and other sensations; with perceptions, apperceptions, and conceptions of every degree of complexity and of infinite variety of content; and, especially, with personal ideas. Meantime the feeling itself does not remain unaltered, but undergoes differentiation and refinement just as does any other sort of crude innate feeling. Thus, while retaining under every phase its characteristic tone or flavor, it breaks up into innumerable self-sentiments. And concrete self-feeling, as it exists in mature persons, is a whole made up of these various sentiments, along with a good deal of primitive emotion not thus broken up. It partakes fully of the general development of the mind, but never loses that peculiar gusto of appropriation that causes us to name a thought with a first-personal pronoun. The other contents of the self-idea are of little use, apparently, in defining it, because they are so extremely various. It would be no more futile, it seems to me, to attempt to define fear by enumerating the things that people are afraid of, than to attempt to define "I" by enumerating the objects with which the word is associated. Very much as fear means primarily a state of feeling, or its expression, and not darkness, fire, lions, snakes, or other things that excite it, so "I" means primarily self-feeling, or its expression, and not body, clothes, treasures, ambition, honors, and the like, with which this feeling may be connected. In either case it is possible and useful to go behind the feeling and inquire what ideas arouse it and why they do so, but this is in a sense a secondary investigation.

Since "I" is known to our experience primarily as a feeling, or as a feeling-ingredient in our ideas, it cannot be described or defined without suggesting that feeling. We are sometimes likely to fall into a formal and empty way of talking regarding questions of emotion, by attempting to define that which is in its nature primary and indefinable. A formal definition of self-feeling, or indeed of any sort of feeling, must be as hollow as a formal definition of the taste of salt, or the color red; we can expect to know what it is only by experiencing it. There can be no final test of the self except the way we feel; it is that toward which we have the "my" attitude. But as this feeling is quite as familiar to us and as easy to recall as the taste of salt or the color red, there should be no difficulty in understanding what is meant by it. One need only imagine some attack on his "me," say ridicule of his dress or an attempt to take away his property or his child, or his good name by slander, and self-feeling immediately appears. Indeed, he need only pronounce, with strong emphasis, one of the selfwords, like "I" or "my," and self-feeling will be recalled by association.

. . .

As many people have the impression that the verifiable self, the object that we name with "I," is usually the material body, it may be well to say

that this impression is an illusion, easily dispelled by any one who will undertake a simple examination of facts. It is true that when we philosophize a
little about "I" and look around for a tangible object to which to attach it,
we soon fix upon the material body as the most available *locus;* but when we
use the word naïvely, as in ordinary speech, it is not very common to think
of the body in connection with it; not nearly so common as it is to think of
other things. There is no difficulty in testing this statement, since the word
"I" is one of the commonest in conversation and literature, so that nothing
is more practicable than to study its meaning at any length that may be
desired. One need only listen to ordinary speech until the word has occurred,
say, a hundred times, noting its connections, or observe its use in a similar
number of cases by the characters in a novel. Ordinarily it will be found that
in not more than ten cases in a hundred does "I" have reference to the body
of the person speaking. It refers chiefly to opinions, purposes, desires, claims,
and the like, concerning matters that involve no thought of the body. *I* think
or feel so and so; *I* wish or intend so and so; *I* want this or that; are typical
uses, the self-feeling being associated with the view, purpose, or object mentioned. It should also be remembered that "my" and "mine" are as much the
names of the self as "I," and these, of course, commonly refer to miscellaneous
possessions.

I had the curiosity to attempt a rough classification of the first hundred
"I's" and "me's" in Hamlet, with the following results. The pronoun was used
in connection with perception, as "I hear," "I see," fourteen times; with
thought, sentiment, intention, etc., thirty-two times; with wish, as "I pray
you," six times; as speaking—"I'll speak to it"—sixteen times; as spoken to,
twelve times; in connection with action, involving perhaps some vague notion
of the body, as "I came to Denmark," nine times; vague or doubtful, ten
times; as equivalent to bodily appearance—"No more like my father than I
to Hercules"—once. Some of the classifications are arbitrary, and another
observer would doubtless get a different result; but he could not fail, I think,
to conclude that Shakespeare's characters are seldom thinking of their bodies
when they say "I" or "me." And in this respect they appear to be representative of mankind in general.

As already suggested, instinctive self-feeling is doubtless connected in
evolution with its important function in stimulating and unifying the special
activities of individuals. It appears to be associated chiefly with ideas of the
exercise of power, of being a cause, ideas that emphasize the antithesis between the mind and the rest of the world. The first definite thoughts that a
child associates with self-feeling are probably those of his earliest endeavors
to control visible objects—his limbs, his playthings, his bottle, and the like.
Then he attempts to control the actions of the persons about him, and so his
circle of power and of self-feeling widens without interruption to the most
complex objects of mature ambition. Although he does not say "I" or "my"
during the first year or two, yet he expresses so clearly by his actions the

feeling that adults associate with these words that we cannot deny him a self even in the first weeks.

The correlation of self-feeling with purposeful activity is easily seen by observing the course of any productive enterprise. If a boy sets about making a boat, and has any success, his interest in the matter waxes, he gloats over it, the keel and stem are dear to his heart, and its ribs are more to him than those of his own frame. He is eager to call in his friends and acquaintances, saying to them, "See what I am doing! Is it not remarkable?" feeling elated when it is praised, and resentful or humiliated when fault is found with it. But so soon as he finishes it and turns to something else, his self-feeling begins to fade away from it, and in a few weeks at most he will have become comparatively indifferent. We all know that much the same course of feeling accompanies the achievements of adults. It is impossible to produce a picture, a poem, an essay, a difficult bit of masonry, or any other work of art or craft, without having self-feeling regarding it, amounting usually to considerable excitement and desire for some sort of appreciation; but this rapidly diminishes with the activity itself, and often lapses into indifference after it ceases.

It may perhaps be objected that the sense of self, instead of being limited to times of activity and definite purpose, is often most conspicuous when the mind is unoccupied or undecided, and that the idle and ineffectual are commonly the most sensitive in their self-esteem. This, however, may be regarded as an instance of the principle that all instincts are likely to assume troublesome forms when denied wholesome expression. The need to exert power, when thwarted in the open fields of life, is the more likely to assert itself in trifles.

.   .   .

In a very large and interesting class of cases the social reference takes the form of a somewhat definite imagination of how one's self—that is any idea he appropriates—appears in a particular mind, and the kind of self-feeling one has is determined by the attitude toward this attributed to that other mind. A social self of this sort might be called the reflected or looking-glass self:

> "Each to each a looking-glass
> Reflects the other that doth pass."

As we see our face, figure, and dress in the glass, and are interested in them because they are ours, and pleased or otherwise with them according as they do or do not answer to what we should like them to be; so in imagination we perceive in another's mind some thought of our appearance, manners, aims, deeds, character, friends, and so on, and are variously affected by it.

A self-idea of this sort seems to have three principal elements: the imagination of our appearance to the other person; the imagination of his judgment of that appearance, and some sort of self-feeling, such as pride or mortification. The comparison with a looking-glass hardly suggests the second element, the imagined judgment, which is quite essential. The thing that moves us to pride or shame is not the mere mechanical reflection of ourselves, but an imputed sentiment, the imagined effect of this reflection upon another's mind. This is evident from the fact that the character and weight of that other, in whose mind we see ourselves, makes all the difference with our feeling. We are ashamed to seem evasive in the presence of a straightforward man, cowardly in the presence of a brave one, gross in the eyes of a refined one, and so on. We always imagine, and in imagining share, the judgments of the other mind. A man will boast to one person of an action—say some sharp transaction in trade—which he would be ashamed to own to another.

.   .   .

The process by which self-feeling of the looking-glass sort develops in children may be followed without much difficulty. Studying the movements of others as closely as they do they soon see a connection between their own acts and changes in those movements; that is, they perceive their own influence or power over persons. The child appropriates the visible actions of his parent or nurse, over which he finds he has some control, in quite the same way as he appropriates one of his own members or a plaything, and he will try to do things with this new possession, just as he will with his hand or his rattle. A girl six months old will attempt in the most evident and deliberate manner to attract attention to herself, to set going by her actions some of those movements of other persons that she has appropriated. She has tasted the joy of being a cause, of exerting social power, and wishes more of it. She will tug at her mother's skirts, wriggle, gurgle, stretch out her arms, etc., all the time watching for the hoped-for effect. These performances often give the child, even at this age, an appearance of what is called affectation, that is, she seems to be unduly preoccupied with what other people think of her. Affectation, at any age, exists when the passion to influence others seems to overbalance the established character and give it an obvious twist or pose. It is instructive to find that even Darwin was, in his childhood, capable of departing from truth for the sake of making an impression. "For instance," he says in his autobiography, "I once gathered much valuable fruit from my father's trees and hid it in the shrubbery, and then ran in breathless haste to spread the news that I had discovered a hoard of stolen fruit."[2]

The young performer soon learns to be different things to different people, showing that he begins to apprehend personality and to foresee its operation. If the mother or nurse is more tender than just she will almost certainly be "worked" by systematic weeping. It is a matter of common observation that children often behave worse with their mother than with other and less sympathetic people. Of the new persons that a child sees it is evident that some make a strong impression and awaken a desire to interest and please them, while others are indifferent or repugnant. Sometimes the reason can be perceived or guessed, sometimes not; but the fact of selective interest, admiration, prestige, is obvious before the end of the second year. By that

[2] *Life and Letters of Charles Darwin,* by F. Darwin, p. 27.

time a child already cares much for the reflection of himself upon one personality and little for that upon another. Moreover, he soon claims intimate and tractable persons as *mine,* classes them among his other possessions, and maintains his ownership against all comers. M., at three years of age, vigorously resented R.'s claim upon their mother. The latter was "*my* mamma," whenever the point was raised.

Strong joy and grief depend upon the treatment this rudimentary social self receives. In the case of M. I noticed as early as the fourth month a "hurt" way of crying which seemed to indicate a sense of personal slight. It was quite different from the cry of pain or that of anger, but seemed about the same as the cry of fright. The slightest tone of reproof would produce it. On the other hand, if people took notice and laughed and encouraged, she was hilarious. At about fifteen months old she had become "a perfect little actress," seeming to live largely in imaginations of her effect upon other people. She constantly and obviously laid traps for attention, and looked abashed or wept at any signs of disapproval or indifference. At times it would seem as if she could not get over these repulses, but would cry long in a grieved way, refusing to be comforted. If she hit upon any little trick that made people laugh she would be sure to repeat it, laughing loudly and affectedly in imitation. She had quite a repertory of these small performances, which she would display to a sympathetic audience, or even try upon strangers. I have seen her at sixteen months, when R. refused to give her the scissors, sit down and make-believe cry, putting up her under lip and snuffling, meanwhile looking up now and then to see what effect she was producing.

In such phenomena we have plainly enough, it seems to me, the germ of personal ambition of every sort. Imagination co-operating with instinctive self-feeling has already created a social "I," and this has become a principal object of interest and endeavor.

Progress from this point is chiefly in the way of a greater definiteness, fulness, and inwardness in the imagination of the other's state of mind. A little child thinks of and tries to elicit certain visible or audible phenomena, and does not go back of them; but what a grown-up person desires to produce in others is an internal, invisible condition which his own richer experience enables him to imagine, and of which expression is only the sign. Even adults, however, make no separation between what other people think and the visible expression of that thought. They imagine the whole thing at once, and their idea differs from that of a child chiefly in the comparative richness and complexity of the elements that accompany and interpret the visible or audible sign. There is also a progress from the naïve to the subtle in socially self-assertive action. A child obviously and simply, at first, does things for effect. Later there is an endeavor to suppress the appearance of doing so; affection, indifference, contempt, etc., are simulated to hide the real wish to affect the self-image. It is perceived that an obvious seeking after good opinion is weak and disagreeable.

I doubt whether there are any regular stages in the development of social self-feeling and expression common to the majority of children. The sentiments of self develop by imperceptible gradations out of the crude appropriative instinct of new-born babes, and their manifestations vary indefinitely in different cases. Many children show "self-consciousness" conspicuously from the first half-year; others have little appearance of it at any age. Still others pass through periods of affectation whose length and time of occurrence would probably be found to be exceedingly various. In childhood, as at all times of life, absorption in some idea other than that of the social self tends to drive "self-consciousness" out.

19   The Self Alone
Henry David Thoreau

This is a delicious evening, when the whole body is one sense, and imbibes delight through every pore. I go and come with a strange liberty in Nature, a part of herself. As I walk along the stony shore of the pond in my shirt sleeves, though it is cool as well as cloudy and windy, and I see nothing special to attract me, all the elements are unusually congenial to me. The bull-frogs trump to usher in the night, and the note of the whippoorwill is borne on the rippling wind from over the water. Sympathy with the fluttering alder and poplar leaves almost takes away my breath; yet, like the lake, my serenity is rippled, but not ruffled. These small waves raised by the evening wind are as remote from storm as the smooth reflecting surface. Though it is now dark, the wind still blows and roars in the wood, the waves still dash, and some creatures lull the rest with their notes. The repose is never complete. The wildest animals do not repose, but seek their prey now; the fox, and skunk, and rabbit, now roam the fields and woods without fear. They are Nature's watchmen,—links which connect the days of animated life.

When I return to my house I find that visitors have been there and left their cards—either a bunch of flowers, or a wreath of evergreen, or a name in pencil on a yellow walnut leaf or a chip. They who come rarely to the woods take some little piece of the forest into their hands to play with by the way, which they leave, either intentionally or accidentally. One has peeled a willow wand, woven it into a ring, and dropped it on my table. I could always tell if visitors had called in my absence, either by the bended twigs or grass, or the print of their shoes, and generally of what sex, or age, or quality they were by some slight trace left, as a flower dropped, or a bunch of grass plucked and thrown away, even as far off as the railroad, half a mile distant,

The essay "Solitude," in *Walden*, by Henry David Thoreau, London, Walter Scott, 1886. This work was first published in 1854.

or by the lingering odour of a cigar or pipe. Nay, I was frequently notified of the passage of a traveller along the highway sixty rods off by the scent of his pipe.

There is commonly sufficient space about us. Our horizon is never quite at our elbows. The thick wood is not just at our door, nor the pond, but somewhat is always clearing, familiar and worn by us, appropriated and fenced in some way, and reclaimed from Nature. For what reason have I this vast range and circuit, some square miles of unfrequented forest, for my privacy, abandoned to me by men? My nearest neighbour is a mile distant, and no house is visible from any place but the hill-tops within half a mile of my own. I have my horizon bounded by woods all to myself; a distant view of the railroad where it touches the pond on the one hand, and of the fence which skirts the woodland road on the other. But for the most part it is as solitary where I live as on the prairies. It is as much Asia or Africa as New England. I have, as it were, my own sun, and moon, and stars, and a little world all to myself. At night there was never a traveller passed my house, or knocked at my door, more than if I were the first or last man, unless it were in the spring, when at long intervals some came from the village to fish for pouts,— they plainly fished much more in the Walden Pond of their own natures, and baited their hooks with darkness,—but they soon retreated, usually with light baskets, and left "the world to darkness and to me," and the black kernel of the night was never profaned by any human neighbourhood. I believe that men are generally still a little afraid of the dark, though the witches are all hung, and Christianity and candles have been introduced.

Yet I experienced sometimes that the most sweet and tender, the most innocent and encouraging society may be found in any natural object, even for the poor misanthrope and most melancholy man. There can be no very black melancholy to him who lives in the midst of Nature, and has his senses still. There was never yet such a storm, but it was Æolian music to a healthy and innocent ear. Nothing can rightly compel a simple and brave man to a vulgar sadness. While I enjoy the friendship of the seasons I trust that nothing can make life a burden to me. The gentle rain which waters my beans and keeps me in the house to-day is not drear and melancholy, but good for me too. Though it prevents my hoeing them, it is of far more worth than my hoeing. If it should continue so long as to cause the seeds to rot in the ground and destroy the potatoes in the low lands, it would still be good for the grass on the uplands, and, being good for the grass, it would be good for me. Sometimes, when I compare myself with other men, it seems as if I were more favoured by the gods than they, beyond any deserts that I am conscious of—as if I had a warrant and surety at their hands which my fellows have not, and were especially guided and guarded. I do not flatter myself, but if it be possible they flatter me. I have never felt lonesome, or in the least oppressed by a sense of solitude, but once, and that was a few weeks after I came to the woods, when, for an hour, I doubted if the near neighbourhood of man was not essential to a serene and healthy life. To be alone was something unpleasant. But I was at the same time conscious of a slight insanity in my mood, and seemed to foresee my recovery. In the midst of a gentle rain, while these thoughts prevailed, I was suddenly sensible of such sweet and beneficent society in Nature, in the very pattering of the drops, and in every sound and sight around my house, an infinite and unaccountable friendliness all at once like an atmosphere sustaining me, as made the fancied advantages of humn neighbourhood insignificant, and I have never thought of them since. Every little pine needle expanded and swelled with sympathy, and befriended me. I was so distinctly made aware of the presence of something kindred to me, even in scenes which we are accustomed to call wild and dreary, and also that the nearest of blood to me and humanest was not a person nor a villager, that I thought no place could ever be strange to me again.

> "Mourning untimely consumes the sad;
> Few are their days in the land of the living,
> Beautiful daughter of Toscar."

Some of my pleasantest hours were during the long rainstorms in the spring or fall, which confined me to the house for the afternoon as well as the forenoon, soothed by their ceaseless roar and pelting; when an early twilight ushered in a long evening in which many thoughts had time to take root and unfold themselves. In those driving north-east rains which tried the village houses so, when the maids stood ready with mop and pail in front entries to keep the deluge out, I sat behind my door in my little house, which was all entry, and thoroughly enjoyed its protection. In one heavy thunder-shower the lightning struck a large pitch-pine across the pond, making a very conspicuous and perfectly regular spiral groove from top to bottom, an inch or more deep, and four or five inches wide, as you would groove a walking-stick. I passed it again the other day, and was struck with awe on looking up and beholding that mark, now more distinct than ever, where a terrific and resistless bolt came down out of the harmless sky eight years ago. Men frequently say to me, "I should think you would feel lonesome down there, and want to be nearer to folks, rainy and snowy days and nights especially." I am tempted to reply to such—This whole earth which we inhabit is but a point in space. How far apart, think you, dwell the two most distant inhabitants of yonder star, the breadth of whose disc cannot be appreciated by our instruments? Why should I feel lonely? Is not our planet in the Milky Way? This which you put seems to me not to be the most important question. What sort of space is that which separates a man from his fellows and makes him solitary? I have found that no exertion of the legs can bring two minds much nearer to one another. What do we want most to dwell near to? Not to many men surely, the depôt, the post office, the bar-room, the meeting-house, the school-house, the grocery, Beacon Hill, or the Five Points, where men most congregate, but to the perennial source of our life, whence in all our experience we have found that to issue, as the willow stands near the water and sends out its roots in that direction. This will vary with different natures, but this is the place where a wise man will dig his cellar. . . . I one evening overtook one of my townsmen, who had accumulated what is called "a handsome property,"—though I never got a *fair* view of it,—on the Walden road, driving a pair of cattle to market, who inquired of me how I could bring my mind to give up so many of the comforts of life. I answered that I was very sure I liked it passably well; I was not joking. And so I went home to my bed, and left him to pick his way through the darkness and the mud to Brighton,—or Bright-town,—which place he would reach some time in the morning.

Any prospect of awakening or coming to life to a dead man makes indifferent all times and places. The place where that may occur is always the same, and indescribably pleasant to all our senses. For the most part we allow only outlying and transient circumstances to make our occasions. They are, in fact, the cause of our distraction. Nearest to all things is that power which fashions their being. *Next* to us the grandest laws are continually being executed. *Next* to us is not the workman whom we have hired, with whom we love so well to talk, but the workman whose work we are.

"How vast and profound is the influence of the subtile powers of Heaven and of Earth!"

"We seek to perceive them, and we do not see them; we seek to hear them, and we do not hear them; identified with the substance of things, they cannot be separated from them."

"They cause that in all the universe men purify and sanctify their hearts, and clothe themselves in their holiday garments to offer sacrifices and oblations to their ancestors. It is an ocean of subtile intelligences. They are everywhere, above us, on our left, on our right; they environ us on all sides."

We are the subjects of an experiment which is not a little interesting to me. Can we not do without the society of our gossips a little while under these circumstances,—have our own thoughts to cheer us? Confucius says truly, "Virtue does not remain as an abandoned orphan; it must of necessity have neighbours."

With thinking we may be beside ourselves in a sane sense. By a conscious effort of the mind we can stand aloof from actions and their consequences; and all things, good and bad, go by us like a torrent. We are not wholly involved in Nature. I may be either the driftwood in the stream, or Indra in the sky looking down on it. I *may* be affected by a theatrical exhibition; on the other hand, I *may not* be affected by an actual event which appears to concern me much more. I only know myself as a human entity; the scene, so to speak, of thoughts and affections; and am sensible of a certain doubleness by which I can stand as remote from myself as from another. However intense my experience, I am conscious of the presence and criticism of a part of me, which, as it were, is not a part of me, but spectator, sharing no experience, but taking note of it; and that is no more I than it is you. When the play, it may be the tragedy, of life is over, the spectator goes his way. It was a kind of fiction, a work of the imagination only, so far as he was concerned. This doubleness may easily make us poor neighbours and friends sometimes.

I find it wholesome to be alone the greater part of the time. To be in company, even with the best, is soon wearisome and dissipating. I love to be alone. I never found the companion that was so companionable as solitude. We are for the most part more lonely when we go abroad among men than when we stay in our chambers. A man thinking or working is always alone, let him be where he will. Solitude is not measured by the miles of space that intervene between a man and his fellows. The really diligent student in one of the crowded hives of Cambridge College is as solitary as a dervish in the desert. The farmer can work alone in the field or the woods all day, hoeing or chopping, and not feel lonesome, because he is employed; but when he comes home at night he cannot sit down in a room alone, at the mercy of his thoughts, but must be where he can "see the folks," and recreate, and, as he thinks, remunerate himself for his day's solitude; and hence he wonders how the student can sit alone in the house all night and most of the day without ennui and "the blues"; but he does not realise that the student, though in the house, is still at work in *his* field, and chopping in *his* woods, as the farmer in his, and in turn seeks the same recreation and society that the latter does, though it may be a more condensed form of it.

Society is commonly too cheap. We meet at very short intervals, not having had time to acquire any new value for each other. We meet at meals three times a-day, and give each other a new taste of that old musty cheese that we are. We have had to agree on a certain set of rules, called etiquette and politeness, to make this frequent meeting tolerable and that we need not come to open war. We meet at the post office, and at the sociable, and about the fireside every night; we live thick and are in each other's way, and stumble over one another, and I think that we thus lose some respect for one another. Certainly less frequency would suffice for all important and hearty communications. Consider the girls in a factory,—never alone, hardly in their dreams. It would be better if there were but one inhabitant to a square mile, as where I live. The value of a man is not in his skin, that we should touch him.

I have heard of a man lost in the woods and dying of famine and exhaustion at the foot of a tree, whose loneliness was relieved by the grotesque visions with which, owing to bodily weakness, his diseased imagination surrounded him, and which he believed to be real. So also, owing to bodily and mental health and strength, we may be continually cheered by a like but more normal and natural society, and come to know that we are never alone.

I have a great deal of company in my house; especially in the morning, when nobody calls. Let me suggest a few comparisons, that some one may convey an idea of my situation. I am no more lonely than the loon in the pond that laughs so loud, or than Walden Pond itself. What company has that lonely lake, I pray? And yet it has not the blue devils, but the blue angels in it, in the azure tint of its waters. The sun is alone, except in thick weather, when there sometimes appear to be two, but one is a mock sun. God is alone, —but the devil, he is far from being alone; he sees a great deal of company; he is legion. I am no more lonely than a single mullein or dandelion in a pasture, or a bean leaf, or sorrel, or a horse-fly, or a humble bee. I am no more lonely than the Mill Brook, or a weathercock, or the north star, or the south wind, or an April shower, or a January thaw, or the first spider in a new house.

I have occasional visits in the long winter evenings, when the snow falls fast and the wind howls in the wood, from an old settler and original proprietor, who is reported to have dug Walden Pond, and stoned it, and fringed it with pine woods: who tells me stories of old time and of new eternity; and between us we manage to pass a cheerful evening with social mirth and pleasant views of things, even without apples or cider,—a most wise and humorous friend, whom I love much, who keeps himself more secret than ever did Goffe or Whalley; and though he is thought to be dead, none can show where he is buried. An elderly dame, too, dwells in my neighbourhood, invisible to most persons, in whose odorous herb garden I love to stroll sometimes, gathering simples and listening to her fables; for she has a genius of unequalled fertility, and her memory runs back farther than mythology, and she can tell me the original of every fable, and on what fact every one is founded, for the incidents occurred when she was young. A ruddy and lusty old dame, who delights in all weathers and seasons, and is likely to outlive all her children yet.

The indescribable innocence and beneficence of Nature,—of sun, and wind, and rain, of summer and winter,—such health, such cheer, they afford for ever! and such sympathy have they ever with our race, that all Nature would be affected, and the sun's brightness fade, and the winds would sigh humanely, and the clouds rain tears, and the woods shed their leaves and put on mourning in midsummer, if any man should ever for a just cause grieve. Shall I not have intelligence with the earth? Am I not partly leaves and vegetable mould myself?

What is the pill which will keep us well, serene, contented? Not my or thy great-grandfather's, but our great-grandmother Nature's universal, vegetable, botanic medicines, by which she has kept herself young always, outlived so many old Parrs in her day, and fed her health with their decaying fatness. For my panacea, instead of one of those quack vials of a mixture dipped from Acheron and the Dead Sea, which come out of those long shallow black-schooner-looking waggons which we sometimes see made to carry bottles, let me have a draught of undiluted morning air. Morning air! If men will not drink of this at the fountain-head of the day, why, then, we must even bottle up some and sell it in the shops, for the benefit of those who have lost their subscription ticket to morning time in this world. But remember, it will not keep quite till noonday even in the coolest cellar, but drive out the stopples long ere that and follow westward the steps of Aurora. I am no worshipper of Hygeia, who was the daughter of that old herb-doctor Æsculapius, and who is represented on monuments holding a serpent in one hand, and in the other a cup out of which the serpent sometimes drinks; but rather of Hebe, cup-bearer to Jupiter, who was the daughter of Juno and wild lettuce, and who had the power of restoring gods and men to the vigour of youth. She was probably the only thoroughly sound-conditioned, healthy, and robust young lady that ever walked the globe, and whenever she came it was spring.

20   The Self in Another Culture
Ruth Benedict

Giri to one's name is the duty to keep one's reputation unspotted. It is a series of virtues—some of which seem to an Occidental to be opposites, but which to the Japanese have a sufficient unity because they are those duties which are not repayments on benefits received; they are "outside the circle of *on*." They are those acts which keep one's reputation bright without reference to a specific previous indebtedness to another person. They include therefore maintaining all the miscellaneous etiquette requirements of "proper station," showing stoicism in pain and defending one's reputation in profession or craft. Giri to one's name also demands acts which remove a slur or an insult; the slur darkens one's good name and should be got rid of. It may be necessary to take vengeance upon one's detractor or it may be necessary to commit suicide, and there are all sorts of possible courses of action between these two extremes. But one does not shrug off lightly anything that is compromising.

The Japanese do not have a separate term for what I call here "giri to one's name." They describe it simply as giri outside the circle of *on*. That is the basis of classification, and not the fact that giri to the world is an obligation to return kindnesses and that giri to one's name prominently includes revenge. The fact that Western languages separate the two into categories as opposite as gratitude and revenge does not impress the Japanese. Why should one virtue not cover a man's behavior when he reacts to another's benevolence and when he reacts to his scorn or malevolence?

From Ch. 8, "Clearing One's Name," with footnote omitted, in *The Chrysanthemum and the Sword*, by Ruth Benedict, Boston Houghton Mifflin, Co. 1946. Reprinted by permission of Houghton Mifflin Co.

In Japan it does. A good man feels as strongly about insults as he does about the benefits he has received. Either way it is virtuous to repay. He does not separate the two, as we do, and call one aggression and one non-aggression. To him aggression only begins outside "the circle of giri"; so long as one is maintaining giri and clearing one's name of slurs, one is not guilty of aggression. One is evening scores. "The world tips," they say, so long as an insult or slur or defeat is not requited or eliminated. A good man must try to get the world back into balance again. It is human virtue, not an all-too-human vice. Giri to one's name, and even the way it is linguistically combined in Japan with gratitude and loyalty, has been a Western virtue in certain periods of European history. It flourished mightily in the Renaissance, especially in Italy, and it has much in common with *el valor Español* in classic Spain and with *die Ehre* in Germany. Something very like it underlay dueling in Europe a hundred years ago. Wherever this virtue of wiping out stains on one's honor has been in the ascendant, in Japan or in Western nations, the very core of it has always been that it transcended profit in any material sense. One was virtuous in proportion as one offered up to "honor" one's possessions, one's family, and one's own life. This is a part of its very definition and is the basis of the claim that these countries always put forward that it is a "spiritual" value. It certainly involves them in great material losses and can hardly be justified on a profit-and-loss basis. In this lies the great contrast between this version of honor and the cut-throat competition and overt hostility that crops up in life in the United States; in America it may be that no holds are barred in some political or financial deal but it is a war to get or to hold some material advantage. It is only in exceptional cases, as, for instance, in the feuds of the Kentucky Mountains, where codes of honor prevail which fall in the category of giri to one's name.

Giri to one's name and all the hostility and watchful waiting that accompany it in any culture, however, is not a virtue that is characteristic of the Asiatic mainland. It is not, as the phrase goes, Oriental. The Chinese do not have it, nor the Siamese, nor the Indians. The Chinese regard all such sensitivity to insults and aspersions as a trait of "small" people—morally small. It is no part of their ideal of nobility, as it is in Japan. Violence which is wrong when a man starts it out of the blue does not become right in Chinese ethics when a man indulges in it to requite an insult. They think it is rather ridiculous to be so sensitive. Nor do they react to a slur by resolving by all that is good and great to prove the aspersion baseless. The Siamese have no place at all for this kind of sensitivity to insult. Like the Chinese they set store by making their detractor ridiculous but they do not imagine that their honor has been impugned. They say "The best way to show an opponent up for a brute is to give in to him."

The full significance of giri to one's name cannot be understood without placing in context all the non-aggressive virtues which are included in it in Japan. Vengeance is only one of the virtues it may require upon occasion. It includes also plenty of quiet and temperate behavior. The stoicism, the self-control that is required of a self-respecting Japanese is part of his giri to his name. A woman may not cry out in childbirth and a man should rise above pain and danger. When floods sweep down upon the Japanese village each self-respecting person gathers up the necessities he is to take with him and seeks higher ground. There is no outcry, no running hither and thither, no panic. When the equinoctial winds and rain come in hurricane strength there is similar self-control. Such behavior is a part of the respect a person has for himself in Japan even granted he may not live up to it. They think American self-respect does not require self-control. There is *noblesse oblige* in this self-control in Japan and in feudal times more was therefore required of the samurai than of the common people but the virtue, though less exigent, was a rule of life among all classes. If the samurai were required to go to extremes in rising above bodily pain, the common people had to go to extremes in accepting the aggressions of the armed samurai.

The tales of samurai stoicism are famous. They were forbidden to give way to hunger but that was too trivial to mention. They were enjoined when they were starving to pretend they had just eaten: they must pick their teeth with a toothpick. "Baby birds," the maxim went, "cry for their food but a samurai holds a toothpick between his teeth." In the past war this became an Army maxim for the enlisted soldier. Nor must they give way to pain. The Japanese attitude was like the boy soldier's rejoinder to Napoleon: "Wounded? Nay, sire, I'm killed." A samurai should give no sign of suffering till he fell dead and he must bear pain without wincing. It is told of Count Katsu who died in 1899 that when he was a boy his testicles were torn by a dog. He was of samurai family but his family had been reduced to beggary. While the doctor operated upon him, his father held a sword to his nose. "If you utter one cry," he told him, "you will die in a way that at least will not be shameful."

Giri to one's name also requires that one live according to one's station in life. If a man fails in this giri he has no right to respect himself. This meant in Tokugawa times that he accepted as part of his self-respect the detailed sumptuary laws which regulated practically everything he wore or had or used. Americans are shocked to the core by laws which define these things by inherited class position. Self-respect in America is bound up with improving one's status and fixed sumptuary laws are a denial of the very basis of our society. We are horrified by Tokugawa laws which stated that a farmer of one class could buy such and such a doll for his child and the farmer of another class could buy a different doll. In America, however, we get the same results by invoking a different sanction. We accept with no criticism the fact that the factory owner's child has a set of electric trains and that the sharecropper's child contents itself with a corncob doll. We accept differences in income and justify them. To earn a good salary is a part of our system of self-respect. If dolls are regulated by income that is no violation of our moral ideas. The person who has got rich buys better dolls for his children. In Japan getting rich is under suspicion and maintaining proper station is not. Even today the poor as well as the rich invest their self-respect in observing the conventions of hierarchy. It is a virtue alien to America, and the Frenchman, de Tocqueville, pointed this out in the eighteen-thirties in his book already quoted.* Born himself in eighteenth-century France, he knew and loved the aristocratic way of life in spite of his generous comments about the egalitarian United States. America, he said, in spite of its virtues, lacked true dignity. "True dignity consists in always taking one's proper station, neither too high nor too low. And this is as much within the reach of the peasant as of the prince." De Tocqueville would have understood the Japanese attitude that class differences are not themselves humiliating.

"True dignity," in this day of objective study of cultures, is recognized as something which different peoples can define differently, just as they always define for themselves what is humiliating. Americans who cry out today that Japan cannot be given self-respect until we enforce our egalitarianism are guilty of ethnocentrism. If what these Americans want is, as they say, a self-respecting Japan they will have to recognize her bases for self-respect. We can recognize, as de Tocqueville did, that this aristocratic "true dignity" is passing from the modern world and that a different and, we believe, a finer dignity is taking its place. It will no doubt happen in Japan too. Meantime Japan will have to rebuild her self-respect today on her own basis, not on ours. And she will have to purify it in her own way.

Giri to one's name is also living up to many sorts of commitments besides those of proper station. A borrower may pledge his giri to his name when he asks for a loan; a generation ago it was common to phrase it that "I agree to be publicly laughed at if I fail to repay this sum." If he failed, he was not literally made a laughingstock; there were no public pillories in Japan. But when the New Year came around, the date on which debts must be paid off, the insolvent debtor might commit suicide to "clear his name." New Year's Eve still has its crop of suicides who have taken this means to redeem their reputations.

All kinds of professional commitments involve giri to one's name. The Japanese requirements are often fantastic when particular circumstances bring one into the public eye and criticism might be general. There are for instance the long list of school principals who committed suicide because fires in their schools—with which they had nothing to do—threatened the picture of the Emperor which was hung in every school. Teachers too have been burned to death dashing into burning schools to rescue these pictures. By their deaths they showed how high they held their giri to their names and their chu to the Emperor. There are also famous stories of persons who were guilty of a slip of the tongue in ceremonious public readings of one of the Imperial Rescripts, either the one on Education or the one for Soldiers and Sailors, and

* [Alexis de Toqueville, Democracy in America—Ed.]

who have cleared their names by committing suicide. Within the reign of the present Emperor, a man who had inadvertently named his son Hirohito —the given name of the Emperor was never spoken in Japan—killed himself and his child.

Giri to one's name as a professional person is very exigent in Japan but it need not be maintained by what an American understands as high professional standards. The teacher says, "I cannot in giri to my name as a teacher admit ignorance of it," and he means that if he does not know to what species a frog belongs nevertheless he has to pretend he does. If he teaches English on the basis of only a few years' school instruction, nevertheless he cannot admit that anyone might be able to correct him. It is specifically to this kind of defensiveness that "giri to one's name as a teacher" refers. The business man too, in giri to his name as a business man, cannot let anyone know that his assets are seriously depleted or that the plans he made for his organization have failed. And the diplomat cannot in giri admit the failure of his policy. In all such giri usages there is extreme identification of a man with his work and any criticism of one's acts or one's competence becomes automatically a criticism of one's self.

These Japanese reactions to imputations of failure and inadequacy can be duplicated over and over again in the United States. We all know persons who are maddened by detraction. But we are seldom so defensive as the Japanese. If a teacher does not know to what species a frog belongs, he thinks it is better behavior to say so than to claim knowledge, even though he might succumb to the temptation to hide his ignorance. If a business man is dissatisfied with a policy he has promoted he thinks he can put out a new and different directive. He does not consider that his self-respect is conditional upon his maintaining that he was right all along and that if he admitted he was wrong he should either resign or retire. In Japan, however, this defensiveness goes very deep and it is the part of wisdom—as it is also universal etiquette—not to tell a person to his face in so many words that he has made a professional error.

This sensitivity is especially conspicuous in situations where one person has lost out to another. It may be only that another person has been preferred for a job or that the person concerned has failed in a competitive examination. The loser "wears a shame" for such failures, and, though this shame is in some cases a strong incentive to greater efforts, in many others it is a dangerous depressant. He loses confidence and becomes melancholy or angry or both. His efforts are stymied. It is especially important for Americans to recognize that competition in Japan thus does not have the same degree of socially desirable effects that it does in our own scheme of life. We rely strongly on competition as a "good thing." Psychological tests show that competition stimulates us to our best work. Performance goes up under this stimulus; when we are given something to do all by ourselves we fall short of the record we make when there are competitors present. In Japan, however, their tests show just the opposite. It is especially marked after childhood is ended, for Japanese children are more playful about competition and not so worried about it. With young men and adults, however, performance deteriorated with competition. Subjects who had made good progress, reduced their mistakes and gained speed when they were working by themselves, began to make mistakes and were far slower when a competitor was introduced. They did best when they were measuring their improvement against their own record, not when they were measuring themselves against others. The Japanese experimenters rightly analyzed the reason for this poor record in competitive situations. Their subjects, they said, when the project became competitive, became principally interested in the danger that they might be defeated, and the work suffered. They felt the competition so keenly as an aggression that they turned their attention to their relation to the aggressor instead of concentrating on the job in hand.

The students examined in these tests tended to be influenced most by the possible shame of failing. Like a teacher or a business man living up to his giri to his professional name they are stung by their giri to their name as students. Student teams who lost in competitive games, too, went to great lengths in abandoning themselves to this shame of failure. Crews might throw themselves down in their boats beside their oars and weep and bewail themselves. Defeated baseball teams might gather in a huddle and cry aloud. In the United States we would say they were bad losers. We have an etiquette that expects them to say that the better team won. It is proper for the defeated to shake hands with the victors. No matter how much we hate to be beaten we scorn people who make an emotional crisis out of it.

The Japanese have always been inventive in devising ways of avoiding direct competition. Their elementary schools minimize it beyond what Americans would think possible. Their teachers are instructed that each child must be taught to better his own record and that he should not be given opportunities to compare himself with others. In their grade schools they do not even keep any students back to repeat a grade and all children who enter together go through their entire elementary education together. Their report cards grade children in elementary schools on marks for conduct but not on their school work: when really competitive situations are unavoidable, as in entrance examinations to the middle schools, the tension is understandably great. Every teacher has stories of the boys who when they know they have failed commit suicide.

This minimizing of direct competition goes all through Japanese life. An ethic that is based on on has small place for competition whereas the American categorical imperative is upon making good in competition with one's fellows. Their whole system of hierarchy with all its detailed rules of class minimizes direct competition. The family system minimizes it too for the father and son are not institutionally in competition as they are in America: it is possible for them to reject each other but not for them to compete.

Japanese comment with amazement on the American family where the father and the son compete both for the use of the family car and for the attention of the mother-wife.

The ubiquitous institution of the go-between is one of the more conspicuous ways in which the Japanese prevent direct confrontation of two persons who are in competition with each other. An intermediary is required in any situation where a man might feel shame if he fell short and consequently go-betweens serve on a great number of occasions—negotiating marriage, offering one's services for hire, leaving a job and arranging countless everyday matters. This go-between reports to both parties, or in case of an important deal like a marriage each side employs its own intermediary and they negotiate the details between themselves before reporting to their side. By dealing in this way at second hand the principals need take no cognizance of claims and charges that would have to be resented in giri to their names if they were in direct communication. The go-between too gains prestige by acting in this official capacity, and gets the respect of the community by his successful manipulation. The chances of a peaceful arrangement are the greater because the go-between has an ego investment in smooth negotiations. The intermediary acts in the same way in feeling out an employer about a job for his client or in relaying to the employer the employee's decision to leave his job.

Etiquette of all kinds is organized to obviate shame-causing situations which might call in question one's giri to one's name. These situations which are thus minimized go far beyond direct competition. The host, they think, should greet his guest with certain ritual welcoming and in his good clothes. Therefore anyone who finds a farmer in his work clothes at home may have to wait a bit. The farmer gives no sign of recognition until he has put on suitable clothes and arranged the proper courtesies. It makes no difference even if the host has to change his clothes in the room where the guest is waiting. He simply is not present until he is there in the proper guise. In the rural areas, too, boys may visit girls at night after the household is asleep and the girl is in bed. Girls can either accept or reject their advances, but the boy wears a towel bound about his face so that if he is rejected he need feel no shame next day. The disguise is not to prevent the girl from recognizing him; it is purely an ostrich technique so that he will not have to admit that he was shamed in his proper person. Etiquette requires too that as little cognizance as possible be taken of any project until success is assured. It is part of the duties of go-betweens arranging a marriage to bring the prospective bride and groom together before the contract is completed. Everything is done to make this a casual meeting for if the purpose of the introduction were avowed at this stage any breaking-off of the negotiations would threaten the honor of one family or of both. Since the young couple must each be escorted by one or both of their parents, and the go-betweens must be the hosts or hostesses, it is most properly arranged when they all "run into each other" casually at the annual chrysanthemum show or at a cherry-blossom viewing or in a well-known park or place of recreation.

In all such ways, and in many more, the Japanese avoid occasions in which failure might be shameful. Though they lay such emphasis on the duty to clear one's name of insult, in actual practice this leads them to arrange events so that insult need be felt as seldom as possible.

The Self As American   21

George Santayana

The language and traditions common to England and America are like other family bonds: they draw kindred together at the greater crises in life, but they also occasion at times a little friction and fault-finding. The groundwork of the two societies is so similar, that each nation, feeling almost at home with the other, and almost able to understand its speech, may instinctively resent what hinders it from feeling at home altogether. Differences will tend to seem anomalies that have slipped in by mistake and through somebody's fault. Each will judge the other by his own standards, not feeling, as in the presence of complete foreigners, that he must make an effort of imagination and put himself in another man's shoes.

In matters of morals, manners, and art, the danger of comparisons is not merely that they may prove invidious, by ranging qualities in an order of merit which might wound somebody's vanity; the danger is rather that comparisons may distort comprehension, because in truth good qualities are all different in kind, and free lives are different in spirit. Comparison is the expedient of those who cannot reach the heart of the things compared; and no philosophy is more external and egotistical than that which places the essence of a thing in its relation to something else. In reality, at the centre of every natural being there is something individual and incommensurable, a seed with its native impulses and aspirations, shaping themselves as best they can in their given environment. Variation is a consequence of freedom, and the slight but radical diversity of souls in turn makes freedom requisite. Instead of instituting in his mind any comparisons between the United States and other nations, I would accordingly urge the reader to forget himself and, in so far as such a thing may be possible for him or for me, to transport himself ideally with me into the outer circumstances of American life, the better to feel its inner temper, and to see how inevitably the American shapes his

Essay "Materialism and Idealism in American Life," in *Character and Opinion in the United States*, George Santayana, New York, Charles Scribner's Sons, 1920. Reprinted by permission of Charles Scribner's Sons. First published in Great Britain by Constable & Co. Ltd. Reprinted by permission of Constable & Co. Ltd.

feelings and judgments, honestly reporting all things as they appear from his new and unobstructed station.

I speak of the American in the singular, as if there were not millions of them, north and south, east and west, of both sexes, of all ages, and of various races, professions, and religions. Of course the one American I speak of is mythical; but to speak in parables is inevitable in such a subject, and it is perhaps as well to do so frankly. There is a sort of poetic ineptitude in all human discourse when it tries to deal with natural and existing things. Practical men may not notice it, but in fact human discourse is intrinsically addressed not to natural existing things but to ideal essences, poetic or logical terms which thought may define and play with. When fortune or necessity diverts our attention from this congenial ideal sport to crude facts and pressing issues, we turn our frail poetic ideas into symbols for those terrible irruptive things. In that paper money of our own stamping, the legal tender of the mind, we are obliged to reckon all the movements and values of the world. The universal American I speak of is one of these symbols; and I should be still speaking in symbols and creating moral units and a false simplicity, if I spoke of classes pedantically subdivided, or individuals ideally integrated and defined. As it happens, the symbolic American can be made largely adequate to the facts; because, if there are immense differences between individual Americans—for some Americans are black—yet there is a great uniformity in their environment, customs, temper, and thoughts. They have all been uprooted from their several soils and ancestries and plunged together into one vortex, whirling irresistibly in a space otherwise quite empty. To be an American is of itself almost a moral condition, an education, and a career. Hence a single ideal figment can cover a large part of what each American is in his character, and almost the whole of what most Americans are in their social outlook and political judgments.

The discovery of the new world exercised a sort of selection among the inhabitants of Europe. All the colonists, except the negroes, were voluntary exiles. The fortunate, the deeply rooted, and the lazy remained at home; the wilder instincts or dissatisfaction of others tempted them beyond the horizon. The American is accordingly the most adventurous, or the descendant of the most adventurous, of Europeans. It is in his blood to be socially a radical, though perhaps not intellectually. What has existed in the past, especially in the remote past, seems to him not only not authoritative, but irrelevant, inferior, and outworn. He finds it rather a sorry waste of time to think about the past at all. But his enthusiasm for the future is profound; he can conceive of no more decisive way of recommending an opinion or a practice than to say that it is what everybody is coming to adopt. This expectation of what he approves, or approval of what he expects, makes up his optimism. It is the necessary faith of the pioneer.

Such a temperament is, of course, not maintained in the nation merely by inheritance. Inheritance notoriously tends to restore the average of a race, and plays incidentally many a trick of atavism. What maintains this temperament and makes it national is social contagion or pressure—something immensely strong in democracies. The luckless American who is born a conservative, or who is drawn to poetic subtlety, pious retreats, or gay passions, nevertheless has the categorical excellence of work, growth, enterprise, reform, and prosperity dinned into his ears: every door is open in this direction and shut in the other; so that he either folds up his heart and withers in a corner—in remote places you sometimes find such a solitary gaunt idealist—or else he flies to Oxford or Florence or Montmartre to save his soul—or perhaps not to save it.

The optimism of the pioneer is not limited to his view of himself and his own future: it starts from that; but feeling assured, safe, and cheery within, he looks with smiling and most kindly eyes on everything and everybody about him. Individualism, roughness, and self-trust are supposed to go with selfishness and a cold heart; but I suspect that is a prejudice. It is rather dependence, insecurity, and mutual jostling that poison our placid gregarious brotherhood; and fanciful passionate demands upon people's affections, when they are disappointed, as they soon must be, breed ill will and a final meanness. The milk of human kindness is less apt to turn sour if the vessel that holds it stands steady, cool, and separate, and is not too often uncorked. In his affections, the American is seldom passionate, often deep, and always kindly. If it were given me to look into the depths of a man's heart, and I did not find goodwill at the bottom, I should say without any hesitation, You are not an American. But as the American is an individualist his goodwill is not officious. His instinct is to think well of everybody, and to wish everybody well, but in a spirit of rough comradeship, expecting every man to stand on his own legs and to be helpful in his turn. When he has given his neighbour a chance he thinks he has done enough for him; but he feels it an absolute duty to do that. It will take some hammering to drive a coddling socialism into America.

As self-trust may pass into self-sufficiency, so optimism, kindness, and goodwill may grow into a habit of doting on everything. To the good American many subjects are sacred: sex is sacred, women are sacred, children are sacred, business is sacred, America is sacred, Masonic lodges and college clubs are sacred. This feeling grows out of the good opinion he wishes to have of these things, and serves to maintain it. If he did not regard all these things as sacred he might come to doubt sometimes if they were wholly good. Of this kind, too, is the idealism of single ladies in reduced circumstances who can see the soul of beauty in ugly things, and are perfectly happy because their old dog has such pathetic eyes, their minister is so eloquent, their garden with its three sunflowers is so pleasant, their dead friends were so devoted, and their distant relations are so rich.

Consider now the great emptiness of America: not merely the primitive physical emptiness, surviving in some regions, and the continental spacing of the chief natural features, but also the moral emptiness of a settlement where men and even houses are easily moved about, and no one, almost, lives where he was born or believes what he has been taught. Not that the American has jettisoned these impedimenta in anger; they have simply slipped from him as he moves. Great empty spaces bring a sort of freedom to both soul and body. You may pitch your tent where you will; or if ever you decide to build anything, it can be in a style of your own devising. You have room, fresh materials, few models, and no critics. You trust your own experience, not only because you must, but because you find you may do so safely and prosperously; the forces that determine fortune are not yet too complicated for one man to explore. Your detachable condition makes you lavish with money and cheerfully experimental; you lose little if you lose all, since you remain completely yourself. At the same time your absolute initiative gives you practice in coping with novel situations, and in being original; it teaches you shrewd management. Your life and mind will become dry and direct, with few decorative flourishes. In your works everything will be stark and pragmatic; you will not understand why anybody should make those little sacrifices to instinct or custom which we call grace. The fine arts will seem to you academic luxuries, fit to amuse the ladies, like Greek and Sanskrit; for while you will perfectly appreciate generosity in men's purposes, you will not admit that the execution of these purposes can be anything but business. Unfortunately the essence of the fine arts is that the execution should be generous too, and delightful in itself; therefore the fine arts will suffer, not so much in their express professional pursuit—for then they become practical tasks and a kind of business—as in that diffused charm which qualifies all human action when men are artists by nature. Elaboration, which is something to accomplish, will be preferred to simplicity, which is something to rest in; manners will suffer somewhat; speech will suffer horribly. For the American the urgency of his novel attack upon matter, his zeal in gathering its fruits, precludes meanderings in primrose paths; devices must be short cuts, and symbols must be mere symbols. If his wife wants luxuries, of course she may have them; if he has vices, that can be provided for too; but they must all be set down under those headings in his ledgers.

At the same time, the American is imaginative; for where life is intense, imagination is intense also. Were he not imaginative he would not live so much in the future. But his imagination is practical, and the future it forecasts is immediate; it works with the clearest and least ambiguous terms known to his experience, in terms of number, measure, contrivance, economy, and speed. He is an idealist working on matter. Understanding as he does the material potentialities of things, he is successful in invention, conservative in reform, and quick in emergencies. All his life he jumps into the train after it has started and jumps out before it has stopped; and he never once gets left behind, or breaks a leg. There is an enthusiasm in his sympathetic handling of material forces which goes far to cancel the illiberal character which it might otherwise assume. The good workman hardly distinguishes his artistic intention from the potency in himself and in things which is about to realise that intention. Accordingly his ideals fall into the form of premonitions and prophecies; and his studious prophecies often come true. So do the happy workmanlike ideals of the American. When a poor boy, perhaps, he dreams of an education, and presently he gets an education, or at least a degree; he dreams of growing rich, and he grows rich—only more slowly and modestly, perhaps, than he expected; he dreams of marrying his Rebecca and, even if he marries a Leah instead, he ultimately finds in Leah his Rebecca after all. He dreams of helping to carry on and to accelerate the movement of a vast, seething, progressive society, and he actually does so. Ideals clinging so close to nature are almost sure of fulfilment; the American beams with a certain self-confidence and sense of mastery; he feels that God and nature are working with him.

Idealism in the American accordingly goes hand in hand with present contentment and with foresight of what the future very likely will actually bring. He is not a revolutionist; he believes he is already on the right track and moving towards an excellent destiny. In revolutionists, on the contrary, idealism is founded on dissatisfaction and expresses it. What exists seems to them an absurd jumble of irrational accidents and bad habits, and they want the future to be based on reason and to be the pellucid embodiment of all their maxims. All their zeal is for something radically different from the actual and (if they only knew it) from the possible; it is ideally simple, and they love it and believe in it because their nature craves it. They think life would be set free by the destruction of all its organs. They are therefore extreme idealists in the region of hope, but not at all, as poets and artists are, in the region of perception and memory. In the atmosphere of civilised life they miss all the refraction and all the fragrance; so that in their conception of actual things they are apt to be crude realists; and their ignorance and inexperience of the moral world, unless it comes of ill-luck, indicates their incapacity for education. Now incapacity for education, when united with great inner vitality, is one root of idealism. It is what condemns us all, in the region of sense, to substitute perpetually what we are capable of imagining for what things may be in themselves; it is what condemns us, wherever it extends, to think *a priori*; it is what keeps us bravely and incorrigibly pursuing what we call the good—that is, what would fulfil the demands of our nature—however little provision the fates may have made for it. But the want of insight on the part of revolutionists touching the past and the present infects in an important particular their idealism about the future; it renders their dreams of the future unrealisable. For in human beings—this may not be true of other animals, more perfectly performed—experience is necessary to pertinent and concrete thinking; even our primitive instincts are blind until they stumble upon some occasion that solicits them; and they can be much transformed or deranged by their first partial satisfactions. Therefore a man who does not idealise his experience, but idealises *a priori,* is incapable of true prophecy; when he dreams he raves, and the more he criticises the less he helps. American idealism, on the contrary, is nothing if not helpful, nothing if not pertinent to practicable transformations; and when the American frets, it is because whatever is useless and impertinent, be it idealism or inertia, irritates him; for it frustrates the good results which he sees might so easily have been obtained.

The American is wonderfully alive; and his vitality, not having often found a suitable outlet, makes him appear agitated on the surface; he is always letting off an unnecessarily loud blast of incidental steam. Yet his vitality is not superficial; it is inwardly prompted, and as sensitive and quick as a magnetic needle. He is inquisitive, and ready with an answer to any question that he may put to himself of his own accord; but if you try to pour instruction into him, on matters that do not touch his own spontaneous life, he shows the most extraordinary powers of resistance and oblivescence; so that he often is remarkably expert in some directions and surprisingly obtuse in others. He seems to bear lightly the sorrowful burden of human knowledge. In a word, he is young.

What sense is there in this feeling, which we all have, that the American is young? His country is blessed with as many elderly people as any other, and his descent from Adam, or from the Darwinian rival of Adam, cannot be shorter than that of his European cousins. Nor are his ideas always very fresh. Trite and rigid bits of morality and religion, with much seemly and antique political lore, remain axiomatic in him, as in the mind of a child; he may carry all this about with an unquestioning familiarity which does not comport understanding. To keep traditional sentiments in this way insulated and uncriticised is itself a sign of youth. A good young man is naturally conservative and loyal on all those subjects which his experience has not brought to a test; advanced opinions on politics, marriage, or literature are comparatively rare in America; they are left for the ladies to discuss, and usually to condemn, while the men get on with their work. In spite of what is old-fashioned in his more general ideas, the American is unmistakably young; and this, I should say, for two reasons: one, that he is chiefly occupied with his immediate environment, and the other, that his reactions upon it are inwardly prompted, spontaneous, and full of vivacity and self-trust. His views are not yet lengthened; his will is not yet broken or transformed. The present moment, however, in this, as in other things, may mark a great change in him; he is perhaps now reaching his majority, and all I say may hardly apply to-day, and may not apply at all to-morrow. I speak of him as I have known him; and whatever moral strength may accrue to him later, I am not sorry to have known him in his youth. The charm of youth, even when it is a little boisterous, lies in nearness to the impulses of nature, in a quicker and more obvious obedience to that pure, seminal principle which, having formed the body and its organs, always directs their movements, unless it is forced by vice or necessity to make them crooked, or to suspend them. Even under the inevitable crust of age the soul remains young, and, wherever it is able to break through, sprouts into something green and tender. We are all as young at heart as the most youthful American, but the seed in his case has fallen upon virgin soil, where it may spring up more bravely and with less respect for the giants of the wood. Peoples seem older when their perennial natural youth is encumbered with more possessions and prepossessions, and they are mindful of the many things they have lost or missed. The American is not mindful of them.

In America there is a tacit optimistic assumption about existence, to the effect that the more existence the better. The soulless critic might urge that quantity is only a physical category, implying no excellence, but at best an abundance of opportunities both for good and for evil. Yet the young soul, being curious and hungry, views existence *a priori* under the form of the good; its instinct to live implies a faith that most things it can become or see or do will be worth while. Respect for quantity is accordingly something more than the childish joy and wonder at bigness; it is the fisherman's joy in a big haul, the good uses of which he can take for granted. Such optimism is amiable. Nature cannot afford that we should begin by being too calculating or wise, and she encourages us by the pleasure she attaches to our functions in advance of their fruits, and often in excess of them; as the angler enjoys catching his fish more than eating it, and often, waiting patiently for the fish to bite, misses his own supper. The pioneer must devote himself to preparations; he must work for the future, and it is healthy and dutiful of him to love his work for its own sake. At the same time, unless reference to an ultimate purpose is at least virtual in all his activities, he runs the danger of becoming a living automaton, vain and ignominious in its mechanical constancy. Idealism about work can hide an intense materialism about life. Man, if he is a rational being, cannot live by bread alone nor be a labourer merely; he must eat and work in view of an ideal harmony which overarches all his days, and which is realised in the way they hang together, or in some ideal issue which they have in common. Otherwise, though his technical philosophy may call itself idealism, he is a materialist in morals; he esteems things, and esteems himself, for mechanical uses and energies. Even sensualists, artists, and pleasure-lovers are wiser than that, for though their idealism may be desultory or corrupt, they attain something ideal, and prize things only for their living effects, moral though perhaps fugitive. Sensation, when we do not take it as a signal for action, but arrest and peruse what it positively brings before us, reveals something ideal—a colour, shape, or sound; and to dwell on these presences, with no thought of their material significance, is an æsthetic or dreamful idealism. To pass from this idealism to the knowledge of matter is a great intellectual advance, and goes with dominion over the world; for in the practical arts the mind is adjusted to a larger object, with more depth and potentiality in it; which is what makes people feel that the material world is real, as they call it, and the ideal world is not. Certainly the material world is real; for the philosophers who deny the existence of matter are like the critics who deny the existence of Homer. If there was never any Homer, there must have been a lot of other poets no less Homeric than he; and if matter does not exist, a combination of other things exists which is just as material. But the intense reality of the material world would not prevent it from being a dreary waste in our eyes, or even an abyss of horror, if it brought forth no spiritual fruits. In fact, it does bring forth spiritual fruits, for otherwise we should not be here to find fault with it, and to set up our ideals over against it. Nature is material, but not materialistic; it issues in life, and breeds all sorts of warm passions and idle beauties. And just as sympathy with the mechanical travail and turmoil of nature, apart from its spiritual fruits, is moral materialism, so the continual perception and love of these fruits is moral idealism—happiness in the presence of immaterial objects and harmonies, such as we envisage in affection, speculation, religion, and all the forms of the beautiful.

The circumstances of his life hitherto have necessarily driven the American into moral materialism; for in his dealings with material things he can hardly stop to enjoy their sensible aspects, which are ideal, nor proceed at once to their ultimate uses, which are ideal, too. He is practical as against the poet, and worldly as against the clear philosopher or the saint. The most striking expression of this materialism is usually supposed to be his love of the almighty dollar; but that is a foreign and unintelligent view. The American talks about money, because that is the symbol and measure he has at hand for success, intelligence, and power; but as to money itself he makes, loses, spends, and gives it away with a very light heart. To my mind the most striking expression of his materialism is his singular preoccupation with quantity. If, for instance, you visit Niagara Falls, you may expect to hear how many cubic feet or metric tons of water are precipitated per second over the cataract; how many cities and towns (with the number of their inhabitants) derive light and motive power from it; and the annual value of the further industries that might very well be carried on by the same means, without visibly depleting the world's greatest wonder or injuring the tourist trade. That is what I confidently expected to hear on arriving at the adjoining town of Buffalo; but I was deceived. The first thing I heard instead was that there are more miles of asphalt pavement in Buffalo than in any city in the world. Nor is this insistence on quantity confined to men of business. The President of Harvard College, seeing me once by chance soon after the beginning of a term, inquired how my classes were getting on; and when I replied that I thought they were getting on well, that my men seemed to be keen and intelligent. He stopped me as if I was about to waste his time. "I meant," said he, "*what is the number* of students in your classes?"

Here I think we may perceive that this love of quantity often has a silent partner, which is diffidence as to quality. The democratic conscience recoils before anything that savours of privilege; and lest it should concede an unmerited privilege to any pursuit or person, it reduces all things as far as possible to the common denominator of quantity. Numbers cannot lie: but if it came to comparing the ideal beauties of philosophy with those of Anglo-Saxon, who should decide? All studies are good—why else have universities? —but those must be most encouraged which attract the greatest number of students. Hence the President's question. Democratic faith, in its diffidence about quality, throws the reins of education upon the pupil's neck, as Don Quixote threw the reins on the neck of Rocinante, and bids his divine instinct choose its own way.

The American has never yet had to face the trials of Job. Great crises, like the Civil War, he has known how to surmount victoriously; and now that he has surmounted a second great crisis victoriously, it is possible that he may relapse, as he did in the other case, into an apparently complete absorption in material enterprise and prosperity. But if serious and irremediable tribulation ever overtook him, what would his attitude be? It is then that we should be able to discover whether materialism or idealism lies at the base of his character. Meantime his working mind is not without its holiday. He spreads humour pretty thick and even over the surface of conversation, and humour is one form of moral emancipation. He loves landscape, he loves mankind, and he loves knowledge; and in music at least he finds an art which he unfeignedly enjoys. In music and landscape, in humour and kindness, he touches the ideal more truly, perhaps, than in his ponderous academic idealisms and busy religions; for it is astonishing how much even religion in America (can it possibly be so in England?) is a matter of meetings, building-funds, schools, charities, clubs, and picnics. To be poor in order to be simple, to produce less in order that the product may be more choice and beautiful, and may leave us less burdened with unnecessary duties and useless possessions—this is an ideal not articulate in the American mind; yet here and there I seem to have heard a sigh after it, a groan at the perpetual incubus of business and shrill society. Significant witness to such aspirations is borne by those new forms of popular religion, not mere variations on tradition, which have sprung up from the soil—revivalism, spiritualism, Christian Science, the New Thought. Whether or no we can tap, through these or other channels, some cosmic or inner energy not hitherto at the disposal of man (and there is nothing incredible in that), we certainly may try to remove friction and waste in the mere process of living; we may relax morbid strains, loosen suppressed instincts, iron out the creases of the soul, discipline ourselves into simplicity, sweetness, and peace. These religious movements are efforts toward such physiological economy and hygiene; and while they are thoroughly plebeian, with no great lights, and no idea of raising men from the most vulgar and humdrum worldly existence, yet they see the possibility of physical and moral health on that common plane, and pursue it. That is true morality. The dignities of various types of life or mind, like the gifts of

various animals, are relative. The snob adores one type only, and the creatures supposed by him to illustrate it perfectly; or envies and hates them,
which is just as snobbish. Veritable lovers of life, on the contrary, like Saint
Francis or like Dickens, knows that in every tenement of clay, with no matter
what endowment or station, happiness and perfection are possible to the soul.
There must be no brow-beating, with shouts of work or progress or revolution, any more than with threats of hell-fire. What does it profit a man to free
the whole world if his soul is not free? Moral freedom is not an artificial condition, because the ideal is the mother tongue of both the heart and the
senses. All that is requisite is that we should pause in living to enjoy life,
and should lift up our hearts to things that are pure goods in themselves, so
that once to have found and loved them, whatever else may betide, may
remain a happiness that nothing can sully. This natural idealism does not
imply that we are immaterial, but only that we are animate and truly alive.
When the senses are sharp, as they are in the American, they are already
half liberated, already a joy in themselves; and when the heart is warm, like
his, and eager to be just, its ideal destiny can hardly be doubtful. It will not
be always merely pumping and working; time and its own pulses will lend
it wings.

Part three

THE SELF IN CLOSE RELATION

Through the Thou a man becomes I

Martin Buber
I AND THOU

INTRODUCTION

To ask you to contemplate your navel may seem facetious, yet the fact that we have navels is a commonplace to which we pay too little serious attention. Consider, for example, what this bodily fact signifies. It suggests that a thread of continuity runs backward in time between you and an infinite number of other human beings. It guarantees that you are part of a family and it marks your origin in and close attachment to another. The umbilicus is the lifeline connecting generations, the "tie" which connects you to a particular family and the "silver cord" between you and a special other. Many linguistic expressions reflect this basic interrelation and a surprising number of human situations use it as an analogy. The primal umbilical situation reverberates throughout our lives, never to be completely eradicated.

Physically, the umbilicus stands for the fact that you are a member of the mammalian tribe and that you, like other mammals, were given birth, fed and nurtured by others of the same kind. The "family" is an animal necessity which gains yet further significance in the human family. Psychologically it causes you to feel related to others, and be disposed to act and react as they do. It predestines you to live in families and to want to start one of your own.

But have you ever considered to what a large family you really belong? Your immediate family is biologically related to countless other families from all parts of the world and with all colors of skin throughout time. In this sense you belong to the family of man—the bipeds who walk erect, who use language to communicate with each other, and who develop ways and rituals to cope with a world. In this sense each man is the genetic repository of thousands of generations.

In another sense, and perhaps more vividly, you belong to a particular family stemming from a given mother and father. This is the family that, in our culture, lives together and engages in fraternal relations. This is the family that visibly stamped you with its monogram of eye color, hair line, length of toe, and pelvic construction.

But your family has given you far more than the idiosyncrasies of your physical structure with its particular strengths and weaknesses, its special beauty and ugliness. Your family has also provided you with a name—both a given name to mark your individuality and a tribal or family name to mark your kinship. Have you considered the uses to which our culture puts a family name? You need a surname to be registered at birth and hence to be recognized as a citizen of a civil state. You need a family name in order to own and inherit property. Your family name largely determines who has what obligations to you. Without a family name you cannot enter into contract, start a business, begin a lawsuit, or marry. In our culture your family name gives you the right to be.

All cultures contrive to identify one's genetic line in some sort of way in order to assign rights, duties, and privileges to each. Of course, not all cultures use the same type of stamp. In some cultures you would be identified with your mother's tribe or clan (a matrilineal culture) while in others, your identity would spring from your father (a patrilineal culture) while in yet others, the particular identity of your father and mother would not be as important as the generation to which you belong. But however the culture chooses to identify you, almost all cultures appeal to some physiological base.

Your family has given you yet another aspect of its culture in your language. Has it occurred to you that you became an apt student of language in your first year of life? In an astonishingly brief time you mastered the language you heard at birth. You probably will never again equal your childhood facility with a strange tongue because your need to communicate will never again be as urgent. Only strong pressures of social need accelerate the process.

In giving you a name and a language your family began enculturating you or preparing you to share in a culture. What is a "culture?" Essentially (as we have already suggested) it is a set of ways of coping with a world. A culture predetermines in large part how you will respond to your experience. Human beings both wittingly and unwittingly construct a culture. Rules of behavior develop which permit the business of life to be transacted. Rituals crystallize which ease the major stressful human experiences, such as birth, coming of age, marriage, and death. Methods of government spring up to permit the group to be peaceful and productive. Ways of punishing offenders, ways of obtaining and distributing wealth, ways of adjudicating disputes, ways of mourning, and ways of rejoicing become the accepted social coin of the realm. In short, your culture determines the limits and boundaries of your entire life: the things you may or must do for a living, what you must contribute to the general social welfare, how you should treat your neighbors, who are your superiors, what you may do for recreation, and when, how, and with whom you may retire. Culture is so enveloping and so ingrained that it is frequently difficult to get an objective glimpse of those forces which deeply etch us. But when one is obliged to live in a culture other than one's own, where people do and see things in a quite different way, one can experience "culture shock" or a feeling of being totally disoriented and out of kilter with the world. A culture is a lens through which we see the world. It can so irrevocably blot out all other cultural possibilities that one can come to consider other people as "barbarians," "savages," and "Gentiles" (outsiders)—they exhibit strange traits and patterns.

How can the human animal so readily forget his kinship with human kind? Reasons are many. The human animal has a very long period of dependency during which those who care for his needs transmit their culture to him and indelibly mark him with it. Not only does the child require physical care and nurture, but in a culture as complex as our own, many years of education and training are necessary for emotional, intellectual, and economic self-sufficiency. Throughout the years from birth to maturity the human being absorbs ways of thinking and feeling, acting and reacting, doing and making, all of which are eventually solidified and made rigid by habit.

Human young, like animal young, learn by emulation. The spirit of "monkey see, monkey do" combines with the powerful social instruments of reward and punishment, praise and blame, acceptance and rejection, to make the child desire to take the ways of his elders as his own. The adults "grow the child up" by encouraging emulation and applying reward and sanction. Since the child needs his parents' care, he eventually exchanges resistance and recalcitrancy for acceptance into the adult community.

But the experience has left its imprint. Not only do we never lose our love of praise and fear of blame but we never lose our craving for a close and deep relationship with another—a relation which reflects and is, to some extent, an analogue to the early primal one. From that time on, each man yearns for maternal care and nurture and paternal protection and strength. Nor can man ever live alone again without becoming anomic or deregulated, rootless and homeless, cut adrift in an empty sea. Having been shaped by social ties, he craves social ties; having been related, he craves relationship.

Some thinkers have traced this profound sense of aloneness in man to a yearning for the parental home; some have traced it to an unconscious desire to return to the parasitic experience within the womb; some have traced it to a cosmic longing for God. But it has been recognized late and early. Literary Existentialists, for instance, have made man's sense of isolation and alienation central to their view of the world. And in the ancient world, Plato's dialogue *Symposium* has Aristophanes, the dramatist, weave a myth to account for it. He relates that "in the beginning" (any beginning) each human being was joined to another at the belly so that they faced one another—a creature with two heads, four legs, and four arms. Thus united, they were fulfilled, satisfied, and without longing. With this felicitous structure, man became so clever and powerful that the species threatened the power of the Gods who protected themselves by cutting the double creatures apart. They then closed the wound by tying each in the middle, thus forming the navel. Thereafter, Aristophanes tells us, each person experiences a sense of aloneness and partiality which he seeks to remedy by reuniting with his "other half."

But whether this phenomenon owes its origin to the cutting of the physical umbilicus, or to long infantile dependency, or to some hidden cosmic cause, each man, without the company of others, feels incomplete. And each seeks to relieve his longing by finding some way to relate to another, to a group or to the forces he believes to be larger and more durable than himself.

The closest and most intense form of this yearning we call "love." In our culture the meaning of this term is highly ambiguous. We use it to cover sentiments as diverse as our feeling for our children, our sexual craving, our desire for three oranges, and our emotion toward God. Perhaps some distinctions would help focus some of the issues involved. The ancient Greek language had different expressions for "love" which have proven immensely important. Writers spoke of *Eros* or sensuous and sensual delight, "desire" in the narrower sense. In *Eros* desire takes a physical form with sexuality at its core and is reflected in the pleasure of the sight and touch of flesh. *Eros*, for the Greeks, was a God, but a God with a lusty appetite and earthy appreciation. The Greeks also spoke of *Philia*, affection or devotion which might take the form of learning or inquiry or the form of tender, nurturing desire for the welfare of another. *Philia* encompasses what we would call "brotherly love"—the desire to give compassion and sympathy, for which the love of a mother for a child is a prototype. Finally, in Plato we learn of the love of man for the good, for the ideal, for the best that can be. This idealized *Eros* was a sublime expression of the love of man for the potentialities of goodness, truth, and beauty in the universe; of the attachment of man to the ultimate fulfillment of all things. In Greek usage and literature the several types of love were often related. Each could presuppose and reverberate with the others; each could represent a facet of the human soul and a dimension of its capacity.

There are other ways to delineate the types of love men experience, foreign though they would have been to the Greeks. In Christianity a distinction is made between sacred and profane love; between love of heavenly as against earthly things. Others have distinguished a domesticated variety of love from an untamed variety called "romantic love." The basis of these distinctions lies in the fact that perhaps all love, even the love of three oranges, has a physical root, that it has a psychic dimension and that it may have an ideal fulfillment. At its physical root, love is a need, even a drive, to connect oneself physically with another; it is linked to procreation. In its psychic dimension, love stems from the social need to want and be wanted, to give and have a place, to like and be liked, and to nourish and be nourished. And insofar as love has an ideal fulfillment, it is the love of another for the sake of the good both may share, for ends held in common, and for goals which interpenetrate. Love springs from community and it returns to enrich community.

In our culture, the epitome of love between men and women is generally understood to be romantic love. Entering the scene with the troubadors in the Middle Ages, romantic love is a breed of sentiment distinguished by certain conspicuous traits. First, the romantic lover overestimates, even worships, the beloved who is believed to be the only possible object of love and, indeed, the exemplar of perfection. In this sense, romantic love isolates the pair from society and puts a monopoly on each by the other. Second, romantic love demands that the feeling of the lover for the beloved be "pure" and undiluted, even by such vagrant sentiments as dislike, disgust, or animosity. Third, it demands that the emotion of the lover for the beloved be absolutely fixed, stable, and unchanging. Fourth, it requires that love so conceived continues, even deepens, when it is nonreciprocal. Though the lover be scorned, he will love forever. Finally, and perhaps most importantly, romantic love has a sacrificial character in that each wishes to die for the other. It is an all-consuming passion in which one or both are consumed. Romantic love aims at fusion; at making two into one. It threatens individuality by demanding a merger.

Romantic love is hostile to the demands of human life. According to Denis de Rougemont, it burgeons when physical and emotional consummation is withheld.[1] The goal of romantic love is not its expression, but its frustration. It thrives on the tension between wanting and not having. Hence, it is antithetical to the experience of marriage and children, to the satisfactions of shared experience, and the sharing of the home. Some have believed that the clash between the romantic love ideal and the goals of family life is the largest single factor in the widespread marital disappointment and failure in our culture. Perhaps the strength and persistence of the ideal of romantic love lies in the fact that it is an unforgettable dream in which man is released from his animal life. Yet since all love has its origin in the facts of animal life, the dream is forever unrealizable. Part of the shaping of each human being is determined by his loves. Each will and must love. The question merely is, "Love whom, what, and how?"

[1] *Love in the Western World*, Denis de Rougemont, New York, Pantheon Books, 1940.

THE FAMILY AS FIRST GROUP

Sympathy in an Animal Base 22

Herbert Spencer

503. If we study the habits of animals of different kinds, with the view of learning what makes the individuals of some species live separately and those of other species live together, we discover two sets of causes uniting or conflicting in various ways and degrees. There are two most general functions, self-maintenance and race-maintenance, to which all more special functions are subservient. Each of these has a share in determining whether the habits shall be solitary or gregarious, or partly the one and partly the other. For according to the circumstances of the species in respect to food, and in respect to rearing of offspring, advantage is gained here by the one habit, here by the other, and here by some alternation of the two. A few instances will make this clear.

An animal of a predatory kind, which has prey that can be caught and killed without help, profits by living alone: especially if its prey is much scattered, and is secured by stealthy approach or by lying in ambush. Gregariousness would here be a positive disadvantage. Hence the tendency of large carnivores, and also of small carnivores that have feeble and widely-distributed prey, to lead solitary lives. Others there are, however, as the wolves and their allies, which, having large prey, profit by co-operation; and gregariousness becomes, in part, their habit. Among herbivorous animals, gregariousness is general for the reason that the distribution of food is not such as would make dispersion decidedly advantageous, while certain benefits arise from living together: more especially the benefit that the eyes and ears of all members of a herd are available for detecting danger; and hence, on the approach of an enemy, each member of the herd has a greater chance of being alarmed in time to escape than if it were alone. Obviously, then, under such conditions as to food, any variety of a herbivorous species which had a tendency for its members to feed within sight of one another, would be the more likely to survive, and gregariousness would be increased and established.

· · ·

From Ch. V, "Sociality and Sympathy" in *The Principles of Psychology*, Vol. II, by Herbert Spencer, New York, D. Appleton and Co., 1905. This was first published in 1872.

504. Recognizing the truth that sociality, while in some cases negatived by the wants of the species, becomes in other cases naturally established as furthering the preservation of the species, we have now to consider what mental traits accompany sociality—what feeling it implies and cultivates.

Sociality can begin only where, through some slight variation, there is less tendency than usual for the individuals to disperse widely. The offspring of the same parents, naturally kept together during their early days, may have their proneness to stay together maintained for a longer time—they may tend to part only at a somewhat later age. If the family profits by this slight modification, dispersion will in subsequent generations be more and more postponed, until it ceases entirely. That slight variations of mental nature sufficient to initiate this process may be fairly assumed, all our domestic animals show us: differences in their characters and likings are conspicuous.

Sociality having thus commenced, and survival of the fittest tending ever to maintain and increase it, it will be further strengthened by the inherited effects of habit. The perception of kindred beings, perpetually seen, heard, and smelt, will come to form a predominant part of consciousness—so predominant a part that absence of it will inevitably cause discomfort. We have but to observe how the caged bird wants to escape, and how the dog, melancholy while chained up, is in ecstasies when liberated, to be reminded that every kind of perceptive activity habitual to a race implies a correlative desire, and a correlative discomfort if that desire is not satisfied. Even during an individual life, as men around us continually show, a trick or habit of quite a special and trivial kind comes to have a corresponding longing which is with difficulty resisted. Clearly, then, in a species to which gregariousness is advantageous, the desire to be together will, generation after generation, be fostered by the habit of being together. How strong this desire does become we see in domestic animals. Horses left alone are often depressed in consequence, and show themselves eager for companionship. A lost sheep is manifestly unhappy until it again finds the flock. The strength of the desire is, indeed, such that in the absence of members of their own species, gregarious animals will form companionships with members of other species.

Without further evidence we may safely infer that among creatures led step by step into gregariousness, there will little by little be established a pleasure in being together—a pleasure in the consciousness of one another's presence—a pleasure simpler than, and quite distinct from, those higher ones which it makes possible. It is a pleasure of like grade with that displayed by the dog on getting off the high road into a field, where the mere sight of grass and contact of the feet with it produce a delight showing itself in scouring around. In the one case, as in the other, there is a set of nervous structures correlated with a set of external conditions. The presence of the external conditions is needful for the exercise of the structures. In the absence of the conditions there arises a craving, and, when the conditions are supplied, a corresponding gratification.

505. From the mental states produced in a gregarious animal by the *presence* of others like itself, we pass to the mental states produced in it by the *actions* of others like itself. The transition is insensible; for consciousness of the presence rarely exists apart from consciousness of the actions. Here, however, we may limit ourselves to actions that have marked significance.

As indicated above, an advantage gained by gregariousness which is probably the first, and remains among many creatures the most important, is the comparative safety secured by earlier detection of enemies. The emotion of fear expresses itself in movements of escape, preceded and accompanied, it may be, by sounds of some kind. Members of a herd simultaneously alarmed by a distant moving object or by some noise it makes—simultaneously making the movements and sounds accompanying alarm—severally see and hear these as being made by the rest at the same time that they are themselves making them, and at the same time that there is present the feeling which prompts them. Frequent repetition inevitably establishes an association between the consciousness of fear and the consciousness of these signs of fear in others—the sounds and movements cannot be perceived without there being aroused the feeling habitually joined with them when they were before perceived. Hence it inevitably happens that what is called the natural language of fear becomes, in a gregarious race, the means of exciting fear in those to whom no fearful object is perceptible. The alarmed members of a flock, seen and heard by the rest, excite in the rest the emotion they are displaying; and the rest, prompted by the emotion thus sympathetically excited, begin to make like movements and sounds. Evidently the process thus initiated must, by inheritance of the effects of habit, furthered by survival of the fittest, render organic a quick and complete sympathy of this simple kind. Eventually a mere hearing of the sound of alarm peculiar to the species, will by itself arouse the emotion of alarm. For the meaning of this sound becomes known not only in the way pointed out but in another way. Each is conscious of the sound made by itself when in fear; and the hearing of a like sound, tending to recall the sound made by itself, tends to arouse the accompanying feeling.

Hence the panics so conspicuous among gregarious creatures. Motions alone often suffice. A flock of birds towards which a man approaches will quietly watch for a while; but when one flies, those near it, excited by its movements of escape, fly also; and in a moment the rest are in the air. The same happens with sheep. Long they stand stupidly gazing, but when one runs, all run; and so strong is the sympathetic tendency among them that they will severally go through the same movement at the same spot—leaping where there is nothing to be leapt over. Commonly, along with these motions of alarm there are sounds of alarm, which may similarly be observed to spread. Rooks on the ground no sooner hear the loud caw of one that suddenly rises, than they join in chorus as they rise.

506. Beyond sympathetic fear, thus readily established in gregarious animals because from hour to hour causes of fear act in common on many, and because the signs of fear are so conspicuous, there are sympathetic feelings of other kinds established after a kindred manner. Creatures living together are simultaneously affected by surrounding conditions of a favourable kind; are therefore liable to be simultaneously thrown into pleasurable states; are therefore habitually witnesses of the sounds and movements accompanying such states, in others as well as in themselves; and hence, in a way like that above explained, are apt to have pleasurable feelings sympathetically excited.

Lambs in the spring show us that the friskiness of one is a cause of friskiness in those near it—if one leaps, others leap. Among horses, pleasurable excitement spreads, as every hunting-field shows. A pack of dogs, too, takes up the cry when a leader begins to give tongue. In the poultry-yard kindred facts may be noticed. Early in the day that quacking of the ducks which is significant of satisfaction, comes and goes in chorus: when one sets the example, the rest follow. The like happens with geese and with fowls. Gregarious birds in a wild state furnish further illustrations. In a rookery the cawing rises into bursts of many voices, and then almost dying away, again suddenly spreads sympathetically; and the like holds with the screaming of parrots and macaws.

This sympathy is most variously exhibited by that most intelligent of the gregarious animals which come under daily observation—the dog. Beyond sympathetic cries of excitement among dogs when chasing their prey in company, there is the sympathetic barking which every quarrel in the streets sets up, and which, under another form, is sometimes so annoying in the night; and there is also the sympathetic howling to be heard from dogs kept together in a kennel. Here, again, the feelings that are communicated from one to another, are feelings often simultaneously produced in many by a common cause. Able, however, as the dog is to perceive more complex and less conspicuous marks of feeling, it displays a degree and variety of sympathy considerably beyond this. Having long had men as well as members of their own species for companions, dogs have acquired tendencies to be sympathetically excited by manifestations of human feeling. I do not refer simply to the fact that sometimes a dog will howl sympathetically when he hears singing, and will even occasionally follow the voice up the gamut; for this is but a slight modification of the effect produced in him by the sounds other dogs make. But I refer to the fact that some dogs are sympathetically affected by the silent manifestations of pain and pleasure in those they are attached to—will stand with drooping tail and grave wistful gaze when the face and attitude of a master show depression, and will display joy on seeing a smile.

507. Here we are naturally introduced to the truth that the degree and range of sympathy depend on the clearness and extent of representation. A

sympathetic feeling is one that is not immediately excited by the natural cause of such a feeling, but one that is mediately excited by the presentation of signs habitually associated with such a feeling. Consequently, it pre-supposes ability to perceive and combine these signs, as well as ability to rep-resent their implications, external or internal, or both. So that there can be sympathy only in proportion as there is power of representation.

For this reason it is that among inferior gregarious animals the range of sympathy is so narrow. The signs of pleasure when it becomes great, and the signs of fear, which is the most common pain, alone arouse in them fellow-feelings. With other emotions there is no sympathy; either because the signs of them are comparatively inconspicuous, or because the causes of them do not act simultaneously on all. A ewe that has lost her lamb, does not by her manifestations of feeling excite like feelings in other ewes; first, for the reason that her bleat does not differ much from the bleat caused by simple discom-fort; second, for the reason that other ewes have not habitually had such slight modifications of bleat associated in themselves with the pains produced by loss of offspring; and third, for the reason that what other manifestations come from the bereaved ewe in the shape of motions and facial modifications, are inappreciable to the rest, and could not be mentally combined even if they were appreciable. There have neither been the requisite experiences, nor does there exist such power of representation as could combine the experi-ences, did they exist into the needful antecedent to the feeling.

Hence increase of intelligence is one condition, though by no means the sole condition, to increase in extent of sympathy. Because they lack intelli-gence, herbivorous creatures, though their habits in scarcely any ways check the growth of sympathy, nevertheless remain unsympathetic in all directions save those above described. While the dog, trained by the habits of his spe-cies in the perception of more complex and varied appearances, has gained a considerably-greater breadth of sympathy, notwithstanding that restraint which the predatory life puts on its extension.

508. One further group of general considerations must be set down. The genesis of sympathy implying in the first place the presence of other beings, and implying in the second place subjection to influences simultaneously operating on these other beings, and calling forth marks of feeling from them; it results that sympathy is cultivated by all relations among individuals which fulfil these conditions. Of such relations we have thus far recognized but one —the relation which gregariousness implies. But there are two others—the sexual relation and the parental relation. These co-operate in various degrees; and the most marked effects are produced where they both act along with simple sociality. A paragraph may be given to each.

The sexual relation can be expected to further the development of sym-pathy in a considerable degree, only if it has considerable permanence. Where the rearing of offspring is so carried on as to keep the parents together during the interval required for bringing up a single brood, and still more where it is so carried on as to keep them together during the rearing of successive broods, there are maintained the conditions under which arise certain sympathetic excitations beyond those entailed by gregariousness alone. As, in their common relation to progeny, parents are liable to have certain pleasurable and painful feelings frequently called out from them by the same cause at the same time in marked ways, they will become sympathetic in respect of such feelings; and in so far as such feelings are in part made up of more general feelings, expressed by more general signs, they will become relatively sympathetic in respect of the more general feelings. Birds furnish instances of the fulfilment of these conditions followed by production of these results. The contrast between polygamous birds, the males of which take no shares in rearing the offspring, and monogamous birds, the males of which take large shares in rearing them, supplies significant evidence. Where the male joins in feeding the young after they are hatched, as among our hedge birds, there is sympathy in fear, when the offspring are in danger; and probably in other feelings not so conspicuous. Among the martins and swifts, the male often feeds the female during incubation; and here we perceive in the simultaneous twittering of groups sitting on the eaves, or in the simultaneous screaming as they fly about together in the evening, that there is a more active sympathy than among barn-door fowls. Most marked, however, is the contrast in the poultry-yard between fowls and pigeons. The same pair of pigeons brings up successive broods, the female while sitting is fed by the male, and the male takes an unusual share in feeding the young: furnishing them with partially-macerated food from his crop. Here, and especially among the variety named doves, the sympathy is so great as to furnish familiar metaphors.

Fellow-feeling is also cultivated in each parent by its direct relations to progeny. Feeling having this origin is so intimately mingled with the parental feeling, which is a primitive and much simpler one, that the two cannot be clearly distinguished. But since parent and offspring are by their intimate relation often exposed to common causes of pleasure and pain, there must be a special exercise of sympathy between them, or rather, of sympathy in the parent towards the offspring; for the offspring, being but partially developed, cannot so interpret the natural language as to make the effects reciprocal. It will habitually happen that the signs of satisfaction consequent on abundance of food, will be shown by offspring and parent together, as well as kindred signs consequent on genial warmth; and the marks of discomfort, say from inclemency, as well as those of alarm from danger, will be frequently simultaneous. Hence there are furnished the conditions under which specialities of sympathy can arise.

These brief indications of an extensive class of facts, will make it adequately clear that there are three causes of sympathy, due respectively to the three relations—between members of a species, between male and female, and between parent and offspring. Co-operating as these causes do in various ways and degrees, according as the circumstances of the species determine one or other set of habits as most conducive to survival, it is inferable that where the circumstances allow co-operation of all the causes, the effects are likely to be the greatest. Among inferior animals, co-operation of all the causes is not frequent: rooks supplying us with one of the few instances easily observable. And even where all the causes co-operate the effect producible depends on the accompanying degree of intelligence; since the capacity for being sympathetically affected, implies the capacity for having an ideal feeling of some kind aroused by perception of the sounds and motions implying a real feeling of the same kind in another.

509. It is only when we come to the highest races of creatures that this last condition is largely fulfilled. Merely noting that among the lower primates, where considerable intelligence goes along with sociality and prolonged care of offspring by the females, sympathy is shown in various ways, we may now limit our attention to the human race. Here we have all three direct causes of sympathy in action, along with the co-essential condition—elevated intelligence.

The lowest types of mankind, exhibiting fellow-feeling in the least-decided and least-varied ways, are those least subject to these co-operating causes, and fulfilling in the least degree the needful condition. Among the Andamanese, there is no permanent marriage: a mother, as soon as her child is born, is left unhelped by the father to rear it; and hence there is wanting that culture of sympathy resulting from the direct paternal relation, as well as that resulting from the joint interest of parents in offspring. Similarly, where polyandry prevails, and paternity is uncertain or wholly unknown, there is not likely to be so active a sympathy of men towards children as where the monogamous relation makes filiation clear. Moreover, between the parents themselves polyandry is less favourable to culture of the sympathies than is monogamy. And when we remember that along with these inferior forms of domestic relations, the social relations are little more than rudimentary, while the intelligence is not great, we have no difficulty in seeing why among the lowest races the sympathies are weak and narrow.

Conversely, the races that have become most sympathetic are those in which monogamy has been long established; those in which the co-operation of parents for rearing children is continued to a comparatively-late period in the lives of children; those in which social development has made the contact of citizens with one another constant, much closer, and more varied; and those in which representativeness of thought has been gradually increased as society has gradually advanced.

And here we are led to remark that the relatively-slow development of sympathy during civilization, notwithstanding the high degree of sociality and the favourable domestic relations, has been in a considerable degree due to the slow development of representative power. The gratuitous infliction of pain, of which so much went on in the past and of which so much goes on now, obviously implies feeble representation of pain in the minds of those who inflict it. Did the signs of the pains they give arouse in them ideal pains of any vividness, they would be deterred. And those in whom the strong language of physical suffering excites so faint a representation of the suffering, cannot be expected to have any sympathy with feelings of which the natural language is complex and not conspicuous.

510. But though inadequacy of intelligence involves limitation of sympathy, and explains absence of sympathy with feelings that are slight in degree and show themselves in obscure or involved ways, it does not by itself explain absence of sympathy in those cases just named, where strong feelings are expressed in conspicuous ways. For this absence of sympathy there is a cause of another order, which it is important ever to remember.

The human race, though a gregarious race, has ever been, and still is, a predatory race. From the beginning, the preservation of each society has depended on fulfilment of two sets of conditions, which, generally considered, are antagonistic. On the one hand, by destructive activities, offensive and defensive, each society has had to maintain itself in the face of external inimical agencies, partly animal but mainly human; and this has required the natures of its members to continue such that the destructive activities are not painful to them, but on the whole pleasurable: it has been necessary that their sympathies with pain should not prevent the infliction of pain. On the other hand, for the furtherance of co-operation between members of the society, and for such maintenance of the domestic relations as insures rearing of offspring, a certain amount of fellow-feeling has been needful; and no great social advance has been possible without an increase of this fellow-feeling. If the members of a tribe cared no more about one another's welfare than they cared about the welfare of their foes, there could be none of that mutual trust and mutual aid required for progress; since the sub-division of functions implied by social evolution, is but another name for mutual aid, which can exist only through mutual trust. So that while the external activities of each society have tended to maintain an unsympathetic nature, its internal activities have demanded sympathy and have tended to make the nature more sympathetic. Noting, as we pass, the fact that under such conditions as have hitherto existed, either set of conflicting activities carried to excess has been fatal—the one by fostering too much in each individual the anti-social character, and the other by rendering the society incapable of successfully resisting aggression; we have here to remark the compromise established in the moral natures of individuals, in adjustment to these opposite requirements.

The compromise is shown in a specialization of the sympathies. Fellow-feeling has been continually repressed in those directions where social safety has involved the disregard of it; while it has been allowed to grow in those directions where it has either positively conduced to the welfare of the society or has not hindered it. The possibility of such a specialization is not at first obvious; but a few illustrations will show its occurrence to be in conformity with known biological principles.

That adaptation by which actions at first disagreeable and even painful are rendered by repetition less disagreeable or painful, is familiar to us both in its bodily and mental forms. We know that a sensitive skin frayed by much friction, becomes thickened and callous if the friction is often repeated; and we know that use eventually makes easy the endurance of a misfortune that seemed at first too great to bear. These instances will call to mind the wide application of this general principle. In the case we are considering its application is obvious. Where the circumstances are such as frequently excite a sympathetic pain, that pain will become less and less excitable sympathetically by those circumstances—there will result in that direction a moral callousness. This is sufficiently shown by the example which surgeons furnish. Though, when he first sees an operation, a student not unfrequently faints from sympathetic pain, he becomes gradually less sensitive; so that he is enabled by and by to perform an operation himself, if not without pain, still with a greatly-diminished amount of it. And the surgeon further shows us how very special this limitation of sympathy may be; since, while ceasing to be so sympathetic as the student in respect of these directly-inflicted physical pains, he retains an equal sympathy, or gains a greater sympathy, with his patients in respect of their general sufferings.

Here, then, is an explanation of the fact that men may be cruel in some directions and kind in others. We are enabled to see how it happens that the shooting of game and the chasing of foxes, is enjoyed by men who are not only tender in their domestic relations but generous and just, even to an unusual degree, in their social relations. And it ceases to seem strange that an old soldier who delights in recollections of battles, nevertheless shows kindness in his dealings with those around him. Sundry of the anomalies in the manifestations of sympathy which are thus made comprehensible, may be fitly grouped together.

Primary Groups 23
Charles Horton Cooley

By primary groups I mean those characterized by intimate face-to-face association and coöperation. They are primary in several senses, but chiefly in that they are fundamental in forming the social nature and ideals of the

From Ch. III, "Primary Groups" and from Ch. IV, "Primary Ideals," with deletions, in *Social Organization*, by Charles Horton Cooley, New York, Charles Scribner's Sons, 1909.

individual. The result of intimate association, psychologically, is a certain fusion of individualities in a common whole, so that one's very self, for many purposes at least, is the common life and purpose of the group. Perhaps the simplest way of describing this wholeness is by saying that it is a "we"; it involves the sort of sympathy and mutual identification for which "we" is the natural expression. One lives in the feeling of the whole and finds the chief aims of his will in that feeling.

It is not to be supposed that the unity of the primary group is one of mere harmony and love. It is always a differentiated and usually a competitive unity, admitting of self-assertion and various appropriative passions; but these passions are socialized by sympathy, and come, or tend to come, under the discipline of a common spirit. The individual will be ambitious, but the chief object of his ambition will be some desired place in the thought of the others, and he will feel allegiance to common standards of service and fair play. So the boy will dispute with his fellows a place on the team, but above such disputes will place the common glory of his class and school.

.   .   .

The most important spheres of this intimate association and coöperation —though by no means the only ones—are the family, the play-group of children, and the neighborhood or community group of elders. These are practically universal, belonging to all times and all stages of development; and are accordingly a chief basis of what is universal in human nature and human ideals. The best comparative studies of the family, such as those of Westermarck[1] or Howard,[2] show it to us as not only a universal institution, but as more alike the world over than the exaggeration of exceptional customs by an earlier school has led us to suppose. Nor can any one doubt the general prevalence of play-groups among children or of informal assemblies of various kinds among their elders. Such association is clearly the nursery of human nature in the world about us, and there is no apparent reason to suppose that the case has anywhere or at any time been essentially different.

As regards play, I might, were it not a matter of common observation, multiply illustrations of the universality and spontaneity of the group discussion and coöperation to which it gives rise. The general fact is that children, especially boys after about their twelfth year, live in fellowships in which their sympathy, ambition and honor are engaged even more, often, than they are in the family. Most of us can recall examples of the endurance by boys of injustice and even cruelty, rather than appeal from their fellows to parents or teachers—as, for instance, in the hazing so prevalent at schools, and so difficult, for this very reason, to repress. And how elaborate the discussion, how cogent the public opinion, how hot the ambitions in these fellowships.

Nor is this facility of juvenile association, as is sometimes supposed, a trait peculiar to English and American boys; since experience among our

[1] The History of Human Marriage.
[2] A History of Matrimonial Institutions.

immigrant population seems to show that the offspring of the more restrictive civilizations of the continent of Europe form self-governing play-groups with almost equal readiness. Thus Miss Jane Addams, after pointing out that the "gang" is almost universal, speaks of the interminable discussion which every detail of the gang's activity receives, remarking that "in these social folk-mores, so to speak, the young citizen learns to act upon his own determination." [3]

Of the neighborhood group it may be said, in general, that from the time men formed permanent settlements upon the land, down, at least, to the rise of modern industrial cities, it has played a main part in the primary, heart-to-heart life of the people. Among our Teutonic forefathers the village community was apparently the chief sphere of sympathy and mutual aid for the commons all through the "dark" and middle ages, and for many purposes it remains so in rural districts at the present day. In some countries we still find it with all its ancient vitality, notably in Russia, where the mir, or self-governing village group, is the main theatre of life, along with the family, for perhaps fifty millions of peasants.

In our own life the intimacy of the neighborhood has been broken up by the growth of an intricate mesh of wider contacts which leaves us strangers to people who live in the same house. And even in the country the same principle is at work, though less obviously, diminishing our economic and spiritual community with our neighbors. How far this change is a healthy development, and how far a disease, is perhaps still uncertain.

Besides these almost universal kinds of primary association, there are many others whose form depends upon the particular state of civilization; the only essential thing, as I have said, being a certain intimacy and fusion of personalities. In our own society, being little bound by place, people easily form clubs, fraternal societies and the like, based on congeniality, which may give rise to real intimacy. Many such relations are formed at school and college, and among men and women brought together in the first instance by their occupations—as workmen in the same trade, or the like. Where there is a little common interest and activity, kindness grows like weeds by the roadside.

But the fact that the family and neighborhood groups are ascendant in the open and plastic time of childhood makes them even now incomparably more influential than all the rest.

·   ·   ·

Primary groups are primary in the sense that they give the individual his earliest and completest experience of social unity, and also in the sense that they do not change in the same degree as more elaborate relations, but form a comparatively permanent source out of which the latter are ever springing. Of course they are not independent of the larger society, but to some extent reflect its spirit; as the German family and the German school bear somewhat distinctly the print of German militarism. But this, after all,

[3] Newer Ideals of Peace, 177.

is like the tide setting back into creeks, and does not commonly go very far. Among the German, and still more among the Russian peasantry, are found habits of free coöperation and discussion almost uninfluenced by the character of the state; and it is a familiar and well-supported view that the village commune, self-governing as regards local affairs and habituated to discussion, is a very widespread institution in settled communities, and the continuator of a similar autonomy previously existing in the clan. "It is man who makes monarchies and establishes republics, but the commune seems to come directly from the hand of God." [4]

In our own cities the crowded tenements and the general economic and social confusion have sorely wounded the family and the neighborhood, but it is remarkable, in view of these conditions, what vitality they show; and there is nothing upon which the conscience of the time is more determined than upon restoring them to health.

These groups, then, are springs of life, not only for the individual but for social institutions. They are only in part moulded by special traditions, and, in larger degree, express a universal nature. The religion or government of other civilizations may seem alien to us, but the children or the family group wear the common life, and with them we can always make ourselves at home.

.   .   .

Life in the primary groups gives rise to social ideals which, as they spring from similar experiences, have much in common throughout the human race. And these naturally become the motive and test of social progress. Under all systems men strive, however blindly, to realize objects suggested by the familiar experience of primary association.

Where do we get our notions of love, freedom, justice, and the like which we are ever applying to social institutions? Not from abstract philosophy, surely, but from the actual life of simple and widespread forms of society, like the family or the play-group. In these relations mankind realizes itself, gratifies its primary needs, in a fairly satisfactory manner, and from the experience forms standards of what it is to expect from more elaborate association. Since groups of this sort are never obliterated from human experience, but flourish more or less under all kinds of institutions, they remain an enduring criterion by which the latter are ultimately judged.

Of course these simpler relations are not uniform for all societies, but vary considerably with race, with the general state of civilization, and with the particular sort of institutions that may prevail. The primary groups themselves are subject to improvement and decay, and need to be watched and cherished with a very special care.

Neither is it claimed that, at the best, they realize ideal conditions; only that they approach them more nearly than anything else in general experience, and so form the practical basis on which higher imaginations are built.

[4] De Tocqueville, Democracy in America, vol. i, chap. 5.

They are not always pleasant or righteous, but they almost always contain elements from which ideals of pleasantness and righteousness may be formed.

The ideal that grows up in familiar association may be said to be a part of human nature itself. In its most general form it is that of a moral whole or community wherein individual minds are merged and the higher capacities of the members find total and adequate expression. And it grows up because familiar association fills our minds with imaginations of the thought and feeling of other members of the group, and of the group as a whole, so that, for many purposes, we really make them a part of ourselves and identify our self-feeling with them.

Children and savages do not formulate any such ideal, but they have it nevertheless; they see it; they see themselves and their fellows as an indivisible, though various, "we," and they desire this "we" to be harmonious, happy, and successful. How heartily one may merge himself in the family and in the fellowships of youth is perhaps within the experience of all of us; and we come to feel that the same spirit should extend to our country, our race, our world. "All the abuses which are the objects of reform . . . are unconsciously amended in the intercourse of friends." [5]

A congenial family life is the immemorial type of moral unity, and source of many of the terms—such as brotherhood, kindness, and the like—which describe it. The members become merged by intimate association into a whole wherein each age and sex participates in its own way. Each lives in imaginative contact with the minds of the others, and finds in them the dwelling-place of his social self, of his affections, ambitions, resentments, and standards of right and wrong. Without uniformity, there is yet unity, a free, pleasant, wholesome, fruitful, common life.

As to the playground, Mr. Joseph Lee, in an excellent paper on Play as a School of the Citizen, gives the following account of the merging of the one in the whole that may be learned from sport. The boy, he says,

"is deeply participating in a common purpose. The team and the plays that it executes are present in a very vivid manner to his consciousness. His conscious individuality is more thoroughly lost in the sense of membership than perhaps it ever becomes in any other way. So that the sheer experience of citizenship in its simplest and essential form—of the sharing in a public consciousness, of having the social organization present as a controlling ideal in your heart—is very intense. . . .

Along with the sense of the team as a mechanical instrument, and unseparated from it in the boy's mind, is the consciousness of it as the embodiment of a common purpose. There is in team play a very intimate experience of the ways in which such a purpose is built up and made effective. You feel, though without analysis, the subtle ways in which a single strong character breaks out the road ahead and gives confidence to the rest to follow; how the creative power of one ardent

[5] Thoreau, A Week on the Concord and Merrimack Rivers, 283.

imagination, bravely sustained, makes possible the putting through of the play as he conceives it. You feel to the marrow of your bones how each loyal member contributes to the salvation of all the others by holding the conception of the whole play so firmly in his mind as to enable them to hold it, and to participate in his single-minded determination to see it carried out. You have intimate experience of the ways in which individual members contribute to the team and of how the team, in turn, builds up their spiritual nature.

And the team is not only an extension of the player's consciousness; it is a part of his personality. His participation has deepened from cooperation to membership. Not only is he now a part of the team, but the team is a part of him." [6]

Moral unity, as this illustration implies, admits and rewards strenuous ambition; but this ambition must either be for the success of the group, or at least not inconsistent with that. The fullest self-realization will belong to the one who embraces in a passionate self-feeling the aims of the fellowship, and spends his life in fighting for their attainment.

The ideal of moral unity I take to be the mother, as it were, of all social ideals.

It is, then, not my aim to depreciate the self-assertive passions. I believe that they are fierce, inextinguishable, indispensable. Competition and the survival of the fittest are as righteous as kindness and coöperation, and not necessarily opposed to them: an adequate view will embrace and harmonize these diverse aspects. The point I wish particularly to bring out in this chapter is that the normal self is moulded in primary groups to be a social self whose ambitions are formed by the common thought of the group.

In their crudest form such passions as lust, greed, revenge, the pride of power and the like are not, distinctively, *human* nature at all, but animal nature, and so far as we rise into the spirit of family or neighborhood association we control and subordinate them. They are rendered human only so far as they are brought under the discipline of sympathy, and refined into sentiments, such as love, resentment, and ambition. And in so far as they are thus humanized they become capable of useful function.

Take the greed of gain, for example, the ancient sin of avarice, the old wolf, as Dante says, that gets more prey than all the other beasts.[7] The desire of possession is in itself a good thing, a phase of self-realization and a cause of social improvement. It is immoral or greedy only when it is without adequate control from sympathy, when the self realized is a narrow self. In that case it is a vice of isolation or weak social consciousness, and indicates a state of mind intermediate between the brutal and the fully human or moral, when

---

[6] Charities and the Commons, Aug. 3, 1907.

[7] Antica lupa,
Che piu che tutte l'altre besttie hai preda.

Purgatorio, xx, 10.

desire is directed toward social objects—wealth or power—but is not social in its attitude toward others who desire the same objects. Intimate association has the power to allay greed. One will hardly be greedy as against his family or close friends, though very decent people will be so as against almost any one else. Every one must have noticed that after frank association, even of a transient character, with another person, one usually has a sense of kindred with him which makes one ashamed to act greedily at his expense.

Those who dwell preponderantly upon the selfish aspect of human nature and flout as sentimentalism the "altruistic" conception of it, make their chief error in failing to see that our self itself is altruistic, that the object of our higher greed is some desired place in the minds of other men, and that through this it is possible to enlist ordinary human nature in the service of ideal aims. The improvement of society does not call for any essential change in human nature, but, chiefly, for a larger and higher application of its familiar impulses.

Enculturation   24
Melville J. Herskovits

In the study of man and his works, it is necessary to distinguish "culture" from its companion term "society." *A culture is the way of life of a people; while a society is an organized, interacting aggregate of individuals who follow a given way of life.* In still simpler terms *a society is composed of people; the way they behave is their culture.*[1] Can we, however, thus separate man as a social animal from man as a creature who has culture? Is not social behavior actually cultural behavior? Indeed, have we not seen that the ultimate reality in the study of man is man himself, rather than the ideas, the institutions, even the material objects that have come into being as a result of man's association in the aggregates we call "societies"?

.   .   .

The process by means of which an individual is integrated into his society is called *socialization.* It involves the adaptation of the individual to the fellow members of his group, which, in turn, gives him status and assigns to

Ch. 17, "Culture and Society," with some footnotes deleted, in Part Three, "The Nature of Culture." From *Cultural Anthropology,* by Melville F. Herskovits. Copyright 1947, 1948, © Copyright 1955 by Melville F. Herskovits. Reprinted by permission of Alfred A. Knopf, Inc.

[1] S. F. Nadel (1951, pp. 79–80) phrases the distinction in this way: "Society, as I see it, means the totality of social facts projected on to the dimension of relationships and groupings; culture, the same totality in the dimension of action."

him the role he plays in the life of the community. He passes through various stages, each distinguished by certain permitted and prohibited forms of behavior, such as playfulness in the young or the manipulation of power among the elders. As sexual maturity is reached, he again participates in a family grouping, but now as parent, protector and teacher. He will also figure as a member of certain groupings not based on kinship at all but on sex or age differences.

Because man alone has the ability to develop and transmit learned behavior, his social institutions exhibit a variety and a degree of complexity greater than the social forms of any other *single species* of animal. By his ability to communicate with his fellows in the symbolic and conceptual forms of speech, he alone has been able to ring the innumerable variations on even such a basic social structure as the family. If we consider the group life of any species of infrahuman animals, we find that their social structures are far more uniform and thus much more predictable than those of man. For each of their generations learns only behavior common to all its contemporaries, whereas man builds on the experience of all who have gone before him.

For animals and man alike, *conditioning,* in its broadest sense, is the essential process involved. Animals can, of course, learn. Countless experiments have shown that canaries brought up among other birds will vary their song, or that cats can be brought up to play with rats rather than to kill them. In one experiment of this latter kind, Kuo even conditioned cats to be afraid of rats; nine of the twenty kittens reared in isolation from rat-killing cats themselves became rat-killers.[2] Yet conscious learning cannot be discarded as a factor, and for kittens brought up under normal circumstances the example of the mother cat is of appreciable importance.

That older animals teach their young is recognized far beyond the limits of scientific inquiry. Such a tale as the following, from Dutch Guiana, shows how recognition of the factor of teaching and learning among animals can be expressed in homely form:

Kitten and little Rat were great friends. Every day they went to play together. But Rat did not know that he was Cat's favorite food, and Kitten did not know that Rat was his favorite food. But one day, when little Rat came home, his mother asked him, "With whom do you play?" He said, "With friend Kitten." And at the same time, when Kitten went home, his mother asked him, "With whom do you play?" He said, "With little Rat." Then Rat's mother said to him, "You must not play with Kitten any more, because you are his favorite food." And at the same time, too, mother Cat was saying to Kitten, "You stupid fellow, don't you know that he is your tidbit? When you play with him, you must strike him." The next day, no sooner did they come out on the street than Kitten called to friend Rat, said, "Aren't you coming to play with me any more?" At once little Rat answered him, "Yes, brother. There are wise people in your village, and there are wise people in my village, too!"[3]

[2] Z. Y. Kuo, 1930.
[3] M. J. and F. S. Herskovits, 1936, p. 281.

The socialization of men is understandably more complex than that of animals, because human social institutions take on such varied and changing forms. This means, moreover, that the process of socialization is only a part of the process by means of which men adjust to their fellows in working with the total body of traditions—economic, social, technological, religious, aesthetic, linguistic—to which they fall heir. Here learning takes on special significance that must be fully grasped if its all-important role in shaping the way of life of a people is to be adequately appreciated.

The aspects of the learning experience that mark off man from other creatures, and by means of which he achieves competence in his culture, may be called *enculturation*. This is in essence a process of conscious or unconscious conditioning, exercised within the limits sanctioned by a given body of custom. From this process not only is all adjustment to social living achieved, but also all those satisfactions, themselves a part of social experience, that derive from individual expression rather than association with others in the group.

Every human being goes through a process of enculturation, for without the adaptations it describes he could not live as a member of society. Like any phenomenon of human behavior, this process is most complex. In the earliest years of an individual's life, it is largely a matter of conditioning to fundamentals—habits of eating, sleeping, speaking, personal cleanliness—whose inculcation has been shown to have special significance in shaping the personality and forming the habit patterns of the adult in later life. Yet the enculturative experience is not terminated at the close of infancy. As an individual continues through childhood and adolescence to adult status, he is continuously exposed to this process of learning, which can be said to end only with his death.

The difference between the nature of the enculturative experience in the early years of life and later is that the range of conscious acceptance or rejection by an individual continuously increases as he grows older. By the time he has reached maturity, a man or woman has been so conditioned that he moves easily within the limits of accepted behavior set by his group. Thereafter, new forms of behavior presented to him are largely those involved in culture change—new inventions or discoveries, or new ideas diffused from outside his society about which, as an individual, he has to "make up his mind" and thus play his role in reorienting his culture.

In truth, we are here touching on one of the most fundamental aspects of the enculturative process, an aspect whose full significance will be probed when we take up such a problem as the relation of the individual to culture, or the question of conservatism and change in culture, the reconciliation of which, it will be recalled, involved the resolution of one of our apparent dilemmas in the understanding of culture. However, the basic principle involved is clear: *The enculturation of the individual in the early years of his life is the prime mechanism making for cultural stability, while the process, as it operates on more mature folk, is highly important in inducing change.*

It is because of the earliest enculturative conditionings that, as we have pointed out, "human beings learn their cultures so well that most behavior rarely rises to the level of consciousness." In our earliest years we are being continuously conditioned to conformity, whether through the exercise of techniques of punishment and reward, as in the inculcation of the moral code of society, or by imitation, as in learning motor habits, such as the gestures, or the cadences of speech. Infantile protest, such as occurs when a child refuses to learn to speak, is not absent. But such protests are individual ones, made against the restraints placed on the infant's freedom of behavior. It is significant that the infantile protest is not rationalized. It cannot be, for the linguistic—that is the symbolic—equipment of the infant does not permit this.

In other words, learning, by inculcating in the new member of society the enculturative disciplines essential for his functioning as a member of his social group, contributes to social stability and cultural continuity. As the individual grows older, these early conditionings become so effective that they settle into the routines of daily behavior. Then the continuing enculturation to which he is exposed is in very large measure a reconditioning process, which lies on the conscious level. A man or woman knows the ways of behavior that are traditionally acceptable to his group in a given situation—in one society, that he must step off a path and turn his back on a passing elder to show respect, in another, that the thing to do with the property of a dead person is to burn it.

But should he have contact with another people who hold that respect is shown by facing a superior rather than by turning away from him, then even with the greatest freedom of choice, an alternative has been presented that must be grappled with. If he accepts the new mode for himself he may meet with resistance at home. But unless he is prevented from carrying on the new way of showing respect, his persistence will make of him a center from which a possible deviation from the sanctioned form of polite behavior radiates, and his fellows will be continuously faced with making the choice he has already made.

The resistances to revisions in economic behavior called into play by the spread of Euroamerican culture over the world demonstrate how this process works. The destruction of the property of the dead, or any other form of destruction of property, is frowned on in our culture. Great pressure to change such customs has been brought upon native peoples by administrators who have no concept of what the social significance of the destruction of property may be. Whether they have succeeded or not, the psychological processes of the natives in making an adjustment to this dictum is of a different order than the early conditioning process to which these same individuals were exposed as infants.

The enculturative experience of later life, however, is only intermittent. It thus presents a further contrast to the continuous conditioning to which the infant and young child are exposed. Nor do these enculturative situations, for the adult, cover as many segments of culture as for the young. The adult knows his language, the systems of etiquette that regulate behavior, the ways of facing the supernatural, the musical forms of his culture—all things that the child must learn. For the adult, enculturation has been completed except where new situations must be met. He projects the decisions he must reach in his daily round against the background of knowledge his culture has provided him. This permits an adult human being to react to the stimuli presented to him by his culture with a minimum of need to traverse ground already covered. Enculturation is thus the process that permits most behavior to be carried on *below the level of conscious thought*. In nontechnical language, it can be taken for granted in the manner in which we accept without question even such complex manifestations of our own culture as automobiles, electricity, and symphony orchestras, to say nothing of the art of writing or such a fundamental technological device as the wheel.

Emotional Development in Adolescence   25
Edgar Z. Friedenberg

Two aspects of growth that contribute most to a clear self-definition are climactic in adolescence. One of these is the capacity for tenderness toward other persons. Since tenderness is fired by sexuality and expresses a primarily sexual feeling, adults are not astonished that it should appear very strongly in the emotional spectrum of adolescence. But we are inclined to underestimate the power and the human value of adolescent love. For one thing, it frightens us and sometimes makes us more envious than we know. For another, we live in a culture which sentimentalizes children and therefore tends to lose sight of the contrasting capacity for tenderness that adolescence brings. Finally—and for reasons which we must subsequently examine rather closely—we regard many of the things and persons beloved by adolescents, including other adolescents, with scorn and utter contempt and so disregard the feeling they arouse. Adolescents tend to be passionate people, and passion is no less real because it is directed toward a hot-rod, a commercialized popular singer, or the leader of a black-jacketed gang. Our exploitive mass culture

From Ch. 2, "Emotional Development in Adolescence," with some footnotes omitted, in *The Vanishing Adolescent*, Edgar Z. Friedenberg, Boston, Beacon Press, 1959. Reprinted by permission of the Beacon Press, copyright © 1959 by Edgar Z. Friedenberg.

makes it terribly hard for youngsters to find or even to identify appropriate objects for love; but it is the new power of adolescence to weave tenderness into the fabric of personality that produces a pattern of life not wholly cynical or expedient.

The other major development is an attitude of respect for competence. Adults often find it hard to see this in adolescent behavior, partly because they lack respect for and disapprove of the kind of competence the adolescent is seeking and partly because adolescent competence tends now to be tapped off for commercial purposes and standardized before it has had much chance to develop or to contribute to the development of the adolescent. But respect for competence in oneself and others is crucial in adolescence, for it is crucial to self-definition. In a world as empirical as ours, a youngster who does not know what he is good *at* will not be sure what he is good *for;* he must know what he can do in order to know who he is. The things he does well may not, of course, be things that win him the esteem of the community; some adolescents, when they get nervous and upset, steal cars and take joy rides in them the way an adult might work off his mood by gardening or a game of golf. But they must be skills that identify him to himself and others, and keep him from getting lost.

In order to understand in detail how tenderness and competence are involved in adolescent growth, we must first establish a basis for interpreting personality development in adolescence as a general process. Because adolescent personality, especially under American social conditions, is so much affected by the feelings and relationships youngsters establish among themselves, I believe that the psychoanalytic system developed by Harry Stack Sullivan and his school will be more useful than the classical Freudian schema. I shall draw freely on Sullivan's work—particularly the *Interpersonal Theory of Psychiatry*.[1]

Sullivan distinguishes two stages of childhood between infancy and adolescence. By "childhood" he refers only to the *first* of these. He considers as a *child* only a person so young that most of his experience occurs in the home. His interpersonal relations are almost entirely with members of his family. Unlike the infant, he has clear interpersonal relations, in that he can consistently tell one person from another and expects different things from them; but these persons all share his essentially private world. They are not strangers, and at this age he does not see them as competitors. As soon as he does —that is, as soon as he begins to approach others expecting to find them impersonal and bent on their own aims to his possible disadvantage—childhood is at an end. When this will be is not a matter of biological age or individual psychodynamics. Childhood ends earlier in lower class, where children may have to fend for themselves almost as soon as they can walk, than it does in

[1] New York, Norton, 1953.

middle class. It ends earlier in this country, with our emphasis on early self-reliance and getting along with others, than in France, where sometimes only sex is strong enough to force parents to recognize childhood's end.

Later childhood, or roughly what Freud called the *latency period*, Sullivan speaks of as the *juvenile era*. The juvenile era begins when social institutions oblige the child to deal *as an individual* with the problems of his relationship to strangers, with the cumulative difficulties that arise from the difference between what he sees in himself and what they see in him, what he needs and what they have to give, what he gives and what they can accept. Sullivan's juvenile, it must be stressed, is *pre-adolescent*; he is not the juvenile of Juvenile Delinquency. He is the youngest person whose fate depends on his ability to communicate with people who have little share in his life, and who are more interested in themselves than in what he is trying to tell them about himself.

Sullivan sees the child as primarily engaged in building concepts which are general enough to permit intelligible communication with other persons. The private symbol system which the infant builds for himself must be modified to permit other persons to understand him; he must consent to a relationship between his language and external phenomena which is fairly consistent with the rules observed in the outer world; he cannot go on calling everything that has fur and moves "doggy." Since these rules are not so important, really, to any of us as our own view of the meaning of our experience, a good deal is lost in the process; but a good deal is gained in not becoming psychotic, which is the other choice. The child learns to talk about what he perceives; that is, he learns to make roughly the same sound other members of his family make to denote similar situations, or at least to say the same thing consistently in response to the same situation. Some of us go through life saying "I'm hungry!" when we mean "Nobody loves me!"; but we say it with as much conviction at three hundred pounds as we did at thirty.

For the fundamental, underlying, feeling-tone—aroused in the infant as a crude response to feeling and perception, and coloring much of his subsequent response to all of life—there is no language; and Sullivan views the most important experiences of life as being permanently incommunicable in language. But between sensitive individuals, feeling is communicated with great precision by empathy, as it was initially from the mother to the infant before the infant had any language.

Neither childhood nor the juvenile era, as Sullivan presents them, does much to advance beyond infancy our capacity for empathy, for precision of *emotional* response; indeed, there is likely to be retrogression. The child who says there are big rats in the alley and gets spanked for lying the third time he says it learns something about how adults use language and the importance they attach to it. He learns what a spanking is and what a rat is not; all this is presumably useful knowledge to take along on the solitary journey toward maturity. But he does not learn, and neither do his parents, what he meant when he said there were rats in the alley. This gets plowed under.

The important point is not that we learn to talk in childhood, but that we learn to repress meanings that are not subject to consensual validation; we learn to keep quiet about what other people cannot see. There are privileged occasions, of course, when storytelling is different from lying; but the discipline of having to distinguish between them reinforces the importance of the distinction. And it is not, of course, primarily a matter of the discipline of formal speech by formally imposed sanction. It is rather that we learn in childhood to sacrifice emotional vividness to intellectual cogency. Both learning and inhibition are involved. The process is necessary; but in blasting wide gateways through the walls of our private world, inscriptions of great significance are obliterated.

And through these gateways, during the juvenile era, the world pours in hordes of Mongolian ferocity and sometimes Mongolian idiocy. To a degree hardly paralleled in what we regard as primitive cultures, which may live by rules of exquisite courtesy, life among juveniles in America is life in the raw. To find anything like it one would have to turn, not to the upper Amazon, but to a prison or a lunatic asylum; that is to say, to a place of resort for individuals whose peculiar distinction is that they are *not* socialized and have little regard for or perception of one another. Juveniles deal with each other with a crudity unparalleled in later life. It is not altogether terrifying if one is a little savage oneself, but a juvenile group is no place for sensitivity. We are inclined as a people to be highly sentimental about children; but I think most thoughtful adults, if they were obliged to sojourn among American eight-to-ten-year-olds, would want to be awfully careful which side of Alice's mushroom they nibbled.

Groups of juveniles are not friendly; and strongly felt friendships do not commonly form among them, though there is often constant association between members of juvenile cliques. They are not there to be friendly; they are there to work out a crude social system and to learn the ropes from one another. To some extent they behave like the gang in an office, jockeying for position within a superficially amiable social group. But if—as seems unlikely —there is still to be found among literate Americans an individual who regards sex as the source of viciousness in human affairs, I would urge him to compare the human relations existing within a juvenile clique to those usually found among adolescents and simply to note what sexual maturation can contribute in a few years to increased sensitivity and tenderness for other persons. Relations *within* the clique, that is, relations between it and the external world, are another matter.

But precisely because of its crudity, the juvenile experience contributes greatly to increased mental cogency, accelerating the processes begun in childhood. It is frank. Juvenile appraisals of other juveniles make up in clarity what they lack in charity; those not too sensitive can learn a great deal about themselves which they would never have learned at home. Juvenile jokes are frank filth cast in the form of jokes as a stratagem to prevent adults —who are terrified of having no sense of humor—from washing the mouth out with soap; but they are explicit and detailed and a welcome relief from the euphemisms of the middle-class bathroom. Juvenile politics is dirty; but it works, and it cuts interfering adults bent on prissiness down to something less than size if they venture beyond their sphere of proper authority.

The juvenile era provides the solid earth of life; the security of having stood up for yourself in a tough and tricky situation; the comparative immunity of knowing for yourself just exactly how the actions that must not be mentioned feel; the safety of knowing the exact margin by which adults are stronger, smarter, or trickier than you; the calm, gained from having survived among comrades, that makes one ready to have friends. You learn a lot being a juvenile.

But in the process it would seem that such vestiges of creative subjectivity as may have survived childhood must certainly be eradicated permanently. So they often are; most of us have lost whatever capacity for poetry we may once have had. In the juvenile era, as that is experienced in the ambience of the American public school, most children will certainly learn to feel severe anxiety at the eruption of any manifestation of their inner life. The eight-year-old who cries, or gives in to a sudden impulse to kiss the teacher, the ten-year-old who uses language differently from his peers—each faces an avalanche of derision. The attack he incurs may be spontaneous; it may also be structured by the teacher as a teaching device or a way of controlling the class. A recent paper describes in sober detail but with lurid effectiveness the specific processes by which the feeling and originality expressed in children's stories and use of language are stamped out in elementary school. The appalling element in the author's observations is the relentless glee with which these juveniles attack one another with what Henry calls "carping criticism"—the intense competitive delight with which they catch one another out. The teachers, being good agents of their culture, encourage this, but they do not have to encourage it much. Henry reports how a teacher, seeing an element of genuine literary quality in a youngster's work, tried to arrest the flow of criticism and mockery long enough to point it out. She was not able to. The difficulty appeared to stem less from the actual hostility of the juveniles than from their inability to comprehend that the teacher's purpose had become momentarily constructive, though they had by this time become highly adept at sensing what kind of response she wanted and giving it to her.

Interpersonal denigration is not, of course, exclusively juvenile. It is rawest among juveniles, unrestrained by either tenderness or sophistication; but it continues through adolescence and for many adults seems to constitute the major source of satisfaction in life. But in adolescence other kinds of interpersonal relations become rather common as well, and among many adolescent groups become dominant. Adolescents jockey for position, pride themselves on knowing their way around, compete bitterly, and play dirty. But they often do much more.

In adolescence, other people begin to make a difference as individuals rather than as sources of support or obstructions to impulse. Shortly before the physical onset of puberty, a different quality of feeling suffuses one's perception of certain other individuals. They are loved.

Children and juveniles do not love, in this sense, because they are rarely interested in the complete personalities of other persons. Their concern is limited to what affects them; as long as their lives run according to custom, they do not care much what other people are really like. Within this area of concern their perception is acute and their judgment sound; children are traditionally known to be all but impossible to fool by cant or hypocrisy. Empathy stands them in good stead in detecting the real predispositions of others toward them. *The Pied Piper,* with its mass deception, is one of the few classical nursery tales which is really silly.

But their penetrating intuition does not permit children to form complete human relationships, since they take no interest in the totality of other persons. Richard Hughes' classic *The Innocent Voyage* (also called *High Wind in Jamaica*), which tells how a group of children cause a band of pirates, who kidnap but do not otherwise harm them, to be hanged as murderers, is not silly at all. The pirates grow to love the children; the children like the pirates, but there is friction; the children get out of hand and are punished occasionally; and in the end they perjure themselves at the pirates' trial because they see no reason for distinguishing between reality and the complex fantasies with which they have been assuaging their feelings. They regard the pirates as friends, more or less; they know that they have been treated as well as the pirates' resources permitted; and they know, more or less, that their testimony is misleading and that it will cause these men's death. But the innocent voyage is over; and the pirates, as individuals, have less interest or value for them than the new melodrama of the trial, which they play out to the hilt.

Children give of themselves freely and have much to give; their feeling and spontaneity are a constant delight to adults. But they hardly love even their parents, much as they need them and however comforting they find them. They see parents as an indispensable institution, not as whole persons. This leads to affection, trust, and loyalty. Love is rounder and more precise.

It begins, and begins with some intensity, in early adolescence. It begins in loving someone *other* than oneself and finishes, if one is fortunate, in loving someone *different* from oneself—as different as man is from woman. The passionate attachments of earliest adolescence are between chums of the same sex. Whether anything sexual happens in the course of them is unimportant, unless someone steps in and makes it important. Indeed, it is largely a matter of definition, though some of the feelings these youngsters arouse in each other are certainly erotic.

Sullivan attributes great developmental value to these attachments of early adolescence. Far from presaging homosexuality in later life, they are notably absent from the case histories of adult homosexuals—a finding expressed also in somewhat different language some years ago by Lewis Terman in his study of *Sex and Personality*. It is evidently much easier to lose oneself in dreams of golden youths if one lacks intimate knowledge of real boys of the kind that only another boy can share. Homophilic love, if not essential to ultimate heterosexual love, certainly tends to pave the way toward it and enrich it.

It does so by restoring a measure of trust in feeling, and combining this with more precise self-perception. Children and juveniles are self-centered; early adolescents, increasingly able to take others to heart, still find this easier at first if the other is not different enough to be threatening. Tenderness, when it is unfamiliar, makes us shy; and shyness dominates relationships with persons beyond our experience; if they are also shy, as girls are in early adolescence, the friendship is likely to be stillborn. Between chums of early adolescence, only tenderness itself is strange.

With love comes trust, which leads to mutual exploration and the confidence to accept intrusion. The feeling of chums in early adolescence for each other is usually their first experience of unconditional acceptance by another person. Once this is established, the two can learn about themselves from each other without the tension of the juvenile proving ground. The learning goes deeper, providing a warm and healing light by which old wounds are examined and old and crumbling defenses abandoned.

This is a genuine therapeutic experience of unique value. Parents cannot help their children in this way, for they are too much involved in the situation which has brought about whatever damage has occurred; if it is severe, the children are quite aware that imprudent self-revelation may lead to further pain and rejection. Children and juveniles cannot help each other in this way; their relationships are too ambivalent and too incomplete. But Tom, at the age of thirteen or fourteen, can say to Dick: "Why do you always have to be such a big wheel?" or "You don't really feel that way any more; you're just trying to make something out of it!" or "That was pretty stupid, what we pulled in school yesterday!" or even just "Well, if that's how you feel about it, screw you, Bud!" And Dick will listen to Tom, when he could hardly afford to listen to anybody else.

Dick does not have to compete with Tom; and he does not have to please him. Their commitment to each other has already been made, without any reservation or purpose of evasion. This is not to say that the friendship between them will run smoothly; it certainly will not and would be less useful if it did. Tom and Dick will fight and bear each other's wounds. Their job is not to be nice to each other, but to be real to each other.

If they are, if there are no traumatic betrayals or intercessions, Dick and Tom help each other very much. Each learns how good it feels to care about another person. Each learns much more about himself from the other; each learns that what makes the other supremely valuable to him is his *difference* from himself. Each confirms the other in masculine self-imagery; each is now ready to risk greater differences for the sake of even greater rewards. The focus of attention shifts. By this time, Dick and Tom are about ready to take Jane and Alice to a high-school dance, though for the first year or so they may all prefer to double-date.

If Jane and Alice are also ready to be real, the exploration and self-definition which tenderness makes possible continue in depth. Dick learns that his relationship to Jane is not a conquest but a process. As they become men and women the process becomes more complex and richer; more is involved, more is constructed, more is maintained. In mature love between adults the process of self-definition, and clarification of the meaning of life and of one's place in it, continues and becomes more abstract. But the basis of this process remains courage to be oneself in all one's imperfection, sustained by a measure of unconditional tenderness; and this is the basis on which Tom and Dick began it together.

LOVE AND SEX

The Procreative Animal　　　　26
Remy de Gourmont

If it is clear that man is an animal, it is also clear that he is a very complex one. One finds in him most of the aptitudes which are distributed one by one among beasts. There is hardly one of his habits, of his virtues, of his vices (to use the conventional terms) which cannot be found either in an insect, a bird or a mammifer: monogamy, adultery, . . . polygamy, polyandry, lasciviousness, laziness, activity, cruelty, courage, devotion, any of these are common to animals, but each as the quality of a whole species. In the state of differentiation to which superior and cultivated human species have attained, each individual forms surely a separate variety determined by what is called, abstractly, "the character." This individual differentiation, very marked in mankind, is less marked in other animal species. Yet we note quite distinct characters in dogs, in horses and even in birds of the same race. It it quite probable that all bees have not the same character, since, for example, they are not all equally prompt to use their stings in analogous circumstances. Even there the difference between man and his brothers in life and in sensibility is but a difference of degree.

"Solidarity" is but an empty ideology if one limit it to the human species. There is no abyss between man and animal; the two domains are separated by a tiny rivulet which a baby could step over. We are animals, we live on animals, and animals live on us. We both have and are parasites. We are predatory, and we are the living prey of the predatory. And when we follow the love act, it is truly, in the idiom of theologians, *more bestiarum*. Love is profoundly animal; therein is its beauty.

·　　·　　·

What is life's aim? Its maintenance.

But the very idea of an aim is a human illusion. There is neither beginning, nor middle, nor end in the series of causes. What is has been caused

From Ch. 1, "The Subject of an Idea" and the whole of Ch. 2, "The Aim of Life" in *The Natural Philosophy of Love*, Remy de Gourmont, New York, Wiley Book Co., 1940. Reprinted by permission of the Wholesale Book Co.

by what was, and what will be has for cause the existent. One can neither conceive a point of rest nor a point of beginning. Born of life, life will beget life eternally. She should, and wants to. Life is characterized on earth by the existence of individuals grouped into species, that is to say having the power, a male being united with a female, to reproduce a similar being. Whether it be the internal conjoining of protozoa, or hermaphrodite fecundation, or the coupling of insects or mammifers, the act is the same: it is common to all that lives, and this not only to animals but to plants, and possibly even to such minerals as are limited by a non-varying form. Of all possible acts, in the possibility that we can imagine, the sexual act is, therefore, the most important of all acts. Without it life comes to an end, and it is absurd to suppose its absence, for in that case thought itself disappears.

Revolt is useless against so evident a necessity. Our finikin scruples protest in vain; man and the most disgusting of his parasites are the products of an identical sexual mechanism. The flowers we have strewn upon love may disguise it as one disguises a trap for wild beasts; all our activities manœuvre along the edge of this precipice and fall over it one after another; the aim of human life is the continuation of human life.

Only in appearance does man escape this obligation of Nature. He escapes as an individual, and he submits as a species. The abuse of thought, religious prejudices, vices sterilize a part of humanity; but this fraction is of merely sociological interest; be he chaste or voluptuary, miserly or prodigal of his flesh, man is in his whole condition subject to the sexual tyranny. All men do not reproduce their species, neither do all animals; the feeble and the late-comers among insects die in their robe of innocence, and many nests laboriously filled by courageous mothers are devastated by pirates or by the inclemency of the sky. Let the ascetic not come boasting that he has freed his blood from the pressure of desire; the very importance which he ascribes to his victory but affirms the same power of the life-will.

A young girl, before the slightest love affair, will, if she is healthy, confess naïvely that she "wants to marry to have children." This so simple formula is the legend of Nature. What an animal seeks is not its own life but reproduction. Doubtless many animals seem, during a relatively long existence, to have but brief sexual periods, but one must make allowance for the period of gestation. In principle the sole occupation of any creature is to renew, by the sex act, the form wherewith it is clothed. To this end it eats, to this end builds. This act is so clearly the aim, unique and definite, that it constitutes the entire life of a very great number of animals, which are, notwithstanding, extremely complex.

The ephemera is born in the evening and copulates, the female lays eggs during the night, both are dead in the morning, without even having looked at the sun. These little animals are so little destined for anything else save love that they have not even mouths. They eat not, neither do they drink. One sees them hovering in clouds above the water, among the reeds. The males, although more numerous than the females, perform a multiple duty and fall exhausted. The *purity* of such a life is to be admired in many butter-flies: the silk-moths, heavy and clumsy, shake their wings for an instant at birth, couple and die. The Great Peacock or Oak Bombyx, much larger than they, eats no more than they do: yet we see him traverse leagues of country in his quest of the female. He has only a rudimentary proboscis and the semblance of a digestive apparatus. Thus his two or three days' existence passes without one egoistic act. The struggle for life, much vaunted, is here the struggle to give life, the struggle for death, for if they can live three days in search of the female they die as soon as the fecundation is accomplished.

Among all solitary bees, scolia, masons, bembex, an anthoporidæ, the males born soonest range about the nests awaiting the birth of the females. As soon as these appear they are seized and fecundated, knowing, thus, life and love in the same shiver. The female osmies and other bees are keenly watched by the males who nab and mount them as they emerge from the natal tube, the hollow stalk of a reed, flying at once with them into the air where the love-feast is finished. Then while the male, drunk with his work, continues his death-flight, the female feverishly hollows the house of her off-spring, partitions it, stores the honey for the larvæ, lays, whirls for an instant and dies. The year following, the same gestures above the same reeds split by the reed-gatherers; and thus in years following, the insect permitted never the least design save the conservation of one fragile form; brief apparition over flowers.

The sitaris is a coleopterous parasite in the nests of the anthoporidæ. Copulation takes place on hatching. Fabre noticed a female still in her wrap-pings, whom a male already free was helping to get loose, waiting only the appearance of the extremity of the abdomen, to hurl himself thereupon. The sitaris's love lasts one minute, long season in a short life: the male drags on for two days before dying, the female lays on the very spot where she has been fecundated, dies having known nothing but the maternal function in the strictest limit of her birthplace.

No one has ever seen the female palingenia. This butterfly is fecundated before even getting rid of her nymph's corset, she dies with her eyes still shut, at once mother and infant in swaddling clothes. Moralists love bees from whom they distil examples and aphorisms. They recommend us work, order, economy, foresight, obedience and divers other virtues. Abandon yourself boldly to labour: Nature wills it. Nature wills everything. She is complacent to all the activities; to our imaginings there is no analogy that she will refuse, not one. She desires the social construction of bees; she desires also the Life All Love of the Great Peacock, of the osmie, of the sitaris. She desires that the forms she has created shall continue indefinitely, and to this end all means are, to her, good. But if she presents us the laborious example of the bee, she does not hide from us the polyandrous example, nor the cruel amours of the mantis. There is not in the will to live the faintest trace of our poor little human morality. If one wishes a unique sole morality, that is to say a universal commandment, which all species may listen to, which they can follow in spirit and in letter, if one wishes in short to know the "aim of life" and the duty of the living, it is necessary, evidently, to find a formula which will totalize all the contradictions, break them and fuse them into a sole affirmation. There is but one, we may repeat it, without fear, and without allowing any objection: the aim of life is life's continuation.

27   The Loving Human
Erich Fromm

Love is not primarily a relationship to a specific person; it is an *attitude,* an *orientation* of *character* which determines the relatedness of a person to the world as a whole, not toward one "object" of love. If a person loves only one other person and is indifferent to the rest of his fellow men, his love is not love but a symbiotic attachment, or an enlarged egotism. Yet, most people believe that love is constituted by the object, not by the faculty. In fact, they even believe that it is a proof of the intensity of their love when they do not love anybody except the "loved" person. This is the same fallacy which we have already mentioned above. Because one does not see that love is an activity, a power of the soul, one believes that all that is necessary to find is the right object—and that everything goes by itself afterward. This attitude can be compared to that of a man who wants to paint but who, instead of learning the art, claims that he has just to wait for the right object, and that he will paint beautifully when he finds it. If I truly love one person I love all persons, I love the world, I love life. If can say to somebody else, "I love you," I must be able to say, "I love in you everybody, I love through you the world, I love in you also myself."

Saying that love is an orientation which refers to all and not to one does not imply, however, the idea that there are no differences between various types of love, which depend on the kind of object which is loved.

A. BROTHERLY LOVE

The most fundamental kind of love, which underlies all types of love, is *brotherly love.* By this I mean the sense of responsibility, care, respect, knowledge of any other human being, the wish to further his life. This is the kind of love the Bible speaks of when it says: love thy neighbor as thyself.

Brotherly love is love for all human beings; it is characterized by its very lack of exclusiveness. If I have developed the capacity for love, then I cannot help loving my brothers. In brotherly love there is the experience of union with all men, of human solidarity, of human at-onement. Brotherly love is based on the experience that we all are one. The differences in talents, intelligence, knowledge are negligible in comparison with the identity of the human core common to all men. In order to experience this identity it is necessary to penetrate from the periphery to the core. If I perceive in another person mainly the differences, that which separates us. If I penetrate to the core, I perceive our identity, the fact of our brotherhood. This relatedness from center to center—instead of that from periphery to periphery—is "central relatedness." Or as Simone Weil expressed it so beautifully: "The same words [e.g., a man says to his wife, "I love you"] can be commonplace or extraordinary according to the manner in which they are spoken. And this manner depends on the depth of the region in a man's being from which they proceed without the will being able to do anything. And by a marvelous agreement they reach the same region in him who hears them. Thus the hearer can discern, if he has any power of discernment, what is the value of the words." [1]

Brotherly love is love between equals; but, indeed, even as equals we are not always "equal"; inasmuch as we are human, we are all in need of help. Today I, tomorrow you. But this need of help does not mean that the one is helpless, the other powerful. Helplessness is a transitory condition; the ability to stand and walk on one's own feet is the permanent and common one.

Yet, love of the helpless one, love of the poor and the stranger, are the beginning of brotherly love. To love one's flesh and blood is no achievement. The animal loves its young and cares for them. The helpless one loves his master, since his life depends on him; the child loves his parents, since he needs them. Only in the love of those who do not serve a purpose, love begins to unfold. Significantly, in the Old Testament, the central object of man's love is the poor, the stranger, the widow and the orphan, and eventually the national enemy, the Egyptian and the Edomite. By having compassion for the helpless one, man begins to develop love for his brother; and in his love for himself he also loves the one who is in need of help, the frail, insecure human being. Compassion implies the element of knowledge and of identification. "You know the heart of the stranger," says the Old Testament, "for you were strangers in the land of Egypt; . . . *therefore love the stranger!*"

B. MOTHERLY LOVE

We have already dealt with the nature of motherly love in a previous chapter which discussed the difference between motherly and fatherly love. Motherly love, as I said there, is unconditional affirmation of the child's life and his

[1] Simone Weil, *Gravity and Grace*, G. P. Putnam's Sons, New York, 1952, p. 117.

needs. But one important addition to this description must be made here. Affirmation of the child's life has two aspects; one is the care and responsibility absolutely necessary for the preservation of the child's life and his growth. The other aspect goes further than mere preservation. It is the attitude which instills in the child a love for living, which gives him the feeling: it is good to be alive, it is good to be a little boy or girl, it is good to be on this earth! These two aspects of motherly love are expressed very succinctly in the Biblical story of creation. God creates the world, and man. This corresponds to the simple care and affirmation of existence. But God goes beyond this minimum requirement. On each day after nature—and man—is created, God says: "It is good." Motherly love, in this second step, makes the child feel: it is good to have been born; it instills in the child the *love for life,* and not only the wish to remain alive. The same idea may be taken to be expressed in another Biblical symbolism. The promised land (land is always a mother symbol) is described as "flowing with milk and honey." Milk is the symbol of the first aspect of love, that of care and affirmation. Honey symbolizes the sweetness of life, the love for it and the happiness in being alive. Most mothers are capable of giving "milk," but only a minority of giving "honey" too. In order to be able to give honey, a mother must not only be a "good mother," but a happy person—and this aim is not achieved by many. The effect on the child can hardly be exaggerated. Mother's love for life is as infectious as her anxiety is. Both attitudes have a deep effect on the child's whole personality; one can distinguish indeed, among children—and adults— those who got only "milk" and those who got "milk and honey."

In contrast to brotherly love and erotic love which are love between equals, the relationship of mother and child is by its very nature one of inequality, where one needs all the help, and the other gives it. It is for this altruistic, unselfish character that motherly love has been considered the highest kind of love, and the most sacred of all emotional bonds. It seems, however, that the real achievement of motherly love lies not in the mother's love for the small infant, but in her love for the growing child. Actually, the vast majority of mothers are loving mothers as long as the infant is small and still completely dependent on them. Most women want children, are happy with the new-born child, and eager in their care for it. This is so in spite of the fact that they do not "get" anything in return from the child, except a smile or the expression of satisfaction in his face. It seems that this attitude of love is partly rooted in an instinctive equipment to be found in animals as well as in the human female. But, whatever the weight of this instinctive factor may be, there are also specifically human psychological factors which are responsible for this type of motherly love. One may be found in the narcissistic element in motherly love. Inasmuch as the infant is still felt to be a part of herself, her love and infatuation may be a satisfaction of her narcissism. Another motivation may be found in a mother's wish for power, or possession. The child, being helpless and completely subject to her will, is a natural object of satisfaction for a domineering and possessive woman.

Frequent as these motivations are, they are probably less important and less universal than one which can be called the need for transcendence. This need for transcendence is one of the most basic needs of man, rooted in the fact of his self-awareness, in the fact that he is not satisfied with the role of the creature, that he cannot accept himself as dice thrown out of the cup. He needs to feel as the creator, as one transcending the passive role of being created. There are many ways of achieving this satisfaction of creation; the most natural and also the easiest one to achieve is the mother's care and love for her creation. She transcends herself in the infant, her love for it gives her life meaning and significance. (In the very inability of the male to satisfy his need for transcendence by bearing children lies his urge to transcend himself by the creation of man-made things and of ideas.)

But the child must grow. It must emerge from mother's womb, from mother's breast; it must eventually become a completely separate human being. The very essence of motherly love is to care for the child's growth, and that means to want the child's separation from herself. Here lies the basic difference to erotic love. In erotic love, two people who were separate become one. In motherly love, two people who were one become separate. The mother must not only tolerate, she must wish and support the child's separation. It is only at this stage that motherly love becomes such a difficult task, that it requires unselfishness, the ability to give everything and to want nothing but the happiness of the loved one. It is also at this stage that many mothers fail in their task of motherly love. The narcissistic, the domineering, the possessive woman can succeed in being a "loving" mother as long as the child is small. Only the really loving woman, the woman who is happier in giving than in taking, who is firmly rooted in her own existence, can be a loving mother when the child is in the process of separation.

Motherly love for the growing child, love which wants nothing for oneself, is perhaps the most difficult form of love to be achieved, and all the more deceptive because of the ease with which a mother can love her small infant. But just because of this difficulty, a woman can be a truly loving mother only if she can *love*; if she is able to love her husband, other children, strangers, all human beings. The woman who is not capable of love in this sense can be an affectionate mother as long as the child is small, but she cannot be a loving mother, the test of which is the willingness to bear separation—and even after the separation to go on loving.

C. EROTIC LOVE

Brotherly love is love among equals; motherly love is love for the helpless. Different as they are from each other, they have in common that they are by their very nature not restricted to one person. If I love my brother, I love all my brothers; if I love my child, I love all my children; no, beyond that, I love all children, all that are in need of my help. In contrast to both types of love is *erotic love*; it is the craving for complete fusion, for union with one other person. It is by its very nature exclusive and not universal; it is also perhaps the most deceptive form of love there is.

First of all, it is often confused with the explosive experience of "falling" in love, the sudden collapse of the barriers which existed until that moment between two strangers. But, as was pointed out before, this experience of sudden intimacy is by its very nature short-lived. After the stranger has become an intimately known person there are no more barriers to be overcome, there is no more sudden closeness to be achieved. The "loved" person becomes as well known as oneself. Or, perhaps I should better say as little known. If there were more depth in the experience of the other person, if one could experience the infiniteness of his personality, the other person would never be so familiar—and the miracle of overcoming the barriers might occur every day anew. But for most people their own person, as well as others, is soon explored and soon exhausted. For them intimacy is established primarily through sexual contact. Since they experience the separateness of the other person primarily as physical separateness, physical union means overcoming separateness.

Beyond that, there are other factors which to many people denote the overcoming of separateness. To speak of one's own personal life, one's hopes and anxieties, to show oneself with one's childlike or childish aspects, to establish a common interest vis-à-vis the world—all this is taken as overcoming separateness. Even to show one's anger, one's hate, one's complete lack of inhibition is taken for intimacy, and this may explain the perverted attraction married couples often have for each other, who seem intimate only when they are in bed or when they give vent to their mutual hate and rage. But all these types of closeness tend to become reduced more and more as time goes on. The consequence is one seeks love with a new person, with a new stranger. Again the stranger is transformed into an "intimate" person, again the experience of falling in love is exhilarating and intense, and again it slowly becomes less and less intense, and ends in the wish for a new conquest, a new love—always with the illusion that the new love will be different from the earlier ones. These illusions are greatly helped by the deceptive character of sexual desire.

Sexual desire aims at fusion—and is by no means only a physical appetite, the relief of a painful tension. But sexual desire can be stimulated by the anxiety of aloneness, by the wish to conquer or be conquered, by vanity, by the wish to hurt and even to destroy, as much as it can be stimulated by love. It seems that sexual desire can easily blend with and be stimulated by any strong emotion, of which love is only one. Because sexual desire is in the minds of most people coupled with the idea of love, they are easily misled to conclude that they love each other when they want each other physically. Love can inspire the wish for sexual union; in this case the physical relationship is lacking in greediness, in a wish to conquer or to be conquered, but is blended with tenderness. If the desire for physical union is not stimulated by love, if erotic love is not also brotherly love, it never leads to union in more than an orgiastic, transitory sense. Sexual attraction creates, for the moment, the illusion of union, yet without love this "union" leaves strangers as far apart as they were before—sometimes it makes them ashamed of each other, or even makes them hate each other, because when the illusion has gone they feel their estrangement even more markedly than before. Tenderness is by no means, as Freud believed, a sublimation of the sexual instinct; it is the direct outcome of brotherly love, and exists in physical as well as in non-physical forms of love.

In erotic love there is an exclusiveness which is lacking in brotherly love and motherly love. This exclusive character of erotic love warrants some further discussion. Frequently the exclusiveness of erotic love is misinterpreted as meaning possessive attachment. One can often find two people "in love" with each other who feel no love for anybody else. Their love is, in fact, an egotism à deux; they are two people who identify themselves with each other, and who solve the problem of separateness by enlarging the single individual into two. They have the experience of overcoming aloneness, yet, since they are separated from the rest of mankind, they remain separated from each other and alienated from themselves; their experience of union is an illusion. Erotic love is exclusive, but it loves in the other person all of mankind, all that is alive. It is exclusive only in the sense that I can fuse myself fully and intensely with one person only. Erotic love excludes the love for others only in the sense of erotic fusion, full commitment in all aspects of life—but not in the sense of deep brotherly love.

Erotic love, if it is love, has one premise. That I love from the essence of my being—and experience the other person in the essence of his or her being. In essence, all human beings are identical. We are all part of One; we are One. This being so, it should not make any difference whom we love. Love should be essentially an act of will, of decision to commit my life completely to that of one other person. This is, indeed, the rationale behind the idea of the insolubility of marriage, as it is behind the many forms of traditional marriage in which the two partners never choose each other, but are chosen for each other—and yet are expected to love each other. In contemporary Western culture this idea appears altogether false. Love is supposed to be the outcome of a spontaneous, emotional reaction, of suddenly being gripped by an irresistible feeling. In this view, one sees only the peculiarities of the two individuals involved—and not the fact that all men are part of Adam, and all women part of Eve. One neglects to see an important factor in erotic love, that of *will*. To love somebody is not just a strong feeling—it is a decision, it is a judgment, it is a promise. If love were only a feeling, there would be no basis for the promise to love each other forever. A feeling comes and it may go. How can I judge that it will stay forever, when my act does not involve judgment and decision?

Taking these views into account one may arrive at the position that love is exclusively an act of will and commitment, and that therefore fundamentally it does not matter who the two persons are. Whether the marriage was arranged by others, or the result of individual choice, once the marriage is concluded, the act of will should guarantee the continuation of love. This view seems to neglect the paradoxical character of human nature and of erotic love. We are all One—yet every one of us is a unique, unduplicable entity. In our relationships to others the same paradox is repeated. Inasmuch as we are all one, we can love everybody in the same way in the sense of brotherly love. But inasmuch as we are all also different, erotic love requires certain specific, highly individual elements which exist between some people but not between all.

Both views then, that of erotic love as completely individual attraction, unique between two specific persons, as well as the other view that erotic love is nothing but an act of will, are true—or, as it may be put more aptly, the truth is neither this nor that. Hence the idea of a relationship which can be easily dissolved if one is not successful with it is as erroneous as the idea that under no circumstances must the relationship be dissolved.

.   .   .

Love is not the result of adequate sexual satisfaction, but sexual happiness—even the knowledge of the so-called sexual technique—is the result of love. If aside from everyday observation this thesis needed to be proved, such proof can be found in ample material of psychoanalytic data. The study of the most frequent sexual problems—frigidity in women, and the more or less severe forms of psychic impotence in men—shows that the cause does not lie in a lack of knowledge of the right technique, but in the inhibitions which make it impossible to love. Fear of or hatred for the other sex are at the bottom of those difficulties which prevent a person from giving himself completely, from acting spontaneously, from trusting the sexual partner in the immediacy and directness of physical closeness. If a sexually inhibited person can emerge from fear or hate, and hence become capable of loving, his or her sexual problems are solved. If not, no amount of knowledge about sexual techniques will help.

28   The Idealizing Human
Plato

Of the nature of the soul, though her true form be ever a theme of large and more than mortal discourse, let me speak briefly, and in a figure. And let the figure be composite—a pair of winged horses and a charioteer. Now the

From the *Phaedrus* in *The Dialogues of Plato,* Vol. I, trans. by B. Jowett, New York, Random House, 1937.

winged horses and the charioteers of the gods are all of them noble and of noble descent, but those of other races are mixed; the human charioteer drives his in a pair; and one of them is noble and of noble breed, and the other is ignoble and of ignoble breed; and the driving of them of necessity gives a great deal of trouble to him. I will endeavour to explain to you in what way the mortal differs from the immortal creature. The soul in her totality has the care of inanimate being everywhere, and traverses the whole heaven in divers forms appearing:—when perfect and fully winged she soars upward, and orders the whole world; whereas the imperfect soul, losing her wings and drooping in her flight at last settles on the solid ground—there, finding a home, she receives an earthly frame which appears to be self-moved, but is really moved by her power; and this composition of soul and body is called a living and mortal creature. For immortal no such union can be reasonably believed to be; although fancy, not having seen nor surely known the nature of God, may imagine an immortal creature having both a body and also a soul which are united throughout all time. Let that, however, be as God wills, and be spoken of acceptably to him. And now let us ask the reason why the soul loses her wings!

The wing is the corporeal element which is most akin to the divine, and which by nature tends to soar aloft and carry that which gravitates downwards into the upper region, which is the habitation of the gods. The divine is beauty, wisdom, goodness, and the like; and by these the wing of the soul is nourished, and grows apace; but when fed upon evil and foulness and the opposite of good, wastes and falls away. Zeus, the mighty lord, holding the reins of a winged chariot, leads the way in heaven, ordering all and taking care of all; and there follows him the array of gods and demi-gods, marshalled in eleven bands; Hestia alone abides at home in the house of heaven; of the rest they who are reckoned among the princely twelve march in their appointed order. They see many blessed sights in the inner heaven, and there are many ways to and fro, along which the blessed gods are passing, every one doing his own work; he may follow who will and can, for jealousy has no place in the celestial choir. But when they go to banquet and festival, then they move up the steep to the top of the vault of heaven. The chariots of the gods in even poise, obeying the rein, glide rapidly; but the others labour, for the vicious steed goes heavily, weighing down the charioteer to the earth when his steed has not been thoroughly trained:—and this is the hour of agony and extremest conflict for the soul. For the immortals, when they are at the end of their course, go forth and stand upon the outside of heaven, and the revolution of the spheres carries them round, and they behold the things beyond. But of the heaven which is above the heavens, what earthly poet ever did or ever will sing worthily? It is such as I will describe; for I must dare to speak the truth, when truth is my theme. There abides the very being with which true knowledge is concerned; the colourless, formless, intangible essence, visible only to mind, the pilot of the soul.

The divine intelligence, being nutured upon mind and pure knowledge, and the intelligence, being nurtured upon mind and pure knowledge, and the intelligence of every soul which is capable of receiving the food proper to it, rejoices at beholding reality, and once more gazing upon truth, is replenished and made glad, until the revolution of the worlds brings her round again to the same place. In the revolution she beholds justice, and temperance, and knowledge absolute, not in the form of generation or of relation, which men call existence, but knowledge absolute in existence absolute; and beholding the other true existences in like manner, and feasting upon them, she passes down into the interior of the heavens and returns home; and there the charioteer putting up his horses at the stall, gives them ambrosia to eat and nectar to drink.

Such is the life of the gods; but of other souls, that which follows God best and is likest to him lifts the head of the charioteer into the outer world, and is carried round in the revolution, troubled indeed by the steeds, and with difficulty beholding true being; while another only rises and falls, and sees, and again fails to see by reason of the unruliness of the steeds. The rest of the souls are also longing after the upper world and they all follow, but not being strong enough they are carried round below the surface, plunging, treading on one another, each striving to be first; and there is confusion and perspiration and the extremity of effort; and many of them are lamed or have their wings broken through the ill-driving of the charioteers; and all of them after a fruitless toil, not having attained to the mysteries of true being, go away, and feed upon opinion. The reason why the souls exhibit this exceeding eagerness to behold the plain of truth is that pasturage is found there, which is suited to the highest part of the soul; and the wing on which the soul soars is nourished with this. And there is a law of Destiny, that the soul which attains any vision of truth in company with a god is preserved from harm until the next period, and if attaining always is always unharmed. But when she is unable to follow, and fails to behold the truth, and through some ill-hap sinks beneath the double load of forgetfulness and vice, and her wings fall from her and she drops to the ground, then the law ordains that this soul shall at her first birth pass, not into any other animal, but only into man; and the soul which has seen most of truth shall come to the birth as a philosopher, or artist, or some musical and loving nature; that which has seen truth in the second degree shall be some righteous king or warrior chief; the soul which is of the third class shall be a politician, or economist, or trader; the fourth shall be a lover of gymnastic toils, or a physician; the fifth shall lead the life of a prophet or hierophant; to the sixth the character of a poet or some other imitative artist will be assigned; to the seventh the life of an artisan or husbandman; to the eighth that of a sophist or demagogue; to the ninth that of a tyrant;—all these are states of probation, in which he who does righteously improves, and he who does unrighteously, deteriorates his lot.

Ten thousand years must elapse before the soul of each one can return to the place from whence she came, for she cannot grow her wings in less; only the soul of a philosopher, guileless and true, or the soul of a lover, who is not devoid of philosophy, may acquire wings in the third of the recurring periods of a thousand years; he is distinguished from the ordinary good man who gains wings in three thousand years:—and they who choose this life three times in succession have wings given them, and go away at the end of three thousand years. But the others [1] receive judgment when they have completed their first life, and after the judgment they go, some of them to the houses of correction which are under the earth, and are punished; others to some place in heaven whither they are lightly borne by justice, and there they live in a manner worthy of the life which they led here when in the form of men. And at the end of the first thousand years the good souls and also the evil souls both come to draw lots and choose their second life, and they may take any which they please. The soul of a man may pass into the life of a beast, or from the beast return again into the man. But the soul which has never seen the truth will not pass into the human form. For a man must have intelligence of universals, and be able to proceed from the many particulars of sense to one conception of reason;—this is the recollection of those things which our soul once saw while following God—when regardless of that which we now call being she raised her head up towards the true being. And therefore the mind of the philosopher alone has wings; and this is just, for he is always, according to the measure of his abilities, clinging in recollection to those things in which God abides, and in beholding which He is what He is. And he who employs aright these memories is ever being initiated into perfect mysteries and alone becomes truly perfect. But, as he forgets earthly interests and is rapt in the divine, the vulgar deem him mad, and rebuke him; they do not see that he is inspired.

Thus far I have been speaking of the fourth and last kind of madness, which is imputed to him who, when he sees the beauty of earth, is transported with the recollection of the true beauty; he would like to fly away, but he cannot; he is like a bird fluttering and looking upward and careless of the world below; and he is therefore thought to be mad. And I have shown this of all inspirations to be the noblest and highest and the offspring of the highest to him who has or shares in it, and that he who loves the beautiful is called a lover because he partakes of it. For, as has been already said, every soul of man has in the way of nature beheld true being; this was the condition of her passing into the form of man. But all souls do not easily recall the things of the other world; they may have seen them for a short time only, or they may have been unfortunate in their earthly lot, and, having had their hearts turned to unrighteousness through some corrupting influence, they may have lost the memory of the holy things which once they

[1] The philosopher alone is not subject to judgment (κρίσις), for he has never lost the vision of truth.

saw. Few only retain an adequate remembrance of them; and they, when they behold here any image of that other world, are rapt in amazement; but they are ignorant of what this rapture means, because they do not clearly perceive. For there is no light of justice or temperance or any of the higher ideas which are precious to souls in the earthly copies of them: they are seen through a glass dimly; and there are few who, going to the images, behold in them the realities, and these only with difficulty. There was a time when with the rest of the happy band they saw beauty shining in brightness,— we philosophers following in the train of Zeus, others in company with other gods; and then we beheld the beatific vision and were initiated into a mystery which may be truly called most blessed, celebrated by us in our state of innocence, before we had any experience of evils to come, when we were admitted to the sight of apparitions innocent and simple and calm and happy, which we beheld shining in pure light, pure ourselves and not yet enshrined in that living tomb which we carry about, now that we are im- prisoned in the body, like an oyster in his shell. Let me linger over the memory of scenes which have passed away.

But of beauty, I repeat again that we saw her there shining in company with the celestial forms; and coming to earth we find her here too, shining in clearness through the clearest aperture of sense. For sight is the most piercing of our bodily senses; though not by that is wisdom seen; her loveli- ness would have been transporting if there had been a visible image of her, and the other ideas, if they had visible counterparts, would be equally lovely. But this is the privilege of beauty, that being the loveliest she is also the most palpable to sight. Now he who is not newly initiated or who has be- come corrupted, does not easily rise out of this world to the sight of true beauty in the other; he looks only at her earthly namesake, and instead of being awed at the sight of her, he is given over to pleasure, and like a brutish beast he rushes on to enjoy and beget; he consorts with wantonness, and is not afraid or ashamed of pursuing pleasure in violation of nature. But he whose initiation is recent, and who has been the spectator of many glories in the other world, is amazed when he sees any one having a godlike face or form, which is the expression of divine beauty; and at first a shudder runs through him, and again the old awe steals over him; then looking upon the face of his beloved as of a god he reverences him, and if he were not afraid of being thought a downright madman, he would sacrifice to his beloved as to the image of a god; then while he gazes on him there is a sort of reaction, and the shudder passes into an unusual heat and perspiration; for, as he receives the effluence of beauty through the eyes, the wing moistens and he warms. And as he warms, the parts out of which the wing grew, and which had been hitherto closed and rigid, and had prevented the wing from shoot- ing forth, are melted, and as nourishment streams upon him, the lower end of the wings begins to swell and grow from the root upwards; and the growth extends under the whole soul—for once the whole was winged. Dur-

ing this process the whole soul is all in a state of ebullition and efferves-
cence,—which may be compared to the irritation and uneasiness in the
gums at the time of cutting teeth,—bubbles up, and has a feeling of uneasiness and tickling; but when in like manner the soul is beginning to grow
wings, the beauty of the beloved meets her eye and she receives the sensible
warm motion of particles which flow towards her, therefore called emotion
(ἵμερος), and is refreshed and warmed by them, and then she ceases from
her pain with joy. But when she is parted from her beloved and her moisture fails, then the orifices of the passage out of which the wing shoots dry
up and close, and intercept the germ of the wing; which, being shut up
with the emotion, throbbing as with the pulsations of an artery, pricks the
aperture which is nearest, until at length the entire soul is pierced and maddened and pained, and at the recollection of beauty is again delighted. And
from both of them together the soul is oppressed at the strangeness of her
condition, and is in a great strait and excitement, and in her madness can
neither sleep by night nor abide in her place by day. And wherever she
thinks that she will behold the beautiful one, thither in her desire she runs.
And when she has seen him, and bathed herself in the waters of beauty, her
constraint is loosened, and she is refreshed, and has no more pangs and pains;
and this is the sweetest of all pleasures at the time, and is the reason why
the soul of the lover will never forsake his beautiful one, whom he esteems
above all; he has forgotten mother and brethren and companions, and he
thinks nothing of the neglect and loss of his property; the rules and proprieties of life, on which he formerly prided himself, he now despises, and is
ready to sleep like a servant, wherever he is allowed, as near as he can to his
desired one, who is the object of his worship, and the physician who can
alone assuage the greatness of his pain. And this state, my dear imaginary
youth to whom I am talking, is by men called love, and among the gods has
a name at which you, in your simplicity, may be inclined to mock; there are
two lines in the apocryphal writings of Homer in which the name occurs.
One of them is rather outrageous, and not altogether metrical. They are as
follows:—

> Mortals call him fluttering love,
> But the immortals call him winged one,
> Because the growing of wings [2] is a necessity to him.

You may believe this, but not unless you like. At any rate the loves of lovers
and their causes are such as I have described.

Now the lover who is taken to be the attendant of Zeus is better able
to bear the winged god, and can endure a heavier burden; but the attendants
and companions of Ares, when under the influence of love, if they fancy
that they have been at all wronged, are ready to kill and put an end to themselves and their beloved. And he who follows in the train of any other god,

---

[2] Or, reading πτερόφοιτου, "the movement of wings."

while he is unspoiled and the impression lasts, honours and imitates him, as far as he is able; and after the manner of his god he behaves in his intercourse with his beloved and with the rest of the world during the first period of his earthly existence. Every one chooses his love from the ranks of beauty according to his character, and this he makes his god, and fashions and adorns as a sort of image which he is to fall down and worship. The followers of Zeus desire that their beloved should have a soul like him; and therefore they seek out some one of a philosophical and imperial nature, and when they have found him and loved him, they do all they can to confirm such a nature in him, and if they have no experience of such a disposition hitherto, they learn of any one who can teach them, and themselves follow in the same way. And they have the less difficulty in finding the nature of their own god in themselves, because they have been compelled to gaze intensely on him; their recollection clings to him, and they become possessed of him, and receive from him their character and disposition, so far as man can participate in God. The qualities of their god they attribute to the beloved, wherefore they love him all the more, and if, like the Bacchic Nymphs, they draw inspiration from Zeus, they pour out their own fountain upon him, wanting to make him as like as possible to their own god. But those who are the followers of Here seek a royal love, and when they have found him they do just the same with him; and in like manner the followers of Apollo, and of every other god walking in the ways of their god, seek a love who is to be made like him whom they serve, and when they have found him, they themselves imitate their god, and persuade their love to do the same, and educate him into the manner and nature of the god as far as they each can; for no feelings of envy or jealousy are entertained by them towards their beloved, but they do their utmost to create in him the greatest likeness of themselves and of the god whom they honour. Thus fair and blissful to the beloved is the desire of the inspired lover, and the initiation of which I speak into the mysteries of true love, if he be captured by the lover and their purpose is effected. Now the beloved is taken captive in the following manner:

As I said at the beginning of this tale, I divided each soul into three—two horses and a charioteer; and one of the horses was good and the other bad: the division may remain, but I have not yet explained in what the goodness or badness of either consists, and to that I will proceed. The right-hand horse is upright and cleanly made; he has a lofty neck and an aquiline nose; his colour is white, and his eyes dark; he is a lover of honour and modesty and temperance, and the follower of true glory; he needs no touch of the whip, but is guided by word and admonition only. The other is a crooked lumbering animal, put together anyhow; he has a short thick neck; he is flat-faced and of a dark colour, with grey eyes and blood-red complexion;[3]

---

[3] Or with grey and blood-shot eyes.

the mate of insolence and pride, shag-eared and deaf, hardly yielding to whip and spur. Now when the charioteer beholds the vision of love, and has his whole soul warmed through sense, and is full of the prickings and ticklings of desire, the obedient steed, then as always under the government of shame, refrains from leaping on the beloved; but the other, heedless of the pricks and of the blows of the whip, plunges and runs away, giving all manner of trouble to his companion and the charioteer, whom he forces to approach the beloved and to remember the joys of love. They at first indignantly oppose him and will not be urged on to do terrible and unlawful deeds; but at last, when he persists in plaguing them, they yield and agree to do as he bids them. And now they are at the spot and behold the flashing beauty of the beloved; which when the charioteer sees, his memory is carried to the true beauty, whom he beholds in company with Modesty like an image placed upon a holy pedestal. He sees her, but he is afraid and falls backwards in adoration, and by his fall is compelled to pull back the reins with such violence as to bring both the steeds on their haunches, the one willing and unresisting, the unruly one very unwilling; and when they have gone back a little, the one is overcome with shame and wonder, and his whole soul is bathed in perspiration; the other, when the pain is over which the bridle and the fall had given him, having with difficulty taken breath, is full of wrath and reproaches, which he heaps upon the charioteer and his fellow-steed, for want of courage and manhood, declaring that they have been false to their agreement and guilty of desertion. Again they refuse, and again he urges them on, and will scarce yield to their prayer that he would wait until another time. When the appointed hour comes, they make as if they had forgotten, and he reminds them, fighting and neighing and dragging them on, until at length he, on the same thoughts intent, forces them to draw near again. And when they are near he stoops his head and puts up his tail, and takes the bit in his teeth and pulls shamelessly. Then the charioteer is worse off than ever; he falls back like a racer at the barrier, and with a still more violent wrench drags the bit out of the teeth of the wild steed and covers his abusive tongue and jaws with blood, and forces his legs and haunches to the ground and punishes him sorely. And when this has happened several times and the villain has ceased from his wanton way, he is tamed and humbled, and follows the will of the charioteer, and when he sees the beautiful one he is ready to die of fear. And from that time forward the soul of the lover follows the beloved in modesty and holy fear.

And so the beloved who, like a god, has received every true and loyal service from his lover, not in pretence but in reality, being also himself of a nature friendly to his admirer,[4] if in former days he has blushed to own his passion and turned away his lover, because his youthful companions or others slanderously told him that he would be disgraced, now as years advance, at

---

4 Omitting εἰς ταὐτὸν ἄγει τὴν φιλίαν.

the appointed age and time, is led to receive him into communion. For fate which has ordained that there shall be no friendship among the evil has also ordained that there shall ever be friendship among the good. And the beloved when he has received him into communion and intimacy, is quite amazed at the good-will of the lover he recognises that the inspired friend is worth all other friends or kinsmen; they have nothing of friendship in them worthy to be compared with his. And when his feeling continues and he is nearer to him and embraces him, in gymnastic exercises and at other times of meeting, then the fountain of that stream, which Zeus when he was in love with Ganymede named Desire, overflows upon the lover, and some enters into his soul, and some when he is filled flows out again; and as a breeze or an echo rebounds from the smooth rocks and returns whence it came, so does the stream of beauty, passing through the eyes which are the windows of the soul, come back to the beautiful one; there arriving and quickening the passages of the wings, watering them and inclining them to grow, and filling the soul of the beloved also with love. And thus he loves, but he knows not what; he does not understand and cannot explain his own state; he appears to have caught the infection of blindness from another; the lover is his mirror in whom he is beholding himself, but he is not aware of this. When he is with the lover, both cease from their pain, but when he is away then he longs as he is longed for, and has love's image, love for love (Anteros) lodging in his breast, which he calls and believes to be not love but friendship only, and his desire is as the desire of the other, but weaker; he wants to see him, touch him, kiss him, embrace him, and probably not long afterwards his desire is accomplished. When they meet, the wanton steed of the lover has a word to say to the charioteer; he would like to have a little pleasure in return for many pains, but the wanton steed of the beloved says not a word, for he is bursting with passion which he understands not;— he throws his arms round the lover and embraces him as his dearest friend; and, when they are side by side, he is not in a state in which he can refuse the lover anything, if he ask him; although his fellow-steed and the charioteer oppose him with the arguments of shame and reason. After this their happiness depends upon their self-control; if the better elements of the mind which lead to order and philosophy prevail, then they pass their life here in happiness and harmony—masters of themselves and orderly—enslaving the vicious and emancipating the virtuous elements of the soul; and when the end comes, they are light and winged for flight, having conquered in one of the three heavenly or truly Olympian victories; nor can human discipline or divine inspiration confer any greater blessing on man than this. If, on the other hand, they leave philosophy and lead the lower life of ambition, then probably, after wine or in some other careless hour, the two wanton animals take the two souls when off their guard and bring them together, and they accomplish that desire of their hearts which to the many is bliss; and this having once enjoyed they continue to enjoy, yet rarely because they have not the approval of the whole soul. They too are dear, but not so dear to one another as the others, either at the time of their love or afterwards. They consider that they have given and taken from each other the most sacred pledges, and they may not break them and fall into enmity. At last they pass out of the body, unwinged, but eager to soar, and thus obtain no mean reward of love and madness. For those who have once begun the heavenward pilgrimage may not go down again to darkness and the journney beneath the earth, but they live in light always; happy companions in their pilgrimage, and when the time comes at which they receive their wings they have the same plumage because of their love.

Thus great are the heavenly blessings which the friendship of a lover will confer upon you, my youth. Whereas the attachment of the non-lover, which is alloyed with a worldly prudence and has worldly and niggardly ways of doling out benefits, will breed in your soul those vulgar qualities which the populace applaud, will send you bowling round the earth during a period of nine thousand years, and leave you a fool in the world below.

The Touchy Balance   29
J. B. Priestley

Our society would be healthier and happier, I believe, if we were not so dangerously confused about eroticism and sex and love. If we could begin to agree about these words and what they mean, we might stop writing and talking at cross-purposes and begin getting our values right.

Now for various reasons, some of them obviously commercial, eroticism flourishes in our society on a scale never known before, not even during the decadence of imperial Rome. One reason for this is that eroticism is a short-cut to masculine interest and curiosity; it is a safe and easy card to play. Let us say you are publishing a cheap edition of a classical novel. The novel may contain no scene in which a blonde is having the clothes torn from her back, but to play safe, commercially, you display a half-ravished blonde on the jacket. The appeal here is not to sex and it is certainly not to love. It is entirely to the eroticism so characteristic of our time.

Eroticism, unlike sex and love, apparently offers something for nothing. It is sexual pleasure without sexual responsibility. It is having your cake and eating it. Unlike sex, it is not completely natural, and it is at the furthest possible remove from love, which is supremely personal. Eroticism is impersonal, which explains why women may lend themselves to it but never

This article by J. B. Priestley appeared in *The Saturday Evening Post*, April 27, 1963. Reprinted by permission of *The Saturday Evening Post* and J. B. Priestley.

believe in it, and it is artificial, man-made, belonging to a technically advanced but very confused civilization.

Eroticism, we might say, is the twanging of a single nerve, concentrating upon a certain kind of excitement and pleasure to the exclusion of everything else. It is solitary and self-regarding, other persons involved in it being treated as instruments, things. Nothing worth calling a relationship can be created by it. One sex cannot do the other sex any good in eroticism. The opposite sex is not really there, so to speak, in its true complementary character.

We have deliberately perverted ourselves, transforming honest sex into this nasty autoerotic stuff. For eroticism makes use of the broad sexual urge, which might lead to love, and narrows it and directs it into a blind alley, turning something that might be fruitful into what is solitary, barren, and forever unrewarding. And we are doing this on a huge and ever-increasing scale.

Let me give you an English example. In England now we have more and more so called clubs entirely devoted to eroticism, displaying not only striptease but also obscene acts of sexual sadism and masochism. If such clubs were patronized only by teen-age lads, naturally curious, it would not be so bad, but in fact their chief patrons, especially in London's Soho, are middle-aged, prosperous men. And when middle-aged businessmen, perhaps entertaining their customers, have to spend their afternoons and their money gaping at such displays, then there is something wrong with our society.

EROTICISM IS A TRAP

It is a mistake to imagine that Western man is so highly sexed that he is incapable of love. He is merely trapped by eroticism, that twanging of a single nerve in the dark. More and more men are crowding into this blind alley, not demanding more life, richer relationships, but only a barren titillation. The encouragement and exploitation of eroticism, sometimes out of hatred of Woman and fear of real sex and love, but mostly for commercial gain, now constitute one of the worst features of our Western civilization.

I must say that, while publishers do not seem as busy with eroticism as they were a few years ago, there are still too many half-ravished blondes and strangled brunettes selling the newer books. I have a weakness for tough "private eye" tales, in the tradition that began with Dashiell Hammett. I enjoy these tales not because they are full of violence but because the best of them are told with uncommon skill, suggest character and background with an economy the ordinary novelist rarely achieves, and keep alive my interest and curiosity. But even in the best of them there is too much suggestion of sadistic eroticism, and on the lower levels there is a deliberate pandering to the worst feelings of the sex-starved and woman-fearing or woman-hating male. The mutilated corpses of voluptuous blondes that turn up so regularly in these stories are not there by accident. They are there to please the customers, men ready to hate what they cannot possess.

Moreover, it is not only on the "private eye" level of fiction that eroticism is offered as a bait. There is plenty of it, spiced with sadism and masochism, in a large proportion of best-selling novels. Some of these are really the old-fashioned novels of American small-town life, with the same background and cast of characters (e.g., the wild girl, the puzzled young man, the envious spinster, the good old doc), with one important difference, that now the people are caught with their pants down, and what was once referred to very vaguely—rape, for instance—is now described in detail. Take the eroticism out of many of these novels, and their sales could be be divided by a hundred. They are using the same bait as the gaudiest of the cheap books.

The movies of course have dealt in eroticism for many years now. But the appeal is more blatant than it used to be. For example, although Garbo was a symbolic figure of mysterious, exotic sex (the best instance I know of what Jung called the *anima* archetype), quite apart from being a superb actress she was not really a figure of obvious eroticism, not simply a lascivious dream creature. She suggested Woman herself, not a thing for secret appetites. But when we arrive at Bardot and the like, we are at once entangled in deliberate eroticism. The movies have gone into the striptease business.

I never knew Marilyn Monroe, but I enjoyed her film performances, not because she was a superb "dish"—I never think of women as dishes, and, if I did, then Monroe would not have been my first choice from the menu— but simply because the attack, the humor, the sparkling vivacity, of the "dumb blondes" she played were enchanting. In short, I enjoyed her as an actress. Within her limits she was an exceptionally fine performer. Her tragedy, it seems to me, was that, feeling basically insecure because of her early background, she wanted to be appreciated as an actress and to be recognized and understood as a person. But she found herself, in and out of the studios, clamped into the role of a symbolic figure, perhaps the supreme symbolic figure in our time, of eroticism. She was offered not as a woman but as a thing to twang that male erotic nerve. And it is my belief that she was so deeply conscious of this humiliating role, so profoundly disturbed by the idea that her huge mass audience never accepted her as a woman, a real person, that she felt herself being destroyed and did nothing to resist that destruction. So she was, as many people realize now, one of the tragic figures of our time.

Now to my mind it is a great mistake to condemn all this eroticism as "sex." I disagree entirely with all those moralists who are always telling us there is "too much sex" in movies, stage shows, fiction. They are confusing two very different things. And it is this confusion that has in fact encouraged eroticism. In other words, eroticism has got away with it just because so many moralists and social reformers have mistakenly condemned it simply as sex. Ordinary people very sensibly feel that there cannot be all that wrong with sex, that while there may be a lot of sex in the movies, shows, fiction, after all there is just as much sex, if not more, down the nearest street.

Sex is not something wickedly thought up since grandma was a girl and the preacher was at college. It is a natural hunger and need, built into us from the beginning and consciously felt as an urge from the age of puberty onward. Of course we can fight it and starve it, just as we can turn ourselves into living skeletons by eating the merest scraps of food, or dangerously de-hydrate ourselves by drinking the barest minimum of fluids. But it is as natural for young people to be deeply concerned with sex as it is for them to use their lungs, arms and legs. To blame them for it is idiotic. They would not have come into existence if it had not been for sex.

I am not going to pretend that there is no difference in our civilization between eating, drinking and making love. We have inherited some very complicated feelings about sex, including some that suggest a strange sort of guilt. As if we ought to know some other and nicer way of producing chil-dren! The truth is, the roots of our civilization—together with all these feel-ings we have inherited—go back about 2,500 years to a time of transition from matriarchal to patriarchal religious and social systems, when men came to believe that Woman was the enemy of man's conscious development, that unchecked sexual indulgence robbed men of the energy, will and purpose necessary for civilization. To this day, I believe, it is largely men, not women, who feel guilty about sex. And there have been many peoples, not necessarily savages but outside our civilization, who have never known these feelings of guilt.

Each sex wants and needs something from the other sex. (I have already shown that this is not true of eroticism, which is entirely self-regarding and does not go out to the other sex.) But it is a mistake, made far more often by men than women, to imagine there is nothing but physical desire here. In-deed, the older I get the more I am convinced that sexual intercourse itself is far more a psychological than a physical act, and that this—really the psycho-logical relationship—explains the seemingly mysterious sexual successes or failures. We are not bulls and cows, so there are innumerable decent couples who are simply not right for each other and do not discover this until they have been married for some time. This is why divorce should be by mutual consent, without any faking of bogus evidence about adultery or cruelty. In Britain you have to make up a dirty story to convince the judge he should grant you a divorce, and then all too often he abuses you as a dirty, low fellow because he believes this story, forgetting that he asked for it.

Now men often persuade themselves that they "want a woman" as they might want a meal or a smoke, but nearly always this is so much cynical self-deception. In fact they need a great deal more than that—unless they have been completely perverted by eroticism—and what they really need is the psychological relationship with Woman herself—the other and complementary sex. Even the roisterer hurrying to the nearest brothel is unconsciously in search of this relationship. But it must be clearly understood that, on this level we are discussing, there is no relationship of persons but simply a relationship between sexes as sexes, not this man and that woman but Man and Woman. When we come to persons, we arrive at love.

Eroticism, closing in on itself, wanting a sensation and not another person, bars love out. Indeed, too much eroticism probably makes real sexual love impossible. Not that this love is easy and entirely effortless, as ten thousand pieces of sentimental claptrap assure us it is. Here it is worth pointing out that as our own age has become more and more insecure, less and less certain of itself, as more and more people have felt bewildered and fearful, there has been an increasing emphasis, not only in fiction and drama and the movies but also even in advertising, upon the value and joy, the magical saving grace, of sexual love. This is not necessarily wrong, but it can be argued that we may now be asking sexual love to shoulder too many burdens, overloading it to the breaking point. It is being offered to us too often as an effortless rescue operation, in a kind of fairy-tale atmosphere in which everybody can "live happily ever after."

But we never get something worth having for nothing. This is the mistake, as we have already seen, of the men who prefer eroticism to love. They dodge responsibility, so pay nothing in human terms, but then they do not get anything worth having. The true lover is ready to pay everything, all that is of value in his life. But we must not confuse love with the state of being in love. It takes two people, in a consciously creative partnership, to love, only one to be in love. A boy or girl, man or woman, can easily fall in love with somebody who is not really there at all—in other words, with a magical image projected from the unconscious onto somebody whose real self may bear no resemblance to that image. All uncontrollable infatuations are in fact self-produced and outside true relationships. The infatuated man is being bewitched by the magic of his own unconscious depths.

THE 100 PERCENT MALE

There is probably some truth in the idea that deep, enduring sexual love is only possible between certain types of men and women. Types that are wrong for each other cannot mate successfully because they are psychologically ill-matched and therefore cannot even be physically aware of each other in a satisfying way. (This accounts for the breakup, often puzzling to relatives and friends, of many marriages.) All this may have something to do with the fact that most of us have an element, to a differing degree, of the opposite sex in us. Perhaps the 100 percent male, an insufferable fellow, can only be happy with the 100 percent female, almost a talking cat. Perhaps a man who is 80 percent male and 20 percent female is happiest with a woman who is 80 percent female, 20 percent male. But this is idle conjecture because we do not know the percentages.

I am myself suspicious of sexual love that appears to rest on no foundation of respect, admiration and genuine liking. This may seem odd, because love is greater than these. Yet I have known a good many married couples who would have been indignant if they had been told they did not love each other, who would have declared at once and in all sincerity that they did, and yet obviously did not like each other. And though sexual love, in all its delight, tenderness and trust, is more than liking, I feel it ought to contain an immense amount of liking. We ought to be married to the kind of person we like enormously—a wonderful magical man, a glowing gem of a woman —a sweetheart and a honey. And if we are, then we can go down the years, not just feeling or accepting love, but consciously creating it, turning a relationship into a glorious work of art. We may have first entered into this relationship, and all the treasures of living it can bestow upon us, by way of an honest sexual attraction. But what is certain is that we shall never find it, or anything else worth having, in the blind alley and dead end of eroticism. Youth, please note!

30   Romantic Love
Albert Ellis

The pattern of courtship in American and in practically all of Western civilized society is, as we have just seen, that of the Sex Tease. In following this pattern, the modern woman, whether she consciously knows it or not, is forcibly striving to do two major things: First, to make herself appear infinitely sexually desirable—but finally approachable only in legal marriage. Second, to use sex as bait and therefore to set it up as something special. If she gives in too easily to sex pleasure, she loses her favorite man-conquering weapon. Hence she must retain sexuality on a special plane, and dole it out only under unusual conditions.

The idealized aspect of this philosophy of let-us-women-stick-together-and-only-employ-sex-for-special-baiting-purposes is what we usually call romantic love. For at the very core of modern romance is a tight rope tautly stretched between, and uneasily dividing as well as soldering, gratified and ungratified, over- and under-evaluated sexuality. Where non-romantic types of love prevail—as they do in numerous primitive, peasant, and Eastern cultures—sex is either enjoyed for its own sake or is hedged in by practical (socio-economic, status-giving, marital, or other) restrictions. Where romance is the rule, sex is virtually never enjoyed for itself. It is invariably hemmed in

From Ch. 5, "Romantic Love," with deletions and some footnotes omitted, in *The American Sexual Tragedy*, Albert Ellis, New York, Lyle Stuart, Inc., 1962. Reprinted by permission of Lyle Stuart, Inc.

by idealistic, nonpractical love restrictions. Romanticism, hand in hand with
the sex tease game of American courtship, often plays up the verbal and plays
down the active expression of human sexuality.

To understand modern romantic love, we should first know a little about
its origins and history. Although the history of love may be traced to the
beginnings of mankind, romantic love seems to have been born in Western
Europe during the Middle Ages. It is, as Finck has pointed out, "A modern
sentiment, less than a thousand years old." [1]

The so-called Dark Ages which preceded the twelfth century was an
epoch of acute socio-economic, religious, philosophic, and esthetic rigidity.
The individual of the day was born into a world which, to the largest possible
extent, predetermined his work, his thoughts, and even his emotions. Against
this church-bound and custom-ridden condition of living, romanticism was
something of a reflexive, and certainly a healthy, rebellion.

Like most rebellious movements, however, romantic love at first tended
to take to extremes its floutings of the established social order. Thus, where
the amorous ideal had emphasized sexual fidelity, *courtoisie* love frequently
glorified adultery. Where eighth century love was based on patriarchal traditions, tenth century troubadours extolled woman-centered, female-worshipping
amour. Where the priests preached divine love, the courtiers deified human
love. Where Christianized conjugality was truly coffined, cabined, and confined, romantic love emphasized freedom of choice—and of parting. As Denis
de Rougement has observed: "The cultivation of passionate love began in
Europe as a reaction to Christianity (and in particular to its doctrine of marriage) by people whose spirit, whether naturally or by inheritance, was still
pagan." [2]

Just as an insurgent political group will often, both prior and subsequent
to its victory, take over many of the trappings of the vested interests it is
undermining, romantic love borrowed from the Christianized version of love
that preceded it. It preempted many of the mystical, irrational, evangelical
aspects of early Christianity. Fighting the restrictions imposed by a mighty
religion, it eventually became almost a religion in its own right.

It should be noted than man achieves so-called free will almost in direct
inverse ratio to his becoming a socialized human being. The mere fact that
one has, and early in one's life is raised by, duly conditioned and biased
parents reduces one's possible free will to meagre amount; the fact that one,
additionally, is raised among hundreds of other human beings, and among
humans who have a long history and an intrenched culture, further reduces
one's potential free will to near-zero proportions. Romanticism, therefore, by

[1] Henry T. Finck, *Romantic Love and Personal Beauty*. New York, Macmillan,
1887, p. 1.

[2] Denis de Rougemont, *Love in the Western World*. New York, Harcourt, Brace,
1940, p. 70; G. R. Taylor, *Sex in History*. New York, Vanguard, 1955.

very virtue of its being a philosophy with quite well-defined rules of the game of living, eventually leads to virtually as much restriction and human determination as do medieval or other non-romantic philosophies. To be human is to be, in one degree or another, predetermined in one's thoughts, feelings, actions. One mainly has a choice of what *kind* of determination one will live by. And even that choice is largely chimerical: since, as it for example happened, early Christianity and its heir-apparent, medievalism, actually determined most of the trappings of the romantic revolt that followed. Small wonder was it, then, that soon after its inception romantic love blanketed itself in religiosity and traditionalism.

Again, although romantic love was in part a reaction against the sexual repressiveness of early Christianity, it quickly took on so many characteristics of the Christianized love that it was trying to replace, that in its own right, it became antisexual. As Emil Lucka observed: "As time went on the barrier erected between true spiritual love and insidious sensuality became more and more clearly defined; the former pervaded the erotic emotion of the whole period. Parallel with chaste love, sensuality continued to exist as something contemptible, unworthy of a noble mind." The cycle, curiously enough, was then complete: romantic love, which originated as a revolt against Christian antisexuality, soon was conquered by its victim: so that, at least in some of its extreme manifestations, it became itself a bulwark against pagan sensuality.

Three notable facts, however, kept the antisexual elements of medieval romantic love within the bounds of practicality and sanity. In the first place, it was not, when it first originated, a mass phenomenon. The troubadours and their ladies followed the romantic patterns, to be sure. But the peasants, footsoldiers, common tradesmen and artisans, and other members of the community tended to remain scrupulously orthodox. In the second place, while the troubadours and lords maintained romantic attachments to the ladies of the day, these were invariably adulterous, and not marital, attachments. Marriages, at this time, were socio-economically arranged, and had little or nothing to do with love either in their courtship or post-courtship stages. In the third place, although the troubadours and courtiers could fall romantically in love with their ladies, they also could, and invariably did, find plenty of girls from the peasant and other classes with whom they could roll in the hay. They could therefore well afford to use love as a special ritual for the unattainable lady while they used sex as a pleasant pastime and an essential ingredient of their relations with women of the lower classes.

Medieval romanticism was in several ways an exceptionally class-limited form of love; and it hardly interfered with sex activity, which the courtier could always have, practically for the asking, with a wife, prostitute, or girl of the lower classes for whom he had very frank sex desire and, usually, no romantic love whatever. Under such conditions, the courtier could easily build love into a mystical, religious, antisexual emotion—while he was gaily, and quite unromantically, fulfilling his sexual needs at the same time.

Up until the twentieth century, vestiges of this medieval pattern of romantic love have persisted. Although the nineteenth century male was supposed to show some degree of romantic love for his wife, several non-romantic aspects of sex and marriage also were so widespread in the 1800's as to be virtually socially sanctioned. Males of the upper class in Europe and America frequently had their regular mistresses; while lower class males often frequented brothels. Marriages, particularly among the gentry, were often arranged by parents, or at least had to be entered into with parental permission; and in a country like the United States, where the frontier still existed and where women tended to bear several children and to work just as hard as their husbands, there was relatively little opportunity for romantic love in marriage, even when some measure of it existed in courtship.

Only in our own day, for the first time in history, has romantic love become ubiquitous. Whereas our forefathers expected only relatively few gentlemen and gentlewomen to love romantically, we expect every male and female to do so. There are several reasons why romantic attitudes have become so democratized today. For one thing, romantic love is facilitated by small families, by weakened religiosity, by the freedom of women, and by social mobility, all of which are considerably more prevalent today than they were a century or more ago. For another thing, modern living arrangements and technological inventions (such as kitchenettes, automobiles, and birth control appliances) make it easy for households to be moved and for families to break up, and this in turn favors romantic views of love. Our present concepts of individual freedom, democracy, and personal adventurousness also encourage romanticism. Finally, we have literally taken up the cudgels for romantic love and actually preach its precepts in our schools, fiction, drama, movies, and television performances. "Romantic love is to a large extent a convention developed by society,"[3] and in our own society we have deliberately adopted this convention and promulgated it with a vengeance.

All love is not, of course, romantic love. Love itself consists of any kind of more or less intense emotional attraction to or involvement with another. It includes many different types and degrees of affection, such as conjugal love, parental love, familial love, religious love, love of humanity, love of animals, love of things, self-love, sexual love, obsessive-compulsive love, etc. Although *romantic* has become, in our day, virtually a synonym for *loving,* romantic love is actually a special type of love, and has several distinguishing features.

A summary description of the characteristics of romantic love—or more accurately of the romantic lover—will help clarify. The romantic lover is unrealistic: he over-evaluates and fictionalizes his beloved. He is verbal and esthetic about his love. As Tolstoy remarked of the lovers of his day, "Many

[3] Arthur Garfield Hays, in V. F. Calverton and Samuel D. Schmalhausen, *Sex in Civilization.* New York, Macaulay, 1929, p. 219.

people's love would be instantly annihilated if they could not speak of it in French." [4] He is aggressively individualistic: he insists, utterly, on his own romantic love choice, and on all but absolute lack of restraint in that choice. This aspect of romantic love was taken so seriously by the famous Comtesse de Champagne's twelfth century Court of Love that it held, in one of its decisions, that "love cannot extend its rights over two married persons. For indeed lovers grant each other all, mutually and freely, without being constrained by any motive of necessity, whereas husband and wife are holden, by their duty, to submit their wills to each other and to refuse each other nothing." [5]

The romantic lover, furthermore, frequently is in love with love rather than with his beloved; and he may well repeat, with Elizabeth Barrett Browning, "If thou must love me, let it be for naught except for love's sake only." He is monopolistic, in that he normally devotes himself to one paramount love object. As Folsom has noted, "Romantic love is intensely monogamous *at any one time*. Yet, essentially, its loyalty is to *love* rather than to a person." [6]

The romantic lover is demanding: he wishes to be loved, in his turn, by his beloved; to be loved madly, completely, monopolistically; and for himself, rather than for his position and accomplishments. He is perfectionistic: he strives for not merely a fine, good, lasting, happy relationship with his beloved, but for the finest, greatest, most lasting, most ecstatic amour.

The romantic lover is, as we have previously noted, antisexual. He acknowledges the value of sexuality only when it is linked to love. He is sentimental and tends to overact and overstate the greatness of his love. He is passionate and intense: he is supposed to love madly and to be violently in love, rather than affectionately loving.

The romantic lover is changeable, and frequently goes from one violent passion to another. He is jealous, often intensely so, of his beloved. He tends to emphasize physical attractiveness above all else. Finally, in today's world, the romantic lover invariably stresses marrying only for love, and is likely to believe that one should never remain married when love dies. For him, too, the death of love from his marriage tends to become sufficient license for every sort of adultery. In the high name of romantic love, he is free to pursue his true passion at any cost.

The romantic lover believes, in sum, two basic propositions which Ernest W. Burgess lists as follows: "1. That the highest personal happiness comes from marriage based upon romantic love. 2. That love and marriage are

[4] Leo Tolstoy, in Frederick W. Morton, *Love in Epigram*. Chicago, McClurg, 1899.
[5] Comtesse de Champagne, in De Stendhal, *On Love*. New York, Liveright, 1947; Alan Watts, *Nature, Man and Woman*. New York, Pantheon, 1958; R. H. Robbins, "Courts of Love," *Sexology*, 1962, 28, 392–396.
[6] Joseph K. Folsom, *The Family*. New York, Harper, 1935, p. 74.

essentially personal and private and are, perhaps, even more than other aspects of life, to be controlled by the individual himself." [7]

.   .   .

Despite these criticisms of romantic love, and for all the jokes current about it, the fact remains that our mass media overwhelmingly favor the belief that romantic amour is incredibly delightful, delicious, and delectable and that a life not rooted in romantic affection is detestable, deleterious, and damnably dull. While not even a dozen non-romantic or anti-romantic views were found in the course of surveying literally hundreds of mass media outlets, several hundred distinctly romantic attitudes were uncovered.

The ubiquity of ultra-romantic philosophies in our mass media, particularly when combined with the unromantic and often harsh realities of modern life, leads to serious (conscious and unconscious) conflicts and disturbances on the part of virtually all the members of our society. Some of the reasons for these conflicts and disturbances are as follows:

1. Romanticism is, almost by definition, passionately untrammeled and unrestricted. But our courtship customs, as we indicated in the previous chapter, are normally hemmed in by many practical and nonromantic considerations. Consequently, the swain who is romantically enamored of his girlfriend must almost necessarily encounter parental objections, financial difficulties, sexual tabus, and other limitations. It may therefore be predicted that, quite aside from his girlfriends' reacting negatively to him, most of his romantic attachments will never get the chance to bud or will be cruelly nipped before they have consequentially flowered. Although the sex tease of courtship which is prevalent in our society nicely dovetails with romanticism's antisexuality, our other courtship restrictions are mainly antithetical to romance: they, to some extent, encourage romantic dreams—but savagely combat the fulfillment of these dreams.

2. The kind of romantic love which is enthusiastically espoused by our mass media is based on many assumptions which, ordinarily, are not sustained by the realities of either living or loving. Thus, it is assumed that romantic love does not change; but, on the contrary, it most often does. It is assumed that romantic love survives the lover's aging process and the beloved's loss of youth and beauty; but, most frequently, it does not. It is assumed that it is easy to tell "true love" from "infatuation"; which, of course, it isn't. It is assumed that romantic love brings nothing but ecstatic joy; when, actually, it often brings worry, responsibility, loss of independence, and all kinds of anguish. It is assumed that having steady sex relations with one's beloved will make one romantically love her more; when, in point of fact, it frequently makes one love her less. It is assumed that if a pair of romantic lovers have children, their offspring will help increase their mutual ardor; when, in

[7] Ernest W. Burgess, "Sociological Aspects of Sex Life in the Unmarried Adult," in Ira S. Wile, Sex Life of the Unmarried Adult. New York, Vanguard, 1934, pp. 153–154.

numerous instances, children seriously sabotage romantic ardor. Similarly, numerous other assumptions about romantic love are made in our popular publications and productions which, in reality, are distinctly false. Consequently, the utter, terrible disillusionment of many or most romantic lovers becomes eventually assured.

3. Romanticism, again almost by definition, implies a considerable degree of fiction, of facing away from instead of toward reality. The romantic lover exaggerates, overestimates, sees his beloved as she really is not. But life, particularly in our technologically influenced world, is hardly fictional; and adjustment to life, as we psychologists have been stressing for many years, means full acceptance of reality. Neurosis, in the last analysis, invariably includes a considerable degree of failure to recognize reality. If, then, romantic love also includes a failure to recognize reality, we should expect it importantly to overlap with neurosis at several points. This means that we, on the one hand, are trying to raise our children to be realistic and, on the other hand, to be non-realistic—that is, romantic. Not only, then, are we directly raising them to be at least semi-neurotic, but we are heading them for a virtually irreconcilable conflict between their romantic and nonromantic aspirations: which conflict, in its turn, is only likely to intensify their neurosis.

4. Many romantic ideals, such as those concerned with purity, dedication, holy affection, and the deification of physical beauty, supply us with perfectionistic goals which will inevitably be unachievable by most of us, and will lead to grim disappointment and disillusionment. The result, particularly where sexuality is at issue, is likely to be neurotic and psychotic feelings of dirtiness, failure, guilt, inadequacy, profanation of what is considered to be holy, and so on. Human happiness, as has long been known, is a ratio between what people expect and what they get from life. When their expectations are ultra-romantic, and hence unrealistic, failure to achieve their level of aspiration must inevitably ensue: with consequent unhappiness and a tendency toward emotional disturbance.

5. Romantic love, in our culture, is supposed to lead to engagement and marriage; but its tenets, actually, are largely opposed to the type of marriage which exists among us. Normal marriage has numerous socio-economic aspects which are antithetical to the maintenance of romantic, (though not necessarily other types of) love. Thus, married couples must be concerned about purchases, repairs, sickness, insurance, child care, entertainment, business success, in-laws, relatives, friends, education, cooking, cleaning, shopping, mending, sleeping facilities, and hundreds of other practical aspects of modern living which are utterly nonromantic and which tend to restrict emotional outpourings of a romantic nature.

Romanticism, moreover, puts a premium on intense amative *feelings*: which are notoriously changeable and fleeting. Romantic courtship usually follows a highly erratic pattern, and includes considerable affectional promiscuity. Romantic marriage, quite logically, tends to follow this same pattern and to result in numerous separations and divorces—at which our society hardly looks with equanimity.

Marriage usually becomes a relatively calm, steady relationship that is not too demanding emotionally: since few married couples have available a great reserve of sustained, intense emotional energy. But romanticism, as Gross has pointed out, demands "constant and unequivocal demonstrations of affection." [8] An individual who is raised to crave romantic love is rarely content with anything but the sustained emotional intensity which is thoroughly non-indigenous to everyday marital domesticity. Hence the almost inevitable dissatisfaction of the arch romanticist who marries.

Romantic love, again, is partly based on the sexual teasing and blocking of modern courtship. Its very intensity, to a large extent, grows out of the generous promises combined with the niggardly actualities of sex fulfillment which exist during the courtship stages. When, after marriage, the sex blockings of the courtship days are necessarily removed, the intensity of romantic love which partly stemmed from these blockings may easily fade; and the result is a relatively (romantically) loveless marriage—which, by the very premises of romanticism, is considered to be worthless and must be broken up.

Romantic love, because it is an idealized, perfectionist emotion, particularly thrives on intermittent rather than steady association between two lovers. During courtship, fellows and girls see each other for relatively few hours per week, when they are well-rested, well-fed, and well-accoutered for having a good time. On such a basis, they are at their best and their handsomest or loveliest, and can reasonably well live up to perfectionist ideals. Marriage, however, invariably means domesticity: meaning, a constant, more or less monotonous, living together on an hour after hour, year after year basis. This type of domesticity, probably, is as well designed to sabotage romantic love as is any other mode of social living. Indeed, if romantic lovers wanted, with perfect logic, to induce their passions to endure for a maximum period of time, they might well ban, under almost any circumstances, marital domesticity. But, in our society, they do just the opposite: they, as it were, condemn themselves to living under the same roof, for perhaps forty or fifty years, with their beloveds. The result, in terms of their own romantic ideals, is almost invariably frightful.

6. Romantic love, in our culture, is essentially opposed to the other modes of love which we also, in one way or another, espouse. It is particularly opposed to conjugal or familial love which our religious institutions and (increasingly) our schools are continually upholding. Moreover, most of our married women, once they see that their early romantic love for their husbands does not last, tend to raise their sons and daughters, and particularly

[8] Llewellyn Gross, "A Belief Pattern Scale for Measuring Attitudes Toward Romanticism." *American Sociological Review*, 1944, 9, 463–472.

perhaps the former, in a Momistic, family-tied manner that brooks little romantic opposition. Mother-centered sons are not encouraged to fall madly in love with the girl next door; and many of them, in point of fact, are raised so that they cannot possibly romantically love anyone. When, because of the pressurizing and pulling influences of their culture (particularly, the novels, films, and television shows of this culture), they do become romantically attached to a woman, they are almost automatically propelled right into the center of a bitter struggle for their souls between their mother and their wife. Since romanticism, with its unrealistic idealizations and demands, can afford no such struggle, it usually gets the worst of the conflict, and the consequent wrestle with reality is often agonizing.

7. Of the several possible logical culminations of romantic love that theoretically may, and presumably should, occur, virtually none are consciously permitted to occur; so that its usual end is desultory, unplanned, and heartbreaking. Some of the possible logical culminations of romantic love are these:

(a) Romantic love may, under some circumstances, be sustained by severely limiting the period of its expression. Thus, Somerset Maugham has the heroine of his play, The Constant Wife, declare that she is going off to stay with her lover only for a period of six weeks: "Because I'm putting a limit to our love it may achieve the perfection of something that is beautiful and transitory." [9]

(b) Romantic love may flower indefinitely if lovers consciously become varietists and change their individual partners while continuing their romantic patterns of attachment.

(c) Romantic lovers may, quite logically, engage in plural love affairs and thus, by having two or more romantic partners simultaneously, avoid much of the monotony and domesticity which normally dooms romanticism.

(d) Romantic lovers may keep their love alive by consciously renouncing its fruition. Thus, Ibsen has his lovers in Love's Comedy break with each other just as they are about to marry, with the heroine ecstatically removing her engagement ring, casting it into the fjord, and exclaiming to her lover: "Now for this earthly life I have forgone thee,—But for the life eternal I have won thee!" [10] George Moore, in his Memoirs of My Dead Life, Andre Gide in Strait is the Gate, Walter Van Tilburg Clark in The City of Trembling Leaves, and Ben Hecht in Erik Dorn solve the problem of longevity of romantic love in precisely the way Ibsen solved it in Love's Comedy.[11] Theophile Gautier, in Mlle. de Maupin, gives one of the best summaries of this renunciation philosophy by having his heroine write a farewell letter to

[9] Somerset Maugham, The Constant Wife. New York, Doubleday, 1932.

[10] Henrik Ibsen, Love's Comedy. New York, Willey Book, pp. 470–71.

[11] George Moore, Memoirs of My Dead Life. London, Heinemann, 1921, p. 72; Andre Gide, Strait is the Gate. New York, Knopf, 1936, pp. 187–89; Walter Van Tilburg Clark, The City of Trembling Leaves. New York, Random House, 1945, p. 395; Ben Hecht, Erik Dorn. New York, Modern Library, 1930, p. 130.

her lover in this wise: "You believe, perhaps, that I do not love you because I am leaving you. Later, you will recognize the truth of the contrary. Had I valued you less, I should have remained, and would have poured out to you the insipid beverage to the dregs. Your love would soon have died of weariness; after a time you would have quite forgotten me, and, as you read over my name on the list of your conquests, would have asked yourself: 'Now, who the deuce was she?' I have at least the satisfaction of thinking that you will remember me sooner than another. Your unsated desire will again spread its wings to fly to me; I shall ever be to you something desirable to which your fancy will love to return, and I hope that in the arms of the mistresses you may have, you will sometimes think of the unrivalled night you spent with me." [12]

(e) Romantic love, most logically perhaps, may be ended in the most drastic of all human acts: death. As Emil Lucka has pointed out: "One thing is certain: the great love cannot find its consummation on earth . . . The love-death is the last and inevitable conclusion of reciprocal love which knows no value but itself, and is resolved to face eternity, so that no alien influence shall reach it." [13] Denis de Rougemont concurs: "The mystic lovers in the Romance are compelled to pursue the *intensification* of passion, not its fortunate appeasement. The keener their passion, the more it can detach them from created things, the more readily do they feel that they are on the way to attaining the death in *endura* which they desire." [14]

Of these logical, or romantically self-consistent, ways of bringing romantic love to a climax, none are consciously espoused by any number of lovers in our culture: for the good reason that the general marital philosophy of our society is quite opposed to such acts as lovers limiting the period of their love, becoming varietists, engaging in plural affairs, consciously renouncing their loves, or arranging a suicide pact with their beloveds. Instead, we espouse what might be called the most illogical climax to romantic courtship and love: consummation. For sexual and marital consummation indubitably, in the vast majority of instances, maims, bloodies, and finally kills romanticism until it is deader than—well, yesterday's romance.

[12] Theophile Gautier, *Mlle. de Maupin*. New York, Three Pay Sales Co., 1900, p. 223.

[13] Emil Lucka, *Eros*. New York, Putnam, 1915.

[14] Denis de Rougemont, *op. cit.*, pp. 123–24.

Part four

THE SELF IN WIDER RELATION

A society has a continuity of life which transcends the lives of men. Men come and go. The society anticipates their coming hither and survives their going hence. It supplies the forms whereby the germ of originality which is in them is either stirred or extinguished.

John Taylor
<small>THE MASKS OF SOCIETY</small>

INTRODUCTION

Few of us have reflected on the actual extent to which our life is shared with others. Though, as a society, we much admire individualism and have legally guaranteed the rights and privileges of the individual, the isolated person is impotent. Our social order has become increasingly "corporate," that is, it consists of autonomous bodies or groups by means of which we carry on the business of living. We inhabit self-governing towns or cities; we become politically efficient by belonging to political parties; we work for corporations, institutions, or government agencies; we live in cooperative apartments, hold group insurance, use group medicine, and belong to the PTA. We even pursue recreation in groups, belonging to golf clubs, yacht clubs, athletic, and dining clubs. In a mammoth, complex society, the person by himself is inept and inefficient. Only in community does he gain strength and influence. A brief review of the groups to which you belong will reveal the network of associations by which your life is structured. The political scientist Robert MacIver has called us a "multi-group" society and the more sardonic have called us "a nation of joiners." In this sense the phrase, "our society," is an abstraction. We belong to many societies with more or less self-determination and self-government.

Why do men want, even need, to belong? The answer is many sided. Historically, first of all the Industrial Revolution brought about commercialism and urbanization, setting the stage for extensive group living. And group living generates further group living. A union of teamsters breeds unions of mechanics, carpenters, and garment workers. Second, persons in groups can better propose and more effectively accomplish mutual goals; they can combine their energy and enhance their mutual strength by concerted effort. Groups present a united front and a spirit of rapport. In fact, it is sometimes thought that part of man's original preference for urban life as against a nomadic existence sprang from this source. A labor union, an NAACP, a Manufacturer's Association can do what no individual can do. These corporate bodies can formulate policy, dictate terms, and apply pressures and sanctions to protect their interests and their rights. In short, many heads can better envisage possibilities and combined strength can better move mountains.

Third, men find security in groups. It is usually easier to carry a shared burden. To do what others do spares the labor of initiative. And, in concert, empathy causes us to absorb, reinforce, and be reinforced by the feeling of others. One of the reasons why a crowd can become a violent mob is that together men can commit acts from which each individual would shrink. Shared feeling, encourages each member of the group to become released from personal responsibility. But groups can act constructively as well as destructively. Security is gained when a town is mutually up-in-arms against a threat, or when group insurance handles the bill, or when group energy accomplishes a task.

Finally, family life has already habituated us toward participation with others. Aristotle pointed out that the family is the core of the state. The family teaches man that he is a social animal, bound by the claims of others. Therefore, it educates him for living in a civil state. Early experience entices men to want to belong; to desire to be "in," part of, and related to. Belonging is native to the human species, arousing emotion which is as intense as it is effective. Children, for example, typically and spontaneously form clubs, gangs, and secret associations. And you, for example, enjoy belonging to fraternities and sororities. You are proud to be part of that "family" of students who call a particular college by the significant name of "Alma Mater." And when a group to which you belong acts in concert on some formal occasion, you may feel an unexpected thrill of being an organic part and may experience a strong sense of loyalty to the whole. Even the G.I. who dislikes the army may find himself in a different frame of mind when his company marches on parade. The worker in a union convalescent home feels the same kind of identity with a larger whole. Even amid alien corn, a member of the Rotary, an Episcopalian, a Mason, can, by virtue of these associations, feel himself rooted. Man is indeed a social animal, and the cloudburst of emotion which so often attends his expressing that fact waters his soul.

You will notice, however, that we have been speaking of voluntary or "functional" groups which men form under their own impetus in order to accomplish goals in common. A functional group is organized with specific ends in view. It is a task group dedicated to common purposes. There are other groups, however, to which men involuntarily belong; groups to which they belong against their wish; groups to which they do not even know they belong. Some groups are "nominal" groups, which are exposed by techniques of classification. The members have no shared purpose but are grouped by the classifier who can select and emphasize them in different ways. For instance, we may select out a group which is red-headed, one which lives in cities, one which wears pajamas, one which speaks Chinese and so on. To speak of a "group" is to classify individuals, and to classify is to arrange units into collections with shared traits.

In order to classify we must select some principle as a basis for distinguishing this group from that. In classifying men, for instance, we may select any imaginable trait—those with long tongues, those who are taciturn, those who are able to thread fine needles, those who are curious, those who are ambitious—depending on what we wish to know or accomplish. In this sense, our principle of selection is arbitrary, for we have decided to classify in terms of this trait rather than any other. In another sense, however, our choice of a principle of discrimination is determined by our purpose in classifying in the first place. We may wish to know whether long-tonguedness aids digestion or if taciturnity is connected with climate. Furthermore, the traits which we have selected are genuinely there. We have simply selected these to the exclusion of others. Moreover, when we classify "courageous men," for example, our group probably consists of members of every ethnic and national group throughout the world. Were we to classify in terms of the principle of being blue-eyed, we would rejuggle the aggregate of mankind and the same national and ethnic diversity would probably hold true.

But, has it not been said that some groups such as racial groups, for instance, are designated by nature herself and are not in the least arbitrarily discriminated by man for his own purposes? And have we not been warned to avoid tampering with nature's own classifications? Indeed, brown-skinnedness is as much an objective trait of some individuals as is short-temperedness. Yet when we select brown-skinnedness as the principle of selection in terms of which to organize our group, we will find that it includes members of varied ethnic backgrounds from many countries and among them those "white" New Yorkers who spend their summer on local beaches. Our group of brown-skinned individuals would include those who are calm-tempered, those who have large appetites, those who are honest, and those who are responsible. To classify in terms of skin color is to determine which members of our aggregate have skins within a specific color range—only that and no more. Were we to classify mankind in terms of "blood," the same situation would obtain. There is type A or type O blood to be found in many geographic areas and among many ethnic and national groups, among men of different colors of skin and among men of different emotional constitution and intellectual capacity. Classification is an especially effective instrument of knowledge. To be able to distinguish one thing from another is a major intellectual feat. But it can be egregiously misused. It can be a fertile source for one of man's most barbaric activities, namely, the designation of an "out" group against an "in" group. It can serve the illegitimate purpose of ostracism and social stigma. It can make it easy for men to express their need to be "better" than another, not on the genuine ground of excelling in some respect, but on the spurious ground of possessing some accidental property, trait, or affiliation. Giving pseudo-justification to name-calling, it can cloak the offender with respectability. It can give rancor free play and can provide a channel for random aggression. It can condemn persons to social alienation regardless of their assets and in defiance of the contribution they might make to society.

A society which tends to emphasize fixed groups and groupings has been called a "status" as against a "contract" society. In a status condition of society one is born irrevocably to a specific place in the social order, a place from which he can never move. In our own culture, where a contract condition of society prevails, by and large, and where stress is placed on the role of individuals, each individual has a right to enter any group he sees fit. Under normal conditions he may go to any school, enter any business or profession, join any fraternal organization, live where he wishes, travel where he wishes, and select or change his religion. Fixed groupings, believed to be stable in the nature of things, belong to less complex societies and inhibit social mobility when they persist in a more variegated culture.

The most significant feature of a contract as against a status condition of society is the importance it places on the rights of the individual. Since he may affiliate or resign affiliation, his relation to the group is not fixed by social code but determined by personal inclination and activity. In a contract condition of society, person and group share equal rights and privileges. When the person is subordinated to the group, individuality may be lost and creativity stifled. When the group is subordinate to the person, anarchy and instability develop. And in either case both person and group lose their integrity as self-determining entities. In an "ideal" society, the group expresses the consensus of all persons within it while the person expresses his will tempered by the claims of others.

One of the most important aspects of the relation of person to group lies in the issue of conformity. Conformity is sometimes a kind of empathy. At its best, it is the basis of socialization in that the person learns by following suit. Without the desire to conform, persons would never become functioning members of society; they would never absorb the social skills necessary to live with others.

Yet conformity, if merely mimetic or even if accommodatingly adaptive, leads to a diminution of the unique powers of the person. When an entire group sings in chorus, any voice which would inform it of possible collective error is drowned out. The urge to conformity can deprive an entire group of whatever penetration and sagacity any of its members might be able to provide. The sincere nonconformist can, as in the fairy tale, remind the entire group that the emperor is actually naked. Since conformity is comfortable habit, the nonconformist alerts the group to its over-simplifications and its oversights.

Of course, nonconformity can be a pose for the attention-seeker. The "beat" can erect nonconformity into a new kind of social ritual where all chorus in aimless protest. Insofar as the beat generation lives in isolate colonies, just insofar will it fail to make contact with the evils it would correct and the stupidities it would rectify. And insofar as the beatnik is ineffectual in his

efforts at personal and societal reform, just insofar is he likely to become defeated, desolate, and drug-ridden. A "potted" Don Quixote can easily mistake
the foundations of civilized society for windmills.

Perhaps the most fundamental problem facing us as a group is that of determining how to work out effective and unencumbered relations between
person and group such that the person's integrity is not submerged under
the weight of the group and the group's integrity is not dissolved by thrusts
of aimless individuality. But the most urgent problem in our day of nuclear
weapons threatening an ever-shrinking globe is that of determining how to
work out constructive and creative relations between diverse national, racial,
and ethnic groups. Harmony amid such dissonance requires a victory over the
troublesome complexities which beset all group life. Only out of courageous
answers proposing how intergroup community might be obtained and enhanced will come, if at all, a brave, new, and hopefully more stable world.

YOU GOT TO TAKE CARE
OF YOURSELF, BABY
NOBODY ELSE WILL.
SO IT'S YOU AND ME
LORD.

THE SOCIAL SITUATION: BELONGING

Why One Must Belong   31
Bertrand Russell

Human beings find it profitable to live in communities, but their desires, unlike those of bees in a hive, remain largely individual; hence arises the difficulty of social life and the need of government. For, on the one hand, government is necessary: without it, only a very small percentage of the population
of civilized countries could hope to survive, and that in a state of pitiable
destitution. But, on the other hand, government involves inequalities of
power, and those who have most power will use it to further their own
desires as opposed to those of ordinary citizens. Thus anarchy and despotism
are alike disastrous, and some compromise is necessary if human beings are to
be happy.

In the present chapter, I wish to consider the organizations concerned
with a given individual, not the individuals concerned with a given organization. This matter is, of course, very different in democratic and in totalitarian States, for in the latter all the organizations concerned, with very few
exceptions, are departments of the State. As far as possible, however, I wish
to ignore this difference in a preliminary survey.

Organizations, both public and private, affect an individual in two ways.
There are those that are designed to facilitate the realization of his own
wishes, or of what are considered to be his interests; and there are those
intended to prevent him from thwarting the legitimate interests of others. The
distinction is not clear-cut: the police exist to further the interests of honest
men, as well as to thwart burglars, but their impact on the lives of burglars is
much more emphatic than their contacts with those who abide by the law. I
shall return to this distinction presently; for the moment, let us consider the
most important points, in the lives of individuals in civilized communities, at
which some organization plays some decisive part.

To begin with birth: the services of a doctor and/or a midwife are considered essential, and although, formerly, a wholly untrained Mrs. Gamp was

Ch. XIII, "Organizations and the Individual" from *Power*, by Bertrand Russell, London, George Allen & Unwin, Ltd., n.d. Reprinted by permission of George Allen &
Unwin.

thought sufficient, a certain level of skill, determined by a public authority, is now exacted. Throughout infancy and childhood, health is to some extent the concern of the State; the extent of the State's concern in various countries is fairly accurately reflected in the infant and juvenile death-rates. If the parents fail too egregiously in their parental duty, the child can be taken from them by the public authority, and assigned to the care of foster-parents or of an institution. At the age of five or six, the child comes under the education authorities, and thenceforward, for a number of years, is compelled to learn those things that the government thinks every citizen should know. At the end of this process, in the majority of cases, most opinions and mental habits are fixed for life.

Meanwhile, in democratic countries, the child comes under other influences which are not exerted by the State. If the parents are religious or political, they will teach the tenets of a creed or a party. As the child grows older, he becomes increasingly interested in organized amusements, such as cinemas and football matches. If he is rather intelligent, but not very, he may be influenced by the Press. If he goes to a school which is not a State school, he acquires an outlook which is in certain ways peculiar—in England, usually an outlook of social superiority to the herd. Meanwhile he imbibes a moral code which is that of his age and class and nation. The moral code is important, but not easy to define, because precepts are of three not sharply differentiated sorts: first, those which must be really obeyed on pain of general obloquy; secondly, those which must not be *openly* disobeyed; and thirdly, those which are regarded as counsels of perfection, only to be obeyed by saints. Moral codes applicable to the whole population are mainly, though by no means wholly, the result of religious tradition, operating through religious organizations, but capable of surviving their decay for a longer or shorter time. There are also professional codes: things which must not be done by an officer, or a doctor, or a barrister, and so on. Such codes, in modern times, are usually formulated by professional associations. They are very imperative: while the Church and the Army conflicted as to duelling, the Army code prevailed among officers; medical and confessional secrecy prevails even against the law.

As soon as a young man or woman begins to earn money, various organizations begin to influence his or her activities. The employer is usually an organization; and there is probably, in addition, a federation of employers. The trade union and the State both control important aspects of the work; and apart from such matters as insurance and Factory Acts, the State can help to decide, by tariffs and by government orders, whether the particular trade that a man has chosen shall prosper or be depressed. The prosperity of an industry may be affected by all kinds of circumstances, such as currency, the international situation, or the ambitions of Japan.

Marriage and duties to children again bring a man into relations with the law, and also with a moral code mainly derived from the Church. If he lives long enough and is sufficiently poor, he may at last enjoy an old age pension; and his death is carefully supervised by the law and the medical profession, to make sure that it has not occurred by his own wish or by any one else's.

Certain matters remain to be decided by personal initiative. A man can marry to please himself, provided the lady is willing; he probably has a certain liberty of choice, in youth, as to his means of livelihood; his leisure can be spent as he chooses, within the limits of what he can afford; if he is interested in religion or politics, he can join whatever sect or party most attracts him. Except in the matter of marriage, he is still dependent upon organizations even when he has freedom of choice: he cannot, unless he is a very exceptional man, found a religion, create a party, organize a football club, or make his own drinks. What he can do is to choose among ready-made alternatives; but competition tends to make all these alternatives as attractive as possible, within what economic conditions permit.

So far, the effect of the organizations characteristic of civilized societies is to increase a man's liberty as compared with (say) a peasant in a comparatively undeveloped community. Consider the life of a Chinese peasant, as compared with that of an Occidental wage-earner. As a child, it is true, he does not have to go to school, but from a very early age he has to work. He is more likely than not to die in early childhood, from hardship and lack of medical care. If he survives, he has no choice as to his means of livelihood, unless he is prepared to become a soldier or a bandit, or to run the risk of migrating to some large town. Custom deprives him of all but a minimum of freedom as to marriage. Of leisure he has practically none, and if he had it there would be nothing very pleasant to do with it. He lives always on the margin of subsistence, and in times of famine a large part of his family is likely to die of hunger. And hard as life is for the man, it is far harder for the wife and daughters. Even the most depressed of the unemployed, in England, have a life which is almost a paradise in comparison with that of the average Chinese peasant.

To come to another class of organizations, those designed to prevent a man from doing injury to others: the most important of these are the police and the criminal law. In so far as these interfere with crimes of violence, such as murder, robbery, and assault, they increase the freedom and happiness of all but a small minority of exceptionally ferocious individuals. Where the police are not in control, gangs of marauders quickly establish a reign of terror, which makes most of the pleasures of civilized life impossible for all except the gangsters. There is, of course, a danger: it is possible for the police themselves to become gangsters, or at any rate to establish some form of tyranny. This danger is by no means imaginary, but the methods of coping with it are well known. There is also the danger that the police may be used by the holders of power to prevent or obstruct movements in favour of desirable reforms. That this should happen to some extent, seems almost inevitable. It is a part of the fundamental difficulty that the measures which are necessary to prevent anarchy are such as make it more difficult to change the *status quo* when it ought to be changed. In spite of this difficulty, few members of civilized communities would think it possible to dispense wholly with the police.

So far, we have taken no account of war and revolution or the fear of them. These involve the State's instinct of self-preservation, and lead to the most drastic forms of control over individual lives. In almost all Continental countries, there is universal compulsory military service. Everywhere, when war breaks out, every male of military age can be called upon to fight, and every adult can be ordered to do the work that the government thinks most conducive to victory. Those whose activities are thought helpful to the enemy are liable to the death penalty. In time of peace, all governments take steps— some more drastically, others less so—to insure willingness to fight when the moment comes, and loyalty to the national cause at all times. Government action in the matter of revolution varies according to the degree of likelihood of it. Other things being equal, the risk of revolution will be greater where government cares little for the welfare of the citizens. But where, as in totali-tarian States, the government has a monopoly, not only of physical coercion, but of moral and economic persuasion, it can go further in disregard of citi-zens than is possible for a less intensive government, since revolutionary sentiment is less easy to propagate and to organize. It is therefore to be ex-pected that, in so far as the State is distinct from the body of the citizens, every increase in its power will make it more indifferent to their welfare.

From the above brief survey it seems to result that, in the main, the effects of organizations, apart from those resulting from governmental self-preserva-tion, are such as to increase individual happiness and well-being. Education, health, productivity of labour, provision against destitution, are matters as to which, in principle, there should be no dispute; and all of them depend upon a very high degree of organization. But when we come to measures intended to prevent revolution or defeat in war, the matter is different. However necessary such measures may be deemed to be, their effects are unpleasant, and they can only be defended on the ground that revolution or defeat would be still more unpleasant. The difference is perhaps only one of degree. It may be said that vaccination, education, and roadmaking are unpleasant, but less so than smallpox, ignorance, and impassable morasses. The difference of degree is, however, so great as to amount almost to a difference in kind. More-over the unpleasantness of the measures involved in peaceful progress need not be more than temporary. Smallpox could be stamped out, and vaccination would then become unnecessary. Education and road-making could both be made fairly agreeable by the employment of enlightened methods. But every technical advance makes war more painful and more destructive, and the prevention of revolution by totalitarian methods more disastrous to humanity and intelligence.

There is another way of classifying the relations of an individual to different organizations: he may be a customer, a voluntary member, an involuntary member, or an enemy.

The organizations of which man is a customer must be thought by him to minister to his comforts, but they do not add much to his feeling of power. He may, of course, be mistaken in his good opinion of their services: the pills he buys may be useless, the beer may be bad, the race-meeting an occasion for losing money to bookmakers. Nevertheless, even in such cases, he gains *something* from the organizations that he patronizes: hope, amusement, and the sense of personal initiative. The prospect of buying a new car gives a man something to think and talk about. On the whole, freedom of choice as to how to spend money is a source of pleasure—affection for one's own furniture, for example, is a very strong and very widespread emotion, which would not exist if the State supplied us all with furnished apartments.

The organizations of which man is a voluntary member include political parties, Churches, clubs, friendly societies, enterprises in which he has invested money, and so on. Many of these are faced by enemy organizations belonging to the same categories: rival political parties, dissident Churches, competing business enterprises, and so on. The resulting contests give to those who are interested in them a sense of drama as well as an outlet for power impulses. Except where the State is weak, such contests are kept within bounds by the law, which punishes violence or gross fraud unless it is a secret accomplice. The battles between opposing organizations, when compelled by the authorities to be bloodless, afford, on the whole, a useful outlet for the feelings of pugnacity and love of power which are likely, otherwise, to seek more sinister forms of satisfaction. There is always the danger, if the State is lax or not impartial, that political contests may degenerate into riot, murder, and civil war. But if this danger is averted they are a wholesome element in the life of individuals and communities.

The most important organization of which a man is an involuntary member is the State. The principle of nationality, so far as it has prevailed, has, however, led to membership of a State being usually in accordance with the will of the citizen, though not due to his will.

> He might have been a Russian,
> A Frenchman, Turk, or Prussian,
> Or perhaps Italian,
> But in spite of all temptations
> To belong to other nations,
> He remains an Englishman.

Most people, given the chance to change their State, would not choose to do so, except when the State represents an alien nationality. Nothing has done more to strengthen the State than the success of the principle of nationality. Where patriotism and citizenship go hand in hand, a man's loyalty to his State usually exceeds his loyalty to voluntary organizations such as Churches and parties.

Loyalty to the State has both positive and negative motives. There is an element which is connected with love of home and family. But this would not take the forms which are taken by loyalty to the State, if it were not reinforced by the twin motives of love of power and fear of foreign aggression. The contests of States, unlike those of political parties, are all-in contests. The whole civilized world was shocked by the kidnapping and murder of the one Lindbergh baby, but such acts, on a vast scale, are to be the commonplaces of the next war, for which we are all preparing, at the cost—in Great Britain—of more than a quarter of our income. No other organization rouses anything like the loyalty aroused by the national State. And the chief activity of the State is preparation for large-scale homicide. It is loyalty to this organization for death that causes men to endure the totalitarian State, and to risk the destruction of home and children and our whole civilization rather than submit to alien rule. Individual psychology and governmental organization have effected a tragic synthesis, from which we and our children must suffer if we continue powerless to find an issue except through disaster.

32   The Classroom As a Society

Emile Durkheim

In order to commit ourselves to collective ends, we must have above all a feeling and affection for the collectivity. Before one gives one's self to a group, he must be fond of life in a group setting. We are beginning to appreciate the gravity of our deficiency in this respect. In the last several years, we have had a new burgeoning of intermediate associations. Hence, we have all sorts of commercial and industrial organizations, scientific societies and congresses in intellectual life, and groups of students in university life. Some persons are even trying to revive, more or less in vain, the vanishing life of local communities. There is more and more talk of town decentralization and of provincial decentralization. Without passing judgment on these very uneven attempts, we are compelled to say that most of them are legal artifacts; they are not an integral part of our way of life. They are most often external arrangements that reveal a felt need for such organizations; but they are not very vital. The central fact is that they cannot become living realities unless they are willed, desired, demanded by grass-roots sentiment—in other

From Ch. 16, "The School Environment; and Teaching the Sciences" in *Moral Education*, trans. by E. K. Wilson and H. Schnurer, ed. by E. K. Wilson. Reprinted by permission of the publisher from *Moral Education* by Emile Durkheim. Copyright © 1961 by the Free Press of Glencoe, Inc. This work was first published in 1925.

words, unless the spirit of association comes alive, not only in a few educated circles, but in the deep mass of the population.

It is here, as we indicated previously, that we seem to be caught in a vicious circle. On the one hand, associations can only spring up again when the feeling for association awakens; and, on the other hand, it cannot awaken except within already existing associations. The only way of getting out of this circle is to get hold of the child when he leaves his family and enters school. It is at that moment that we can instill in him the inclination for collective life. For the school is a society, a natural group capable of branching out in derivative groupings and in all sorts of ramifications. If the child, at this decisive time, is carried along in the current of social life, the chances are strong that he will remain oriented in this way throughout his life. If he develops the habit of expressing his interests and activities in various groups, he will keep the habit in his post-school life; and then the action of the lawmaker will really be fruitful, for it will emerge from soil that education will have prepared. This is what accounts for the tremendous social significance of the school today. And this is why the nation hopes for so much in the teacher. It is not simply because of the intellectual training that he can give. What many people feel strongly is that we have here an unexcelled opportunity to exert a kind of influence on the child which nothing else can replace.

What should the school be, what should the class be, to fulfill this expectation? The entire problem consists of how to take advantage of that association in which children of the same class perforce find themselves. How to make them acquire a liking for a collective life both more extensive and impersonal than the one to which they are accustomed? There is nothing insurmountable in this problem. As a matter of fact, there is nothing more agreeable than collective life if one has had a little experience with it at an early age. It has the effect of enhancing the vitality of each individual. The child feels himself stronger, more confident, when he feels that he is not alone. There is something in all common activities that warms the heart and fortifies the will.

Religious minorities are an interesting example of the tempering of character, of the training in life that a strongly cohesive group communicates to its members. Wherever a church is in the minority it is obliged to fall back on itself, to fight against hostility or ill will from outside. There are much tighter bonds of solidarity among the faithful than when external resistance is no longer a factor and the church can function freely—a condition that brings about a loosening of the social bonds. With the religious minority, there is a backlog of solidarity, of mutual aid and comfort; there is something unifying, which sustains the faithful against the difficulties of life. That is why the tendency to suicide in given religions varies according to its minority status. There is pleasure in saying "we," rather than "I," because anyone in a position to say "we" feels behind him a support, a force on which he can count, a force that is much more intense than that upon which isolated individuals can rely. The pleasure grows in proportion as we can say "we" with more assurance and conviction.

The whole point is to give the child a taste for this pleasure and to instill in him the need for it. We will succeed the more easily because in certain respects he is much more amenable than the adult. For the greatest obstacle to this fusion, this joining of minds in a common consciousness, is the individual personality. The more decided that personality is, the more clearly its contours are outlined, the more difficult for it to merge into something other than itself. To experience the pleasure of saying "we," it is important not to enjoy saying "I" too much. At least to the extent that the idiosyncratic is emphasized, only a very complex solidarity is possible; and it implies an organization skilled enough to connect the different parts of the whole all the while leaving to each his autonomy. We do not have to inquire here how these contrasting requirements can be reconciled. We do have to realize that the problem is difficult. But for the child, there is no such problem; today, as in the past, he is suggestible and malleable. The characteristic traits of the individual have not yet asserted themselves to the point of masking the general traits of the species. Life in common requires no sacrifice of his individuality. It gives him more than it takes from him; consequently, it has much greater attractions for him. The observer has only to note the moral transformation that takes place in the child who, after a solitary upbringing in his family, enters a lively and well-organized class for the first time. He comes out of it entirely changed. He is alert, his face is expressive, he talks with animation; for the first time the child has had a tonic experience—he has known a new life far more intense than the one he knew before; he is happy with it. He is no longer supported by his own energy alone: to his own strength that of others is added. He participates in the collective life, and his whole being is enhanced. (I assume that he has not run afoul of a teacher who thinks it is his duty to make a somber business of school life. But I will come back to this point.)

To achieve this tonic effect on the child, the class must really share in a collective life. The instructor must therefore exert every effort to bring that about. Such phrases as *the class*, the *spirit of the class*, and the *honor of the class* must become something more than abstract expressions in the student's mind. Everybody knows that almost spontaneously, without anyone's intervention, every class has its own characteristic features, its ways of being, of feeling and thinking—its temperament—which persist from year to year. A class is a personal being, a genuine "individual," whose identity may be recognized several years later. When one says of a class that it is good or bad, that it has a good or bad spirit, that it has warmth or life, or that on the contrary it is dull and dead, it is the collective individuality that is being judged and qualified. What gives it this character are the conditions under which it is recruited and the extent to which it is morally and intellectually homogeneous; a class is altogether different depending on whether its members have a common background or, on the contrary, quite different ones— e.g., classes in elementary mathematics. The collective life, which comes into being by itself and which results from the exchange of ideas and sentiments among associated children, takes shape haphazardly. Such a community could arise just as easily on the basis of undesirable sentiments as on the basis of precise ideas and good habits. It is the teacher's responsibility to direct it into normal channels. How should he go about it?

It is a fact, and one resulting from what we have just said, that we must be on our guard in thinking that the class can be molded and fashioned at will. A teacher can no more make the temper of a class than a king can fashion that of a nation. As we have just shown, the composition of a class partly determines its character. Although each of the classes that passes through the hands of the same teacher reflects his influence, they nevertheless differ from each other. There is an entirely spontaneous collective life that cannot be created out of whole cloth and that nothing can replace.

The role of the teacher, although thus limited, is very important: he directs the class. His task is above all to multiply the circumstances in which a free elaboration of common ideas and sentiments can take place, to bring out the positive results, to co-ordinate them, and give them stable shape. Preventing the spread of destructive sentiments; discouraging their expression; re-enforcing wholesome ones with the full weight of his authority, by taking advantage of all the incidents of school life; awakening them in such a manner that they become crystallized and durable—these are the procedures he may use. In a word, he must lie in wait for everything that causes the children of a given class to sense their unity in a common enterprise. The opportunities to achieve this goal are abundantly present if we watch for them. It may be a common emotion that grips the class upon reading a touching piece. It may be a judgment passed on some historical character or event after general discussion of its moral value and social bearing. It may be a common impulse of esteem or blame, which any of a thousand events in everyday life may suggest—reprehensible or praiseworthy behavior. It has been suggested that the class itself could become a sort of court, which would judge the conduct of its members with the teacher acting only as the chief justice. The idea is not compatible with the dominant role that the teacher must play in the moral life of the school. On the other hand, a class in which justice is dispensed by the teacher alone, without securing the support of the group, would be like a society in which the judges render sentence against actions that the public does not condemn. Such judgments would lack both influence and authority. The teacher must gain the support of the class when he punishes or rewards.

Clearly, there are many sources of the collective life of a class. But if the emotions of all sorts that thus pervade this small group disappear as fast as they are felt, the collective life would immediately be too chaotic and un-

stable to have any impact on the child. Therefore, it is well for the collective
sentiments of the class not to remain at the level of fugitive impressions, producing no ties between the students and lacking any sequel. Something of
them must remain, something durable, something that recalls them. In the
ideas evoked by a historical narration or an event in the life of the school,
there is always something that transcends the particular case. There is a
general conclusion to draw. It must be drawn, and it must be impressed on
the group. If this is done, the child will have the feeling that he sees here,
not a series of unconnected incidents, but a consistent and unified life. At
the same time, he will acquire the eminently social habit of emulating in the
future types of conduct or ways of thinking worked out collectively. It is thus
that in adult society collective sentiments are crystallized in the form of popular proverbs, apothegms, and moral or legal maxims. Similarly, each class
should have its little code of precepts, worked out in the course of everyday
life—a sort of condensed summary of its collective experiences. In the turn
of these maxims, quite naturally, the spirit of the teacher and the spirit of the
class would stand revealed, as the spirit of a people is revealed by its laws,
its familiar precepts, its proverbs, and so on.

Another means that could awaken in the child the feeling of solidarity
is the very discreet and deliberate use of collective punishments and rewards.
Such a proposition, it is true, encounters certain prejudices. It seems to be
agreed that all responsibility must necessarily be individual. However, strictly
individual responsibility is only justified as long as the individual is completely and solely the author of his action. In fact, it is nearly impossible that
the community of which we are a part should not have a smaller or greater
share in what we do. Thus, it is impossible that it be free of responsibility
for the actions of the individual. Neither our temperament nor the ideas and
habits that our education have inculcated in us are strictly our own. It cannot
be said, then, that collective responsibility is a thing of the past, an archaic
conception never to be revived. On the contrary, it is important that the
group be conscious of its responsibility for the morality of its members. What
is true of civil society is equally applicable to the classroom. It would even
seem that, because of the smaller scale of the school society and the resulting
closeness of each person to every other, phenomena of social contagion should
be more intense here than in other situations. There are many actions in the
school that result from the general situation and are not attributable to any
one person in particular. There are times when a class is particularly restive,
showing a general impatience of all discipline. That impatience often shows
most markedly in those least responsible for initiating it. The excitement
reverberates through the students and is amplified and exaggerated through
them, although they did nothing to start it. They are the prime targets of
punishment, although they are not the most guilty. Conversely, there is such
a thing as a general atmosphere of moral health, which contributes to the
development of good students although they themselves do not personally
deserve the entire credit. Everybody contributes to the whole. Normally,

therefore, collective sanctions play a very important part in the life of the classroom. What is the most powerful means to instill in children the feeling of solidarity that binds them to their companions, a sense of sharing in a common life? Nothing can draw them out of their narrow individualism as much as making them feel that the value of each is a function of the worth of all; and that our actions are at the same time causes and consequences, which transcend the sphere of our individual personalities. There is no better way of instilling the feeling that we are not self-sufficient, but a part of a whole that envelops, penetrates, and supports us.

Once acknowledged, this principle demands that we apply it with restraint and judgment. We cannot, of course, discriminate between individual and collective responsibility for every misdeed. Collective responsibility is reduced to very little in each particular act isolated from all the others. In reality it is felt only in the whole pattern of actions performed by everybody during a given period of time—in the general temper of the class. To evaluate it one must set up, as it were, a moral balance sheet at regular intervals, not for such and such an individual, but for the class taken collectively. We must judge it as a whole and impose appropriate sanctions. For example, the teacher might make an inventory of everything accomplished—good and bad —during the week, sum up notes and observations made from day to day; and, on the general impression that emerges from this summary he could grant or withhold certain rewards from the entire class—a game everyone enjoys, an exceptional type of recreation or reading, a desirable trip, etc. A reward would go to everyone without any distinction between individuals since everyone had earned it. I am not here inquiring into the detailed rules that apply to this evaluation—how to assess the seriousness or the frequency of good or bad behavior. Experience will easily take care of that. The important thing is for the child to realize clearly that to a certain extent he is working for everybody and everybody is working for him. The availability of collective rewards helps us in the solution of a problem of schoolroom casuistry that often plagues the conscience of the teacher: namely, whether to punish an entire class for the misdeed of a single person when that person is unknown. To allow that misdeed to go unpunished is a serious thing; to punish innocent people is cruelty. Nothing is more natural than to withhold a gratification that is justified only when things go well. The denial of collective rewards is the best sanction against anonymous offenses.

Common ideas, common feeling, common responsibilities—we have enough here to nurture the collective life of the class. But a class is a group of young people of the same age and generation. Society, on the contrary, comprises a plurality of generations superimposed on each other and connected with each other. When we start life we find already established and all around us a complex of ideas, beliefs, and behaviors, which others have acknowledged and practiced before us. These are the legacy of our forebears and will not change very much in the course of our lives. In this matter we are bound, not only to our contemporaries, but to those who came before us;

and we have the feeling that there is an impersonal force beyond us, one which took shape before we were born, which will outlast us, and which dominates us; and that force is society. Without this feeling of the bond thus joining generation to generation—sense of continuity that makes of each generation a phase in the development of the collective being—social solidarity would be singularly precarious, since its life would not, perforce, outlast that of a single man, and since it would have to be renewed with each generation. Therefore, it would be well for the child if, upon entering the class, he realized that the group of which he is a member is not a mere improvisation just sprung into being from the time of his arrival. He should be made aware of the legacy of those who preceded him. Collections of the best work done in the class by students in past years would be one of the best ways of giving each class an identification with the past and some sense of continuity. In the same manner it would be well to record and collect all the unusual awards, all the exceptional actions, and all the special celebrations that have taken place in the past. In short, each class would have its history, would learn that it has a past and the meaning of that past. For the same reason, each teacher would have to know the history of the class he is taking over—the students and the events that marked its past. Thus, the child would not feel at the end of each year that a bond is severed and, at the beginning of each year, that an altogether new one is being created, which will itself only last for a time. He would feel that the entire school, the succession of classes through which he passes, forms a continuous whole and a coherent moral environment, enveloping and sustaining him and re-enforcing his sense of solidarity.

It is true that, to forestall discontinuity in school life, it has been suggested that a given teacher should continue with the same class. Indeed, this practice is followed in a number of places. We have gone over its disadvantages and dangers. The authority of the teacher is too great to allow children to be exposed to the influence of one and the same teacher throughout the course of their studies. It is important that the diversity of teachers succeeding each other prevent the influence of any one from being too exclusive and therefore too restricting to the individuality of the child.

But it is also important that these successive influences do not cancel each other. To some degree, it is necessary to establish a bond between them, to instill in the child a sense of the continuity of that influence, diverse though it is, to which he is exposed. It is especially the principal of the school who must insure this continuity. Not that he must do the entire job himself, in an authoritarian manner—just as the teacher does not have the entire job of fashioning the spirit of the classroom. However, he must put the teachers in contact with each other to prevent them from acting autonomously rather than in concert. In brief, the principal is responsible for the spirit and the moral unity of the school, as the teacher is responsible for the spirit and moral unity of the class.

Thus, the school possesses everything it needs to awaken in the child the feeling of solidarity, of group life. If this collective life were to end abruptly upon leaving the closely knit school society, the person's sense of social solidarity would be jeopardized in the context of the larger society. Fortunately, in recent times school groups have felt a need to carry on beyond school life itself, to continue into the life of adult groups. We now have alumni activities of all sorts, in which recent and former graduates get together and take part in a common life. Not only are they wholesome civic organizations, but they are invaluable in providing for the child encouragement, stimulation, and protection from the depressing influence of moral isolation. Generally speaking, everything that can multiply contacts between successive generations—which is what alumni organizations do—is of the greatest social service. Indeed, every generation has its own spirit, its own way of thinking and feeling, its own needs, and its special aspirations. We have a fact here whose causes are as yet not well known, but an indisputable fact, nonetheless. There are linguistic changes in each generation, changes in fashion, in aesthetic appreciation, and in philosophical views. A cosmopolitan generation is succeeded by a very nationalistic generation, or vice versa. Optimism follows pessimism. Anarchism follows religious dogmatism, and so on. Such moral discontinuity between generations runs the risk of giving social evolution a jerky and erratic character, promoting chaotic impulses, if precautions are not taken to bring differing generations together as soon and as completely as possible, so as to encourage their interpenetration and so closing the moral gaps between them.

A Deviant Society   33

Richard A. Cloward
and Lloyd E. Ohlin

As we have noted, there appear to be three major types of delinquent subculture typically encountered among adolescent males in lower-class areas of large urban centers. One is based principally upon criminal values; its members are organized primarily for the pursuit of material gain by such illegal means as extortion, fraud, and theft. In the second, violence is the keynote; its members pursue status ("rep") through the manipulation of force or threat of force. These are the "warrior" groups that attract so much attention in the press. Finally, there are subcultures which emphasize the consumption

From Ch. 1, "Delinquent Subcultures" with most footnotes omitted and from Ch. 5, "The Evolution of Delinquent Subcultures" with footnotes omitted. Reprinted by permission of the publisher from *Delinquency and Opportunity* by Richard A. Cloward and Lloyd E. Ohlin. Copyright © 1961 by the Free Press of Glencoe, Inc.

of drugs. The participants in these drug subcultures have become alienated from conventional roles, such as those required in the family or the occupational world. They have withdrawn into a restricted world in which the ultimate value consists in the "kick." We call these three subcultural forms "criminal," "conflict," and "retreatist," respectively.

These shorthand terms simply denote the *principal* orientation of each form of adaptation from the perspective of the dominant social order; although one can find many examples of subcultures that fit accurately into one of these three categories, subcultures frequently appear in somewhat mixed form. Thus members of a predominantly conflict subculture may also on occasion engage in systematic theft; members of a criminal subculture may sometimes do combat in the streets with rival gangs. But this should not obscure the fact that these subcultures tend to exhibit essentially different orientations.

The extent to which the delinquent subculture organizes and controls a participant's allegiance varies from one member to another. Some members of the gang are almost totally immersed in the perspectives of the subculture and bring them into play in all their contacts; others segregate this aspect of their lives and maintain other roles in the family, school, and church. The chances are relatively slight, however, that an adolescent can successfully segregate delinquent and conforming roles for a long period of time. Pressures emanate from the subculture leading its members to adopt unfavorable attitudes toward parents, school teachers, policemen, and other adults in the conventional world. When he is apprehended for delinquent acts, the possibility of the delinquent's maintaining distinctly separate role involvements breaks down, and he is confronted with the necessity of choosing between law-abiding and delinquent styles of life. Since family, welfare, religious, educational, law-enforcement, and correctional institutions are arrayed against the appeal of his delinquent associates, the decision is a difficult one, frequently requiring either complete acceptance or complete rejection of one or the other system of obligations.

At any one point in time, however, the extent to which the norms of the delinquent subculture control behavior will vary from one member to another. Accordingly, descriptions of these subcultures must be stated in terms of the fully indoctrinated member rather than the average member. Only in this way can the distinctiveness of delinquent styles of life be made clear. It is with this understanding that we offer the following brief empirical characterizations of the three main types of delinquent subculture.

THE CRIMINAL PATTERN

The most extensive documentation in the sociological literature of delinquent behavior patterns in lower-class culture describes a tradition which integrates youthful delinquency with adult criminality. In the central value orientation of youths participating in this tradition, delinquent and criminal behavior is accepted as a means of achieving success-goals. The dominant criteria of in-group evaluation stress achievement, the use of skill and knowledge to get results. In this culture, prestige is allocated to those who achieve material gain and power through avenues defined as illegitimate by the larger society. From the very young to the very old, the successful "haul"—which quickly transforms the penniless into a man of means—is an ever-present vision of the possible and desirable. Although one may also achieve material success through the routine practice of theft or fraud, the "big score" remains the symbolic image of quick success.

The means by which a member of a criminal subculture achieves success are clearly defined for the aspirant. At a young age, he learns to admire and respect older criminals and to adopt the "right guy" as his role-model. Delinquent episodes help him to acquire mastery of the techniques and orientation of the criminal world and to learn how to cooperate successfully with others in criminal enterprises. He exhibits hostility and distrust toward representatives of the larger society. He regards members of the conventional world as "suckers," his natural vicitms, to be exploited when possible. He sees successful people in the conventional world as having a "racket"—e.g., big businessmen have huge expense accounts, politicians get graft, etc. This attitude successfully neutralizes the controlling effect of conventional norms. Toward the in-group the "right guy" maintains relationships of loyalty, honesty, and trustworthiness. He must prove himself reliable and dependable in his contacts with his criminal associates although he has no such obligations toward the out-group of noncriminals.

One of the best ways of assuring success in the criminal world is to cultivate appropriate "connections." As a youngster, this means running with a clique composed of other "right guys" and promoting an apprenticeship or some other favored relationship with older and successful offenders. Close and dependable ties with income-producing outlets for stolen goods, such as the wagon peddler, the junkman, and the fence, are especially useful. Furthermore, these intermediaries encourage and protect the young delinquent in a criminal way of life by giving him a jaundiced perspective on the private morality of many functionaries in conventional society. As he matures, the young delinquent becomes acquainted with a new world made up of predatory bondsmen, shady lawyers, crooked policemen, grafting politicians, dishonest businessmen, and corrupt jailers. Through "connections" with occupants of these half-legitimate, half-illegitimate roles and with "big shots" in the underworld, the aspiring criminal validates and assures his freedom of movement in a world made safe for crime.

THE CONFLICT PATTERN

The role-model in the conflict pattern of lower-class culture is the "bopper" who swaggers with his gang, fights with weapons to win a wary respect from other gangs, and compels a fearful deference from the conventional adult world by his unpredictable and destructive assaults on persons and property. To other gang members, however, the key qualities of the bopper are those of the successful warrior. His performance must reveal a willingness to defend his personal integrity and the honor of the gang. He must do this with great courage and displays of fearlessness in the face of personal danger.

The immediate aim in the world of fighting gangs is to acquire a reputation for toughness and destructive violence. A "rep" assures not only respectful behavior from peers and threatened adults but also admiration for the physical strength and masculinity which it symbolizes. It represents a way of securing access to the scarce resources for adolescent pleasure and opportunity in underprivileged areas.

Above all things, the bopper is valued for his "heart." He does not "chicken out," even when confronted by superior force. He never defaults in the face of a personal insult or a challenge to the integrity of his gang. The code of the bopper is that of the warrior who places great stress on courage, the defense of his group, and the maintenance of honor.

Relationships between bopping gang members and the adult world are severely attenuated. The term that the bopper uses most frequently to characterize his relationships with adults is "weak." He is unable to find appropriate role-models that can designate for him a structure of opportunities leading to adult success. He views himself as isolated and the adult world as indifferent. The commitments of adults are to their own interests and not to his. Their explanations of why he should behave differently are "weak," as are their efforts to help him.

Confronted by the apparent indifference and insincerity of the adult world, the ideal bopper seeks to win by coercion the attention and opportunities he lacks and cannot otherwise attract. In recent years the street-gang worker who deals with the fighting gang on its own "turf" has come to symbolize not only a recognition by conventional adult society of the gang's toughness but also a concession of opportunities formerly denied. Through the alchemy of competition between gangs, this gesture of attention by the adult world to the "worst" gangs is transformed into a mark of prestige. Thus does the manipulation of violence convert indifference into accommodation and attention into status.

THE RETREATIST PATTERN

Retreatism may include a variety of expressive, sensual, or consummatory experiences, alone or in a group. In this analysis, we are interested only in those experiences that involve the use of drugs and that are supported by a subculture. We have adopted these limitations in order to maintain our focus on subcultural formations which are clearly recognized as delinquent, as drug use by adolescents is. The retreatist preoccupation with expressive experiences creates many varieties of "hipster" cult among lower-class adolescents which foster patterns of deviant but not necessarily delinquent conduct.

Subcultural drug-users in lower-class areas perceive themselves as culturally and socially detached from the life-style and everyday preoccupations of members of the conventional world. The following characterization of the "cat" culture, observed by Finestone in a lower-class Negro area in Chicago, describes drug use in the more general context of "hipsterism." [1] Thus it should not be assumed that this description in every respect fits drug cultures found elsewhere. We have drawn heavily on Finestone's observations, however, because they provide the best descriptions available of the social world in which lower-class adolescent drug cultures typically arise.

The dominant feature of the retreatist subculture of the "cat" lies in the continuous pursuit of the "kick." Every cat has a kick—alcohol, marijuana, addicting drugs, unusual sexual experiences, hot jazz, cool jazz, or any combination of these. Whatever its content, the kick is a search for ecstatic experiences. The retreatist strives for an intense awareness of living and a sense of pleasure that is "out of this world." In extreme form, he seeks an almost spiritual and mystical knowledge that is experienced when one comes to know "it" at the height of one's kick. The past and the future recede in the time perspective of the cat, since complete awareness in present experience is the essence of the kick.

The successful cat has a lucrative "hustle" which contrasts sharply with the routine and discipline required in the ordinary occupational tasks of conventional society. The many varieties of the hustle are characterized by a rejection of violence or force and a preference for manipulating, persuading, outwitting, or "conning" others to obtain resources for experiencing the kick. The cat begs, borrows, steals, or engages in some petty con-game. He caters to the illegitimate cravings of others by peddling drugs or working as a pimp. A highly exploitative attitude toward women permits the cat to view pimping as a prestigeful source of income. Through the labor of "chicks" engaged in prostitution or shoplifting, he can live in idleness and concentrate his entire attention on organizing, scheduling, and experiencing the esthetic pleasure of the kick. The hustle of the cat is secondary to his interest in the kick. In this respect the cat differs from his fellow delinquents in the criminal subculture, for whom income-producing activity is a primary concern.

The ideal cat's appearance, demeanor, and taste can best be characterized as "cool." The cat seeks to exhibit a highly developed and sophisticated taste for clothes. In his demeanor, he struggles to reveal a self-assured and unruffled manner, thereby emphasizing his aloofness and "superiority" to the "squares." He develops a colorful, discriminating vocabulary and ritualized gestures which express his sense of difference from the conventional world and his solidarity with the retreatist subculture.

The word "cool" also best describes the sense of apartness and detachment which the retreatist experiences in his relationships with the conventional world. His reference group is the "society of cats," an "elite" group in

[1] Harold Finestone, "Cats, Kicks and Color," *Social Problems*, Vol. 5 (July 1957), pp. 3–13.

which he becomes isolated from conventional society. Within this group, a new order of goals and criteria of achievement are created. The cat does not seek to impose this system of values on the world of the squares. Instead, he strives for status and deference within the society of cats by cultivating the kick and the hustle. Thus the retreatist subculture provides avenues to success-goals, to the social admiration and the sense of well-being or oneness with the world which the members feel are otherwise beyond their reach.

.   .   .

When a social system generates severe problems of adjustment for occupants of a particular social status, it is possible that a collective challenge to the legitimacy of the established rules of conduct will emerge. As we have noted, this is especially likely to occur where a democratic ideology exists, espousing equality of opportunity and universally high aspirations for success. Since discrepancies between aspiration and opportunity are likely to be experienced more intensely at some social positions than at others, persons in status locations where the discrepancy is most acute may develop a common perception and sense of indignation about their disadvantages as contrasted with the advantages of others. Interaction among those sharing the same problem may provide encouragement for the withdrawal of sentiments in support of the established system of norms. Once freed of allegiance to the existing set of rules, such persons may devise or adopt delinquent means of achieving success.

A collective delinquent solution to an adjustment problem is more likely to evolve by this process in a society in which the legitimacy of social rules can be questioned apart from their moral validity. For example, it would be relatively unlikely to develop in a tradition-bound, self-sufficient folk society where a complex network of closely integrated moral sentiments reinforce acceptance of the dominant norms. In such a society an intricate interweaving of sacred and secular motivations defines whatever is as right. In the secular, competitive, impersonal, mass society of the modern Western world, on the other hand, the necessity for highly specialized activities has enormously complicated the task of maintaining a cohesive and stable order. It has become more and more difficult to identify universally shared moral sentiments which will guarantee allegiance to the dominant norms of the society. The long, complex chains of relationships required to integrate the social and economic life of the society permit the development of special beliefs, values, and norms at different social locations and the dissolution of links in the established structure of beliefs, values, and norms. What seems expedient, rational, and efficient often becomes separable from what is traditional, sacred, and moral as a basis for the imputation of legitimacy. Under such conditions it is difficult for persons at different social positions to agree about the forms of conduct that are both expedient and morally right. Once this separation takes place, the supporting structure of the existing system of norms becomes highly vulnerable. When the individual defines his commitment to the dominant system of norms on the basis of expediency rather than moral validity, his sentiments may become attached to some competing set of norms more to his advantage. It is even possible that he may attribute legitimacy on the grounds of expediency to rules of conduct that he regards at the same time as morally inferior to some competing set of norms.

To understand the growth of delinquent subcultures, we must identify more explicitly the social conditions within which this alienation from established norms and acceptance of illegitimate models of behavior occurs. It seems evident that the members of a newly emerging delinquent subculture must pass through a complex process of change in attitudes toward themselves, other persons, and the established social order before such a major shift in allegiance can take place. First, they must be freed from commitment to and belief in the legitimacy of certain aspects of the existing organization of means. They must be led to question the validity of various conventional codes of conduct as an appropriate guide for their own actions before accepting a model of behavior involving forbidden acts. Secondly, they must join with others in seeking a solution to their adjustment problems rather than attempt to solve them alone. Thirdly, they must be provided with appropriate means for handling the problems of guilt and fear which new recruits to the subculture sometimes experience as a result of engaging in acts of deviance. Finally, they must face no obstacles to the possibility of joint problem-solving.

Race: A Modern Myth   34

Clyde Kluckhohn

Until recently physical anthropologists were, more than anything else, describers and classifiers of the physical varieties of man. All living types of man belong to the same species. No populations have been completely isolated reproductively since their differentiation. Throughout human history there has been exchange of genes between different varieties of man. Some authorities are convinced that even the most ancient fossil men of Java, China, and Europe represented only geographical varieties or races of the same species.

In general biology the term "race" or "variety" is used to designate a group of organisms that physically resemble one another by virtue of their descent from common ancestors. Most living species of animals are more or less clearly differentiated into geographic races. When races are separated by migration barriers, the distinction between them are definite and consistent. If two or more races come to inhabit the same territory over a long period of time, the differences are gradually erased, and the races are fused into a single population that is more variable than any of the original constituent elements.

There are undoubtedly human races. However, the make-up of breeding populations has shifted so frequently in the course of migrations that sharp demarcations are few. Moreover, human inheritance is so complex and so imperfectly known as yet that differences in visible physical features are not always sure guides to differences in ancestry. The extent of present confusion is indicated by the fact that the numbers of races distinguished by competent students range from two to two hundred. Hence, though the concept of race is genuine enough, there is perhaps no field of science in which the misunderstandings among educated people are so frequent and so serious. Racial classifications still published by certain physical anthropologists are in some respects meaningless or actually misleading in the light of contemporary knowledge about human inheritance. The significance of a sound genetic classification, if we had one, is not yet clear. The one thing certain is that in the modern world many peoples react suspiciously, defensively, or hostilely toward individuals who differ in obvious physical characteristics such as skin color, hair form, and nose shape.

Throughout human history, societies and individuals have been conscious of the differences that set them off from other societies and other individuals. Group spokesmen have been concerned to assert that their way of dressing, or marrying, or believing was intrinsically superior. Sometimes the existence of other customs has been treated as an insupportable affront to the pride of the group or the laws of its gods. This threat to the dominance of the one true way of life has stimulated wars or has, at least, provided handy rationalizations for them. Seldom, prior to the nineteenth century, however, were such differences in group habits explained as due to variations in the biological heredity of human societies.

Although ties of "blood" were certainly much invoked to support community loyalty, differences in custom were usually linked to divine gifts or instructions, to the inventions of bygone human leaders, or to other historical experiences of the group rather than to physical inheritance. In the ancient and medieval religions the idea of race had little or no place. Most of the great world religions have been deeply committed to the concept of universal brotherhood. Often this concept has included the explicit or implicit premise that brotherhood was a feasible goal because all human beings were the physical descendants of a single pair of original ancestors. The messianic religions have necessarily held the view that heathens were in error not because they were inherently inferior, but because they had known no opportunity to learn the true way.

In the past it has usually been the culturally alien rather than the biologically alien that has borne the brunt of religious as well as political antagonisms. The Bible describes vividly the drastic disillusionment resulting from marriages to non-Jews in the time of Ezra, but "blood" is treated as the secondary and accidental factor, culture as the essential. The self-isolation of the Jew in Christian Europe during the Middle Ages was more a matter of culture than of biology. Jewish motivations arose from the fervent desire to preserve intact a way of life, and especially a religion, and not from the wish to keep a line of blood unsullied—even though there were occasional references to "the seed of Abraham."

Only in the small primitive or folk society where almost everyone is in fact biologically related to almost everyone else have the primary loyalties been frequently anchored to blood kinship. In the cosmopolitan societies of the ancient world, in the nations that gradually emerged toward the close of the Middle Ages in Europe, the major shiftings of individuals and whole peoples were too numerous and too recent for any national or regional population to be victimized by the illusion of descent from common ancestors distinct from the ancestors of its neighbors.

It is true that, before the dawn of history, the Bushmen and other groups depicted the physical types of foreign peoples and that the Egyptians, three thousand years ago, pictured "the four races of man." Probably there has never been a time when any people was completely indifferent to the physical differences between itself and other peoples. But it is a historical fact that in the last hundred and fifty years awareness of these variations and emotional reactions to them have heightened enormously. The first Negroes in modern Europe were received in aristocratic households as equals; nor was intermarriage frowned upon. Certain racial classifications of the seventeenth and eighteenth centuries lumped American Indians with Europeans. Until the beginning of the nineteenth century all inhabitants of Europe, except the Lapps, were considered a single race.

Why, then, in the late nineteenth and early twentieth centuries has a naïve biologism become rampant? An underlying condition to the flowering of this new mythology was undoubtedly the tremendous advance made by biological science. Men's minds were intoxicated by the revolutionary theories of Darwin, and by the immediately practical discoveries of Mendel, Pasteur, Lister, and a host of others. Most men, and especially Americans, want simple answers. In a world where living, however joyous at times, is always precarious and happiness is always threatened by present problems and unforeseen contingencies, men lust after certainty. The absolutes of religion were weakened by the schisms within the Christian Church, on the one hand, and by historical criticism of the Bible and scientific findings, on the other. The movement was by no means complete, of course, but Western humanity tended to seek in science the security formerly supplied by religious faith. Physical science was to bring about a millennium of ease and comfort; biological science was to abolish all the ills to which flesh had been heir. The twain would rapidly answer all the riddles of the universe. What was more natural than to assume that the puzzling question of differences in the behavior of individuals and whole groups had been solved?

Prior to the mid-nineteenth century Europeans and Americans had theories that satisfied them as explanations of observed facts. The story of the sons of Noah helped to explain the presence of humans of different skin colors and general physical appearance. Other variations were dismissed as the will of God. There were no authoritative descriptions of biological mechanisms. In the seventeenth and eighteenth centuries there were many widely current speculations about the influence of climate on physique. The American Indians, for instance, were held by some to be the descendants of Phoenicians or of Welsh adventurers or of the lost tribes of Israel, with their distinctive appearance explained as having been produced by the physical environment of the New World.

The discoveries of Darwin, Mendel, and others put everything on a new footing. From the popular point of view, laws had been evolved that stated immutable and watertight connections between biological processes and all sorts of other phenomena. A magic key had been created which unlocked all previous perplexities about human behavior. Unfortunately, the step from science to mythology is short and all too attractive.

An investigation by A. M. Tozzar of a large number of contemporary biographies showed very dramatically the hold biological mythology has upon our thinking. In every case the biographer seized upon physical heredity as the explanation of the personality traits of his subject. Where no plausible ancestors were available, legends were used or invented. Perhaps the most farfetched of these was the fantasy that the true father of Abraham Lincoln was Chief Justice John Marshall.

The fact that the human beings usually acquire their physical and most of their culture heritage from their parents has helped perpetuate these beliefs. It is part of common experience that peculiar traits do "run in families," but this does necessarily prove that these traits are inherited in the genetic sense. Parents train their children by the same standards that were invoked when they were children; happy children take their parents as models. In homogeneous and relatively stable cultures, family traits may be perpetuated for generations, even though "the blood line" is broken again and again—as is evidenced by Japanese and Roman lineages where remarkable continuity of character was preserved in spite of frequent adoptions to keep the family line intact.

Misconception is also generated by the circumstance that personality development ordinarily goes on at the same time that the child is growing up physically; both types of development usually stop or at least slow up at about the same time. In general, the status of adulthood implies both physical and social maturity. Since the two forms of development occur side by side, there is a tendency to assume that both are the expression of the same process, that is, biological maturation. A human animal, however, can easily come to physical maturity without learning to speak, use table utensils, or keep himself clean. Children do not stop crying over frustration because of progressive atrophy of the tear ducts or change in the vocal cords, but because they are taught to respond in other ways. In the process of getting food, shelter, and other prerequisites for normal physical growth, most individuals encounter conditions, both social and physical, which force them to accept those responsibilities and restraints which are considered the hallmarks of socialized adults. If children become responsible adults through the operation of biological processes, home and school training is a waste of energy. Every parent and teacher knows that children do not automatically become socially mature as they mature physically.

The same exaggeration of the role of biological forces may be noted in popular notions about different peoples. Here also, the fact that "race" and life habits vary together has fostered the impression that both are due to the common cause of biological heredity. However, a closer inspection of the facts shows that this inference is untenable. Not only do Canadians, Australians, and New Zealanders show different typical personality structures from each other and from their relatives in Britain, but the British stock in the same environment has had a different character at various historical periods. Between the sixteenth and nineteenth centuries there were no successful invasions of Britain, no substantial introduction of new materials of physical heredity. And yet Franz Boas rightly contrasts "the boisterous joy of life of Elizabethan England and the prudery of the Victorian age; the transition from the rationalism of the eighteenth century to the romanticism of the beginning of the nineteenth century." In American Indian tribes where the percentage of mixed bloods is still trifling, the personality types most frequently encountered today are not all those described by writers at the time of the original contact with white men. Furthermore, it has been demonstrated again and again that a child brought up in a foreign society acquires the life ways and the characteristic personality traits of the foreign "race." If pigmentation or other physical differences are obvious, these may create special problems for him in his new social group, but where these are not conspicuous he fits in as well as the native-born.

However, this argument must not be made to explain too much. Overemphasis upon social conditioning is just as harmful and one-sided as making a magic key of biology. Nothing can be more certain than that any individual's physical characteristics resemble those of his relatives more than those of a random sample of the population at large—and obviously this resemblance cannot be due to training or to imitation. Good predictions can be made as to what proportion of the descendants of an original couple will manifest a certain physical peculiarity of the parents—provided the number involved is large. Anyone's temperamental and intellectual traits are partially determined by the genes supplied by his ancestors, but it is definitely established that these are not the only influences of importance.

As usual, however, the generalization of a scientific theory is too simply conceived and explains too much. The fact that simple questions can be put does not mean that there are simple answers. To say that physical heredity is enormously important in understanding the appearance and behavior of human beings is one thing. But it is quite another to jump from this correct statement to the implications: (*a*) that biological inheritance is the only important factor and (*b*) that one may pass easily from talking about the heredity equipment of individuals to that of groups.

Superficially, biology might seem to give scientific support to racist theories. If physical heredity admittedly sets limits to the potentialities of individuals, "isn't it just common sense to believe that the peculiarities of various groups of individuals are the consequence of their genetic equipment?" The thinking, often completely sincere, of those who follow this line of reasoning is weakened by a number of major errors. They forget that race is strictly a biological concept; they erroneously transfer what is known about individual inheritance to group inheritance; they greatly underestimate biological complexities and their interactions with nonbiological processes; they overestimate present knowledge of the mechanisms of inheritance.

To classify human beings as a race on other than a purely biological basis destroys the proper meaning of the term and removes even the support provided by the one-sided biological argument. "Aryan" is a linguistic designation. Hence "the Aryan race" is a contradiction in terms. As Max Müller remarked long ago it makes about as much sense as a "brachycephalic dictionary" or a "dolicocephalic grammar." Unless there were grounds for believing—which there most certainly are not—that all individuals who speak "Aryan" (Indo-European) languages are descendants of the same ancestors, there could be no justification for confusing linguistic and biological classifications. Similarly, nationality and "race" must not be confused. To speak of "the Italian race" is nonsense, for there is every reason to assume that the Italians of Piedmont share more ancestors with persons who are French or Swiss than they do with their fellow Italians of Sicily. "The Jewish race" is equally a misnomer because there is great diversity in physical type among those who practice or whose parents or grandparents have practiced the Jewish religion and because the physical stereotype which is popularly considered Jewish is actually common among all sorts of Levantine and Near Eastern peoples who are not and have never been Jewish.

Jews have mixed so much with the varying physical types of the different countries in which they have lived that by no single physical or physiological feature nor by any group of such features can they be distinguished as a race. Huntington regards them as a kith, like the Icelanders, the Parsis, and the Puritans. That some Jews can be identified on sight is due less to physically inherited traits, than as Jacobs says, to "those emotional and other reactions and conditionings which take the form of distinctive facial behavior, bodily posturings and mannerisms, sentence tone, and temperamental and character peculiarity" which can be traced to Jewish customs and to the treatment of Jews at the hands of non-Jews.

In the light of the biological preoccupation of our recent thinking, the naïve view that there *must* be a connection between physical type and character type is understandable. The "personality" of the poodle *is* different from that of the police dog. The temperament of the Percheron *is* different from that of the Arabian race horse.

Men are animals. But *man* is a very special kind of animal, and the transfer of observations from nonhumans to humans dare not be made so glibly. In the first place, nonhuman animals derive their character and personality mainly from their physical heredity, though domestic animals are also influenced by training. While animals learn from experience, they learn hardly more than crude survival techniques from each other. The factor of social heredity is unimportant. A diving bird brought up in complete isolation from all other birds of its species will still dive like its ancestors when released near a body of water. A Chinese boy, however, brought up in an English-speaking American household, will speak English and be awkward at using chopsticks.

And so, though the fact that nonhuman animals of similar physical appearance behave in about the same way is correctly interpreted as due mainly to their genetic relationship, the matter is not so simple when it comes to the human animal. The existence of physical stereotypes for human groups that live in the same area or speak the same language or practice the same religion is probably to be traced to the preconception that organisms that resemble each other in action ought to resemble each other in physique. In any such group there are large numbers of individuals who are closely related biologically and who approximate a certain physical norm. The lay observer focuses his attention on these similar persons and either fails even to notice the others or dismisses them as exceptions. We thus get the persistent stereotype of the Swede as blond and blue-eyed. Dark Swedes are commented upon with surprise, though, in fact, blond individuals are in the minority in a number of districts in Sweden.

Among nonhuman animals resemblance in physical appearance is a fair basis for assuming close relationship. If two dogs who look like pure Dachshunds breed, we are amazed if any of the puppies look like fox terriers, police dogs, or Airedales. But if a man and a woman whom ten competent physical anthropologists classify as "pure Mediterranean" marry, their ten children may approach in varying degrees the Mediterranean, Alpine, and Atlanto-Mediterranean types.

Wild animals ordinarily breed only with others of the same type. The lines of most domestic animals are kept pure by human control of breeding. There are exceptions, such as mongrel dogs. But virtually all human beings are mongrels! For countless thousand of years human beings have been wandering over the surface of the globe, mating with whomever opportunity afforded or fancy dictated.

The significance of physical heredity in family lines is not to be minimized. But heredity acts only in lines of direct descent, and there is no full unity of descent in any of the existing races. The observable physical types, just as the varieties of non-human animals, arose mainly as a consequence of geographic isolation. Physical differences which characterize all animal races are in large measure the product of chance samplings which took place at the time ancestral groups separated, plus accumulated variations that have occurred since the groups became isolated, plus certain inherent trends.

It should not be forgotten, furthermore, that we know much less about the details of human heredity than about animal heredity. This is due partly to the greater complexities involved, and partly to the fact that we do not experiment with human beings. Also, men mature so slowly that the statistics of ordinary matings do not accumulate as rapidly as those of laboratory animals. Since the beginnings of recorded history in Egypt there have been only 200 human generations; the mouse has had 24,000.

One difference between humans and nonhumans is the fact of preferential mating. In some societies one is expected to marry one's maternal first cousin; in others one may not marry so close a relative. But the important difference is that animal races tended to remain in geographical isolation, and did not interbreed with other races of the same species. With humans, however, continual intermixture, often among the most diverse types, has been the rule in history's broad perspective. Looking at particular societies within the framework of a narrower time span, one can indeed point to populations isolated on islands, in inaccessible valleys, or infertile deserts where inbreeding in a relatively small group has prevailed over some hundreds of years. The same has been true for royal families and other special groups. Lorenz has shown that in 12 generations the last German emperor had only 533 actual ancestors as compared with a theoretical 4,096.

Undoubtedly there are local physical types. This is true not only of populations of small islands and of peasant groups. Hooton's studies of American criminals have revealed the existence of fairly well-differentiated regional types in the United States. In such instances relative genetic homogeneity and stability have been attained. This, however, is recent. A longer time perspective shows that such homogeneity is based upon an underlying heterogeneity. If one compared the number of different ancestors such groups had during the past ten thousand years with the number of different ancestors of a horde of South American monkeys or of African zebras during the same period, the human population would prove to have drawn from a significantly larger number of genetic lines. In any case the total of such recently isolated and inbreeding populations is small. Throughout Europe, the Americas, Africa, and Asia, constant formation of new and largely unstable blends has been the keynote of the past thousand years. This means that the diversity of genetic strains in even a superficially similar population is great. It means also that outward resemblance in two or more individuals is not necessarily indicative of common descent, for the similarities may be the product of chance combinations of characters derived from an altogether different set of ancestors. Practically no one can even name all of his ancestors for seven generations. If we except connection through the dynastic line of Charlemagne, there is probably not a single European family, save the Byzantine Palaeologues and Spanish Jews such as the de Solas, that has a pedigree going back before A.D. 800.

Europeans or Americans who can place those ancestors from whom they take their family names are all too likely to underestimate ludicrously the mixed nature of their ancestry. They feel that the statement, "Oh, we come of English stock," is an adequate description of "racial affiliation." If pressed, they will admit that the recent population of England represents an amalgam of physical strains brought in by Stone Age, Bronze Age, Saxon, Dane, Norman, and other invaders. But few of us can even imagine the tremendous diversity that would be represented by the total assemblage of our ancestors, during even the past thousand years. Charles Darwin was a member of a middle-class family:

> . . . we think of his mind as a typical English mind, working in a typical English manner, yet when we come to study his pedigree we seek in vain for "purity of race." He is descended in four different lines from Irish kinglets; he is descended in as many lines from Scottish and Pictish Kings. He had Manx blood. He claims descent in at least three lines from Alfred the Great, and so links up with Anglo-Saxon blood, but he links up also in several lines with Charlemagne and the Carlovingians. He sprang also from the Saxon Emperors of Germany, as well as from Barbarossa and the Hohenstaufens. He had Norwegian blood and much Norman blood. He had descent from the Dukes of Bavaria, of Saxony, of Flanders, the Princes of Savoy, and the Kings of Italy. He had the blood in his veins of Franks, Alamans, Merovingians, Burgundians, and Longobards. He sprang in direct descent from the Hun rulers of Hungary and the Greek Emperors of Constantinople. If I recollect rightly, Ivan the Terrible provided a Russian link. There is probably not one of the races of Europe concerned in the folk wanderings which has not a share in the ancestry of Charles Darwin. If it has been possible in the case of one Englishman of this kind to show in a considerable number of lines how impure is his race, can we venture to assert that if the like knowledge were possible of attainment, we could expect greater purity of blood in any of his countrymen? [If] what we are able to show may occur by tracing an individual in historic times, have we any valid reason for supposing [this same thing] did not occur in prehistoric times, wherever physical barriers did not isolate a limited section of mankind?
> —KARL PEARSON

When I was a student in England, I used to be annoyed at advertisements in British newspapers: "Americans! Descent traced to Edward III, £100!" I felt this was another evidence of the European playing upon the gullibility of my fellow countrymen. But, if the American could name a single ancestor in an English parish registry, the chances were good that his ancestry could be traced to Edward III, or to any other Englishman living at that period who left a number of adult children in a place where records were preserved.

By the laws of chance, essentially every person whose ancestry is at least half European can include Charlemagne in his "family tree." But he is equally descended from the bandit hanged on the hill, from the half-witted serf, and from every other person living in A.D. 800 who left as many descendants as did Charlemagne. The principal difference between the family of the snob and the "lower-class" citizen is that the former has the money to pay a genealogist to trace or to fake a lineage. The amusing thing about those who maintain that "blood will tell" (over the distance of eleven centuries) is that they are usually too ignorant to realize that a man of 1948 may be able truly to claim Charlemagne as a forefather without having any trace of Charlemagne's "blood." The child gets not all but only a random assortment of the genes of the father and mother. A person could have Charlemagne as his own great-grandfather and still not have inherited a single one of Charlemagne's genes. Over more than thirty generations the betting odds are excellent that few of that fabled emperor's genes exist at all in certain localities where he has many descendants, whereas some of them may well constitute part of the genetic equipment of practically all peasants in isolated Swiss valleys.

In Darwin's time heredity was thought to be a matter of continuous aggregates of materials. A new organism's inheritance was the result of blending the total hereditary potential of the father with that of the mother. In these terms it made a little sense to believe that any descendant of Charlemagne had a portion (albeit diluted) of what had made the emperor great.

But the studies of the famous monk, Gregor Mendel, led to the discovery that each child got part and only part of the germ plasm of each parent. This meant that the children of the same parents (except multiple births formed from a single egg) had a different heredity. In fact, geneticists estimate that if a man and his wife had thousands of children no two would look exactly alike. This is because the particular heredity which a new organism gets from the two genetic lines that are crossing depends upon the accidental way in which the two germ cells exchange parts of chromosomes.

From the standpoint of the modern science of heredity (genetics), all snobbism that is supposed to be founded upon biological heredity from one or a few distant ancestors is essentially absurd. We have at present no techniques for determining all the genes an individual actually possesses. Human beings reproduce too slowly and have too few offspring to make it possible to use the methods that have been successfully applied to establishing genetic charts for other animals. With men we must go entirely by the appearance of the organism, if we wish to assign the individual to a race. In non-human animals this gives good results in practice. But the human beings of the great peoples and nations of the contemporary world have had ancestors of too diverse physical strains to make it likely that classifications on the basis of similarities in appearance correspond to the true genetic picture.

Human populations are too mongrel and too variable to be grouped into races as meaningful as animal varieties. A classification on the basis of their genes is not yet possible. The classifications by appearance are not consistent. There are almost as many different groupings as there are physical anthropologists. The difficulties physical anthropologists have in reaching agreement on race classification is testimony that the data do not fall neatly and nicely into line as they ought to do if they truly represent an order in nature. Of course in all biological classifications there are some borderline instances and some disagreements among specialists as to what the standards for a separate variety, species, or genus should be. Among anthropologists one too often gets the impression that almost every case is a borderline case; and, even when there is agreement as to standards, there is dispute as to whether a given individual or group of individuals meet them. With some qualifications and exceptions, one may say that, if all living people were ranged in a single sequence according to degree of resemblance, there would be no sharp breaks in the line but rather a continuum where each specimen differed from the next by almost imperceptible variation.

Prejudice 35

Gordon Allport

In Rhodesia a white truck driver passed a group of idle natives and muttered, "They're lazy brutes." A few hours later he saw natives heaving two-hundred pound sacks of grain onto a truck, singing in rhythm to their work. "Savages," he grumbled. "What do you expect?"

In one of the West Indies it was customary at one time for natives to hold their noses conspicuously whenever they passed an American on the street. And in England, during the war, it was said, "The only trouble with the Yanks is that they are over-paid, over-sexed, and over here."

Polish people often called the Ukrainians "reptiles" to express their contempt for a group they regarded as ungrateful, revengeful, wily, and treacherous. At the same time Germans called their neighbors to the east "Polish cattle." The Poles retaliated with "Prussian swine"—a jibe at the presumed uncouthness and lack of honor of the Germans.

From Ch. 1, "What is the Problem?" and Ch. 2, "The Normality of Prejudgment," with some footnotes omitted. From G. W. Allport, *The Nature of Prejudice*, 1954, Addison-Wesley, Reading, Mass. Reprinted by permission.

In South Africa, the English, it is said, are against the Afrikaner; both are against the Jews; all three are opposed to the Indians; while all four conspire against the native black.

In Boston, a dignitary of the Roman Catholic Church was driving along a lonesome road on the outskirts of the city. Seeing a small Negro boy trudging along, the dignitary told his chauffeur to stop and give the boy a lift. Seated together in the back of the limousine, the cleric, to make conversation, asked, "Little Boy, are you a Catholic?" Wide-eyed with alarm, the boy replied, "No sir, it's bad enough being colored without being one of those things."

Pressed to tell what Chinese people really think of Americans, a Chinese student reluctantly replied, "Well, we think they are the best of the foreign devils." This incident occurred before the Communist revolution in China. Today's youth in China are trained to think of Americans as the *worst* of the foreign devils.

In Hungary, the saying is, "An anti-Semite is a person who hates the Jews more than is absolutely necessary."

No corner of the world is free from group scorn. Being fettered to our respective cultures, we, like Charles Lamb, are bundles of prejudice.

TWO CASES

An anthropologist in his middle thirties had two young children, Susan and Tom. His work required him to live for a year with a tribe of American Indians in the home of a hospitable Indian family. He insisted, however, that his own family live in a community of white people several miles distant from the Indian reservation. Seldom would he allow Tom and Susan to come to the tribal village, though they pleaded for the privilege. And on rare occasions when they made the visit, he sternly refused to allow them to play with the friendly Indian children.

Some people, including a few of the Indians, complained that the anthropologist was untrue to the code of his profession—that he was displaying race prejudice.

The truth is otherwise. This scientist knew that tuberculosis was rife in the tribal village, and that four of the children in the household where he lived had already died of the disease. The probability of infection for his own children, if they came much in contact with the natives, was high. His better judgment told him that he should not take the risk. In this case, his ethnic avoidance was based on rational and realistic grounds. There was no feeling of antagonism involved. The anthropologist had no generally negative attitude toward the Indians. In fact he liked them very much.

Since this case fails to illustrate what we mean by racial or ethnic prejudice, let us turn to another.

In the early summer season two Toronto newspapers carried between them holiday advertisements from approximately 100 different resorts. A Canadian social scientist, S. L. Wax, undertook an interesting experiment. To each of these hotels and resorts he wrote two letters, mailing them at the same time, and asking for room reservations for exactly the same dates. One letter he signed with the name "Mr. Greenberg," the other with the name "Mr. Lockwood." Here are the results:

To "Mr. Greenberg":
    52 percent of the resorts replied;
    36 percent offered him accommodations.
To "Mr. Lockwood":
    95 percent of the resorts replied;
    93 percent offered him accommodations.

Thus, nearly all of the resorts in question welcomed Mr. Lockwood as a correspondent and as a guest; but nearly half of them failed to give Mr. Greenberg the courtesy of a reply, and only slightly more than a third were willing to receive him as a guest.

None of the hotels knew "Mr. Lockwood" or "Mr. Greenberg." For all they knew "Mr. Greenberg" might be a quiet, orderly gentleman, and "Mr. Lockwood" rowdy and drunk. The decision was obviously made not on the merits of the individual, but on "Mr. Greenberg's" supposed membership in a group.

Unlike our first case, this incident contains the two essential ingredients of ethnic prejudice. (1) There is definite hostility and rejection. The majority of the hotels wanted nothing to do with "Mr. Greenberg." (2) The basis of the rejection was categorical. "Mr. Greenberg" was not evaluated as an individual. Rather, he was condemned on the basis of his presumed group membership.

A close reasoner might at this point ask the question: What basic difference exists between the cases of the anthropologist and the hotels in the matter of "categorical rejection?" Did not the anthropologist reason from the high probability of infection that it would be safer not to risk contact between his children and the Indians? And did not the hotelkeepers reason from a high probability that Mr. Greenberg's ethnic membership would in fact bring them an undesirable guest? The anthropologist knew that tubercular contagion was rampant; did not the innkeepers know that "Jewish vices" were rampant and not to be risked?

This question is legitimate. If the innkeepers were basing their rejection on facts (more accurately, on a high probability that a given Jew will have undesirable traits), their action would be as rational and defensible as the anthropologist's. But we can be sure that such is not the case.

Some managers may never have had any unpleasant experiences with Jewish guests—a situation that seems likely in view of the fact that in many cases Jewish guests had never been admitted to the hotels. Or, if they have had such experiences, they have not kept a record of their frequency in comparison with objectionable non-Jewish guests. Certainly they have not consulted scientific studies concerning the relative frequency of desirable and undesirable traits in Jews and non-Jews. If they sought such evidence, they would, as we shall learn in Chapter 6, find no support for their policy of rejection.

It is, of course, possible that the manager himself was free from personal prejudice, but, if so, he was reflecting the anti-Semitism of his gentile guests. In either event our point is made.

DEFINITION

The word *prejudice*, derived from the Latin noun *praejudicium*, has, like most words, undergone a change of meaning since classical times. There are three stages in the transformation.

1. To the ancients, *praejudicium* meant a *precedent*—a judgment based on previous decisions and experiences.
2. Later, the term, in English, acquired the meaning of a judgment formed before due examination and consideration of the facts—a premature or hasty judgment.
3. Finally the term acquired also its present emotional flavor of favorableness or unfavorableness that accompanies such a prior and unsupported judgment.

Perhaps the briefest of all definitions of prejudice is: *thinking ill of others without sufficient warrant*. This crisp phrasing contains the two essential ingredients of all definitions—reference to unfounded judgment and to a feeling-tone. It is, however, too brief for complete clarity.

In the first place, it refers only to *negative* prejudice. People may be prejudiced in favor of others; they may think *well* of them without sufficient warrant. The wording offered by the New English Dictionary recognizes positive as well as negative prejudice:

A feeling, favorable or unfavorable, toward a person or thing, prior to, or not based on, actual experience.

While it is important to bear in mind that biases may be *pro* as well as *con*, it is none the less true that *ethnic* prejudice is mostly negative. A group of students was asked to describe their attitudes toward ethnic groups. No suggestion was made that might lead them toward negative reports. Even so, they reported eight times as many antagonistic attitudes as favorable attitudes. In this volume, accordingly, we shall be concerned chiefly with prejudice *against*, not with prejudice *in favor of*, ethnic groups.

The phrase "thinking ill of others" is obviously an elliptical expression that must be understood to include feelings of scorn or dislike, of fear and aversion, as well as various forms of antipathetic conduct: such as talking against people, discriminating against them, or attacking them with violence.

Similarly, we need to expand the phrase "without sufficient warrant." A judgment is unwarranted whenever it lacks basis in fact. A wit defined prejudice as "being down on something you're not up on."

It is not easy to say how much fact is required in order to justify a judgment. A prejudiced person will almost certainly claim that he has sufficient warrant for his views. He will tell of bitter experiences he has had with refugees, Catholics, or Orientals. But, in most cases, it is evident that his facts are scanty and strained. He resorts to a selective sorting of his own few memories, mixes them up with hearsay, and overgeneralizes. No one can possibly know *all* refugees, Catholics, or Orientals. Hence any negative judgment of these groups *as a whole* is, strictly speaking, an instance of thinking ill without sufficient warrant.

Sometimes, the ill-thinker has no first-hand experience on which to base his judgment. A few years ago most Americans thought exceedingly ill of Turks—but very few had ever seen a Turk nor did they know any person who had seen one. Their warrant lay exclusively in what they had heard of the Armenian massacres and of the legendary crusades. On such evidence they presumed to condemn all members of a nation.

Ordinarily, prejudice manifests itself in dealing with individual members of rejected groups. But in avoiding a Negro neighbor, or in answering "Mr. Greenberg's" application for a room, we frame our action to accord with our categorical generalization of the group as a whole. We pay little or no attention to individual differences, and overlook the important fact that Negro X, our neighbor, is not Negro Y, whom we dislike for good and sufficient reason; that Mr. Greenberg, who may be a fine gentleman, is not Mr. Bloom, whom we have good reason to dislike.

So common is this process that we might define prejudice as:

an avertive or hostile attitude toward a person who belongs to a group, simply because he belongs to that group, and is therefore presumed to have the objectionable qualities ascribed to the group.

This definition stresses the fact that while ethnic prejudice in daily life is ordinarily a matter of dealing with individual people it also entails an unwarranted idea concerning a group as a whole.

We can never hope to draw a hard and fast line between "sufficient" and "insufficient" warrant. For this reason we cannot always be sure whether we are dealing with a case of prejudice or nonprejudice. Yet no one will deny that often we form judgments on the basis of scant, even nonexistent, probabilities.

Overcategorization is perhaps the commonest trick of the human mind. Given a thimbleful of facts we rush to make generalizations as large as a tub.

One young boy developed the idea that all Norwegians were giants because he was impressed by the gigantic stature of Ymir in the saga, and for years was fearful lest he meet a living Norwegian. A certain man happened to know three Englishmen personally and proceeded to declare that the whole English race had the common attributes that he observed in these three.

There is a natural basis for this tendency. Life is so short, and the demands upon us for practical adjustments so great, that we cannot let our ignorance detain us in our daily transactions. We have to decide whether objects are good or bad by classes. We cannot weigh each object in the world by itself. Rough and ready rubrics, however coarse and broad, have to suffice.

Not every overblown generalization is a prejudice. Some are simply *misconceptions,* wherein we organize wrong information. One child had the idea that all people living in Minneapolis were "monopolists." And from his father he had learned that monopolists were evil folk. When in later years he discovered the confusion, his dislike of dwellers in Minneapolis vanished.

Here we have the test to help us distinguish between ordinary errors of prejudgment and prejudice. If a person is capable of rectifying his erroneous judgments in the light of new evidence he is not prejudiced. *Prejudgments become prejudices only if they are not reversible when exposed to new knowledge.* A prejudice, unlike a simple misconception, is actively resistant to all evidence that would unseat it. We tend to grow emotional when a prejudice is threatened with contradiction. Thus the difference between ordinary prejudgments and prejudice is that one can discuss and rectify a prejudgment without emotional resistance.

Taking these various considerations into account, we may now attempt a final definition of negative ethnic prejudice—one that will serve us throughout this book. Each phrase in the definition represents a considerable condensation of the points we have been discussing:

Ethnic prejudice is an antipathy based upon a faulty and inflexible generalization. It may be felt or expressed. It may be directed toward a group as a whole, or toward an individual because he is a member of that group.

The net effect of prejudice, thus defined, is to place the object of prejudice at some disadvantage not merited by his own misconduct.

IS PREJUDICE A VALUE CONCEPT?

Some authors have introduced an additional ingredient into their definitions of prejudice. They claim that attitudes are prejudiced only if they violate some important norms or values accepted in a culture.[1, 2] They insist that

[1] CF. R. M. Williams, Jr., "The Reduction of Intergroup Tensions," New York, *Social Science Research Council,* 1947, Bulletin 57, p. 37.

[2] H. S. Dyer, "The Usability of the Concept 'Prejudice'" *Psychometrika,* 1945, 10, pp. 219–224.

prejudice is only that type of prejudgment that is ethically disapproved in a society.

If we use the term in this sense we should have to say that the older caste system in India—which is now breaking down—involved no prejudice. It was simply a convenient stratification in the social structure, acceptable to nearly all citizens because it clarified the division of labor and defined social prerogatives. It was for centuries acceptable even to the untouchables because the religious doctrine of reincarnation made the arrangement seem entirely just. An untouchable was ostracized because in previous existences he failed to merit promotions to a higher caste or to a supermortal existence. He now has his just deserts and likewise an opportunity through an obedient and spiritually directed life to win advancement in future reincarnations. Assuming that this account of a happy caste system really marked Hindu society at one time, was there then no question of prejudice?

Or take the Ghetto system. Through long stretches of history Jews have been segregated in certain residential zones, sometimes with a chain around the region. Only inside were they allowed to move freely. The method had the merit of preventing unpleasant conflict, and the Jew, knowing his place, could plan his life with a certain definiteness and comfort. It could be argued that his lot was much more secure and predictable than in the modern world. There were periods in history when neither the Jew nor gentile felt particularly outraged by the system. Was prejudice then absent?

Even today, in certain states, a *modus vivendi* has been worked out between white and colored people. A ritual of relations is established, and most people abide unthinkingly by the realities of social structure. Since they merely follow the folkways they deny that they are prejudiced. The Negro simply knows his place, and white people know theirs. Shall we then say, as some writers have, that prejudice exists only when actions are *more* condescending, *more* negative, than the accepted culture itself prescribes? Is prejudice to be regarded merely as deviance from common practice?

What shall we say about this line of argument? It has impressed some critics so much that they hold the whole problem of prejudice to be nothing more than a value-judgment invented by "liberal intellectuals."

These critics, it would seem, confuse two separate and distinct problems. Prejudice in the simple psychological sense of negative, overgeneralized judgment exists just as surely in caste societies, slave societies, or countries believing in witchcraft as in ethically more sensitive societies. The second problem —whether prejudice is or is not attended by a sense of moral outrage—is a separate issue altogether.

There is not the slightest justification for confusing the objective facts of prejudice with cultural or ethical judgment of these facts. The unpleasant flavor of a word should not mislead us into believing that it stands only for a value-judgment. Take the word *epidemic*. It suggests something disagreeable. No doubt Pasteur, the great conqueror of epidemics, hated them. But his value-judgment did not affect in the slightest degree the objective facts with which he dealt so successfully. *Syphilis* is a term flavored with opprobrium in our culture. But the emotional tinge has no bearing whatever upon the operations of the spirochete within the human frame.

Some cultures, like our own, abjure prejudice; some do not; but the fundamental psychological analysis of prejudice is the same whether we are talking about Hindus, Navahos, the Greeks of antiquity, or Middletown, U.S.A. Whenever a negative attitude toward persons is sustained by a spurious overgeneralization we encounter the syndrome of prejudice. It is not essential that people deplore this syndrome. It has existed in all ages in every country. It constitutes a bona fide psychological problem. The degree of moral indignation engendered is irrelevant.

.   .   .

Why do human beings slip so easily into ethnic prejudice? They do so because the two essential ingredients that we have discussed—*erroneous generalization* and *hostility*—are natural and common capacities of the human mind. For the time being we shall leave hostility and its related problems out of account. Let us consider only those basic conditions of human living and thinking that lead naturally to the formation of erroneous and categorical prejudgment—and which therefore deposit us on the very threshold of ethnic and group antagonism.

The reader is warned that the full story of prejudice cannot be told in this—or in any other—single chapter of this book. Each chapter, taken by itself, is one-sided. This is the inevitable defect of any *analytical* treatment of the subject.

THE SEPARATION OF HUMAN GROUPS

Everywhere on earth we find a condition of separateness among groups. People mate with their own kind. They eat, play, reside in homogeneous clusters. They visit with their own kind, and prefer to worship together. Much of this automatic cohesion is due to nothing more than convenience. There is no need to turn to out-groups for companionship. With plenty of people at hand to choose from, why create for ourselves the trouble of adjusting to new languages, new foods, new cultures, or to people of a different educational level?

Thus most of the business of life can go on with less effort if we stick together with our own kind. Foreigners are a strain. So too are people of a higher or lower social and economic class than our own. We don't play bridge with the janitor. Why? Perhaps he prefers poker; almost certainly he would not grasp the type of jests and chatter that we and our friends enjoy; there would be a certain awkwardness in blending our differing manners. It is not that we have class prejudice, but only that we find comfort and ease in our own class. And normally there are plenty of people of our own class, or race, or religion to play, live, and eat with, and to marry.

It is not always the dominant majority that forces minority groups to remain separate. They often prefer to keep their identity, so that they need not strain to speak a foreign language or to watch their manners. Like the old grads at a college reunion, they can "let down" with those who share their traditions and presuppositions.

One enlightening study shows that high school students representing American minorities display even greater ethnocentrism than do native white Americans. Negro, Chinese, and Japanese young people, for example, are much more insistent upon choosing their friends, their work companions, and their "dates" from their own group than are white students. It is true that they do not select "leaders" from their own group, but prefer the non-Jewish white majority. But while agreeing that class leaders should come from the dominant group, they then seek the greater comfort of confining their intimate relations to their own kind.[3]

The initial fact, therefore, is that human groups tend to stay apart. We need not ascribe this tendency to a gregarious instinct, to a "consciousness of kind," or to prejudice. The fact is adequately explained by the principles of ease, least effort, congeniality, and pride in one's own culture.

Once this separatism exists, however, the ground is laid for all sorts of psychological elaboration. People who stay separate have few channels of communication. They easily exaggerate the degree of difference between groups, and readily misunderstand the grounds for it. And, perhaps most important of all, the separateness may lead to genuine conflicts of interests, as well as to many imaginary conflicts.

THE PROCESS OF CATEGORIZATION

The human mind must think with the aid of categories (the term is equivalent here to *generalizations*). Once formed, categories are the basis for normal prejudgment. We cannot possibly avoid this process. Orderly living depends upon it.

We may say that the process of categorization has five important characteristics.

1. *It forms large classes and clusters for guiding our daily adjustments.* We spend most of our waking life calling upon preformed categories for this purpose. When the sky darkens and the barometer falls we prejudge that rain will fall. We adjust to this cluster of happenings by taking along an umbrella. When an angry looking dog charges down the street, we categorize him as a "mad dog" and avoid him. When we go to a physician with an ailment we expect him to behave in a certain way toward us. On these, and

[3] A. Lundberg and Lenore Dickson, "Selective Association Among Ethnic Groups in a High School Population," *American Sociological Review*, 1952, 17, pp. 23–34.

countless other occasions, we "type" a single event, place it within a familiar rubric, and act accordingly. Sometimes we are mistaken: the event does not fit the category. It does not rain; the dog is not mad; the physician behaves unprofessionally. Yet our behavior was rational. It was based on high probability. Though we used the wrong category, we did the best we could.

What all this means is that our experience in life tends to form itself into clusters (concepts, categories), and while we may call on the right cluster at the wrong time, or the wrong cluster at the right time, still the process in question dominates our entire mental life. A million events befall us every day. We cannot handle so many events. If we think of them at all, we type them.

Open-mindedness is considered to be a virtue. But, strictly speaking, it cannot occur. A new experience *must* be redacted into old categories. We cannot handle each event freshly in its own right. If we did so, of what use would past experience be? Bertrand Russell, the philosopher, has summed up the matter in a phrase, "a mind perpetually open will be a mind perpetually vacant."

2. *Categorization assimilates as much as it can to the cluster.* There is a curious inertia in our thinking. We like to solve problems easily. We can do so best if we can fit them rapidly into a satisfactory category and use this category as a means of prejudging the solution. The story is told of the pharmacist's mate in the Navy who had only two categories into which he fitted every ailment that came to his attention on sick call: if you can *see* it put iodine on it; if you *can't,* give the patient a dose of salts. Life was simple for this pharmacist's mate; he ran his whole professional life with the aid of only two categories.

The point may be stated in this way: the mind tends to categorize environmental events in the "grossest" manner compatible with the need for action. If the pharmacist's mate in our story were called to task for his over-crude practice of medicine, he might then mend his ways and learn to employ more discriminated categories. But so long as we can "get away" with coarse overgeneralizations we tend to do so. (Why? Well, it takes less effort, and effort, except in the area of our most intense interests, is disagreeable.)

The bearing of this tendency on our problem is clear. It costs the Anglo employer less effort to guide his daily behavior by the generalization "Mexicans are lazy," than to individualize his workmen and learn the real reasons for their conduct. If I can lump thirteen million of my fellow citizens under a simple formula, "Negroes are stupid, dirty, and inferior," I simplify my life enormously. I simply avoid them one and all. What could be easier?

3. *The category enables us quickly to identify a related object.* Every event has certain marks that serve as a cue to bring the category of prejudgment into action. When we see a red-breasted bird, we say to ourselves "robin." When we see a crazily swaying automobile, we think, "drunken driver," and act accordingly. A person with dark brown skin will activate

whatever concept of Negro is dominant in our mind. If the dominant category is one composed of negative attitudes and beliefs we will automatically avoid him, or adopt whichever habit of rejection is most available to us.

Thus categories have a close and immediate tie with what we see, how we judge, and what we do. In fact, their whole purpose seems to be to facilitate perception and conduct—in other words, to make our adjustment to life speedy, smooth, and consistent. This principle holds even though we often make mistakes in fitting events to categories and thus get ourselves into trouble.

4. *The category saturates all that it contains with the same ideational and emotional flavor.* Some categories are almost purely intellectual. Such categories we call concepts. *Tree* is a concept made up of our experience with hundreds of kinds of trees and with thousands of individual trees, and yet it has essentially one ideational meaning. But many of our concepts (even *tree*) have in addition to a "meaning" also a characteristic "feeling." We not only know what *tree* is but we *like* trees. And so it is with ethnic categories. Not only do we know what Chinese, Mexican, Londoner mean, but we may have a feeling tone of favor or disfavor accompanying the concept.

5. *Categories may be more or less rational.* We have said that generally a category starts to grow up from a "kernel of truth." A rational category does so, and enlarges and solidifies itself through the increment of relevant experience. Scientific laws are examples of rational categories. They are backed up by experience. Every event to which they pertain turns out in a certain way. Even if the laws are not 100 percent perfect, we consider them rational if they have a high probability of predicting a happening.

Some of our ethnic categories are quite rational. It is probable a Negro will have dark skin (though this is not always true). It is probable that a Frenchman will speak French better than German (though here, too, are exceptions). But is it true that the Negro will be superstitious, or that the Frenchman will be morally lax?

To make a rational prejudgment of members of a group requires considerable knowledge of the characteristics of the group. It is unlikely that anyone has sound evidence that Scots are more penurious than Norwegians, or that Orientals are more wily than Caucasians, yet these beliefs grow as readily as do more rational beliefs.

In a certain Guatemalan community there is fierce hatred of the Jews. No resident has ever seen a Jew. How did the Jew-is-to-be-hated category grow up? In the first place, the community was strongly Catholic. Teachers had told the residents that the Jews were Christ-killers. It also so happened that in the local culture was an old pagan myth about a devil who killed a god. Thus two powerfully emotional ideas converged and created a hostile prejudgment of Jews.

We have said that irrational categories are formed as easily as rational categories. Probably they are formed *more* easily, for intense emotional feelings have a property of acting like sponges. Ideas, engulfed by an overpowering emotion, are more likely to conform to the emotion than to objective evidence.

There is a story of an Oxford student who once remarked, "I despise all Americans, but have never met one I didn't like." In this case the categorization went against even his firsthand experience. Holding to a prejudgment when we know better is one of the strangest features of prejudice. Theologians tell us that in prejudgments based on ignorance there is no question of sin; but that in prejudgments held in deliberate disregard of evidence, sin is involved.

CONFORMITY AS SOCIALIZATION

Conformity with Self: Habit   36
William James

It is very important that teachers should realize the importance of habit, and psychology helps us greatly at this point. We speak, it is true, of good habits and of bad habits; but, when people use the word "habit," in the majority of instances it is a bad habit which they have in mind. They talk of the smoking-habit and the swearing-habit and the drinking-habit, but not of the abstention-habit or the moderation-habit or the courage-habit. But the fact is that our virtues are habits as much as our vices. All our life, so far as it has definite form, is but a mass of habits—practical, emotional, and intellectual—systematically organized for our weal or woe, and bearing us irresistibly toward our destiny, whatever the latter may be.

Since pupils can understand this at a comparatively early age, and since to understand it contributes in no small measure to their feeling of responsibility, it would be well if the teacher were able himself to talk to them of the philosophy of habit in some such abstract terms as I am now about to talk of it to you.

I believe that we are subject to the law of habit in consequence of the fact that we have bodies. The plasticity of the living matter of our nervous system, in short, is the reason why we do a thing with difficulty the first time, but soon do it more and more easily, and finally, with sufficient practice, do it semi-mechanically, or with hardly any consciousness at all. Our nervous systems have (in Dr. Carpenter's words) *grown* to the way in which they have been exercised, just as a sheet of paper or a coat, once creased or folded, tends to fall forever afterward into the same identical folds.

Habit is thus a second nature, or rather, as the Duke of Wellington said, it is "ten times nature"—at any rate as regards its importance in adult life; for the acquired habits of our training have by that time inhibited or strangled most of the natural impulsive tendencies which were originally

From Ch. VIII, "The Laws of Habit" in *Talks to Teachers on Psychology,* William James, New York, Henry Hall and Co., 1908.

there. Ninety-nine hundredths or, possibly, nine hundred and ninety-nine thousandths of our activity is purely automatic and habitual, from our rising in the morning to our lying down each night. Our dressing and undressing, our eating and drinking, our greetings and partings, our hat-raisings and giving way for ladies to precede, nay, even most of the forms of our common speech, are things of a type so fixed by repetition as almost to be classed as reflex actions. To each sort of impression we have an automatic, ready-made response. My very words to you now are an example of what I mean; for having already lectured upon habit and printed a chapter about it in a book, and read the latter when in print, I find my tongue inevitably falling into its old phrases and repeating almost literally what I said before.

So far as we are thus mere bundles of habit, we are stereotyped creatures, imitators and copiers of our past selves. And since this, under any circumstances, is what we always tend to become, it follows first of all that the teacher's prime concern should be to ingrain into the pupil that assortment of habits that shall be most useful to him throughout life. Education is for behavior, and habits are the stuff of which behavior consists.

To quote my earlier book directly, the great thing in all education is to *make our nervous system our ally instead of our enemy.* It is to fund and capitalize our acquisitions, and live at ease upon the interest of the fund. *For this we must make automatic and habitual, as early as possible, as many useful actions as we can,* and as carefully guard against the growing into ways that are likely to be disadvantageous. The more of the details of our daily life we can hand over to the effortless custody of automatism, the more our higher powers of mind will be set free for their own proper work. There is no more miserable human being than one in whom nothing is habitual but indecision, and for whom the lighting of every cigar, the drinking of every cup, the time of rising and going to bed every day, and the beginning of every bit of work are subjects of express volitional deliberation. Fully half the time of such a man goes to the deciding or regretting of matters which ought to be so ingrained in him as practically not to exist for his consciousness at all. If there be such daily duties not yet ingrained in any one of my hearers, let him begin this very hour to set the matter right.

In Professor Bain's chapter on "The Moral Habits" there are some admirable practical remarks laid down. Two great maxims emerge from the treatment. The first is that in the acquisition of a new habit, or the leaving off of an old one, we must take care to *launch ourselves with as strong and decided an initiative as possible.* Accumulate all the possible circumstances which shall reinforce the right motives; put yourself assiduously in conditions that encourage the new way; make engagements incompatible with the old; take a public pledge, if the case allows; in short, envelope your resolution with every aid you know. This will give your new beginning such a momentum that the temptation to break down will not occur as soon as it otherwise might; and every day during which a breakdown is postponed adds to the chances of its not occurring at all.

I remember long ago reading in an Austrian paper the advertisement of a certain Rudolph Somebody, who promised fifty gulden reward to any one who after that date should find him at the wine-shop of Ambrosius So-and-so. "This I do," the advertisement continued, "in consequence of a promise which I have made my wife." With such a wife, and such an understanding of the way in which to start new habits, it would be safe to stake one's money on Rudolph's ultimate success.

The second maxim is, *Never suffer an exception to occur till the new habit is securely rooted in your life*. Each lapse is like the letting fall of a ball of string which one is carefully winding up: a single slip undoes more than a great many turns will wind again. Continuity of training is the great means of making the nervous system act infallibly right. As Professor Bain says:

"The peculiarity of the moral habits, contradistinguishing them from the intellectual acquisitions, is the presence of two hostile powers, one to be gradually raised into the ascendant over the other. It is necessary above all things, in such a situation, never to lose a battle. Every gain on the wrong side undoes the effect of many conquests on the right. The essential precaution, therefore, is so to regulate the two opposing powers that the one may have a series of uninterrupted successes, until repetition has fortified it to such a degree as to enable it to cope with the opposition, under any circumstances. This is the theoretically best career of mental progress."

A third maxim may be added to the preceding pair: *Seize the very first possible opportunity to act on every resolution you make, and on every emotional prompting you may experience in the direction of the habits you aspire to gain*. It is not in the moment of their forming, but in the moment of their producing motor effects, that resolves and aspirations communicate the new "set" to the brain.

No matter how full a reservoir of maxims one may possess, and no matter how good one's sentiments may be, if one has not taken advantage of every concrete opportunity to act, one's character may remain entirely unaffected for the better. With good intentions, hell proverbially is paved. This is an obvious consequence of the principles I have laid down. A "character," as J. S. Mill says, "is a completely fashioned will"; and a will, in the sense in which he means it, is an aggregate of tendencies to act in a firm and prompt and definite way upon all the principal emergencies of life. A tendency to act only becomes effectively ingrained in us in proportion to the uninterrupted frequency with which the actions actually occur, and the brain "grows" to their use. When a resolve or a fine glow of feeling is allowed to evaporate without bearing practical fruit, it is worse than a chance lost: it works so as positively to hinder future resolutions and emotions from taking the normal path of discharge.

Conformity with the Group
Ralph Linton

In spite of the functional interrelations of the individual, society and culture, these three entities may, and indeed must, be differentiated for descriptive purposes. Although any particular individual is rarely of great importance to the survival and functioning of the society to which he belongs or the culture in which he participates, *the individual,* his needs and potentialities, lies at the foundation of all social and cultural phenomena. Societies are organized groups of individuals, and cultures are, in the last analysis, nothing more than the organized repetitive responses of a society's members. For this reason the individual is the logical starting point for any investigation of the larger configuration.

It may be assumed that it is the needs of the individual which provide the motivations for his behavior and which are, through this, responsible for the operation of society and culture. The needs of human beings appear to be more numerous and more varied than those of any other species. In addition to those which can be traced directly to physiological tensions, as the needs for food, for sleep, for escape from pain and for sexual satisfaction, man has a whole series of other needs whose connection with such tensions cannot be clearly demonstrated. These, for lack of a better term, we may call the *psychic needs.* Although the physiologically determined needs of the individual are usually called primary and the psychic ones secondary, such a distinction is justifiable mainly in terms of a genetic approach. The physiologically determined needs unquestionably appear first in the general course of evolution and are the first to manifest themselves in the individual life cycle. However, as motivations of adult behavior, physical and psychic needs seem to stand very much on a par. Perhaps in any long-continued conflict between the two the odds are on the physical needs, but the victory of the body's demands is never assured. Hunger strikers do persist to the end, and, as in Europe today, men die under torture rather than betray a friend or even give up an opinion. In the less violent exigencies of daily life we find the psychic needs again and again given precedence over the physical ones. Everyone knows the old proverb, "One must suffer to be beautiful."

In spite of the importance of psychic needs as motivations of behavior, we still know very little about them. Their genesis is obscure, and they have not even been adequately described or classified. Psychological states are

From Ch. 1, "The Individual, Culture and Society," with most footnotes omitted, in *The Cultural Background of Personality,* Ralph Linton, New York, Appleton-Century-Crofts, 1945. Reprinted with permission of Appleton-Century-Crofts.

tenuous things exceedingly difficult to deal with by exact objective methods. The nature and even the presence of psychic needs can only be deduced from the behavior to which they give rise. This behavior is so varied that it becomes largely a matter of choice whether it is to be referred to a small number of general motivations or a great number of specific ones. If the latter method is followed, the psychic needs can be expanded almost to infinity and most of the value inherent in taxonomic systems is thereby lost. A further difficulty in the development of an adequate classification of psychic needs arises from the fact that any human need, whether physical or psychic, rarely stands in a clear-cut one-to-one relationship with any pattern of overt behavior. When people act, especially if they do so in accordance with an established culture pattern, the action usually contributes toward satisfying several different needs simultaneously. Thus when we dress we do so partly to protect the body and partly to satisfy vanity or at least avoid censure. Under the circumstances it seems safest not to try to set up any classification of psychic needs, contenting ourselves with a brief discussion of a few of those which seem to be most general and most significant for the understanding of human behavior.

Perhaps the most outstanding and most continuously operative of man's psychic needs is that for emotional response from other individuals. The term emotional response is used advisedly, since the eliciting of mere behavioral responses may leave this need quite unsatisfied. Thus in a modern city it is quite possible for the individual to interact in formal, culturally established terms with a great number of other individuals and to obtain necessary services from them without eliciting any emotional responses. Under such circumstances his psychic need for response remains unsatisfied and he suffers from feelings of loneliness and isolation which are almost as acute as though no one else were present. In fact the experience tends to be more frustrating than genuine solitude. We all know what it means to be alone in a crowd. It is this need for response, and especially for favorable response, which provides the individual with his main stimulus to socially acceptable behavior. People abide by the mores of their societies quite as much because they desire approval as because they fear punishment.

This need for emotional response from others is so universal and so strong that many social scientists have regarded it as instinctive in the sense of being inborn. Whether it actually is so or whether it is a product of conditioning is a problem which may never be solved. The individual is so completely dependent upon others during infancy that he cannot survive without eliciting response from them. Such response would, therefore, come to be associated with the satisfaction of even his most elementary needs, and the desire for it might well survive even when he had developed techniques for satisfying them without assistance. On the other hand, there is good evidence that even young infants require a certain amount of emotional response for their well-being. Lack of it seems to be the only explanation for the high infant death-rate in even the best-run and most sanitary institutions, which far exceeds that under even unsanitary conditions of home life. As a leading psychoanalyst has succinctly phrased it in his lectures: "Babies who aren't loved don't live." [1] Since all individuals go through the experiences of infancy, the question of whether this need is innate or acquired is really an academic one. In either case its presence is universal.

A second and equally universal psychic need is that for security of the long-term sort. Thanks to the human ability to perceive time as a continuum extending beyond past and present into the future, present satisfactions are not enough as long as future ones remain uncertain. We are in constant need of reassurance, although the same time sense which makes it possible for us to worry about what may happen also makes it possible for us to postpone the satisfaction of present needs and put up with current discomforts in the expectation of future rewards. This need for security and for reassurance is reflected in innumerable forms of culturally patterned behavior. It leads the primitive craftsman to mingle magic with his technology and men at all levels of culture to imagine heavens in which the proper behavior of the present will be properly rewarded. In the light of our present very limited knowledge of psychological processes it seems idle to speculate as to the origins of this need. It is enough to recognize its importance as a motivation of forward-looking behavior.

The third and last psychic need which deserves mention at this time is that for novelty of experience. This is probably less compulsive than the needs which have just been discussed; at least it rarely seems to come into play until most other needs have been satisfied. It finds its expression in the familiar phenomenon of boredom and leads to all sorts of experimental behavior. Just as in the case of the need for response, there is a possible explanation for it in terms of early conditioning. During early childhood the individual is constantly having new experiences, and, since many of these are pleasurable, the qualities of novelty and of pleasurableness may very well come to be linked in anticipation. On the other hand, the roots of this need may lie deeper. Even very small children show experimental tendencies, and Pavlov has recognized what he calls the exploratory reflex in animals.

·   ·   ·

Whatever the genesis of human societies may have been, all of them have certain features in common. The first and perhaps most important of these is that the society, rather than the individual, has become the significant unit in our species struggle for survival. Except by some unhappy accident, like that of Robinson Crusoe, all human beings live as members of organized groups and have their fate inextricably bound up with that of the group to which they belong. They cannot survive the hazards of infancy or satisfy their adult needs without the aid and coöperation of other indi-

[1] Dr. S. Ferenczi, quoted by Dr. Abram Kardiner.

viduals. Human life has passed long since from the stage of the individual workman to that of the assembly line in which each person makes his small, specfic contribution to the finished product.

A second characteristic of societies is that they normally persist far beyond the life span of any one individual. Each of us is brought, by the accident of birth, into an organization which is already a going concern. Although new societies may come into being under certain conditions, most people are born, live and die as members of old ones. Their problem as individuals is not to assist in the organization of a new society but to adjust themselves to a pattern of group living which has long since crystallized. It may seem hardly necessary to point this out, but one finds in many writings a confusion between the genesis of social forms and the genesis of social behavior in the individual. How such an institution as the family originated is a problem of quite a different sort from that of how the individual becomes a functional, fully integrated member of a family.

Third, societies are functional, operative units. In spite of the fact that they are made up of individuals, they work as wholes. The interests of each of their component members are subordinated to those of the entire group. Societies do not even hesitate to eliminate some of these members when this is to the advantage of the society as a whole. Men go to war and are killed in war that the society may be protected or enriched, and the criminal is destroyed or segregated because he is a disturbing factor. Less obvious but more continuous are the daily sacrifices of inclinations and desires which social living requires of those who participate in it. Such sacrifices are rewarded in many ways, perhaps most of all by the favorable responses of others. Nevertheless, to belong to a society is to sacrifice some measure of individual liberty, no matter how slight the restraints which the society consciously imposes. The so-called free societies are not really free. They are merely those societies which encourage their members to express their individuality along a few minor and socially acceptable lines. At the same time they condition their members to abide by innumerable rules and regulations, doing this so subtly and completely that these members are largely unconscious that the rules exist. If a society has done its work of shaping the individual properly, he is no more conscious of most of the restrictions it has imposed than he is of the restraints which his habitual clothing imposes on his movements.

Fourth, in every society the activities necessary to the survival of the whole are divided and apportioned to the various members. There is no society so simple that it does not distinguish at least between men's and women's work, while most of them also set aside certain persons as intermediaries between man and the supernatural and as leaders to organize and direct the group's activities along certain lines. Such a division represents the absolute minimum, and in most societies we find it carried far beyond that point, with an assignment of various crafts to specialists and the appointment of social functionaries. This formal division of activities serves to give the society structure, organization and cohesion. It transforms the group of individuals who constitute the society from a mere amorphous mass into an organism. With each step in the differentiation of functions the individuals who perform these functions become increasingly dependent upon the whole. The merchant cannot exist without customers or the priest without a congregation.

CONFORMITY AS SLAVERY

Opinions and Social Pressure   38
Solomon E. Asch

That social influences shape every person's practices, judgments and beliefs is a truism to which anyone will readily assent. A child masters his "native" dialect down to the finest nuances; a member of a tribe of cannibals accepts cannibalism as altogether fitting and proper. All the social sciences take their departure from the observation of the profound effects that groups exert on their members. For psychologists, group pressure upon the minds of individuals raises a host of questions they would like to investigate in detail.

How, and to what extent, do social forces constrain people's opinions and attitudes? This question is especially pertinent in our day. The same epoch that has witnessed the unprecedented technical extension of communication has also brought into existence the deliberate manipulation of opinion and the "engineering of consent." There are many good reasons why, as citizens and as scientists, we should be concerned with studying the ways in which human beings form their opinions and the role that social conditions play.

Studies of these questions began with the interest in hypnosis aroused by the French physician Jean Martin Charcot (a teacher of Sigmund Freud) toward the end of the 19th century. Charcot believed that only hysterical patients could be fully hypnotized, but this view was soon challenged by two other physicians Hyppolyte Bernheim and A. A. Liébault, who demonstrated that they could put most people under the hypnotic spell. Bernheim proposed that hypnosis was but an extreme form of a normal psychological process which became known as "suggestibility." It was shown that monotonous reiteration of instructions could induce in normal persons in the waking state involuntary bodily changes such as swaying or rigidity of the arms, and sensations such as warmth and odor.

It was not long before social thinkers seized upon these discoveries as a basis for explaining numerous social phenomena, from the spread of opinion to the formation of crowds and the following of leaders. The sociologist Gabriel Tarde summed it all up in the aphorism: "Social man is a somnambulist."

When the new discipline of social psychology was born at the beginning of this century, its first experiments were essentially adaptations of the suggestion demonstration. The technique generally followed a simple plan. The subjects, usually college students, were asked to give their opinions or preferences concerning various matters; some time later they were again asked to state their choices, but now they were also informed of the opinions held by authorities or large groups of their peers on the same matters. (Often the alleged consensus was fictitious.) Most of these studies had substantially the same result: confronted with opinions contrary to their own, many subjects apparently shifted their judgments in the direction of the views of the majorities or the experts. The late psychologist Edward L. Thorndike reported that he had succeeded in modifying the esthetic preferences of adults by this procedure. Other psychologists reported that people's evaluations of the merit of a literary passage could be raised or lowered by ascribing the passage to different authors. Apparently the sheer weight of numbers or authority sufficed to change opinions, even when no arguments for the opinions themselves were provided.

Now the very ease of success in these experiments arouses suspicion. Did the subjects actually change their opinions, or were the experimental victories scored only on paper? On grounds of common sense, one must question whether opinions are generally as watery as these studies indicate. There is some reason to wonder whether it was not the investigators who, in their enthusiasm for a theory, were suggestible, and whether the ostensibly gullible subjects were not providing answers which they thought good subjects were expected to give.

The investigations were guided by certain underlying assumptions, which today are common currency and account for much that is thought and said about the operations of propaganda and public opinion. The assumptions are that people submit uncritically and painlessly to external manipulation by suggestion or prestige, and that any given idea or value can be "sold" or "unsold" without reference to its merits. We should be skeptical, however, of the supposition that the power of social pressure necessarily implies uncritical submission to it: independence and the capacity to rise above group passion are also open to human beings. Further, one may question on psychological grounds whether it is possible as a rule to change a person's judgment of a situation or an object without first changing his knowledge or assumptions about it.

In what follows I shall describe some experiments in an investigation of the effects of group pressure which was carried out recently with the help of a number of my associates. The tests not only demonstrate the operations of group pressure upon individuals but also illustrate a new kind of attack on the problem and some of the more subtle questions that it raises.

A group of seven to nine young men, all college students, are assembled in a classroom for a "psychological experiment" in visual judgment. The experimenter informs them that they will be comparing the lengths of lines. He shows two large white cards. On one is a single vertical black line—the standard whose length is to be matched. On the other card are three vertical lines of various lengths. The subjects are to choose the one that is of the same length as the line on the other card. One of the three actually is of the same length; the other two are substantially different, the difference ranging from three quarters of an inch to an inch and three quarters.

The experiment opens uneventfully. The subjects announce their answers in the order in which they have been seated in the room, and on the first round every person chooses the same matching line. Then a second set of cards is exposed; again the group is unanimous. The members appear ready to endure politely another boring experiment. On the third trial there is an unexpected disturbance. One person near the end of the group disagrees with all the others in his selection of the matching line. He looks surprised, indeed incredulous, about the disagreement. On the following trial he disagrees again, while the others remain unanimous in their choice. The dissenter becomes more and more worried and hesitant as the disagreement continues in succeeding trials; he may pause before announcing his answer and speak in a low voice, or he may smile in an embarrassed way.

What the dissenter does not know is that all the other members of the group were instructed by the experimenter beforehand to give incorrect answers in unanimity at certain points. The single individual who is not a party to this pre-arrangement is the focal subject of our experiment. He is placed in a position in which, while he is actually giving the correct answers, he finds himself unexpectedly in a minority of one, opposed by a unanimous and arbitrary majority with respect to a clear and simple fact. Upon him we have brought to bear two opposed forces: the evidence of his senses and the unanimous opinion of a group of his peers. Also, he must declare his judgments in public, before a majority which has also stated its position publicly.

The instructed majority occasionally reports correctly in order to reduce the possibility that the naïve subject will suspect collusion against him. (In only a few cases did the subject actually show suspicion; when this happened, the experiment was stopped and the results were not counted.) There are 18 trials in each series, and on 12 of these the majority responds erroneously.

How do people respond to group pressure in this situation? I shall report first the statistical results of a series in which a total of 123 subjects from three institutions of higher learning (not including my own, Swarthmore College) were placed in the minority situation described above.

Two alternatives were open to the subject: he could act independently, repudiating the majority, or he could go along with the majority, repudiating the evidence of his senses. Of the 123 put to the test, a considerable percentage yielded to the majority. Whereas in ordinary circumstances individuals matching the lines will make mistakes less than 1 per cent of the time, under group pressure the minority subjects swung to acceptance of the misleading majority's wrong judgments in 36.8 per cent of the selections.

Of course individuals differed in response. At one extreme, about one quarter of the subjects were completely independent and never agreed with the erroneous judgments of the majority. At the other extreme, some individuals went with the majority nearly all the time. The performances of individuals in this experiment tend to be highly consistent. Those who strike out on the path of independence do not, as a rule, succumb to the majority even over an extended series of trials, while those who choose the path of compliance are unable to free themselves as the ordeal is prolonged.

The reasons for the startling individual differences have not yet been investigated in detail. At this point we can only report some tentative generalizations from talks with the subjects, each of whom was interviewed at the end of the experiment. Among the independent individuals were many who held fast because of staunch confidence in their own judgment. The most significant fact about them was not absence of responsiveness to the majority but a capacity to recover from doubt and to re-establish their equilibrium. Others who acted independently came to believe that the majority was correct in its answers, but they continued their dissent on the simple ground that it was their obligation to call the play as they saw it.

Among the extremely yielding persons we found a group who quickly reached the conclusion: "I am wrong, they are right." Others yielded in order "not to spoil your results." Many of the individuals who went along suspected that the majority were "sheep" following the first responder, or that the majority were victims of an optical illusion; nevertheless, these suspicions failed to free them at the moment of decision. More disquieting were the reactions of subjects who construed their difference from the majority as a sign of some general deficiency in themselves, which at all costs they must hide. On this basis they desperately tried to merge with the majority, not realizing the longer-range consequences to themselves. All the yielding subjects underestimated the frequency with which they conformed.

Which aspect of the influence of a majority is more important—the size of the majority or its unanimity? The experiment was modified to examine this question. In one series the size of the opposition was varied from one to 15 persons. The results showed a clear trend. When a subject was confronted with only a single individual who contradicted his answers, he was swayed little: he continued to answer independently and correctly in nearly all trials. When the opposition was increased to two, the pressure became substantial: minority subjects now accepted the wrong answer 13.6 per cent of the time. Under the pressure of a majority of three, the subjects' errors jumped to 31.8

per cent. But further increases in the size of the majority apparently did not increase the weight of the pressure substantially. Clearly the size of the opposition is important only up to a point.

Disturbance of the majority's unanimity had a striking effect. In this experiment the subject was given the support of a truthful partner—either another individual who did not know of the pre-arranged agreement among the rest of the group, or a person who was instructed to give correct answers throughout.

The presence of a supporting partner depleted the majority of much of its power. Its pressure on the dissenting individual was reduced to one fourth: that is, subjects answered incorrectly only one fourth as often as under the pressure of a unanimous majority. The weakest persons did not yield as readily. Most interesting were the reactions to the partner. Generally the feeling toward him was one of warmth and closeness; he was credited with inspiring confidence. However, the subjects repudiated the suggestion that the partner decided them to be independent.

Was the partner's effect a consequence of his dissent, or was it related to his accuracy? We now introduced into the experimental group a person who was instructed to dissent from the majority but also to disagree with the subject. In some experiments the majority was always to choose the worst of the comparison lines and the instructed dissenter to pick the line that was closer to the length of the standard one; in others the majority was consistently intermediate and the dissenter most in error. In this manner we were able to study the relative influence of "compromising" and "extremist" dissenters.

Again the results are clear. When a moderate dissenter is present, the effect of the majority on the subject decreases by approximately one third, and extremes of yielding disappear. Moreover, most of the errors the subjects do make are moderate, rather than flagrant. In short, the dissenter largely controls the choice of errors. To this extent the subjects broke away from the majority even while bending to it.

On the other hand, when the dissenter always chose the line that was more flagrantly different from the standard, the results were of quite a different kind. The extremist dissenter produced a remarkable freeing of the subjects; their errors dropped to only 9 per cent. Furthermore, all the errors were of the moderate variety. We were able to conclude that dissent *per se* increased independence and moderated the errors that occurred, and that the direction of dissent exerted consistent effects.

In all the foregoing experiments each subject was observed only in a single setting. We now turned to studying the effects upon a given individual of a change in the situation to which he was exposed. The first experiment examined the consequences of losing or gaining a partner. The instructed partner began by answering correctly on the first six trials. With his support the subject usually resisted pressure from the majority: 18 of 27 subjects were completely independent. But after six trials the partner joined the majority. As soon as he did so, there was an abrupt rise in the subjects' errors. Their submission to the majority was just about as frequent as when the minority subject was opposed by a unanimous majority throughout.

It was surprising to find that the experience of having had a partner and of having braved the majority opposition with him had failed to strengthen the individuals' independence. Questioning at the conclusion of the experiment suggested that we had overlooked an important circumstance; namely, the strong specific effect of "desertion" by the partner to the other side. We therefore changed the conditions so that the partner would simply leave the group at the proper point. (To allay suspicion it was announced in advance that he had an appointment with the dean.) In this form of the experiment the partner's effect outlasted his presence. The errors increased after his departure, but less markedly than after a partner switched to the majority.

In a variant of this procedure the trials began with the majority unanimously giving correct answers. Then they gradually broke away until on the sixth trial the naïve subject was alone and the group unanimously against him. As long as the subject had anyone on his side, he was almost invariably independent, but as soon as he found himself alone, the tendency to conform to the majority rose abruptly.

As might be expected, an individual's resistance to group pressure in these experiments depends to a considerable degree on how wrong the majority is. We varied the discrepancy between the standard line and the other lines systematically, with the hope of reaching a point where the error of the majority would be so glaring that every subject would repudiate it and choose independently. In this we regretfully did not succeed. Even when the difference between the lines was seven inches, there were still some who yielded to the error of the majority.

The study provides clear answers to a few relatively simple questions, and it raises many others that await investigation. We would like to know the degree of consistency of persons in situations which differ in content and structure. If consistency of independence or conformity in behavior is shown to be a fact, how is it functionally related to qualities of character and personality? In what ways is independence related to sociological or cultural conditions? Are leaders more independent than other people, or are they adept at following their followers? These and many other questions may perhaps be answerable by investigations of the type described here.

Life in society requires consensus as an indispensable condition. But consensus, to be productive, requires that each individual contribute independently out of his experience and insight. When consensus comes under the dominance of conformity, the social process is polluted and the individual at the same time surrenders the powers on which his functioning as a feeling and thinking being depends. That we have found the tendency to conformity in our society so strong that reasonably intelligent and well-meaning young people are willing to call white black is a matter of concern. It raises questions about our ways of education and about the values that guide our conduct.

Yet anyone inclined to draw too pessimistic conclusions from this report would do well to remind himself that the capacities for independence are not to be underestimated. He may also draw some consolation from a further observation: those who participated in this challenging experiment agreed nearly without exception that independence was preferable to conformity.

Groups into Crowds 39
Gustave Le Bon

In its ordinary sense the word "crowd" means a gathering of individuals of whatever nationality, profession, or sex, and whatever be the chances that have brought them together. From the psychological point of view the expression "crowd" assumes quite a different signification. Under certain given circumstances, and only under those circumstances, an agglomeration of men presents new characteristics very different from those of the individuals composing it. The sentiments and ideas of all the persons in the gathering take one and the same direction, and their conscious personality vanishes. A collective mind is formed, doubtless transitory, but presenting very clearly defined characteristics. The gathering has thus become what, in the absence of a better expression, I will call an organised crowd, or, if the term is considered preferable, a psychological crowd. It forms a single being, and is subjected to the *law of the mental unity of crowds.*

It is evident that it is not by the mere fact of a number of individuals finding themselves accidentally side by side that they acquire the character of an organised crowd. A thousand individuals accidentally gathered in a public place without any determined object in no way constitute a crowd from the psychological point of view. To acquire the special characteristics of such a crowd, the influence is necessary of certain predisposing causes of which we shall have to determine the nature.

The disappearance of conscious personality and the turning of feelings and thoughts in a different direction, which are the primary characteristics of a crowd about to become organised, do not always involve the simultaneous presence of a number of individuals on one spot. Thousands of isolated individuals may acquire at certain moments, and under the influence of certain

From Book I, "The Mind of Crowds," (from Ch. I, "The Mind of Crowds" and from Ch. II "The Sentiments and Morality of Crowds") in *The Crowd*, Gustave Le Bon, London, T. Fisher Unwin, 1896.

violent emotions—such, for example, as a great national event—the characteristics of a psychological crowd. It will be sufficient in that case that a mere
chance should bring them together for their acts to at once assume the characteristics peculiar to the acts of a crowd. At certain moments half a dozen
men might constitute a psychological crowd, which may not happen in the
case of hundreds of men gathered together by accident. On the other hand,
an entire nation, though there may be no visible agglomeration, may become
a crowd under the action of certain influences.

A psychological crowd once constituted, it acquires certain provisional
but determinable general characteristics. To these general characteristics there
are adjoined particular characteristics which vary according to the elements
of which the crowd is composed, and may modify its mental constitution.
Psychological crowds, then, are susceptible of classification; and when we
come to occupy ourselves with this matter, we shall see that a heterogeneous
crowd—that is, a crowd composed of dissimilar elements—presents certain
characteristics in common with homogeneous crowds—that is, with crowds
composed of elements more or less akin (sects, castes, and classes)—and side
by side with these common characteristics particularities which permit of the
two kinds of crowds being differentiated.

But before occupying ourselves with the different categories of crowds,
we must first of all examine the characteristics common to them all. We shall
set to work like the naturalist, who begins by describing the general characteristics common to all the members of a family, before concerning himself
with the particular characteristics which allow the differentiation of the
genera and species that the family includes.

It is not easy to describe the mind of crowds with exactness, because its
organisation varies not only according to race and composition, but also
according to the nature and intensity of the exciting causes to which crowds
are subjected. The same difficulty, however, presents itself in the psychological study of an individual. It is only in novels that individuals are found to
traverse their whole life with an unvarying character. It is only the uniformity
of the environment that creates the apparent uniformity of characters. I have
shown elsewhere that all mental constitutions contain possibilities of character which may be manifested in consequence of a sudden change of environment. This explains how it was that among the most savage members of the
French Convention were to be found inoffensive citizens who, under ordinary circumstances, would have been peaceable notaries or virtuous magis-
trates. The storm past, they resumed their normal character of quiet, law-
abiding citizens. Napoleon found amongst them his most docile servants.

It being impossible to study here all the successive degrees of organisation of crowds, we shall concern ourselves more especially with such crowds
as have attained to the phase of complete organisation. In this way we shall
see what crowds may become, but not what they invariably are. It is only
in this advanced phase of organisation that certain new and special charac-

teristics are superposed on the unvarying and dominant character of the race; then takes place that turning already alluded to of all the feelings and thoughts of the collectivity in an identical direction. It is only under such circumstances too, that what I have called above the *psychological law of the mental unity of crowds* comes into play.

Among the psychological characteristics of crowds there are some that they may present in common with isolated individuals, and others, on the contrary, which are absolutely peculiar to them and are only to be met with in collectivities. It is these special characteristics that we shall study, first of all, in order to show their importance.

The most striking peculiarity presented by a psychological crowd is the following: Whoever be the individuals that compose it, however like or unlike be their mode of life, their occupations, their character, or their intelligence, the fact that they have been transformed into a crowd puts them in possession of a sort of collective mind which makes them feel, think, and act in a manner quite different from that in which each individual of them would feel, think, and act were he in a state of isolation. There are certain ideas and feelings which do not come into being, or do not transform themselves into acts except in the case of individuals forming a crowd. The psychological crowd is a provisional being formed of heterogeneous elements, which for a moment are combined, exactly as the cells which constitute a living body form by their reunion a new being which displays characteristics very different from those possessed by each of the cells singly.

Contrary to an opinion which one is astonished to find coming from the pen of so acute a philosopher as Herbert Spencer, in the aggregate which constitutes a crowd there is in no sort a summing-up of or an average struck between its elements. What really takes place is a combination followed by the creation of new characteristics, just as in chemistry certain elements, when brought into contact—bases and acids, for example—combine to form a new body possessing properties quite different from those of the bodies that have served to form it.

It is easy to prove how much the individual forming part of a crowd differs from the isolated individual, but it is less easy to discover the causes of this difference.

To obtain at any rate a glimpse of them it is necessary in the first place to call to mind the truth established by modern psychology, that unconscious phenomena play an altogether preponderating part not only in organic life, but also in the operations of the intelligence. The conscious life of the mind is of small importance in comparison with its unconscious life. The most subtle analyst, the most acute observer, is scarcely successful in discovering more than a very small number of the unconscious motives that determine his conduct. Our conscious acts are the outcome of an unconscious substratum created in the mind in the main by hereditary influences. This substratum consists of the innumerable common characteristics handed down from generation to generation, which constitute the genius of a race. Behind the avowed causes of our acts there undoubtedly lie secret causes that we do not avow, but behind these secret causes there are many others more secret still which we ourselves ignore. The greater part of our daily actions are the result of hidden motives which escape our observation.

It is more especially with respect to those unconscious elements which constitute the genius of a race that all the individuals belonging to it resemble each other, while it is principally in respect to the conscious elements of their character—the fruit of education, and yet more of exceptional hereditary conditions—that they differ from each other. Men the most unlike in the matter of their intelligence possess instincts, passions, and feelings that are very similar. In the case of everything that belongs to the realm of sentiment—religion, politics, morality, the affections and antipathies, etc.—the most eminent men seldom surpass the standard of the most ordinary individuals. From the intellectual point of view an abyss may exist between a great mathematician and his bootmaker, but from the point of view of character the difference is most often slight or non-existent.

It is precisely these general qualities of character, governed by forces of which we are unconscious, and possessed by the majority of the normal individuals of a race in much the same degree—it is precisely these qualities, I say, that in crowds become common property. In the collective mind the intellectual aptitudes of the individuals, and in consequence their individuality, are weakened. The heterogeneous is swamped by the homogeneous, and the unconscious qualities obtain the upper hand.

This very fact that crowds possess in common ordinary qualities explains why they can never accomplish acts demanding a high degree of intelligence. The decisions affecting matters of general interest come to by an assembly of men of distinction, but specialists in different walks of life, are not sensibly superior to the decisions that would be adopted by a gathering of imbeciles. The truth is, they can only bring to bear in common on the work in hand those mediocre qualities which are the birthright of every average individual. In crowds it is stupidity and not mother-wit that is accumulated. It is not all the world, as is so often repeated, that has more wit than Voltaire, but assuredly Voltaire that has more wit than all the world, if by "all the world" crowds are to be understood.

If the individuals of a crowd confined themselves to putting in common the ordinary qualities of which each of them has his share, there would merely result the striking of an average, and not, as we have said is actually the case, the creation of new characteristics. How is it that these new characteristics are created? This is what we are now to investigate.

Different causes determine the appearance of these characteristics peculiar to crowds, and not possessed by isolated individuals. The first is that the individual forming part of a crowd acquires, solely from numerical considerations, a sentiment of invincible power which allows him to yield to instincts which, had he been alone, he would perforce have kept under restraint. He will be the less disposed to check himself from the consideration that, a crowd being anonymous, and in consequence irresponsible, the sentiment of responsibility which always controls individuals disappears entirely.

The second cause, which is contagion, also intervenes to determine the manifestation in crowds of their special characteristics, and at the same time the trend they are to take. Contagion is a phenomenon of which it is easy to establish the presence, but that it is not easy to explain. It must be classed among those phenomena of a hypnotic order, which we shall shortly study. In a crowd every sentiment and act is contagious, and contagious to such a degree that an individual readily sacrifices his personal interest to the collective interest. This is an aptitude very contrary to his nature, and of which a man is scarcely capable, except when he makes part of a crowd.

A third cause, and by far the most important, determines in the individuals of a crowd special characteristics which are quite contrary at times to those presented by the isolated individual. I allude to that suggestibility of which, moreover, the contagion mentioned above is neither more nor less than an effect.

To understand this phenomenon it is necessary to bear in mind certain recent physiological discoveries. We know to-day that by various processes an individual may be brought into such a condition that, having entirely lost his conscious personality, he obeys all the suggestions of the operator who has deprived him of it, and commits acts in utter contradiction with his character and habits. The most careful observations seem to prove that an individual immerged for some length of time in a crowd in action soon finds himself— either in consequence of the magnetic influence given out by the crowd, or from some other cause of which we are ignorant—in a special state, which much resembles the state of fascination in which the hypnotised individual finds himself in the hands of the hypnotiser. The activity of the brain being paralysed in the case of the hypnotised subject, the latter becomes the slave of all the unconscious activities of his spinal cord, which the hypnotiser directs at will. The conscious personality has entirely vanished; will and discernment are lost. All feelings and thoughts are bent in the direction determined by the hypnotiser.

Such also is approximately the state of the individual forming part of a psychological crowd. He is no longer conscious of his acts. In his case, as in the case of the hypnotised subject, at the same time that certain faculties are destroyed, others may be brought to a high degree of exaltation. Under the influence of a suggestion, he will undertake the accomplishment of certain acts with irresistible impetuosity. This impetuosity is the more irresistible in the case of crowds than in that of the hypnotised subject, from the fact that, the suggestion being the same for all the individuals of the crowd, it gains in strength by reciprocity. The individualities in the crowd who might possess a personality sufficiently strong to resist the suggestion are too few in number to struggle against the current. At the utmost, they may be able to attempt a diversion by means of different suggestions. It is in this way, for instance, that a happy expression, an image opportunely evoked, have occasionally deterred crowds from the most bloodthirsty acts.

We see, then, that the disappearance of the conscious personality, the predominance of the unconscious personality, the turning by means of suggestion and contagion of feelings and ideas in an identical direction, the tendency immediately to transform the suggested ideas into acts; these we see, are the principal characteristics of the individual forming part of a crowd. He is no longer himself, but has become an automaton who has ceased to be guided by his will.

Moreover, by the mere fact that he forms part of an organised crowd, a man descends several rungs in the ladder of civilisation. Isolated, he may be a cultivated individual; in a crowd, he is a barbarian—that is, a creature acting by instinct. He possesses the spontaneity, the violence, the ferocity, and also the enthusiasm and heroism of primitive beings, whom he further tends to resemble by the facility with which he allows himself to be impressed by words and images—which would be entirely without action on each of the isolated individuals composing the crowd—and to be induced to commit acts contrary to his most obvious interests and his best-known habits. An individual in a crowd is a grain of sand amid other grains of sand, which the wind stirs up at will.

It is for these reasons that juries are seen to deliver verdicts of which each individual juror would disapprove, that parliamentary assemblies adopt laws and measures of which each of their members would disapprove in his own person. Taken separately, the men of the French Revolutionary Convention were enlightened citizens of peaceful habits. United in a crowd, they did not hesitate to give their adhesion to the most savage proposals, to guillotine individuals most clearly innocent, and, contrary to their interests, to renounce their inviolability and to decimate themselves.

It is not only by his acts that the individual in a crowd differs essentially from himself. Even before he has entirely lost his independence, his ideas and feelings have undergone a transformation, and the transformation is so profound as to change the miser into a spendthrift, the sceptic into a believer, the honest man into a criminal, and the coward into a hero. The renunciation of all its privileges which the French nobility voted in a moment of enthusiasm during the celebrated night of August 4, 1789, would certainly never have been consented to by any of its members taken singly.

The conclusion to be drawn from what precedes is, that the crowd is always intellectually inferior to the isolated individual, but that, from the point of view of feelings and of the acts these feelings provoke, the crowd may, according to circumstances, be better or worse than the individual. All depends on the nature of the suggestion to which the crowd is exposed. This is the point that has been completely misunderstood by writers who have only studied crowds from the criminal point of view. Doubtless a crowd is often criminal, but also it is often heroic. It is crowds rather than isolated individuals that may be induced to run the risk of death to secure the triumph of a creed or an idea, that may be fired with enthusiasm for glory and honour, that are led on—almost without bread and without arms, as in the age of the Crusades—to deliver the tomb of Christ from the infidel, or, as in '93, to defend the fatherland. Such heroism is without doubt somewhat unconscious, but it is of such heroism that history is made. Were peoples only to be credited with the great actions performed in cold blood, the annals of the world would register but few of them.

.   .   .

Having indicated in a general way the principal characteristics of crowds, it remains to study these characteristics in detail.

It will be remarked that among the special characteristics of crowds there are several—such as impulsiveness, irritability, incapacity to reason, the absence of judgment and of the critical spirit, the exaggeration of the sentiments, and others besides—which are almost always observed in beings belonging to inferior forms of evolution—in women, savages, and children, for instance. However, I merely indicate this analogy in passing; its demonstration is outside the scope of this work. It would, moreover, be useless for persons acquainted with the psychology of primitive beings, and would scarcely carry conviction to those in ignorance of this matter.

I now proceed to the successive consideration of the different characteristics that may be observed in the majority of crowds.

1. IMPULSIVENESS, MOBILITY, AND IRRITABILITY OF CROWDS

When studying the fundamental characteristics of a crowd we stated that it is guided almost exclusively by unconscious motives. Its acts are far more under the influence of the spinal cord than of the brain. In this respect a crowd is closely akin to quite primitive beings. The acts performed may be perfect so far as their execution is concerned, but as they are not directed by the brain, the individual conducts himself according as the exciting causes to which he is submitted may happen to decide. A crowd is at the mercy of all external exciting causes, and reflects their incessant variations. It is the slave of the impulses which it receives. The isolated individual may be submitted to the same exciting causes as the man in a crowd, but as his brain shows him the inadvisability of yielding to them, he refrains from yielding. This truth may be physiologically expressed by saying that the isolated individual possesses the capacity of dominating his reflex actions, while a crowd is devoid of this capacity.

The varying impulses which crowds obey may be, according to their exciting causes, generous or cruel, heroic or cowardly, but they will always be so imperious that the interest of the individual, even the interest of self-preservation, will not dominate them. The exciting causes that may act on crowds being so varied, and crowds always obeying them, crowds are in consequence extremely mobile. This explains how it is that we see them pass in a moment from the most bloodthirsty ferocity to the most extreme generosity and heroism. A crowd may easily enact the part of an executioner, but not less easily that of a martyr. It is crowds that have furnished the torrents of blood requisite for the triumph of every belief. It is not necessary to go back to the heroic ages to see what crowds are capable of in this latter direction. They are never sparing of their life in an insurrection, and not long since a general,[1] becoming suddenly popular, might easily have found a hundred thousand men ready to sacrifice their lives for his cause had he demanded it.

Any display of premeditation by crowds is in consequence out of the question. They may be animated in succession by the most contrary sentiments, but they will always be under the influence of the exciting causes of the moment. They are like the leaves which a tempest whirls up and scatters in every direction and then allows to fall. When studying later on certain revolutionary crowds we shall give some examples of the variability of their sentiments.

This mobility of crowds renders them very difficult to govern, especially when a measure of public authority has fallen into their hands. Did not the necessities of everyday life constitute a sort of invisible regulator of existence, it would scarcely be possible for democracies to last. Still, though the wishes of crowds are frenzied they are not durable. Crowds are as incapable of willing as of thinking for any length of time.

A crowd is not merely impulsive and mobile. Like a savage, it is not prepared to admit that anything can come between its desire and the realisation of its desire. It is the less capable of understanding such an intervention, in consequence of the feeling of irresistible power given it by its numerical strength. The notion of impossibility disappears for the individual in a crowd. An isolated individual knows well enough that alone he cannot set fire to a palace or loot a shop, and should he be tempted to do so, he will easily resist the temptation. Making part of a crowd, he is conscious of the power given him by number, and it is sufficient to suggest to him ideas of murder or pillage for him to yield immediately to temptation. An unexpected obstacle will be destroyed with frenzied rage. Did the human organism allow of the perpetuity of furious passion, it might be said that the normal condition of a crowd baulked in its wishes is just such a state of furious passion.

The fundamental characteristics of the race, which constitute the unvarying source from which all our sentiments spring, always exert an influence on the irritability of crowds, their impulsiveness and their mobility, as

[1] General Boulanger.

on all the popular sentiments we shall have to study. All crowds are doubtless always irritable and impulsive, but with great variations of degree. For instance, the difference between a Latin and an Anglo-Saxon crowd is striking. The most recent facts in French history throw a vivid light on this point. The mere publication, twenty-five years ago, of a telegram, relating an insult supposed to have been offered an ambassador, was sufficient to determine an explosion of fury, whence followed immediately a terrible war. Some years later the telegraphic announcement of an insignificant reverse at Langson provoked a fresh explosion which brought about the instantaneous overthrow of the Government. At the same moment a much more serious reverse undergone by the English expedition to Khartoum produced only a slight emotion in England, and no ministry was overturned. Crowds are everywhere distinguished by feminine characteristics, but Latin crowds are the most feminine of all. Whoever trusts in them may rapidly attain a lofty destiny, but to do so is to be perpetually skirting the brink of a Tarpeian rock, with the certainty of one day being precipitated from it.

2. THE SUGGESTIBILITY AND CREDULITY OF CROWDS

When defining crowds, we said that one of their general characteristics was an excessive suggestibility, and we have shown to what an extent suggestions are contagious in every human agglomeration; a fact which explains the rapid turning of the sentiments of a crowd in a definite direction. However indifferent it may be supposed, a crowd, as a rule, is in a state of expectant attention, which renders suggestion easy. The first suggestion formulated which arises implants itself immediately by a process of contagion in the brains of all assembled, and the identical bent of the sentiments of the crowd is immediately an accomplished fact.

As is the case with all persons under the influence of suggestion, the idea which has entered the brain tends to transform itself into an act. Whether the act is that of setting fire to a palace, or involves self-sacrifice, a crowd lends itself to it with equal facility. All will depend on the nature of the exciting cause, and no longer, as in the case of the isolated individual, on the relations existing between the act suggested and the sum total of the reasons which may be urged against its realisation.

In consequence, a crowd perpetually hovering on the borderland of unconsciousness, readily yielding to all suggestions, having all the violence of feeling peculiar to beings who cannot appeal to the influence of reason, deprived of all critical faculty, cannot be otherwise than excessively credulous. The improbable does not exist for a crowd, and it is necessary to bear this circumstance well in mind to understand the facility with which are created and propagated the most improbable legends and stories.[2]

[2] Persons who went through the siege of Paris saw numerous examples of this credulity of crowds. A candle alight in an upper storey was immediately looked upon as a signal given the besiegers, although it was evident, after a moment of reflection,

The creation of the legends which so easily obtain circulation in crowds is not solely the consequence of their extreme credulity. It is also the result of the prodigious perversions that events undergo in the imagination of a throng. The simplest event that comes under the observation of a crowd is soon totally transformed. A crowd thinks in images, and the image itself immediately calls up a series of other images, having no logical connection with the first. We can easily conceive this state by thinking of the fantastic succession of ideas to which we are sometimes led by calling up in our minds any fact. Our reason shows us the incoherence there is in these images, but a crowd is almost blind to this truth, and confuses with the real event what the deforming action of its imagination has superimposed thereon. A crowd scarcely distinguishes between the subjective and the objective. It accepts as real the images evoked in its mind, though they most often have only a very distant relation with the observed fact.

The ways in which a crowd perverts any event of which it is a witness ought, it would seem, to be innumerable and unlike each other, since the individuals composing the gathering are of very different temperaments. But this is not the case. As the result of contagion the perversions are of the same kind, and take the same shape in the case of all the assembled individuals.

---

that it was utterly impossible to catch sight of the light of the candle at a distance of several miles.

40   Total Conformity

Joost A. M. Meerloo

During the last thirty years several political agencies have tried to misuse psychological and psychiatric experience to further their private aims. Active psychological warfare and mental torture are now accepted concepts in totalitarian countries. A prime result of the political pressure, both overt and unobtrusive, has been a cynical re-evaluation of human values. A new profession of specialists has emerged whose task it is not to cure, but to aggravate and manipulate the weaknesses of selected victims so that they might become more easily amenable to influence, and to prescribed political ideologies.

We may define such planned enforcement of ideas and mental coercion applied as a political tool as "thought control." The provocation of false confessions in the service of political propaganda can be defined as "brainwashing" or "menticide." The United Nations defined the systematic suppression,

From the article, "Brainwashing and Menticide: Some Implications of Conscious and Unconscious Thought Control," *Psychoanalysis and Psychoanalytic Review*, Vol. XLV, No. 1, 1958, pp. 38–90. Reprinted by permission of the National Psychological Association for Psychoanalysis, Inc. and Joost A. M. Meerloo.

starvation, and killing of minorities as the crime of *genocide*, the murder of a species. The new, more subtle crime is *menticide*, the murder of the potentialities of the free creative mind.

I wish to say no more at this time concerning the obviously sensational impact of this problem of brainwashing. It is interesting to know, however, why people reacted so hysterically and dramatically to the first detailed news on brainwashing. Terrible fears were aroused in them: especially the fear of conformity and the fear of the evil eye that can see through the person and magically dig the truth out of him.

The psychiatric problem of thought control can be approached from different angles. One may ask "what is the political technique of mental and spiritual terror?" One may make a survey of the political variations in coercive strategy. Various psychiatric and psychological schools have given different explanations of psychodynamics involved in political thought control and brainwashing.

I am here concerned, above all, with the more general question: "What do we clinicians learn from this extensive political experiment on human guinea pigs?"

Enforced interrogation, inquisition, persuasion, and mental coercion in the service of thought control and thought reform exist in many places. What lessons can be derived from the cynical political experiment with human beings? What are its implications?

There is overwhelming evidence that dictatorial regimes have improved their techniques of mental terror and mental coercion in the last quarter-century. I have followed this problem since 1933 when I along with a number of others suspected that one of the psychopathic patients in the Netherlands was used as a political tool and scapegoat in starting the Reichstag fire —the signal Hitler needed so badly in order to take dictatorial power into his own hands. At that time we had hardly any notion that a man could be changed into a servile robot with a built-in gramophone record, speaking his master's voice. When Marinus Van der Lubbe came before a German court and world forum in order to confess his crime in public, psychiatric observers thought that he had been treated with special narcotics and sedatives. At least they felt that he behaved very strangely—as if he were "punch-drunk." There was, of course, no possibility of further study after his conviction and hanging. It was not until the confession at the Nüremberg trials that we heard how Van der Lubbe had been used as a willing political tool and that the very men who had punished and killed him had been the ones who had urged him to start the fire.

True, we know of the Pavlovian technique of conditioning animals as a kind of scientific training, but, in those days, it was impossible for us psychiatrists to believe that such a laboratory experiment could be used to transform a human's mind, even temporarily, into an imitative voice speaking only the thoughts of the master.

Yet, we must not forget that enforced persuasion and inquisition by means of subtle or not so subtle intimidation had existed as long as mankind itself. As a matter of fact, every time two people meet in exchange of thought, a subtle dialectic battle starts about who is the stronger one in his capacity to communicate and dominate and who is the weaker; who is the more persuasive one and who the more submissive. When, however, psychic arguments are not sufficient, often a different kind of talk with iron fists may start. Religious wars often occurred in the service of enforced persuasion and conversion. The more subtle techniques of coercive interrogation we learned, for example, from the Inquisition of the Middle Ages. Many witches were finally made to "confess" their sexual union with the devil Beelzebub.

What then is new about this question of coercive persuasion and brainwashing?

Two big developments made these old problems of enforced persuasion of decisive importance in our era:

In the first place, the modern strategy of totalitarian governments developed a systematic political thought control and thought reform as a strategy of absolute control over the minds of people. Without such control of man's mind, no dictatorship can remain in existence.

In the second place, the technical development of the means of communication made mankind much more susceptible and sensitive to the influence and mental manipulations by political ideologies and to strange absurd suggestions from the outside. We all live daily in a web of noises and suggestions.

Let us make a survey of the most prominent points that come to the fore in this new development. I prefer to treat the general implications of the problem because they bring the clinical aspects to the fore more clearly, namely: (1) the technique of individual mental coercion and brainwashing; (2) the technique of mass-coercion and mass-seduction; (3) the problem of unobtrusive and unconscious mental coercion, and (4) ways by which a free society can resist, neutralize, and counteract these strange mental intrusions.

THE TECHNIQUES OF INDIVIDUAL MENTAL COERCION

The totalitarian brainwashing technique involves a double task. First, the mind of the victim has to be broken down—made empty according to the brainwasher's terminology; then a clean gramophone record has to be filled with new grooves, a new ideology.

The methods used are simple enough. Soldiers and officers who were prisoners of war in Korea and China were submitted to a systematic regime of mental submission followed by political propaganda in which hunger and isolation played the most important part in breaking down the victim's mental resistance. If perceptual isolation and coercive persuasion are applied day in and day out, most people will lose their individual critical distinctions and gradually follow the suggestions of their inquisitors. This happens especially when a clever alternation of hunger and giving food is used as a system of Pavlovian conditioning and training. Then new ideas are hammered in with repetitious ideological catchwords, launched after enforced, long-lasting interrogation and sleeplessness.

Especially, however, when the interrogators are able to arouse a man's deep-seated feelings of guilt can they make him even more abject and dependent, more willing to confess any crime. This subtle manipulation of man's feelings of shame and guilt was also the old coercive tool of the inquisitor but is also one of the prominent modern instruments of brainwashing. The prisoners of war in Korea were invited in a seemingly innocent way to write down their autobiographies and to describe their own mistakes and failures in life. In doing so, they inadvertently surrendered to their inquisitors details concerning personal weakness and confusion, which were investigated and analyzed again and again and finally led to mental submission, confession, and conversion. We may also say it this way: The brainwasher blackmails man's inner need to communicate. The need to talk and to communicate in days of loneliness and great boredom gradually becomes a need to confess. Abject dependency arouses all man's masochistic traits.

In the new military regulations, we have to guide the soldiers to adhere strictly to the rules and to give no information at all, and they must learn that willful silence affords better protection than their infantile need to talk and to communicate.

The official data indicate that nearly 70 per cent of the prisoners of war in Korea, unprepared for such subtle psychic attacks on their integrity, communicated with the enemy in a way not permitted by military rules. This does not mean, however, that they may be regarded as real collaborators or traitors.

For psychiatry and social psychology a few facts came to the fore which were rather surprising:

How weak and submissive is the human mind under such abnormal, stressful circumstances! Hunger can break the mental dignity and integrity of most people. When man is alone, without sufficient food, without his daily work and without his usual human contacts, he easily breaks down. He unconsciously accepts the verdict of the inquisitor and accepts the self-image imposed on him by this new father image. In brainwashing, man's masochism is the victor. Psychiatrists could have gathered some of this from previous studies of prison-psychoses and contagious delusions in isolated communities but they had to learn it anew from this political experiment.

In the laboratory this inner breakdown of man can be provoked in a rather short time by the exclusion of sensory contact with the outside world. In many a student—serving as a human guinea pig—such extreme isolation, sensory deprivation and lack of verification of reality caused fearful dreams and actual hallucinations *within twelve hours.*

When the normal sensory stimulation from the outside world fails to enter the mind and the sense of time and space disappears, the inner world of primary unconscious processes begins to take over. These experiments revealed that most men need a continual verification of and confrontation with reality lest their infantile anxieties and fantasies begin to dominate them. We now have a more exact picture of why the lonely and isolated man breaks down so easily especially in the age of advertised togetherness. Isolation and living on one's own inner resources is a state for which one has to be carefully trained.

The methods of political thought control have also directed our attention to the importance of the process of interrogation of patients. We are more convinced now that the ways and methods of interrogation and interviewing are able to influence patients and to bias the information we obtain.

Experiences with brainwashed soldiers have greatly improved our understanding. We are consequently able now to inform the courts of justice how easy it is to imprint subjective feelings on some of the accused. With the help of third degree and even with the threat of so-called truth serum or lie detector one can coerce people into false confessions.

This poses many questions concerning our own communication with patients, our own ways of interrogation and subsequent treatment. Are we sufficiently aware of the fact that the rhythmic, repeated, intimate talks and therapeutic sessions inadvertently can have a subtle, coercive action on patients? Even our benevolent silent attitude can have this effect. What we ascribe as positive and negative transference towards our patients—and from the patients toward us—has a much greater persuasive and suggestive action than many therapists would want to admit.

Unobtrusively we can transplant our ideas to the patients. Current psychotherapy and psychoanalysis are well aware of these facts and try to prevent them by emphasizing the final analysis of the transference as one of the most basic processes in every therapeutic encounter. This awareness of subjectivity and prejudice cannot be granted, however, to other more physical, medical methods where patients are just as much submitted to psychic persuasion and conditioning with neither doctor nor patient being aware of it. Take, for instance, the habit of taking tranquillizers, sedatives, and sleeping drugs. Not only mental and physical health can be affected by it, but, at the same time, the mild addict can gradually become a more submissive, masochistic personality, dependent on the physician and his chemical magic.

In the initial phases of brainwashing technique, narcotics were used as additional means of breaking down mental resistance. The old device "*in vino veritas*"—the truth is in the wine—was the first aphorism dedicated to such forms of coercive thought control. But the totalitarian inquisitor discovered rather soon that hunger, lack of sleep, cold, dirt, and isolation brought about with greater rapidity the regression and mental breakdown they wanted. This is not completely true for the application of pain and physical torture so often used by the inquisition of the Middle Ages. Experience showed that pain more often aroused rebellion and resistance in the person while the "hunger-isolation" treatment led more easily to a submissive form of dependency.

THE TECHNIQUES OF MASS–COERCION AND MASS SEDUCTION

The art of convincing other groups and nations of the subjective truth of the "chosen tribe or country" is as old as human history. Most religions have wanted to convert the nonbelievers, often forcefully and with the sword. Napoleon changed such persuasion into a military science in his "Bureau de l'Opinion Publique." In the meantime the science of advertising and propaganda discovered new methods by which to imprint onto the public favorable suggestions before actual selling of the product. Even when people are skeptical about ads, the repeated clichés and slogans have an impact. A gradual penetration into man's unconsciousness takes place no matter how much he may criticize the cheap suggestion. In the end he buys the commodity he did not first need or want.

As far as our subject of thought control is concerned it is not so important that one soap outsells another. Much day-to-day advertising and public-opinion engineering makes use of the psychological experience that a repeated suggestion, no matter how far-fetched, may gradually creep through the barriers of our critical defenses into the deeper layers of our psyche and leave some "memento" behind. The next time we hear the familiar slogan combined with the same musical jingle, our recognition acts automatically. Inwardly we say "Aha," and without critical awareness we buy the soap we will perhaps never use. The advertiser does not even need the trick of subliminal advertising to make some imprint on the minds, provided his product arouses some basic need.

The unobtrusive penetration and unconscious leakage through man's critical barriers that occurs even in a free democracy becomes, however, a thousandfold stronger persuasion when the suggestions are backed by political terror. Then, man's unconscious urge to surrender and merge with the stronger party easily takes over. The passive defense of identification with the aggressor takes hold of man.

The collective terror in a totalitarian state with the help of secret police and concentration camps makes people much more submissive and obedient to the partisans in power. Under such strain and stress the spirit may seem to be critical but the will yields.

Such are the two sides of our problem. On one side we see the engineers of mass opinion trying to use our best psychoanalytic knowledge in the service of propaganda and advertising. On the other side we discover political systems that not only use this unconscious penetration into the psyche to sell products but also to implant and imprint ideologies and slogans in the public mind.

The current Chinese program of thought reform and thought control is an example of how far this idea of mental mass submission may be executed. Hitler's idea of equalization and merging (*Gleichschaltung*) was based on the same coercive principle. In a totalitarian system the luxury of having an individual ego and an individual opinion is superfluous. All thinking and feeling belongs to the monolithic party.

It is not my task here to describe the ways in which the conductor of enforced pessimism and despair relate to the psychological warfare and actual cold war now in progress. A few illustrations may be given of what happens, however, of special affects worked on the individual psyche by such continual mental attack.

Totalitarian strategy in its tactical description of the techniques of mass intimidation and collective control discovered that the arousing of simple panic, fear and terror do not suffice. Too great a mental pressure exerted over a long period of time loses its frightening impact and often stirs rebellion and critical resistance in the people, militating against the final aim of producing obedient automatic thought machines out of human beings.

In order to better reach its goal, the more scientific strategy makes use of *waves of terror* "with in-between periods of relative calm and freedom"— the so-called "*breathing spell*," (*peredishka*). These intervals of relative freedom and lack of overt tensions can be used to much better advantage for political persuasion and mass-hypnosis provided some new wave of terror is anticipated. It is completely comparable with the patient in hypnotherapy who becomes easier to hypnotize at every session. The alternation of terror and breathing spell, for example, the alternation of a cold war of hatred with the opposite propaganda for harmonious, peaceful coexistence, can gradually cause confusion and increased anxious anticipation in people.

The Nazis had already been playing that psychological cat-and-mouse game very cleverly in the occupied countries. People ask themselves: "But what will happen tomorrow?" Gradually a silent panic saps their critical potentials and the passive expectation of renewed terror makes them easy marks for ideological slogans. According to totalitarian strategists, well-applied waves of terror are the best recipes for terrorizing people into co-operation and collaboration. It is the latent silent panic in people that makes them into more submissive and suggestible beings. On the other hand, overwhelming fear and acute fright may make rebels of them.

I make a special point of this strategy of *fractionalized panic* because its paralyzing influence is not enough known, and in actual politics we can easily be surprised by it.

Human Prospects 41
Lewis Mumford

The development of a world culture concerns mankind at large and each individual human being. Every community and society, every association and organization, has a part to play in this transformation; and no domain of life will be unaffected by it. This effort grows naturally out of the crisis of our time: the need to redress the dangerous overdevelopment of technical organization and physical energies by social and moral agencies equally far-reaching and even more commanding. In that sense, the rise of world culture comes as a measure to secure human survival. But the process would lose no small part of its meaning were it not also an effort to bring forth a more complete kind of man than history has yet disclosed. That we need leadership and participation by unified personalities is clear; but the human transformation would remain desirable and valid, even if the need were not so imperative.

The kind of person called for by the present situation is one capable of breaking through the boundaries of culture and history, which have so far limited human growth. A person not indelibly marked by the tattooings of his tribe or restricted by the taboos of his totem: not sewed up for life in the stiff clothes of his caste and calling or encased in vocational armor he cannot remove even when it endangers his life. A person not kept by his religious dietary restrictions from sharing spiritual food that other men have found nourishing; and finally, not prevented by his ideological spectacles from ever getting more than a glimpse of the world as it shows itself to men with other ideological spectacles, or as it discloses itself to those who may, with increasing frequency, be able without glasses to achieve normal vision.

The immediate object of world culture is to break through the premature closures, the corrosive conflicts, and the cyclical frustrations of history. This breakthrough would enable modern man to take advantage of the peculiar circumstances today that favor a universalism that earlier periods could only dream about. But the ultimate purpose of One World culture is to widen the human prospect and open up new domains—on earth, not in interstellar space—for human development. If the chief result of a world civilization were only to provide each individual with a television set, a motor car, a social security card, and a one-way ticket on a spaceship, one might as well turn the planet over at once to post-historic man.

The resources for this human transformation have been available for only little more than a century; and many of the technical instruments and corporate agencies have still to be shaped. But for the first time in history, man now begins to know his planet as a whole and to respond to all the peoples who inhabit it: that is, he begins to see his own multiple image in a common mirror, or rather, in a moving picture that traverses backward and forward the dimension of time. Since the exploration of the earth was undertaken by Western man before he was spiritually prepared for it, the peoples and regions that were drawn together by trade, colonization, and conquest lost many of the most precious attributes of their cultures and their personalities. The New World expansion barbarized the conquerors instead of civilizing the conquered. By the same token, Western man impoverished his own future development, too, for the heritage he mangled and often extirpated was also his own, as a member of the human race. In his land hunger, in his greed for gold and silver, for coal and iron and oil, Western man overlooked far greater riches.

Though our dawning sense of interdependence and unity comes too belatedly to repair all the damage that has been done, we see that even the residue of past cultures still holds more values than any single nation has yet created or expressed. By his very consciousness of history, modern man may free himself at last from unconscious compulsions, derived from situations he has outlived, which continue to push him off the highway of development into rubbish-filled blind alleys. Yet if he achieves a fresh understanding of the potentialities he has buried through his own failure to know himself, he may repair his shattered confidence in his future and throw open new vistas.

The survey of human existence as a whole that has gone on systematically only for the last four centuries has not alone naturalized man by bringing him within the cycle of cosmic, geological, and biological processes: it has likewise humanized nature and made it more closely than ever before an integral part of human consciousness. Man's own creative works, whether they are a temple, an atomic pile, or a mathematical theorem, are themselves expressions of nature and witnesses of potentialities that were latent in the atom and in the formative process that built up, in rhythmic series, the stable elements.

Whatever the ultimate realities, that which man knows of nature is conditioned by his self, and it changes from moment to moment and age to age as his experience matures and his capacity for symbolic interpretation grows. His feelings are as much a part of this reality as his thoughts, for his very concept of an "objective," neutral world without feelings and values was itself the product of a particular moment in his own self-development and is no longer as important as it once seemed. Yet whatever man knows of himself is conditioned by nature: so that the more exact, the more self-detached, becomes his perception of natural processes, the more fully does he free himself from the delusions of arbitrary subjectivity. Brahman and Atman are indeed one, once they are conceived in dynamic interaction: the self-creating world and the world-creating self.

This exploration of nature has naturally opened up man's inner history, too. Within the individual soul man finds in symbolic form a whole universe that seems to contain the scattered debris of past cultures and the germinal nodes of future ones. Here, within himself, he finds primitive urges and civilized constraints, tribal fixations and axial liberations, animal lethargies and angelic flights. Through the agency of culture, if not through any more direct impress upon the psyche, all of man's past selves remain disconcertingly alive. Just as man's interpretation of the so-called physical world has now become multidimensional spanning the whole distance from interstellar to intra-atomic space, and including an exact knowledge of phenomena, like ultraviolet rays, which are outside his sensory experience, so with the inner world of man: it ranges from the depths of the unconscious to the highest levels of conscious ideation, disciplined feeling, and purposeful action.

Our view of the self now includes earlier interpretations that New World science, in its confident externalism, had discarded. Augustine's picture of the mind is closer to Freud's than is John Locke's, and St. Paul's description of human nature seems far more adequate than Jeremy Bentham's. Heaven and hell, as the ultimate destinations of creativity or disintegration, are necessary cardinal points in any description of the human soul. It is not through scientific description, but through sympathy and empathy, through parallel acts of re-creation, that one explores this world, even after it has been opened up to other men in the symbols and forms of art.

Now the persistence of old biological or historic residues, whether active or inert, does not mean, as many still falsely suppose, that they have a pre-appointed or fated outcome. If certain aspects of man's nature are relatively fixed, since they are structured in his organs, they function like the warp in the loom: not merely is there considerable play in the fixed threads themselves, but the shuttle that weaves the fabric lies in man's hands, and by his conscious efforts, introducing new colors and figures, he modifies even the over-all design. Every culture attaches different estimates to man's nature and history; and in its creative moments, it adds new values that enlarge the human personality and give it new destinations. Though man's release from nature's conditions or his own past selves can never be complete, the effort to achieve it is what gives individuality to every historic form: this indeed is what keeps even the most repetitive movements of history from being entirely meaningless. The making of the future is an essential part of man's self-revelation.

The problem for man today is to use his widened consciousness of natural processes and of his own historic nature to promote his own further growth. Such knowledge must now be turned to fuller uses, in the projection of a fresh plan of life and a new image of the self, which shall be capable of rising above man's present limitations and disabilities. This effort, as we have seen, is an old one; for even before man achieved any degree of self-consciousness, he was actively engaged in self-fabrication. If "Be yourself"is nature's first injunction to man, "Transform yourself" was her second—even as "Transcend yourself" seems, at least up to now, to be her final imperative. What will distinguish the present effort to create world culture, if once it takes form, is the richness and variety of the resources that are now open, and the multitude of people now sufficiently released from the struggle for existence to play a part in this new drama.

Part five

THE ARTS

*the artist plunges with abandon
into the unknown
in order to render visible, palpable, audible,
   perceptible
new life approaching*

Willem Sandberg
"The Creative Use of Leisure"
AMERICAN SCHOLAR

Quick Watson, the Culture

Jacques Barzun
TEACHER IN AMERICA

INTRODUCTION

If you have ever attended a play, a concert, or an exhibition and examined your feelings, you will undoubtedly recall experiencing some unpleasant sensations of puzzlement. What should you say? How should you respond? What is "good?" And have you heard others express enthusiasm about some work which left you embarrassingly unmoved? Has an accepted critic pronounced as inferior a work which you have found strongly and hauntingly attractive? Have you encountered a "masterpiece" and silently wondered what others have liked about it? Do you listen to what others say before risking a comment, having a vague feeling that since you know so little, they must know more? Besides, what is there to "know?" Is appreciation a matter of knowledge or of feeling; of wisdom or of sensitivity?

If you have had such disconcerting experiences, perhaps you may not have realized that you are not an isolated sufferer from ignorance and insecurity in aesthetics, but that our culture is especially unclear regarding whether the right of personal taste is a legitimate human right. Furthermore, you might have noticed that everyone has "taste," however poor it may be. As you probably know, some declare their preferences justified by such invincible clichés as, "I don't know what is good in art, but I know what I like."

But is what we like what we would like were we more familiar with the particular work or with the specific art form in which the work was created? Is taste inborn, or is it educatable? And isn't diversity of taste a patent fact? If you reflect for a moment, you may recall the tremendous historical diversity in art. There are the attenuated, greenish madonnas of the Middle Ages; the plump and healthy ones of the Renaissance who often look like courtesans; and the madonnas of this day who are distorted and sometimes dismembered as in a nightmare. There are the archaic and thin sounds of the vielles playing ancient dances; the perfection of Bach's many-voiced harmonies; the sombre, ominous, or violent sounds of the romantics; and the dissonant effects of contemporary music.

Art is a social as well as an individual product, reflecting and identifying the particular temper of a culture. Perhaps one of the reasons why the music of Buxtehude sounds so different from that of Bartok is that the daily sounds which Buxtehude might have heard were so different from those which we hear, who live today. Music, like every other art, changes as the experience of men changes.

Standards of beauty—personal, natural, utilitarian, and artistic—not only differ radically across cultures but change within a culture in an astonishingly rapid way. But you probably can recall your early "art appreciation" course which seemed to suggest quite the reverse. It seemed to be taken for granted that responses to art should not be either a personal or even a cultural matter, but that some works are masterpieces whether one responds to them favorably or not. The notion of a "masterpiece" assumes that taste, if "good," ought to command general agreement and that it is governed by certain unassailable standards. According to this view, if one's taste in art is abominable, it can be educated to conform to the authoritative opinion. (You may have wondered whether aesthetic education could be accomplished by simple exposure to art.) What is good taste which supposedly selects "great art" automatically? Where do the standards of "goodness" and "greatness" come from?

The question regarding the origin, basis, and justification of standards for artistic excellence is a crucial one. It presumes that there *are* standards or measuring rods by which we can determine artistic worth. It indirectly presumes agreement regarding these. Are there such standards or is beauty and aesthetic excitement actually only in the eye of the beholder? Are there objectively determinable criteria for aesthetic excellence or is our choice of objects with which to decorate ourselves and our homes simply a matter of prejudicial feeling? And if it is, are some persons more sensitive than others? Is sensitivity inborn or must it be educated?

If standards of artistic excellence have produced a host of questions and problems, so have standards of impiety and obscenity. The heavy hand of culture has often intervened to declare some things legitimate and others not. Just what is the case for limiting experience by means of censorship? Who ought to have the right to impose it? If art reflects experience, should it concern itself only with what society considers "proper" experience? But are not all human experiences legitimately explorable by science? And should not the same freedom be accorded to art?

Some have claimed that communication in art differs radically from that in science: we tend to be moved by and to emulate that which the artist shows us, and for this reason the artist should be denied the right to expose us to all things. But, of course, one might equally argue that men have been moved by and emulated the work of science as well, and sometimes with serious results. Have they not concocted homemade bombs? Have they not learned the properties of drugs? Have they not imagined themselves superior to other men? Are there some especially compelling reasons then, why we should be protected from things artistically displayed? What should be censored? And how should we select those in charge of protecting us from the dark corners of experience? Aesthetic appreciation surely seems to be a special kind of response, but what makes it special?

The question of the nature of our response to art is a knotty one. First, what is one supposed to be appreciating? Should our interest center on the line, design, sound, color, and texture of the object; or on the story it tells; or on the way it is told, lighted, presented, or staginated?

Second, what are the essential traits of aesthetic experience? It can not be solely an experience of beauty if we consider the fact that the terrible, the ugly, the revolting, and the frightening have always played a role in art and play a major role in contemporary art. Is a typically aesthetic experience one of excitement and vividness? Or is it some vaguely discriminated feeling for which we have no name?

Third, if you examine the experience closely enough, you will see that you have prepared yourself for it. Entering the gallery, waiting for the curtain, seeing the conductor on the podium is a sign that something special is going to happen and that it is to be received in a particular way. In some sense your everyday perspective changed into one appropriate to the reception of art. You may have been aware of this phenomenon at other times and places, for example, when purchasing clothing, cars, houses, or dishes. While you may have asked how well it will wear or how efficiently it will run you might also have asked whether you found it attractive. This question can bring such a radical change of viewpoint that you might have found yourself balancing factors of utility against those of beauty. Attractiveness and ugliness involve a new kind of looking, a new way of seeing, an alternation in approach from that of practical life. What distinguishes a daily perspective from an artistic one?

Finally, reflection will reveal that aesthetic appreciation brings a special relation between you and the object. For you to like it, it has to "strike home," to haunt your memory. It may even cause you, if the relation has been strong, to wish to possess it, to buy it, to take it home, to make it yours. In some way the work has become "part" of you. Writers of aesthetics have called this phenomenon psychic "empathy." Just why you should empathize with one painting, poem, or quartet and not another is itself a mystery. As a creature of this century you probably know that Freud would have accounted for your special response in terms of your previous experiences, your early encounters, traumas, and fulfillments. And while this may or may not be so, the character of the empathetic relation is still more difficult to account for. What are the traits of this odd experience in which you seem to share the fate of the characters you are watching or reading about while yet being aware that you are part of the audience? You identify with them, yet are discrete from them. Such empathy may take many forms. You may have held your breath at a crescendo of music or unwittingly moved in time with it. You may have wept at a movie; you may have felt the jagged sense of a contemporary design as you looked at a landscape; or recalled the lines of a poem at an appropriate moment. In some sense, the work of art has crept into your awareness to sharpen and focus it. Obviously, it has been caught up into your experience and become part of your memory.

But if appreciation of any work of art requires empathy, it also requires the opposite psychic movement of "distance." You have probably seen children living the excitement of a celluloid duel. Later, tired and spent, they no longer savor the movie as an art form. When empathy is thus excessive, the experience is no longer one of art but of life. It is an aesthetic fact that a bereaved wife can hardly enjoy a poem on death, and that a jealous one can hardly savor *Medea*. Lacking distance, aesthetic experience becomes too vivid and too painful. Empathy and distance seem to be twin psychic movements, closely yet inversely related. Some have said that the greatest appreciation requires as much empathy as is possible while yet permitting distance. Perhaps it is lack of distance which moves a society to censorship. Perhaps one is especially apt to censor the things which one fears. For whatever reason, Russians curb what they call "capitalistic art" while Americans censor aberrant sexual behavior.

One of the major questions of aesthetics surrounds the issue of the social function of art and the obligation of the artist to his society. It has been said that art communicates more vividly and directly than any other mode of interpersonal exchange and, hence, artistic censorship is justified on these grounds. Unlike other foods which we can examine to determine their salubriousness before we swallow them, the work of art is ingested immediately and is therefore potentially more dangerous to the body politic. Some have believed that art can arouse emotions of love and hate of man for man; that it can propagandize and be put into servitude to a cause. Advertising art gives evidence of the power of art to make us want to buy, to do, and to become. It might be argued that advertising is not "art," but this is, like any attempt to rule out by definition, a sophistic verbalism. Commercial art is as much a selected arrangement as any other art form. And if it has other motives, so did Tolstoy's *War and Peace,* Picasso's *Guernica,* and Bach's *Goldberg Variations.* What, then, is the difference between "fine" and commercial art? And how do these differ from the arts of silver making or rug making or any of the other so-called "practical" arts?

Much of the material customarily known as "aesthetics" has been devoted to the question, "What is art?" But different things have been meant by this question. Sometimes it has meant, "What does the artist do and why does he do it?" Sometimes it has meant, "How does the work of art affect the appreciator and why does it move him as it does?" As a result of this ambiguity, many types of answers to the question have been given, none of which actually "defines" art as such, but each of which uncovers some fundamental and distinguishing trait of art as a human enterprise. Some have said that the artist manipulates and experiments with his materials for their own sake and, hence, that art is a form of "play." Others have said that art is the most elevated form of human activity. Some have believed that art expresses the emotions the artist wishes to share; others have believed that it expresses feelings he doesn't even know, much less wishes to share. Some have said that the work of art is a form of wish-fulfillment in which the artist gratifies his particular desires. Others have said that art crystallizes, focusses, and clarifies common social experience. Such a diversity of opinion must seem confusing indeed. Yet, each answer points to an aspect of the truth; to an insight which contributes to a more detailed and ramified view of the matter than is found in common opinion and everyday discourse.

One of the most influential views of our day is that which supports the right of art to be "abstract," formalized, and not *about* anything, nor to represent anything in any literal sense. This view is an old one which stems from human interest in exploring the intrinsic qualities and properties of things. Contemporary painting may be a blaze of juxtaposed colors; it may be a series of intersecting lines. Contemporary sculpture may consist of a mass of wires or of dismembered automobile parts. Contemporary music may include the banging of spoons and hammers or accidental, never-to-be-repeated sounds produced at irregular intervals. Such "abstractionism" is actually a selection of certain qualities from a world in order to remove them from ordinary perspective so that they may be highlighted and put into sharp focus. In one sense, every work of art in every age is just such an abstraction and distortion designed to awaken and enliven awareness.

Art is generated out of the entire range of human experience and reflects man's response to the qualitative richness of things. Since experience shapes the substance of art, both appreciator and artist encounter this raw material. But the artist possesses the skill and imagination to embody this wealth vividly.

If we examine our own experience, we will see that we have been responding aesthetically to many things. We are struck by the design of a face or the grace of a body. We struggle to increase our own personal attractiveness. These reactions, which might be said to comprise "personal aesthetic," have many things in common with our responses to art. What might be called "practical aesthetic" dominates our taste in cars, houses, and furniture. Moreover, the career of the aesthetic in everyday life must be expanded to include "natural aesthetic" or our responses to the roar of the wind, the surge of the sea, the design of a fern, or the color of a sunset. It should not be surprising, then, that we respond as well to works of art which are objects contrived to exhibit the qualities of the world.

AESTHETIC EXPERIENCE

Art and Experience   42
Irwin Edman

Whatever life may be, it is an experience; whatever experience may be, it is a flow through time, a duration, a many-colored episode in eternity. Experience may be simple as it is among babies and simple people; it may be complex as it is in the case of a scientist or poet or man of affairs. It may range from the aimless movement of a baby's hands and the undisciplined distraction of its eyes to the controlled vision and deliberate movements of the champion marksman. It may move from the beholding and manipulation of physical things to the invention and organization of ideas tenuous and abstract. But between birth and death, this much may be averred of life, it is the stimulation and response of a living body, of "five little senses startling with delight," of muscle twitching to answer with action, of hands eager and restless, of a tongue moved to utterance and a mind provoked to thought. Portions or aspects of that experience may be remembered and recorded. Totally considered, it may be aimless or purposeful. It may be merely the veil or revelation of something behind or beyond experience itself. It may be merely a systematic transient delusion. It may be a nightmare or a dream. Philosophers and poets have espoused at one time or another all these hypotheses.

But whatever experience may portend or signify, veil or reveal, it is irretrievably there. It may be intensified and heightened or dulled and obscured. It may remain brutal and dim and chaotic; it may become meaningful and clear and alive. For a moment in one aspect, for a lifetime in many, experience may achieve lucidity and vividness, intensity and depth. To effect such an intensification and clarification of experience is the province of art. So far from having to do merely with statues, pictures, and symphonies, art is the name for that whole process of intelligence by which life, understanding its own conditions, turns them to the most interesting or exquisite account. An art, properly important, would be, as Aristotle pointed out, politics.

Its theme would be the whole of experience; its materials and its theater the whole of life.

Such a comprehensive art is still the statesman's dream. The conditions of life, especially of life together, are as complex as they are precarious. We do not know enough about them to be sure of our touch, nor has any man enough power to be sure his touch is translated into action. An artist bent on turning the whole of life into an art would have to be at once a universal despot and a universal genius, a Goethe, a Newton, and an Alexander rolled into one. The art of life is an aspiration and a prophecy, not a history or a fact.

The artist de facto has had to deal with segments of experience, though he may suggest or imply it all. Experience, apart from art and intelligence, is capricious and confused. It is matter without form, movement without direction. The passing sounds are a vague noise unattended or undesired; the colors and shapes about us are unnoticed or unpleasant. The words we hear are signals to action; if they are that. Now to a certain extent life has achieved form. As we shall try to point out in the succeeding chapter, civilization itself is an art form, highly successful and fortuitous, but none the less an art.

To the extent that life has form, it is an art, and to the extent that the established disorder of civilization has some coherence, it is a work of art. All that goes by the name of custom or technique or institution is the working of intelligence or its perhaps dilapidated heritage. The realm of art is identical with the realm of man's deliberate control of that world of materials and movements among which he must make his home, of that inner world of random impulses and automatic processes which constitute his inner being. The breaking of a stick, the building of a hut, a skyscraper, or a cathedral, the use of language for communication, the sowing or the harvesting of a crop, the nurture and education of children, the framing of a code of law or morals, the weaving of a garment, or the digging of a mine—all these are alike examples of art no less than the molding of a relief or the composition of a symphony.

It is for purely accidental reasons that the fine arts have been singled out to be almost identical with Art. For in painting and sculpture, music and poetry, there is so nice and so explicit a utilization of materials, intelligence has so clear and complete a sway over materials at once so flexible and delightful, that we turn to examples of these arts for Art and in them find our aesthetic experience most intense and pure. But wherever materials are given form, wherever movement has direction, wherever life has, as it were, line and composition, there we have intelligence and there we have that transformation of a given chaos into a desired and desirable order that we call Art. Experience, apart from art and intelligence, is wild and orderless. It is formless matter, aimless movement.

It is difficult to realize how much of our diurnal experience is what

William James called it, "a big blooming buzzing confusion." It is hard to realize how much of it is a semistupor. Life has often enough been described as a waking dream. But not much of it has the vividness, though a great deal of it may have the incoherence or the horror of a dream. For most people most of the time it is a heavy lethargy. They have eyes, yet they do not, in any keen and clear sense, see. They have ears, yet they do not finely and variously hear. They have a thousand provocations to feeling and to thought, but out of their torpor comes no response. Only the pressure of some animal excitement, instant and voluminous, rouses them for a moment to an impulsive clouded answer. Life is for most of us what someone described music to be for the uninitiate, "a drowsy reverie, interrupted by nervous thrills."

How is this dazed basking in the sun, or this hurried passage from an unwilled stimulus to an uncontrolled response, transformed? How does an artist remake experience into something at once peaceful and intense, domestic and strange? What does the artist do to the world to render it arresting? What part do the arts play in our experience that gives them a special seduction and delight?

Ordinary experience, that of practical or instinctive compulsion, is at once restless and dead. Our equipment of habits and impulses is such that we see and hear just so much of objects, partake imaginatively just so much in events as is necessary for the immediate satisfaction of impulses or the fulfillment of practical intentions. Our instincts and our necessities hasten us from object to object. From each we select just as much as is requisite to our desires or to our purposes, the bare minimum of all that to free and complete aesthetic apprehension would be there. Just as meat to the dog is something to be eaten, and the cat simply something to be chased, so the chair to a tired man or an executive is simply something to be sat on; and to the thirsty man water, however lovely its flow or sparkle, simply something to be drunk. The man of affairs intent upon future issues or the next step, the scientist interested in some special consequence of the combination of two elements, the hungry or the lustful intent upon the fulfillment of one absorbing and immediate desire—all these hasten from moment to moment, from object to object, from event to event. Experience is a minimum and that minimum is bare. Only one aspect of its momentary practical or impulsive urgency is remembered; all else is forgotten or more precisely ignored.

It is one of the chief functions of the artist to render experience arresting by rendering it alive. The artist, be he poet, painter, sculptor, or architect, does something to objects, the poet and novelist do something to events, that compel the eye to stop and find pleasure in the beholding, the ear to hear for the sheer sake of listening, the mind to attend for the keen, impractical pleasure of discovery or suspense or surprise. The chair ceases to be a signal to a sitter; it becomes a part and a point in a composition, a focus of color and form. It becomes in a painting pictorially significant; it becomes alive. That passing face is not something to be persuaded or conquered or for-

gotten. It is to be looked at; it is an object of pictorial interest, at once satisfying and exciting. It ceases to be an incident or an instrument; it is not a
precipitate to action, a signal to anger or to lust. It is a moment crowded
with vitality and filled with order; it is knowledge for its own sweet sake of
something living and composed; it is beautiful, as we say, to look at, and its
beholding is a pleasure.

Painters sometimes speak of dead spots in a painting: areas where the
color is wan or uninteresting, or the forms irrelevant and cold. Experience
is full of dead spots. Art gives it life. A comprehensive art, as has been in-
timated, would render the whole of life alive. The daily detail of doing or
undergoing would be delightful, both in its immediate quality, and for the
meaning that it held. Our relations with others would all have something of
the quality of friendship and affection; what we did would be stimulating as
it is stimulating to a writer to write or to a painter to paint. What we encountered would be like an encounter with music or with painting or poetry.
To live would be a constant continuum of creative action and aesthetic appreciation. All that we did would be an art, and all that we experienced
would be an appreciation and a delight. Living would be at once ordered and
spontaneous, disciplined and free.

.   .   .

Nor is it only the madder moments of passionate assertion that find
their expression in the arts. Nuances of feeling, subtleties of thought that
practical experience keeps us too gross or too busy to observe, that words are
too crude to express, and affairs too crude to exhaust, have in the arts their
moment of being. For these reasons, too, for the observer, they are absorbing
flights from life. But they may—in major instances they do—clarify, intensify, and interpret life.

First, as to the intensification: our senses, we learn from the biologists,
are adaptations to a changing and precarious environment. They were developed, in the long animal history of the race, as instruments by which a
troubled animal might adjust itself to a constantly shifting experience. A
pigmented spot sensitive to light becomes eventually the eye. That organ
enables the animal to estimate at a distance the dangerous and desirable
object too far removed for touch. The ear, similarly the product of a long
evolutionary history, likewise originated as an instrument that rendered the
animal advertent to the dangers and promises in a mysterious and uncertain
environment. Smell, in its animal origin, was likewise a warning of the
noxious, a signal of edible or otherwise promising things. Taste, too, developed as a rough guide to the poisonous and the nourishing. Touch began
as that near and immediate sensitivity closely bound up with self-preserving
and procreative lusts.

In their origin our senses are thus practical, not aesthetic. They remain
in diurnal living, essentially practical still. There is, as it were, a myopia to

which we are all subject. Rather we are all subject to a blindness, instinctive and compulsive. We become anaesthetic to all phases of objects save those in which our immediate fortunes or actions are concerned.

The artist's function, the success of a work of art, are both partly measurable by the extent to which our senses become not signals to action but revelations of what is sensibly and tangibly there. Somewhere Stephen Crane has a story of three men shipwrecked in a small boat on a wide and stormy sea. The first sentence is, "They did not see the color of the sky." So intent were they upon the possibilities of being saved that they had no time, interest, or impulse for seeing the color of the sky above them.

In the fine arts, then, the experience becomes intensified by the arresting of sensations. We become aware with tingling pleasure of the colors and shapes on a canvas, of the sounds of a voice or a violin. The other senses, too, have their possible aesthetic exploitation, but touch, taste, and smell are not as finely manipulable, not as easily incorporated in objects or detached from practical biological interests as are sight and sound. The peculiar function of the fine arts lies, therefore, chiefly in the realm of these two subtle and finely discriminated organs, the eye and the ear. Color, which for practical purposes is usually the most negligible aspect of an object, is the painter's special material. Differences in rhythm and tone, negligible in practical communication, become for the musician the source of all his art, for the music lover the source of all his pleasure. The senses from being incitements to action are turned into avenues of delight.

It is in this respect that the basis and the ultimate appeal of all art is sensuous. We become engaged, as it were, by the amiable and intensified surfaces of things. The charm of a still life is certainly in its composition, but it is the blues and greens and yellows of the fruit that arrest us; our body becomes alive to what the senses present. Those moralists who have regarded art as a sensuous distraction have sourly stated the truth. Eyes dulled and routinated become keen again in the observation of painting; the ear becomes a subtilized organ of precise and intense sensation. We move in painting and in music not among the abstract possibilities of action but among the concrete actualities of what is there to be seen and heard.

The arts do more, however, than simply intensify sensations. In the routine of our lives, successively similar situations have produced successively similar emotional reactions. We become dulled emotionally as well as sensuously. In the clear and artful discipline of a novel or a drama, our emotions become reinstated into a kind of pure intensity. It might appear on the surface that the actualities of life, the impingements of those so very real crises of birth and death and love, are more intense than any form of art provides. That is true. But we do not live always amid crises, and the ordinary run of our experiences gives us only emotions that are dull and thin. A tragedy like *Hamlet*, a novel like *Anna Karenina*, clarify and deepen for us emotional incidents of familiar human situations. For many people, it is literature rather than life that teaches them what their native emotions are. And ideas themselves, which in the abstractions of formal reasoning may be thin and cold and external, in the passionate presentation of poetry and drama may become intimate and alive. Those would fall asleep over Godwin's *Political Justice* who might be inflamed to passion by the political poetry of Shelley. Whom the formulas of friendship enunciated by Aristotle leave cold, would be stirred to living emotion by dialogues gracious and humane in which Plato illuminates that amiable theme.

The second function of the arts noted above was the clarification of experience. This holds true likewise from the direct level of the senses to that of speculation and reflection. Our experience, through the pressure of impulses on the one hand, and the conditions of living on the other, is conventionalized into logical and practical patterns; we are likely to forget how diverse and miscellaneous experience in its immediacy is. It consists of patches of color and fragments of form; it lives as a moment transient and confused in a vanishing flux. Our senses, our instincts, and our world give some form to the undiscriminated blur. Were there no pattern at all to follow we could not live. Every blur of vision forms itself into some kind of landscape: the chaos of impressions and impulses at any moment has for that moment some coherency and shape. Our habits and our institutions canalize life. Even insanity has its own, if irrelevant, kind of order. Except in drowsiness or semistupor, and hardly even there, absolute chaos does not exist.

But in works of art sensations are more profoundly and richly clarified through some deliberate and explicit pattern; emotions are given a sequence and a development such as the exigencies of practical life scarcely or rarely permit. Our reveries, amiable and wandering, are disciplined to the pathway of some controlled, logical sequence.

An illustration of each may be of service. Others than painters of still life have seen fruit in a bowl on a table. But it requires a Cézanne or a Vermeer to organize the disordered sensations of color and form into something lucid and harmonious and whole. Everyone has experienced the blindness of human pride, or the fatal possessiveness of love. But it requires a Sophocles to show him the tragic meaning of the first in such a play as *Oedipus*, a Shakespeare to exhibit to him the latter in *Othello*. Even the most unreflective have at some time or other harbored scattered and painful thoughts on the vanity of life or the essential beauty and goodness of Nature. A few have formulated these scattered insights into a system. But a poet like Lucretius can turn that vague intuition into a major and systematic insight; Dante can exhibit the latter in a magnificent panorama of life and destiny. The kaleidoscope of our sensations falls into an eternal pattern; a mood half articulate and half recognized in its confused recurrence becomes, as it were, clarified forever in a poem or a novel or a drama. A floating impression becomes fixed in the vivid system of music or letters.

In a sense, therefore, all art is idealization, even where it pretends to be realistic. For no experience could possibly have the permanent order, the pattern, the changeless integration of a work of art. The mere permanence of a painting as compared with the vision of a passing moment, the mere dramatic logic of a drama as compared with the incongruous juxtapositions of life are illustrations of the point. But the idealization which is art has the benefit of holding a clarifying mirror up to Nature. It shows us by deliberate artifice what is potentially in Nature to be seen, in life to be felt, in speculation to be thought.

Now, to return to the interpretation of experience. Psychologists and logicians are fond of pointing out how much of what seems to be mere and sheer sensation is a matter of judgment and inference. We do not see cabbages and kings; we thus interpret blurs of vision. Our intelligence and our habits are, in their way, artists. They enable us to respond to things not simply as sheer physical stimuli but as meanings. The fine arts simply accentuate the process or perhaps merely italicize the process which all intelligence exemplifies. Those separate spots of color become significant items in the total pattern in a painting, the pattern itself is significant of a face, the face of some passion or its tragic frustration. In a novel the words are significant as well as vibrant: they tell with significant detail of some life, some experience, some destiny.

All the arts in one way or another, to some greater or lesser extent, interpret life. They may "interpret" nothing more than the way in which a bowl of fruit "appears" to the ordered imagination of a painter. They may "interpret" nothing more than sensation. Or they may interpret, as *Hamlet* does, or *War and Peace,* or *Ode on the Intimations of Immortality from Recollections of Early Childhood,* the confused intuitions of millions of men, bringing to a focus an obscure burden of human emotion. A poem like *The Divine Comedy* or Goethe's *Faust* may be a commentary upon the whole human scene, its nature, its movement, and its destiny. When Matthew Arnold defined poetry as a criticism of life, he might well have extended his definition to the whole of the fine arts. For criticism is a judgment upon, an interpretation of, a given section of life. Explicit interpretation, of course, is to be found chiefly in literature. But a statue by Michelangelo or Rodin, a piece of music by Beethoven or Debussy, is by virtue of its comprehensive and basic quality, its mood, its tempo, and its essential timbre, an interpretation of experience. One hears more than an arrangement of sounds in Beethoven's Fifth Symphony. One hears the comment of a great spirit on the world in which it lives. In Rembrandt's pictures of old rabbis, or El Greco's of Spanish grandees, there is more than meets the simply pictorial eye. These works are the language of men who not only saw and heard with the external eye and ear, but put into sound a hearing, into canvas a vision of what life essentially meant to them.

These three functions, intensification, clarification, and interpretation of experience, the arts fulfill in various degree. For many observers the arts are simply sensuous excitements and delights. For many they are the language in which the human spirit has clarified to itself the meanings of its world. For many the arts are the sensuously enticing and emotionally moving vehicles of great total visions of experience. The arts, in fragments as it were, suggest the goal toward which all experience is moving: the outer world of things, the inner world of impulse mastered thoroughly by intelligence, so that whatever is done is itself delightful in the doing, delightful in the result. The Utopia of the philosopher of which Plato dreamed is foreshadowed in those moments of felicity which the fine arts at moments provide. A symphony in its ordered perfection, a drama in its tragic logic, a poem in its sensuously moving grace, is a foretaste of what an ordered world might be. Art is another name for intelligence, which in an ordered society would function over the whole of men's concerns, as it functions happily now in those scattered works we call beautiful, in those happy moments we call aesthetic pleasure.

43   On Good Taste

David Hume

The great variety of Taste, as well as of opinion, which prevails in the world, is too obvious not to have fallen under everyone's observation. Men of the most confined knowledge are able to remark a difference of taste in the narrow circle of their acquaintance, even where the persons have been educated under the same government, and have early imbibed the same prejudices. But those, who can enlarge their view to contemplate distant nations and remote ages, are still more surprised at the great inconsistence and contrariety. We are apt to call *barbarous* whatever departs widely from our own taste and appehension; but soon find the epithet of reproach retorted on us. And the highest arrogance and self-conceit is at last startled, on observing an equal assurance on all sides, and scruples, amidst such a contest of sentiment, to pronounce positively in its own favor.

As this variety of taste is obvious to the most careless inquirer; so will it be found, on examination, to be still greater in reality than in appearance. The sentiments of men often differ with regard to beauty and deformity of all kinds, even while their general discourse is the same. There are certain terms in every language, which import blame, and others praise; and all men, who use the same tongue, must agree in their application of them. Every voice is united in applauding elegance, propriety, simplicity, spirit in writing;

From Essay XXIII "Of the Standard of Taste" in *Philosophical Works of David Hume* (Vol. III) Boston, Little, Brown & Co., 1854.

and in blaming fustian, affectation, coldness, and a false brilliancy: But when critics come to particulars, this seeming unanimity vanishes; and it is found, that they had affixed a very different meaning to their expressions. In all matters of opinion and science, the case is opposite: The difference among men is there oftener found to lie in generals than in particulars; and to be less in reality than in appearance. An explanation of the terms commonly ends the controversy; and the disputants are surprised to find, that they have been quarreling, while at bottom they agreed in their judgment.

.   .   .

It is natural for us to seek a *Standard of Taste;* a rule, by which the various sentiments of men may be reconciled; at least, a decision afforded, confirming one sentiment, and condemning another.

There is a species of philosophy, which cuts off all hopes of success in such an attempt, and represents the impossibility of ever attaining any standard of taste. The difference, it is said, is very wide between judgment and sentiment. All sentiment is right; because sentiment has a reference to nothing beyond itself, and is always real, wherever a man is conscious of it. But all determinations of the understanding are not right; because they have a reference to something beyond themselves, to wit, real matter of fact; and are not always conformable to that standard. Among a thousand different opinions which different men may entertain of the same subject, there is one, and but one, that is just and true; and the only difficulty is to fix and ascertain it. On the contrary, a thousand different sentiments, excited by the same object, are all right: Because no sentiment represents what is really in the object. It only marks a certain conformity or relation between the object and the organs or faculties of the mind; and if that conformity did not really exist, the sentiment could never possibly have being. Beauty is no quality in things themselves: It exists merely in the mind which contemplates them; and each mind perceives a different beauty. One person may even perceive deformity, where another is sensible of beauty; and every individual ought to acquiesce in his own sentiment, without pretending to regulate those of others. To seek the real beauty, or real deformity, is as fruitless an inquiry as to pretend to ascertain the real sweet or real bitter. According to the disposition of the organs, the same object may be both sweet and bitter: and the proverb has justly determined it to be fruitless to dispute concerning tastes. It is very natural, and even quite necessary, to extend this axiom to mental, as well as bodily taste; and thus common sense, which is so often at variance with philosophy, especially with the skeptical kind, is found, in one instance at least, to agree in pronouncing the same decision.

But though this axiom, by passing into a proverb, seems to have attained the sanction of common sense; there is certainly a species of common sense, which opposes it, at least serves to modify and restrain it. Whoever would assert an equality of genius and elegance between Ogilby and Milton, or

Bunyan and Addison, would be thought to defend no less an extravagance, than if he had maintained a mole-hill to be as high as Teneriffe, or a pond as extensive as the ocean. Though there may be found persons, who give the preference to the former authors; no one pays attention to such a taste; and we pronounce, without scruple, the sentiment of these pretended critics to be absurd and ridiculous. The principle of the natural equality of tastes is then totally forgot, and while we admit it on some occasions, where the objects seem near an equality, it appears an extravagant paradox, or rather a palpable absurdity, where objects so disproportioned are compared together.

It is evident that none of the rules of composition are fixed by reasonings *a priori,* or can be esteemed abstract conclusions of the understanding, from comparing those habitudes and relations of ideas, which are eternal and immutable. Their foundation is the same with that of all the practical sciences, experience; nor are there anything but general observations, concerning what has been universally found to please in all countries and in all ages. Many of the beauties of poetry, and even of eloquence, are founded on falsehood and fiction, on hyperboles, metaphors, and an abuse or perversion of terms from their natural meaning. To check the sallies of the imagination, and to reduce every expression to geometrical truth and exactness, would be the most contrary to the laws of criticism; because it would produce a work, which, by universal experience, has been found the most insipid and disagreeable. But though poetry can never submit to exact truth, it must be confined by rules of art, discovered to the author either by genius or observation. If some negligent or irregular writers have pleased, they have not pleased by their transgressions of rule or order, but in spite of these transgressions: They have possessed other beauties, which were conformable to just criticism; and the force of these beauties has been able to overpower censure, and give the mind a satisfaction superior to the disgust arising from the blemishes. Ariosto pleases; but not by his monstrous and improbable fictions, by his bizarre mixture of the serious and comic styles, by the want of coherence in his stories, or by the continual interruptions of his narration. He charms by the force and clearness of his expression, by the readiness and variety of his inventions, and by his natural pictures of the passions, especially those of the gay and amorous kind: And however his faults may diminish our satisfaction, they are not able entirely to destroy it. Did our pleasure really arise from those parts of his poem, which we denominate faults, this would be no objection to criticism in general: It would only be an objection to those particular rules of criticism, which would establish such circumstances to be faults, and would represent them as universally blameable. If they are found to please, they cannot be faults; let the pleasure, which they produce, be ever so unexpected and unaccountable.

But though all the general rules of art are founded only on experience, and on the observation of the common sentiments of human nature, we must not imagine, that, on every occasion, the feelings of men will be conformable to these rules. Those finer emotions of the mind are of a very tender and delicate nature, and require the concurrence of many favorable circumstances to make them play with facility and exactness, according to their general and established principles. The least exterior hindrance to such small springs, or the least internal disorder, disturbs their motion, and confounds the operation of the whole machine. When we would make an experiment of this nature, and would try the force of any beauty or deformity, we must choose with care a proper time and place, and bring the fancy to a suitable situation and disposition. A perfect serenity of mind, a recollection of thought, a due attention to the object; if any of these circumstances be wanting, our experiment will be fallacious, and we shall be unable to judge of the catholic and universal beauty. The relation, which nature has placed between the form and the sentiment, will at least be more obscure; and it will require greater accuracy to trace and discern it. We shall be able to ascertain its influence, not so much from the operation of each particular beauty, as from the durable admiration, which attends those works, that have survived all the caprices of mode and fashion, all the mistakes of ignorance and envy.

The same Homer, who pleased at Athens and Rome two thousand years ago, is still admired at Paris and at London. All the changes of climate, government, religion, and language, have not been able to obscure his glory. Authority or prejudice may give a temporary vogue to a bad poet or orator; but his reputation will never be durable or general. When his compositions are examined by posterity or by foreigners, the enchantment is dissipated, and his faults appear in their true colors. On the contrary, a real genius, the longer his works endure, and the more wide they are spread, the more sincere is the admiration which he meets with. Envy and jealousy have too much place in a narrow circle; and even familiar acquaintance with his person may diminish the applause due to his performances: But when these obstructions are removed, the beauties, which are naturally fitted to excite agreeable sentiments, immediately display their energy; while the world endures, they maintain their authority over the minds of men.

It appears then, that, amidst all the variety and caprice of taste, there are certain general principles of approbation or blame, whose influence a careful eye may trace in all operations of the mind. Some particular forms or qualities, from the original structure of the internal fabric, are calculated to please, and others to displease; and if they fail of their effect in any particular instance, it is from some apparent defect or imperfection in the organ. A man in a fever would not insist on his palate as able to decide concerning flavors; nor would one, affected with the jaundice, pretend to give a verdict with regard to colors. In each creature, there is a sound and a defective state; and the former alone can be supposed to afford us a true standard of taste and sentiment. If, in the sound state of the organ, there be an entire or a considerable uniformity of sentiment among men, we may thence derive an idea of the perfect beauty; in like manner as the appearance of objects in daylight, to the eye of a man in health, is denominated their true and real color, even while color is allowed to be merely a phantasm of the senses.

Many and frequent are the defects in the internal organs, which prevent or weaken the influence of those general principles, on which depends our sentiment of beauty or deformity. Though some objects, by the structure of the mind, be naturally calculated to give pleasure, it is not to be expected, that in every individual the pleasure will be equally felt. Particular incidents and situations occur, which either throw a false light on the objects, or hinder the true from conveying to the imagination the proper sentiment and perception.

One obvious cause, why many feel not the proper sentiment of beauty, is the want of that *delicacy* of imagination, which is requisite to convey a sensibility of those finer emotions. This delicacy everyone pretends to: Everyone talks of it; and would reduce every kind of taste or sentiment to its standard. But as our intention in this essay is to mingle some light of the understanding with the feelings of sentiment, it will be proper to give a more accurate definition of delicacy than has hitherto been attempted. And not to draw our philosophy from too profound a source, we shall have recourse to a noted story in Don Quixote.

It is with good reason, says Sancho to the squire with the great nose, that I pretend to have a judgment in wine: This is a quality hereditary in our family. Two of my kinsmen were once called to give their opinion of a hogshead, which was supposed to be excellent, being old and of a good vintage. One of them tastes it; considers it; and, after mature reflection, pronounces the wine to be good, were it not for a small taste of leather, which he perceived in it. The other, after using the same precautions, gives also his verdict in favor of the wine; but with the reserve of a taste of iron, which he could easily distinguish. You cannot imagine how much they were both ridiculed for their judgment. But who laughed in the end? On emptying the hogshead, there was found at the bottom an old key with a leathern thong tied to it.

The great resemblance between mental and bodily taste will easily teach us to apply this story. Though it be certain, that beauty and deformity, more than sweet and bitter, are not qualities in objects, but belong entirely to the sentiment, internal or external; it must be allowed, that there are certain qualities in objects, which are fitted by nature to produce those particular feelings. Now as these qualities may be found in a small degree, or may be mixed and confounded with each other, it often happens that the taste is not affected with such minute qualities, or is not able to distinguish all the particular flavors, amidst the disorder in which they are presented. Where the organs are so fine, as to allow nothing to escape them; and at the same time so exact, as to perceive every ingredient in the composition: This we call delicacy of taste, whether we employ these terms in the literal or metaphorical sense. Here then the general rules of beauty are of use, being drawn from established models, and from the observation of what pleases or displeases, when presented singly and in a high degree: And if the same qualities, in a continued composition, and in a smaller degree, affect not the organs with a sensible delight or uneasiness, we exclude the person from all pretensions to this delicacy. To produce these general rules or avowed patterns of composition, is like finding the key with the leathern thong; which justified the verdict of Sancho's kinsmen, and confounded those pretended judges who had condemned them. Though the hogshead had never been emptied, the taste of the one was still equally delicate, and that of the other equally dull and languid: But it would have been more difficult to have proved the superiority of the former, to the conviction of every bystander. In like manner, though the beauties of writing had never been methodized, or reduced to general principles; though no excellent models had ever been acknowledged; the different degrees of taste would still have subsisted, and the judgment of one man been preferable to that of another; but it would not have been so easy to silence the bad critic, who might always insist upon his particular sentiment, and refuse to submit to his antagonist. But when we show him an avowed principle of art; when we illustrate this principle by examples, whose operation, from his own particular taste, he acknowledges to be conformable to the principle; when we prove that the same principle may be applied to the present case, where he did not perceive or feel its influence: He must conclude, upon the whole, that the fault lies in himself, and that he wants the delicacy, which is requisite to make him sensible of every beauty and every blemish, in any composition or discourse.

It is acknowledged to be the perfection of every sense or faculty, to perceive with exactness its most minute objects, and allow nothing to escape its notice and observation. The smaller the objects are, which become sensible to the eye, the finer is that organ, and the more elaborate its make and composition. A good palate is not tried by strong flavors, but by a mixture of small ingredients, where we are still sensible of each part, notwithstanding its minuteness and its confusion with the rest. In like manner, a quick and acute perception of beauty and deformity must be the perfection of our mental taste; nor can a man be satisfied with himself while he suspects that any excellence or blemish in a discourse has passed him unobserved. In this case, the perfection of the man, and the perfection of the sense or feeling, are found to be united. A very delicate palate, on many occasions, may be a great inconvenience both to a man himself and to his friends: But a delicate taste of wit or beauty must always be a desirable quality, because it is the source of all the finest and most innocent enjoyments of which human nature is susceptible. In this decision the sentiments of all mankind are agreed. Wherever you can ascertain a delicacy of taste, it is sure to meet with approbation; and the best way of ascertaining it is to appeal to those models and principles which have been established by the uniform consent and experience of nations and ages.

But though there be naturally a wide difference in point of delicacy between one person and another, nothing tends further to increase and improve this talent, than *practice* in a particular art, and the frequent survey or contemplation of a particular species of beauty. When objects of any kind are first presented to the eye or imagination, the sentiment which attends them is obscure and confused; and the mind is, in a great measure, incapable of pronouncing concerning their merits or defects. The taste cannot perceive the several excellencies of the performance, much less distinguish the particular character of each excellency, and ascertain its quality and degree. If it pronounce the whole in general to be beautiful or deformed, it is the utmost that can be expected; and even this judgment, a person so unpracticed will be apt to deliver with great hesitation and reserve. But allow him to acquire experience in those objects, his feeling becomes more exact and nice: He not only perceives the beauties and defects of each part, but marks the distinguishing species of each quality, and assigns it suitable praise or blame. A clear and distinct sentiment attends him through the whole survey of the objects; and he discerns that very degree and kind of approbation or displeasure which each part is naturally fitted to produce. The mist dissipates which seemed formerly to hang over the object: The organ acquires greater perfection in its operations; and can pronounce, without danger or mistake, concerning the merits of every performance. In a word, the same address and dexterity, which practice gives to the execution of any work, is also acquired by the same means, in the judging of it.

So advantageous is practice to the discernment of beauty, that, before we can give judgment on any work of importance, it will even be requisite that that very individual performance be more than once perused by us, and be surveyed in different lights with attention and deliberation. There is a flutter or hurry of thought which attends the first perusal of any piece, and which confounds the genuine sentiment of beauty. The relation of the parts is not discerned: The true characters of style are little distinguished. The several perfections and defects seem wrapped up in a species of confusion, and present themselves indistinctly to the imagination. Not to mention, that there is a species of beauty, which, as it is florid and superficial, pleases at first; but being found incompatible with a just expression either of reason or passion, soon palls upon the taste, and is then rejected with disdain, at least rated at a much lower value.

It is impossible to continue in the practice of contemplating any order of beauty, without being frequently obliged to form *comparisons* between the several species and degrees of excellence, and estimating their proportion to each other. A man, who had had no opportunity of comparing the different kinds of beauty, is indeed totally unqualified to pronounce an opinion with regard to any object presented to him. By comparison alone we fix the epithets of praise or blame, and learn how to assign the due degree of each. The coarsest daubing contains a certain lustre of colors and exactness of imitation, which are so far beauties, and would affect the mind of a peasant or Indian

with the highest admiration. The most vulgar ballads are not entirely destitute of harmony or nature; and none but a person familiarized to superior
beauties would pronounce their numbers harsh, or narration uninteresting. A
great inferiority of beauty gives pain to a person conversant in the highest
excellence of the kind, and is for that reason pronounced a deformity: As the
most finished object with which we are acquainted is naturally supposed to
have reached the pinnacle of perfection, and to be entitled to the highest
applause. One accustomed to see, and examine, and weigh the several performances, admired in different ages and nations, can alone rate the merits of
a work exhibited to his view, and assign its proper rank among the productions of genius.

But to enable a critic the more fully to execute this undertaking, he must
preserve his mind free from all *prejudice,* and allow nothing to enter into his
consideration but the very object which is submitted to his examination. We
may observe, that every work of art, in order to produce its due effect on the
mind, must be surveyed in a certain point of view, and cannot be fully
relished by persons, whose situation, real or imaginary, is not conformable to
that which is required by the performance. An orator addresses himself to a
particular audience, and must have a regard to their particular genius, interests, opinions, passions, and prejudices; otherwise he hopes in vain to govern
their resolutions, and inflame their affections. Should they even have entertained some prepossessions against him, however unreasonable, he must not
overlook this disadvantage; but, before he enters upon the subject, must endeavour to conciliate their affection, and acquire their good graces. A critic
of a different age or nation, who should peruse this discourse, must have all
these circumstances in his eye, and must place himself in the same situation
as the audience, in order to form a true judgment of the oration. In like
manner, when any work is addressed to the public, though I should have a
friendship or enmity with the author, I must depart from this situation; and
considering myself as a man in general, forget, if possible, my individual
being, and my peculiar circumstances. A person influenced by prejudice,
complies not with this condition, but obstinately maintains his natural position, without placing himself in that point of view which the performance
supposes. If the work be addressed to persons of a different age or nation, he
makes no allowance for their peculiar views and prejudices; but, full of the
manners of his own age and country, rashly condemns what seemed admirable in the eyes of those for whom alone the discourse was calculated. If
the work be executed for the public, he never sufficiently enlarges his comprehension, or forgets his interest as a friend or enemy, as a rival or com-
mentator. By this means, his sentiments are perverted; nor have the same
beauties and blemishes the same influence upon him, as if he had imposed a
proper violence on his imagination, and had forgotten himself for a moment.
So far his taste evidently departs from the true standard, and of consequence
loses all credit and authority.

It is well known, that in all questions submitted to the understanding, prejudice is destructive of sound judgment, and perverts all operations of the intellectual faculties: It is no less contrary to good taste; nor has it less influence to corrupt our sentiment of beauty. It belongs to *good sense* to check its influence in both cases; and in this respect, as well as in many others, reason, if not an essential part of taste, is at least requisite to the operations of this latter faculty. In all the nobler productions of genius, there is a mutual relation and correspondence of parts; nor can either the beauties or blemishes be perceived by him, whose thought is not capacious enough to comprehend all those parts, and compare them with each other, in order to perceive the consistence and uniformity of the whole. Every work of art has also a certain end or purpose for which it is calculated; and is to be deemed more or less perfect, as it is more or less fitted to attain this end. The object of eloquence is to persuade, of history to instruct, of poetry to please, by means of the passions and the imagination. These ends we must carry constantly in our view when we peruse any performance; and we must be able to judge how far the means employed are adapted to their respective purposes. Besides, every kind of composition, even the most poetical, is nothing but a chain of propositions and reasonings; not always indeed, the justest and most exact, but still plausible and specious, however disguised by the coloring of the imagination. The persons introduced in tragedy and epic poetry, must be represented as reasoning, and thinking, and concluding, and acting, suitably to their character and circumstances; and without judgment, as well as taste and invention, a poet can never hope to succeed in so delicate an undertaking. Not to mention, that the same excellence of faculties which contributes to the improvement of reason, the same clearness of conception, the same exactness of distinction, the same vivacity of apprehension, are essential to the operations of true taste, and are its infallible concomitants. It seldom or never happens, that a man of sense, who has experience in any art, cannot judge of its beauty; and it is no less rare to meet with a man who has a just taste without a sound understanding.

Thus, though the principles of taste be universal, and nearly, if not entirely, the same in all men; yet few are qualified to give judgment on any work of art, or establish their own sentiment as the standard of beauty. The organs of internal sensation are seldom so perfect as to allow the general principles their full play, and produce a feeling correspondent to those principles. They either labor under some defect, or are vitiated by some disorder; and by that means, excite a sentiment, which may be pronounced erroneous. When the critic has no delicacy, he judges without any distinction, and is only affected by the grosser and more palpable qualities of the object: The finer touches pass unnoticed and disregarded. Where he is not aided by practice, his verdict is attended with confusion and hesitation. Where no comparison has been employed, the most frivolous beauties, such as rather merit the name of defects, are the object of his admiration. Where he lies under the influence of prejudice, all his natural sentiments are perverted. Where good sense is wanting, he is not qualified to discern the beauties of design and reasoning, which are the highest and most excellent. Under some or other of these imperfections, the generality of men labor; and hence a true judge in the finer arts is observed, even during the most polished ages, to be so rare a character: Strong sense, united to delicate sentiment, improved by practice, perfected by comparison, and cleared of all prejudice, can alone entitle critics to this valuable character; and the joint verdict of such, wherever they are to be found, is the true standard of taste and beauty.

But where are such critics to be found? By what remarks are they to be known? How distinguish them from pretenders? These questions are embarrassing; and seem to throw us back into the same uncertainty, from which, during the course of this essay, we have endeavored to extricate ourselves.

But if we consider the matter aright, these are questions of fact, not of sentiment. Whether any particular person be endowed with good sense and a delicate imagination, free from prejudice, may often be the subject of dispute, and be liable to great discussion and inquiry: But that such a character is valuable and estimable, will be agreed in by all mankind. Where these doubts occur, men can do no more than in other disputable questions which are submitted to the understanding: They must produce the best arguments that their invention suggests to them; they must acknowledge a true and decisive standard to exist somewhere, to wit, real existence and matter of fact; and they must have indulgence to such as differ from them in their appeals to this standard. It is sufficient for our present purpose, if we have proved that the taste of all individuals is not upon an equal footing, and that some men in general, however difficult to be particularly pitched upon, will be acknowledged by universal sentiment to have a preference above others.

But, in reality, the difficulty of finding, even in particulars, the standard of taste, is not so great as it is represented.

.   .   .

Though men of delicate taste be rare, they are easily to be distinguished in society by the soundness of their understanding, and the superiority of their faculties above the rest of mankind. The ascendant, which they acquire, gives a prevalence to that lively approbation with which they receive any productions of genius, and renders it generally predominant. Many men, when left to themselves, have but a faint and dubious perception of beauty, who yet are capable of relishing any fine stroke which is pointed out to them. Every convert to the admiration of the real poet or orator is the cause of some new conversion. And though prejudices may prevail for a time, they never unite in celebrating any rival to the true genius, but yield at last to the force of nature and just sentiment. Thus, though a civilized nation may easily be mistaken in the choice of their admired philosopher, they never have been found long to err, in their affection for a favorite epic or tragic author.

But notwithstanding all our endeavors to fix a standard of taste, and reconcile the discordant apprehensions of men, there still remain two sources of variation which are not sufficient indeed to confound all the boundaries of beauty and deformity, but will often serve to produce a difference in the degrees of our approbation or blame. The one is the different humors of particular men; the other, the particular manners and opinions of our age and country. The general principles of taste are uniform in human nature: Where men vary in their judgments, some defect or perversion in the faculties may commonly be remarked; proceeding either from prejudice, from want of practice, or want of delicacy: and there is just reason for approving one taste, and condemning another. But where there is such a diversity in the internal frame or external situation as is entirely blameless on both sides, and leaves no room to give one the preference above the other; in that case a certain degree of diversity in judgment is unavoidable, and we seek in vain for a standard by which we can reconcile the contrary sentiments.

ART AND THE CURRICULUM

Art and Education   44

Herbert Read

THE THESIS

The thesis which is to be put forward in this book is not original. It was very explicitly formulated by Plato many centuries ago, and I have no other ambition than to translate his view of the function of art in education into terms which are directly applicable to our present needs and conditions.

It is surely one of the curiosities of the history of philosophy that one of the most cherished notions of this great man has never been taken seriously by any of his followers, Schiller alone being an exception. Scholars have played with his thesis as with a toy: they have acknowledged its beauty, its logic, its completeness; but never for a moment have they considered its feasibility. They have treated Plato's most passionate ideal as an idle paradox, only to be understood in the context of a lost civilization.

The thesis is: that art should be the basis of education.

Stated so briefly it has admittedly an air of paradox. But a paradox may owe its apparent absurdity to an unfamiliar use of language, and my first care will be to give a general definition of the two terms here involved—art and education. I believe that Plato's reasonable thesis has been misunderstood, firstly because for centuries there has been no understanding of what he meant by art; and secondly because there has been an almost contemporaneous uncertainty about the purpose of education.

Of the nature of art I might conceivably persuade my readers that there can be no two opinions, for the definition I offer is objective. It implies no "views," no transcendental elements whatsoever: it brings art within the world of natural phenomena and makes it in certain essentials subject to the measurements upon which scientific laws are based. But it is not likely that I shall carry general agreement on the purpose I ascribe to education, for here there are at least two irreconcilable possibilities: one, that man should be educated to become what he is; the other, that he should be educated to become what

From Ch. One, "The Purpose of Education" and Ch. Seven, "The Natural Form of Education," with some footnotes deleted: Reprinted from *Education Through Art,* by Herbert Read, by permission of Pantheon Books, a Division of Random House, Inc. All rights reserved.

he is not. The first view assumes that each individual is born with certain potentialities which have a positive value for that individual and that it is his proper destiny to develop these potentialities within the framework of a society liberal enough to allow for an infinite variation of types. The second view assumes that whatever idiosyncrasies the individual may possess at birth, it is the duty of the teacher to eradicate them unless they conform to a certain ideal of character determined by the traditions of the society of which the individual has involuntarily become a member.

.   .   .

A PRELIMINARY DEFINITION

Having made clear the choice I make between these necessary and fundamental assumptions, I can now give the first of the general definitions promised: it can best take the form of an answer to the question: *What is the purpose of education?*

An answer to this question is implied in a libertarian conception of democracy. The purpose of education can then only be to develop, at the same time as the uniqueness, the social consciousness or reciprocity of the individual. As a result of the infinite permutations of heredity, the individual will inevitably be unique, and this uniqueness, because it is something not possessed by anyone else, will be of value to the community. It may be only a unique way of speaking or of smiling—but that contributes to life's variety. But it may be a unique way of seeing, of thinking, of inventing, of expressing mind or emotion—and in that case, one man's individuality may be of incalculable benefit to the whole of humanity. But uniqueness has no practical value in isolation. One of the most certain lessons of modern psychology and of recent historical experiences, is that education must be a process, not only of individuation, but also of *integration,* which is the reconciliation of individual uniqueness with social unity. From this point of view, the individual will be "good" in the degree that his individuality is realized within the organic wholeness of the community. His touch of colour contributes, however imperceptibly, to the beauty of the landscape—his note is a necessary, though unnoticed, element in the universal harmony.

.   .   .

Having established the relevance of aesthetics to the processes of perception and imagination, I shall then pass on to the less disputed ground of expression. Education is the fostering of growth, but apart from physical maturation, growth is only made apparent in expression—audible or visible signs and symbols. Education may therefore be defined as the cultivation of modes of expression—it is teaching children and adults how to make sounds, images, movements, tools and utensils. A man who can make such things well is a well educated man. If he can make good sounds, he is a good speaker, a good musician, a good poet; if he can make good images, he is a good painter or sculptor; if good movements, a good dancer or labourer; if good tools or utensils, a good craftsman. All faculties, of thought, logic, memory, sensibility and intellect, are involved in such processes, and no aspect of education is excluded in such processes. And they are all processes which involve art, for art is nothing but the good making of sounds, images, etc. The aim of education is therefore the creation of artists—of people efficient in the various modes of expression.

. . .

FROM PLAY TO ART

It will be found that the varieties of children's play are capable of being co-ordinated and developed in four directions, corresponding to the four basic mental functions, and that when so developed, the play activity naturally incorporates all the subjects appropriate to the primary phase of education.

From the aspect of *feeling* play may be developed by personification and objectivation towards DRAMA.

From the aspect of *sensation* play may be developed by modes of self-expression towards visual or plastic DESIGN.

From the aspect of *intuition* play may be developed by rhythmic exercises towards DANCE and MUSIC.

From the aspect of *thought* play may be developed by constructive activities towards CRAFT.

These four aspects of development, DRAMA, DESIGN, DANCE (including MUSIC) and CRAFT, are the four divisions into which a primary system of education naturally falls, but together they form a unity which is the unity of the harmoniously developing personality.[1]

Actually they include all the subjects normally taught in elementary schools in separate and unrelated classes. Drama includes the various modes of communication, such as elocution, reading and English. Dance incorporates music and physical training. Design includes painting, drawing and modelling. Craft includes measurement (elementary arithmetic and geometry), gardening, biology, farming, needlework, and some elementary physics and chemistry, structure of materials, composition of foodstuffs, fertilizers, etc.

These aspects of education are aspects of one process, and cannot be departmentalized without harm to one another. The fundamental play is a drama, the unfolding drama of creation and discovery, a drama called GROWTH, and it involves craft, design and dance as necessary co-operative activities.

As a child grows, he will develop a bias, according to his temperamental disposition, along one of the four directions of originating activity. The ideal is, of course, the harmonious development of all the mental functions, but there is not one ideal of human personality, nor even four, but four main

[1] Cf. Aristotle. *Politics* (V, iii). 'The customary branches of education are in number four; they are—(1) reading and writing, (2) gymnastic, (3) music, and, although this is not universally admitted, (4) the art of design.'

groups with different combinations of the three subordinate functions under the dominant trait. But it is not until adolescence that the combination assumes its final pattern, and until that phase of development is reached it is not practicable to partition the educational system according to temperamental disposition—that is to say, to start vocational education. But this does not, of course, exempt a teacher at the primary stage from the necessity of adapting a general system to the requirements of particular types.

Primary education should have as its ideal an individual in whom all the mental functions grow harmoniously together. It is in this sense that we can return with deeper understanding to Edmond Holmes's statement, that the function of education is to foster growth. At the beginning the growth may seem to be uniform, but sooner or later, and at the latest at the stage marked by the end of primary and the beginning of secondary education, branches stem from the trunk, personality is differentiated according to innate disposition, and teaching must follow along the diverse directions in which the human psyche splits and spreads out into the social environment.

.   .   .

There are teachers who by disposition and capability are more suited to the teaching of infants, and others who are more suited to the teaching of adolescent youths, and the hierarchy should be differentiated to provide for a variety of vocational aptitudes. But it should be one hierarchy, related to one system of training, and providing within its limits the possibilities of promotion and development which should be characteristic of all democratic institutions. Even from the point of view of the children, it should be possible for a teacher to carry on through the various stages into which the educational system is divided. It is conceivable, that is to say, that the same teacher (of drawing, for example) would move with his or her class through all the stages of primary or secondary education. We want a conception of the teacher as group guardian, rather than as a dispenser of information about a particular subject; and the integrity of the group is probably a far more powerful educational factor than a progressive grading of teachers. This is a subject which must be discussed at greater length on another occasion, the only point which it is necessary to stress now being the continuity of the process of education. We must desist from the common habit of regarding the elementary and the secondary school child as two different animals, for whom different cages and different keepers must be provided. It is the same child, from birth to maturity, and its education should be a single undivided process.

It follows, therefore, that the fourfold method which began in the infant school should continue in the primary school. The child is maturing, absorbing new experiences, new sensations; his eidetic world is beginning to crystallize around concepts, growing in number and utility. His education must keep pace with these organic processes, increasing in range of materials, complexity of movements, scope of discipline. But the moulds do not break: they expand. Drawing, as we have seen, expands and develops naturally; its richness of content compensating for the blankness of conceptual knowledge. Verbal and musical expression increase in the same ratio of complexity, with unity or integration as the continuing aim. But the greatest development will be in dramatic expression and in constructive activities. The "project," taking in wider and wider aspects of experience and relevant knowledge, will dominate whole weeks and even terms of the school programme. It will begin to embrace history and geography, economics and sociology. It will call upon the constructive abilities of the children, and these in their turn will involve increasingly difficult problems in measurement and calculation, in surveying and building, in physics and chemistry. Incidentally, the school itself, as a theatre, arena or background, becomes an element in education; and its care, its heating and lighting and ventilation, and above all the cultivation of the school garden or farm, provide the opportunity for teaching those elements of science and natural history which are appropriate to the primary stage.

This, it will be said (now as always) is fine in theory, but is it practicable? Its practicability has been proved by many experiments, which only fail to reach the ideal because they are partial, and unco-ordinated by any general theory of human development or social organization. But as evidence of the practicability of this kind of education I would prefer to quote, not any of those experiments in progressive education carried out under artificial conditions of selection and environment (whose value is not questioned), but a description of a one-room school inspected by an American educationalist. It comes from an unpublished study carried out by Florence Tilton under the direction of Dr. Leo Brueckner and Dr. Wesley Peik, of the University of Minnesota: [2]

I am thinking now of a lovely little white schoolhouse set on a hill surrounded by a wood in Hennepin County, Minnesota. The instant I entered that doorway I knew I had entered a school where art was a part of daily living. The formal set arrangement of desks, so common in one-room schools, was banished. Instead, desks were grouped. All along one wall was a large frieze with figures painted in what was very evidently child work. The colour scheme was restful; the teacher was dressed in good taste; well-arranged books added colour to the room; there was an air of happy comradeship as the children made covers for a history booklet. The teacher began plying me with art questions. She was concerned about how appreciation was to be developed without pictures. She expressed the opinion I had long held that arranging a display of child work was something children should do themselves because they could learn thus how to balance sizes and shapes of paper in a given space. She was aware of the opportunities for teaching colour in their daily life. When questioned about how she organized her work, she said she taught one subject such as lettering to the entire group, but varied the work, giving simple applications to the small children, more difficult ones to the fourth, fifth and sixth grades, and the most difficult applications to the seventh and eighth grade children.

2 *A Field Study of Art Teaching in One-Room Rural Schools of Hennepin County, Minnesota*, 1936. Quoted in the Fortieth Yearbook of the National Society for the Study of Education (1941), pp. 587–8.

In this school art is an integral part of living. Children are taught to be conscious of beauty in all things. They endeavour to make their environment beautiful. They accept appraisals of school work for its artistic merit as naturally as they accept appraisals of speech. They believe that all things, to be effective, must be beautiful. They learn how to create beauty through daily choices in dress, the arrangement of their books and playthings. They enjoy colour, simplicity of line, dark and light pattern and forms of many kinds through association with beauty. These they find in nature, in pictures, in sculpture, in architecture, and in manufactured articles. They experiment with modelling in clay, in wood, and in plaster. They weave simple patterns on looms they themselves have made. They express their imaginative ideas both as individuals and as groups. Through working together to accomplish common objectives of beauty for their school, they learn how to subordinate selfish desires to group objectives. They are developing hobbies and interests. When a study is made of a foreign country, they learn what types of costumes are worn, what are the typical colour arrangements, how the forms of artistic expression of a people are influenced by their geographical background, the facts of their history, their emotional characteristics, and their economic status. In all social studies the contributions of art are studied. The teacher thinks of art as one of the areas of learning, developed through four approaches; namely, the appreciative, the creative, the informational, and the technical. There is a well-adjusted balance between work designed to foster self-expression and opportunities to make art choices. All work is child-originated. There is no dictation, no tracing, very little copy-work; but much more imagination, much work for the development of mental images. The power to do things skillfully is kept growing throughout the school period. The children are taught those knowledges and abilities judged by experts to be most socially useful. This teaching is by the rural teacher, not by a special art teacher.

Such, it seems to me, is the realizable pattern of education, in London or New York as well as in Hennepin County, Minnesota. That single-handed rural teacher, working in a one-room school, is the model for all teachers, elementary or secondary, even university. I will add nothing to the force and Platonic truth of this one example.

45 What Art Can Do for You

Curt J. Ducasse

Not so many decades ago, the admissibility of the natural sciences to the curriculum of our colleges was a live question. These sciences had to argue their right to share the noble company of the humanities. But nowadays the question often raised is rather whether the study of the humanities is worth

From Curt J. Ducasse: Art, the Critics and You, copyright © 1944 by Oskar Piest, 1955 by The Liberal Arts Press, Inc., reprinted by permission of the Liberal Arts Press Division of the Bobbs-Merrill Company, Inc.

retaining, or at least on what grounds. The natural sciences have put into the hands of men unprecedented power to harness to his ends the forces of nature. The telephone, the airplane, the conquest of disease, mass production, and other inventions of our age, which these sciences alone have made possible, are very generally held to show that their study is worth while. But the study of the humanities bears no fruits of comparably obvious sorts. What, then, justifies the pursuit of humanistic studies?

I believe that the case for these studies is even stronger today than in the past, but it cannot be adequately presented unless we are first agreed as to what exactly the humanities shall be held to embrace. The application of that term has grown in rather haphazard fashion. Originally, it included the study of the classics—that is, of the finest literature of ancient Greece and Rome. But today it includes study of the masterpieces also of other great literatures, and more besides. Grammar, philology, linguistics, and other subjects that, although distinct from literature, are more or less closely connected with it are classed among the humanities. Archaeology, the history of art, and in general the history of civilization would be examples.

It appears, then, that the term "humanities" has been applied with but little thought as to what it should imply; and, as its application has become more and more heterogeneous, its implication has correspondingly dwindled more and more to nearly nothing. Our only hope of rescuing the term from its present vagueness and of finding for it a meaning both definite and rooted in realities lies in approaching the problem, on the one hand, through a conception of what the education of a complete human being involves; and, on the other, through an understanding of the specific contributions to it that certain subjects and modes of study alone can make.

When education is mentioned, the idea that most readily presents itself is perhaps that education consists in acquiring knowledge of a variety of facts and their relations, and in developing the intellectual powers required for the acquisition, organization, and application of this knowledge. But evidently this constitutes only what may be called intellectual education. For the development of a complete human being, education of several other sorts is needed in addition—physical education, to unfold the powers of his body; religious education, to foster in him goodness of heart; moral education, to establish in him the habit of dealing justly with all. But there is need also for education of a kind less often explicitly mentioned but just as important, namely, pathetic education—that is, education of the feelings. This seeks to open up to man and to sensitize him to ranges and subtleties of feeling for which he has the capacity, but which he would not ordinarily discover unaided.

The term "feelings" is used in the present connection to refer to two large groups of experiences. One of them, to be called for short the sensations, consists both of sensory impressions and of images of imagination. The other group consists of the feelings that may be called the sentiments and includes emotions, moods, attitudes, as well as longings, impulses, dispositions, aspirations, inclinations, and aversions—all of these, however, as felt directly, rather than as intellectually analyzed.

This qualification is important, for language has no names for most impulses or dispositions as immediately experienced, and therefore is compelled to refer to them as impulses or dispositions *to do so and so*. But such a description of an impulse, by riveting our attention on the actions in which it eventuates, easily deludes us into believing that to experience an impulse is to contemplate some course of action; whereas the fact is that every impulse has its own peculiar "feel," which we instantly experience, whether or not we have as yet learned what action it leads to. The impulse to sneeze, for example, has its own characteristic feel, which is experienced even by an infant who, never before having sneezed, does not yet know that the action—sneezing—follows upon the particular feeling he is experiencing at the moment.

The common character of the sensations and the sentiments, and that which accounts for the common name "feelings" being applied to both, is thus their immediacy or intuitiveness—the fact that, however much we may learn *about* them, yet we do not know *them* unless we ourselves have felt their intrinsic quality. Feeling, that is to say, is here contrasted with intellectual knowledge, as in French *"connaître"* is contrasted with *"savoir,"* or in German *"kennen"* with *"wissen."* To express this contrast in English, William James, it will be recalled, proposed the two terms, "knowledge of acquaintance" and "knowledge about."

Education of the feelings, which requires acquaintance with an increasingly wide variety of feelings, brings about development of the capacity to discriminate among feelings—the capacity to discern among them differences, likenesses, and other relations of which we were before unconscious. Discrimination or discernment is commonly described as "the capacity to tell the difference," which is substantially correct. But more accurately it is the capacity, not so much to tell, as to notice a difference; and, indeed, not exclusively a difference, but equally a likeness or other relation to which persons not having had the sort of education now being considered would be blind.

Only a moment's reflection is needed to perceive how essential a part of the education of a complete man and how important, not only to the sensibilities, but often even to the happiness of those with whom he comes in contact is this capacity to distinguish nuances of feeling more subtle and relationships between them less obvious than those that spontaneously thrust themselves upon everyone. As it concerns the sensations, this sensitiveness and capacity for fine discrimination constitutes what is meant by possession of a developed or cultivated aesthetic taste. And as it concerns the sentiments, it alone is what makes possible intuitive apprehension of another's temperament and sympathetic insight into his scheme of values, his motives, his problems, his ideals and aspirations; or, in general, into the emotional meaning or puzzle that life presents from his unique point of view.

This ability to discriminate is thus the indispensable foundation for tactful dealing with others, and for accurate appreciation of the endless variety of human relationships and human situations. Hence, however greatly we may admire a man's moral character and his intellectual attainments, we perceive an unmistakable lack in him if we cannot also say that he is a man of taste and gifted with delicacy of sentiment. A man is not fully human if he is undeveloped in the feeling dimension of his being. The saying that "the road to hell is paved with good intentions" and the remark that "some men of brilliant intellect are yet scoundrels" are but ways of expressing the fact that piety, righteousness, and intelligence are not enough. This is brought sharply home to us when we meet, as we occasionally do, someone who has all these qualities but who is yet crude of taste, uncouth of manner, clumsy of speech, tactless, emotionally immature, or incapable of sympathetic discernment.

How, then, may sublety and delicacy of sentiment and a sensitive, discriminating taste be developed? Man's daily experience in the natural course of his life normally contributes something to this development, just as it contributes something also to the growth of his intellectual equipment. But precisely because the range of development that comes thus unaided is usually very limited, there is a universally recognized necessity for deliberately planned education that shall go beyond that range. This leads us to ask what particular subjects of study and what particular modes of studying them are especially adapted to the education of the feelings.

The answer is not hard to discern. Art is the language of feeling; and the works of the various arts are the expression and record, in communicable form, of the feelings with which their creators were inspired. Works of art, that is to say, provide the means to the desired greater breadth and depth of acquaintance with the immense variety of human feelings. Contemplation by an individual of the things artists have created makes it possible for him to experience and discriminate many of the endlessly numerous feelings with which the unaided course of his life would certainly have left him unacquainted. The products of the various arts, then, are to pathetic education what scientific, historical, or philosophical books are to intellectual education.

But to the distinction made among feelings between the sentiments and the sensations, there corresponds one between the *dramatic* components of a work of art and its *design* components. The word "dramatic" is here used to refer to those aspects of the work that, either through representation of persons and things and of relations that bear on their purposes, or in some more direct manner, express and excite sentiments. The design aspect of a work of art, on the other hand, is impersonal, in the sense that its material is sense qualities themselves; and that the relations used in their arrangement are simply spatial, temporal, or qualitative ones, and not, as in the dramatic aspect of the work, interrelations of human purposes. In some works of art, the design aspect is emphasized, and the dramatic minimized or disregarded; in others, the converse is the case; and in yet others, both are made to play essential parts.

DESIGNS AS MATERIALS FOR
EDUCATING THE SENSATIONS

Evidently designs, or the design component of works that are not simply designs, will furnish us with the best material for educating our sensuous discrimination and our appreciation of the qualitative and spatio-temporal organization of sensations. We shall gain this education from the study of works of painting, sculpture, architecture, music, poetry; and of art objects such as tapestries, furniture, fabrics, jades and ivories, lacquers, wood carvings, book bindings, and the like.

But it cannot be too much emphasized that, for the purpose of developing the discrimination that constitutes taste, study must here mean primarily the direct, personal, intimate, repeated, and prolonged contemplation and comparison of diversified examples of objects of the kinds just mentioned. For discursive "knowledge about" such objects has, for the purpose now in view, no importance except insofar as it may prove an aid or a stimulus to contemplation. Although reading, hearing, or talking about works of art may enliven our interest in them and move us to sharper observation of them, nevertheless discourse concerning works of art is never a possible substitute for firsthand observation if our purpose is to develop in ourselves genuine sensuous discrimination and discernment of design form, and not just to stock our memories, for conversational or lecture purposes, with the recorded results of other people's direct observations.

As pointed out earlier, this is something that scholars who teach "art appreciation" need constantly to remember; for scholars are persons whose central interest is in scholarship, and whose inveterate tendency it therefore is to conceptualize whatever their attention touches and turn it into a subject of discourse. In the realm of art, however, this means erecting into an end the pursuit of information that, at best, can be only an aid to the sensitization of taste. It should never be forgotten in this connection that a man blind from birth, but who had studied many books, could give a learned lecture about the history and appreciation of painting, although himself totally incapable even of telling one color from another; and that, on the other hand, even exquisitely sensitive painters have, for the most part, possessed little book knowledge about painting.

DRAMATIC LITERATURE AS EDUCATOR
OF THE SENTIMENTS

For the education of the sentiments, as distinguished from the sensations, the appropriate study material will be works of art considered in respect to their dramatic component—dramatic, that is, in the sense already stated of embodying hopes or fears, desires or aversions, or other of the countless varieties and subtleties of human sentiments. Painting, through the representation of persons, human relations and situations, or objects of use, has considerable resources for this purpose. So, too, has music, independently of representation, through its power to express moods and emotions directly, as do the intonations of the human voice. But the art whose dramatic resources probably exceed those of all the others is literature, including thereunder naturally what is specifically called the drama; but also all poetry, the story, the novel, and indeed also biography and much of history, if considered as stories rather than as stocks of factual information.

Such literature makes it possible for the reader who lives in imagination in the situations it depicts and identifies himself imaginatively with the characters it describes to experience vicariously all the diverse human sentiments that such human beings in such situations and relations would experience. Obviously, there could be no opportunity in the reader's own real life for experience so varied or so costly. And it is worth while to note that, although the situations and roles that literature thus permits the reader to enter or play are entered or played by him, not really, but only in imagination, nevertheless *the psychological insights obtained by him in this way are in no way imaginary, but as genuine and real as any*. A man, for example, may imagine his beloved to be faithless without believing that she is; but when he dwells on this image, the feeling of jealousy, which may hitherto have remained utterly unknown to him, is none the less then genuinely discovered by him and as really, even if not as intensely, experienced as if he believed what he imagines.

The study of literature thus makes it possible for us to broaden immensely our horizon of sympathetic insight into human sentiments and into the human problems or relations to which they relate; but it must be stressed that, for this, the manner of study is again all-important. It must be the manner that alone procures to the student personal experience of the sentiments packed into the literary works he reads. It consists in his entering imaginatively into and living emotionally in the characters, situations, and relations depicted. On the other hand, study that consists in reading about such literature or in technical analysis of it is, for the purpose of education of the sentiments, never a possible substitute for the reading of the works themselves in the manner just described. For this purpose, lectures or reading about a literary work have importance only insofar as they actually aid us to understand more adequately the situations into which, through reading the work itself, we attempt to project ourselves in imagination.

. . .

SOME OTHER THINGS ART DOES FOR MAN

That the works of the various arts are instruments *par excellence* fitted to serve as educators of the feelings will have been made evident by what precedes. But art can do for men a number of other things also, which are no less deserving of attention.

The most obvious of them, perhaps, is to introduce into the environment of man objects whose beauty delights him. Although, as we have seen, an object may be genuinely a work of art without being beautiful, nevertheless the fact is that, as judged by the taste of most men, the majority of works of art have some beauty. This, of course, is true especially of the works of the decorative arts, since in their case there is positive attempt to make the object produced aesthetically pleasing. At all events, works of art which lack beauty in the eyes of those who behold them are neglected and automatically tend soon to disappear unless their failure to give aesthetic pleasure is compensated by merit of some other kind. The craving for beauty is strong and widespread among human beings; and, since it is so no less among those who create works of art than among those who behold them, it naturally tends to function in the artist as does a censor, which determines not so much what he shall do as, negatively, that he shall not do this or that unbeautiful thing unless some positive reason for it compels.

The beauty of beautiful works of art yields aesthetic delight not only when attention is deliberately turned on them, as with paintings in galleries or symphonies in concert halls, but also when they gain only the margin instead of the focus of attention. This is what occurs at times when works of decorative art, such as furniture, silverware, and the like, are being used for the practical functions they were also expected to serve, rather than being attentively contemplated. The same thing occurs also when works of "free" art are being employed, deliberately, as decorative context of some of the activities of ordinary life—for example, when songs are being sung while marching; or, again, when music is being played during dinner; or, as in some factories, while monotonous work is being done.

Works of art, however, function not only as aesthetically pleasing contexts of various activities, but also sometimes, through the feelings they express, as ancillary to certain activities to which these feelings are related. Examples would be the religiously stimulating or inspiring effect of religious music, religious paintings or statues or stained glass, or religious dramas, as contexts of religious exercises in places of worship; or, again, martial music as context of some military exercises.

For the artist—and let it be remembered that most of us do at times engage in creative activity in some art medium, even if at humble levels—art serves not only to relieve the pressure of the emotion which inspires him to create, but also, by objectifying that emotion, his creative activity clarifies it for him and gives him the opportunity to judge it.

A poem one has written, for example, is an objective, scrutinizable record of one's state of soul at the time. On reading it later, one may admire still the sentiments it expresses; or, on the contrary, one may judge them tawdry or naïve or otherwise unfit to own, and one may then repudiate them as being no part of the self one chooses to be henceforth. The creation of things that express the artist's inner state in objective form thus in part serves him as a means of self-knowledge. But it is not to himself only that it reveals what sort of person he is. Others, who contemplate his works and read the feelings expressed in them, learn it also. In this way, art serves to attract to the artist as a person those who find the soul he expresses congenial to their own. But it functions equally to repel from him those who find it uncongenial, and this is no less important. Thus, as pointed out in passing in an earlier chapter, art is an instrument of social assortment, rather than, as H. R. Marshall said, of social consolidation.

It is worth noting, moreover, that the function of art as a means of revealing aspects of one's inner self to others is not confined to the cases where the work they contemplate is of one's own making. The comments two persons exchange concerning the music they both hear, the paintings they both look at, the poems or other works of literature they both read, and so on, likewise reveal each of the two persons to the other, even when the works on which they comment were created by neither of them. Works of art thus are, indirectly but quite effectively, a means of getting acquainted with another person's taste, with the directions of his imaginative interest, and with the nature of his emotional aspirations and aversions.

That art can also serve, for artist or consumer alike, as a form of escape —as temporary vacation from worry, from pain, or from the drab monotony of routine duties—is likewise true. This, however, is not a capacity peculiar to art but rather one it shares with many other activities, and it therefore need not here be more than mentioned.

The Role of Art in Society   46
Lewis Mumford

During the last two centuries there has been a vast expansion of the material means of living throughout the world. But instead of our thus producing a state of widely distributed leisure, favorable to the cultivation of the inner life and the production and enjoyment of the arts, we find ourselves more absorbed than ever in the process of mechanization. Even a large part of our fantasies are no longer self-begotten: they have no reality, no viability, until they are harnessed to the machine, and without the aid of the radio and television they would hardly have the energy to maintain their existence. Compare our present situation with that which accompanied the relatively technical primitive era of the seventeenth century. In that time a good London burgher, like Samuel Pepys, a practical man, a hard-working administrator, would select the servants in his household partly on the basis of

From "Art and the Symbol" in *Art and Technics*, by Lewis Mumford, New York, Columbia University Press, 1952. Reprinted by permission of Columbia University Press.

their having a good voice, so that they might sit down with the family in the evening to take part in domestic singing. Such people not merely listened passively to music, but could produce it, or at least reproduce it, in their own right. Today, in contrast, we often see people wandering around with a portable radio set on Riverside Drive, listening to a radio musical program, with no thought that they might sing a song freely in the open air without invoking any mechanical aid.

Even worse, the very growth of mechanical facilities has given people a false ideal of technical perfectionism, so that unless they can compete with the products of the machine or with those whose professional training qualifies them for such a public appearance, they are all too ready to take a back seat. And, to complete this process, not in the least to offset it, in those special realms of art, above all painting, that once recorded the greatest freedom and creativeness, we find that the symbols that most deeply express the emotions and feelings of our age are a succession of dehumanized nightmares, transposing into esthetic form either the horror and violence or the vacuity and despair of our time. Undoubtedly one of the great paintings of our day is Picasso's Guernica mural, just as he himself is one of the great artists of our time, with a capacity for beautiful rhythmic expression like that of a dancer; a gift that the stroboscopic camera has recently revealed. But the fresh symbols that come forth from his masterly hand reveal chiefly the wounds and scars of our time, with not even the faintest hint of a new integration. At times, as in the preliminary sketches for the Guernica mural, the emotion is so lacerating that the next step beyond would be either insanity or suicide.

Violence and nihilism: the death of the human personality. This is the message that modern art brings to us in its freest and purest moments; and that, obviously, is no counterpoise to the dehumanization wrought by technics.

Most of the great artists of the last two centuries—and this has been equally true, I think, in music and poetry and painting, even in some degree in architecture—have been in revolt against the machine and have proclaimed the autonomy of the human spirit: its autonomy, its spontaneity, its inexhaustible creativeness. Actually, the religious impulse, suppressed by the institutionalism of the Churches, manifested itself during this period chiefly in the arts, so that the great saints of the last century were as often as not artists, like Van Gogh or Ryder or Tolstoy. This strong reaction against a too-singleminded commitment to mechanical invention and practical effort helped produce great works of music and painting, perhaps as great as any other age could show. In the great symphonic music of the nineteenth century the human spirit utilized its characteristic division of labor, its specialization of functions, and its intricate organization of time and rhythm to express the tragic yearnings and joyful triumphs of this new epoch. Because of the traditional separation of art and technics we have yet sufficiently to realize that the symphony orchestra is a triumph of engineering, and that its products, such as the music of Mozart and Beethoven, etherealized into symbols, will probably outlast all our steel bridges and automatic machines.

But that protest was possible, those triumphs could be expressed, only so long as a belief in the human person, and particularly in the inner life, the creative moment, remained dominant, carried over from the older cultures that had nourished the human spirit. By the end of the nineteenth century, this evocative protest began to die away. In a mood of submission and self-abnegation, sensitively recorded by Henry Adams, people began to worship the machine and its masters. If anyone was *unreal*, Adams wrote, it was the poet, not the businessman. We had created a topsyturvy world in which machines had become autonomous and men had become servile and mechanical: that is, thing-conditioned, externalized, de-humanized—disconnected from their historic values and purposes. And so it has come about that one whole part of man's life, springing from his innermost nature, his deepest desires and impulses, his ability to enjoy and bestow love, to give life to and receive life from his fellow men, has been suppressed. Those deep organic impulses for which art is both the surrogate in immediate action and the ultimate expression of that action as transferred to the life of other men—all this part of man's nature has become progressively empty and meaningless. The maimed fantasies, the organized frustrations, that we see in every comprehensive exhibition of modern painting today are so many symptoms of this deep personal abdication. Pattern and purpose have progressively disappeared, along with the person who once, in his own right, embodied them. Man has become an exile in this mechanical world: or rather, even worse, he has become a Displaced Person.

On one hand, through the advance of technics, we have produced a new kind of environment and a highly organized routine of life, which satisfies, to a fabulous degree, man's need to live in an orderly and predictable world. There is something noble, as Emerson recognized long ago, in the fact that our railroads, our ocean steamships, our planes, run on a time-schedule almost as regular as the movement of the heavenly bodies. Uniformity, regularity, mechanical accuracy and reliability all have been advanced to a singular degree of perfection. And just as the autonomic nervous system and the reflexes in the human body free the mind for its higher functions, so this new kind of mechanical order should bring about a similar freedom, a similar release of energy for the creative processes. Because of our achievement of mechanical order throughout the planet, the dream of Isaiah might in fact come true: the dream of a universal society in which men shall be weaned from habits of hostility and war. Originally these aggressions were perhaps the natural outcome of anxiety for the future, in periods when there was never enough food or goods to go round: periods when only the powerful could arrogate to themselves all the resources men needed to be fully human.

But the good fairy who presided over the development of technics did not succeed in forestalling the curse that accompanied this genuine gift: a

curse that came from this very overcommitment to the external, the quantitative, the measurable, the external. For our inner life has become impoverished: as in our factories, so throughout our society, the automatic
machine tends to replace the person and to make all his decisions—while,
for its smoother working, it anesthetizes every part of the personality that
will not easily conform to its mechanical needs.

All these are the veriest commonplaces of our "interesting age;" I remind you only of what you already know. On one side, the highest degree
of scientific and technical refinement, as in the atomic bomb; on the other
side, moral depravity, as in the use of that bomb not to conquer armies, but
to exterminate defenseless people at random. On one side, intellectual maturity, as in the cooperative activities of science; on the other, crass emotional immaturity—the kind painfully exhibited by the traitorous physicist
Fuchs. External order: internal chaos. External progress: internal regression.
External rationalism: internal irrationality. In this impersonal and over-
disciplined machine civilization, so proud of its objectivity, spontaneity too
often takes the form of criminal acts, and creativeness finds its main open
outlet in destruction. If this seems like an exaggeration, that is due only to
the illusion of security. Open your eyes and look around you!

Now I put these paradoxes and contradictions before you at the beginning, dismaying though they may be, because I believe that the relations
between art and technics give us a significant clue to every other type of
activity, and may even provide an understanding of the way to integration.
The great problem of our time is to restore modern man's balance and
wholeness: to give him the capacity to command the machines he has
created instead of becoming their helpless accomplice and passive victim;
to bring back, into the very heart of our culture, that respect for the essential attributes of personality, its creativity and autonomy, which Western
man lost at the moment he displaced his own life in order to concentrate on
the improvement of the machine. In short, the problem of our time is how
to prevent ourselves from committing suicide, precisely at the height and
climax of our one-sided mechanical triumphs.

There are doubtless many other excellent reasons for studying the relation of art and technics; and in a happier period of history I might have
been tempted to dwell on them more extensively than I propose to do in the
present lectures. By now, however, every intelligent observer knows—as
Mr. Arnold Toynbee, among others, has impressively demonstrated—that
our civilization cannot go on indefinitely in the present fashion. Like a
drunken locomotive engineer on a streamlined train, plunging through the
darkness at a hundred miles an hour, we have been going past the danger
signals without realizing that our speed, which springs from our mechanical
facility, only increases our danger and will make more fatal the crash. If
we are to find a different destination for our civilization, every part of our
life must be re-examined and overhauled, every activity must undergo criti-

cism and revaluation; every institution must seek its own renovation and re-newal. Precisely in those areas where modern man has seemed most prosperous and secure, most efficient in action, most adept in thought, we begin to realize that something has been left out of his regimen, something essential to his organic balance and development.

What is that missing element? That missing element, I suggest, is the human person. Our power and knowledge, our scientific discoveries and our technical achievements, have all been running wild because Western man turned his back upon the very core and center of his own life. He has not merely lost confidence in himself: he has made his proper life insignificant, and so he finds the rest of the world equally empty of values, equally insignificant. More and more, from the sixteenth century on, modern man patterned himself upon the machine. Despite sentimental compunctions of various sorts, compunctions expressed in the romantic movement, in nationalism, in the reactivation of Christian theology, Western man has sought to live in a nonhistoric and impersonal world of matter and motion, a world with no values except the value of quantities; a world of causal sequences, not human purposes. Even when he has added depth to his life by his exploration of the human soul, as Sigmund Freud and his followers undoubtedly have done in psychology, he has used his new-found knowledge to a large degree only to continue the general process of self-devaluation.

In such a world, man's spiritual life is limited to that part of it which directly or indirectly serves science and technics: all other interests and activities of the person are suppressed as "non-objective," emotional, and therefore unreal. This decision in effect banished art, because art is one of the essential spheres of man's autonomous and creative activities. Art as the domain of symbol and form, of pattern and significance became the blighted area of modern life, within whose dilapidated mansions a few pious caretakers and family servants fought a hopeless battle against neglect and the final abandonment of the deserted homes themselves. That is why, with all our boasted efficiency of machines, with all our super-abundance of energy, food, materials, products, there has been no commensurate improvement in the quality of our daily existence; why the great mass of comfortable well-fed people in our civilization live lives of emotional apathy and mental torpor, of dull passivity and enfeebled desire—lives that belie the real potentialities of modern culture. *Art degraded, imagination denied, war governed the nations.* Thus spoke William Blake; and we have lived to understand the truth of that aphorism.

My special purpose in these lectures, then, springs out of our common responsibility to restore order and value and purpose, on the widest scale, to human life. This means two things. We must find out how to make our subjective life more disciplined and resolute, endowed with more of the qualities that we have poured into the machine, so that we shall not equate our subjectivity with the trivial and the idle, the disorderly and the irra-

tional, as if the only road to free creativity lay through a complete withdrawal from the effort to communicate and cooperate with other men. When
society is healthy, the artist reinforces its health; but when it is ailing, he
likewise reinforces its ailments. This is probably the reason that the artists
and the poets are looked upon with suspicion by moralists like Plato or
Tolstoy, who write in a time of decay. Though the esthetic movements of
our time—post-impressionism, futurism, cubism, primitivism, surrealism—
have taught us much about the actual nature of our civilization, they themselves, from this point of view, are so conditioned by the very disintegration
they draw upon for nourishment that they are incapable, without themselves
undergoing a profound spiritual change, of bringing a new balance and
security into our life.

Fortunately, here and there, one still finds truly integrated artists. Sur-
vivors of a better past, precursors of a better future can in fact be found:
people like Naum Gabo in sculpture and Frank Lloyd Wright in architecture; artists whose work begins once more to have fresh meaning for the
younger generation. But if our life as a whole is to take on the qualities foreshadowed in the work of these artists, the world of technics itself must be
transformed: salvation lies, not in the pragmatic adaptation of the human
personality to the machine, but in the readaptation of the machine, itself a
product of life's needs for order and organization, to the human personality.
A human pattern, a human measure, a human tempo, above all, a human
goal must transform the activities and processes of technics, curbing them,
when they become dangerous to man's development, even cutting them off
for a while—as a more prudent world statesmanship would have cut off our
present developments of atomic energy—until the appropriate political instruments and social institutions had been created for directing technics into the
channels of human development. If our civilization is not to go further in
the disintegration now manifested in the state of art and technics, we must
salvage and redeem the Displaced Person; and that means that we must pour
once more into the arts some of the vitality and energy now almost wholly
drained off by a depersonalized technics.

Already, by my use of the terms art and technics, I have partly defined
them; but now let me make their definition a little more precise. Technics is
a word that has only lately come into use in English; people still sometimes
try to Frenchify it into "techniques" and thereby give it a quite different
meaning. We ordinarily use the word technology to describe both the field
of the practical arts and the systematic study of their operations and products.
For the sake of clarity, I prefer to use technics alone to describe the field
itself, that part of human activity wherein, by an energetic organization of
the process of work, man controls and directs the forces of nature for his own
purposes.

Technics began when man first used his fingers for pincers or a stone
for a projectile: like art itself, it is rooted in man's use of his own body. But

man has gone on developing his technical facilities, slowly, fitfully, only rarely in such rapid spurts as we have seen during the last century; so that by now he has extended the range and power of many of his organic aptitudes: he can kill at a distance of five thousand yards and converse at a distance of five thousand miles; and in certain complicated mathematical calculations he can, by the aid of an electronic brain, perform in a few seconds operations that might otherwise take a lifetime of strenuous effort. All these magnified human powers are the result of human desires, human contrivances, human efforts. However formidably automatic the machine may look, there is always a man lurking in the background, adjusting it, correcting it, nursing it; and the machine itself is half slave, half god. You might in fact call the machine modern man's totem animal.

Art, in the only sense in which one can separate art from technics, is primarily the domain of the person; and the purpose of art, apart from various incidental technical functions that may be associated with it, is to widen the province of personality, so that feelings, emotions, attitudes, and values, in the special individualized form in which they happen in one particular person, in one particular culture, can be transmitted with all their force and meaning to other persons or to other cultures. Sympathy and empathy are the characteristic ways of art: a feeling with, a feeling into, the innermost experiences of other men. The work of art is the visible, potable spring from which men share the deep underground sources of their experience. Art arises out of man's need to create for himself, beyond any requirement for mere animal survival, a meaningful and valuable world: his need to dwell on, to intensify, and to project in more permanent forms those precious parts of his experience that would otherwise slip too quickly out of his grasp, or sink too deeply into his unconscious to be retrieved.

CREATIVITY

47   Art and Inspiration
                Plato

Soc. And you say that Homer and the other poets, such as Hesiod and Archilochus, speak of the same things, although not in the same way; but the one speaks well and the other not so well?

Ion. Yes; and I am right in saying so.

Soc. And if you knew the good speaker, you would also know the inferior speakers to be inferior?

Ion. That is true.

Soc. Then, my dear friend, can I be mistaken in saying that Ion is equally skilled in Homer and in other poets, since he himself acknowledges that the same person will be a good judge of all those who speak of the same things; and that almost all poets do speak of the same things?

Ion. Why then, Socrates, do I lose attention and go to sleep and have absolutely no ideas of the least value, when any one speaks of any other poet; but when Homer is mentioned, I wake up at once and am all attention and have plenty to say?

Soc. The reason, my friend, is obvious. No one can fail to see that you speak of Homer without any art or knowledge. If you were able to speak of him by rules of art, you would have been able to speak of all other poets; for poetry is a whole.

Ion. Yes.

Soc. And when any one acquires any other art as a whole, the same may be said of them. Would you like me to explain my meaning, Ion?

Ion. Yes, indeed, Socrates; I very much wish that you would: for I love to hear you wise men talk.

Soc. O that we were wise, Ion, and that you could truly call us so; but you rhapsodes and actors, and the poets whose verses you sing, are wise; whereas I am a common man, who only speak the truth. For consider what a very commonplace and trivial thing is this which I have said—a thing

From the *Ion* in *The Dialogues of Plato,* Vol. I, trans. by B. Jowett, New York, Random House, 1937.

which any man might say: that when a man has acquired a knowledge of a whole art, the enquiry into good and bad is one and the same. Let us consider this matter; is not the art of painting a whole?

Ion. Yes.

Soc. And there are and have been many painters good and bad?

Ion. Yes.

Soc. And did you ever know any one who was skilful in pointing out the excellences and defects of Polygnotus the son of Aglaophon, but incapable of criticizing other painters; and when the work of any other painter was produced, went to sleep and was at a loss, and had no ideas; but when he had to give his opinion about Polygnotus, or whoever the painter might be, and about him only, woke up and was attentive and had plenty to say?

Ion. No indeed, I have never known such a person.

Soc. Or did you ever know of any one in sculpture, who was skilful in expounding the merits of Daedalus the son of Metion, or of Epeius the son of Panopeus, or of Theodorus the Samian, or of any individual sculptor; but when the works of sculptors in general were produced, was at a loss and went to sleep and had nothing to say?

Ion. No indeed; no more than the other.

Soc. And if I am not mistaken, you never met with any one among flute-players or harp-players or singers to the harp or rhapsodes who was able to discourse of Olympus or Thamyras or Orpheus, or Phemius the rhapsode of Ithaca, but was at a loss when he came to speak of Ion of Ephesus, and had no notion of his merits or defects?

Ion. I cannot deny what you say, Socrates. Nevertheless I am conscious in my own self, and the world agrees with me in thinking that I do speak better and have more to say about Homer than any other man. But I do not speak equally well about others—tell me the reason of this.

Soc. I perceive, Ion; and I will proceed to explain to you what I imagine to be the reason of this. The gift which you possess of speaking excellently about Homer is not an art, but, as I was just saying, an inspiration; there is a divinity moving you, like that contained in the stone which Euripides calls a magnet, but which is commonly known as the stone of Heraclea. This stone not only attracts iron rings, but also imparts to them a similiar power of attracting other rings; and sometimes you may see a number of pieces of iron and rings suspended from one another so as to form quite a long chain: and all of them derive their power of suspension from the original stone. In like manner the Muse first of all inspires men herself; and from these inspired persons a chain of other persons is suspended, who take the inspiration. For all good poets, epic as well as lyric, compose their beautiful poems not by art, but because they are inspired and possessed. And as the Corybantian revellers when they dance are not in their right mind, so the lyric poets are not in their right mind when they are composing their beautiful strains: but when falling under the power of music and metre they are inspired and possessed; like Bacchic maidens who draw milk and honey from the rivers when they are under the influence of Dionysus but not when they are in their right mind. And the soul of the lyric poet does the same, as they themselves say; for they tell us that they bring songs from honeyed fountains, culling them out of the gardens and dells of the Muses; they, like the bees, winging their way from flower to flower. And this is true. For the poet is a light and winged and holy thing, and there is no invention in him until he has been inspired and is out of his senses, and the mind is no longer in him: when he has not attained to this state, he is powerless and is unable to utter his oracles. Many are the noble words in which poets speak concerning the actions of men; but like yourself when speaking about Homer, they do not speak of them by any rules of art: they are simply inspired to utter that to which the Muse impels them, and that only; and when inspired, one of them will make dithyrambs, another hymns of praise, another choral strains, another epic or iambic verses—and he who is good at one is not good at any other kind of verse: for not by art does the poet sing, but by power divine. Had he learned by rules of art, he would have known how to speak not of one theme only, but of all; and therefore God takes away the minds of poets, and uses them as his ministers, as he also uses diviners and holy prophets, in order that we who hear them may know them to be speaking not of themselves who utter these priceless words in a state of unconsciousness, but that God himself is the speaker, and that through them he is conversing with us. And Tynnichus the Chalcidian affords a striking instance of what I am saying: he wrote nothing that any one would care to remember but the famous paean which is in every one's mouth, one of the finest poems ever written, simply an invention of the Muses, as he himself says. For in this way the God would seem to indicate to us and not allow us to doubt that these beautiful poems are not human, or the work of man, but divine and the work of God; and that the poets are only the interpreters of the Gods by whom they are severally possessed. Was not this the lesson which the God intended to teach when by the mouth of the worst of poets he sang the best of songs? Am I not right, Ion?

Ion. Yes, indeed, Socrates, I feel that you are; for your words touch my soul, and I am persuaded that good poets by a divine inspiration interpret the things of the Gods to us.

Soc. And you rhapsodists are the interpreters of the poets?

Ion. There again you are right.

Soc. Then you are the interpreters of interpreters?

Ion. Precisely.

Soc. I wish you would frankly tell me, Ion, what I am going to ask of you: When you produce the greatest effect upon the audience in the recitation of some striking passage, such as the apparition of Odysseus leaping forth on the floor, recognized by the suitors and casting his arrows at his feet, or the description of Achilles rushing at Hector, or the sorrows of Andromache, Hecuba, or Priam,—are you in your right mind? Are you not carried out of yourself, and does not your soul in an ecstasy seem to be among the persons or places of which you are speaking, whether they are in Ithaca or in Troy or whatever may be the scene of the poem?

Ion. That proof strikes home to me, Socrates. For I must frankly confess that at the tale of pity my eyes are filled with tears, and when I speak of horrors, my hair stands on end and my heart throbs.

Soc. Well, Ion, and what are we to say of a man who at a sacrifice or festival, when he is dressed in holiday attire, and has golden crowns upon his head, of which nobody has robbed him, appears weeping or panic-stricken in the presence of more than twenty thousand friendly faces, when there is no one despoiling or wronging him;—is he in his right mind or is he not?

Ion. No indeed, Socrates, I must say that, strictly speaking, he is not in his right mind.

Soc. And are you aware that you produce similar effects on most spectators?

Ion. Only too well; for I look down upon them from the stage, and behold the various emotions of pity, wonder, sternness, stamped upon their countenances when I am speaking: and I am obliged to give my very best attention to them; for if I make them cry I myself shall laugh, and if I make them laugh I myself shall cry when the time of payment arrives.

Soc. Do you know that the spectator is the last of the rings which, as I am saying, receive the power of the original magnet from one another? The rhapsode like yourself and the actor are intermediate links, and the poet himself is the first of them. Through all these the God sways the souls of men in any direction which he pleases, and makes one man hang down from another. Thus there is a vast chain of dancers and masters and undermasters of choruses, who are suspended, as if from the stone, at the side of the rings which hang down from the Muse. And every poet has some Muse from whom he is suspended, and by whom he is said to be possessed, which is nearly the same thing; for he is taken hold of. And from these first rings, which are the poets, depend others, some deriving their inspiration from Orpheus, others from Musaeus; but the greater number are possessed and held by Homer. Of whom, Ion, you are one, and are possessed by Homer; and when any one repeats the words of another poet you go to sleep, and know not what to say; but when any one recites a strain of Homer you wake up in a moment, and your soul leaps within you, and you have plenty to say; for not by art or knowledge about Homer do you say what you say, but by divine inspiration and by possession; just as the Corybantian revellers too have a quick perception of that strain only which is appropriated to the God by whom they are possessed, and have plenty of dances and words for that, but take no heed of any other. And you, Ion, when the name of Homer is mentioned have plenty to say, and have nothing to say of others. You ask,

'Why is this?' The answer is that you praise Homer not by art but by divine inspiration.

Ion. That is good, Socrates; and yet I doubt whether you will ever have eloquence enough to persuade me that I praise Homer only when I am mad and possessed; and if you could hear me speak of him I am sure you would never think this to be the case.

48   What Makes a Person Creative
Donald W. MacKinnon

Six years ago, a group of psychologists began a nationwide study of human creativity. They wanted the scientific answers to the mystery of human personality, biology, intelligence, and intuition that makes some persons more creative than others.

Working under a grant by the Carnegie Corporation of New York, the researchers were faced with the usual stereotypes that picture the highly creative person as a genius with an I.Q. far above average, an eccentric not only in thinking but in appearance, dress, and behavior, a Bohemian, an egghead, a longhair. According to these unproved stereotypes, he was not only introverted but a true neurotic, withdrawn from society, inept in his relations with others, totally unable to carry on a conversation with others less gifted than himself. Still others held that the creative person might be profound but that his intelligence was highly one-sided, in a rather narrow channel, and that he was emotionally unstable. Indeed, one of the most commonly held of these images was that he lived just this side of madness.

The psychological researchers who sought a more precise picture of the creative person conducted their investigations on the Berkeley campus of the University of California in the Institute of Personality Assessment and Research. At the Institute, the persons to be studied have been brought together, usually ten at a time, for several days, most often a three-day weekend. There they have been examined by a variety of means—by the broad problem posed by the assessment situation itself, by problem-solving experiments, by tests designed to discover what a person does not know or is unable to reveal about himself, by tests and questionnaires that permit a person to manifest various aspects of his personality and to express his attitudes, interests, and values, by searching interviews.

The professional groups whose creative members were chosen for study

"What Makes a Person Creative," by Donald W. MacKinnon, in *The Saturday Review,* February 10, 1962. Reprinted by permission of the *Saturday Review* and Donald W. MacKinnon.

were writers, architects, research workers in the physical sciences and engineering, and mathematicians. In no instance did the psychological assessors decide which highly creative persons should be studied. Rather, they were nominated by experts in their own fields; and to insure that the traits found to characterize the highly creative were related to their creativity rather than indigenous to all members of the profession, a wider, more representative sample of persons in each of the professional groups was also chosen, though for somewhat less intensive study. All told, some 600 persons participated.

As the study has progressed it has become abundantly clear that creative persons seldom represent fully any of the common stereotypes, and yet in some respects and to some degree there are likenesses. It is not that such images of the creative person are fantastic but that they are caricatures rather than characterizations, heightening and sharpening traits and dispositions so as to yield a picture recognizable, yet still out of accord with reality. There are, of course, some stereotypes that reflect only error, but more often the distortion of the reality would seem to be less complete.

As for intellectual capacity, it will come as no surprise that highly creative persons have been found to be, in the main, well above average. But the relation between intelligence and creativity is not as clear-cut as this would suggest, if for no other reason than that intelligence is a many-faceted thing. There is no single psychological process to which the term "intelligence" applies; rather, there are many types of intellective functioning. There is verbal intelligence, and on a well-known test of this factor creative writers on the average score higher than any of the other groups. But there is also spatial intelligence—the capacity to perceive and to deal with spatial arrangements—and on a test of this aspect of intelligence creative writers as a group earn the lowest average score, while creative architects as a group are the star performers. There are, of course, many elements of intelligence in addition to these two.

If for the moment we ignore those patterns of intellective functioning which clearly and most interestingly differentiate one creative group from another, there are some more general observations that may be noted. It is quite apparent that creative persons have an unusual capacity to record and retain and have readily available the experiences of their life history. They are discerning, which is to say that they are observant in a differentiated fashion; they are alert, capable of concentrating attention readily and shifting it appropriately; they are fluent in scanning thoughts and producing those that serve to solve the problems they undertake; and, characteristically, they have a wide range of information at their command. As in the case of any intelligent person, the items of information which creative persons possess may readily enter into combinations, and the number of possible combinations is increased for such persons because of both a greater range of information and a greater fluency of combination. Since true creativity is defined by the adaptiveness of a response as well as its unusualness, it is apparent that intelligence alone will tend to produce creativity. The more combinations that are found, the more likely it is on purely statistical grounds that some of them will be creative.

Yet intelligence alone does not guarantee creativity. On a difficult, high-level test of the more general aspects of intelligence, creative persons score well above average, but their individual scores range widely, and in several of the creative groups the correlation of intelligence as measured by this test and creativity as rated by the experts is essentially zero.

Certainly this does not mean that over the whole range of creative endeavor there is no relation between general intelligence and creativity. No feeble-minded persons appeared in any of the creative groups. Clearly a certain degree of intelligence, and in general a rather high degree, is required for creativity, but above that point the degree of intelligence does not seem to determine the level of one's creativeness. In some fields of endeavor, mathematics and theoretical physics for example, the requisite intelligence for highly creative achievement is obviously high. But it does not follow that the theoretical physicist of very superior I.Q. will necessarily be creative, and in many fields of significant creative endeavor it is not necessary that a person be outstanding in intelligence to be recognized as highly creative, at least as intelligence is measured by intelligence tests.

Regardless of the level of his measured intelligence, what seems to characterize the creative person—and this is especially so for the artistically creative—is a relative absence of repression and suppression as mechanisms for the control of impulse and imagery. Repression operates against creativity, regardless of how intelligent a person may be, because it makes unavailable to the individual large aspects of his own experience, particularly the life of impulse and experience which gets assimilated to the symbols of aggression and sexuality. Dissociated items of experience cannot combine with one another; there are barriers to communication among different systems of experience. The creative person, given to expression rather than suppression or repression, thus has fuller access to his own experience, both conscious and unconscious. Furthermore, because the unconscious operates more by symbols than by logic, the creative person is more open to the perception of complex equivalences in experience, facility in metaphor being one specific consequence of the creative person's greater openness to his own depths.

This openness to experience is one of the most striking characteristics of the highly creative person, and it reveals itself in many forms. It may be observed, for example, in the realm of sexual identifications and interests, where creative males give more expression to the feminine side of their nature than do less creative men. On a number of tests of masculinity-femininity, creative men score relatively high on femininity, and this despite the fact that, as a group, they do not present an effeminate appearance or give evidence of increased homosexual interests or experiences. Their elevated scores on femininity indicate rather an openness to their feelings and emotions, a sensitive intellect and understanding self-awareness, and wide-ranging interests including many which in the American culture are thought of as more feminine, and these traits are observed and confirmed by other techniques of assessment. If one were to use the language of the Swiss psychiatrist C. G. Jung, it might be said that creative persons are not so completely identified with their masculine *persona* roles as to blind themselves to or deny expression to the more feminine traits of the *anima*. For some, of course, the balance between masculine and feminine traits, interests, and identifications is a precarious one, and for several it would appear that their presently achieved reconciliation of these opposites of their nature has been barely achieved and only after considerable psychic stress and turmoil.

It is the creative person's openness to experience and his relative lack of self-defensiveness that make it possible for him to speak frankly and critically about his childhood and family, and equally openly about himself and his problems as an adult.

One gets the impression that by and large those persons who as adults are widely recognized for their creative achievements have had rather favorable early life circumstances, and yet they often recall their childhood as not having been especially happy.

In studying adult creative persons, one is dependent upon their own reports for the picture they give of their early years. Although they may often describe their early family life as less harmonious and happy than that of their peers, one cannot know for certain what the true state of affairs was. In reality the situation in their homes may not have been appreciably different from that of their peers. The differences may reside mainly in their perceptions and memories of childhood experiences, and it seems the more likely since one of the most striking things to be noted about creative persons is their unwillingness to deny or to repress things that are unpleasant or troubling.

The theme of remembered unhappiness in childhood is so recurrent that one is led to speculate about its role in fostering creative potential. In the absence of a sensitive awareness of one's own experience and of the world around one, without considerable development of and attention to one's own inner life, and lacking an interest in ideational, imaginal, and symbolic processes, highly creative responses can hardly be expected to occur. Something less than complete satisfaction with oneself and one's situation in childhood, if not a prerequisite for the development of a rich inner life and a concern for things of the mind and spirit, may nevertheless play an important contributory role.

There is no doubt, too, that some of the highly creative persons had, as children, endured rather cruel treatment at the hands of their fathers. These, to be sure, constitute the minority, but they appear today to be no less creative than those who could more easily identify with their fathers. There is some evidence, however, that those who were harshly treated in childhood have not been so effective or so successful in the financial and business (masculine) aspects of their profession as the others. There is in these persons more than a hint that they have had some difficulty in assuming an aggressive professional role because, through fear of their fathers, their masculine identifications were inhibited.

Both in psychiatric interviews that survey the individual's history and present psychological status, and in clinical tests of personality, creative persons tend to reveal a considerable amount of psychic turbulence. By and large they freely admit the existence of psychological problems and they speak frankly about their symptoms and complaints. But the manner in which they describe their problems is less suggestive of disabling psychopathology than of good intellect, richness and complexity of personality, and a general candor in self-description. They reveal clearly what clinical psychologists have long contended: that personal soundness is not an absence of problems but a way of reacting to them.

We may resort again to Jung's theory of the psychological functions and types of personality as an aid in depicting the psychology of the creative person. According to this view it might be said that whenever a person uses his mind for any purpose he either perceives (becomes aware of something) or he judges (comes to a conclusion about something). Everyone perceives and judges, but the creative person tends to prefer perceiving to judging. Where a judging person emphasizes the control and regulation of experience, the perceptive creative person is inclined to be more interested and curious, more open and receptive, seeking to experience life to the full. Indeed, the more perceptive a person is, the more creative he tends to be.

In his perceptions, both of the outer world and of inner experiences, one may focus upon what is presented to his senses, upon the facts as they are, or he may seek to see, through intuition, their deeper meanings and possibilities. One would not expect creative persons in their perceptions to be bound to the presented stimulus or object but rather to be intuitively alert to that which is capable of occurring, to that which is not yet realized; this capacity is, in fact, especially characteristic of the creative person.

One judges or evaluates experience with thought or with feeling, thinking being a logical process aimed at an impersonal analysis of the facts, feeling, on the other hand, being a process of appreciation and evaluation of things which gives them a personal and subjective value. The creative person's preference for thinking or for feeling in his making of judgments is less related to his creativeness as such than it is to the type of material or concepts with which he deals. Artists, in general, show a preference for feeling, scientists and engineers a preference for thinking, while architects are more divided in their preference for one or the other of these two functions.

Everyone, of course, perceives and judges, senses and intuits, thinks and feels. It is not a matter of using one of the opposed functions to the exclusion of the other. It is rather a question of which of them is preferred, which gets emphasized, and which is most often used. So also is it with introversion and extroversion of interest, but two-thirds or more of each of the creative groups which have participated in the study have shown a rather clear tendency toward introversion. Yet, interestingly enough, extroverts, though they are in the minority in our samples, are rated as high on creativity as the introverts.

Whether introvert or extrovert, the creative individual is an impressive person, and he is so because he has to such a large degree realized his potentialities. He has become in great measure the person he was capable of becoming. Since he is not preoccupied with the impression he makes on others, and is not overconcerned with their opinion of him, he is freer than most to be himself. To say that he is relatively free from conventional restraints and inhibitions might seem to suggest that he is to some degree socially irresponsible. He may seem to be, and in some instances he doubtless is if judged by the conventional standards of society, since his behavior is dictated more by his own set of values and by ethical standards that may not be precisely those of others around him.

The highly creative are not conformists in their ideas, but on the other hand they are not deliberate nonconformists, either. Instead, they are genuinely independent. They are often, in fact, quite conventional in matters and in actions that are not central to their areas of creative endeavor. It is in their creative striving that their independence of thought and autonomy of action are revealed. Indeed, it is characteristic of the highly creative person that he is strongly motivated to achieve in situations in which independence in thought and action are called for, but much less inclined to strive for achievement in situations where conforming behavior is expected or required. Flexibility with respect to means and goals is a striking characteristic of the groups we have studied.

On a test that measures the similarity of a person's expressed interests with the known interests of individuals successful in a variety of occupations and professions, creative persons reveal themselves as having interests similar to those of psychologists, architects, artists, writers, physicists, and musicians, and quite unlike those of purchasing agents, office men, bankers, farmers, carpenters, policemen, and morticians. These similarities and dissimilarities of interest are in themselves less significant than the abstractions and inferences that may be drawn from them. They suggest strongly that creative persons are relatively less interested in small details, in facts as such, and more concerned with their meanings and implications, possessed of considerable cognitive flexibility, verbally skillful, eager to communicate with others with nicety and precision, open to experience, and relatively uninterested in policing either their own impulses and images or those of others.

With respect to philosophical values—the theoretical, economic, esthetic, social, political, and religious as measured on one of our tests—there are two values most emphasized by all the creative groups. They are the theoretical and esthetic. One might think that there is some incompatibility and conflict between a cognitive and rational concern with truth and an emotional concern with form and beauty. If this is so, it would appear that the creative person has the capacity to tolerate the tension created in him by opposing strong values, and in his life and work he effects some reconciliation of them. Perhaps a less dramatic and more cautious interpretation of the simultaneous high valuing of the theoretical and the esthetic would be that for the truly creative person the solution of a problem is not sufficient; there is the further demand that it be elegant. The esthetic viewpoint permeates all of a creative person's work. He seeks not only truth but also beauty.

Closely allied to his strong theoretical and esthetic values is another pervasive trait of the creative, his preference for complexity, his delight in the challenging and unfinished, which evoke in him an urge, indeed a need, to discover unifying principles for ordering and integrating multiplicity.

In so brief a report, emphasis has had to be placed upon the generality of research findings. What needs to be equally emphasized is that there are many paths along which persons travel toward the full development and expression of their creative potential, and that there is no single mold into which all who are creative will fit. The full and complete picturing of the creative person will require many images. But if, despite this caution, one still insists on asking what most generally characterizes the creative individual as he has revealed himself in the Berkeley studies, it is his high level of effective intelligence, his openness to experience, his freedom from crippling restraints and impoverishing inhibitions, his esthetic sensitivity, his cognitive flexibility, his independence in thought and action, his high level of creative energy, his unquestioning commitment to creative endeavor, and his unceasing striving for solutions to the ever more difficult problems that he constantly sets for himself.

49   The Creative Process
D. W. Gotshalk

I. INTRODUCTORY

In many respects the creative process in the arts is indistinguishable from innumerable other types of creative activity. It consists of a series of interactions between an agent and a material. The agent is seeking to shape the material in certain ways for certain purposes. He is a center of impulse, of striving, of tendency toward ends; and he possesses causal powers that implement the realization of these ends and a nature, environmentally nurtured, that colors the form of the realization. The material, for its part, is in certain ways resistant and in other ways plastic to the efforts of the agent. It has its own nature, its own possibilities, its own limitations, its resident self-determinacy. All this, however, is true of many other creative situations: e.g., agricultural experimentation or technological invention. They consist of an agent or set of agents in interaction with a material, each endowed with such general characteristics as those just enumerated. What, then, is peculiar in the case of the fine arts? There seem to me to be two major peculiarities.

First, the material of the arts, generally speaking, is material of great intrinsic perceptual interest. The great poet's words are not the flat stereotypes of a business letter. The sculptor's stone is not the lustreless shale of a river bed. The dancer's body is not the ungainly and ill-co-ordinated organism of the ordinary ten-year-old schoolgirl. The musician's tones are not the screeching noises of a city street, and the architect's blocks are not the ill-shaped boulders of a vacant lot. In the overwhelming majority of cases the material of each art exhibits, or under transformation is easily capable of exhibiting, vivid intrinsic values for perception. It is alive with all the possibilities of great art. The second peculiarity concerns the artist himself. "The artist is not distinguished either by the quality or the amount of his feeling, but by the intensity and comprehensiveness of his unifying perception." [1] "Genius, considered in itself, is but superior perceptive power, coming from exaggerated excitability and elasticity in the nervous centres." [2] More precisely, the peculiarity of the artist is an extraordinarily keen interest in, and power to assimilate phases of, the perceptual world—sounds, colors, lines, motions, the perceptible oddities of people—together with the capacity to create diverse perceptual systems which extend his original interest and power and satisfy in a superior way the deeply innate craving for novel and internally complete intrinsic perceptions.

The key terms of the creative process in the arts, then, are a certain kind of agent and a certain type of material. Nevertheless, it seems impossible to give an adequate description of this creative process merely by depicting the overt interactions between the agent and the material. The agent, for example, has a complex inner consciousness, in which a great deal often occurs before overt interaction with the material takes place. In part, the development of all human consciousness consists of the acquisition of an elaborate set of symbols or imagery representative of the physicosocial world and the reintegration of these symbols as a preparation for overt "action."

---

[1] Leo Stein, *A B C of Aesthetics* (New York: Boni & Liveright, 1927), p. 206.
[2] Eugène Véron, *Aesthetics*, trans. W. H. Armstrong (London: Chapman & Hall, 1879), p. 73; cf. also George Santayana, *Reason in Art* (New York: Charles Scribner's Sons, 1905), p. 181.

This is especially true in the case of the artist. Indeed, it has been so true here that some thinkers, such as Croce, have reduced the creative process of the artist to the mere subjective reintegration of symbols. Leonardo's creation of the "Last Supper," according to this view, consisted not in the overt act of painting but in that "arranging" of the colors, lines, shapes, and figures on the wall at Santa Maria delle Grazie that took place during the hours in which the artist merely gazed studiously upon the surface to be painted.

.   .   .

II. THE SUBJECTIVE PHASE

Besides the instance of Leonardo at Santa Maria, there are other famous examples of the visionary manipulation of symbols. "Kubla Khan" is said to have been dreamed as it is, then written down. Mozart is quoted as saying: "My ideas come as they will, I don't know how, all in a stream. If I like them I keep them in my head, and people say that I often hum them over to myself. Well, if I can hold on to them, they begin to join on to one another, as if they were bits that a pastry cook should join together in his pantry. And now my soul gets heated, and if nothing disturbs me the piece grows larger and brighter, until, however long it is, it is all finished at once in my mind, so that I can see it at a glance as if it were a pretty picture or a pleasing person. Then I don't hear the notes one after another, as they are hereafter to be played, but it is as if in my fancy they were all at once. And that *is* a revel [*das ist nun ein Schmaus*]. While I'm inventing, it all seems to me like a fine vivid dream, but that hearing it all at once [when the invention is done], that's the best. When I have once so heard I forget not again, and perhaps this is the best gift that God has granted me." [4]

Inner creation, such as this, presupposes, as I have suggested in the case of Leonardo, antecedent experience. Such creation may occur suddenly and most unexpectedly. But it does not arise from nothing. It springs from a soil usually prepared by technical training and always stocked with symbols acquired from interactions with artistic material and with a physicosocial world. Even the six-year-old musical prodigy bursts into creative invention only after antecedent social and musical observation and experience. "We know that one of the conditions most favorable to invention is. . . . accumulated experience, knowledge." [5] "To become an artist the most highly gifted must go through a long course of hard practice and experiment." [6] Testimony of this sort from all quarters is almost endless. A well-known detailed treatise on the acquisition of symbols from antecedent interactions is Lowes's *Road to*

[4] Josiah Royce, *The Spirit of Modern Philosophy* (Boston: Houghton Mifflin Co., 1892), p. 457. This letter has been suspected of being apocryphal, but, apocryphal or not, it describes a process which might have occurred, and so illustrates a real possibility in artistic creation.

[5] Th. Ribot, *Essai sur l'imagination créatrice* (Paris: Félix Alcan, 1900), p. 135.

[6] J. Littlejohns, *How To Enjoy Pictures* (New York: Macmillan Co., 1927), p. 6.

Xanadu, in which words and phrases in *The Rime of the Ancient Mariner* and "Kubla Khan" are traced to books of travel and adventure that Coleridge had been reading before composing the poems. "A work of pure imagination," Lowes remarks, "is not something fabricated by a *tour de force* from nothing, and suspended, without anchorage in fact, in the impalpable ether of a visionary world. No conception could run more sharply counter to the truth." Supposedly a mere vision, *The Rime of the Ancient Mariner* is steeped in the factual lore of the day. "It has swept within its assimilating influence a bewildering diversity of facts in which contemporary interest was active. The facts are forgotten, and the poem stays." But the acquisition of the "facts" was a precondition both of the poem and of the vision which it embodies.[7]

The capacity to be keenly affected by the perceptual world, to gather "facts," and to lay up memories convertible into a great symbolic repertory is usually called "sensitivity." The power to reintegrate this repertory, to construct from it images of novel perceptual systems, to shape "the facts into the fabric of a vision," [8] is usually called "imagination," creative as distinct from reproductive imagination. Sensitivity and creative imagination are the basic powers of the subjective phase of creation.

Sensitivity in artists is usually uneven. Some artists are extraordinarily sensitive to words or tones but not to lines or colors. Others are extraordinarily senstive to lines and colors but not to words or tones. Still others are extraordinarily sensitive to the motives and basic characteristics of human beings but not to tones or colors. This unevenness of sensitivity conditions imagination, explaining in part the different directions that imagination takes and why there are different arts—an art of words, an art of tones, an art of colors, etc. Nor is this unevenness of sensitivity altogether regrettable in other respects. If artists were extraordinarily affected by all the perceptual facets of the physical and social world, they would probably be suffocated by experience, overwhelmed by its sheer massiveness. In any case artists need merely sensitivity enough to provide their powers of symbolic reorganization with an unusually ample and fertile field for action, and great depth of sensitivity in one direction only is ordinarily sufficient to do this.

Sensitivity is the point of contact between the inner consciousness of the artist and the outer world. It is almost public. More inward and secretive is the other basic power of the subjective phase—creative imagination. Imagination, as it operates in aesthetic appreciation, we have defined as the power to connect the absent with the present. It is a process of synthesis of the "not-given" with the "given." Creative imagination, as it operates in subjective symbolic manipulations, is also a process of synthesis. It might be defined as the power to connect a multiplicity of assimilated items into a novel synthetical unity. At its weakest, where imagination is what Coleridge called "fancy," this unity is like an aggregate in which the items have some

[7] John L. Lowes, *The Road to Xanadu* (Boston: Houghton Mifflin Co., 1927), p. 241.
    [8] *Ibid.*, p. 241.

superficial interrelevance that gives them the appearance of going effectively together, as when a person compares the frost to icing on a cake or a child draws an ensemble in which a candle and a doll stand as high as a house. Such facile combinations are often momentarily startling and pleasing, but they are not particularly rewarding to closer scrutiny. On the other hand, at its best, where imagination is what Coleridge meant by the term, the unity created is like an organism in which the parts have a complex, mutually sustaining interrelevance that gives the whole a dense and durable set of values, as when the poet compares the frost to a white assassin or a painter arranges the colors and shapes of the objects in a small picture so as to create subtly contrasting or parallel rhythms within a unified realistic design. In forms larger than metaphor or miniature patterns, the elements of highly imaginative wholes mutually enhance one another in more complex, and often in seemingly miraculous, ways. These combinations not only suggest the daring and audacity romantically associated with genius but sometimes also exhibit a wealth of connections so rich as to reach indefinitely beyond the grasp of the keenest analytic attention. They suggest the inexhaustible and the infinite in the manner of Kant's Aesthetical Ideas.[9] In all cases, however, creative imagination is the power to connect a diversity into a novel synthetical unity, the rank accorded the result being ultimately a function of the wealth of perceptual value that is found in the unified diversity.

Sensitivity, then, is the material principle of the symbolic or subjective phase of creation, and imagination is the form principle; and, at its best, imagination weaves the symbols derived from sensitivity into designs of great suggestiveness and power. Yet other factors besides these two inner capacities enter into the subjective manipulatory process. Abstractly, sensitivity is pure receptivity, the power to record indiscriminately anything impinging on the organism, while, abstractly, creative imagination is pure madness, the power to combine anything with anything.[10] Both require control principles, governance, and guidance for the emergence of the results which they help attain. What are the subjective control factors which modify sensitivity in its acquisitive role and govern imagination in its formal shaping?

First and foremost is the personality of the artist. By "personality of the artist" I do not mean merely his superficial whims and striking mannerisms, although these are a part and, with minor artists, a great part of its meaning. More basic than these is the artist's fund of inborn drives and needs as these have been released and transformed by environment and education into a system of purposes and aspirations manifesting a set of standards or a "scale of values." Personality is a fruition of heredity modified by environment, but its essence is the fruition emerging from the heredity and expressed in relation

[9] I. Kant, *Critique of Judgement,* trans. Bernard (2d ed.; London: Macmillan & Co., Ltd., 1914), pp. 201 ff.

[10] I. A. Richards, *Coleridge on Imagination* (London: Kegan Paul, Trench, Trubner & Co., Ltd., 1934), pp. 74, 172.

to the environment. Its essence is the system of inclinations and aspirations of the artist underlying his mannerisms and manifesting through his actions and mannerisms a scale of values.

Personality in the sense of the basic underlying value inclinations and aspirations of the artist is a fundamental control factor of the subjective creative process. It exerts a control over sensitivity and the symbolic material acquired through sensitivity. In part, sensitivity and the material it acquires are a function of native endowment and training, i.e., of the mechanical agility of the receptor mechanism. In part, however, they are a function of the underlying value inclinations and aspirations of the artist. These value inclinations and aspirations tend to determine the paths into which the receptor powers are directed, the zest with which they respond, and the items that interest the artist in these paths. Moreover, these value inclinations and aspirations generally determine the selections for symbolic use, "instinctive" and reflective, that the artist makes from the total acquisitions of his receptor mechanism. Indeed, personality so determines these selections or, with imagination, so modifies them that certain material items in a work—tone clusters, lines, words, shapes, and so on—sometimes immediately and unmistakably signalize a particular artist, independent of the larger form of the work. Hearing or seeing these, we realize at once that the work is by Debussy, Cézanne, Poe, Pope, Delacroix, Rodin, Michelangelo, and so on.

Personality equally controls imagination, the great forming power. The personality of the artist regulates the act of unification in such a way that the created product exhibits a characteristic system of accents and emphases which leads one to associate it with the artist and even with his age. Sometimes in given works this system of accents and emphases is incompletely definitive of the creator. Apprentice and imitation work, work in some type of form or material ably used by other artists, or work of short span often illustrates incompletely definitive creations. But the more vigorously creative a work is, the more definitely personal do its accents and emphases usually become. Even in music—the art in which the condition of personal indeterminacy is likely to be most pronounced because the materials and forms of music have been highly conventionalized and the expressive substance of the art is so general and "abstract"—the modifications by personality are frequently crystal clear. Certain music by Wagner is as different in its accentual system from certain music by Haydn as the two men or their two epochs are. The one is surging, ponderous, ruthlessly declarative, endlessly persistent, while the other is mechanically elegant and graciously artificial, its sprightliness and melancholy and playful surprises confined within fixed bounds as if restricted a priori to certain clear and unalterable limits. And this is a statement not merely of certain accentual qualities of the pieces of music but also of certain personal qualities of Wagner and Haydn and of certain widespread qualities of the surging bourgeois nineteenth century and of the courtly eighteenth-century mid-Continental Europe.

The personality of the artist also affects the aesthetic "depth" of a creation. Everyone is familiar with the fact that violin tones sound mellow or thin according to the nature of the sound chamber over which the strings are stretched. Now personality in the subjective phase of creation has a role similar to the sound chamber or resonator in tone production. It serves as an amplifier or denudator of undertones and overtones of value. The result is an imaginative structure that is aesthetically subtle and rich or arid and commonplace. Two artists of equally facile sensitivity and imagination go to work on the same subject, producing results utterly different not only in vocabulary and accent but in expressive depth. They may paint before the same model, one producing a "fancy" magazine-cover painting and the other a landmark in pictorial art. The greater wealth of expressive values in the one work reflects a greater depth of value penetration of its creator. It is a product of his "realizations" of the subject and springs from the system of value inclinations and aspirations that he brings to the interpretation of the subject. Thus personality is influential in supplying not only a peculiar idiom and accentual structure to a symbolic system but also an expressive wealth and richness or an expressive bareness and poverty. It may, indeed, mark a difference as wide as that between glitter and gold. Two works may brilliantly bespeak in vocabulary and syntax the unmistakable characteristics of two artists. Yet they may be the opposite in expressive density, one meretricious and thin, the other solid and mellow-toned.

Personality, then, is a basic control factor in the subjective creative process, modifying sensitivity and imagination, and the symbolic material, the form and the expression. Usually these modifications are "underground" events, occurring without the artist's explicit will or awareness at the time. But, as we shall see in the next section, there is no fixed rule on this point. Besides personality, there are other control factors in the subjective process. Some of these are fortuitous conditions: a spell of very good or of very bad health, a temporary lazy streak or a sudden disposition for hard work, personal good fortune or a great misfortune, a period of inner peace or of inner tumult. Sometimes these "scratches" on the surface of the artist's existence impair or enhance creation considerably. Sometimes you would never know from the created product that they had existed at all. More uniform and usually more profound in their effects are two other control factors, the "subject" of a work and its functional end. Both frequently control the selection of material and the shaping of the form as vigorously as personality. The subject of the "Last Supper" certainly exercised control over Leonardo's choice of colors, lines, and shapes and even more control over his arrangement of these materials into a form suitable to articulate the dramatic moment that was the subject. In general, a subject has certain broad or typic characteristics that allow a certain latitude to its treatment, e.g., a material, formal, and expressive range for personality. But the artist must keep within the broad generic bounds of these characteristics if his work is to be at all a recognizable treatment of the subject.

The other control factor here—the functional end of the work—may be simple or complex. In either case it is usually an explicit type of control factor. At its simplest it is subjectively aesthetic, i.e., the functional end of the work is simply that of satisfying the artist's private aesthetic interest. Here the selection of the material and the shaping process have maximum freedom, being governed from above solely by a purpose which the work can fulfill independently of all explicit extrinsic considerations. Usually, however, the functional end of a work is much more complex than this. Most works of art have come into existence not merely to discharge a private end but also to perform a public function, as a statue to fit a public square, a painting to decorate a church, a piece of music to fit a certain concert program. Shakespeare, writing his plays, presumably sought not merely to articulate a vision satisfying to his own private perception but to write plays fitting the requirements of his theater, the needs of his players, and the demands of his audience. The functional end of his plays was very complex, and, for him to create successfully under the circumstances, his symbols and forms had to be governed to some extent by each element of this functional complex. The imagination of the professional artist particularly, far from a free and roving fancy, is usually regulated by a number of explicit functional considerations, social in origin and character, which powerfully modify his materials as well as his forms, just as this imagination is regulated and the materials and forms modified by a number of the most obscure personal traits, reaching back into the heredity and the earliest environment of the artist.

THE ARTS SPEAK FOR THEMSELVES

[movement]

50   ## On Dance

Curt Sachs

The dance is the mother of the arts. Music and poetry exist in time; painting and architecture in space. But the dance lives at once in time and space. The creator and the thing created, the artist and the work are still one and the same thing. Rhythmical patterns of movement, the plastic sense of space, the vivid representation of a world seen and imagined—these things man creates in his own body in the dance before he uses substance and stone and word to give expression to his inner experiences.

The word art does not altogether express this idea. Indeed, one almost fears to use the word, for its present-day significance, exaggerated and at the same time circumscribed, is not sufficient to explain what the dance in all its richness really is. The dance breaks down the distinctions of body and soul, of abandoned expression of the emotions and controlled behavior, of social life and the expression of individuality, of play, religion, battle, and drama—all the distinctions that a more advanced civilization has established. The body, which in ecstasy is conquered and forgotten and which becomes merely a receptacle for the superhuman power of the soul, and the soul, which achieves happiness and bliss in the accelerated movements of a body freed of its own weight; the need to dance, because an effervescent zest for life forces the limbs from sloth, and the desire to dance, because the dancer gains magic powers, which bring him victory, health, life; a mystic tie binding the tribe when it joins hands in the choral dance, and the unconstrained dance of the individual in utter devotion to self—there is no "art" which includes so much.

Repressed powers are loosed and seek free expression; an innate sense of rhythm orders them into lively harmony. Harmony deadens and dissipates the will. Delivered then from his will, the dancer gives himself over to the supreme delight of play prescribed by custom, gives himself over to the exhilaration, which carries him away from the monotony of everyday life, from palpable reality, from the sober facts of his experience—thither where imagination, fancy, and vision waken and become creative.

In the ecstasy of the dance man bridges the chasm between this and the other world, to the realm of demons, spirits, and God. Captivated and entranced he bursts his earthly chains and trembling feels himself in tune with all the world. "Whosoever knoweth the power of the dance, dwelleth in God," cries the Persian dervish poet Rumi impulsively. The dance, inherited from savage ancestors as an ordered expression in motion of the exhilaration of the soul, develops and broadens into the search for God, into a conscious effort to become a part of those powers beyond the might of man which control our destinies. The dance becomes a sacrificial rite, a charm, a prayer, and a prophetic vision. It summons and dispels the forces of nature, heals the sick, links the dead to the chain of their descendants; it assures sustenance, luck in the chase, victory in battle; it blesses the fields and the tribe. It is creator, preserver, steward, and guardian.

From its deep and far-reaching influence it will be apparent that in the life of primitive peoples and of ancient civilizations scarcely anything approaches the dance in importance. It is no art that disregards bread; on the contrary, it provides bread and everything else that is needed to sustain life. It is not a sin, proscribed by the priest or at best merely accepted by him, but rather a sacred act and priestly office; not a pastime to be tolerated only, but a very serious activity of the entire tribe. On no occasion in the life of primitive peoples could the dance be dispensed with. Birth, circumcision, and the consecration of maidens, marriage and death, planting and harvest, the celebrations of chieftains, hunting, war, and feasts, the changes of the moon and sickness—for all of these the dance is needed. But it is not a question here of display and festivity in our sense. We know that in New Caledonia the merchants in the market house dance out in turn to show off their wares, and that the inhabitants of North Queensland pick lice off one another in a festive round dance. We read that the American Indian divorces his wife in the dance and when he is ill, dances himself to dispel the disease; further, that a chieftain in the Cameroons, condemned to death for revolt, walked up to the gallows singing and dancing, and that once, in front of the Turkish soldiers, sixty Greek maidens and mothers with children danced the old *romaiika* as they threw themselves one after another into an abyss. Only when we take into account such examples do we begin to comprehend that the dance in its essence is simply life on a higher level.

The dance is life on a higher level simply—this statement points out its all-inclusive character and its ultimate significance. Yet while it might extend the scope of a scientific consideration, it is nevertheless not a definition upon which to base such a consideration. Such a definition is not easy to formulate; indeed, in the last analysis, perhaps impossible. For all human activity eludes hard and fast classification; work and play, law and liberty, merge and the imperceptibility of the transition may be its chief characteristic. Thus from a positive approach it is almost impossible to define the dance more narrowly than as "rhythmic motion." What is lacking in this definition is that it does not exclude other rhythmic movements, such as running, rowing, turning a handle, working a treadle. These may be excluded only if we adopt a negative approach. For no positive expression is valid. "Playful" would exclude all the religious dances; "purposeless," the magic dances. That which is to be excluded might perhaps best be designated as anything having to do with work. By this we would mean everything which we describe in everyday life as "practical;" all kinds of rhythmical handwork, but also walking and marching, the playing of a violinist as well as the gestures of the orchestra conductor. The rhythmic features of sport and of gymnastics are, to be sure, included in the work motif, and there is a gap here. But we shall leave this gap open deliberately; otherwise we should be ruling out the important power dances, skill dances, and war dances, thus cutting into the whole elastic organism of the dance. Therefore let us consider as dance all rhythmical motion not related to the work motif.

This is still not art in the usual sense. But art is included in this concept, provided it means the re-creating of things seen and heard, the giving of form and substance to the intangible and irrational perceptions of the half conscious, and the experiencing in the creative process of the divine rapture of another world and of self-forgetfulness. As early as the Stone Age, dances become works of art; and on the threshold of the Metal Ages, legend seizes the dance and raises it into drama. But when in higher cultures it becomes art in the narrower sense, when it becomes a spectacle, when it seeks to influence men rather than spirits, then its universal power is broken. It disintegrates. Play and physical exercise renounce rhythm and break away, the drama itself denies its father, and the new religions become estranged from rounds and dances. What was left to the higher civilizations, especially to the European, was divided between guild art and social enjoyment. To pray with the feet like Gottfried Keller's little Musa, like the beautiful gypsy Preciosa of Cervantes, and like the old juggler who knew no Latin quotation to say to the Mother of God—all that is lost to us. But every high culture still has as a spiritual inheritance from a distant past, the lofty conception that all supermundane and superhuman motion is dance. Turning about in divine rhythm, Siva creates the world; for the Chinese, cosmic harmony originates in the dance; planets and gods swing through the universe in the dance; and late Jewish theology, indeed even Christianity, ever hostile to the dance, cannot visualize the lot of the redeemed except in a picture of an ethereal round about the shining throne of God.

On Music 51

Leopold Stokowski

Just as men and women can have various kinds and degrees of physical beauty—just as mountains, forests, lakes, deserts, rivers, oceans, the stars, the moon, the sunset can have a thousand variations of physical beauty that thrill us—so the mere physical sound of voices and instruments can delight us, quite apart from the deeper aspects of the music they may be singing or playing.

If we take each instrument separately, we will find it has wonderful characteristics, much as all people have—if we take the trouble to find them. Each instrument is capable of producing many tone colors or timbres, according to the expression of the melody being played at the moment. Every instrument has its deep sounds—its high, brilliant tones—and, midway, more mellow sounds. This is a kind of trinity which exists for every instrument, but some instruments have still more variations of tone color which lie between the three tonal registers described. For example, the clarinet has a soft, dovelike group of tones in the middle register, sounds typical of the clarinet. In this part of its tonal range are some technical and structural difficulties, but a good player knows how to turn these into one of the most beautiful tonal characteristics of that instrument. The bassoon has an extremely high register of a strange, veiled, intense quality which can be highly expressive. The opening phrase of Stravinsky's *Rite of Spring* is a masterly example of this strange, exotic timbre—the primitive, solitary character of the melody is expressed to perfection by the fantastic coloring of the register of the bassoon. The bassoon also has a low register which, in the hands of an artist, can sound dry and grotesque and mocking.

The string instruments all have a different timbre, each string having its own individual quality of tone. For example, the lowest string of the violin can sound rich and golden, the highest string brilliant and penetrating. The two middle strings have different nuances of soft, rich, velvety, dark tone quality. The high string of the viola can have a biting, acid quality which alone can express certain kinds of music. The lowest string is somber and melancholy, with an indescribable beauty of tone. The high string of the

Ch. 5, "The Physical Beauty of Music," with deletions, Ch. 7, "Freedom of Response to Music," and Ch. 8, "All Sound Can be Music" in *Music For All of Us*, by Leopold Stokowski, New York, Simon and Schuster, 1943. Reprinted by permission of Leopold Stokowski.

cello is extremely rich, ardent, expressive, full of sunshine. Each of the four strings of the double bass has a different character. Each individual instrument is different from every other instrument, so that there is a never-ending variety of tone in each section of the orchestra, and an inexhaustible range of color in the complete orchestra.

Some musicians believe that there is one ideal tonal beauty for each instrument. Others believe there is infinity in the variety of tone color or timbre. They try to find the particular ideal timbre for each tone, each phrase, each harmony, and this quest of the most eloquent tone color, for each moment of the music, is to them a never-ending source of musical delight.

Some kinds of music are tonal paintings of certain poetic ideas and dream pictures. At the same time, they are wonderful music in their flowing harmonies and melodies, subtle tangles of interwoven rhythms, masterly counterpoint, and all the purely musical elements which make up the heart and substance of great music. But in addition to all this, some music can give us the most intense delight just as sound and combinations of sound— simply for its sensuous and physical beauty. For example, Debussy's *Afternoon of a Faun* is a masterpiece of tonal painting—of suggestion in the dim twilight of a remote and exotic land—of the voluptuous interplay of melodies and counter-melodies—the gliding succession of harmonies—where each tone seems to caress the next in the melody and the nearest tones in the harmony —where all the tone colors and timbres enrich each other by a kind of soft-colored light which glows from them. Another outstanding example is Ravel's *Daphnis and Chloë*, in which savage, leaping rhythms and eager, rushing streams of sound are contrasted with soft, distant music painted in pale, transparent hues—like the memory of an antique Elysian world, vaguely discerned in our dreams. Both of these show the instinctive feeling of great musicians for the purely physical beauty of tone—its sensuous loveliness—its unending variety of color.

Even when instruments are not playing any particular music—but when good players in an orchestra are tuning their instruments, the sheer sound of the tones can be a delight, just as are the pure colors on the palette of a painter. Orchestral tuning is a confused tangle of tones—a stampede of colored sound, like a jungle in Africa or India. Various individual instruments shoot up high like a rocket and then fall again into the agitated sea of sound. Each time they become lost as they dive beneath the tonal surface, but again they come up and are clear against the sky like a soaring eagle. This interwoven tumultuous mass of sound is like a complex Chinese silk weaving of the Han dynasty or the *mille-fleurs* tapestries of Arras.

We can fill our souls with this physical beauty of tone, its limitless combinations of melodies, harmonies, rhythms, tone colors. Or we can look more deeply into music and seek its inner message. Each lover of music will decide for himself, according to his temperament. Perhaps the ideal is to fuse the profound spiritual significance of music with the highest tonal and physical beauty.

. . .

We all are sensitive in our own way to what is beautiful *for us*. If we respond to some form of beauty, it is ours as a birthright. A second person may not find beauty in that same thing, which only means that he does not respond to it—not that either person is right or wrong. These differences of opinion are liberty—the variety in life which gives it zest—the thrill of adventure—of constantly discovering new things. Everything that moves us deeply in Nature or Art is significant and beautiful *for us*. We call Shakespeare great because thousands have responded to the magic of his words. But if few had responded, those words would still be the same. A wild flower may bloom in a remote valley in the mountains. Whether anyone passes by to enjoy it or not, the flower gives of its perfume and the beauty of its color and form. Sometimes a soul has existed ahead of its time and few have realized its greatness. The music of Bach is now loved all over the world by millions who respond to its nobility, depth of feeling, and spiritual beauty. But in Bach's own time, even in the city of Leipzig, where he lived and made music so many years, he was appreciated only to a comparatively small degree. A few individuals realized his greatness during his lifetime—now millions all over the world respond deeply and powerfully to the inner spirit of this music.

There is no question of right or wrong here—it is simply a question of individual response. For a person to say that certain music is good, and other music bad, is an attempt at mental and spiritual dictatorship. Such dictatorship of the mind and spirit is in some ways more destructive than the tyranny of men who exploit individuals and nations on the material plane. In music and art of every kind, dictatorship is quite unnecessary and definitely stultifying. It is interesting and instructive to hear the opinions of educated and experienced musicians about various kinds of music, but we must always be free to feel about music in our own way—with sincerity and spontaneity. Let us all love, in music, where we find loveliness. Then our feeling will be sincere and simple. The music itself will create in us the emotions of which we are capable. Sincerity in response to music is as much to be valued as sincerity in every form of life. Freedom of thought about music and freedom of reaction to music are indispensable to true culture. Just as each of us must be free in this, so we must insist on everyone else being free. Tolerance and generosity of spirit are absolutely essential to art of all kinds—in us as individuals—in our community—our nation—and the whole world.

It makes no difference whether a man or woman in whose life music plays a large part is a professional musician or not—we all react to music differently because of the difference in our heredity and environment. If we were able to trace back our ancestors for about three centuries—and that is a mere fraction of time in the full span of man's evolution—we would find that we have thousands of ancestors. Our mental and emotional characteristics are inherited in varying degrees from some, or possibly all, of these ancestors, according to laws and processes of Nature of which at present we know little. This explains why no two music lovers in the world respond to music exactly alike. Nature does not standardize, but is unendingly fertile in creating new forms and new combinations.

Just as we are all influenced by the past through our ancestors, so we are influenced in the present through our environment. All of us who love music live in different environments. We come under greatly varying influences. If we look back to the earliest days of our childhood, we realize that we have had numberless different impressions of music—the music made by man, and the music of Nature—such as the sound of wind, waves, waterfalls, the soft clashing of the leaves of trees, the rhythmic sounds of insects, the songs of birds. Not only do we all have different musical experiences, but our emotional responses to these experiences are different in every individual. These differences are a glorious thing. They are an expression of our individuality. If we were to try to standardize ourselves, we would become mechanical automata. But if we give free expression to these spontaneous outpourings of our inner nature, we will be our true selves, grow in every direction, enlarge our personality, and find richer and more varied delight in all our experiences of life and music.

It is important to distinguish clearly between the unity of basic principles in music and the immense diversity of our individual reactions to music. Although the fundamental principles of music are unified, there is no end to the diversity of our personal *feeling* about music. Some enjoy the beauty of its sounds—others look beneath the surface into the profound depths of music—still others combine both of these. It is all a matter of temperament.

Differences of temperament and differences of emotional response to music add to its variety and unlimited range of color and character. Two players or two singers may do exactly the same thing and yet the musical result will be quite different. The reason is that one may do it to follow tradition—the other from spontaneous feeling. When it is done as tradition, it may be the result of an intellectual conception, or of a knowledge of musical history, or of a desire to conform to what is thought to be "good taste." When it is done from spontaneous feeling, it will be music coming from the heart. It will ring true—have conviction—be eloquent. Even though it is "wrong," it will sound authentic and be true to character—like a hungry workman who eats lustily with his knife.

It is important to realize that our individual reactions to music are completely relative. How we *feel* about music, and what it really *is*, may be two totally different things. How we feel about music is our personal reaction and is purely subjective. What the music is by its character is a fact and objective. If we are willing to regard our feeling about music as something individual, it will be sincere and spontaneous. But if we try to transform our subjective impression of any particular music into an objective fact, and insist that others have the same impression of the music as ourselves, we not only show disrespect for the spontaneous reactions of others, but we also show ignorance of those laws of Nature which govern the subjective impressions of all men to objective realities. We must all be free to react to music according to our inner nature—any attempt to force ourselves to react to music according to another person's feelings may spoil for a time the freshness and truth of our reaction. If a hundred persons listen to Beethoven's "Eroica" Symphony, the rhythms and tones heard are the same for every one of the hundred—but their impressions and emotional reactions will be different for each one of the hundred. This difference of reaction to music and all art is fundamental and eternal. It is of great importance not to tamper with the honesty of this, or to try to enslave the reaction of music lovers by any so-called authority. No one can enjoy music for us—we can do it only for ourselves.

In this individual approach to music, we shall naturally wish to enjoy the full meaning and potentialities of the music. When we listen to music, we sometimes feel that its complete message and spirit have been expressed. At other times we feel that we have only heard a mechanical rendering of the music, and that there is far more significance in the music than has been expressed. True music is always spontaneous—glowing with the fire of creation. Mechanical routine and convention are fatal to music. Spontaneity, deep feeling, sincerity, and inspiration are the very life of music. Music inspires the musician, who is the channel through which music flows to us—and music inspires the listener, who absorbs the inspiration to the degree that he is sensitive to the music. Music demands of us all—musician and listener—the highest that is in us.

There is no exception to this. If the composer is inspired—but the performance of his music is uninspired—the music will sound dull, mechanical, at best note perfect. It will be like an electric current which begins with high voltage but somewhere along its route is reduced to lower voltage—so that the current received at the end will be at the lowest voltage along its route, no matter how high the voltage was at its initial point of transmission. This is not an exact analogy, but it suggests how greatly the inspiration of the composer can be reduced and almost completely nullified by a performance which may be literally perfect, but which entirely misses the spirit of the music because it lacks the great essential—inspiration.

How are we to know what is good or bad in music? One man likes *The Last Rose of Summer* but finds a symphony of Brahms meaningless and dry. Another man likes the symphonies of Brahms but smiles with disdain at such simple melodies as *Drink to Me Only with Thine Eyes* or *My Old Kentucky Home*. But a third man likes all of this music. His range is greater. He does not disdain simple folk music, but loves it. With another part of his being he is capable of understanding and feeling intensely the profound music of Brahms. Another man might regard the fugues of Bach as great music and be quite sincere in detesting the intoxicated, ecstatic dance rhythms of the Negro musician. He might say, "That is bad music—in fact it is not music at all." But there are others who find that type of African dance music exciting, and who would find the fugues of Bach cold and monotonous—particularly if they are played, as sometimes happens, in a dull, uninspired way, with little variation of timbre, with clumsy phrasing, with small understanding of the architectonics and organic growth of the music. How can we know what is right and wrong about all this? What is good music? What is bad music? To make this judgment with certainty, we should find out whether there exists a *norm* or *standard* or *criterion* for measuring the quality of music. We can measure the length of things—is it possible to measure the quality of music?

In the Place Vendôme in Paris is a strip of metal designed to give the exact length of the meter. Somewhere in Washington is a similar standard measure for the yard. By these two, we have an attempt at standardized measurement for length. Is there such a standard for music? If so, we can apply this standard to all music and find out whether it is good or bad.

Fortunately there is no such norm or standard, because if there were a norm, music could not grow and evolve in new directions but would always be circling around that norm—like an animal in captivity chained to a post. Music is free and limitless—it is forever expanding in new directions. Each one of us feels music differently because of that sacred thing inside us—our individuality. Music will never stop evolving, but century after century will become richer in variety, richer in life experience, in unending difference of feeling. If we compare the opinions of a thousand persons from different countries all over the world, we will find immense variations of opinion as to what is good or bad music. They will sometimes contradict each other completely, with scarcely any two people feeling and thinking exactly alike. Even professional teachers in conservatories of music do not always agree, but each one has his own idea of what is good and bad. We all remember the episode in Beethoven's life when a friend objected to consecutive fifths in one of his symphonies. Beethoven replied "What of it?" The friend said, "But they are not allowed." Beethoven roared, "I allow them." It is this spontaneity in Beethoven—this truth to himself—this disregard of academic rules—which was one of Beethoven's greatest qualities and which has made his music of such lasting value to the culture of the whole world.

This lasting value is an important element in all music. There is music that has lasted a long time and is still loved by millions of people—for example, the music of Bach. Some prefer not to dogmatize and say this is "good" music, but that it is music that millions of people have enjoyed for a period of about two centuries and still are enjoying. This is a matter of great cultural importance, because just as we must be free to live our lives our own way, provided we do not harm others, so we must be free to enjoy that kind of music which appeals to us—which is of immense value to the thought and feeling of our cultural lives—and to the development of world culture.

There are several conceptions of the value of any particular music—

1. The music we personally like as individuals.
2. The music liked by large numbers of music lovers.
3. The music liked by experts, musicologists, musicians, and writers who have given much time and thought to the study of music.
4. The music liked by large numbers over a long period.

Sometimes music that at first was regarded as the ravings of a madman is accepted by later generations as normal and even as on a high level of beauty and inspiration. This complete change of opinion has happened many times in the history of music. Beethoven and Wagner were misunderstood in their time, but far more appreciated by later generations. Debussy's *Afternoon of a Faun* is understood and intensely enjoyed by almost everyone today. Not long ago it was regarded by many as amorphous, unintelligible, and immoral.

There is another reason why it is of vital importance that we all respond to music in our own way. The development and evolution of our character and faculties can take place only when we do our own thinking—our own feeling—with freedom and full intensity. We must do this ourselves—no one else can do it for us. Upon this evolution of the individual depends the evolution of all mankind. Only through the evolution of all mankind can we raise the level of living from life governed by force to life ruled by our higher faculties.

Just as a radio can be made sensitive by dialing to different wave lengths covering an extended frequency range—so some music lovers are sensitive to many types of music, from the most simple to the most exalted. Our degree of sensitivity to music can grow with experience—experience of life—experience of listening to many kinds of music. This sensitivity can be broadened and enlarged, if the desire is strong enough in us. It is always possible for the listener to enjoy more keenly and absorb more richly the meaning of great music. One way is by clearing the mind of all previous judgments concerning the music to which we are listening. Another is by trying to make the inner self more sensitive to the sounds and meaning of the music. Still another is by remembering that there are no limits to music—only the limits we ourselves create. If we open our souls to the music, there is always still more that we can absorb.

It may be that the future holds for us two major lines of development—one, greater freedom of the individual, so that he can develop all his faculties—the other, a psychology in which everyone is willing and eager to contribute to others whatever he is able to do best. The greater the opportunity given to each individual to develop all his faculties, the greater can be his contribution.

As we are all different as human beings, and all respond differently to music, so there are numberless kinds of music and unlimited variation of expression and feeling through music. Underlying the differences which seem to separate these various kinds of music are universal principles which are alike—just as underlying the superficial differences of various kinds of men —white, black, yellow—are fundamental life essentials which are basically similar. So to understand the deep-lying principles of music and mankind— how they are alike, how they are related—will help us to understand the essential unity of life. Through this understanding, we shall wish all men to have as nearly as possible equal joy in living, and equal opportunity to enjoy and be inspired by great music.

.   .   .

All sound can be music to some—to them every sound has some kind of tonal design, no matter how irregular. Some enjoy only the formal music of the eighteenth century—others, romantic music—still others respond only to the modern music of today. There are those who enjoy none of this kind of music,but like the simple folk music of the countryside. There is no right or wrong in this—it is simply a matter of varying sensitivity of different personalities to various kinds of music.

It is like the varying range of consciousness. Some are to a degree conscious of the whole cosmos, including cosmic thought and feeling. Others are conscious in a broad general way of what is happening all over this relatively small planet on which we live. Others are conscious of what is happening all over their own country, but pay little attention to other continents. Others are city conscious and seldom let their thoughts range outside of their home town—or are class conscious and confine their thoughts to a group of friends and acquaintances. Others are completely egocentric and take little interest in anything that does not concern them personally.

These variations of range of consciousness have their parallel in our sensitivity to music. There are some who respond to every kind, and at the opposing pole there are those who respond only to one or a few kinds of music. Between these two are many degrees and variations. Apart from formal music, there are those who find in the street sounds of a great metropolis an irregular but fascinating rhythm, which is to them a kind of music. The same is true of a forest—where the rustling of leaves in the wind—the minute pattern of insect noises—and perhaps the sound of a river or waterfall in the distance makes a complex design of sounds which is music to some. The forest has still more beautiful sounds—the singing of birds—which many find thrilling music. These songs are a spontaneous blending of rhythm and melody. The nightingale and the lark are glorious singers to almost everyone.

Even birds that are imprisoned in cages sometimes sing when they are shown kindness, or when someone they like enters the room. Most birds show such a high degree of awareness that it is possible they enjoy their own singing, just as men and women sing when they are happy and absorbed in some interesting occupation.

The sounds of the ocean have an immense range of rhythm and dynamics. On a calm day, the lapping of water against rocks and sand is a kind of lyrical music. Another day, great waves will roll in and crash on the shore—their rhythm is asymmetric, but has something of the same depth of sound and hypnotic fascination as the great drums of Africa or Haiti. In a furious storm, the shrieking of the wind and the terrifying violence of the ocean make for some of us a music that is heroic and sublime. Wagner organized these sounds in rhythmic and tonal design in *The Flying Dutchman*.

One of the strangest sounds I ever heard was in Tibet. I was permitted to enter the temple of one of the Lamaist monasteries which was famous for an immense drum in front of the central altar. The moment I entered the monastery I was conscious of a deep agitated sound that seemed to be coming from a great distance and yet was within the temple. Never in my life had I heard such a mysterious and complex sound. In addition to the central altar, this temple has an enclosed altar on each side. I asked permission to go into these enclosures, and there I found monks seated Lama fashion on the ground, chanting to themselves from ancient books. Each one was chanting in a different key and singing a different chant, but they were all singing with deep voice and extremely softly, so that the temple was filled with a kind of agitated murmur. This was not music in the ordinary sense, but it was one of the most fascinating sounds I have ever heard, with all the rhythms of the chants crossing each other like the mazes of a labyrinth.

Machinery sometimes makes cross-rhythms, accents and frequencies that form a highly complex tapestry of sound. A fascinating kind of rhythmic sound is the galloping, cantering, or trotting of a horse. Sometimes in the mountains when it is very silent, the creaking of the leather of the saddle makes sounds which have a rhythmic relation to the swaying motion as the horse walks. Trains have regular pulsations as the wheels pass over the small spaces between the rails. These pulsations can set up in us a rhythm that for some persons stimulates mental concentration. There are thousands of other forms of sound—such as those made by automobiles, planes, sailing ships—which are interesting to those whose sound-consciousness is relatively universal. One of the most beautiful is the sound of a canoe gliding over the peaceful surface of a lake—the dipping of the paddle—the lapping of the water against the side of the canoe—the Glockenspiel-like sound of globes of water dropping from the paddle. To me almost all sound can have rhythmic and vibrational designs and patterns which are a kind of music.

52   On Architecture

Frank Lloyd Wright

THE EARTH LINE

At last we come to the analysis of the principles that became so solidly basic to my sense and practice of architecture. How do these principles, now beginning to be recognized as the centerline of American democracy, work?

PRINCIPLE ONE: KINSHIP OF BUILDING TO GROUND. This basic inevitability in organic architecture entails an entirely new sense of proportion. The human figure appeared to me, about 1893 or earlier, as the true *human* scale of architecture. Buildings I myself then designed and built—Midwest— seemed, by means of this new scale, to belong to man and at the moment especially as he lived on rolling Western prairie. Soon I had occasion to observe that every inch of height there on the prairie was exaggerated. All breadths fell short. So in breadth, length, height and weight, these buildings belonged to the prairie just as the human being himself belonged to it with his gift of speed. The term "streamlined" as my own expression was then and there born.

As result, the new buildings were rational: low, swift and clean, and were studiously adapted to machine methods. The quiet, intuitional, horizontal line (it will always be the line of human tenure on this earth) was thus humanly interpreted and suited to modern machine-performance. Machine-methods and these new streamlined, flat-plane effects first appeared together in our American architecture as expression of new ways to reach true objectives in building. The main objective was gracious appropriation of the art of architecture itself to the Time, the Place, and Modern Man.

What now is organic "design?" Design appropriate to modern tools, the machine, and this new human scale. Thus, design was opportune, and well within the architect's creative hand if his mind was receptive to these relatively new values: moving perception at this time with reverential spirit toward the understanding of the "nature of nature." The nature of the machine, studied by experiment and basically used in structural design, was still to be limited to a tool, and proved to be a powerful new medium of expression. Buildings before long were evidencing beautiful simplicity, a fresh exuberance of countenance. Originality.

From Book Two, "A New Architecture," Part one, "Principles," with deletions, in *A Testament*, by Frank Lloyd Wright, New York, Horizon Press, 1957. Reprinted by permission of Horizon Press.

Never did I allow the machine to become "motif"—always machine for man and never man for the machine. Ever since, in organic architecture I have used the machine and evolved a system of building from the inside out, always according to the nature of both man and machine—as I could see it— avoiding the passing aspects now characteristic of urban architecture. The machine I found a better means to broaden the humane interest in modern architecture. Nor, in point of style, have I once looked upon the machine as in itself an end, either in planning or building or style. Quantity has never superseded quality.

The Modular of the Kindergarten Table

Kindergarten training, as I have shown, proved an unforeseen asset: for one thing, because later all my planning was devised on a properly proportional unit system. I found this would keep all to scale, ensure consistent proportion throughout the edifice, large or small, which thus became—like tapestry —a consistent fabric woven of interdependent, related units, however various.

So from the very first this system of "fabrication" was applied to planning even in minor buildings. Later, I found technological advantages when this system was applied to heights. In elevation, therefore, soon came the vertical module as experience might dictate. All this was very much like laying warp on the loom. The woof (substance) was practically the same as if stretched upon this predetermined warp. This basic practice has proved indispensable and good machine technique must yield its advantages. Invariably it appears in organic architecture as visible feature in the fabric of the design—insuring unity of proportion. The harmony of texture is thus, with the scale of all parts, within the complete ensemble.

. . .

CHARACTER IS A NATURAL

THREE: Appropriate "character" is inevitable to all architecture if organic. Significance of any building would clearly express its objective, its purpose— whether store, apartment building, bank, church, hotel or pie-club, factory, circus or school. Fundamental requirement, this should apply to all building, in ground-planning and, especially, relative to human life and its site. This means sane appropriation of imaginative design to specific human purposes, by the natural use of nature-materials or synthetics, and appropriate methods of construction. Our new resources already evolved by science, especially glass and steel wrought by the machine, are bound continually to develop new forms. Continually new ways and shapes of building will continue to give fresh character and true significance to all modern structure.

Poetic tranquility instead of a more deadly "efficiency," should be the consequence in the art of Building: concordant, sane, exuberant, and appropriate to purpose. Durable, serviceable, economical. Beautiful. In the ever-changing circumstances of complex modern existence all this is not too easy to accomplish and the extent of these evolving changes may not yet be fully seen but as architects we may thus reconstitute architecture in our hearts and minds and act to re-write our dated "codes" and refrain from disfiguring our American landscape by buildings or "service" systems.

TENUITY PLUS CONTINUITY

FOUR: Completely new character by these simple means came to architecture; came to view, not by haphazard use, but by organic interpretation, of steel and glass. Steel gave rise to a new property: I call it *tenuity*. Tenuity is simply a matter of tension (pull), something never before known in the architecture of this world. No building could withstand a pull. Push it you might and it would stay together but pull on it and it would fall apart. With tensile strength of steel, this pull permits free use of the cantilever, a projectile and tensile at the same time, in building-design. The outstretched arm with its hand (with drooping fingers for walls) is a cantilever. So is the branch of a tree.

The cantilever is essentially steel at its most economical level of use. The principle of the cantilever in architecture develops tenuity as a wholly new human expression, a means, too, of placing all loads over central supports, thereby balancing extended load against opposite extended load. This brought into architecture for the first time another principle in construction—I call it *continuity*—a property which may be seen as a new, elastic, cohesive *stability*. The creative architect finds here a marvelous new inspiration in design. A new freedom involving far wider spacings of more slender supports. Thus architecture arrived at construction from within outward rather than from outside inward; much heightening and lightening of proportions throughout all building is now economical and natural, space extended and utilized in a more liberal planning than the ancients could ever have dreamed of. This is now a prime characteristic of the new architecture called organic.

Rigid box shapes, outsides steel-framed, belong strictly to the nineteenth century. They cannot be twentieth century architecture. Support at rigid corners becomes mere obstruction: corners themselves now insignificant become extravagant waste, mere accents of enclosure. Construction lightened by means of cantilevered steel in tension, makes continuity a most valuable characteristic of architectural enlightenment. Our new architectural freedom now lies within this province. In the character of this new circumstance buildings now may proceed *from within outward*: Because push or pull may be integral to building design.

.   .   .

SPACE

SIX: Space, elemental to architecture, has now found architectural expression. Glass: air in air, to keep air out or keep it in. Steel, a strand slight and strong as the thread of the spider spinning, is able now to span extraordinary spaces. By new products of technology and increased inventive ingenuity in applying them to building-construction many superlative new space-forms have already come alive: and, because of them, more continually in sight. Some as a matter of course will be novel but insignificant; some will be significant and really new. But more important, modern building becomes the solid creative art which the poetic principle can release and develop. Noble, vital, exuberant forms are already here. Democracy awakes to a more spiritual expression. Indigenous culture will now awaken. Properly focused upon needs of twentieth century life, new uses of livable space will continually evolve, improved; more exuberant and serene. A new security and a new tranquility. Enlightened enjoyment of fresh beauty is here or due. As for the future: encouraging to me are the many letters, coming continually, country-wide, from teen-agers now in high school, asking for help with the term theses they have chosen to write upon organic architecture. This widening of the awareness of the coming generation's interest in architecture can only mean a new American architecture. When these youngsters become fathers and mothers, say a generation hence, they are going to demand appropriate space-homes on these modern terms. We will soon see the house as a work of art and because of its intrinsic beauty more a home than ever.

FORM

SEVEN: Anyone anything of an architect will never be content to design a building merely (or chiefly) for the picture it makes—any more than a man would buy a horse merely by its color. What kind of intellect must the critic have who seeing a building judges it by "the look of it," ignorant of the nature of its construction?

For the first time in 500 years a sense of architectural form appears as a new spiritual integrity.

Heavy walls, senseless overheads and overloads of every sort, vanish— let us be glad. Light and thin walls may now depend from cantilever slabs supported from the interior on shallow, dry-wall footings, walls themselves becoming slender screens, entirely independent of use as support. Centralized supports may stand isolated, balancing load against load—seen not as walls at all, but as integral pattern; walls may be slender suspension from point to point, in fascinating pendant forms. In general, structure now becomes an affair from the inside outward instead of from the outside inward. Various geometrical forms (circular especially) in planning structure become more economical than the square of the box. Building loads may be suspended, suspension supported by slender, isolated uprights. Glass or light plastics may be used to fill in and make the whole habitable. Sheet metal and light metal castings afford a permanent material for the exteriors of such structures. Enclosures extremely light in weight combined with such structural elements relieve all modern building of surplus static; structure no longer an obesity or likely to fall of its own weight. Walls require little or no floor space. Spaces hitherto concealed or wasted or made impossible by heavy walls are revealed and made useful. Arrangements for human occupation in comfort may be so well aimed that spaciousness becomes economical as well as beautiful, appearing where it was never before thought to exist. Space now gives not only charm and character to practical occupation but beauty to the countenance and form of a valid new kind of habitation for mankind. Buildings, at long last—like their occupants—may be themselves free and wear the shining countenance of principle and directly say honestly, by free expression, yet becomingly, what they really are, what they really mean. The new sense of interior space as reality may characterize modern building. Style will be the consequence of integral character. Intellect thus reinforces and makes Spirit effective. An art as flexible, as various, as infinite in its possibilities as the spirit of man.

Organic Unit

Thus environment and building are one: Planting the grounds around the building on the site as well as adorning the building take on new importance as they become features harmonious with the space-within-to-be-lived-in. Site, structure, furnishing—decoration too, planting as well—all these become as one in organic architecture. What was once called "decorating"—landscaping, lighting, etc.—and modern gadgetry (mechanical fixtures like air-conditioning) all are within the building structure as features of the building itself. Therefore all are elements of this synthesis of features of habitation and harmonious with environment. This is what *posterity* will call "modern architecture."

SHELTER: INHERENT HUMAN FACTOR

EIGHT: As interior space to be lived in becomes the reality of building so shelter thus emphasized becomes more than ever significant in character and important as a feature. Shelter is still a strange disorder when reduced to a flat lid—though a common desire on account of economy. *To qualify this common-sense desire for shelter* as a most significant feature of architecture is now in organic architecture of greatly increased importance. Witness, for instance: The new sense of spaciousness requires, as inherent human factor, significant cover as well as shade. Cover therefore now becomes in itself a feature more important as architectural form: Solidity of walls vanishing to reappear as imaginative screens involving light, and as inevitable consequence leaving more responsibility to the shapes and shaping of the whole building "overhead" with direct reference to the elements. Radical structural changes too now make the overhead lighter, less an imposition, more graceful, more harmonious feature of environment. Organic architecture sees shelter not only as a quality of space but of spirit, and the prime factor in any concept of building man into his environment as a legitimate feature of it. Weather is omnipresent and buildings must be left out in the rain. Shelter is dedicated to these elements. So much so that almost all other features of design tend to lead by one another to this important feature, shelter, and its component shade. In order to complete the building, protecting all within it from every changing circumstance of light, of cold and heat, of wear and tear and usage, we require shelter. The occupants of a building readily discover greater opportunity for comfort and more gracious, expanded living wherever shelter is becoming shade. By shade, charm has been added to character; style to comfort; significance to form.

[the word]

On Poetry

53

Gilbert Highet

Children ask lots and lots of questions, about religion, about sex, about the stars. But there are some questions which they never ask: they leave grown-ups to ask them and to answer them. Often this means the questions are silly: that they are questions about nonexistent problems, or questions to which the answer is obvious. Sometimes it means that the question *should* be asked, but that the answer is difficult or multiplex.

So children never ask what is the good of music. They just like singing and dancing, and even drumming on a low note of the piano. In the same way, they never ask what is the use of poetry. They all enjoy poems and songs, and very often come to like them before they can even talk properly; but it never occurs to them that they ought to find reasons for their enjoyment. But grown-ups do inquire about the justification of poetry: they ask what is the point of putting words in a special order and extracting special sound effects from them, instead of speaking plainly and directly. And often —because they get no adequate answer, either from the poets or from the professors—they conclude that poetry is only a set of tricks like conjuring, or a complicated game like chess; and they turn away from it in discouragement . . . until, perhaps, a poetic film like *Henry V* shocks them into realizing something of its power; or, as they grow older, they find that a poem learned in childhood sticks in their mind and becomes clearer and more beautiful with age.

What is the use of poetry?

There must be a number of different answers to the question. Just as a picture can be meant to give pleasure, or to carry a puzzle, or to convey information, so poems are meant for many different things. We can begin to get some of the answers if we look at the poetry that children themselves naturally enjoy, and then see how it is connected with the most famous grown-up poems.

The first pleasure of poetry is the simplest. It is the same pleasure that we have in music—the pleasure of following a pattern of sound. Everyone loves talking, and most people like what might be called doodling in sound. So, if you look through the *Oxford Dictionary of Nursery Rhymes,* you will find several tongue-twisters, like this:

> Peter Piper picked a peck of pickled pepper;
> A peck of pickled pepper Peter Piper picked;
> If Peter Piper picked a peck of pickled pepper,
> Where's the peck of pickled pepper Peter Piper picked?

On a grown-up level, many a famous poem is little more than a pattern of sound: for instance, Shakespeare's love song:

> It was a lover and his lass,
>   With a hey and a ho and a hey nonino,
> That o'er the green cornfield did pass,
>   In the spring time, the only pretty ring time,
>   When birds do sing, hey ding a ding ding;
>   Sweet lovers love the spring.

Much of the best poetry of Swinburne is pattern-making in sound, with a very light core of meaning. Here are four exquisite lines which really mean very little more than the sound of spring showers:

> When the hounds of spring are on winter's traces,
>   The mother of months in meadow or plain
> Fills the shadows and windy places
>   With lisp of leaves and ripple of rain.

Small meaning, but lovely rhythm and melody.

Now, there is a second pleasure in poetry. This is that it is sometimes better than prose for telling a story. It even gives authority to a story which is illogical or incredible, or even gruesome. That is one reason children love the poem that tells of the tragic fate of Jack and Jill. There is an interesting variant of it: the cumulative story, in which one detail is piled up on another until the whole story has been set forth with the simple exactitude of a primitive painting: for instance, "The House That Jack Built," and the funeral elegy, "Who Killed Cock Robin?" and the famous old Jewish rhyme, "Had Gadyo," about the kid bought for two pieces of money—which is said to symbolize a vast stretch of the history of the Jewish people. Another variant is the limerick, which is simply a funny story in verse. Many a man who would protest that he knew no poetry, and cared nothing for it, could recite eight or ten limericks in the right company.

In serious adult poetry there are many superb stories, including the two oldest books in Western literature, the *Iliad* and the *Odyssey*. Every good collection of poems will include some of the most dramatic tales ever told, the English and Scottish ballads, which are still occasionally sung in our own southern states. One of the strangest things about the stories told as ballads is their terrible abruptness and directness. They leave out a great deal. They give only a few details, a name or two; they draw the outlines, harsh and black or blood-red, and they concentrate on the actions and the passions. Such is the ballad about an ambush in which a knight was killed by his own wife's brother. It is called "The Dowie Houms of Yarrow" (that means the sad fields beside the river Yarrow, in the Scottish borders), and it opens immediately with the quarrel, almost with the clash of swords:

> Late at een, drinkin' the wine,
>   And ere they paid the lawin',
> They set a combat them between,
>   To fight it in the dawin'.

Within only a few verses, the knight has been surrounded, and treacherously murdered, fighting against heavy odds; and when his widow goes out to find his body, her anguish is described in one of the most terrible stanzas in all poetry:

> She kissed his cheek, she kamed his hair,
>   As oft she did before, O;
> She drank the red blood frae him ran,
>   On the dowie houms o' Yarrow.

That story in poetry and a few others like "Edward, Edward"—in which a mother persuades her son to kill his own father, and drives him mad—are absolutely unforgettable.

But besides storytelling, poetry has another use, known all over the world. This is mnemonic. Put words into a pattern, and they are easier to remember. I should never have known the lengths of the months if I had not learned:

> Thirty days hath September,
> April, June, and November;
> All the rest have thirty-one,
> Excepting February alone,
> And that has twenty-eight days clear
> And twenty-nine in each leap year.

This is certainly four hundred years old, for it occurs in an English manuscript dated about 1555, and there is a French poem, with the same rhyme scheme, written three hundred years earlier. (It might be easier to change the calendar, but mankind is by nature conservative.) On a simpler level there are many nursery rhymes in every language which are designed to teach children the very simplest things; for instance, counting and performing easy actions:

> One, two,
> Buckle my shoe,
> Three, four,
> Shut the door.

And even earlier, before the child can speak, he is lucky if his mother can recite the poem that goes over his five toes or fingers, one after another:

> This little pig went to market,
> This little pig stayed at home,

up to the comical climax when the child is meant to squeak too, and to enjoy staying at home.

Adults also remember facts better if they are put into verse. Nearly every morning I repeat to myself:

> Early to bed and early to rise
> Makes a man healthy and wealthy and wise.

And nearly every evening I change it to Thurber's parody:

> Early to rise and early to bed
> Makes a male healthy and wealthy and dead;

or occasionally to George Ade's variant:

> Early to bed and early to rise
> Will make you miss all the regular guys.

This is the source of what they call didactic poetry, poetry meant to teach. The best-known example of it is the Book of Proverbs in the Bible, which ought to be translated into rhythmical prose, or even verse. The third oldest book in Greek literature, not much younger than Homer, is a farmer's handbook all set out in poetry, so that it could be learned off by heart and remembered: it is the *Works and Days* by Hesiod. To teach has long been one of the highest functions of the poet: great poetry can be written in order to carry a message of philosophical or practical truth—or sometimes an ironical counsel, as in this strange poem by Sir Walter Scott:

> Look not thou on beauty's charming;
> Sit thou still when kings are arming;
> Taste not when the winecup glistens;
> Speak not when the people listens;
> Stop thine ear against the singer;
> From the red gold keep thy finger;
> Vacant heart and hand and eye,
> Easy live and quiet die.

There is one peculiar variation on the poem that conveys information. This is the riddle poem, which tells you something—but only if you are smart enough to see through its disguise. There are some such riddles in the Bible: Samson created a good one, about the dead lion with a hive of wild bees inside it. Legend has it that Homer died of chagrin because he could not solve a rather sordid poetic puzzle. The nursery rhyme "Humpty Dumpty" was really a riddle to begin with (before Lewis Carroll and his illustrator gave it away). We are supposed to guess what was the mysterious person or thing which fell down, and then could not possibly be put together again, not even by all the king's horses and all the king's men, and nowadays by all the republic's scientific experts: the answer is an egg. There is a beautiful folk song made up of three such riddles: the cherry without a stone, the chicken without a bone, and the baby that does not cry. It is at least five hundred years old, and yet for four hundred years it was passed on from one singer to another, without ever being printed.

Again, there are some famous and splendid poems that deal with mystical experience in riddling terms, phrases which have two meanings, or three, or one concealed: these are also didactic, informative, and yet riddles. One such poem, by an American poet, deals with the paradox of God—the complete God, who includes all the appearances of the universe, both the appearance of good and the appearance of evil. This is Emerson's "Brahma."

> If the red slayer think he slays,
>   Or if the slain think he is slain,
> They know not well the subtle ways
>   I keep, and pass, and turn again.
>
> Far or forgot to me is near;
>   Shadow and sunlight are the same;
> The vanished gods to me appear;
>   And one to me are shame and fame.
>
> They reckon ill who leave me out;
>   When me they fly, I am the wings;
> I am the doubter and the doubt,
>   And I the hymn the Brahmin sings.
>
> The strong gods pine for my abode,
>   And pine in vain the sacred Seven;
> But thou, meek lover of the good!
>   Find me, and turn thy back on heaven.

This is a riddle which is meant not for children but for adults. There are similar riddles in the Bible, sometimes equally beautiful. Such is the meditation on old age at the end of that mysterious and rather unorthodox book called *Koheleth*, or *Ecclesiastes*:

Remember now thy Creator in the days of thy youth,
  while the evil days come not,
  nor the years draw nigh, when thou shalt say, I have no pleasure in them;

while the sun or the light or the moon or the stars be
  not darkened, nor the clouds return after the rain;

in the day when the keepers of the house shall tremble,
  and the strong men shall bow themselves,
  and the grinders cease because they are few,
  and those that look out of the windows be darkened,
and the doors shall be shut in the streets,
  when the sound of the grinding is low,
  and he shall rise up at the voice of the bird,
  and all the daughters of music shall be brought low,
also when they shall be afraid of that which is high,
  and fears shall be in the way,
  and the almond tree shall flourish,
  and the grasshopper shall be a burden,
and desire shall fail:
  because man goeth to his long home
  and the mourners go about the streets;

or ever the silver cord be loosed,
  or the golden bowl be broken,
  or the pitcher be broken at the fountain
  or the wheel broken at the cistern.
Then shall the dust return to the earth as it was;
  and the spirit shall return unto God who gave it.

All these enigmatic and memorable phrases are descriptions of the symptoms of the last and almost the bitterest fact in life, old age. They show that it is pathetic, and yet they make it beautiful.

Such poetry is unusual. Or rather, its manner is unusual and its subject is a fact of common experience. It is possible for poets to speak plainly and frankly about everyday life; and that is one more of the uses of poetry—one of the best known. Poetry can express general experience: can say what many men and women have thought and felt. The benefit of this is that it actually helps ordinary people, by giving them words. Most of us are not eloquent. Most of us—especially in times of intense emotion—cannot say what we feel; often we hardly know what we feel. There, in our heart, there is the turmoil, be it love or protest or exultation or despair: it stirs us, but all our gestures and words are inadequate. As the emotion departs, we know that an opportunity was somehow missed, an opportunity of realizing a great moment to the full. It is in this field that poetry comes close to religion. Religion is one of the experiences which the ordinary man finds most difficult to compass in words. Therefore he nearly always falls back on phrases which have been composed for him by someone more gifted. Many, many thousands of times, in battles and concentration camps and hospitals, beside death beds, and even on death beds, men and women have repeated a very ancient poem only six verses long, and have found comfort in it, such as no words of their own would have brought them. It begins, "The Lord is my shepherd; I shall not want."

If we look at poetry or any of the arts from this point of view, we shall gain a much greater respect for them. They are not amusements or decorations; they are aids to life. Ordinary men and women find living rather difficult. One of their chief difficulties is to apprehend their own thoughts and feelings, and to respond to them by doing the right things and saying the right sentences. It is the poets who supply the words and sentences. They too have felt as we do, but they have been able to speak, while we are dumb.

Not only that. By expressing common emotions clearly and eloquently, the poets help us to understand them in other people. It is difficult to understand—for any grown-up it is difficult to understand—what goes on in the mind of a boy or girl. Parents are often so anxious and serious that they have forgotten what it was like to be young, and vague, and romantic. It is a huge effort, rather an unpleasantly arduous effort, to think oneself back into boyhood. Yet there are several poems which will allow us to understand it, and even to enjoy the experience. One of them is a fine lyric by Longfellow, called "My Lost Youth":

> I remember the gleams and glooms that dart
>   Across the schoolboy's brain;
> The song and the silence in the heart,
> That in part are prophecies, and in part
>   Are longings wild and vain.
>   And the voice of that fitful song
>   Sings on, and is never still:
>   "A boy's will is the wind's will,
> And the thoughts of youth are long, long thoughts."
>
> There are things of which I may not speak;
>   There are dreams that cannot die;
> There are thoughts that make the strong heart weak,
> And bring a pallor into the cheek,
>   And a mist before the eye.
>   And the words of that fatal song
>   Come over me like a chill:
>   "A boy's will is the wind's will,
> And the thoughts of youth are long, long thoughts."

If you have a young son who seems to be woolgathering half the time, and who sometimes does not even answer when he is spoken to, you should read and reflect on that poem of Longfellow.

This function of poetry is not the only one, but it is one of the most vital: to give adequate expression to important general experiences. In 1897, when Queen Victoria celebrated her Diamond Jubilee, the Poet Laureate was that completely inadequate little fellow, Alfred Austin; but the man who wrote the poem summing up the emotions most deeply felt during the Jubilee was Rudyard Kipling. It is called "Recessional." It is a splendid poem, almost a hymn—Biblical in its phrasing and deeply prophetic in its thought:

> The tumult and the shouting dies—
>   The captains and the kings depart—
> Still stands Thine ancient sacrifice,
>   An humble and a contrite heart.
> Lord God of Hosts, be with us yet,
> Lest we forget, lest we forget!

However, as you think over the poems you know, you will realize that many of them seem to be quite different from this. They are not even trying to do the same thing. They do not express important general experiences in universally acceptable words. On the contrary, they express strange and individual experiences in abstruse and sometimes unintelligible words. We enjoy them not because they say what we have often thought but because they say what we should never have dreamed of thinking. If a poem like Kipling's "Recessional" or Longfellow's "Lost Youth" is close to religion, then this other kind of poetry is close to magic: its words sound like spells; its subjects are often dreams, visions, and myths.

Such are the two most famous poems by Coleridge: "The Ancient Mariner" and "Kubla Khan." They are scarcely understandable. They are unbelievable. Beautiful, yes, and haunting, yes, but utterly illogical; crazy. Coleridge himself scarcely knew their sources, deep in his memory and his sub-conscious—sources on which a modern scholar has written a superb book. Both of them end with a mystical experience that none of us has ever had: "The Ancient Mariner" telling how, like the Wandering Jew, he must travel forever from country to country, telling his story with "strange power of speech;" and "Kubla Khan" with the poet himself creating a magical palace:

> I would build that dome in air,
> That sunny dome! those caves of ice!
> And all who heard should see them there,
> And all should cry, Beware! Beware!
> His flashing eyes, his floating hair!
> Weave a circle round him thrice,
>   And close your eyes with holy dread,
>   For he on honey-dew hath fed,
> And drunk the milk of Paradise.

Not long after those fantastic verses were written, young Keats was composing a lyric, almost equally weird, which is now considered one of the finest odes in the English language. It ends with the famous words which we all know, and which few of us believe:

> Beauty is truth, truth beauty,—that is all
> Ye know on earth, and all ye need to know.

It is the "Ode on a Grecian Urn;" but how many of us have ever stood, like Keats, meditating on the paintings that surround a Greek vase? and, even if we have, how many of us have thought that,

> Heard melodies are sweet, but those unheard
> Are sweeter?

It is a paradox. The entire ode is a paradox: not an expression of ordinary life, but an extreme extension of it, almost a direct contradiction of usual experience.

Most modern poetry is like this. It tells of things almost unknown to ordinary men and women, even to children. If it has power over them at all, it is because it enchants them by its strangeness. Such is the poetry of Verlaine, and Mallarmé, and Rimbaud; of the difficult and sensitive Austrian poet Rilke; in our own language, such is most of Auden's poetry, and Ezra Pound's; and what could be more unusual than most of T. S. Eliot— although he is the most famous poet writing today? Suppose we test this. Let us take something simple. Spring. What have the poets said about the first month of spring, about April? Most of them say it is charming and frail:

> April, April,
> Laugh thy girlish laughter;
> Then, the moment after,
> Weep thy girlish tears!

That is Sir William Watson: turn back, and see Shakespeare talking of

> The uncertain glory of an April day;

turn forward, and hear Browning cry

> O to be in England
> Now that April's there!

and then hundreds of years earlier, see Chaucer beginning his *Canterbury Tales* with a handshake of welcome to "Aprille, with his shoures soote." Indeed, that is what most of us feel about April: it is sweet and delicate and youthful and hopeful. But T. S. Eliot begins *The Waste Land* with a grim statement which is far outside ordinary feelings:

> April is the cruellest month, breeding
> Lilacs out of the dead land, mixing
> Memory and desire, stirring
> Dull roots with spring rain.

And the entire poem, the best known of our generation, is a description of several agonizing experiences which most of us not only have never had but have not even conceived as possible. Yet there is no doubt that it is good poetry, and that it has taken a permanent place in our literature, together with other eccentric and individual visions.

But some of us do not admit it to be poetry—or rather claim that, if it is so extreme and unusual, poetry is useless. This is a mistake. The universe is so vast, the universe is so various, that we owe it to ourselves to try to understand every kind of experience—both the usual and the remote, both the intelligible and the mystical. Logic is not enough. Not all the truth about the world, or about our own lives, can be set down in straightforward prose, or even in straightforward poetry. Some important truths are too subtle even to be uttered in words. A Japanese, by arranging a few flowers in a vase, or Rembrandt, by drawing a dark room with an old man sitting in it, can convey meanings which no one could ever utter in speech. So also, however extravagant a romantic poem may seem, it can tell us something about our world which we ought to know.

It is easier for us to appreciate this nowadays than it would have been for our grandfathers in the nineteenth century, or for their great-grandfathers in the eighteenth century. Our lives are far less predictable; and it is far less possible to use logic alone in organizing and understanding them. Therefore there are justifications, and good ones, for reading and memorizing not only what we might call universal poetry but also strange and visionary poetry. We ourselves, at some time within the mysterious future, may well have to endure and to try to understand some experience absolutely outside our present scope: suffering of some unforeseen kind, a magnificent and somber duty, a splendid triumph, the development of some new power within us. We shall be better able to do so if we know what the poets (yes, and the musicians) have said about such enchantments and extensions of life. Many a man has lived happily until something came upon him which made him, for the first time, think of committing suicide. Such a man will be better able to understand himself and to rise above the thought if he knows the music that Rachmaninoff wrote when he, too, had such thoughts and conquered them, or if he reads the play of *Hamlet,* or if he travels through Dante's *Comedy,* which begins in utter despair and ends in the vision of

love, that moves the sun and the other stars.

And even if we ourselves are not called upon to endure such extremes, there may be those around us, perhaps very close to us, who are faced with situations the ordinary mind cannot assimilate: sudden wealth, the temptations of great beauty, the gift of creation, profound sorrow, unmerited guilt. The knowledge of what the poets have said about experiences beyond the frontiers of logic will help us at least to sympathize with them in these experiences. Such understanding is one of the most difficult and necessary efforts of the soul. Shelley compared the skylark, lost in the radiance of the sun, to

> a Poet hidden
> In the light of thought
> Singing hymns unbidden,
> Till the world is wrought
> To sympathy with hopes and fears it heeded not.

To create such sympathy is one of the deepest functions of poetry, and one of the most bitterly needed.

Part six

THE SCIENCES

"The winds of February are not colder to a featherless chick than are the surprises which nature and truth bring to our dreaming egoism."

George Santayana
SOLILOQUIES IN ENGLAND

INTRODUCTION

We can look at ourselves and our world in many ways: through the plastic arts, through music, through literature, and certainly through science. Having looked, we have tampered, collectively, through the ages, so that the world we move in (and that is getting bigger every day) is a different world for our having been there. And since our first fumbling attempts to comprehend our world, nothing man has done or thought has been unaffected by that growing understanding. From the dullest clod to the greatest genius, from the most menial to the most inspired person, each has felt in every aspect of his living the impact of this intellectual perception of our universe we call science.

We can hardly call ourselves educated, then, if we have no awareness of the unseen intellectual potency that has wrought these changes; for science lives in the mind of man, not in the material manifestations we see around us. What is there about science that fosters such accomplishment, for good or ill? As an approach to man's problems, has it any limitations? Can it be applied with equal success to all areas of knowledge and understanding? In short, what should we know about science if we are to function as intelligent, responsible human beings in our society?

This is a formidable challenge; yet the case is not hopeless. Take this simple analogy. You can learn much about all symphonies by studying the nature of a few. You can discover in their foundations the order that distinguishes a symphony from a random collection of sounds and makes a whole out of many bits and pieces. So it is with science, if we but look with discernment.

Imagine that you stand on the plateau of the directly observable, and that standing beside you are an artist and a scientist. With minor variations, you each have the same built-in instruments to make you aware of your surroundings, that is, your senses. They are ultimately all you have, with all their unbelievable acuities and their frustrating weaknesses. Each of you will *sense* the same world, yet each will *describe* a different world, and in your own language. As Francis Bacon put it long ago,

. . . all perceptions . . . are according to the measure of the individual and not according to the measure of the universe. And the human understanding is like a false mirror, which, receiving rays irregularly, distorts and discolours the nature of things by mingling its own nature with it.[1]

If we can get some idea of how the scientist "sees" the world, and how he communicates his observations, we will be well started toward understanding science, since observation is the foundation on which all science rests and, paradoxically, the capstone that crowns the whole scientific structure.

Back on your imaginary plateau you will soon be frustrated by the limitations of your senses just as every scientist has been. Much of what we consider scientific knowledge today rests on data gathered by ingenious and imaginative extensions of our senses; telescopes, microscopes, electronic devices, and spectroscopes of all sorts. The list seems endless and hopelessly confusing to the layman if he tries to understand all these instruments in detail. Fortunately that is not the important point, fascinating as it is to learn all you can about them. Rather it is important to try to discover why the scientist is willing to accept the evidence from these instruments as the equivalent of direct observation, and to what degree he should do so. Where does he start dealing with the interpretation of evidence, rather than the evidence itself?

Suppose, for example, you want to find the depth of a hole in the earth. You reach your arm down and find that your fingers cannot touch bottom. What do you do? Just what the scientist does, you devise an instrument to help you. You find a stick long enough to touch bottom. But just a moment. How do you know the stick has touched bottom? Why do you believe this evidence? To complicate things a bit, suppose that this hole is filled with a clay-like sludge of increasing viscosity, so that you have to push the stick downward with ever-increasing force. At what point will you decide that you have reached bottom? This is precisely the kind of question the scientist must answer for all his measurements.

Remembering that such measurements form the foundation upon which all science rests, it becomes important for all of us to undertand why the scientist puts such faith in apparently arbitrary judgements. You will find, as you proceed, that individual belief in scientific evidence and its interpretation rests to a great degree upon acceptance by the scientific community and, ultimately, by the entire human community. Paradoxically, you will also discover that in science, as elsewhere, a mark of genius is the ability and courage to go beyond common beliefs and interpretations. Thus science exists on conformity, but grows on nonconformity. In our better newspapers and periodicals you will see constant evidence of controversies raging over such scientific matters. Is the evidence valid? Was it collected under proper conditions? What does it mean? Does it threaten our beliefs?

[1] From *The Works of Francis Bacon* edited by James Spedding, Robert Ellis, and Douglas Heath (N.Y.: Hurd and Houghon, 1869) VIII, pp. 76–90.

But assembling the evidence is only a beginning. I think you would all agree that there seems to be more to science than the gathering of data, important as that is. The history of science will show that, as the repetitive nature of a particular phenomenon becomes apparent with the accumulation of data, there will be attempts to express all these related results in terms of a generalization and in the language of contemporary science—mathematics. Such generalizations, if they survive further and exhaustive verification, become what we call "the laws" of science.

Here, then, is an attempt to simplify and create order in what might otherwise seem to be a chaotic assembly of unrelated facts. In all of man's intellectual and artistic endeavors this striving toward order is constantly present. So strong is this urge that we perhaps see order and relation where none exists. To quote Francis Bacon again,

The human understanding is of its own nature prone to suppose the existence of more order and regularity in the world than it finds. And though there be many things in nature which are singular and unmatched, yet it devises for them parallels and conjugates and relatives which do not exist . . . And these fancies affect not dogmas only, but simple notions also.

Be that as it may, we go on searching for order and the simpler the better, as though there were some virtue in simplicity. You will find that the structural order devised by scientists rests heavily on the almost monotonous repetition of events. In fact, it is this aspect of man's sensing of nature that gives the physical scientist confidence to predict future events. Can the biologist be equally successful at predicting results? How about the psychologist, or the social scientist? What is there about a simple physical system, such as a gas in a container, that allows one to predict its behavior? The answer seems to lie in the realm of statistical probability. Even a modest understanding of this branch of mathematics can give you a new and perhaps more rational perspective on its application to areas other than the physical sciences.

Man is inherently inquisitive, and even the firm establishment of a scientific law leaves him dissatisfied. True, when he does A to this system, B happens, but why does it happen? How can he "explain" these events? To the scientist, and I suppose to everyone, "explanation" in the simplest terms consists of expressing the unfamiliar, the mysterious, in terms of the familiar, or the accepted. You can find examples of these attempts at clarification in all areas of human knowledge, and in all periods of history: in religion, in mythology, in art, as well as in science.

In science, such an explanation, if it is to be accepted, must first provide a "reasonable" answer to questions. Secondly, it must enable the scientist to predict unobserved behavior for the relevant system. Finally, this predicted behavior must stand the test of experimental verification. Then, and only then, does the explanation warrant being called a theory. This is important, be-

cause we popularly call almost any wild guess a theory. To the scientist, however, a theory must be both a unifying principle and a powerful tool for
expanding understanding, or it is rejected.

Once again an historical perspective is peculiarly revealing. You will find
theories change with the times, that there is a kind of inherent obsolescence
in theoretical explanations, which makes one wonder if we can ever attain
ultimate answers to the puzzling questions of nature.

So, you see, we have come full circle in our discussion. We started with
observation, and we end with observation. This is the eternal cycle of science,
and if you can experience some sense of this through your studies, you will
be on your way to becoming scientifically literate.

THE SPIRIT OF SCIENCE

Primitive Science

54

Bronislaw Malinowski

The problem of primitive knowledge has been singularly neglected by anthropology. Studies on savage psychology were exclusively confined to early religion, magic and mythology. Only recently the work of several English, German, and French writers, notably the daring and brilliant speculations of Professor Lévy-Bruhl, gave an impetus to the student's interest in what the savage does in his more sober moods. The results were startling indeed: Professor Lévy-Bruhl tells us, to put it in a nutshell, that primitive man has no sober moods at all, that he is hopelessly and completely immersed in a mystical frame of mind. Incapable of dispassionate and consistent observation, devoid of the power of abstraction, hampered by "a decided aversion towards reasoning," he is unable to draw any benefit from experience, to construct or comprehend even the most elementary laws of nature. "For minds thus orientated there is no fact purely physical." Nor can there exist for them any clear idea of substance and attribute, cause and effect, identity and contradiction. Their outlook is that of confused superstition, "prelogical," made of mystic "participations" and "exclusions." I have here summarized a body of opinion, of which the brilliant French sociologist is the most decided and competent spokesman, but which numbers besides, many anthropologists and philosophers of renown.

But there are also dissenting voices. When a scholar and anthropologist of the measure of Professor J. L. Myres entitles an article in *Notes and Queries* "Natural Science," and when we read there that the savage's "knowledge based on observation is distinct and accurate," we must surely pause before accepting primitive man's irrationality as a dogma. Another highly competent writer, Dr. A. A. Goldenweiser, speaking about primitive "discoveries, inventions and improvements"—which could hardly be attributed to any pre-empirical or prelogical mind—affirms that "it would be unwise to ascribe to the primitive mechanic merely a passive part in the origination of

From Bronislaw Malinowski, "Magic, Science, and Religion," in J. Needham, ed., *Science, Religion* and *Reality*, London, S.P.C.K.

inventions. Many a happy thought must have crossed his mind, nor was he wholly unfamiliar with the thrill that comes from an idea effective in action." Here we see the savage endowed with an attitude of mind wholly akin to that of a modern man of science!

To bridge over the wide gap between the two extreme opinions current on the subject of primitive man's reason, it will be best to resolve the problem into two questions.

First, has the savage any rational outlook, any rational mastery of his surroundings, or is he, as M. Lévy-Bruhl and his school maintain, entirely "mystical?" The answer will be that every primitive community is in possession of a considerable store of knowledge, based on experience and fashioned by reason.

The second question then opens: Can this primitive knowledge be regarded as a rudimentary form of science or is it, on the contrary, radically different, a crude empiry, a body of practical and technical abilities, rules of thumb and rules of art having no theoretical value? This second question, epistemological rather than belonging to the study of man, will be barely touched upon at the end of this section and a tentative answer only will be given.

In dealing with the first question, we shall have to examine the "profane" side of life, the arts, crafts and economic pursuits, and we shall attempt to disentangle in it a type of behavior, clearly marked off from magic and religion, based on empirical knowledge and on the confidence in logic. We shall try to find whether the lines of such behavior are defined by traditional rules, known, perhaps even discussed sometimes, and tested. We shall have to inquire whether the sociological setting of the rational and empirical behavior differs from that of ritual and cult. Above all we shall ask, do the natives distinguish the two domains and keep them apart, or is the field of knowledge constantly swamped by superstition, ritualism, magic or religion?

Since in the matter under discussion there is an appalling lack of relevant and reliable observations, I shall have largely to draw upon my own material, mostly unpublished, collected during a few years' field work among the Melanesian and Papuo-Melanesian tribes of Eastern New Guinea and the surrounding archipelagoes. As the Melanesians are reputed, however, to be specially magic-ridden, they will furnish an acid test of the existence of empirical and rational knowledge among savages living in the age of polished stone.

These natives, and I am speaking mainly of the Melanesians who inhabit the coral atolls to the N.E. of the main island, the Trobriand Archipelago and the adjoining groups, are expert fishermen, industrious manufacturers and traders, but they rely mainly on gardening for their subsistence. With the most rudimentary implements, a pointed digging-stick and a small axe, they are able to raise crops sufficient to maintain a dense population and even yielding a surplus, which in olden days was allowed to rot unconsumed, and which at present is exported to feed plantation hands. The success in their agriculture depends—besides the excellent natural conditions with which they are favored—upon their extensive knowledge of the classes of the soil, of the various cultivated plants, of the mutual adaptation of these two factors, and, last not least, upon their knowledge of the importance of accurate and hard work. They have to select the soil and the seedlings, they have appropriately to fix the times for clearing and burning the scrub, for planting and weeding, for training the vines of the yam plants. In all this they are guided by a clear knowledge of weather and seasons, plants and pests, soil and tubers, and by a conviction that this knowledge is true and reliable, that it can be counted upon and must be scrupulously obeyed.

Yet mixed with all their activities there is to be found magic, a series of rites performed every year over the gardens in rigorous sequence and order. Since the leadership in garden work is in the hands of the magician, and since ritual and practical work are intimately associated, a superficial observer might be led to assume that the mystic and the rational behavior are mixed up, that their effects are not distinguished by the natives and not distinguishable in scientific analysis. Is this so really?

Magic is undoubtedly regarded by the natives as absolutely indispensable to the welfare of the gardens. What would happen without it no one can exactly tell, for no native garden has ever been made without its ritual, in spite of some thirty years of European rule and missionary influence and well over a century's contact with white traders. But certainly various kinds of disaster, blight, unseasonable droughts, rains, bush-pigs and locusts, would destroy the unhallowed garden made without magic.

Does this mean, however, that the natives attribute all the good results to magic? Certainly not. If you were to suggest to a native that he should make his garden mainly by magic and scamp his work, he would simply smile on your simplicity. He knows as well as you do that there are natural conditions and causes, and by his observations he knows also that he is able to control these natural forces by mental and physical effort. His knowledge is limited, no doubt, but as far as it goes it is sound and proof against mysticism. If the fences are broken down, if the seed is destroyed or has been dried or washed away, he will have recourse not to magic, but to work, guided by knowledge and reason. His experience has taught him also, on the other hand, that in spite of all his forethought and beyond all his efforts there are agencies and forces which one year bestow unwonted and unearned benefits of fertility, making everything run smooth and well, rain and sun appear at the right moment, noxious insects remain in abeyance, the harvest yields a superabundant crop; and another year again the same agencies bring ill luck and bad chance, pursue him from beginning till end and thwart all his most strenuous efforts and his best-founded knowledge. To control these influences and these only he employs magic.

Thus there is a clear-cut division: there is first the well-known set of conditions, the natural course of growth, as well as the ordinary pests and dangers to be warded off by fencing and weeding. On the other hand there is the domain of the unaccountable and adverse influences, as well as the great unearned increment of fortunate coincidence. The first conditions are coped with by knowledge and work, the second by magic.

This line of division can also be traced in the social setting of work and ritual respectively. Though the garden magician is, as a rule, also the leader in practical activities, these two functions are kept strictly apart. Every magical ceremony has its distinctive name, its appropriate time and its place in the scheme of work, and it stands out of the ordinary course of activities completely. Some of them are ceremonial and have to be attended by the whole community, all are public in that it is known when they are going to happen and anyone can attend them. They are performed on selected plots within the gardens and on a special corner of this plot. Work is always tabooed on such occasions, sometimes only while the ceremony lasts, sometimes for a day or two. In his lay character the leader and magician directs the work, fixes the dates for starting, harangues and exhorts slack or careless gardeners. But the two roles never overlap or interfere: they are always clear, and any native will inform you without hesitation whether the man acts as magician or as leader in garden work.

What has been said about gardens can be paralleled from any one of the many other activities in which work and magic run side by side without ever mixing. Thus in canoe building empirical knowledge of material, of technology, and of certain principles of stability and hydrodynamics, function in company and close association with magic, each yet uncontaminated by the other.

For example, they understand perfectly well that the wider the span of the outrigger the greater the stability yet the smaller the resistance against strain. They can clearly explain why they have to give this span a certain traditional width, measured in fractions of the length of the dugout. They can also explain, in rudimentary but clearly mechanical terms, how they have to behave in a sudden gale, why the outrigger must be always on the weather side, why the one type of canoe can and the other cannot beat. They have, in fact, a whole system of principles of sailing, embodied in a complex and rich terminology, traditionally handed on and obeyed as rationally and consistently as is modern science by modern sailors. How could they sail otherwise under eminently dangerous conditions in their frail primitive craft?

But even with all their systematic knowledge, methodically applied, they are still at the mercy of powerful and incalculable tides, sudden gales during the monsoon season and unknown reefs. And here comes in their magic, performed over the canoe during its construction, carried out at the beginning and in the course of expeditions and resorted to in moments of real danger. If the modern seaman, entrenched in science and reason, provided with all sorts of safety appliances, sailing on steel-built steamers, if even he has a singular tendency to superstition—which does not rob him of his knowledge or reason, nor make him altogether prelogical—can we wonder that his savage colleague, under much more precarious conditions, holds fast to the safety and comfort of magic?

An interesting and crucial test is provided by fishing in the Trobriand Islands and its magic. While in the villages on the inner lagoon fishing is done in an easy and absolutely reliable manner by the method of poisoning, yielding abundant results without danger and uncertainty, there are on the shores of the open sea dangerous modes of fishing and also certain types in which the yield greatly varies according to whether shoals of fish appear beforehand or not. It is most significant that in the lagoon fishing, where man can rely completely upon his knowledge and skill, magic does not exist, while in the open-sea fishing, full of danger and uncertainty, there is extensive magical ritual to secure safety and good results.

Again, in warfare the natives know that strength, courage, and agility play a decisive part. Yet here also they practice magic to master the elements of chance and luck.

Nowhere is the duality of natural and supernatural causes divided by a line so thin and intricate, yet, if carefully followed up, so well marked, decisive, and instructive, as in the two most fateful forces of human destiny: health and death. Health to the Melanesians is a natural state of affairs and, unless tampered with, the human body will remain in perfect order. But the natives know perfectly well that there are natural means which can affect health and even destroy the body. Poisons, wounds, burns, falls, are known to cause disablement or death in a natural way. And this is not a matter of private opinion of this or that individual, but it is laid down in traditional lore and even in belief, for there are considered to be different ways to the nether world for those who died by sorcery and those who met "natural" death. Again, it is recognized that cold, heat, overstrain, too much sun, over-eating, can all cause minor ailments, which are treated by natural remedies such as massage, steaming, warming at a fire and certain potions. Old age is known to lead to bodily decay and the explanation is given by the natives that very old people grow weak, their oesophagus closes up, and therefore they must die.

But besides these natural causes there is the enormous domain of sorcery and by far the most cases of illness and death are ascribed to this. The line of distinction between sorcery and the other causes is clear in theory and in most cases of practice, but it must be realized that it is subject to what could be called the personal perspective. That is, the more closely a case has to do with the person who considers it, the less will it be "natural," the more "magical." Thus a very old man, whose pending death will be considered natural by the other members of the community, will be afraid only of sorcery and never think of his natural fate. A fairly sick person will diagnose sorcery in his own case, while all the others might speak of too much betel nut or overeating or some other indulgence.

But who of us really believes that his own bodily infirmities and the approaching death is a purely natural occurrence, just an insignificant event in the infinite chain of causes? To the most rational of civilized men health, disease, the threat of death, float in a hazy emotional mist, which seems to become denser and more impenetrable as the fateful forms approach. It is indeed astonishing that "savages" can achieve such a sober, dispassionate outlook in these matters as they actually do.

Thus in his relation to nature and destiny, whether he tries to exploit the first or to dodge the second, primitive man recognizes both the natural and the supernatural forces and agencies, and he tries to use them both for his benefit. Whenever he has been taught by experience that effort guided by knowledge is of some avail, he never spares the one or ignores the other. He knows that a plant cannot grow by magic alone, or a canoe sail or float without being properly constructed and managed, or a fight be won without skill and daring. He never relies on magic alone, while, on the contrary, he sometimes dispenses with it completely, as in fire-making and in a number of crafts and pursuits. But he clings to it, whenever he has to recognize the impotence of his knowledge and of his rational technique.

I have given my reasons why in this argument I had to rely principally on the material collected in the classical land of magic, Melanesia. But the facts discussed are so fundamental, the conclusions drawn of such a general nature, that it will be easy to check them on any modern detailed ethnographic record. Comparing agricultural work and magic, the building of canoes, the art of healing by magic and by natural remedies, the ideas about the causes of death in other regions, the universal validity of what has been established here could easily be proved. Only, since no observations have methodically been made with reference to the problem of primitive knowledge, the data from other writers could be gleaned only piecemeal and their testimony though clear would be indirect.

I have chosen to face the question of primitive man's rational knowledge directly: watching him at his principal occupations, seeing him pass from work to magic and back again, entering into his mind, listening to his opinions. The whole problem might have been approached through the avenue of language, but this would have led us too far into questions of logic, semasiology, and theory of primitive languages. Words which serve to express general ideas such as *existence, substance,* and *attribute, cause* and *effect,* the *fundamental* and the *secondary;* words and expressions used in complicated pursuits like sailing, construction, measuring and checking; numerals and quantitative descriptions, correct and detailed classifications of natural phenomena, plants and animals—all this would lead us exactly to the same conclusion: that primitive man can observe and think, and that he possesses, embodied in his language, systems of methodical though rudimentary knowledge.

Similar conclusions could be drawn from an examination of those mental schemes and physical contrivances which could be described as diagrams or formulas. Methods of indicating the main points of the compass, arrangements of stars into constellations, co-ordination of these with the seasons, naming of moons in the year, of quarters in the moon—all these accomplishments are known to the simplest savages. Also they are all able to draw diagrammatic maps in the sand or dust, indicate arrangements by placing small stones, shells, or sticks on the ground, plan expeditions or raids on such rudimentary charts. By co-ordinating space and time they are able to arrange big tribal gatherings and to combine vast tribal movements over extensive areas.[1] The use of leaves, notched sticks, and similar aids to memory is well known and seems to be almost universal. All such "diagrams" are means of reducing a complex and unwieldy bit of reality to a simple and handy form. They give a man a relatively easy mental control over it. As such are they not—in a very rudimentary form no doubt—fundamentally akin to developed scientific formulas and "models," which are also simple and handy paraphrases of a complex or abstract reality, giving the civilized physicist mental control over it?

This brings us to the second question: Can we regard primitive knowledge, which, as we found, is both empirical and rational, as a rudimentary stage of science, or is it not at all related to it? If by science be understood a body of rules and conceptions, based on experience and derived from it by logical inference, embodied in material achievements and in a fixed form of tradition and carried on by some sort of social organization—then there is no doubt that even the lowest savage communities have the beginnings of science, however rudimentary.

Most epistemologists would not, however, be satisfied with such a "minimum definition" of science, for it might apply to the rules of an art or craft as well. They would maintain that the rules of science must be laid down explicitly, open to control by experiment and critique by reason. They must not only be rules of practical behavior, but theoretical laws of knowledge. Even accepting this stricture, however, there is hardly any doubt that many of the principles of savage knowledge are scientific in this sense. The native shipwright knows not only practically of buoyancy, leverage, equilibrium, he has to obey these laws not only on water, but while making the canoe he must have the principles in his mind. He instructs his helpers in them. He gives them the traditional rules, and in a crude and simple manner, using his hands, pieces of wood, and a limited technical vocabulary, he explains some general laws of hydrodynamics and equilibrium. Science is not detached from the craft, that is certainly true, it is only a means to an end, it is crude, rudimentary, and inchoate, but with all that it is the matrix from which the higher developments must have sprung.

If we applied another criterion yet, that of the really scientific attitude, the disinterested search for knowledge and for the understanding of causes

[1] Cf. the writer's *Argonauts of the Western Pacific,* chap. xvi.

and reasons, the answer would certainly not be in a direct negative. There is, of course, no widespread thirst for knowledge in a savage community, new things such as European topics bore them frankly and their whole interest is largely encompassed by the traditional world of their culture. But within this there is both the antiquarian mind passionately interested in myths, stories, details of customs, pedigrees, and ancient happenings, and there is also to be found the naturalist, patient and painstaking in his observations, capable of generalization and of connecting long chains of events in the life of animals, and in the marine world or in the jungle. It is enough to realize how much European naturalists have often learned from their savage colleagues to appreciate this interest found in the native for nature. There is finally among the primitives, as every fieldworker well knows, the sociologist, the ideal informant, capable with marvelous accuracy and insight to give the *raison d'être*, the function, and the organization of many a simpler institution in his tribe.

Science, of course, does not exist in any uncivilized community as a driving power, criticizing, renewing, constructing. Science is never consciously made. But on this criterion, neither is there law, nor religion, nor government among savages.

The question, however, whether we should call it *science* or only *empirical and rational knowledge* is not of primary importance in this context. We have tried to gain a clear idea as to whether the savage has only one domain of reality or two, and we found that he has his profane world of practical activities and rational outlook besides the sacred region of cult and belief.

55   An Example of a Problem—
The Behavior of the Nile River

*Morris R. Cohen
and Ernest Nagel*

1. THE OCCASION AND THE FUNCTION OF INQUIRY

In the second book of his fascinating *History,* Herodotus recounts the sights that met him on his travels to Egypt. The river Nile aroused his attention:

"Now the Nile, when it overflows, floods not only the Delta, but also the tracts of country on both sides the stream which are thought to belong to Libya and Arabia, in some places reaching to the extent of two days' journey from its banks, in some even exceeding that distance, but in others falling short of it.

"Concerning the nature of the river, I was not able to gain any information either from the priests or from others. I was particularly anxious to learn from them why the Nile, at the commencement of the summer solstice, begins to rise, and continues to increase for a hundred days—and why, as soon as that number is past, it forthwith retires and contracts its stream, continuing low during the whole of the winter until the summer solstice comes around again. On none of these points could I obtain any explanation from the inhabitants, though I made every inquiry, wishing to know what was commonly reported—they could neither tell me what special virtue the Nile has which makes it so opposite in its nature to all other streams, nor why, unlike every other river, it gives forth no breezes from its surface.

"Some of the Greeks, however, wishing to get a reputation for cleverness, have offered explanations of the phenomena of the river, for which they have accounted in three different ways. Two of these I do not think it worth while to speak of, further than simply to mention what they are. One pretends that the Etesian winds [the northwest winds blowing from the Mediterranean] cause the rise of the river by preventing the Nile-water from running off into the sea. But in the first place it has often happened, when the Etesian winds did not blow, that the Nile has risen according to its usual wont; and further, if the Etesian winds produced the effect, the other rivers which flow in a direction opposite to those winds ought to present the same phenomena as the Nile, and the more so as they are all smaller streams, and have a weaker current. But these rivers, of which there are many both in Syria and in Libya, are entirely unlike the Nile in this respect.

"The second opinion is even more unscientific than the one just mentioned, and also, if I may so say, more marvellous. It is that the Nile acts so strangely because it flows from the ocean, and that the ocean flows all round the earth.

"The third explanation, which is very much more plausible than either of the others, is positively the furthest from the truth; for there is really nothing in what it says, any more than in the other theories. It is, that the inundation of the Nile is caused by the melting of snows. Now, as the Nile flows out of Libya [Central Africa], through Ethiopia, into Egypt, how is it possible that it can be formed of melting snow, running, as it does, from the hottest regions of the world into cooler countries? Many are the proofs whereby anyone capable of reasoning on the subject may be convinced that it is most unlikely this should be the case. The first and strongest argument is furnished by the winds, which always blow hot from these regions. The second is, that rain and frost are unknown there. Now, whenever snow falls, it must of necessity rain within five days; so that, if there were snow, there must be rain also in those parts. Thirdly, it is certain that the natives of the country are black with the heat, that the kites and the swallows remain there the whole year, and that the cranes, when they fly from the rigors of a Scythian winter, flock thither to pass the cold season. If then, in the country whence the Nile has its source, or in that through which it flows, there fell ever so little snow, it is absolutely impossible that any of these circumstances could take place.

"As for the writer who attributes the phenomenon to the ocean, his account is involved in such obscurity, that it is impossible to disprove it by argument. For my part I know of no river called Ocean, and I think that Homer, or one of the earlier poets, invented the name and introduced it into his poetry." [1]

Herodotus then goes on to state his own explanation of the behavior of the Nile.

Has the reader ever been guilty of believing or saying that the way to find out what the truth is, is to "study the facts" or to "let the facts speak for themselves?" Then let him examine this quotation for the light it may throw on the nature of the circumstances under which contributions to knowledge are made. We have suggested in the introductory chapter of the present Book that unless habitual beliefs are shaken into doubt by alterations in our familiar environment or by our curiosity, we either do no thinking at all, or our thinking, such as it is, has a routine character. We wish now to reinforce this suggestion and indicate its importance in understanding the nature of reflective or scientific method.

This excerpt from Herodotus illustrates clearly the Greek zest for scientific knowledge and speculation. But it also illustrates the great difference between the habit of simple acceptance of apparently stray, disconnected information, and the attitude that searches for some order in facts which are only superficially isolated. The observable inundation of the Nile was to many a brute fact, unconnected with other familiar but isolated facts. For Herodotus, however, the behavior of the Nile was not simply a brute fact. It presented a *problem* that could be resolved only by finding some general *connection* between the periodic inundation of the Nile and *other* facts.

It is an utterly superficial view, therefore, that the truth is to be found by "studying the facts." It is superficial because no inquiry can even get under way until and unless *some difficulty is felt* in a practical or theoretical situation. It is the difficulty, or problem, which guides our search for some *order among the facts,* in terms of which the difficulty is to be removed. We could not possibly discover the *reasons* for the inundation of the Nile unless we first recognized in the inundation a *problem* demanding solution.

If some problem is the occasion for inquiry, the *solution* of the problem is the goal and function of the inquiry. What constitutes a satisfactory solution of a problem, and in particular of the problem: Why does the Nile overflow its banks? The sort of answer for which Herodotus was looking was the

[1] *History,* tr. by George Rawlinson, 1859, 4 vols., Vol. II, pp. 24–29.

discovery of a connection between the fact of the Nile's behavior and *other* facts; in virtue of that connection, apparently isolated facts would be seen to be *ordered* facts. And in general, scientific investigations must begin with some problem, and aim at an order connecting what at first sight may seem unrelated facts. But the ability to perceive in some brute experience the occasion for a problem, and especially a problem *whose solution has a bearing on the solution of other problems,* is not a common talent among men. For no rule can be given by means of which men can learn to ask significant questions. It is a mark of scientific genius to be sensitive to difficulties where less gifted people pass by untroubled with doubt.

2. THE FORMULATION OF RELEVANT HYPOTHESIS

How does such a search for an order among facts proceed? The reader must note in the first place that a problem cannot even be *stated* unless we are somewhat familiar with the subject matter in which we discover the problem. The Greeks found a problem in the behavior of the Nile because, among other reasons, they were acquainted with the behavior of other rivers, and because the behavior of these other rivers was known to them to be connected with such things as wind, snowfall, and evaporation.

In order to state some obscurely felt difficulty in the form of a determinate problem, we must be able to *pick out,* on the basis of *previous knowledge,* certain elements in the subject matter as *significant.* Thus Herodotus noted the *distance covered* by the overflowing waters, the *time* at which the inundation *begins,* the *time* at which the overflow reaches its *maximum,* and the absence of *breezes* at the river's surface. It was in terms of such distinguishable and repeatable elements in the total situation known as "the inundation of the Nile" that Herodotus stated his difficulty. But his attention was drawn to these elements, rather than to others, because he was familiar with certain *theories* dealing with the behavior of rivers. It was his familiarity with such theories which made him look to facts like the winds, snowfall, or evaporation rather than to other facts in order to find a connection between them and the Nile's behavior.

We cannot take a single step forward in any inquiry unless we begin with a *suggested* explanation or solution of the difficulty which originated it. Such tentative explanations are suggested to us by something in the subject matter and by our previous knowledge. When they are formulated as propositions, they are called *hypotheses.*

The function of a hypothesis is to *direct* our search for the order among facts. The suggestions formulated in the hypothesis *may* be solutions to the problem. *Whether* they are, is the task of the inquiry. No one of the suggestions need necessarily lead to our goal. And frequently some of the suggestions are incompatible with one another, so that they cannot all be solutions to the same problem.

We shall discuss below the formal conditions a satisfactory hypothesis must fulfill. The reader should note at this point that Herodotus examined three hypotheses (besides his own) for solving the problem of the Nile's periodic inundation. He accepted his own, after rejecting the other three. As a matter of fact, all four explanations are false. Nevertheless, the procedure he followed in rejecting some hypotheses and accepting others is still a model of scientific method.

How important hypotheses are in directing inquiry will be seen clearly if we reflect once more on the frequent advice: "Let the facts speak for themselves." For what *are* the facts, and *which* facts should we study? Herodotus could have observed the rise and retreat of the Nile until the end of time without finding in that particular repeated fact the sort of connections he was looking for—the relations of the inundation to the rainfall in Central Africa, for example. His problem could receive a solution only with the discovery of an invariable connection between the overflow of the Nile and some other fact. But *what* other fact? The number of other facts is endless, and an undirected observation of the Nile may never reveal either the other facts or their mode of connection. Facts must be *selected* for study on the basis of a hypothesis.

In directing an inquiry, a hypothesis must of necessity regard some facts as *significant* and others as not. It would have been humanly impossible for Herodotus to examine the relations of the Nile to *every other* class of events. Such a task, however, would have been regarded by him as preposterous. For most of these other facts, such as the number of prayers offered by the Egyptians every day, or the number of travelers visiting Naucratis each season, were judged by him to be *irrelevant*.

What is meant by saying that some hypotheses express "relevant" connection of facts, and others do not? The melting of snows is a relevant fact for understanding the Nile's behavior, Herodotus might have explained, because *on the basis of previous knowledge* melting snow can be regarded as related more or less constantly and in some determinate manner with the volume of rivers. But the number of visitors in Naucratis each season is not relevant to the Nile's behavior, because no such relation is known to exist between changes in the visiting population of a city and variations in the volume of rivers. A hypothesis is believed to be relevant to a problem if it expresses determinate modes of connections between a set of facts, including the fact investigated; it is irrelevant otherwise.

No rules can be stated for "hitting upon" relevant hypotheses. A hypothesis may often be believed to be relevant which subsequent inquiry shows to be not so. Or we may believe that certain facts are irrelevant to a problem although subsequent inquiry may reveal the contrary. *In the absence of knowledge concerning a subject matter, we can make no well-founded judgments of relevance.*

It follows that the valuable suggestions for solving a problem can be made only by those who are familiar with the kinds of connections which the subject matter under investigation is capable of exhibiting. Thus the explanation of the Nile's periodic overflow as due to heavy rainfall would not be very likely to occur to anyone not already familiar with the relation between rain and swollen rivers. The hypotheses which occur to an investigator are therefore a function, in part at least, of his previous knowledge.

3. THE DEDUCTIVE DEVELOPMENT OF HYPOTHESES

Let us now reëxamine the procedure of Herodotus in terms of the distinctions already familiar.

The search for an explanation of the Nile's behavior was a search for a *general rule* which asserts a *universal* connection between facts of that kind and other facts of different kind. The task of Herodotus was to show that the general rule which was suggested to him in the form of a hypothesis *did truly and in fact* apply to the specific problem at hand. How did he perform it?

The argument which Herodotus employed to reject the first theory may be stated as follows: The defender of the theory offers the following argument:

If the Etesian winds blow, the Nile rises (*general rule*).
The Nile rises for one hundred days beginning with the summer solstice (*observed fact*).
∴ The Etesian winds blow, beginning with the summer solstice (*inferred event*).

The inference is, of course, invalid as a conclusive proof. But its proponent may claim that the reasoning is a *presumptive probable inference*, so that the conclusion is probable on the evidence. Herodotus shows that this is not the case. He points out that we can find an occasion when the Nile rises (*observed case*) and the Etesian winds do not blow. Such a case is obviously not explained by our general rule. He therefore concludes that the hypothesis of the winds will not *always* account for the inundation of the river. But he is not content with this, for the defender of the theory may perhaps be satisfied with an explanation of the overflow which is not invariable. Herodotus showed further that the logical consequences of the Etesian wind theory were *contrary* to the known facts. In order to do this, he had therefore to point out some of the other consequences of that theory by discovering what it *implied*.

His argument continues:

If the blowing of the Etesian winds produced inundations, other rivers should behave as the Nile does (*elaborated rule*).
These other rivers do not overflow their banks (*observed fact*).
∴ The blowing of the Etesian winds does not invariably produce inundations.

This inference is a valid mixed hypothetical syllogism. Herodotus has therefore shown that the Etesian-wind theory cannot be regarded as a satisfactory explanation of the problem.

In this rejection of the first theory, Herodotus was compelled to elaborate it deductively. The importance of this step can be seen even more clearly by considering his rejection of the third theory. This may be stated as follows: If there are periodic melting snows in the interior of Africa, then the Nile will inundate periodically. Herodotus rejects this explanation not because he can *actually observe* the absence of snow in Central Africa, but because he can observe what he believes to be the consequences of Central Africa's being a warm country. And since he rejects the possibility of snowfall in warm places, he also rejects the theory of melting snows as the cause of the Nile's behavior. Let us restate part of his argument:

If hot winds blow from a region, then that region itself is hot (*general rule*).
Hot winds blow from the interior of Africa (*observed fact*).
∴ The interior of Africa is hot (*inferred fact*).
If snow falls in a region, then that region cannot have a hot climate (*rule*).
The interior of Africa *is* hot (*inferred from the previous inference*).
∴ Snow does not fall in the interior of Africa (*inferred fact*).

From this analysis we may conclude that the deductive elaboration of a hypothesis must follow its formulation. For we can discover the full meaning of a hypothesis, whether it is relevant and whether it offers a satisfactory solution of the problem, only by discovering what it *implies*. It is worth noting that Herodotus rejected the second theory simply on the ground that it was obscurely stated, so that it was impossible to find out what it did imply.

We are therefore already in the position to appreciate how important the technique of deduction is for scientific method. In the chapter on mathematics we have seen how a complex set of assumptions may be explored for their implications. The techniques we have discussed there are relevant for the deductive elaboration of any theory. Without writing a textbook on some special science one cannot illustrate the full scope of those methods in a particular subject matter. But by attending to a few more relatively simple examples the reader can appreciate the indispensability for scientific procedure of developing a hypothesis deductively.

Galileo's study on falling bodies is one of the most far-reaching in modern times. He had shown that if we neglect the resistance of air, the velocity with which bodies fall to the ground does not depend on their weight. It was known that bodies pick up speed as they approach the ground. But it was not known what the relation is between the velocity, the space traveled, and the time required for the fall. Of what general law could the fall of a body be regarded as an instance?

Galileo considered two hypotheses. According to the first, the increase in the velocity of a freely falling body is proportional to the *space* traversed. But Galileo argued (mistakenly, as we now know) that one consequence of this assumption is that a body should travel *instantaneously* through a portion of its path. He believed this was impossible, and therefore rejected the proposed law of the increase in velocity.

Galileo next considered the hypothesis that the change in velocity of a freely falling body during an interval of time is proportional to that interval. This assumption may be expressed in modern notation as: $v = at$, where v represents the velocity, a the velocity acquired in one second, and t the number of seconds the body has fallen. It may also be expressed by saying that the acceleration of a falling body (defined as the change in velocity during any unit interval of time) is constant.

But the assumption that the acceleration is constant could not be put to the test *directly*. Galileo was compelled to strengthen his argument by *deducing other consequences* from the acceleration hypothesis, and showing that these consequences were capable of direct verification. The argument was strengthened because these consequences had not previously been known to be true. For example, he deduced from the hypothesis $v = at$, the proposition: The distances freely falling bodies traverse are proportional to the square of the time of their fall.

Instances of this rule can be established experimentally. Thus a body which falls for two seconds travels four times as far as a body which falls only one second; and a body falling three seconds travels nine times as far as a body falling one second. This, therefore, strengthens the evidence for the hypothesis that bodies fall so that their acceleration is constant.

In a similar fashion, Galileo deduced other propositions from the acceleration hypothesis, all of which he could verify with much precision. In this way the evidence for that hypothesis was increased. *But it was possible to increase it only after exploring its directly verifiable implications.*

Nevertheless, the evidence for the acceleration hypothesis always remains only *probable*. The hypothesis is only probable on the evidence because it is always logically possible to find some other hypothesis from which all the verified propositions are consequences. Nevertheless, it shows itself the best available so long as it enables us to infer and discover an ever greater variety of true propositions. A comprehensive theory is established as true with a high probability by showing that various *samplings* from its logical consequences are empirically true.

Let us now summarize the general features of Galileo's procedure. We find that he *selected* some *portion* of his experiences for study. His experiments from the Tower of Pisa resolved some of his doubts. But the resolution of these doubts only raised others. If the behavior of freely falling bodies did not depend upon their weight, upon what did it depend? The ancients, as well as his own contemporaries, had already isolated some properties of bodies as *irrelevant* to their behavior in falling. The temperature, the smell, the color, the shapes of the bodies, were tacitly assumed to be irrelevant qualities. The ancients also regarded the distance and the duration of fall as unimportant. But this assumption Galileo refused to make. And he ventured to formulate hypotheses in which these properties of bodies were the determining factors of their behavior.

This selection of the relevant factors was in part based on his previous knowledge. Galileo, like the ancients, neglected the color and smell of bodies because general experience seemed to indicate that their color or smell could vary without corresponding changes in their behavior when falling. In part, however, the selection was based on a tentative guess that properties heretofore regarded as unimportant were in fact relevant. Galileo had already made successful researches in physics, in which the quantitative relations exclusively studied by the mathematics of his day played a fundamental rôle. He was also well read in ancient philosophy, and had an unbounded confidence that the "Book of Nature" was written in geometric characters. It was not, therefore, with an *unbiased* mind, it was not with a mind empty of strong convictions and interesting suggestions, that Galileo tried to solve for himself the problems of motion. It was a conviction with him that the only relevant factors in the study of motion were velocity, time, distance, and certain constant proportions.

We may thus distinguish two sets of ideas which Galileo employed in studying the motions of bodies. One set, by far the larger, consisted of his mathematical, physical, and philosophical convictions, which determined his choice of subjects and their relevant properties. The other set consisted of the *special* hypotheses he devised for discovering the relations between the relevant factors. The first set was a relatively stable collection of beliefs and prejudices. It is very likely Galileo would have held on to these, even if neither of his two hypotheses on falling bodies had been confirmed by experiment. The second set, especially at the stage of scientific development in Galileo's time, was a more unsettled collection of suggestions and beliefs. Thus Galileo might easily have sacrificed his very simple equations between velocity, time, distance, and acceleration for somewhat more complex ones if his experiments had demanded the latter.

It is these special assumptions which become formulated consciously as hypotheses or theories. And it is to a more careful study of the conditions which such hypotheses must meet that we now turn.

56   Facts into Laws
Hermann Von Helmholtz

In discussing the progress of physical science as a whole, the first question which presents itself is, By what standard are we to estimate this progress?

To the uninitiated, this science of ours is an accumulation of a vast

From "The Aim and Progress of Physical Science," with deletions, in *Popular Lectures on Scientific Subjects,* by H. Von Helmholtz, trans. by W. Flight, New York, D. Appleton & Co., 1873. From an address delivered in 1869.

number of facts, some of which are conspicuous for their practical utility, while others are merely curiosities, or objects of wonder. And, if it were possible to classify this unconnected mass of facts, as was done in the Linnean system, or in encyclopaedias, so that each may be readily found when required, such knowledge as this would not deserve the name of science, nor satisfy either the scientific wants of the human mind, or the desire for progressive mastery over the powers of nature. For the former requires an intellectual grasp of the connection of ideas, the latter demands our anticipation of a result in cases yet untried, and under conditions that we propose to introduce in the course of our experiment. Both are obviously arrived at by a knowledge of the *law* of the phenomena.

Isolated facts and experiments have in themselves no value, however great their number may be. They only become valuable in a theoretical or practical point of view when they make us acquainted with the *law* of a series of uniformly recurring phenomena, or, it may be, only give a negative result showing an incompleteness in our knowledge of such a law, till then held to be perfect. From the exact and universal conformity to law of natural phenomena, a single observation of a condition that we may presume to be rigorously conformable to law, suffices, it is true, at times to establish a rule with the highest degree of probability; just as, for example, we assume our knowledge of the skeleton of a prehistoric animal to be complete if we find only one complete skeleton of a single individual. But we must not lose sight of the fact that the isolated observation is not of value in that it is isolated, but because it is an aid to the knowledge of the conformable regularity in bodily structure of an entire species of organisms. In like manner, the knowledge of the specific heat of one small fragment of a new metal is important because we have no grounds for doubting that any other pieces of the same metal subjected to the same treatment will yield the same result.

To find the *law* by which they are regulated is to *understand* phenomena. For law is nothing more than the general conception in which a series of similarly recurring natural processes may be embraced. Just as we include in the conception "mammal" all that is common to the man, the ape, the dog, the lion, the hare, the horse, the whale, &c., so we comprehend in the law of refraction that which we observe to regularly recur when a ray of light of any colour passes in any direction through the common boundary of any two transparent media.

A law of nature, however, is not a mere logical conception that we have adopted as a kind of *memoria technica* to enable us to more readily remember facts. We of the present day have already sufficient insight to know that the laws of nature are not things which we can evolve by any speculative method. On the contrary, we have to *discover* them in the facts; we have to test them by repeated observation or experiment, in constantly new cases, under ever-varying circumstances; and in proportion only as they hold good under a constantly increasing change of conditions, in a constantly increasing number of cases and with greater delicacy in the means of observation, does our confidence in their trustworthiness rise.

Thus the laws of nature occupy the position of a power with which we are not familiar, not to be arbitrarily selected and determined in our minds, as one might devise various systems of animals and plants one after another, so long as the object is only one of classification. Before we can say that our knowledge of any one law of nature is complete, we must see that *it holds good without exception,* and make this the test of its correctness. If we can be assured that the conditions under which the law operates have presented themselves, the result must ensue without arbitrariness, without choice, without our co-operation, and from the very necessity which regulates the things of the external world as well as our perception. The law then takes the form of an objective power, and for that reason we call it *force.*

.   .   .

On looking back over the history of our sciences, the first great example we find of the subjugation of a wide mass of facts to a comprehensive law, occurred in the case of theoretical mechanics, the fundamental conception of which was first clearly propounded by Galileo. The question then was to find the general propositions that to us now appear so self-evident, that all substance is inert, and that the magnitude of force is to be measured not by its velocity, but by changes in it. At first the operation of a continually acting force could only be represented as a series of small impacts. It was not till Leibnitz and Newton, by the discovery of the differential calculus, had dispelled the ancient darkness which enveloped the conception of the infinite, and had clearly established the conception of the Continuous and of continuous change, that a full and productive application of the newly-found mechanical conceptions made any progress. The most singular and most splendid instance of such an application was in regard to the motion of the planets, and I need scarcely remind you here how brilliant an example astronomy has been for the development of the other branches of science. In its case, by the theory of gravitation, a vast and complex mass of facts were first embraced in a single principle of great simplicity, and such a reconciliation of theory and fact established as has never been accomplished in any other department of science, either before or since. In supplying the wants of astronomy, have originated almost all the exact methods of measurement as well as the principal advances made in modern mathematics; the science itself was peculiarly fitted to attract the attention of the general public, partly by the grandeur of the objects under investigation, partly by its practical utility in navigation and geodesy, and the many industrial and social interests arising from them.

Galileo began with the study of terrestrial gravity. Newton extended the application, at first cautiously and hesitatingly, to the moon, then boldly to all the planets. And, in more recent times, we learn that these laws of the common inertia and gravitation of all ponderable masses hold good of the movements of the most distant double stars of which the light has yet reached us.

During the latter half of the last and the first half of the present century came the great progress of chemistry which conclusively solved the ancient problem of discovering the elementary substances, a task to which so much metaphysical speculation had been devoted. Reality has always far exceeded even the boldest and wildest speculation, and, in the place of the four primitive metaphysical elements—fire, water, air, and earth—we have now the sixty-five simple bodies of modern chemistry. Science has shown that these elements are really indestructible, unalterable in their mass, unalterable also in their properties; in short, that from every condition into which they may have been converted, they can invariably be isolated, and recover those qualities which they previously possessed in the free state. Through all the varied phases of the phenomena of animated and inanimate nature, so far as we are acquainted with them, in all the astonishing results of chemical decomposition and combination, the number and diversity of which the chemist with unwearied diligence augments from year to year, the one law of the *immutability of matter* prevails as a necessity that knows no exception. And chemistry has already pressed on into the depths of immeasurable space, and detected in the most distant suns or nebulae indications of well-known terrestrial elements, so that doubts respecting the prevailing homogeneity of the matter of the universe no longer exist, though certain elements may perhaps be restricted to certain groups of the heavenly bodies.

From this invariability of the elements follows another and wider consequence. Chemistry shows by actual experiment that all matter is made up of the elements which have been already isolated. These elements may exhibit great differences as regards combination or mixture, the mode of aggregation or molecular structure—that is to say, they may vary the mode of their *distribution in space*. In their *properties*, on the other hand, they are altogether unchangeable; in other words, when referred to the same compound, as regards isolation, and to the same state of aggregation, they invariably exhibit the same properties as before. If, then, all elementary substances are unchangeable in respect to their properties, and only changeable as regards their combination and their states of aggregation—that is, in respect to their distribution in space—it follows that all changes in the world are changes in the local distribution of elementary matter, and are eventually brought about through *Motion*.

If, however, motion be the primordial change which lies at the root of all the other changes occurring in the world, every elementary force is a force of motion, and the ultimate aim of physical science must be to determine the movements which are the real causes of all other phenomena and discover the motive powers on which they depend; in other words, to merge itself into mechanics.

Though this is clearly the final consequence of the qualitative and quantitative immutability of matter, it is after all an ideal proposition, the realization of which is still very remote. The field is a prescribed one, in which we have succeeded in tracing back actually observed changes to motions and forces of motion of a definite kind. Besides astronomy, may be mentioned the purely mechanical part of physics, then acoustics, optics, and electricity; in the science of heat and in chemistry, strenuous endeavours are being made towards perfecting definite views respecting the nature of the motion and position of molecules, while physiology has scarcely made a definite step in this direction.

This renders all the more important, therefore, a noteworthy advancement of the most general importance made during the last quarter of a century in the direction we are considering. If all elementary forces are forces of motion, and all, consequently, of similar nature, they should all be measurable by the same standard, that is, the standard of the mechanical forces. And that this is actually the fact is now regarded as proved. The law expressing this is known under the name of *the law of the Conservation of Force.*

.   .   .

Physical science has made active progress, not only in this or that direction, but as a vast whole, and what has been accomplished may warrant the attainment of further progress. Doubts respecting the entire conformity to law of nature are more and more dispelled; laws more general and more comprehensive have revealed themselves. That the direction which scientific study has taken is a healthy one, its great practical issues have clearly demonstrated; and I may here be permitted to direct particular attention to the branch of science more especially my own. In physiology particularly scientific work had been crippled by doubts respecting the necessary conformity to law, which means, as we have shown, the intelligibility of vital phenomena, and this naturally extended itself to the practical science directly dependent on physiology, namely, medicine. Both have received an impetus, such as had not been felt for thousands of years, from the time that they seriously adopted the method of physical science, the exact observation of phenomena and experiment. As a practising physician, in my earlier days, I can personally bear testimony to this. I was educated at a period when medicine was in a transitional stage, when the minds of the most thoughtful and exact were filled with despair. It was not difficult to recognise that the old predominant theorising methods of practising medicine were altogether untenable; with these theories, however, the facts on which they had actually been founded had become so inextricably entangled that they also were mostly thrown overboard. How a science should be built up anew had already been seen in the case of the other sciences; but the new task assumed colossal proportions; few steps had been taken towards accomplishing it, and these first efforts were in some measure but crude and clumsy. We need feel no astonishment that many sincere and earnest men should at that time have abandoned medicine as unsatisfactory, or on principle given themselves over to an exaggerated empiricism.

But well directed efforts produced the right result more quickly even than many had hoped for. The application of the mechanical ideas to the doctrine of circulation and respiration, the better interpretation of thermal phenomena, the more refined physiological study of the nerves, soon led to practical results of the greatest importance; microscopic examination of parasitic structures, the stupendous development of pathological anatomy, irresistibly led from nebulous theories to reality. We found that we now possessed a much clearer means of distinguishing, and a clearer insight into the mechanism of the process of disease than the beats of the pulse, the urinary deposit, or the fever type of older medical science had ever given us. If I might name one department of medicine in which the influence of the scientific method has been, perhaps, most brilliantly displayed, it would be in ophthalmic medicine. The peculiar constitution of the eye enables us to apply physical modes of investigation as well in functional as in anatomical derangements of the living organ. Simple physical expedients, spectacles, sometimes spherical, sometimes cylindrical or prismatic, suffice, in many cases, to cure disorders which in earlier times left the organ in a condition of chronic incapacity; a great number of changes on the other hand, which formerly did not attract notice till they induced incurable blindness, can now be detected and remedied at the outset. From the very reason of its presenting the most favourable ground for the application of the scientific method, ophthalmology has proved attractive to a peculiarly large number of excellent investigators, and rapidly attained its present position, in which it sets an example to the other departments of medicine, of the actual capabilities of the true method, as brilliant as that which astronomy for long had offered to the other branches of physical science.

Measurement 57

Norman Campbell

WHAT IS MEASUREMENT?

Measurement is one of the notions which modern science has taken over from common sense. Measurement does not appear as part of common sense until a comparatively high stage of civilization is reached; and even the common-sense conception has changed and developed enormously in historic times. When I say that measurement belongs to common sense, I only mean that it is something with which every civilized person to-day is entirely familiar. It may be defined, in general, as the assignment of numbers to represent proper-

From Ch. VI, "Measurement," in *What is Science?*, with footnote omitted. From Norman Campbell: *What Is Science?*, Dover Publications, Inc., New York, 1921, 1952. Reprinted through permission of the publisher.

ties. If we say that the time is 3 o'clock, that the price of coal is 56 shillings a ton, and that we have just bought 2 tons of it—in all such cases we are using numbers to convey important information about the "properties" of the day, of coal in general, of the coal in our cellar, or so on; and our statement depends somehow upon measurement.

The first point I want to notice is that it is only some properties and not all that can be thus represented by numbers. If I am buying a sack of potatoes I may ask what it weighs and what it costs; to those questions I shall expect a number in answer; it weighs 56 lbs. and costs 5 shillings. But I may also ask of what variety the potatoes are, and whether they are good cookers; to those questions I shall not expect a number in answer. The dealer may possibly call the variety "No. 11" in somebody's catalogue; but even if he does, I shall feel that such use of a number is not real measurement, and is not of the same kind as the use in connexion with weight or cost. What is the difference? Why are some properties measurable and others not? Those are the questions I want to discuss. And I will outline the answer immediately in order that the reader may see at what the subsequent discussion is aiming. The difference is this. Suppose I have two sacks of potatoes which are identical in weight, cost, variety, and cooking qualities; and that I pour the two sacks into one so that there is now only one sack of potatoes. This sack will differ from the two original sacks in weight and cost (the measurable properties), but will not differ from them in variety and cooking qualities (the properties that are not measurable). The measurable properties of a body are those which are changed by the combination of similar bodies; the non-measurable properties are those that are not changed. We shall see that this definition is rather too crude, but it will serve for the present.

NUMBERS

In order to see why this difference is so important we must inquire more closely into the meaning of "number." And at the outset we must note that confusion is apt to arise because that word is used to denote two perfectly different things. It sometimes means a mere name or word or symbol, and it sometimes means a property of an object. Thus, besides the properties which have been mentioned, the sack of potatoes has another definite property, namely the number of potatoes in it, and the number is as much a property of the object which we call a sack of potatoes as its weight or its cost. This property can be (and must be) "represented by a number" just as the weight can be; for instance, it might be represented by 200. But this "200" is not itself a property of the sack; it is a mere mark on the paper for which would be substituted, if I was speaking instead of writing, a spoken sound; it is a name or symbol for the property. When we say that measurement is the representation of properties by "numbers," we mean that it is the representation of properties, other than number, by the symbols which are always used to represent number. Moreover, there is a separate word for these symbols; they are called "numerals." We shall always use that word in future and confine "number" to the meaning of the property which is always represented by numerals.

These considerations are not mere quibbling over words; they bring out clearly an important point, namely, that the measurable properties of an object must resemble in some special way the property number, since they can be fitly represented by the same symbols; they must have some quality common with number. We must proceed to ask what this common quality is, and the best way to begin is to examine the property number rather more closely.

The number of a sack of potatoes, or, as it is more usually expressed, the number of potatoes contained in it, is ascertained by the process of counting. Counting is inseparably connected in our minds to-day with numerals, but the process can be, and at an earlier stage of civilization was, carried on without them. Without any use of numerals I can determine whether the number of one sack of potatoes is equal to that of another. For this purpose I take a potato from one sack, mark it in some way to distinguish it from the rest (e.g. by putting it into a box), and then perform a similar operation on a potato from the other sack. I then repeat this double operation continually until I have exhausted the potatoes from one sack. If the operation which exhausts the potatoes from one sack exhausts also the potatoes from the other, then I know that the sacks had the same number of potatoes; if not, then the sack which is not exhausted had a larger number of potatoes than the other.

THE RULES FOR COUNTING

This process could be applied equally well if the objects counted against each other were not of the same nature. The potatoes in a sack can be counted, not only against another collection of potatoes, but also against the men in a regiment or against the days in the year. The "mark," which is used for distinguishing the objects in the process of counting, may have to be altered to suit the objects counted, but some other suitable mark could be found which would enable the process to be carried out. If, having never heard of counting before, we applied the process to all kinds of different objects, we should soon discover certain rules which would enable us to abbreviate and simplify the process considerably. These rules appear to us to-day so obvious as to be hardly worth stating, but as they are undoubtedly employed in modern methods of counting, we must notice them here. The first is that if two sets of objects, when counted against a third set, are found to have the, same number as that third set, then, when counted against each other they will be found to have the same number. This rule enables us to determine whether two sets of objects have the same number without bringing them together;

if I want to find out whether the number of potatoes in the sack I propose to buy is the same as that in a sack I have at home, I need not bring my sack to the shop; I can count the potatoes at the shop against some third collection, take this collection home, and count it against my potatoes. Accordingly the discovery of this first rule immediately suggests the use of portable collections which can be counted, first against one collection and then against another, in order to ascertain whether these two have the same number.

The value of this suggestion is increased greatly by the discovery of a second rule. It is that by starting with a single object and continually adding to it another single object, we can build up a series of collections of which one will have the same number as any other collection whatsoever. This rule helps us in two ways. First, since it states that it is possible to make a standard series of collections one of which will have the same number as any other collection, it suggests that it might be well to count collections, not against each other, but against a standard series of collections. If we could carry this standard series about with us, we could always ascertain whether any one collection had the same number as any other by observing whether the member of the standard series which had the same number as the first had also the same number as the second. Next, it shows us how to make such a standard series with the least possible cumbrousness. If we had to have a totally different collection for each member of the standard series, the whole series would be impossibly cumbrous; but our rule shows that the earlier members of the series (that is those with the smaller number) may be all parts of the later members. Suppose we have a collection of objects, each distinguishable from each other, and agree to take one of these objects as the first member of the series; this object together with some other as the next member; these objects with yet another as the next member; and so on. Then we shall obtain, according to our rule, a series, some member of which has the same number as any other collection we want to count, and yet the number of objects, in all the members of the standard series taken together, will not be greater than that of the largest collection we want to count.

And, of course, this is the process actually adopted. For the successive members of the standard series compounded in this way, primitive man chose, as portable, distinguishable objects, his fingers and toes. Civilized man invented numerals for the same purpose. Numerals are simply distinguishable objects out of which we build our standard series of collections by adding them in turn to previous members of the series. The first member of our standard series is 1, the next 1, 2, the next 1, 2, 3 and so on. We count other collections against these members of the standard series and so ascertain whether or no two collections so counted have the same number. By an ingenious convention we describe which member of the series has the same number as a collection counted against it by quoting simply the last numeral in that member; we describe the fact that the collection of the days of the week has the same number as the collection 1, 2, 3, 4, 5, 6, 7, by saying "that the number" of the days of the week is 7. But when we say that what we really mean, and what is really important, is that this collection has the same number as the collection of numerals (taken in the standard order) which ends in 7 and the same number as any other collection which also has the same number as the collection of numerals which ends in 7.[1]

The two rules that have been mentioned are necessary to explain what we mean by "the number" of a collection and how we ascertain that number. There is a third rule which is of great importance in the use of numbers. We often want to know what is the number of a collection which is formed by combining two other collections of which the numbers are known, or, as it is usually called, adding the two collections. For instance we may ask what is the number of the collection made by adding a collection of 2 objects to a collection of 3 objects. We all know the answer, 5. It can be found by arguing thus: The first collection can be counted against the numerals 1, 2; the second against the numerals 1, 2, 3. But the numerals 1, 2, 3, 1, 2, a collection formed by adding the two first collections, can be counted against 1, 2, 3, 4, 5. Therefore the number of the combined collection is 5. However, a little examination will show that in reaching this conclusion we have made use of another rule, namely that if two collections A and a, have the same number, and two other collections B and b, have the same number, then the collection formed by adding A to B has the same number as that formed by adding a to b; in other words, equals added to equals produce equal sums. This is a third rule about numbers and counting; it is quite as important as the other two rules; all three are so obvious to us to-day that we never think about them, but they must have been definitely discovered at some time in the history of mankind, and without them all, our habitual use of numbers would be impossible.

WHAT PROPERTIES ARE MEASURABLE?

And now, after this discussion of number, we can return to the other measurable properties of objects which, like number, can be represented by numerals. We can now say more definitely what is the characteristic of these properties which makes them measurable. It is that there are rules true of these properties, closely analogous to the rules on which the use of number depends. If a property is to be measurable it must be such that (1) two

---

[1] Numerals have also an immense advantage over fingers and toes as objects of which the standard series may be formed, in that the series can be extended indefinitely by a simple rule which automatically gives names to any new numerals that may be required. Even if we have never hitherto had reason to carry the series beyond (say) 131679 in order to count all the collections we have met with, when we do meet at last with a larger collection, we know at once that the objects we must add to our standard series are 131680, 131681, and so on. This is a triumph of conventional nomenclature, much more satisfactory than the old convention that when we have exhausted our fingers we must begin on our toes, but it is not essentially different.

objects which are the same in respect of that property as some third object are the same as each other; (2) by adding objects successively we must be able to make a standard series one member of which will be the same in respect of the property as any other object we want to measure; (3) equals added to equals produce equal sums. In order to make a property measurable we must find some method of judging equality and of adding objects, such that these rules are true.

Let me explain what is meant by using as an example the measurable property, weight.

Weight is measured by the balance. Two bodies are judged to have the same weight if, when they are placed in opposite pans, neither tends to sink; and two bodies are added in respect of weight when they are both placed on the same pan of the balance. With these definitions of equality and addition, it is found that the three rules are obeyed. (1) If the body A balances the body B, and B balances C, then A balances C. (2) By placing a body in one pan and continually adding it to others, collections can be built up which will balance any other body placed in the other pan. (3) If the body A balances the body B, and C balances D, then A and C in the same pan will balance B and D in the other pan. To make the matter yet clearer let us take another measurable property, length. Two straight rods are judged equal in length, if they can be placed so that both ends of one are contiguous to both ends of the other; they are added in respect of length, when they are placed with one end of one contiguous with one end of the other, while the two form a single straight rod. Here again we find the three rules fulfilled. Bodies which are equal in length to the same body are equal in length to each other. By adding successively rods to each other, a rod can be built up which is equal to any other rod. And equal rods added to equal rods produce equal rods. Length is therefore a measurable property.

It is because these rules are true that measurement of these properties is useful and possible; it is these rules that make the measurable properties so similar to numbers, that it is possible and useful to represent them by numerals the primary purpose of which is to represent numbers. It is because of them that it is possible to find one, and only one numeral, which will fitly represent each property; and it is because of them, that these numerals, when they are found, tell us something useful about the properties. One such use arises in the combination of bodies possessing the properties. We may want to know how the property varies when bodies possessing it are added in the way characteristic of measurement. When we have assigned numerals to represent the property we shall know that the body with the property 2 added to that with the property 3 will have the same property as that with the property 5, or as the combination of the bodies with properties 4 and 1. This is not the place to examine exactly how these conclusions are shown to be universally valid; but they are valid only because the three rules are true.

THE LAWS OF MEASUREMENT

But what is the nature of these rules? They are laws established by definite experiment. The word "rule" has been used hitherto, because it is not quite certain whether they are truly laws in their application to number; but they certainly are laws in their application to other measurable properties, such as weight or length. The fact that the rules are true can be, and must be, determined by experiment in the same way as the fact that any other laws are true. Perhaps it may have appeared to the reader that the rules must be true; that it requires no experiment to determine that bodies which balance the same body will balance each other; and that it is inconceivable that this rule should not be true. But I think he will change his opinion, if it is pointed out that the rule is actually true only in certain conditions; for instance, it is only true if the balance is a good one, and has arms of equal length and pans of equal weight. If the arms were unequal, the rule would not be found to be true unless it were carefully prescribed in which pan the bodies were placed during the judgment of equality. Again, the rules would not be true of the property length, unless the rods were straight and were rigid. In implying that the balance is good, and the rods straight and rigid, we have implied definite laws which must be true if the properties are to be measurable, namely that it is possible to make a perfect balance, and that there are rods which are straight and rigid. These are experimental laws; they could not be known apart from definite experiment and observation of the external world; they are not self-evident.

Accordingly the process of discovering that a property is measurable in the way that has been described, and setting up a process for measuring it, is one that rests entirely upon experimental inquiry. It is a part, and a most important part, of experimental science. Whenever a new branch of physics is opened up (for, as has been said, physics is the science that deals with such processes of measurement), the first step is always to find some process for measuring the new properties that are investigated; and it is not until this problem has been solved, that any great progress can be made along the branch. Its solution demands the discovery of new laws. We can actually trace the development of new measurable properties in this way in the history of science. Before the dawn of definite history, laws had been discovered which made measurable some of the properties employed by modern science. History practically begins with the Greeks, but before their time the properties, weight, length, volume, and area had been found to be measurable; the establishment of the necessary laws had probably occurred in the great period of Babylonian and Egyptian civilization. The Greeks, largely in the person of Archimedes, found how to measure force by establishing the laws of the lever, and other mechanical systems. Again from the earliest era, there have been rough methods of measuring periods of time,[2] but a true method, really obeying the three rules, was not discovered till the seventeenth century; it arose out of Galileo's laws of the pendulum. Modern science has added greatly to the list of measurable properties; the science of electricity is based on the discovery, by Cavendish and Coulomb, of the law necessary to measure an electric charge; on the laws, discovered by Œrsted and Ampère, necessary to measure an electric current; and on the laws, discovered by Ohm and Kirchhoff, necessary to measure electrical resistance. And the discovery of similar laws has made possible the development of other branches of physics.

But, it may be asked, has there ever been a failure to discover the necessary laws? The answer is that there are certainly many properties which are not measurable in the sense that we have been discussing; there are more properties, definitely recognized by science, that are not so measurable than are so measurable. But, as will appear presently, the very nature of these properties makes it impossible that they should be measured in this way. For the only properties to which this kind of measurement seems conceivably applicable, are those which fulfil the condition stated provisionally on p. 111; they must be such that the combination of objects possessing the property increases that property. For this is the fundamental significance of the property number; it is something that is increased by addition; any property which does not agree with number in this matter cannot be very closely related to number and cannot possibly be measured by the scheme that has been described. But it will be seen that fulfilment of this condition only makes rule (2) true; it is at least conceivable that a property might obey rule (2) and not rules (1) and (3). Does that ever happen, or can we always find methods of addition and of judging equality such that, if rule (2) is true, the laws are such that rules (1) and (3) are also true? In the vast majority of cases we can find such methods and such laws; and it is a very remarkable fact that we can; it is only one more instance of the way in which nature kindly falls in with our ideas of what ought to be. But I think there is one case in which the necessary methods and laws have not yet been found and are not likely to be found. It is a very difficult matter concerning which even expert physicists might differ, and so no discussion of it can be entered on here. But it is mentioned in order to impress the reader with the fact that measurement does depend upon experimental laws; that it does depend upon the facts of the external world; and that it is not wholly within our power to determine whether we will or will not measure a certain property. That is the feature of measurement which it is really important to grasp for a proper understanding of science.

[2] By a period of time I mean the thing that is measured when we say that it took us 3 hours to do so-and-so. This is a different "time" from that which is measured when we say it is 3 o'clock. The difference is rather abstruse and cannot be discussed here; but it may be mentioned that the "measurement" involved in "3 o'clock" is more like that discussed later in the chapter.

The Scientific Attitude

Charles Sanders Peirce

THE SCIENTIFIC ATTITUDE

43. If we endeavor to form our conceptions upon history and life, we remark three classes of men. The first consists of those for whom the chief thing is the qualities of feelings. These men create art. The second consists of the practical men, who carry on the business of the world. They respect nothing but power, and respect power only so far as it [is] exercized. The third class consists of men to whom nothing seems great but reason. If force interests them, it is not in its exertion, but in that it has a reason and a law. For men of the first class, nature is a picture; for men of the second class, it is an opportunity; for men of the third class, it is a cosmos, so admirable, that to penetrate to its ways seems to them the only thing that makes life worth living. These are the men whom we see possessed by a passion to learn, just as other men have a passion to teach and to disseminate their influence. If they do not give themselves over completely to their passion to learn, it is because they exercise self-control. Those are the natural scientific men; and they are the only men that have any real success in scientific research.

44. If we are to define science, not in the sense of stuffing it into an artificial pigeon-hole where it may be found again by some insignificant mark, but in the sense of characterizing it as a living historic entity, we must conceive it as that about which such men as I have described busy themselves. As such, it does not consist so much in *knowing,* nor even in "organized knowledge," as it does in diligent inquiry into truth for truth's sake, without any sort of axe to grind, nor for the sake of the delight of contemplating it, but from an impulse to penetrate into the reason of things. This is the sense in which this book is entitled a History of *Science.* Science and philosophy seem to have been changed in their cradles. For it is not knowing, but the love of learning, that characterizes the scientific man; while the "philosopher" is a man with a system which he thinks embodies all that is best worth knowing. If a man burns to learn and sets himself to comparing his ideas with experimental results in order that he may correct those ideas, every

From Ch. 2 "Lessons from the History of Science" and Ch. 3 "Notes on Scientific Philosophy," with deletions and some footnotes omitted, in *Collected Papers of Charles Sanders Peirce,* Vol. I. Reprinted by permission of the publishers from Charles Hartshorne & Paul Weiss, eds. *Collected Papers of Charles Sanders Peirce,* Vol. 1. Cambridge, Mass.: Harvard University Press, Copyright 1931, 1932, 1959, 1960, by the President and Fellows of Harvard College.

scientific man will recognize him as a brother, no matter how small his knowledge may be.

45. But if a man occupies himself with investigating the truth of some question for some ulterior purpose, such as to make money, or to amend his life, or to benefit his fellows, he may be ever so much better than a scientific man, if you will—to discuss that would be aside from the question—but he is not a scientific man. For example, there are numbers of chemists who occupy themselves exclusively with the study of dyestuffs. They discover facts that are useful to scientific chemistry; but they do not rank as genuine scientific men. The genuine scientific chemist cares just as much to learn about erbium—the extreme rarity of which renders it commercially unimportant—as he does about iron. He is more eager to learn about erbium if the knowledge of it would do more to complete his conception of the Periodic Law, which expresses the mutual relations of the elements.

THE SCIENTIFIC IMAGINATION

46. When a man desires ardently to know the truth, his first effort will be to imagine what that truth can be. He cannot prosecute his pursuit long without finding that imagination unbridled is sure to carry him off the track. Yet nevertheless, it remains true that there is, after all, nothing but imagination that can ever supply him an inkling of the truth. He can stare stupidly at phenomena; but in the absence of imagination they will not connect themselves together in any rational way. Just as for Peter Bell a cowslip was nothing but a cowslip, so for thousands of men a falling apple was nothing but a falling apple; and to compare it to the moon would by them be deemed "fanciful."

47. It is not too much to say that next after the passion to learn there is no quality so indispensable to the successful prosecution of science as imagination. Find me a people whose early medicine is not mixed up with magic and incantations, and I will find you a people devoid of all scientific ability. There is no magic in the medical Papyrus Ebers. The stolid Egyptian saw nothing in disease but derangemnet of the affected organ. There never was any true Egyptian science.

48. There are, no doubt, kinds of imagination of no value in science, mere artistic imagination, mere dreaming of opportunities for gain. The scientific imagination dreams of explanation and laws.

.   .   .

THE STUDY OF THE USELESS

75. . . . . The old-fashioned political economist adored, as alone capable of redeeming the human race, the glorious principle of individual greed, although, as this principle requires for its action hypocrisy and fraud, he gen-

erally threw in some dash of inconsistent concessions to virtue, as a sop to the vulgar Cerberus. But it is easy to see that the only kind of science this principle would favor would be such as is immediately remunerative with a great preference for such as can be kept secret, like the modern sciences of dyeing and perfumery. Kepler's discovery rendered Newton possible, and Newton rendered modern physics possible, with the steam engine, electricity, and all the other sources of the stupendous fortunes of our age. But Kepler's discovery would not have been possible without the doctrine of conics. Now contemporaries of Kepler—such penetrating minds as Descartes and Pascal —were abandoning the study of geometry (in which they included what we now call the differential calculus, so far as that had at that time any existence) because they said it was so UTTERLY USELESS. There was the future of the human race almost trembling in the balance; for had not the geometry of conic sections already been worked out in large measure, and had their opinion that only sciences apparently useful ought to be pursued, [prevailed] the nineteenth century would have had none of those characters which distinguish it from the *ancien régime*.

76. True science is distinctively the study of useless things. For the useful things will get studied without the aid of scientific men. To employ these rare minds on such work is like running a steam engine by burning diamonds.

. . .

THE UNCERTAINTY OF SCIENTIFIC RESULTS

120. It is a great mistake to suppose that the mind of the active scientist is filled with propositions which, if not proved beyond all reasonable cavil, are at least extremely probable. On the contrary, he entertains hypotheses which are almost wildly incredible, and treats them with respect for the time being. Why does he do this? Simply because any scientific proposition whatever is always liable to be refuted and dropped at short notice. A hypothesis is something which looks as if it might be true and were true, and which is capable of verification or refutation by comparison with facts. The best hypothesis, in the sense of the one most recommending itself to the inquirer, is the one which can be the most readily refuted if it is false. This far outweighs the trifling merit of being likely. For after all, what is a *likely* hypothesis? It is one which falls in with our preconceived ideas. But these may be wrong. Their errors are just what the scientific man is out gunning for more particularly. But if a hypothesis can quickly and easily be cleared away so as to go toward leaving the field free for the main struggle, this is an immense advantage.

121. Retroduction goes upon the hope that there is sufficient affinity between the reasoner's mind and nature's to render guessing not altogether

hopeless, provided each guess is checked by comparison with observation. It is true that agreement does not show the guess is right; but if it is wrong it must ultimately get found out. The effort should therefore be to make each hypothesis, which is practically no more than a question, as near an even bet as possible.

.   .   .

THE FIRST RULE OF REASON

135. Upon this first, and in one sense this sole, rule of reason, that in order to learn you must desire to learn, and in so desiring not to be satisfied with what you already incline to think, there follows one corollary which itself deserves to be inscribed upon every wall of the city of philosophy:

Do not block the way of inquiry.

136. Although it is better to be methodical in our investigations, and to consider the economics of research, yet there is no positive sin against logic in *trying* any theory which may come into our heads, so long as it is adopted in such a sense as to permit the investigation to go on unimpeded and undiscouraged. On the other hand, to set up a philosophy which barricades the road of further advance toward the truth is the one unpardonable offence in reasoning, as it is also the one to which metaphysicians have in all ages shown themselves the most addicted.

Let me call your attention to four familiar shapes in which this venomous error assails our knowledge:

137. The first is the shape of absolute assertion. That we can be sure of nothing in science is an ancient truth. The Academy taught it. Yet science has been infested with overconfident assertion, especially on the part of the third-rate and fourth-rate men, who have been more concerned with teaching than with learning, at all times. No doubt some of the geometries still teach as a self-evident truth the proposition that if two straight lines in one plane meet a third straight line so as to make the sum of the internal angles on one side less than two right angles, those two lines will meet on that side if sufficiently prolonged. Euclid, whose logic was more careful, only reckoned this proposition as a *Postulate*, or arbitrary Hypothesis. Yet even he places among his axioms the proposition that a part is less than its whole, and falls into several conflicts with our most modern geometry in consequence. But why need we stop to consider cases where some subtlety of thought is required to see that the assertion is not warranted when every book which applies philosophy to the conduct of life lays down as positive certainty propositions which it is quite as easy to doubt as to believe?

138. The second bar which philosophers often set up across the roadway of inquiry lies in maintaining that this, that, and the other never can be known. When Auguste Comte was pressed to specify any matter of positive

fact to the knowledge of which no man could by any possibility attain, he instanced the knowledge of the chemical composition of the fixed stars; and you may see his answer set down in the *Philosophie positive*.[1] But the ink was scarcely dry upon the printed page before the spectroscope was discovered and that which he had deemed absolutely unknowable was well on the way of getting ascertained. It is easy enough to mention a question the answer to which is not known to me today. But to aver that that answer will not be known tomorrow is somewhat risky; for oftentimes it is precisely the least expected truth which is turned up under the ploughshare of research. And when it comes to positive assertion that the truth never will be found out, that, in the light of the history of our time, seems to me more hazardous than the venture of Andrée.[2]

139. The third philosophical stratagem for cutting off inquiry consists in maintaining that this, that, or the other element of science is basic, ultimate, independent of aught else, and utterly inexplicable—not so much from any defect in our knowing as because there is nothing beneath it to know. The only type of reasoning by which such a conclusion could possibly be reached is *retroduction*. Now nothing justifies a retroductive inference except its affording an explanation of the facts. It is, however, no explanation at all of a fact to pronounce it *inexplicable*. That, therefore, is a conclusion which no reasoning can ever justify or excuse.

140. The last philosophical obstacle to the advance of knowledge which I intend to mention is the holding that this or that law or truth has found its last and perfect formulation—and especially that the ordinary and usual course of nature never can be broken through. "Stones do not fall from heaven," said Laplace, although they had been falling upon inhabited ground every day from the earliest times. But there is no kind of inference which can lend the slightest probability to any such absolute denial of an unusual phenomenon.

FALLIBILISM, CONTINUITY, AND EVOLUTION

141. All positive reasoning is of the nature of judging the proportion of something in a whole collection by the proportion found in a sample. Accordingly, there are three things to which we can never hope to attain by reasoning, namely, absolute certainty, absolute exactitude, absolute universality. We cannot be absolutely certain that our conclusions are even approximately true; for the sample may be utterly unlike the unsampled part of the collection. We cannot pretend to be even probably exact; because the sample consists of but a finite number of instances and only admits special values of the proportion sought. Finally, even if we could ascertain with absolute certainty

---

[1] 19me leçon.
[2] In 1897 Salomon August Andrée attempted to fly over the polar regions in a balloon. He died in the attempt.

and exactness that the ratio of sinful men to all men was as 1 to 1; still among the infinite generations of men there would be room for any finite number of sinless men without violating the proportion. The case is the same with a seven legged calf.

59 Fifty Years of Poaching in Science

Albert Szent-Györgyi

I have always been an amateur scientist but a professional poacher. I have never been married to any single principle, and my relations to science have been most promiscuous. This is perhaps the reason why I was chosen to discuss here The Relationship Between the Biological and Physical Sciences.

That title suggests some basic difference between the animate and inanimate world, and so at the outset we find ourselves in a contradiction. We probably all feel that there *is* some basic difference between the living and the non-living, while as scientists we cannot believe that the laws of the universe should lose their validity at the surface of our skin. Life must actually have been created by these laws. So our first step has to be to clear our minds about this contradiction.

They can be so cleared, to a great extent, by the simple fact that things can be put together in two different ways, at random or meaningfully. This is a cardinal point. I would like to illustrate it by an example. Six toothpicks and two corks on a table will be but six toothpicks and two corks. Their qualities are additive. However, if I put these toothpicks and corks together in a specific way, they will make a (somewhat symbolic) horse which can no longer be fully described in terms of the constituents. New qualities are developed which are no longer additive. With a few more pieces I could set a man on this horse; then I would again have something new—neither a horse nor a man but a man-on-a-horse. This is what is called "organization," putting things together in a meaningful way; it is one of the basic features of nature. If elementary particles are put together to form an atomic nucleus, something new is created which can no longer be described in terms of elementary particles. The same happens over again if you surround this nucleus by electrons and build an atom, when you put atoms together to form a molecule, etc. Inanimate nature stops at the low level of organization of simple molecules.

This article by Albert Szent-Györgyi appeared in the Graduate Faculties News-letter, Columbia University, March, 1966. The article is based on a lecture that Dr. Szent-Györgyi delivered (on October 25, 1965) at Columbia University for The Symposium on the Relationship between the Biological and Physical Sciences. The Symposium is supported by The New York State Science and Technology Foundation. Reprinted by permission of Columbia University and Dr. Szent-Györgyi.

But living systems go on and combine molecules to form macromolecules, macromolecules to form organelles (such as nuclei, mitochondria, chloroplasts, ribosomes or membranes) and eventually put all these together to form the greatest wonder of creation, a cell, with its astounding inner regulations. Then it goes on putting cells together to form "higher organisms" and increasingly more complex individuals, of which you are an example. At every step new, more complex and subtle qualities are created, and so in the end we are faced with properties which have no parallel in the inanimate world, though the basic rules remain unchanged.

It is most important for the biologist to give himself an account of these relations when he asks himself on which level of organization to work when embarking on research with the desire to understand life. Those who like to express themselves in the language of mathematics do well to keep to lower levels. Any level of organization is fascinating and offers new vistas and horizons, but we must not lose our bearings or else we may fall victim to the simple idea that any level of organization can best be understood by pulling it to pieces, by a study of its components—that is, the study of the next lower level. This may make us dive to lower and lower levels in the hope of finding the secret of life there. This made, out of my own life, a wild-goose chase. I started my experimental work with rabbits, but I found rabbits too complex, so I shifted to a lower level and studied bacteria; I became a bacteriologist. But soon I found bacteria too complex, and shifted to molecules and became a biochemist. So I spent my life in the hunt for the secret of life.

We do not know what life is but, all the same, know life from death. I know that my cat is dead when it moves no more, has no reflexes and leaves my carpet clean—that is, no longer transforms chemical energy into mechanic, electric or osmotic work. These transformations of energy are most closely linked up with the very nature of life. We, ourselves, get our energies by burning our food and transducing its chemical energy into heat and various sorts of work.

So for twenty years I studied energy transformations by going to the source of the vital energies and worked on biological oxidation on the molecular level. These studies netted me a Nobel Prize (which was most pleasant) but left me eventually high and dry without a better understanding. So I turned to muscle, the seat of the most violent and massive energy transformations. This study led me and my associates to the discovery of a new muscle protein, and we could then ourselves make little muscles and make them jump outside the body. To see these little artificial muscles jump for the first time was, perhaps, the most exciting experience of my scientific life, and I felt sure that in a fortnight I would understand everything. Then I worked for twenty more years on muscle and learned not a thing. The more I knew, the less I understood; and I was afraid to finish my life with knowing everything and understanding nothing. Evidently something very basic was missing. I thought that in order to understand I had to go one level lower, to electrons, and—with graying hair—I began to muddle in quantum mechanics. So I finished up with electrons. But electrons are just electrons and have no life at all. Evidently on the way I lost life; it had run out between my fingers.

I do not regret this wild-goose chase—because it made me wiser and I know, now, that all levels of organization are equally important and we have to know something about all of them if we want to approach life. The biologist wants to read in the book of creation. If there was a creator, he could not have been a molecular biologist only. He must have known a great deal of quantum mechanics and mathematics, too, and must have been a good geneticist and physiologist. He must have been all of that, and so if we want to follow his trail and read in the book of creation, we must be a bit of everything. Even if limiting our work to a single level, we have to keep the whole in mind. Naturally, the higher we climb on the ladder of organization and complexity, the less our material becomes accessible to mathematical analysis, but we must not think ourselves to be scientists only when speaking in equations.

To finish my life's story, now I am climbing up again on the ladder of organization on which I worked my way down through half a century, and am working on the cellular level—for the cell is the cornerstone, the greatest wonder, of living nature, and is, today, a somewhat neglected dimension. Not only do I not regret my earlier climbing down to electrons; I even feel I might not have climbed down far enough, and it is possible that we have to wait for discovery of new science, some sort of super-wave-mechanics, till we can really approach life; but electrons and quantum mechanics are the limit set to the biologist by physics today.

Quantum mechanics, which deals with the electronic structure of molecules, taught me something most important: how wonderfully subtle and complex is a structure of even a simple molecule. As a student I learned that the benzene ring is a hexagon, and this was all there was to it. Quantum mechanics has taught me that in the simplest aromatic molecule every C atom has its individuality which can be described only by half a dozen electronic indices, which give to the molecule a very sharp profile, a very specific individuality, most complex in the very complex molecules of the living edifice. This brings me to the problem on which I plan to spend the next fifty years of my research. The problem is this: most biological reactions are chain reactions. To interact in a chain, these precisely built molecules must fit together most precisely, as the cogwheels of a Swiss watch do. But if this is so, then how can such a system develop at all? For if any one of the very specific cogwheels in these chains is changed, then the whole system must simply become inoperative. Saying that it can be improved by random mutation of one link sounds to me like saying that you could improve a Swiss watch by dropping it and thus bending one of its wheels or axles. To get a better watch all the wheels must be changed simultaneously to make a good fit again.

There is no need to descend into the electronic world for examples on this line. In the winter, at Woods Hole, the sea gulls are my main company. These gulls, the "herring gulls," have a red patch on their beaks. This red patch has an important meaning, for the gull feeds its babies by going out fishing and swallowing the fish it has caught. Then, on coming home, the hungry baby gull knocks at the red spot. This elicits a reflex of regurgitation in mama, and the baby takes the fish from her gullet. All this may sound very simple, but it involves a whole series of most complicated chain reactions with a horribly complex underlying nervous mechanism. How could such a system develop? The red spot would make no sense without the complex nervous mechanism of the knocking baby and that of the regurgitating mother. All this had to be developed simultaneously, which, as a random mutation, has a probability of zero. I am unable to approach this problem without supposing an innate *drive* in living matter to perfect itself.

I know that many of my colleagues, especially the molecular biologists, will be horrified, if not disgusted, to hear me talk about a "drive" and will call me a "vitalist," which is worse than to be called a communist. But I think that the use of such words as "drive" does no harm if we do not imagine we have found an explanation by finding a name. If we look upon such words as simply denoting great unsolved problems of science, they can even lead to useful experimentation. By "drive" I denote here simply the ability of life to maintain and improve itself. You know this from your daily life. You know well that if you use your car too much and your legs too little, your car gets worn out while your legs atrophy, just fade away. This is one of the most characteristic differences between the living and non-living. The non-living is worn out by use, while the living is improved, developed by it. Life keeps life going, building up and improving itself, while inactivity makes it go to pieces.

An early American physiologist, [Henry Pickering] Bowditch, discovered an unexpected phenomenon which reflects these relations and makes them accessible to experimentation. I am alluding to his "staircase." If I ask you what you expect if I make the heart rest for a little while and then make it go again, your guess will probably be that the first beat after the rest will be stronger than the last one before it. But the opposite is true: it will be weaker, and the tension developed will gradually rise to its original level in the subsequent beats. Here is the same problem in a nutshell. Dr. Hajdu and I have tried to find out what is behind this "staircase" phenonemon and found that what happens is simply that, in rest, potassium leaks out of the muscle fibers, and is pumped back in the subsequent contractions. As you all know, for the muscle to work well the potassium must have a high concentration inside the fibers and low outside them. What happens in rest is an increase in randomness; the entropy of the potassium increases in rest and decreases again in function. Function thus keeps the living system on its low entropy state, in its highly specialized spatial structure—puts or keeps everything in its place. Life thus keeps life going, building up itself. These are not merely abstruse problems of biology. We could show, with Dr. Hajdu, that if your heart fails in some infectious disease and you die, this is because it behaves like a heart which rested too much; and if digitalis pulls you through, it is by doing to it what work should have done.

But the heart may be too complex to allow a more detailed analysis, and according to the rules of my life I should take you lower down from the molecular to the electronic dimension. So I will talk about "charge transfer." It has become clear during the last decades that under certain conditions an electron of a molecule, say molecule A, can go over to an orbital of another molecule, molecule B. For this the two molecules must be in very intimate contact; electronic orbitals must overlap. Evidently the electron goes over because by its doing so the free energy of the system decreases and the system becomes more stable. The "charge transfer energy" will thus contribute to the forces keeping the two molecules together. Without it the system would be less stable, would tend more to go to pieces. Here then is a simple example of function maintaining structure. We could continue this spirited game and add molecules $C, D, E,$ and F to the system and imagine the electrons flowing from B to C, and from there to D, E and F continuously.

This is not a meaningless speculation, a "jeux d'esprit," for all of our vital energies are actually derived from such an electron flow. The energies which are driving you are the energies which these "flowing" electrons gradually lose in this transfer from one molecule to the other. Finally this energy is translated into "high energy-phosphate," the immediate source of the energy by which your cells live. This flow of electrons can be expected to help keep the molecules of the chain together, in their very specific steric relations, and we can expect the system to tend to go to pieces as soon as the electron flow stops. We have thus a clear-cut example of life being kept in the living condition by life itself, kept by work in good working order. We can even expect the system of our molecules A and B to tend to add further molecules, to decrease free energy further, and thereby to become more stable, better and more complex. So actually we arrive at a "drive" to improvement, to building up.

In thermodynamics such a system as I just described would be called an "open system," which reaches its energy minimum—that is, its greatest stability—by working. So the "drive" can even be expressed in the idioms of accredited science.

These problems are so fascinating that I would like to spend a few more minutes with them. Many years ago I proposed, with my colleagues, Isenberg and McLaughlin, that electrons may be transferred by certain molecules at specific points only, and showed that indoles will probably transfer their electron at Carbon No. 3. Many of the drugs which provoke hallucination, the "hallucinogens," contain an indole ring. With Karreman and Isenberg we also showed that hallucinogens have a strong tendency to give off electrons, are good "electron donors." We concluded that hallucination, in this case, may be caused by transfer of electrons from the drug to the nerve cell. Both our assumptions have found corroboration very recently—the first by Green and Martieu in Pullman's laboratory, the latter by Snyder and Merrill, who showed that the hallucinogenic property goes parallel to the electron-donating ability in a great number of hallucinogens and related compounds.

In order to be able to pass an electron on at a certain point, the molecules must be fitted together most accurately, and linked together strongly in two dimensions to form a "membrane" as in the case of mitochondria, where all our vital energies are generated by the flow of electrons. So these considerations may lead even to an answer of one of the most puzzling problems of biology: what is a membrane? The knowledge gained might also help to cure mysterious diseases, answer problems of everyday medicine.

Since I was not afraid to use the word *drive,* I might as well be even more audacious and use the word *wisdom.* I am not the first to do so. The great American physiologist, Walter B. Cannon, talked and wrote a great deal about the "wisdom of the body." He never talked about the "wisdom of the mind." (He seems to have found little of it there.)

I would like to illustrate with one example what I call "wisdom." If you look at a motor nerve cell, which gives the immediate command to your muscles to contract, you will find a great number of fibers from other nerve cells, hundreds of them, ending at its surface. These fibers bring messages from faraway nerve centers and modify the action of this motor nerve cell and the motion this nerve cell will induce.

Perhaps I could make this clearer by a little story about a kitten which shared my tent once in Cornwall, England. One day a snake crept into our tent. My kitten stiffened in horror. When I touched its tail, the kitten jumped up vertically about two feet high. This happened because the nerve fibers which ended on the motor nerve cells conveyed the message that there was danger of life and any motion had to be fast and violent. These messages came, as I said, from faraway complex nerve centers which worked up and evaluated the visual impressions of my kitten.

The problem I want to bring out here is this: how could these hundreds of nerve fibers, coming from faraway nerve centers, ever find the right motor nerve cell? All this could not have been coded into the egg cell from which my kitten grew. Of course, this egg cell must have contained (in conjunction with the sperm) all the information which is necessary to build such a wondrous organism as a cat. But all those excessively complex networks which make a brain could not have been inscribed into the egg cell. The egg cell cannot be a blueprint; it can only be an instruction manual, which contains instructions on how to build macromolecular systems with sufficient wisdom to find their place and function. That all this could not have been inscribed in the egg cell we could show by cutting these nerve fibers and introducing a new factor of which the egg did not know. We could expect that the fibers would again find their severed ends through their own wisdom. As suggested by the experiments of Sperry, even if we should cut a great number of these fibers simultaneously, they would not get mixed up and each of them would find its very own ending again—a really remarkable wisdom.

This "wisdom" may be even much more difficult to understand than the "drive," but also must have its well-defined mechanism. Perhaps this "wisdom" and "drive" are essentially the same, and may be the property of living matter in general—the property that has driven matter to generate life, which then tends to build its own mechanisms. I feel strongly that, for instance, the human speech center was not developed by random mutation, but had to be developed as soon as man had something to say—the function generating its own mechanism. Of course I know that to make any such change permanent, the change must be communicated by some sort of feedback mechanism from periphery to DNA. We do not know of any such feedback, but it was only a few years ago that we had not the least idea of how DNA communicates with the periphery either.

Maybe this drive is not an exclusive property of living systems, but is the property of matter in general. We know today that fairly complex organic molecules can be built without the intervention of living matter, while by the word "organic" our scientific fathers wanted to express the idea that it is only life which can build such molecules. Sidney Fox in Florida even builds protein-like substances without life. It may have been this innate drive of matter which led to the origin of life and played, later, an important hand in its evolution.

I have tried to show that many of the greatest problems of biology are unsolved, if not untouched, and that we can expect to solve them by applying physics. But whether physics in its present state allows us the analysis of the underlying mechanisms, I do not know. I rather doubt it, and we may have to wait for the discovery of entirely new physical sciences till we can penetrate deeper into the nature of life. In my student days we hardly knew more than the structure of a few amino acids and sugars, and we felt obliged to explain life. It was not so long ago that the young Max Planck was advised by one of the best physicists to become a pianist rather than a physicist because physics was a finished and closed subject to which nothing could be added. So we biologists have to look out most anxiously for any new development in physics and any new instrument physics may give into our hands. Meanwhile, we must not feel obliged to explain life with our present knowledge, and we should not shy away from admitting our ignorance—the first step towards new knowledge being to recognize ignorance.

I have been often reproached for being a vitalist, mysticist, obscurist, and teleologist while the real situation was clear and simple, there being a complete interdependence between structure and function. Since every function must have its underlying structure which must be of physical nature, all we have to do is to apply physics to structure. This may be so, but, all the same, I feel we must be careful with this interdependence as we don't know how many unknowns our equations still contain. Certainly there is such an interdependence as there is complete interdependence between the needle of your gramophone and the groove on your record; and once the needle follows the groove, your victrola must produce the sound it does. All you have forgotten is only Beethoven or Bach, whose music you might have been playing, and without whose genius your gramophone would be useless. Of course, Bach and Beethoven, too, were built of macromolecules, but, all the same, we do well to keep our reverence before their genius, which is still far beyond the possibility of detailed physical analysis. Such a speechless deep reverence and amazement before the wonders of nature is the main result of my half a century's poaching, and if I were to sum up my summary now, I would do it in Shakespeare's words, saying: "There are more things in heaven and earth, Horatio, than are dreamt of in your philosophy."

SCIENCE AND THE CURRICULUM

60   The Teaching of Science

Jean Jacques Rousseau

... Children are first restless, then curious; and this curiosity, rightly directed, is the means of development for the age with which we are dealing. Always distinguish between natural and acquired tendencies. There is a zeal for learning which has no other foundation than a wish to appear learned, and there is another which springs from man's natural curiosity about all things far or near which may affect himself. The innate desire for comfort and the impossibility of its complete satisfaction impel him to the endless search for fresh means of contributing to its satisfaction. This is the first principle of curiosity; a principle natural to the human heart, though its growth is proportional to the development of our feeling and knowledge. If a man of science were left on a desert island with his books and instruments and knowing that he must spend the rest of his life there, he would scarcely trouble himself about the solar system, the laws of attraction, or the differential calculus. He might never even open a book again; but he would never rest till he had explored the furthest corner of his island, however large it might be. Let us therefore omit from our early studies such knowledge as has no natural attraction for us, and confine ourselves to such things as instinct impels us to study.

Our island is this earth; and the most striking object we behold is the sun. As soon as we pass beyond our immediate surroundings, one or both of these must meet our eye. Thus the philosophy of most savage races is mainly directed to imaginary divisions of the earth or to the divinity of the sun.

What a sudden change you will say. Just now we were concerned with what touches ourselves, with our immediate environment, and all at once we are exploring the round world and leaping to the bounds of the universe. This change is the result of our growing strength and of the natural bent of the mind. While we were weak and feeble, self-preservation concentrated our

From the book *Emile; or, Education* by Jean Jacques Rousseau. Translated by Barbara Foxley. Everyman's Library. Reprinted by permission of E. P. Dutton & Co., Inc. Also reprinted by permission of J. M. Dent & Sons Ltd.: Publishers. This book was first published in 1762.

attention on ourselves; now that we are strong and powerful, the desire for a wider sphere carries us beyond ourselves as far as our eyes can reach. But as the intellectual world is still unknown to us, our thoughts are bounded by the visible horizon, and our understanding only develops within the limits of our vision.

Let us transform our sensations into ideas, but do not let us jump all at once from the objects of sense to objects of thought. The latter are attained by means of the former. Let the senses be the only guide for the first workings of reason. No book but the world, no teaching but that of fact. The child who reads ceases to think, he only reads. He is acquiring words not knowledge.

Teach your scholar to observe the phenomena of nature; you will soon rouse his curiosity, but if you would have it grow, do not be in too great a hurry to satisfy this curiosity. Put the problems before him and let him solve them himself. Let him know nothing because you have told him, but because he has learnt it for himself. Let him not be taught science, let him discover it. If ever you substitute authority for reason he will cease to reason; he will be a mere plaything of other people's thoughts.

You wish to teach this child geography and you provide him with globes, spheres, and maps. What elaborate preparations! What is the use of all these symbols; why not begin by showing him the real thing so that he may at least know what you are talking about?

One fine evening we are walking in a suitable place where the wide horizon gives us a full view of the setting sun, and we note the objects which mark the place where it sets. Next morning we return to the same place for a breath of fresh air before sun-rise. We see the rays of light which announce the sun's approach; the glow increases, the east seems afire, and long before the sun appears the light leads us to expect its return. Every moment you expect to see it. There it is at last! A shining point appears like a flash of lightning and soon fills the whole space; the veil of darkness rolls away, man perceives his dwelling place in fresh beauty. During the night the grass has assumed a fresher green; in the light of early dawn, and gilded by the first rays of the sun, it seems covered with a shining network of dew reflecting the light and colour. The birds raise their chorus of praise to greet the Father of life, not one of them is mute; their gentle warbling is softer than by day, it expresses the languor of a peaceful waking. All these produce an impression of freshness which seems to reach the very soul. It is a brief hour of enchantment which no man can resist; a sight so grand, so fair, so delicious, that none can behold it unmoved.

Fired with this enthusiasm, the master wishes to impart it to the child. He expects to rouse his emotion by drawing attention to his own. Mere folly! The splendour of nature lives in man's heart; to be seen, it must be felt. The child sees the objects themselves, but does not perceive their relations, and cannot hear their harmony. It needs knowledge he has not yet acquired, feelings he has not yet experienced, to receive the complex impression which results from all these separate sensations. If he has not wandered over arid plains, if his feet have not been scorched by the burning sands of the desert, if he has not breathed the hot and oppressive air reflected from the glowing rocks, how shall he delight in the fresh air of a fine morning? The scent of flowers, the beauty of foliage, the moistness of the dew, the soft turf beneath his feet, how shall all these delight his senses? How shall the song of the birds arouse voluptuous emotion if love and pleasure are still unknown to him? How shall he behold with rapture the birth of this fair day, if his imagination cannot paint the joys it may bring in its track? How can he feel the beauty of nature, while the hand that formed it is unknown?

Never tell the child what he cannot understand: no descriptions, no eloquence, no figures of speech, no poetry. The time has not come for feeling or taste. Continue to be clear and cold; the time will come only too soon when you must adopt another tone.

Brought up in the spirit of our maxims, accustomed to make his own tools and not to appeal to others until he has tried and failed, he will examine everything he sees carefully and in silence. He thinks rather than questions. Be content, therefore, to show him things at a fit season; then, when you see that his curiosity is thoroughly aroused, put some brief question which will set him trying to discover the answer.

On the present occasion when you and he have carefully observed the rising sun, when you have called his attention to the mountains and other objects visible from the same spot, after he has chattered freely about them, keep quiet for a few minutes as if lost in thought and then say, "I think the sun set over there last night; it rose here this morning. How can that be?" Say no more; if he asks questions, do not answer them; talk of something else. Let him alone, and be sure he will think about it.

To train a child to be really attentive so that he may be really impressed by any truth of experience, he must spend anxious days before he discovers that truth. If he does not learn enough in this way, there is another way of drawing his attention to the matter. Turn the question about. If he does not know how the sun gets from the place where it sets to where it rises, he knows at least how it travels from sunrise to sunset, his eyes teach him that. Use the second question to throw light on the first; either your pupil is a regular dunce or the analogy is too clear to be missed. This is his first lesson in cosmography.

As we always advance slowly from one sensible idea to another, and as we give time enough to each for him to become really familiar with it before we go on to another, and lastly as we never force our scholar's attention, we are still a long way from a knowledge of the course of the sun or the shape of the earth; but as all the apparent movements of the celestial bodies depend on the same principle, and the first observation leads on to all the rest, less effort is needed, though more time, to proceed from the diurnal revolution to the calculation of eclipses, than to get a thorough understanding of day and night.

Since the sun revolves round the earth it describes a circle, and every circle must have a centre; that we know already. This centre is invisible, it is in the middle of the earth, but we can mark out two opposite points on the earth's surface which correspond to it. A skewer passed through the three points and prolonged to the sky at either end would represent the earth's axis and the sun's daily course. A round teetotum revolving on its point represents the sky turning on its axis, the two points of the teetotum are the two poles; the child will be delighted to find one of them, and I show him the tail of the Little Bear. Here is another game for the dark. Little by little we get to know the stars, and from this comes a wish to know the planets and observe the constellations.

We saw the sun rise at midsummer, we shall see it rise at Christmas or some other fine winter's day; for you know we are no lie-a-beds and we enjoy the cold. I take care to make this second observation in the same place as the first, and if skilfully lead up to, one or other will certainly exclaim, "What a funny thing! The sun is not rising in the same place; here are our landmarks, but it is rising over there. So there is the summer east and the winter east, etc." Young teacher, you are on the right track. These examples should show you how to teach the sphere without any difficulty, taking the earth for the earth and the sun for the sun.

As a general rule—never substitute the symbol for the thing signified, unless it is impossible to show the thing itself; for the child's attention is so taken up with the symbol that he will forget what it signifies.

I consider the armillary sphere a clumsy disproportioned bit of apparatus. The confused circles and the strange figures described on it suggest witchcraft and frighten the child. The earth is too small, the circles too large and too numerous, some of them, the colures, for instance, are quite useless, and the thickness of the pasteboard gives them an appearance of solidity so that they are taken for circular masses having a real existence, and when you tell the child that these are imaginary circles, he does not know what he is looking at and is none the wiser.

We are unable to put ourselves in the child's place, we fail to enter into his thoughts, we invest him with our own ideas, and while we are following our own chain of reasoning, we merely fill his head with errors and absurdities.

Should the method of studying science be analytic or synthetic? People dispute over this question, but it is not always necessary to choose between them. Sometimes the same experiments allow one to use both analysis and synthesis, and thus to guide the child by the method of instruction when he fancies he is only analysing. Then, by using both at once, each method confirms the results of the other. Starting from opposite ends, without thinking of following the same road, he will unexpectedly reach their meeting place and this will be a delightful surprise. For example, I would begin geography at both ends and add to the study of the earth's revolution the measurement of its divisions, beginning at home. While the child is studying the sphere and is thus transported to the heavens, bring him back to the divisions of the globe and show him his own home.

His geography will begin with the town he lives in and his father's country house, then the places between them, the rivers near them, and then the sun's aspect and how to find one's way by its aid. This is the meeting place. Let him make his own map, a very simple map, at first containing only two places; others may be added from time to time, as he is able to estimate their distance and position. You see at once what a good start we have given him by making his eye his compass.

No doubt he will require some guidance in spite of this, but very little, and that little without his knowing it. If he goes wrong let him alone, do not correct his mistakes; hold your tongue till he finds them out for himself and corrects them, or at most arrange something, as opportunity offers, which may show him his mistakes. If he never makes mistakes he will never learn anything thoroughly. Moreover, what he needs is not an exact knowledge of local topography, but how to find out for himself. No matter whether he carries maps in his head provided he understands what they mean, and has a clear idea of the art of making them. See what a difference there is already between the knowledge of your scholars and the ignorance of mine. They learn maps, he makes them. Here are fresh ornaments for his room.

Remember that this is the essential point in my method—Do not teach the child many things, but never to let him form inaccurate or confused ideas. I care not if he knows nothing provided he is not mistaken, and I only acquaint him with truths to guard him against the errors he might put in their place. Reason and judgment come slowly, prejudices flock to us in crowds, and from these he must be protected. But if you make science itself your object, you embark on an unfathomable and shoreless ocean, an ocean strewn with reefs from which you will never return. When I see a man in love with knowledge, yielding to its charms and flitting from one branch to another unable to stay his steps, he seems to me like a child gathering shells on the sea-shore, now picking them up, then throwing them aside for others which he sees beyond them, then taking them again, till overwhelmed by their number and unable to choose between them, he flings them all away and returns empty handed.

Time was long during early childhood; we only tried to pass our time for fear of using it ill; now it is the other way; we have not time enough for all that would be of use. The passions, remember, are drawing near, and when they knock at the door your scholar will have no ear for anything else. The peaceful age of intelligence is so short, it flies so swiftly, there is so much to be done, that it is madness to try to make your child learned. It is not your business to teach him the various sciences, but to give him a taste for them and methods of learning them when this taste is more mature. That is assuredly a fundamental principle of all good education.

This is also the time to train him gradually to prolonged attention to a given object; but this attention should never be the result of constraint, but of interest or desire; you must be very careful that it is not too much for his strength, and that it is not carried to the point of tedium. Watch him, therefore, and whatever happens, stop before he is tired, for it matters little what he learns; it does matter that he should do nothing against his will.

If he asks questions let your answers be enough to whet his curiosity but not enough to satisfy it; above all, when you find him talking at random and overwhelming you with silly questions instead of asking for information, at once refuse to answer; for it is clear that he no longer cares about the matter in hand, but wants to make you a slave to his questions. Consider his motives rather than his words. This warning, which was scarcely needed before, becomes of supreme importance when the child begins to reason.

There is a series of abstract truths by means of which all the sciences are related to common principles and are developed each in its turn. This relationship is the method of the philosophers. We are not concerned with it at present. There is quite another method by which every concrete example suggests another and always points to the next in the series. This succession, which stimulates the curiosity and so arouses the attention required by every object in turn, is the order followed by most men, and it is the right order for all children.

.   .   .

Undoubtedly the notions of things thus acquired for oneself are clearer and much more convincing than those acquired from the teaching of others; and not only is our reason not accustomed to a slavish submission to authority, but we develop greater ingenuity in discovering relations, connecting ideas and inventing apparatus, than when we merely accept what is given us and allow our minds to be enfeebled by indifference, like the body of a man whose servants always wait on him, dress him and put on his shoes, whose horse carries him, till he loses the use of his limbs. Boileau used to boast that he had taught Racine the art of rhyming with difficulty. Among the many short cuts to science, we badly need some one to teach us the art of learning with difficulty.

The most obvious advantage of these slow and laborious inquiries is this: the scholar, while engaged in speculative studies, is actively using his body, gaining suppleness of limb, and training his hands to labour so that he will be able to make them useful when he is a man. Too much apparatus, designed to guide us in our experiments and to supplement the exactness of our senses, makes us neglect to use those senses. The theodolite makes it unnecessary to estimate the size of angles; the eye which used to judge distances with much precision, trusts to the chain for its measurements; the steel yard dispenses with the need of judging weight by the hand as I used to do. The more ingenious our apparatus, the coarser and more unskilful our senses. We surround ourselves with tools and fail to use those with which nature has provided every one of us.

But when we devote to the making of these instruments the skill which did instead of them, when for their construction we use the intelligence which enabled us to dispense with them, this is gain not loss, we add art to nature, we gain ingenuity without loss of skill. If instead of making a child stick to his books I employ him in a workshop, his hands work for the development of his mind. While he fancies himself a workman he is becoming a philosopher. Moreover, this exercise has other advantages of which I shall speak later; and you will see how, through philosophy in sport, one may rise to the real duties of man.

I have said already that purely theoretical science is hardly suitable for children, even for children approaching adolescence; but without going far into theoretical physics, take care that all their experiments are connected together by some chain of reasoning, so that they may follow an orderly sequence in the mind, and may be recalled at need; for it is very difficult to remember isolated facts or arguments, when there is no cue for their recall.

In your inquiry into the laws of nature always begin with the commonest and most conspicuous phenomena, and train your scholar not to accept these phenomena as causes but as facts. I take a stone and pretend to place it in the air; I open my hand, the stone falls. I see Emile watching my action and I say, "Why does this stone fall?"

What child will hesitate over this question? None, not even Emile, unless I have taken great pains to teach him not to answer. Every one will say, "The stone falls because it is heavy." "And what do you mean by heavy?" "That which falls." "So the stone falls because it falls?" Here is a poser for my little philosopher. This is his first lesson in systematic physics, and whether he learns physics or no it is a good lesson in common-sense.

As the child develops in intelligence other important considerations require us to be still more careful in our choice of his occupations. As soon as he has sufficient self-knowledge to understand what constitutes his well-being, as soon as he can grasp such far-reaching relations as to judge what is good for him and what is not, then he is able to discern the difference between work and play, and to consider the latter merely as relaxation. The objects of real utility may be introduced into his studies and may lead him to more prolonged attention than he gave to his games. The ever-recurring law of necessity soon teaches a man to do what he does not like, so as to avert evils which he would dislike still more. Such is the use of foresight, and this foresight, well or ill used, is the source of all the wisdom or the wretchedness of mankind.

Every one desires happiness, but to secure it he must know what happiness is. For the natural man happiness is as simple as his life; it consists in the absence of pain; health, freedom, the necessaries of life are its elements. The happiness of the moral man is another matter, but it does not concern us at present. I cannot repeat too often that it is only objects which can be perceived by the senses which can have any interest for children, especially children whose vanity has not been stimulated nor their minds corrupted by social conventions.

As soon as they foresee their needs before they feel them, their intelligence has made a great step forward, they are beginning to know the value of time. They must then be trained to devote this time to useful purposes, but this usefulness should be such as they can readily perceive and should be within the reach of their age and experience. What concerns the moral order and the customs of society should not yet be given them, for they are not in a condition to understand it. It is folly to expect them to attend to things vaguely described as good for them, when they do not know what this good is, things which they are assured will be to their advantage when they are grown up, though for the present they take no interest in this so-called advantage, which they are unable to understand.

Let the child do nothing because he is told; nothing is good for him but what he recognises as good. When you are always urging him beyond his present understanding, you think you are exercising a foresight which you really lack. To provide him with useless tools which he may never require, you deprive him of man's most useful tool—common-sense. You would have him docile as a child; he will be a credulous dupe when he grows up. You are always saying, "What I ask is for your good, though you cannot understand it. What does it matter to me whether you do it or not; my efforts are entirely on your account." All these fine speeches with which you hope to make him good, are preparing the way, so that the visionary, the tempter, the charlatan, the rascal, and every kind of fool may catch him in his snare or draw him into his folly.

A man must know many things which seem useless to a child, but need the child learn, or can he indeed learn, all that the man must know? Try to teach the child what is of use to a child and you will find that it takes all his time. Why urge him to the studies of an age he may never reach, to the neglect of those studies which meet his present needs? "But," you ask, "will it not be too late to learn what he ought to know when the time comes to use it?" I cannot tell; but this I do know, it is impossible to teach it sooner, for our real teachers are experience and emotion, and man will never learn what befits a man except under its own conditions. A child knows he must become a man; all the ideas he may have as to man's estate are so many opportunities for his instruction, but he should remain in complete ignorance of those ideas which are beyond his grasp. My whole book is one continued argument in support of this fundamental principle of education.

As soon as we have contrived to give our pupil an idea of the word "Useful," we have got an additional means of controlling him, for this word

makes a great impression on him, provided that its meaning for him is a
meaning relative to his own age, and provided he clearly sees its relation to
his own well-being. This word makes no impression on your scholars because
you have taken no pains to give it a meaning they can understand, and because other people always undertake to supply their needs so that they never
require to think for themselves, and do not know what utility is.

"What is the use of that?" In future this is the sacred formula, the formula by which he and I test every action of our lives. This is the question
with which I invariably answer all his questions; it serves to check the stream
of foolish and tiresome questions with which children weary those about
them. These incessant questions produce no result, and their object is rather
to get a hold over you than to gain any real advantage. A pupil, who has been
really taught only to want to know what is useful, questions like Socrates;
he never asks a question without a reason for it, for he knows he will be required to give his reason before he gets an answer.

See what a powerful instrument I have put into your hands for use with
your pupil. As he does not know the reason for anything you can reduce him
to silence almost at will; and what advantages do your knowledge and experience give you to show him the usefulness of what you suggest. For, make no
mistake about it, when you put this question to him, you are teaching him to
put it to you, and you must expect that whatever you suggest to him in the
future he will follow your example and ask, "What is the use of this?"

Perhaps this is the greatest of the tutor's difficulties. If you merely try
to put the child off when he asks a question, and if you give him a single
reason he is not able to understand, if he finds that you reason according to
your own ideas, not his, he will think what you tell him is good for you but
not for him; you will lose his confidence and all your labour is thrown away.
But what master will stop short and confess his faults to his pupil? We all
make it a rule never to own to the faults we really have. Now I would make
it a rule to admit even the faults I have not, if I could not make my reasons
clear to him; as my conduct will always be intelligible to him, he will never
doubt me and I shall gain more credit by confessing my imaginary faults than
those who conceal their real defects.

In the first place do not forget that it is rarely your business to suggest
what he ought to learn; it is for him to want to learn, to seek and to find it.
You should put it within his reach, you should skillfully awaken the desire
and supply him with means for its satisfaction. So your questions should be
few and well-chosen, and as he will always have more questions to put to you
than you to him, you will always have the advantage and will be able to ask
all the oftener, "What is the use of that question?" Moreover, as it matters
little what he learns provided he understands it and knows how to use it, as
soon as you cannot give him a suitable explanation give him none at all. Do
not hesitate to say, "I have no good answer to give you; I was wrong, let us
drop the subject." If your teaching was really ill-chosen there is no harm in

dropping it altogether; if it was not, with a little care you will soon find an opportunity of making its use apparent to him.

I do not like verbal explanations. Young people pay little heed to them, nor do they remember them. Things! Things! I cannot repeat it too often. We lay too much stress upon words; we teachers babble, and our scholars follow our example.

Suppose we are studying the course of the sun and the way to find our bearings, when all at once Emile interrupts me with the question, "What is the use of that?" what a fine lecture I might give, how many things I might take occasion to teach him in reply to his question, especially if there is any one there. I might speak of the advantages of travel, the value of commerce, the special products of different lands and the peculiar customs of different nations, the use of the calendar, the way to reckon the seasons for agriculture, the art of navigation, how to steer our course at sea, how to find our way without knowing exactly where we are. Politics, natural history, astronomy, even morals and international law are involved in my explanation, so as to give my pupil some idea of all these sciences and a great wish to learn them. When I have finished I shall have shown myself a regular pedant, I shall have made a great display of learning, and not one single idea has he understood. He is longing to ask me again, "What is the use of taking one's bearings?" but he dare not for fear of vexing me. He finds it pays best to pretend to listen to what he is forced to hear. This is the practical result of our fine systems of education.

The Ivory Lab 61

Jacques Barzun

Most of the excitement about "higher education" in the last three years has been about the teaching of history, languages, and "great books." But the most serious and pressing need in colleges today seems to me to be the teaching of science. It may appear paradoxical that I speak of a "need" which everyone believes to be adequately met, but paradox disappears when the point of view changes. From one point of view, science is taught in every American college; from another point of view, it is taught in none, or very few. Looked at in a certain light, science teaching today is the most efficient, up to date, and worldly-wise. In another light, it is backward, wasteful and "escapist." Let me explain these contrasts.

Fifty or sixty years ago, science was a new academic subject. People mistrusted its power to educate, and many of its proponents seemed as if they could never be educated themselves. The tradition of liberal studies had always included mathematics, because mathematics was supposed to train the mind; but the new physical sciences were first seen as manual arts, messy and expensive, and with no more "discipline" to them than a pair of elastic-sided boots. At the time of the fight for adding science to the curriculum, the defensive position was held by Greek and Latin, which unfortunately adopted a "scorched earth" policy. I mean that they allowed themselves to be invaded by the "scientific spirit" and in trying to compete with it reduced their field to a wasteland of verbal criticism, grammar, and philology. Literature was relegated to a second place and studying the classics came to mean research into the uses of *utor, fruor,* and *fungor.*

Naturally the classics were exterminated, for science could beat them at their own game. A young man trained in science could on graduation get any of a hundred desirable jobs in industry. A young "scientific" classicist could only hope to teach his own subject to a dwindling number of students. That is what invariably comes of trying to put belles-lettres into utilitarian envelopes. As Dean Briggs of Harvard said when the Bachelor of Science degree was established: "It does not guarantee that the holder knows any science, but it does guarantee that he does *not* know any Latin." When the study of classical literature in translation was reintroduced for freshmen at Columbia College a few years ago, the undergraduate department of classics was surprised to find its enrollment in beginning Greek increased 150 per cent: they now had ten students.

But the bitter joke is not on the Classics alone. Having stepped into Greek's vacated place, Science now occupies its position, not with respect to size of enrollment, but with respect to educational attitude. It is now in power and it acts disdainful, holier-than-thou, and prudish. Someone once asked, "What is it that our men of science are guarding like a threatened virginity?" "Oh," was the answer, "they have a Vestal interest in their subject." Considered—somewhat unfairly—in the mass, science teachers may be said to contribute the greatest proportion of backward-looking, anti-intellectual, mechanic-minded members to the faculty. Characteristically, single departments of physical science have in certain institutions tried to set up separate schools, where only their one science would be taught for four years and rewarded with some kind of Bachelor's degree. The intention was to monopolize the student's time, cram him full of "practical" knowledge, and sell him to the highest bidder the moment he had clutched his diploma and redeemed his ten-dollar deposit for apparatus.

Doubtless there is a demand for such prefabricated industrial robots and I see no reason why such schools should not function in a manner useful to the commonwealth—off the campus. But departments that once clamored for admission to university status and have had it for fifty years are unwilling to give up all the *douceurs* of the association. They would still like to profit from the university connection, to color their degree with a faint tincture of liberal teaching—perhaps they would require a year of English and a year of history and economics—and to boast that their own subject, be it chemistry or geology, is also one of the "humanities." They want to eat their cake as many times over as a cow does her cud.

A crowd of evils springs from this ambiguous mood in the present college curriculum. There is an undignified scramble for the student's time, with broad hints on the part of the scientist that the rest of the program is folderol. Repressed antagonisms divide teachers of the humanities (vague, pointless, unpractical subjects—except economics) from teachers of the real stuff represented by science. Moreover, departments of physics and chemistry require mathematical preparation in strict amount and order of time, with the result that all scheduling revolves around their claims. Since most young Americans discover their vocational bent while undergraduates, the wish to qualify for a profession is a powerful lever to make everyone study science for one or two years under these barbaric conditions. The doctor, the engineer, the research man in any science must gobble up as many courses as he can; and the man uninterested in science must "fulfill the requirement." Both are often judged on their science record, in the belief that it unmistakably reveals "real brains" or the lack of them.

The worst of all this is that neither group of students learns much about science but goes to swell the ranks of the two great classes of modern men— the single-track expert and the scientific ignoramus. Could anything more plainly demonstrate the failure of science to become a subject fit for college teaching? What makes a subject fit for the higher curriculum is surely no novelty: it is that it shall enlighten all the corners of the mind and teach its own uses. The humble three R's begin in strict utility and end up in poetry, science, and the search for the Infinite. They can and should therefore be taught indefinitely. Men have known for three thousand years that other matters of knowledge naturally divide themselves into special and general, that both are needful, but that whereas the special *add* to one's powers, the general *enhance the quality* of all of them.

At a recent educational conference, the Dean of a Midwestern university complained humorously that he was always being asked to give credits for impossible subjects—subjects that, he said, deserved to be called *in-credible*. A transfer student, for example, wanted "points" for seven hours of saw filing. Undeniably saw filing is a necessary art, but its merits as a general enhancer of power and personality stop accruing so soon after study is begun that it is not properly a branch of academic learning. The same is true of still more complex matters like shorthand, typewriting, and dress designing. Farther on in the series, it becomes harder to draw the line: stamp collecting is sub-educational, but numismatics is a province of history.

Fortunately there is no doubt whatever about the place of the sciences:

they *are* humanities and they belong in the college curriculum. Accordingly, they should be introduced into it *as humanities,* at the earliest possible moment. How? I have some tentative suggestions to make, but first I want to stress the danger of further delay and of the continuance of our present malpractice.

The worst danger is the creation of a large, powerful, and complacent class of college-trained uneducated men at the very heart of our industrial and political system. We may be too near to judge, but it strikes me that one of the conditions that made possible the present folly in Germany was the split among three groups: the technicians, the citizens, and the irresponsible rabble. This becomes persuasively plain if you consider the professional army caste as a group of unthinking technicians. The rabble together with the technicians can cow the citizenry; the technicians—wedded solely to their workbench—will work for any group that hires; and the rabble, worshiping "science" to the exclusion of less tangible necessaries, are perfectly willing to sacrifice the citizen. They probably think that, if necessary, "science" could manufacture German citizens—out of wolfram.

Such principles will hardly give long life and happiness to a democracy. The only hope for a democratic state is to have more citizens than anything else. Hence technicians must not be allowed to hibernate between experiments, but must become conscious, responsible, politically and morally active men. Otherwise they will find not only that representative government has slipped out of their fingers, but that they have also lost their commanding position. They will be paid slaves in the service of some rabble, high or low. Meanwhile our present stock of citizens must not simply gape at the wonders of science, but must understand enough of its principles to criticize and value the results. As for the rabble, it must be transmuted as fast as it forms, by science and morals both.

All this clearly depends on teaching our easygoing, rather credulous college boys and girls what science is. If they leave college thinking, as they usually do, that science offers a full, accurate, and literal description of man and Nature; if they think scientific research by itself yields final answers to social problems; if they think scientists are the only honest, patient, and careful workers in the world; if they think that Copernicus, Galileo, Newton, Lavoisier, and Faraday were unimaginative plodders like their own instructors; if they think theories spring from facts and that scientific authority at any time is infallible; if they think that the ability to write down symbols and read manometers is fair grounds for superiority and pride, and if they think that science steadily and automatically makes for a better world—then they have wasted their time in the science lecture room; they live in an Ivory Laboratory more isolated than the poet's tower[1] and they are a plain menace to the society they belong to. They are a menace whether they believe all

[1] To judge by results, it would seem that the poet climbs to the top of his tower to look out on the world and write about it. Why cavil at the building material—at once durable and attractive and requiring no upkeep?

this by virtue of being engaged in scientific work themselves or of being disqualified from it by felt or fancied incapacity.

I return to what might perhaps be done preventively and constructively. To begin with, a change of direction must be imparted to the teaching of science. The fact must be recognized that most students still do not make science their profession.[2] Consequently, for future lay citizens the compulsory science requirement in force nearly everywhere must be justified by a course explicitly designed for them. Such a course must not play at making physicists or biologists, but must explain the principles of the physical sciences in a coherent manner. A "survey" of all the sciences is out of the question. It would be at once superficial and bewildering. But an intelligent introduction to principles can be given. The assumptions that connect and that differentiate the sciences of matter, of living beings, and of logical relation can be taught; the meaning and the grounds of great unifying theories can be explained, and significant demonstrations and experiments can be shown to and made by the students.

Out of such a course there would surely come a changed attitude on the part of teachers and indeed a change in teaching personnel. At present, side by side with wise men and ripe teachers in the sciences, one finds many highly trained and absolutely uneducated practitioners. One also finds fanatics of the order that Dickens described in Professor Dingo, who, being caught defacing houses with his geological hammer, replied that "he knew of no building save the Temple of Science." Many university scientists openly scorn teaching and use their appointment to boil the pot of individual research. Now a life of research is a worthy one, but no amount of worthy motive justifies false pretenses and fraudulent impersonation—in this case the pretense of imparting knowledge and the impersonation of a teacher.

In the classroom, such men usually are neither civil, nor literate, nor even scientific, for their knowledge of science is purely from inside—a limitation equally bad but more misleading than the limitation of knowing it purely from outside. "What do they know of science who only science know?" They teach it as a set of rules, and speak of the profession as a "game." Drill in manual dexterity they entrust to laboratory assistants, who are only younger editions of themselves, and for whom a good notebook or speed in performing repetitious experiments is the passport to approval. There is seldom any consideration of the students as thinking minds, of the proper allocation of effort among the many interests legitimate at their time of life, nor of the philosophical implications which the words, the history, and the processes of the particular science disclose.

To offset this lamentable state of things, it must be said that two of the professions most concerned with scientific training—engineering and medi-

---

[2] Statistics for the Middle West, based on large freshman enrollments, show that 50 per cent of those taking Chemistry 1, 60 per cent of those taking Geology 1, 73 per cent of those taking Physics 1, 75 per cent of those taking Biology 1, and 82 per cent of those taking Botany 1, never go further into the science.

cine—have lately amended their outlook and made overtures to the humanities. The medical schools have declared that cramming the student with science in college was a poor thing. He had better study other, less "practical," more formative subjects and postpone advanced chemistry and biology until medical school, where they will be taught him again in a fashion better tailored to his needs. This new policy is excellent, but it is not yet sufficiently enforced. The lesser medical schools—and some others—do not trust their own belief in the principle; they still appeal to "practical" views and judge applicants by A's in science.

Similarly, the Society for the Promotion of Engineering Education has passed splendid resolutions approving what they call the "social-humanistic stem"—by which they mean a few branches of non-engineering study; more accurately then, the "social-humanistic faggots." But here again, engineering thought is ahead of the engineer's emotions. When it comes to the test, the student or the program is pushed around to suit engineering subject matter.

If you add to this the important fact that many young Americans choose "engineering" in the belief that this means a career of research in pure science, you may form some notion of the present anarchical mess. The would-be engineer of seventeen finds that what he really wants to work at is pure research in electricity, that is, to be a physicist. He must therefore back water, change his course, and take some new prerequisites. Meanwhile his upbringing as a man and citizen goes by the board. He is caught between two grindstones, each indifferent to the effect of its motion, just as if the boy being put through this mill were not a human being, a student of the university, and a future citizen of the nation. Who is being "practical" now?

Some would probably still maintain that the professional schools in contact with "the world" know best what is the practical view, and that the college is as ever utopian. But there is one curious fact to be added. It is that the scientific professional schools have a way of relaxing their jaws into a smile whenever the market demand for their product decreases: it is a reflex action. They fall in love with the humanities all over again and raise the amount they require for admission, until outside pressure once again lowers the floodgates and the frown succeeds the smile. This self-regulating action is a feat of engineering in itself—or shall I say of doctoring the supply for public consumption?

The question is not whether this is the easy way to go about marketing young men, but whether it is a responsible grownup way of replenishing the professional class of society. Granted that practice is the test of all schemes and ideals, is this the most practical scheme that American ingenuity can devise? I concede that in the present state of mind of the American public, desire for vocational training takes the lead over anything else. But are the directing members of the university world to follow other people's untutored impulses or to guide and redirect them? We may well ask when we reflect that the first victims of the system are the children of the unthinking public and the public itself. For it is the oldest fallacy about schooling to suppose that it can train a man for "practical" life. Inevitably, while the plan of study is being taught, "practical life" has moved on. "They did it this way three months ago, now they do it this way." No employer who knows anything about men will value a beginner because he knows the ropes of a particular changeable routine. It would be as sensible to require that newcomers know the floor plan of the factory ahead of time.[3]

The corporations employing the largest numbers of engineers and scientific research men are on this matter way ahead of the colleges. One such firm conducted a survey last year to find out where and how its first-rate executives had been prepared. They came from the most unexpected places— including small liberal arts colleges, the teaching profession, the stage, and the Baptist ministry. It was found that the engineering schools—particularly those sensible ones that make no pretense at intellectual *cachet*—turned out a good average product, but few leaders. The company's own institutes and night courses raised the chance of foremen and district managers—but only up to a point. The survey concluded that what it wanted as material to shape future executives was graduates of liberal arts colleges, trained in history and economics, in philosophy and in good English, and likewise possessed of *an intelligent interest in science and technology*. Gentlemen, the path lies open.

---

[3] The S.P.E.E. reports: "From its very nature, engineering education operates under changing conditions which constantly challenge its processes and test its results . . . so as to adapt itself to changing needs." (*Draft of a Report*, etc. November 16, 1939, p. 1.) This is fine and good, but it holds true of every other professional subject and most academic ones. The old belief that only a few schools are in touch with the "real world" is untrue, even if the newer belief should prove true that it is best for the world to have the school conform to every change outside.

SCIENCE AND SOCIETY

62   A Survival Technique
Marshall Walker

The scientific method is merely a formalization of *learning by experience.*
Anything that learns by experience is using the scientific method in a primitive form. Learning by experience is not limited to humans, animals, or even
living things; certain devices can learn by experience. The essential steps in
the process are these:

1. A first stimulus causes an animal (or device) to act in a specific pattern.
2. While following this pattern, the animal or device encounters a second stimulus.
3. This second stimulus is recorded as a *memory.*
4. When the first stimulus is applied again, the animal or device follows a different pattern of action because of the *memory.*

As an example, consider a child who reacts to a first stimulus of thirst by
drinking from his glass of milk. One day the glass is filled with buttermilk,
and the child receives an unexpected second stimulus. The next time he is
thirsty he may refuse his milk until convinced that it is not buttermilk.

As an example of a nonliving device that learns by experience, consider
an ordinary household electric outlet and its fuse. When a household appliance is plugged in, the outlet provides the necessary electric current. This
is normal behavior; it corresponds to the child habitually drinking his milk.
Then one day a defective lamp is plugged in and the fuse burns out. The
burnt fuse corresponds to the child's memory of the buttermilk. The outlet
will no longer provide current to appliances until the memory has been removed by inserting a new fuse. Both the child and the electric circuit have
"learned by experience." The brain and nerve circuits of the child are much
more complicated than the electrical circuits of the electric outlet and fuse,
but the same sort of process has occurred in each. In a primitive way, both

From Ch. II, "A Survival Technique": Marshall Walker, *The Nature of Scientific
Thought,* © 1963. Reprinted by permission of Prentice-Hall, Inc., Englewood Cliffs,
New Jersey.

the child and the electric circuit have used the scientific method and for the same purpose—self-preservation. The child's response to strange-tasting milk is part of the organism's defense mechanism against being destroyed by spoiled food. This mechanism was developed during the evolution of the human body by natural selection. The response of the fused circuit to an overload current is the circuit's defense mechanism against being destroyed by the overload. It also arose by a sort of natural selection because designers found that unfused circuits did not survive.

The phrase *scientific method* has usually been applied only to cases where it was used consciously. One tends to think of a professional scientist testing model after model until he finds a successful one. But the child with the milk is obviously using the scientific method even though he can hardly talk. He has a model based on experience and predicts from his model that the glass of white stuff will taste good. For a large number of instances his predictions are correct. Then he encounters a glass of white stuff that does *not* taste good, alters his model accordingly, and predicts that the next glass of white stuff will taste bad. And he will retain this second model until further experience leads him to modify it. It is very unlikely that he has been consciously following the steps of the scientific method. Nevertheless, it seems a reasonable inference that the steps of the scientific method have been followed automatically.

We now have three instances of the scientific method in action. The scientist is conscious himself and uses the method consciously. The child is conscious himself and uses the method automatically. The electric circuit is not conscious and uses the method automatically. The scientist and the electric circuit represent two extreme examples of the same process; between them lie a whole series of instances differing in degrees of consciousness.

It is the point of view of this chapter that the scientific method is a survival technique that developed during the biological evolution of living things. Any organism or device that includes a suitably connected memory unit can "learn by experience," and this learning by experience contains the basic elements of the scientific method. In order that the origin of the scientific method can be seen in its historical setting, we will consider briefly the current models of physical and biological evolution.

Measurements made in recent years have been extrapolated into the past to yield models of the early development of the universe. The interpretation of our astronomical measurements as numbers that describe stars and planets existing in space and time is, of course, itself a model. However, it is a model of such long standing that one tends to ascribe reality to it. In writing about such long-established models as space and time, we shall use ordinary language which regards space and time as aspects of reality, and remind the reader only occasionally that even these basic concepts are conceptual models used to correlate stimuli.

Careful measurements of the position and motion of the nearby stars show that our sun and its planets are located in one of the spiral arms of a great pinwheel of stars called the *local galaxy*. The Milky Way is our view of the stars in the arms of this galaxy. Millions of other such galaxies scattered through space can be seen on the photograph taken with the great telescopic cameras of the astronomical observatories. The nearest of these other spiral nebulas can be seen with the naked eye in the constellation Andromeda.

The common unit of distance, the mile, is much too small for use in expressing astronomical distances. A more convenient unit is the *light-year*, the distance light travels in a year. Since light has a speed of 186,000 miles per second, the *light-year* is a distance of about six million miles. Expressed in this unit, the distance from the earth to the sun is about one sixty-thousandth of a light-year, the distance to the center of our local galaxy is about 30,000 light years, and the distance to the next nearest spiral galaxy is about two million light-years.

During the last forty years careful measurements have been made on the light coming to us from many of these distant spiral galaxies. From such measurements one can infer the distances of these galaxies. The color of light emitted by hydrogen gas in a distant galaxy is more reddish than the light emitted by hydrogen gas in a laboratory on earth. This red-shift can be interpreted in three ways: (1) the hydrogen gas observed in the distant galaxy is different from hydrogen gas on earth; (2) the light from the distant galaxy changed color during the millions of years of travel since it left the galaxy; (3) the distant galaxy is moving away from the earth at a speed of thousands of miles per second. The consensus of astronomers favors the third interpretation, presumably because such an expansion of galactic space is consistent with one of the solutions of the equations of general relativity. No direct experimental observation has yet been devised which can differentiate among the three interpretations.

According to the third interpretation, the current model of the universe pictures the galaxies as flying apart from each other. The galaxies nearest to the earth are receding at a rate of about a thousand miles per second. The more distant galaxies recede progressively faster as the distance increases. This description sounds as though all the galaxies were running away from the observer on the earth, but an observer in any other galaxy would get the same impression. Imagine a race in which all the runners start together, but run at different (but constant) speeds. From the view point of any one runner, all the other runners seem to be moving away from him—those in front seem to move forward and those behind get further behind.

It is natural to extrapolate this model backward and try to infer what the universe was like billions of years ago. This backward extrapolation can be done in two ways. If one assumes that the total amount of matter in the universe remained constant during the expansion, the Gamow model results.

If one assumes that the total amount of matter in the universe increased during expansion, then the Hoyle model results.[1]

The Gamow model pictures the universe as originating in a giant explosion several thousand million years ago. At that time all the matter in the universe was packed into a small space, and the temperature was very high. The spiral galaxies as we see them today are regarded as fragments from the original explosion. The fastest galaxies are most distant because it is their great speed that took them out to such great distances in the time that has elapsed since the explosion. The slower galaxies, correspondingly, are not so far away.

The Hoyle model pictures the universe of the remote past as looking the same as the universe looks today. Although the galaxies are pictured as moving away from each other continually, matter appears in the universe and eventually forms new galaxies so that the average separation of the galaxies remains about the same. No one has yet devised a measurable experiment that can distinguish between the Hoyle and Gamow models. We will therefore leave this phase of evolution of the universe and proceed to the phase of biological evolution on the earth.

Suppose a scientist wishes to experiment with a simple form of living thing such as bacteria. First, he must arrange a place that has the right temperature for them. He usually constructs a water bath for them to grow in because it is hard to change the temperature of water, and once the temperature is set at the right value it is fairly easy to keep the temperature constant. To help keep the temperature constant he surrounds the water bath with a layer of insulating material—perhaps a wall of cork. He then provides a source of heat to keep the bath warm. He usually puts an electric immersion heater in the bath, and provides a thermostat to turn it on and off as needed. However, he could provide a heat lamp and adjust its distance from the water until the heat arriving from the lamp just balanced the heat lost by the water to the room. The water would then stay at a constant temperature until the lamp burned out or the water evaporated. He could prevent the evaporation of water by covering the tank so the evaporating water would condense and flow back into the bath.

A few hundred million years ago conditions on earth resembled such a constant temperature bath. The ocean was the water bath, the vacuum of space provided a good insulator, the sun acted as a heat lamp, and the force of gravitation returned the evaporated water to the ocean through rainfall and rivers. One should not thereby assume that our planet was designed for the support of living things. If a particular sun has a series of planets at different distances, one or more of them may be located so that the proper conditions for living things exist there. We observe that life does exist on our

---

[1] See George Gamow, *The Creation of the Universe* (New York: The Viking Press, 1952), and Fred Hoyle, *Frontiers of Astronomy* (New York: Harper & Row, Publishers, 1955); both available in paperback form.

planet, and can only infer thereby that conditions favorable to life have existed for some time.

The early ocean was warm, about 70° Fahrenheit. Over the ocean there was an atmosphere, which probably contained (among other gases) water vapor, methane, ammonia, and hydrogen. Lightning storms doubtless occurred then as they do now. Harold Urey and S. L. Miller have shown that electrical discharges in such a mixture of gases cause amino acids to be formed. These amino acids are the building blocks of proteins, the stuff from which all living things are constructed. Once these amino acids were present in the ocean, it was only a matter of time for chance collisions between them to build up the giant protein molecules that make up viruses and other more complicated living things.

This model has been criticized by du Noüy, who computed that the probability of a protein molecule's being formed by chance encounters is very small. The details of his calculation are not given, but it appears that the computation is for the case of building a protein molecule *in one step* by accidental placement of its constituent atoms. The resulting probability is, of course, very small. Scientists have never suggested that proteins were formed in this way. The actual process is pictured as occurring in steps, two single particles joining to become a double particle, two double particles to become a quadruple particle, and so on. The colliding particles do not even need any particular orientation in most cases since the attractive forces will pull them into the proper position. The probabilities involved are nearly certainties rather than otherwise, and an essentially similar process would occur in any organic chemistry laboratory if a complicated compound were synthesized from its elements. The chemist is useful only in producing an economic yield of a pure product. Nature dispenses with the chemist and uses low yields of impure products.

The essence of this increase in complexity is that it is a *one-way* process. Owing to the prevailing ambient temperature, components that join together *stay* together. They can easily become more complex by collision, but special conditions are needed to break them apart again. The reactions themselves are reversible, but the surrounding conditions favor the survival of the complex molecule. Some doors are built to swing either way, and people can pass through one way as easily as the other, but other conditions—say an open elevator shaft behind the door—can easily convert the two-way door into a one-way trap.

The transition from complex inert molecular aggregates to even more complex living molecular aggregates is a series of almost imperceptible steps. The self-repair, reproduction, and response to stimuli characteristic of living aggregates have been found over a considerable range of colloid and virus structures in such various degrees that the distinction between living and nonliving matter is no longer a sharp line but a diffuse region.

As time went on, these aggregates, in activity described by biological laws yet unformulated, increased in complexity and size and became adapted to wider ranges of living conditions. Some crawled out of the ocean onto the shore, and, as time went on developed into amphibians, reptiles, and mammals; some took to the air and developed eventually into birds. Despite the controversies over the details of natural selection, the basic idea is unquestioned: those structure changes that favored survival persisted. One such structure that favored survival was a device to store records of the surrounding environment. Then, when the current environment resembled a previous threat, the organism could attempt to change it by flight or attack.

This device eventually developed into the brain. The ability to predict future events obviously increases the probability of survival, and thus natural selection tends to favor the development of the brain. One can imagine a small animal running desperately from a large carnivore. By chance the little animal dashes across some swampy ground, and the large animal bogs down in the mud. The next time the small animal seeks to evade such a luncheon engagement he may streak for the nearest swamp. Competence in such elementary mental activity is well rewarded—by survival. Incompetence is also rewarded—by death. Presumably, this small ancestor of ours did not outline the steps of the scientific method as he ran, but the essential steps were there whether he was conscious of them or not.

As time went on, various living things evolved specializations that increased their probability of survival. Antelopes specialized in escape by running, cats specialized in skillful stalking, turtles specialized in armament, skunks specialized in defensive gas warfare. Man specialized in predicting the future, and the systemization of this process is called *science*. An explorer in a strange land would infer the presence of skunk from an odor in the air; he would infer the presence of man from the discovery of a scientifically designed trap: science is the stink of man.

Attributes or techniques favor survival with respect to a certain environment. If the environment changes fairly suddenly, the attributes evolved to favor survival under the old conditions may actually oppose survival under the new conditions. An animal that has adapted to desert conditions may die if the desert, through some geologic cataclysm, becomes a swamp. An elderly immigrant may bury his money in the traditional way to keep it safe. In his new country it would probably be safer to keep it in a bank. He intends to keep his money safe, but it is his behavior, not his intention, that influences the probability of safety. Although all normal behavior is intended to favor survival, an act may actually oppose survival if the actor is unaware of new factors in the situation.

Science, like all other weapons of survival, is a double-edged tool. The same knowledge that can be used to help society survive can be used to destroy it. A small dose of radiation can sometimes retard cancer; a large dose of radiation can kill the patient. Any survival technique can be misused and become a technique of destruction.

The human organism has drawn far enough ahead in its race for survival so that the luxury of *comfort* is possible. Comfort is the state of an organism when there appears to be no immediate threat to its survival. A man is said to be in "comfortable circumstances" when his physiological and psychological needs of the moment and foreseeable future seem assured. Clearly, the man must have well-validated knowledge of his immediate and future needs or his "comfort" will be an illusion. The unprotected happy moron does not live long.

In the everyday life of man today, the desire for survival takes on the more sophisticated form of the desire for comfort. The natural selection that favored the development of the brain in the struggle for bare survival still favors the development of the brain today when man is engaged in the competition of economic and social survival. The degree of comfort, provided it is not an illusion, is a measure of successful competition because the degree of comfort measures the probability of future survival.

The scientific method is valued by man because it contributes to man's struggle for survival as an individual and as a species, and beyond survival to man's desire for comfort. Clearly the society that can predict what vaccine will kill poliomyelitis virus is more likely to survive (other things being equal) than the society that cannot make such predictions.

The operation of the brain is a rapid repetition of the cycle of the scientific method applied to successive instantaneous situations. A child who wants to cross the street predicts that he can do so before the approaching truck arrives and then submits his prediction to experimental validation. The brain processes of an Einstein as he works on the unified field theory differ only in degree from the brain processes of the child crossing the street. The method is essentially the same in both instances, and both processes persist because they increase the probability of survival of the individual and the species.

ARGUMENT

The scientific method is a formalization of the process of learning by experience. Any organism or device with a memory can learn by experience. The operation of the brain of any living thing is a rapid, automatic repetition of the basic steps of the scientific method applied to successive instantaneous situations. Some men use the scientific method consciously, but the same basic process goes on in men and animals automatically in everyday life. The scientific method is a survival technique that first appeared in primitive form in the first organism that included a memory. As the brain and nervous system increased in complexity through evolutionary processes, the sophistication of the scientific method increased. Man has the most complex brain and nervous system known, and the scientific method in its most sophisticated form is used by man as he strives for survival and comfort.

Science, the Destroyer or Creator? 63

J. Bronowski

We all know the story of the sorcerer's apprentice; or *Frankenstein* which Mary Shelley wrote in competition with her husband and Byron; or some other story of the same kind out of the macabre invention of the nineteenth century. In these stories, someone who has special powers over nature conjures or creates a stick or a machine to do his work for him; and then finds that he cannot take back the life he has given it. The mindless monster overwhelms him; and what began as an invention to do the housework ends by destroying the master of the house.

These stories have become the epitome of our own fears. We have been inventing machines at a growing pace now for about three hundred years. This is a short span even in our recorded history, and it is not a thousandth part of our history as men. In that short moment of time we have found a remarkable insight into the working of nature. We have used it to make ourselves far more flexible in our adaptation to the outside world than any other animal has ever been. We can survive in climates which even germs find difficult. We can grow our own food and meat. We can travel overland and we can tunnel and swim and fly, all in the one body. More important than any of these, we have come nearest to the dream which Lamarck had, that animals might inherit the skills which their parents learned. We have discovered the means to record our experience so that others may live it again.

The history of other animal species shows that the most successful in the struggle for survival have been those which were most adaptable to changes in their world. We have made ourselves by means of our tools beyond all measure more adaptable than any other species, living or extinct; and we continue to do so with gathering speed. Yet today we are afraid of our own shadow in the nine o'clock news; and we wonder whether we shall survive so over-specialized a creature as the Pekinese.

Everyone likes to blame his sense of defeat on someone else; and for some time scientists have been a favorite scapegoat. I want to look at their responsibility, and for that matter at everybody's, rather more closely. They do have a special responsibility; do not let us argue that out of existence; but it is a complicated one, and it is not the whole responsibility. For example,

Ch. 9, "Science, the Destroyer or Creator?": Reprinted by permission of the publishers from J. Bronowski, *The Common Sense of Science*, Cambridge, Mass.: Harvard University Press, 1953. Also by permission of Heinemann Educational Books Ltd.

science obviously is not responsible for the readiness of people, who do not take their private quarrels beyond the stage of insult, to carry their public quarrels to the point of war. Many animals fight for their needs, and some for their mere greeds, to the point of death. Bucks fight for females, and birds fight for their territories. The fighting habits of man are odd because he displays them only in groups. But they were not supplied by scientists. On the contrary, science has helped to end several kinds of group murder, such as witch hunting and the taboos of the early nineteenth century against disinfecting hospitals.

Neither is science responsible for the existence of groups which believe themselves to be in competition: for the existence above all of nations. And the threat of war today is always a national threat. Some bone of contention and competition is identified with a national need: Fiume or the Polish corridor or the dignity of the Austrian Empire; and in the end nations are willing to organize and to invite the death of citizens on both sides in order to reach these collective aims. Science did not create the nations; on the contrary, it has helped to soften those strong national idiosyncrasies which it seems necessary to exploit if war is to be made with enthusiasm. And wars are not made by *any* traditional groups: they are made by highly organized societies, they are made by nations. Most of us have seen Yorkshiremen invade Old Trafford, and a bloody nose or two if the day was thirsty. But no Yorkshireman would have grown pale if he had been told that Lancashire had the atomic bomb.

The sense of doom in us today is not a fear of science; it is a fear of war. And the causes of war were not created by science; they do not differ in kind from the known causes of the War of Jenkins' Ear or the Wars of the Roses, which were carried on with only the most modest scientific aids. No, science has not invented war; but it has turned it into a very different thing. The people who distrust it are not wrong. The man in the pub who says "It'll wipe out the world," the woman in the queue who says "It isn't natural"— they do not express themselves very well; but what they are trying to say does make sense. Science has enlarged the mechanism of war, and it has distorted it. It has done this in at least two ways.

First, science has obviously multiplied the power of the warmakers. The weapons of the moment can kill more people more secretly and more unpleasantly than those of the past. This progress, as for want of another word I must call it—this progress has been going on for some time; and for some time it has been said, of each new weapon, that it is so destructive or so horrible that it will frighten people into their wits, and force the nations to give up war for lack of cannon fodder. This hope has never been fulfilled, and I know no one who takes refuge in it today. The acts of men and women are not dictated by such simple compulsions; and they themselves do not stand in any simple relation to the decisions of the nations which they compose. Grapeshot and TNT and gas have not helped to outlaw war; and I see no sign that the hydrogen bomb or a whiff of bacteria will be more successful in making men wise by compulsion.

Secondly, science at the same time has given the nations quite new occasions for falling out. I do not mean such simple objectives as someone else's uranium mine, or a Pacific Island which happens to be knee-deep in organic fertilizer. I do not even mean merely another nation's factories and her skilled population. These are all parts of the surplus above our simple needs which they themselves help to create and which gives our civilization its character. And war in our world battens on this surplus. This is the object of the greed of nations, and this also gives them the leisure to train and the means to arm for war. At bottom, we have remained individually too greedy to distribute our surplus, and collectively too stupid to pile it up in any more useful form than the traditional mountains of arms. Science can claim to have created the surplus in our societies, and we know from the working day and the working diet how greatly it has increased it in the last two hundred years. Science has created the surplus. Now put this year's budget beside the budget of 1750, anywhere in the world, and you will see what we are doing with it.

I myself think there is a third dimension which science has added to modern war. It has created war nerves and the war of nerves. I am not thinking about the technical conditions for a war of nerves: the camera man and the radio and the massed display of strength. I am thinking of the climate in which this stage lightning flickers and is made to seem real. The last twenty years have given us a frightening show of these mental states. There is a division in the mind of each of us, that has become plain, between the man and the brute; and the rift can be opened, the man submerged, with a cynical simplicity, with the meanest tools of envy and frustration, which in my boyhood would have been thought inconceivable in a civilized society. I shall come back to this cleavage in our minds, for it is much more than an item in a list of war crimes. But it is an item. It helps to create the conditions for disaster. And I think that science has contributed to it. Science; the fact that science is there, mysterious, powerful; the fact that most people are impressed by it but ignorant and helpless—all this seems to me to have contributed to the division in our minds. And scientists cannot escape the responsibility for this. They have enjoyed acting the mysterious stranger, the powerful voice without emotion, the expert and the god. They have failed to make themselves comfortable in the talk of people in the street; no one taught them the knack, of course, but they were not keen to learn. And now they find the distance which they enjoyed has turned to distrust, and the awe has turned to fear; and people who are by no means fools really believe that we should be better off without science.

These are the indictments which scientists cannot escape. Of course, they are often badly phrased, so that scientists can side-step them with generalities about the common responsibility, and who voted the credits for atomic research anyway; which are prefectly just, but not at all relevant. That is not the heart of the matter; and the people in queues and pubs are humbly groping for the heart. They are not good at saying things and they do not give model answers to interviewers. But when we say "We've forgotten what's right," when they say "We're not fit to handle such things," what is in their minds is perfectly true. Science and society are out of joint. Science has given to no one in particular a power which no one in particular knows how to use. Why do not scientists invent something sensible? Wives say it every time they stub their toe on the waste bin, and husbands say it whenever a fuse blows. Why is it the business of no one in particular to stop fitting science for death and to begin fitting it into our lives? We will agree that warlike science is no more than a by-product of a warlike society. Science has merely provided the means, for good or for bad; and society has seized it for bad. But what are we going to do about it?

The first thing to do, it seems to me, is to treat this as a scientific question: by which I mean as a practical and sensible question, which deserves a factual approach and a reasoned answer. Now that I have apologized on behalf of scientists, and this on a scale which some of them will certainly think too ample, let us cut out what usually happens to the argument at this point, the rush of recriminations. The scientists are conscious of their mistakes; and I do not want to discuss the mistakes of non-scientists—although they have made a great many—except those which we all must begin to make good.

I have said that a scientific answer must be practical as well as sensible. This really rules out at once the panaceas which also tend to run the argument into a blind alley at this stage; the panaceas which say summarily "Get rid of them." Naturally, it does not seem to me to be sensible to get rid of scientists; but in any case, it plainly is not practical. And whatever we do with our own scientists, it very plainly is not practical to get rid of the scientists of rival nations; because if there existed the conditions for agreement among nations on this far-reaching scheme, then the conditions for war would already have disappeared. If there existed the conditions for international agreement, say to suspend all scientific research, or to abandon warlike research, or in any other way to forgo science as an instrument of nationalism —if such agreements could be reached, then they would already be superfluous; because the conditions for war would already have disappeared. So, however we might sigh for Samuel Butler's panacea in *Erewhon,* simply to give up all machines, there is no point in talking about it. I believe it would be a disaster for mankind like the coming of the Dark Ages. But there is no point in arguing this. It just is not practical, nationally or internationally.

There are no panaceas at all; and we had better face that. There is nothing that we can do overnight, in a week or a month, which can straighten by a laying on of hands the ancient distortion of our society. Do not let us fancy that any one of us out of the blue will concoct that stirring letter to

The Times which will change the black mood of history—and the instructions to diplomats. Putting scientists in the Cabinet will not do that, and women in the War Office will not, nor will bishops in the Privy Council. There are no panaceas. We are the heirs to a tradition which has left science and society out of step. The man in the street is right: we have never learned to handle such things. Nothing will do but that we learn. But learning is not done in a year. Our ultimate survival is in our own hands. Our survival while we are learning is a much chancier thing. We had better be realistic about that.

Meanwhile we had better settle down to work for our ultimate survival; and we had better start now. We have seen that the diagnosis has turned out to be not very difficult. Science and our social habits are out of step. And the cure is no deeper either. We must learn to match them. And there is no way of learning this unless we learn to understand *both*.

Of the two, of course, the one which is strange is science. I have already blamed the scientist for that. He has been the monk of our age, timid, thwarted, anxious to be asked to help; and with a secret ambition to play the Grey Eminence. Through years of childhood poverty he dreamed of this. Scientific skill was a blue door beckoning to him, which would open into the society of dignitaries of state. But the private motives of scientists are not the trend of science. The trend of science is made by the needs of society: navigation before the eighteenth century, manufacture thereafter; and in our age I believe the liberation of personality. Whatever the part which scientists like to act, or for that matter which painters like to dress, science shares the aims of our society just as art does. The difficulties of understanding either are not fundamental; they are difficulties only of language. To grow familiar with the large ideas of science calls for patience and an effort of attention; and I hope I have shown that it repays them.

For two hundred years, these ideas have been applied to technical needs; and they have made our world anew, triumphantly, from top to toe. Our shoes are tanned and stitched, our clothes are spun and dyed and woven, we are lighted and carried and doctored by means which were unknown to neat Mr. Pope at Twickenham in 1740. We may not think that is much to put against the eighty thousand dead in Hiroshima, or we may. We may not think it recompenses us for the absence of any Mr. Pope from Twickenham today; we may even hold it responsible. It is certainly not a spiritual achievement. But it has not yet tried to be. It has applied its ideas monotonously to shoe-leather and bicycle bells. And it has made a superb job of them. Compare its record in its own field with that of any other ideas of the same age: Burke's ideas of the imagination, or Bentham's on government, or Adam Smith on political economy. If any ideas have a claim to be called creative, because they have created something, then certainly it is the ideas of science.

We may think that all that science has created is comfort; and it certainly has done that—the very word "comfortable" in the modern sense dates from the Industrial Revolution. But have we always stopped to think what science has done not to our mode of living but to our life? We talk about research for death, the threat of war and the number of civilians who get killed. But have we always weighed this against the increase in our own life span? Let us do a small sum. The number of people killed in Great Britain in six years of war by German bombs, flying bombs, and V2's was sixty thousand. They were an average lot of people, which means that on an average they lost half their expectation of life. Quite an easy long division shows that the effect of this in our population of fifty million people was to shorten the average span of life by less than one tenth of one per cent. This is considerably less than a fortnight. Put this on the debt side. And on the credit side, we know that in the last hundred years the average span of life in England has increased by twenty years. That is the price of science, take it or leave it —a fortnight for twenty years of life. And these twenty years have been created by applying to daily life, to clothing and bedding, to hygiene and infection, to birth and death, the simple ideas of science—the fundamental ideas I have been talking about: order, cause, and chance. If any ideas have a claim to be called creative, because they have created life, it is the ideas of science.

We have not neglected these ideas altogether in our social organization. But, it is a point I have made several times, we have got hopelessly behind with them. The idea or order is now old enough to have reached at least our filing cabinets. The idea of cause and effect has entered our habits, until it has become the new *a priori* in the making of administrative plans. The difficulty is to dislodge it, now that it is hardening into a scholastic formula. For the idea which has given a new vigor to science in our generation is larger than the machinery of cause and effect. It stipulates no special mechanism between the present and the future. It is content to predict the future, without insisting that the computation must follow the steps of causal law. I have called this the idea of chance, because its method is statistical, and because it recognizes that every prediction carries with it its own measurable uncertainty. A good prediction is one which defines its area of uncertainty; a bad prediction ignores it. And at bottom this is no more than the return to the essentially empirical, the experimental nature of science. Science is a great many things, and I have called them a great many names; but in the end they all return to this: science is the acceptance of what works and the rejection of what does not. That needs more courage than we might think.

It needs more courage than we have ever found when we have faced our worldly problems. This is how society has lost touch with science: because it has hesitated to judge itself by the same impersonal code of what works and what does not. We have clung to Adam Smith and Burke, or we have agitated for Plato or Aquinas, through wars and famine, through rising and falling birth-rates, and through libraries of learned argument. And in the end, our eyes have always wandered from the birth-rate to the argument: from the birth-rate to what we have wanted to believe. Here is the crux of what I have been saying. Here is our ultimate hope of saving ourselves from extinction. We must learn to understand that the content of all knowledge is empirical; that its test is whether it works; and we must learn to act on that understanding in the world as well as in the laboratory.

This is the message of science: our ideas must be realistic, flexible, un-bigoted—they must be human, they must create their own authority. If any ideas have a claim to be called creative, because they have liberated that creative impulse, it is the ideas of science.

This is not only a material code. On the contrary, my hope is that it may heal the spiritual cleft which two wars have uncovered. I have seen in my lifetime an abyss open in the human mind: a gulf between the endeavor to be man, and the relish in being brute. The scientist has indeed had a hand in this, and every other specialist too, with his prim detachment and his oracular airs. But of course, the large strain which has opened this fault is social. We have made men live in two halves, a Sunday half and a workday half. We have ordered them to love their neighbor and to turn the other cheek, in a society which has constantly compelled them to shoulder their neighbor aside and to turn their backs. So we have created a savage sense of failure which, as we know now to our cost, can be tapped with an ease which is frightening; and which can thrust up, with an explosive force, a symbol to repeat to an unhappy people its most degrading dream.

Can science heal that neurotic flaw in us? If science cannot, then nothing can. Let us stop pretending. There is no cure in high moral precepts. We have preached them too long to men who are forced to live how they can: *that* makes the strain which they have not been able to bear. We need an ethic which is moral *and* which works. It is often said that science has destroyed our values and put nothing in their place. What has really happened of course is that science has shown in harsh relief the division between our values and our world. We have not begun to let science get into our heads; where then was it supposed to create these values? We have used it as a machine without will, the conjured spirit to do the chores. I believe that science can create values: and will create them precisely as literature does, by looking into the human personality; by discovering what divides it and what cements it. That is how great writers have explored man, and this whether they themselves as men have been driven by the anguish in *Gulliver's Travels* or the sympathy in *Moll Flanders*. The insight of science is not different from that of the arts. Science will create values, I believe, and discover virtues, when it looks into man; when it explores what makes him man and not an animal, and what makes his societies human and not animal packs.

I believe that we can reach this unity in our culture. I began this book by recalling that nations in their great ages have not been great in art or science, but in art and science. Rembrandt was the contemporary of Huygens and Spinoza. At that very time, Isaac Newton walked with Dryden and Christopher Wren. We know that ours is a remarkable age of science. It is for us to use it to broaden and to liberate our culture. These are the marks of science: that it is open for all to hear, and all are free to speak their minds in it. They are marks of the world at its best, and the human spirit at its most challenging.

SCIENCE IN ACTION

The Three Forms of Water   64
Michael Faraday

And now—to go into the history of this wonderful production of water from combustibles, and by combustion—I must first of all tell you that this water may exist in different conditions, and although you may now be acquainted with all its forms, they still require us to give a little attention to them for the present; so that we may perceive how the water, whilst it goes through its Protean changes, is entirely and absolutely the same thing, whether it is produced from a candle, by combustion, or from the rivers or ocean.

First of all, water, when at the coldest, is ice. Now, we philosophers— I hope that I may class you and myself together in this case—speak of water as water, whether it be in its solid, or liquid, or gaseous state—we speak of it chemically as water. Water is a thing compounded of two substances, one of which we have derived from the candle; and the other we shall find elsewhere. Water may occur as ice; and you have had most excellent opportunities lately of seeing this. Ice changes back to water—for we had on our last Sabbath a strong instance of this change, by the sad catastrophe which occurred in our own house, as well as in the houses of many of our friends— ice changes back into water when the temperature is raised: water also changes into steam when it is warmed enough. The water which we have here before us, is in its densest state, and although it changes in weight, in condition, in form, and in many other qualities, it still is water; and whether we alter it into ice by cooling, or whether we change it into steam by heat, it increases in volume—in the one case very strangely and powerfully, and in the other case very largely and wonderfully. For instance, I will now take

From Lecture III, "Products: Water From the Combustion—Nature of Water— A Compound—Hydrogen," with illustrations omitted, in *Chemical History of a Candle*, by Michael Faraday, London, The Scientific Book Guild, 1960. Reprinted by permission of The Scientific Book Guild. The lectures were delivered in 1849 and were first published in 1861.

this tin cylinder, and pour a little water into it, and seeing how much water I pour in, you may easily estimate for yourselves how high it will rise in the vessel: it will cover the bottom about two inches. I am now about to convert the water into steam, for the purpose of showing to you the different volumes which water occupies in its different states of water and steam.

Let us now take the case of water changing into ice: we can effect that by cooling it in a mixture of salt and pounded ice—and I shall do so to show you the expansion of water into a thing of larger bulk when it is so changed. These bottles [holding one] are made of strong cast iron, very strong and very thick—I suppose they are the third of an inch in thickness; they are very carefully filled with water, so as to exclude all air, and then they are screwed down tight. We shall see that when we freeze the water in these iron vessels, they will not be able to hold the ice, and the expansion within them will break them in pieces as these [pointing to some fragments] are broken, which have been bottles of exactly the same kind. I am about to put these two bottles into that mixture of ice and salt, for the purpose of showing that when water becomes ice, it changes in volume in this extraordinary way.

In the meantime look at the change which has taken place in the water to which we have applied heat; it is losing its fluid state. You may tell this by two or three circumstances. I have covered the mouth of this glass flask, in which water is boiling, with a watch-glass. Do you see what happens? It rattles away like a valve chattering, because the steam rising from the boiling water sends the valve up and down, and forces itself out, and so makes it clatter. You can very easily perceive that the flask is quite full of steam, or else it would not force its way out. You see also that the flask contains a substance very much larger than the water, for it fills the whole of the flask over and over again, and there it is blowing away into the air; and yet you cannot observe any great diminution in the bulk of the water, which shows you that its change of bulk is very great when it becomes steam.

I have put our iron bottles containing water into this freezing mixture, that you may see what happens. No communication will take place, you observe, between the water in the bottles and the ice in the outer vessel. But there will be a conveyance of heat from the one to the other, and if we are successful—we are making our experiment in very great haste—I expect you will by and by, so soon as the cold has taken possession of the bottles and their contents, hear a pop on the occasion of the bursting of the one bottle or the other, and, when we come to examine the bottles, we shall find their contents masses of ice, partly enclosed by the covering of iron which is too small for them, because the ice is larger in bulk than the water. You know very well that ice floats upon water; if a boy falls through a hole into the water, he tries to get on the ice again to float him up. Why does the ice float?—think of that, and philosophize. Because the ice is larger than the quantity of water which can produce it, and therefore the ice weighs the lighter and the water is the heavier.

To return now to the action of heat on water. See what a stream of vapour is issuing from this tin vessel. You observe, we must have made it quite full of steam to have it sent out in that great quantity. And now, as we can convert the water into steam by heat, we convert it back into liquid water by the application of cold. And if we take a glass, or any other cold thing, and hold it over this steam, see how soon it gets damp with water; it will condense it until the glass is warm—it condenses the water which is now running down the sides of it. I have here another experiment to show the condensation of water from a vaporous state back into a liquid state, in the same way as the vapour, one of the products of the candle, was condensed against the bottom of the dish and obtained in the form of water; and to show you how truly and thoroughly these changes take place, I will take this tin flask, which is now full of steam, and close the top. We shall see what takes place when we cause this water or steam to return back to the fluid state by pouring some cold water on the outside. [The Lecturer poured the cold water over the vessel, when it immediately collapsed.] You see what has happened. If I had closed the stopper, and still kept the heat applied to it, it would have burst the vessel; yet when the steam returns to the state of water, the vessel collapses, there being a vacuum produced inside by the condensation of the steam. I show you these experiments for the purpose of pointing out that in all these occurrences there is nothing that changes the water into any other thing, it still remains water; and so the vessel is obliged to give way, and is crushed inwards, as, in the other case, by the further application of heat, it would have blown outwards.

And what do you think the bulk of that water is when it assumes the vapour condition? You see that cube [pointing to a cubic foot]. There, by its side, is a cubic inch, exactly the same shape as the cube foot, and that bulk of water [the cubic inch] is sufficient to expand into that bulk [the cubic foot] of steam; and, on the contrary, the application of cold will contract that large quantity of steam into this small quantity of water. [One of the iron bottles burst at that moment.] Ah! There is one of our bottles burst, and here you see is a crack down one side an eighth of an inch in width. [The other now exploded, sending the freezing mixture in all directions.] This other bottle is also broken; although the iron was nearly half an inch thick, the ice has burst it asunder. These changes always take place in water; they do not require to be always produced by artificial means—we only use them here because we want to produce a small winter round that little bottle instead of a long and severe one. But if you go to Canada, or to the North, you will find the temperature there out of doors will do the same thing as has been done here by the freezing mixture.

65 The Sex of Plants

Carl Von Linne

The organs common in general to all plants are: 1st. The root, with its capillary vessels, extracting nourishment from the ground. 2nd. The leaves, which may be called the limbs, and which, like the feet and wings of animals, are organs of motion; for being themselves shaken by the external air, they shake and exercise the plant. 3rd. The trunk, containing the medullary substance, which is nourished by the bark, and for the most part multiplied into several compound plants. 4th. The fructification, which is the true body of the plant, set at liberty by a metamorphosis, and consists only of the organs of generation; it is often defended by a calyx, and furnished with petals, by means of which it in a matter flutters in the air.

Many flowers have no calyx, as several of the lily tribe, the Hippuris, etc., many want the corolla, as grasses, and the plants called apetalous; but there are none more destitute of stamina and pistilla, those important organs destined to the formation of fruit. We therefore infer from experience that the stamina are the male organs of generation, and the pistilla of the female; and as many flowers are furnished with both at once, it follows that such flowers are hermaphrodites. Nor is this so wonderful, as that there should be any plants in which the different sexes are distinct individuals; for plants being immovably fixed to one spot, cannot like animals, travel in search of a mate. There exists, however, in some plants a real difference of sex. From seeds of the same mother, some individuals shall be produced, whose flowers exhibit stamina without pistilla, and may therefore properly be called male; while the rest being furnished with pistilla without stamina are therefore denominated females; and so uniformly does this take place, that no vegetable was ever found to produce female flowers without flowers furnished with stamina being produced, either on the same individual or on another plant of the same species, and *vice versa*.

As all seed vessels are destined to produce seeds, so are the stamina to bear the pollen, or fecundating powder. All seeds contain within their membranes a certain medullary substance, which swells when dipped into warm water. All pollen, likewise, contains in its membrane an elastic sub-

"The Sex of Plants," by Linnaeus (Carl Von Linne), with deletions, is from a publication of the Linnaean Society. It appears in Ch. XI in *Classics of Modern Science,* edited by William S. Knickerbocker, New York, F. S. Crofts, Inc., 1927. Von Linne lived between 1707–1778.

stance, which, although very subtle, and almost invisible, by means of warm water often explodes with great vehemence. While plants are in flower, the pollen falls from their antheræ, and is dispersed abroad, as seeds are dislodged from their situation when the fruit is ripe. At the same time that the pollen is scattered, the pistillum presents its stigma, which is then in its highest vigour, and, for a portion of the day at least, is moistened with a fine dew. The stamina either surround this stigma, or if the flowers are of the drooping kind, they are bent towards one side, so that the pollen can easily find access to the stigma, where it not only adheres by means of the dew of that part, but the moisture occasions its bursting, by which means its contents are discharged. That issued from it being mixed with the fluid of the stigma, is conveyed to rudiments of the seed. Many evident instances of this present themselves to our notice; but I have nowhere seen it more manifest than in the Jacobean Lily (*Amarylis formosissima*), the pistillum of which, when sufficient heat is given the plant to make it flower in perfection, is bent downwards and from its stigma issues a drop of limpid fluid, so large that one would think it in danger of falling to the ground. It is, however, gradually reabsorbed into the style about three or four o'clock and becomes invisible until about ten the next morning, when it appears again; by noon it attains its largest dimensions; and in the afternoon, by a gentle and scarcely perceptible decrease it returns to its source. If we shake the antheræ over the stigma, so that the pollen may fall on this limpid drop, we see the fluid soon after become turbid and assume a yellow color; and we perceive little rivulets, or opaque streaks running from the stigma towards the rudiments of the seed. Some time afterwards, when the drop has totally disappeared, the pollen may be observed adhering to the stigma, but of an irregular figure, having lost its original form. No one, therefore, can assent to what Morland and others have asserted, that the pollen passes into the stigma, pervades the style and enters the tender rudiments of the seed, as Leeuwenhoeck supposed his worms to enter the ova. A most evident proof of the falsehood of this opinion may be obtained from any species of *Mirabilis* (Marvel of Peru), whose pollen is so very large that it almost exceeds the style itself in thickness, and, falling on the stigma, adheres firmly to it; that organ sucking and exhausting the pollen, as a cuttle fish devours everything that comes within its grasp. One evening in the month of August, I removed all the stamina from three flowers of the *Mirabilis Longiflora*, at the same time destroying all the rest of the flowers which were expanded; I sprinkled these three flowers with the pollen of *Mirabilis Jalappa*; the seed-buds swelled, but did not ripen. Another evening I performed a similar experiment, only sprinkling the flowers with the pollen of the same species; all these flowers produced ripe seeds.

Some writers have believed that the stamina are parts of the fructification, which serve only to discharge an impure or excrementitious matter, and by no means formed for so important a work as generation. But it is very evident that these authors have not sufficiently examined the subject; for, as in many vegetables, some flowers are furnished with stamina only, and others only with pistilla; it is altogether impossible that stamina situated at so very great a distance from the fruit, as on a different branch, or perhaps on a separate plant, should serve to convey any impurities from the embryo.

No physiologist could demonstrate, *a priori*, the necessity of the masculine fluid to the rendering the eggs of animals prolific, but experience has established it beyond a doubt. We therefore judge *a posteriori* principally, of the same effect in plants.

In the month of January, 1760, the *Antholyza Cunonia* flowered in a pot in my parlour, but produced no fruit, the air of the room not being sufficiently agitated to waft the pollen to the stigma. One day, about noon, feeling the stigma very moist, I plucked off one of the antheræ, by means of a fine pair of forceps, and gently rubbed it on one part of the expanded stigmata. The spike of flowers remained eight or ten days longer; when I observed, in gathering the branch for my herbarium, that the fruit of that flower only on which the experiment had been made, had swelled to the size of a bean. I then dissected this fruit and discovered that one of the three cells contained seeds in considerable number, the other two being entirely withered.

In the month of April I sowed the seeds of hemp (*Cannabis*) in two different pots. The young plants came up so plentifully, that each pot contained thirty or forty. I placed each by the light of a window, but in different and remote apartments. The hemp grew extremely well in both pots. In one of them I permitted the male and female plants to remain together, to flower and bear fruit, which ripened in July, being macerated in water, and committed to the earth, sprung up in twelve days. From the other, however, I removed all the male plants, as soon as they were old enough for me to distinguish them from the females. The remaining females grew very well, and presented their long pistilla in great abundance, these flowers continuing a very long time, as if in expectation of their mates; while the plants in the other pot had already ripened their fruit, their pistilla having, quite in a different manner, faded as soon as the males had discharged all their pollen. It was truly a beautiful and truly admirable spectacle to see the unimpregnated females preserve their pistilla so long green and flourishing, not permitting them to begin to fade till they had been for a very considerable time exposed in vain, to the access of the male pollen.

Afterwards, when these virgin plants began to decay through age, I examined all their calyces in the presence of several botanists and found them large and flourishing, although every one of the seed-buds was brown, compressed, membranaceous, and dry, not exhibiting any appearance of cotyledons or pulp. Hence I am perfectly convinced that the circumstance which authors have recorded, of the female hemp having produced seeds, although deprived of the male, could only have happened by means of pollen brought by the wind from some distant place. No experiment can be more easily performed than the above; none more satisfactory in demonstrating the generation of plants.

The *Clutia tenella* was in like manner kept growing in my window during the months of June and July. The male plant was in one pot, the female in another. The latter abounded with fruit, not one of its flowers proving abortive. I removed the two pots into different windows of the same apartment; still all the female flowers continued to become fruitful. At length I took away the male entirely, leaving the female alone, and cutting off all the flowers which it had already borne. Every day new ones appeared from the axila of every leaf; each remained eight or ten days, after which their foot stalks turning yellow, they fell barren to the ground. A botanical friend, who had amused himself with observing this phenomenon with me, persuaded me to bring, from the stove in the garden, a single male flower, which he placed over one of the female ones, then in perfection, tying a piece of red silk around its pistillum. The next day the male flower was taken away, and this single seed-bud remained, and bore fruit. Afterwards I took another male flower out of the same stove, and with a pair of slender forceps pinched off one of its antheræ, which I afterwards gently scratched with a feather, so that a very small portion of its pollen was discharged upon one of the three stigmata of a female flower, the other two stigmata being covered with paper. This fruit likewise attained its due size, and on being cut transversely, exhibited one cell filled with a large seed, and the other two empty. The rest of the flowers, being unimpregnated, faded and fell off. This experiment may be performed with as little trouble as the former.

The *Datisca cannabina* came up in my garden from seed ten years ago, and has every year been plentifully increased by means of its perennial root. Flowers in great number have been produced by it; but, being all female, they proved abortive. Being desirous of producing male plants, I obtained more seeds from Paris. Some more plants were raised; but these likewise to my great mortification, all proved females, and bore flowers, but no fruit. In the year 1757 I received another parcel of seeds. From these I obtained a few male plants, which flowered in 1758. These were planted at a great distance from the females; and when their flowers were just ready to emit their pollen, holding a paper under them, I gently shook the spike of panicle with my finger, till the paper was almost covered with the yellow powder. I carried this to the females, which were flowering in another part of the garden, and placed it over them. The cold nights of the year in which this experiment was made, destroyed these Datiscas, with many other plants, much earlier than usual. Nevertheless, when I examined the flowers of those plants, which I had sprinkled with the fertilizing powder, I found the seeds of their due magnitude; while in the more remote Datiscas, which had not been impregnated with pollen, no traces of seeds were visible.

Several species of Momordica, cultivated by us, like other Indian vegetables, in close stoves, have frequently borne female flowers; which, although at first very vigorous, after a short time have constantly faded and turned yellow, without perfecting any seed, till I instructed the gardener, as soon as he observed a female flower, to gather a male one, and place it above the female. By this contrivance we are so certain of obtaining fruit that we dare pledge ourselves to make any female flowers fertile that shall be fixed on.

The *Jatropha urens* has flowered every year in my hot-house; but the female flowers coming before the males, in a week's time dropped their petals and faded before the latter were opened; from which cause no fruit has been produced, but the *germina* themselves have fallen off. We have therefore never had any fruit of the Jatropha till the year 1752, when the male flowers were in vigour on a tall tree, at the same time that the females began to appear on a small Jatropha which was growing in a garden-pot. I placed this pot under the other tree, by which means the female flowers bore seeds, which grew on being sown. I have frequently amused myself with taking the male flowers from one plant, and scattering them over the female flowers of another, and have always found the seeds of the latter impregnated by it.

Two years ago I placed a piece of paper under some of these male flowers and afterwards folded up the pollen which had fallen upon it, preserving it so folded up, if I remember right, four or six weeks, at the end of which time another branch of the same Jatropha was in flower. I then took the pollen, which I had so long preserved in paper, and strewed it over three female flowers, the only ones at that time expanded. The three females proved fruitful, while all the rest, which grew in the same bunch, fell off abortive.

. . .

The Neapolitan star flower (*Ornithogalum nutans*) has six broad stamina, which stand close together in the form of a bell, the three external ones being but half the length of the others; so that it seems impossible for their antheræ ever to convey their pollen to the stigma; but nature, by an admirable contrivance, bends the summits of these external stamina inwards between the other filaments, so that they are enabled to accomplish their purpose.

The Plaintain tree (*Musa*) bears two kinds of hermaphrodite flowers; some have imperfect antheræ, others only the rudiments of stigmata; as the last mentioned kind appear after the others, they cannot impregnate them, consequently no seeds are produced in our gardens, and scarcely ever on the plants cultivated in India. An event happened this year, which I have long wished for; two plaintain-trees flowering with me so fortunately that one of them brought forth its first female blossoms at the time that male ones began to appear on the other. I eagerly ran to collect antheræ from the first plant, in order to scatter them over the newly-expanded females, in hopes of obtaining seed from them, which no botanist has yet been able to do. But when I came to examine the antheræ I found even the largest of them absolutely empty and void of pollen, consequently unfit for impregnating the females; the seeds of this plant, therefore, can never be perfected in our gardens. I do not doubt, however, that real male plants of this species may be found in its native country, bearing flowers without fruit, which the gardeners have neglected; while the females in this country produce imperfect fruit, without seeds, like the female fig; and, like that tree, are increased easily by suckers. The fruit, therefore, of the plaintain-tree scarcely attains anything like its due size, the larger seed-buds only ripening, without containing anything in them.

The day would sooner fail me than examples. A female date-bearing palm flowered many years at Berlin, without producing any seeds. But the Berlin people taking care to have some of the blossoms of the male tree, which was then flowering at Leipsic, sent them by the post, they obtained fruit by that means; and some dates, the offspring of this impregnation, being planted in my garden, sprung up, and to this day continue to grow vigorously. Kœmpfer formerly told us how necessary it was found by the oriental people, who live upon the produce of palm-trees, and are the true Lotophagi, to plant some male trees among the females, if they hoped for any fruit; hence, it is the practice of those who make war in that part of the world to cut down all the male palms, that a famine may afflict their proprietors; sometimes even the inhabitants themselves destroy the male trees, when they dread an invasion, that their enemies may find no sustenance in the country.

Leaving these instances, and innumerable others, which are so well known to botanists that they would by no means bear the appearance of novelty, and can only be doubted by those persons who neither have observed nature, nor will they take the trouble to study her, I pass to a fresh subject, concerning which much new light is wanted; I mean hybrid, or mule vegetables, the existence and origin of which we shall now consider.

I shall enumerate three or four real mule plants, to whose origin I have been an eye-witness.

1. *Veronica spuria*, described in Amœnitates Acad. vol. III. p. 35, came from the impregnation of *Veronic maratima* by *Verbena officinalis*; it is easily propagated by cuttings, and agrees perfectly with its mother in fructification, and with its father in leaves.

2. *Delphinium hybridum*, sprung up in a part of the garden where *Delphinium clatum* and *Aconitum Napellus* grew together; it resembles its mother as much in its internal parts, that is, in fructification as it does its father (the *Aconitum*) in outward structure, or leaves; and, owing its origin

to plants so nearly allied to each other, it propagates itself by seed; some of which I now send with this Dissertation.

3. *Hieracium Taraxici,* gathered in 1753 upon our mountains by Dr. Solander, in its thick, brown, woolly calyx; in its stem being hairy towards the top, and in its bracteæ, as well as in every part of its fructification, resembles so perfectly its mother, *Hieracium alpinum,* that an inexperienced person might mistake one for the other; but in the smoothness of its leaves, in their indentations and whole structure, it so manifestly agrees with its father, *Leontodon Taraxacum* (Dandelion), that there can be no doubt of its origin.

4. *Tragopogon hybridum* attracted my notice the autumn before last, in a part of the garden where I had planted *Tragopogon pratense,* and *Tragopogon porrifolium;* but winter coming on, destroyed its seeds. Last year, while the *Tragopogon pratense* was in flower I rubbed off its pollen early in the morning, and about eight o'clock sprinkled its stigmata with some pollen of the *Tragopogon porrifolium,* marking the calyces by tying a thread round them. I afterwards gathered the seeds when ripe, and sowed them that autumn in another place; they grew, and produced this year, 1759, purple flowers yellow at the base, seeds of which I now send. I doubt whether any experiment demonstrates the generation of plants more certainly than this.

There can be no doubt that these are all new species produced by hybrid generation. And hence we learn, that a mule offspring is the exact image of its mother in its medullary substance, internal nature, or fructification, but resembles its father in leaves. This is a foundation upon which naturalists may build much. For it seems probable that many plants, which now appear different species of the same *genus,* may in the beginning have been but one plant, having arisen merely from hybrid generation. Many of those Geraniums which grow at the Cape of Good Hope, and have never been found wild anywhere but in the south parts of Africa, and which, as they are distinguished from all other Geraniums by their single-leaved calyx, many-flowered foot-stalk, irregular corolla, seven fertile stamina, and three mutilated ones, and by their naked seeds furnished with downy awns; so they agree together in all these characters, although very various in their roots, stems and leaves; these Geraniums, I say, would almost induce a botanist to believe that the species of one *genus* in vegetables are only so many different plants as there have been different associations with the flowers of one species, and consequently a *genus* is nothing else than a number of plants sprung from the same mother by different fathers. But whether all these species be the offspring of time; whether, in the beginning of all things, the Creator limited the number of future species, I dare not presume to determine. I am, however, convinced this mode of multiplying plants does not interfere with the system or general scheme of nature; as I daily observe that insects, which live upon one species of a particular *genus,* are contented with another of the same *genus.*

A person who has once seen the *Achyranthes aspera,* and remarked its spike, the parts of its flower, its small and peculiarly formed nectaria, as well as its calyces bent backwards as the fruit ripens, would think it very easy at any time to distinguish these flowers from all others in the universe; but when he finds the flowers of *Achyranthes indica* agreeing with them even in their minutest parts, and at the same time observes the large, thick, obtuse, undulated leaves of the last-mentioned plant, he will think he sees *Achyranthes aspera* masked in the foliage of *Xanthium strumarium.* But I forbear to mention any more instances.

Here is a new employment for botanists, to attempt the production of new species of vegetables by scattering the pollen of various plants over various widowed females. And if these remarks should meet with a favourable reception, I shall be the more induced to dedicate what remains of my life to such experiments, which recommend themselves by being at the same time agreeable and useful. I am persuaded by many considerations that those numerous and most valuable varieties of plants which are used for culinary purposes, have been produced in this manner, as the several kinds of cabbages, lettuces, etc.; and I apprehend this is the reason of their not being changed by a difference of soil. Hence I cannot give my assent to the opinion of those who imagine all varieties to have been occasioned by change of soil; for, if this were the case, the plants would return to their original form, if removed again to their original situation.

[the animal world]
From Embryo to Child 66
Sir Charles Sherrington

We dismiss wonder commonly with childhood. Much later we may return. Then the whole world becomes wonderful. But, greatest wonder, our wonder soon lapses. A rainbow every morning who would pause to look at? The wonderful which comes often is soon taken for granted. That is practical enough. It allows us to get on with life. But it may stultify if it cannot on occasion be thrown off. To recapture now and then childhood's wonder is a driving force for occasional grown-up thoughts. Among the workings of this planet, there is a *tour de force,* if such term befits the workings of a planet.

From Ch. IV, "The Wisdom of the Body," with deletions, in *Man on his Nature,* by Sir Charles Sherrington, Cambridge, Cambridge University Press, 1963. Reprinted by permission of Cambridge University Press.

The body is made up of cells, thousands of millions of them, in our own instance about 1000 billions. It is a unity which has become multiplicity while keeping its unity (Carrel).[1] At its beginning it is just one cell, and the whole body is the progeny of that one. Its ancestry converges back to that one ancestral cell. And that, in its turn, was from the ancestral cell of a next preceding family of cells.

In each generation the impetus for the initial cell to produce its organized family is supplied by the coming together of it and another cell, outside its own familial stock, but not too far outside. In our own case and in the case of all our nearer kind, these two cells come from individuals of like species. The two individuals have to be complemental in sex. The fertilization-process which is preliminary to the train of growth of a new individual we can dispense with. The story of growth from a rounded microscopic speck to a shaped creature, is what we will glance at in outline. Before the coming of the microscope the earliest chapters of this life-story baffled the wisest. They were mere conjecture. When the microscope did come it set itself to trace this Odyssey, this journey from a pin's-head egg to a grown man. Some saw as the starting-point of it an infinitesimal man. The truth was stranger still. All there was to see was a speck of granular jelly, bearing no likeness to either parent or to man at all.

Then at its outsetting that speck grew and, presently tearing its tiny self in two, made an adhering pair. Then they 4, 8, 16, 32 and so on; only to slow down after reaching millions upon millions. Not to stop altogether until by misadventure or, after years, by natural term, there falls on the whole assembly that subversive change called "death." Each of the cells from the beginning besides shaping itself takes up for itself a right station in the total assembly according to the stage which the assembly has by that time attained. Thus each cell helps to shape, and to construct as by design, the total assembly. So it is that those early thirty-two cells dispose themselves as a little ball, hollow and filled with water. These thirty-two cells then are a beginning stage of the individual to be, and the beginning whether beast or man.

Their visible arrangement taken at that stage gives no obvious hint of what the ultimate will be. Thence quickly, though gradually, change sweeps onward to later stage on stage. Darwin quoted the naturalist who wrote, "I have two little embryos in spirit, to which I have omitted to attach names. I am now quite unable to say to what class of animals they belong." Lizards or birds or mammals, they might be any of them. That kind of thing must have confronted Aristotle as a biologist; it was a *final* cause. He insisted that to know a thing its final cause must have been explored. That was an injunction which Jean Fernel accepted from him and endorsed. In biology to jump at the final causes has many times led to mistakes. It did so notably with Galen. But it has also often solved problems. It opened clues to Harvey. But in fol-

[1] *Methods of Tissue Culture* (1938), by R. C. Parker, foreword by Alexis Carrel.

lowing it, Harvey never forgot that its following as a clue demands control by other evidence at every step.

The successive chapters of the story of the little ball of cells is like a serial transformation scene. The little ball can be likened, crudely enough, to a set of magic bricks. The one cell, the original fertilized cell, grows into two and those two each into two, and so forth. When that has gone on in the aggregate some 45 times there are 26 million magic bricks all of a family. That is about the number in the human child at birth. They have arranged themselves into a complex, which is a human child. Each has assumed its required form and size in the right place. The whole is not merely specific but is a particular individual within the limits of the specific.

Each cell, we remember, is blind; senses it has none. It knows not "up" from "down;" it works in the dark. Yet the nerve-cell, for instance, "finds" even to the fingertips the nerve-cell with which it should touch fingers. It is as if an immanent principle inspired each cell with knowledge for the carrying out of a design. And this picture which the microscope supplies to us, conveying this impression of prescience and intention, supplies us after all, because it is but a picture, with only the static form. That is but the outward and visible sign of a dynamic activity, which is a harmony in time as well as space. "Never the time and the place and the loved one all together." Here all three and always, save for disease.

In its earliest stage the embryo's cells are not notably different one from another. Later a finished muscle-cell and a finished nerve-cell and a finished liver-cell are as far apart in visible structure as in what they do. They become so in spite of being by descent all members of one family. On the other hand, take of each similarly-functioning cells a pair, one from man and one from fish, and, though by descent worlds apart, the observer can read at a glance that members of a pair, alike in what they do, conform to the same pattern. The nerve-cell is as obviously a nerve-cell whether from man or fish. The cells of the various parts of the systematized assembly assume special shapes, octagonal, stellate, threadlike, or what not. They, as the case may require, pour out cement which binds, or fluid in which they shall move free. Some will have changed their stuff and become rigid bone or, harder still, the enamel of a tooth; some become fluid, so to flow along tubes too fine for the eye to see. Some become clear as glass, some opaque as stone, some colourless, some red, some black. Some become factories of a furious chemistry, some become inert as death. Some become engines of mechanical pull, some scaffoldings of static support. Some a system transmitting electrical signs. It might serve as a text for democracy. It is as if the life of each one of all those millions has understood its special part. Thus arises the new integral individual to be.

To this there seems at first sight one exception. One cell-type which, out of all the myriads, alone remains its original self and does not specialize. It retains the old original nature of the ancestral cell. Its sisters and their progeny pass on through chains of metamorphoses to form a world of different shapes and activities. But this one persists still unmodified and true to its own primitive forbear. It must be so, or there would be no future generation of the entire stock. To begin again there must be a return to the beginning. All its sisters with their flights into far-fetched specializations, including the brain with its mysteries of mind, are powerless to produce again a germ such as they sprang from. From no one of them all, let them be ever so human, can any fertilization produce their like again in the shape of man or human child. For that their sister cell, still generalized like the ancestral cell, is the sole means remaining. Hence from the old ancestral cell one narrow derivative line of descendants, nested in the rest of the immense specialized collateral progeny, retains its original germinal and general nature; and even this has to ripen. Significantly enough it then sets itself free from all the others. And so from generation on to generation. This limited cell-stock which can be called exceptional in that unlike its congeners, it does not specialize away from the parent germinal form, can be thought of as no exception after all. It is specialized for reproduction. It is clearly specialized in so far that only a special fertilizer can fertilize it. Its own specialization, as though by foreknowledge, anticipates among other anticipations what the nature of that special fertilizer will be. The whole astonishing process achieving the making of a new individual is thus an organized adventure in specialization on the part of countless co-operating units. It does more than complete the new individual; it provides for the future production of further individuals from that one.

More than half a million different species of pattern of creature are, I believe, listed as current life. And each, as we say, "breeds true." This particular one we have followed is that to which the pair of cells, which made it, themselves belong, and they will make no other kind. But although of their species it is not quite like any other that ever was. It is not only man but it is the man John Brown, or the woman Mary Smith, whose exact like never was yet.

But that procession of change which for instance abuts in the human child has never come within the role of the actual ancestry of the fertilized cell which sets about it. All that has come within the experience of that ancestry has been the launching from generation to generation of that side-adventure which now terminates in fully completed man. An explanation once offered for the evolutionary process traced it to "memory" in the ancestral cell. But such an explanation rests, even as analogy, on a misapprehension of the actual circumstances. It would be imagination rather than memory which we must assume for the ancestral cell; memory could not recall experience it never had.

The few early units which formed the family when it was but a tiny ball take into their counsel water. The ball they form is filled with it. The growing membrane, half-floating, can then fold. It shapes itself, it feeds, water is a generous solvent; and it admits electrical activities, chemical compounds separating with opposite charge. Water is the very menstruum and habitat of each and every cell. Water, within and without, allows the cell free scope for action. Water is a wonderful "surround" and the germinal cell seems to appreciate that.

Water within and water without. The cell-surface becomes at once a boundary and a medium of exchange between two chemical worlds, one inside the cell, "alive," the other outside it, lifeless. The cells divide and divide and differentiate and differentiate. The total aggregate of the surface between alive and not alive becomes greater and greater, and endlessly qualitatively graded.

Step by step things shape. There appear, tiny at first, what to the eye of the expert are recognizable as rudiments of parts of the future creature. The brain is a set of three little hollow chambers, and, thrust from the hindmost, a short tube, the spinal cord. They were formed by the membrane folding over right and left, the side-flaps merging and so making a tube. Their membrane will come to be a patterned nest of branching cells all in touch directly or indirectly one with the other and, in man, approaching in number our planet's human population. The tubular chamber with its watery content persists, buried within the greatly enriched membrane. It persists throughout life, a primitive vestige, a dumb witness to far primeval times when not only man, but bird and mammal and even reptile had not yet come to be. That early step of folding to make a tube-like brain belongs to the opening chapter of the story of the human embryo growing into a child, but it is a primordial step, which foreran by aeons the advent of the human form itself.

.   .   .

We speak of nerves *for* doing this and that. This is the Galen in us. To do so comes unbidden to the lips. And Galen in this was thinking as everyone thinks and was speaking for Mr. Everyman, not merely of his own time but for practically ever since. Muscles seem made for what will be wanted of them. In the foetus a short channel joins the root of the lung-artery with that of the main artery of the body. Immediately following birth the lung enters activity, and this side-tracking of its blood-supply would be disadvantageous. A little before the foetus is actually born this channel is shut by a special small muscle. This muscle "as far as is known never used in the foetus," "springs into action at birth"[1] and shuts the channel. "Having performed its function it degenerates" and disappears, the channel having in due course become obliterated under disuse. Sir Joseph Barcroft adds "it would seem very difficult to claim that the muscle which closes the ductus at birth has been differentiated as the result of any specific conditions to which it has been subjected—much less any specific use which it has subserved."[2] It is an instance of a final cause.

[1] *The Brain and its Environment,* by Sir Joseph Barcroft (Yale University Press, 1938), pp. 73–81.
[2] *Ibid.* p. 73.

Nerves seem *for* their purpose, constructed in view of what *will* be "wanted" of them. Before ever they function they grow where they *will* be wanted, they make the "right" connections. We all drop into this mode of thought; we adopt it as we dissect. In the particular prodigy before us now, that of a microscopic cell becoming a man, we incline to read the whole story in that way. We say "it grows into" a child. Grows? Levers laid down in gristle, becoming bone when wanted for the heavier pull of muscle which *will* clothe them. Lungs, solid glands, yet arranged to hollow out at a few minutes' notice when the necessary air shall enter. Limb-buds, futile at their appearing and yet deliberately appearing, in order to become limbs in readiness for an existence where they will be all-important. A pseudo-aquatic parasite, voiceless as a fish, yet constructing within itself an instrument of voice against the time when it *will* talk. Organs of skin, ear, eye, nose, tongue, superfluous all of them in the watery dark where formed, yet each unhaltingly preparing to enter a daylit, airy, object-full manifold world which they *will* be wanted to report on. A great excrescence at one end of a nerve-tube, an outrageously outsized brain, of no avail at the moment but where the learning of a world which is *to be* experienced will go forward. Living structure is a mass of Aristotle's final causes. All is remembered; no detail is forgotten, even to the criss-cross hairs at entrance to a cat's ear which keep out water and flies (Pl. V*a*). Had antiquity or the middle ages been acquainted with the facts, they would have been set down to Natural Magic. Fernel's Preface (1542) wrote "as Aristotle says to know the end of a thing is to know the why of it." And similarly today the biologist writes, "we can only understand an organism if we regard it *as though* produced under the guidance of thought for an end," [3] as a final cause at work.

[3] R. C. Punnett, "Forty years of evolution theory," in Needham and Pagel, *Background to Modern Science* (Cambridge, 1938), p. 196.

[the heavens]

67   The Expanding Universe
Fred Hoyle

At the risk of seeming a little repetitive I should like to begin this chapter by recalling some of our previous results. One of the things I have been trying to do is to break up our survey of the Universe into distinct parts. We started with the Sun and our system of planets. To get an idea of the size of this system we took a model with the Sun represented by a ball about six inches in diameter. In spite of this enormous reduction of scale we found that our model would still cover the area of a small town. On the same scale the Earth has to be represented by a speck of dust, and the nearest stars are 2,000 miles away. So it is quite unwieldly to use this model to describe the positions or even the closest stars.

Some other means had to be found to get to grips with the distances of the stars in the Milky Way. Choosing light as our measure of distance, we saw that light takes several years to travel to us from near-by stars, and that many of the stars in the Milky Way are at a distance of as much as 1,000 light years. But the Milky Way is only a small bit of a great disk-shaped system of gas and stars that is turning in space like a great wheel. The diameter of the disk is about 60,000 light years. This distance is so colossal that there has only been time for the disk to turn round about twenty times since the oldest stars were born—about 4,000,000,000 years ago. And this is in spite of the tremendous speed of nearly 1,000,000 miles an hour at which the outer parts of the disk are moving. We also saw that the Sun and our planets lie together near the edge of our Galaxy, as this huge disk is called.

Now we shall go out into the depths of space far beyond the confines of our own Galaxy. Look out at the heavens on a clear night; if you want a really impressive sight do so from a steep mountainside or from a ship at sea. As I have said before, by looking at any part of the sky that is distant from the Milky Way you can see right out of the disk that forms our Galaxy. What lies out there? Not just scattered stars by themselves, but in every direction space is strewn with whole galaxies, each one like our own. Most of these other galaxies—or extragalactic nebulae as astronomers often call them —are too faint to be seen with the naked eye, but vast numbers of them can be observed with a powerful telescope. When I say that these other galaxies are similar to our Galaxy, I do not mean that they are exactly alike. Some are much smaller than ours, others are not disk-shaped but nearly spherical in form. The basic similarity is that they are all enormous clouds of gas and stars, each one with anything from 100,000,000 to 10,000,000,000 or so members.

Although most of the other galaxies are somewhat different from ours, it is important to realize that some of them are indeed very like our Galaxy even so far as details are concerned. By good fortune one of the nearest of them, only about 700,000 light years away, seems to be practically a twin of our Galaxy. You can see it for yourself by looking in the constellation of Andromeda. With the naked eye it appears as a vague blur, but with a powerful telescope it shows up as one of the most impressive of all astronomical objects. On a good photograph of it you can easily pick out places where there are great clouds of dust. These clouds are just the sort of thing that in our own Galaxy produces the troublesome fog I mentioned in earlier talks. It is this fog that stops us seeing more than a small bit of our own Galaxy. If you want to get an idea of what our Galaxy would look like if it were seen from outside, the best way is to study this other one in Andromeda. If the truth be known I expect that in many places there living creatures are looking out across space at our Galaxy. They must be seeing much the same spectacle as we see when we look at their galaxy.

It would be possible to say a great deal about all these other galaxies: how they are spinning round like our own; how their brightest stars are supergiants, just like those of our Galaxy; and how in those where supergiants are common, wonderful spiral patterns are found. A question that interests me very much is whether these spiral patterns are connected with the tunneling process I discussed in a previous chapter. We can also find exploding stars in these other galaxies. In particular, supernovae are so brilliant that they show up even though they are very far off. Now the existence of supernovae in other galaxies has implications for our cosmology. You will remember that in a previous chapter I described the way in which planetary systems like our own come into being; the basic requirement of the process was the supernova explosion. So we can conclude, since supernovae occur in the other galaxies, planetary systems must exist there just as in our own. Moreover, by observing the other galaxies we get a far better idea of the rate at which supernovae occur than we could ever get from our Galaxy alone. A general survey by the American observers Baade and Zwicky has shown that on the average there is a supernova explosion every four or five hundred years in each galaxy. So, remembering one previous argument, you will see that on the average each galaxy must contain more than 1,000,000 planetary systems.

How many of these gigantic galaxies are there? Well, they are strewn through space as far as we can see with the most powerful telescopes. Spaced apart at an average distance of rather more than 1,000,000 light years, they certainly continue out to the fantastic distance of 1,000,000,000 light years. Our telescopes fail to penetrate further than that, so we cannot be certain that the galaxies extend still deeper into space, but we feel pretty sure that they do. One of the questions we shall have to consider later is what lies beyond the range of our most powerful instruments. But even within the range of observation there are about 100,000,000 galaxies. With upward of 1,000,000 planetary systems per galaxy the combined total for the parts of the Universe that we can see comes out at more than a hundred million million. I find myself wondering whether somewhere among them there is a cricket team that could beat the Australians.

We now come to the important question of where this great swarm of galaxies has come from. Perhaps I should first remind you of what was said when we were discussing the origin of the stars. We saw that in the space between the stars of our Galaxy there is a tenuous gas, the interstellar gas. At one time our Galaxy was a whirling disk of gas with no stars in it. Out of the gas, clouds condensed, and then in each cloud further condensations were formed. This went on until finally stars were born. Stars were formed in the other galaxies in exactly the same way. But we can go further than this and extend the condensation idea to include the origin of the galaxies themselves. Just as the basic step in explaining the origin of the stars is the recognition that a tenuous gas pervades the space within a galaxy, so the basic step in explaining the origin of the galaxies is the recognition that a still more tenuous gas fills the whole of space. It is out of this general background material, as I shall call it, that the galaxies have condensed.

Here now is a question that is important for our cosmology. What is the present density of the background material? The average density is so low that a pint measure would contain only about one atom. But small as this is, the total amount of the background material exceeds about a thousandfold the combined quantity of material in all the galaxies put together. This may seem surprising but it is a consequence of the fact that the galaxies occupy only a very small fraction of the whole of space. You see here the characteristic signature of the New Cosmology. We have seen that inside our Galaxy the interstellar gas outweighs the material in all the stars put together. Now we see that the background material outweighs by a large margin all the galaxies put together. And just as it is the interstellar gas that controls the situation inside our Galaxy, so it is the background material that controls the Universe as a whole. This will become increasingly clear as we go on.

The degree to which the background material has to be compressed to form a galaxy is not at all comparable with the tremendous compression necessary to produce a star. This you can see by thinking of a model in which our Galaxy is represented by a fifty-cent piece. Then the blob of background material out of which our Galaxy condensed would be only about a foot in diameter. This incidentally is the right way to think about the Universe as a whole. If in your mind's eye you take the average galaxy to be about the size of a bee—a small bee, a honeybee, not a bumblebee—our Galaxy, which is a good deal larger than the average, would be roughly represented in shape and size by the fifty-cent piece, and the average spacing of the galaxies would be about three yards, and the range of telescopic vision about a mile. So sit back and imagine a swarm of bees spaced about three yards apart and stretching away from you in all directions for a distance of about a mile. Now for each honeybee substitute the vast bulk of a galaxy and you have an idea of the Universe that has been revealed by the large American telescopes.

Next I must introduce the idea that this colossal swarm is not static: it is expanding. There are some people who seem to think that it would be a good idea if it was static. I disagree with this idea, if only because a static universe would be very dull. To show you what I mean by this I should like to point out that the Universe is wound up in two ways—that is to say, energy can be got out of the background material in two ways. Whenever a new galaxy is formed, gravitation supplies energy. For instance, gravitation supplies the energy of the rotation that develops when a galaxy condenses out of the background material. And gravitation again supplies energy during every subsequent condensation of the interstellar gas inside a galaxy. It is because of this energy that a star becomes hot when it is born. The second source of energy lies in the atomic nature of the background material. It seems likely that this was originally pure hydrogen. This does not mean that the background material is now entirely pure hydrogen, because it gets slightly adulterated by some of the material expelled by the exploding supernovae. As a source of energy hydrogen does not come into operation until high temperatures develop—and this only arises when stars condense. It is this second source of energy that is more familiar and important to us on the Earth.

Now, why would a Universe that was static on a large scale, that was not expanding in fact, be uninteresting? Because of the following sequence of events. Even if the Universe were static on a large scale it would not be locally static: that is to say, the background material would condense into galaxies, and after a few thousand million years this process would be completed—no background would be left. Furthermore, the gas out of which the galaxies were initially composed would condense into stars. When this stage was reached hydrogen would be steadily converted into helium. After several hundreds of thousands of millions of years this process would be everywhere completed and all the stars would evolve toward the black dwarfs I mentioned in a previous chapter. So finally the whole Universe would become entirely dead. This would be the running down of the Universe that was described so graphically by Jeans.

One of my main aims will be to explain why we get a different answer to this when we take account of the dynamic nature of the Universe. You might like to know something about the observational evidence that the Universe is indeed in a dynamic state of expansion. Perhaps you've noticed that a whistle from an approaching train has a higher pitch, and from a receding train a lower pitch, than a similar whistle from a stationary train. Light emitted by a moving source has the same property. The pitch of the light is lowered, or as we usually say reddened, if the source is moving away from us. Now we observe that the light from the galaxies is reddened, and the degree of reddening increases proportionately with the distance of a galaxy. The natural explanation of this is that the galaxies are rushing away from each other at enormous speeds, which for the most distant galaxies that we can see with the biggest telescopes become comparable with the speed of light itself.

My nonmathematical friends often tell me that they find it difficult to picture this expansion. Short of using a lot of mathematics I cannot do better than use the analogy of a balloon with a large number of dots marked on its surface. If the balloon is blown up the distances between the dots increase in the same way as the distances between the galaxies. Here I should give a warning that this analogy must not be taken too strictly. There are several important respects in which it is definitely misleading. For example, the dots on the surface of a balloon would themselves increase in size as the balloon was being blown up. This is not the case for the galaxies, for their internal gravitational fields are sufficiently strong to prevent any such expansion. A further weakness of our analogy is that the surface of an ordinary balloon is two dimensional—that is to say, the points of its surface can be described by two co-ordinates; for example, by latitude and longitude. In the case of the Universe we must think of the surface as possessing a third dimension. This is not as difficult as it may sound. We are all familiar with pictures in per-spective—pictures in which artists have represented three-dimensional scenes on two-dimensional canvases. So it is not really a difficult conception to imagine the three dimensions of space as being confined to the surface of a balloon. But then what does the radius of the balloon represent, and what does it mean to say that the balloon is being blown up? The answer to this is that the radius of the balloon is a measure of time, and the passage of time has the effect of blowing up the balloon. This will give you a very rough, but useful, idea of the sort of theory investigated by the mathematician.

The balloon analogy brings out a very important point. It shows we must not imagine that we are situated at the center of the Universe, just because we see all the galaxies to be moving away from us. For, whichever dot you care to choose on the surface of the balloon, you will find that the other dots all move away from it. In other words, whichever galaxy you happen to be in, the other galaxies will appear to be receding from you.

Now let us consider the recession of the galaxies in a little more detail. The greater the distance of a galaxy the faster it is receding. Every time you double the distance you double the speed of recession. The speeds come out as vast beyond all precedent. Near-by galaxies are moving outward at several million miles an hour, whereas the most distant ones that can be seen with our biggest telescopes are receding at over 200,000,000 miles an hour. This leads us to the obvious question: If we could see galaxies lying at even greater distances, would their speeds be still vaster? Nobody seriously doubts that this would be so, which gives rise to a very curious situation that I will now describe.

Galaxies lying at only about twice the distance of the furthest ones that actually can be observed with the new telescope at Mount Palomar would be moving away from us at a speed that equalled light itself. Those at still greater distances would have speeds of recession exceeding that of light. Many people find this extremely puzzling because they have learned from Einstein's special theory of relativity that no material body can have a speed greater than light. This is true enough in the special theory of relativity which refers to a particularly simple system of space and time. But it is not true in Einstein's general theory of relativity, and it is in terms of the general theory that the Universe has to be discussed. The point is rather difficult, but I can do something toward making it a little clearer. The further a galaxy is away from us the more its distance will increase during the time required by its light to reach us. Indeed, if it is far enough away the light never reaches us at all because its path stretches faster than the light can make progress. This is what is meant by saying that the speed of recession exceeds the velocity of light. Events occurring in a galaxy at such a distance can never be observed at all by anyone inside our Galaxy, no matter how patient the observer and no matter how powerful his telescope. All the galaxies that we actually see are ones that lie close enough for their light to reach us in spite of the expansion of space that's going on. But the struggle of the light against the expansion of space does show itself, as I said before, in the reddening of the light.

As you will easily guess, there must be intermediate cases where a galaxy is at such a distance that, so to speak, the light it emits neither gains ground nor loses it. In this case the path between us and the galaxy stretches at just such a rate as exactly compensates for the velocity of the light. The light gets lost on the way. It is a case, as the Red Queen remarked to Alice, of "taking all the running you can do to keep in the same place." We know fairly accurately how far away a galaxy has to be for this special case to occur. The answer is about 2,000,000,000 light years, which is only about twice as far as the distances that we expect the giant telescope at Mount Palomar to penetrate. This means that we are already observing about half as far into space as we can ever hope to do. If we built a telescope a million times as big as the one at Mount Palomar we could scarcely double our present range of vision. So what it amounts to is that owing to the expansion of the Universe we can never observe events that happen outside a certain quite definite finite region of space. We refer to this finite region as the observable Universe. The word "observable" here does not mean what we actually observe, but what we could observe if we were equipped with perfect telescopes.

So far we have been entirely concerned with the rich fruits of twentieth century observational astronomy and in particular with the results achieved by Hubble and his colleagues. We have seen that all space is strewn with galaxies, and we have seen that space itself is continually expanding. Further questions come crowding in: What causes the expansion? Does the expansion mean that as time goes on the observable Universe is becoming less and less occupied by matter? Is space finite or infinite? How old is the Universe? To settle these questions we shall now have to consider new trains of thought. These will lead us to strange conclusions.

First I will consider the older ideas—that is to say, the ideas of the nineteen-twenties and the nineteen-thirties—and then I will go on to offer my own opinion. Broadly speaking, the older ideas fall into two groups. One of them is distinguished by the assumption that the Universe started its life a finite time ago in a single huge explosion. On this supposition the present expansion is a relic of the violence of this explosion. This big bang idea seemed to me to be unsatisfactory even before detailed examination showed that it leads to serious difficulties. For when we look at our own Galaxy there is not the smallest sign that such an explosion ever occurred. This might not be such a cogent argument against the explosion school of thought if our Galaxy had turned out to be much younger than the whole Universe. But this is not so. On the contrary, in some of these theories the Universe comes out to be younger than our astrophysical estimates of the age of our own Galaxy. Another really serious difficulty arises when we try to reconcile the idea of an explosion with the requirement that the galaxies have condensed out of diffuse background material. The two concepts of explosion and condensation are obviously contradictory, and it is easy to show, if you postulate an explosion of sufficient violence to explain the expansion of the Universe, that condensations looking at all like the galaxies could never have been formed.

And so we come to the second group of theories that attempt to explain the expansion of the Universe. These all work by monkeying with the law of gravitation. The conventional idea that two particles attract each other is only accepted if their distance apart is not too great. At really large distances, so the argument goes, the two particles repel each other instead. On this basis it can be shown that if the density of the background material is sufficiently small, expansion must occur. But once again there is a difficulty in reconciling all this with the requirement that the background material must condense to form the galaxies. For once the law of gravitation has been modified in this way the tendency is for the background material to be torn apart rather than for it to condense into galaxies. Actually there is just one way in which a theory along these lines can be built so as to get round this difficulty. This is a theory worked out by Lemaître which was often discussed by Eddington in his popular books. But we now know that on this theory the galaxies would have to be vastly older than our astrophysical studies show them actually to be. So even this has to be rejected.

I should like now to approach more recent ideas by describing what would be the fate of our observable universe if any of these older theories had turned out to be correct. According to them every receding galaxy will eventually increase its distance from us until it passes beyond the limit of the observable universe—that is to say, they will move to a distance beyond the critical limit of about 2,000,000,000 light years that I have already mentioned. When this happens they will disappear—nothing that then occurs within them can ever be observed from our Galaxy. So if any of the older theories were right we should end in a seemingly empty universe, or at any rate in a universe that was empty apart perhaps from one or two very close galaxies that became attached to our Galaxy as satellites. Nor would this situation take very long to develop. Only about 10,000,000,000 years—that is to say, about a fifth of the lifetime of the Sun—would be needed to empty the sky of the 100,000,000 or so galaxies that we can now observe there.

My own view is very different. Although I think there is no doubt that every galaxy we observe to be receding from us will in about 10,000,000,000 years have passed entirely beyond the limit of vision of an observer in our Galaxy, yet I think that such an observer will be able to see about the same number of galaxies as we do now. By this I mean that new galaxies will have condensed out of the background material at just about the rate necessary to compensate for those that are being lost as a consequence of their passing beyond our observable universe. At first sight it might be thought that this could not go on indefinitely because the material forming the background would ultimately become exhausted. The reason why this is not so, is that new material appears to compensate for the background material that is constantly being condensed into galaxies. This is perhaps the most surprising of all the conceptions of the New Cosmology. For I find myself forced to assume that the nature of the Universe requires continuous creation—the perpetual bringing into being of new background material.

The idea that matter is created continuously represents our ultimate goal in this book. It would be wrong to suppose that the idea itself is a new one. I know of references to the continuous creation of matter that go back more than twenty years, and I have no doubt that a close inquiry would show that the idea, in its vaguest form, goes back very much further than that. What is new about it is this: it has now been found possible to put a hitherto vague idea in a precise mathematical form. It is only when this has been done that the consequences of any physical idea can be worked out and its scientific value assessed. I should perhaps explain that besides my personal views, which I shall now be putting forward, there are two other lines of thought on this matter. One comes from the German scientist P. Jordan, whose views differ from my own by so wide a gulf that it would be too wide a digression to discuss them. The other line of attack has come from the Cambridge scientists H. Bondi and T. Gold, who, although using quite a different form of argument from the one I adopted, have reached conclusions almost identical with those I am now going to discuss.

The most obvious question to ask about continuous creation is this: Where does the created material come from? It does not come from anywhere. Material simply appears—it is created. At one time the various atoms composing the material do not exist, and at a later time they do. This may seem a very strange idea and I agree that it is, but in science it does not matter how strange an idea may seem so long as it works—that is to say, so long as the idea can be expressed in a precise form and so long as its consequences are found to be in agreement with observation. Some people have argued that continuous creation introduces a new assumption into science—and a very startling assumption at that. Now I do not agree that continuous creation is an additional assumption. It is certainly a new hypothesis, but it only replaces a hypothesis that lies concealed in the older theories, which assume, as I have said before, that the whole of the matter in the Universe was created in one big bang at a particular time in the remote past. On scientific grounds this big bang assumption is much the less palatable of the two. For it is an irrational process that cannot be described in scientific terms. Continuous creation, on the other hand, can be represented by precise mathematical equations whose consequences can be worked out and compared with observation. On philosophical grounds too I cannot see any good reason for preferring the big bang idea. Indeed it seems to me in the philosophical sense to be a distinctly unsatisfactory notion, since it puts the basic assumption out of sight where it can never be challenged by a direct appeal to observation.

Perhaps you may think that the whole question of the creation of the Universe could be avoided in some way. But this is not so. To avoid the issue of creation it would be necessary for all the material of the Universe to be infinitely old, and this it cannot be for a very practical reason. For if this were so, there could be no hydrogen left in the Universe. As I think I demonstrated when I talked about the insides of the stars, hydrogen is being steadily converted into helium throughout the Universe and this conversion is a one-way process—that is to say, hydrogen cannot be produced in any appreciable quantity through the breakdown of the other elements. How comes it then that the Universe consists almost entirely of hydrogen? If matter were infinitely old this would be quite impossible. So we see that the Universe being what it is, the creation issue simply cannot be dodged. And I think that of all the various possibilities that have been suggested, continuous creation is easily the most satisfactory.

Now what are the consequences of continuous creation? Perhaps the most surprising result of the mathematical theory is that the average density of the background material must stay constant. The new material does not appear in a concentrated form in small localized regions but is spread throughout the whole of space. The average rate of appearance of matter amounts to no more than the creation of one atom in the course of about a year in a volume equal to that of a moderate-sized skyscraper. As you will realize, it would be quite impossible to detect such a rate of creation by direct experiment. But although this seems such a slow rate when judged by ordinary ideas, it is not small when you consider that it is happening everywhere in space. The total rate for the observable universe alone is about a hundred million, million, million, million, million tons per second. Do not let this surprise you because, as I have said, the volume of the observable universe is very large. Indeed I must now make it quite clear that here we have the answer to our question, Why does the Universe expand? For it is this creation that drives the Universe. The new material produces an outward pressure that leads to the steady expansion. But it does much more than that. With continuous creation the apparent contradiction between the expansion of the Universe and the requirement that the background material shall be able to condense into galaxies is completely overcome. For it can be shown that once an irregularity occurs in the background material a galaxy must eventually be formed. Such irregularities are constantly being produced by the gravitational effect of the galaxies themselves. For the gravitational field of the galaxies disturbs the background material and causes irregularities to form within it. So the background material must give a steady supply of new galaxies. Moreover, the created material also supplies unending quantities of atomic energy, since by arranging that newly created material should be composed of hydrogen we explain why in spite of the fact that hydrogen is being consumed in huge quantities in the stars, the Universe is nevertheless observed to be overwhelmingly composed of it.

We must now leave this extraordinary business of continuous creation for a moment to consider the question of what lies beyond the observable part of the Universe. In the first place you must let me ask, Does this question have any meaning? According to the theory it does. Theory requires the galaxies to go on forever, even though we cannot see them. That is to say, the galaxies are expanding out into an infinite space. There is no end to it all. And what is more, apart from the possibility of there being a few freak galaxies, one bit of this infinite space will behave in the same way as any other bit.

The same thing applies to time. You will have noticed that I have used the concepts of space and time as if they could be treated separately. According to the relativity theory this is a dangerous thing to do. But it so happens that it can be done with impunity in our Universe, although it is easy to imagine other universes where it could not be done. What I mean by this is that a division between space and time can be made and this division can be used throughout the whole of our Universe. This is a very important and special property of our Universe, which I think it is important to take into account in forming the equations that decide the way in which matter is created.

Perhaps you will allow me a short diversion here to answer the question: How does the idea of infinite space fit in with the balloon analogy that I mentioned earlier? Suppose you were blowing up a balloon that could never burst. Then it is clear that if you went on blowing long enough you could make its size greater than anything I cared to specify, greater for instance than a billion billion miles or a billion billion billion miles and so on. This is what is meant by saying that the radius of the balloon tends to infinity. If you are used to thinking in terms of the balloon analogy, this is the case that gives you what we call an infinite space.

Now let us suppose that a film is made from any space position in the Universe. To make the film, let a still picture be taken at each instant of time. This, by the way, is what we are doing in our astronomical observations. We are actually taking the picture of the Universe at one instant of time—the present. Next, let all the stills be run together so as to form a continuous film. What would the film look like? Galaxies would be observed to be continually condensing out of the background material. The general expansion of the whole system would be clear, but though the galaxies seemed to be moving away from us there would be a curious sameness about the film. It would be only in the details of each galaxy that changes would be seen. The overall picture would stay the same because of the compensation whereby the galaxies that were constantly disappearing through the expansion of the Universe were replaced by newly forming galaxies. A casual observer who went to sleep during the showing of the film would find it difficult to see much change when he awoke. How long would our film show go on? It would go on forever.

There is a complement to this result that we can see by running our film backward. Then new galaxies would appear at the outer fringes of our picture as faint objects that come gradually closer to us. For if the film were run backward the Universe would appear to contract. The galaxies would come closer and closer to us until they evaporated before our eyes. First the stars of a galaxy would evaporate back into the gas from which they were formed. Then the gas in the galaxy would evaporate back into the general background from which it had condensed. The background material itself would stay of constant density, not through matter being created, but through matter disappearing. How far could we run our hypothetical film back into the past? Again according to the theory, forever. After we had run backward for about 5,000,000,000 years our own Galaxy itself would disappear before our eyes. But although important details like this would no doubt be of great interest to us there would again be a general sameness about the whole proceeding. Whether we run the film backward or forward the large-scale features of the Universe remain unchanged.

It is a simple consequence of all this that the total amount of energy that can be observed at any one time must be equal to the amount observed at any other time. This means that energy is conserved. So continuous creation does not lead to nonconservation of energy as one or two critics have suggested. The reverse is the case for without continuous creation the total energy observed must decrease with time.

We see, therefore, that no large-scale changes in the Universe can be expected to take place in the future. But individual galaxies will change and you may well want to know what is likely to happen to our Galaxy. This issue cannot be decided by observation because none of the galaxies that we observe can be much more than 10,000,000,000 years old as yet, and we need to observe much older ones to find out anything about the ultimate fate of a galaxy. The reason why no observable galaxy is appreciably older than this is that a new galaxy condensing close by our own would move away from us and pass out of the observable region of space in only about 10,000,000,000 years. So we have to decide the ultimate fate of our Galaxy again from theory, and this is what theory predicts. It will become steadily more massive as more and more background material gets pulled into it. After about 10,000,000,000 years it is likely that our Galaxy will have succeeded in gathering quite a cloud of gas and satellite bodies. Where this will ultimately lead is difficult to say with any precision. The distant future of the Galaxy is to some extent bound up with an investigation made about thirty years ago by Schwarzschild, who found that very strange things happen when a body grows particularly massive. It becomes difficult, for instance, for light emitted by the body ever to get out into surrounding space. When this stage is reached, further growth is likely to be strongly inhibited. Just what it would then be like to live in our Galaxy I should very much like to know.

To conclude, I should like to stress that so far as the Universe as a whole is concerned the essential difference made by the idea of continuous creation of matter is this: Without continuous creation the Universe must evolve toward a dead state in which all the matter is condensed into a vast number of dead stars. The details of the way this happens are different in the different theories that have been put forward, but the outcome is always the same. With continuous creation, on the other hand, the Universe has an infinite future in which all its present very large-scale features will be preserved.

Part seven

THE IDEA OF SUCCESS

If a man has important work, and enough leisure and income to enable him to do it properly, he is in possession of as much happiness as is good for any of the children of Adam.

R. H. Tawney
THE ACQUISITIVE SOCIETY

INTRODUCTION

Even a brief perusal of the readings which follow should enable you to appreciate how difficult it is to define, much less achieve, success. While psychiatrists, sociologists, anthropologists, historians, journalists, and others tempt you to grapple with the problem, its dimensions remain elusive. Are we to regard success as a universal aspiration, valued through the ages in all times and climes or do we limit our attention to the here and now? If you think you have a satisfactory definition of success, is your view shared equally by the city-dweller, the inhabitant of a small rural community, and the sub-urbanite; by white and Negro, by people differing in culture, religion, or social class?

If you live in a traditional society, success may still mean following the folk-ways of your ancestors without deviation. If the society is changing as a result of contact with others, the goal of your efforts may be to become literate, to leave the land, go to the cities, and work for money. For the traditional Buddhist, success implies the attainment of *Nirvana*, getting "off the wheel of life," the denial of self, whereas the medieval Christian constructed a world view out of his hope for other-worldly salvation. If you measure success in material terms—increasingly the case in the East as well as here in the West—success might mean various things. Here in America it might mean a secure job with the assurance of frequent promotions, a high-powered car, a suitable wife and children, a variety of credit cards, and a tax-proof expense account. To a Pakistani villager, on the other hand, it might mean a transistor radio, even if what it broadcasts is government-controlled; or a wrist watch, even if the time it measures is largely irrelevant to his daily concerns. If you were an Indonesian farmer, success might mean owning a water buffalo instead of using your wife as a beast of burden. The catalogue of possible meanings of the term "success" is almost endless. Let us therefore begin with the assumption that there are as many connotations to the word as there are cultures and sub-cultures and human situations on the earth, and limit our-selves to a few observations and reflections on success in contemporary twentieth-century America, in which the social context of success can be described with such words as "urban," "industrial," "secular," and "middle-class." But let us keep in mind the lessons derived from the fact of culture variability and the attitude of cultural relativism, *viz.*, that ours is not the only approach to a definition of success; that, important as the problem is to us, it is only one of many and indeed the most recent of many even in Western society.

The present social and cultural perspectives of success as a goal to be prized are a product of long evolution. We had to move from rural to urban, from preindustrial to industrial, from sacred to secular society, and from upper-class to middle-class dominance—a series of transitions which for America did not begin to be accomplished until the period between the Civil War and World War I. Up to then, it was still possible for many people to live by traditional or inner standards of what was right. Only as this type of customary faith began to be shaken did we begin to look to others for direction, only to find that they were in the same quandary, equally in need of assurance.

At this point, you might ask what is wrong with striving for success in worldly terms? Isn't this the path to power and wealth, to status and prestige? America, as a nation of immigrants, it is argued, had to strive for success. Isn't this a part of the "American Dream," the desire to transcend lowly origins, to remove barriers to the achievement of status? Questions such as these must be repeatedly raised because of one very complicating factor—*the cost of success.*

If the class system is viewed as a pyramid, it becomes rapidly apparent that, other things being equal, there are fewer positions at the apex than at the base. This means that success involves *competition,* and in our society the conditions and incentives for competing are not equal. What the social scientist calls "ascribed status" limits equality of opportunity. For example, if you were born into a low-income family in a society that measures success in monetary terms, if you were born female into a male-dominated social system, or if you are a member of a racial or religious minority, does this alter the basis for competing successfully? What happens to the middle-aged in a youth-centered society, to the products of divorce and desertion in a milieu preaching "togetherness," to the school dropout in a setting that extols the virtues of education?

Robert K. Merton, the sociologist, has argued that the conformist is the one who employs legitimate means for the attainment of his goals. If your goal is success, there will be pressure upon you throughout your life cycle—by parents, teachers, peer groups, and others—to use these customary means in competing for success, even if at the price of neurosis, ulcers, and aimlessness. For those who are blocked from equal access to legitimate means, illegitimate means may be resorted to as long as the goal of success is prized. Thus, illegal and unethical expedients equalize the competitive rules of the game for some. There is also another level of adaptation, which Merton calls "retreatism," in which the goal itself is rejected. One becomes progressively alienated from accepted goals. Such withdrawal may be symptomatized by the beat generation as a social movement, by the cultist practice as Zen Buddhism, and by drugs. May not the purpose of a drug be withdrawal from the pressures and problems of the world of reality into a temporary realm of fantasy in which the need to compete for success is erased from consciousness? And it is not merely the drug addict who is under discussion, but also the occasional user, who in a manner akin to the Sunday painter, will take drugs infrequently in order to help cope with the burdens of a competitive social system.

If we grant that aspiring to success can create as well as solve problems, we must reflect on the following issues: Is it possible to achieve success and yet reduce the social costs of success? Can legitimate means for attaining success be made possible for unprivileged groups? Is it possible to be successful cooperatively, not competitively—or at least equalize opportunities to compete?

If it is the society and culture, rather than the individual, which defines success both as an end and as the means to its attainment, even more basic questions have to be asked. Can the child be motivated to succeed for reasons intrinsic to his own autonomy as a person rather than act to fulfill parental ambitions or compensate for parental frustrations? Can the school and college assist in redefining success in terms not limited to the economic value of the diploma? Can the student be motivated to redefine success in school not alone by a competitive grading system, but in more broadly humanistic terms? Is it possible for an affluent society to cease linking economic success with psychological insecurity? On the level of interpersonal relations, is it possible to define success as the "art of loving" rather than demanding love as a balm for the traumas of a competitive world? Is it necessary to tolerate the confusion of romantic love with the standards of the market place, as illustrated by the recent series of automobile advertisements in which a girl is depicted in a pensive mood and saying hesitantly: "Don, I might—if you drove a Chrysler."

As final commentary on the context and cost of success, it is hoped that excerpts from a recent provocative speech by Erich Fromm will furnish you with an occasion for creative thought and—hopefully—action. Addressing a meeting of the American Orthopsychiatric Association in San Francisco on the theme of alienation, he had occasion to make the following cogent observations:

(We are) . . . not concerned enough with the pathology of normalcy—the drive to conform—that prevents a man from knowing his own fears, his angers, his hopelessness. . . .

In the last 50 years . . . sexual desires and fantasies, which Freud assumed to be the vital contents of the unconscious, have become less and less repressed. Not only has there been a change in mores, but sex and love have also become part of the "consumer culture."

Sex is something to "get," something cheap and relatively accessible, and love is something that, if you don't "get" it, you're deprived, like a baby without milk. . . .

In psychoanalytic terms, an individual's repressed unconscious feelings govern his behavior. . . . the underlying anxiety, depression, loneliness, boredom and pain about the meaningless of life.

A man sits in front of a bad television program and does not know he is bored; he reads of Vietcong casualties in the newspaper and does not recall the teachings of religion; he learns of the dangers of nuclear holocaust and does not feel fear; he joins the rat race of commerce, where personal worth is measured in terms of market values, and is not aware of his anxiety. Ulcers speak louder than the mind. . . .

Theologians and philosophers have been saying for a century that God is dead, but what we confront now is the possibility that man is dead, transformed into a thing, a producer, a consumer, an idolator of other things.[1]

Is this the portrait of success? Must it be purchased at such a price?

[1] *The New York Times*, April 14, 1966.

THE DESIRE FOR SUCCESS

The Marketing Orientation   68
Erich Fromm

The marketing orientation developed as a dominant one only in the modern era. In order to understand its nature one must consider the economic function of the market in modern society as being not only analogous to this character orientation but as the basis and the main condition for its development in modern man.

Barter is one of the oldest economic mechanisms. The traditional local market, however, is essentially different from the market as it has developed in modern capitalism. Bartering on a local market offered an opportunity to meet for the purpose of exchanging commodities. Producers and customers became acquainted; they were relatively small groups; the demand was more or less known, so that the producer could produce for this specific demand.

The modern market is no longer a meeting place but a mechanism characterized by abstract and impersonal demand. One produces for this market, not for a known circle of customers; its verdict is based on laws of supply and demand; and it determines whether the commodity can be sold and at what price. No matter what the *use value* of a pair of shoes may be, for instance, if the supply is greater than the demand, some shoes will be sentenced to economic death; they might as well not have been produced at all. The market day is the "day of judgment" as far as the *exchange value* of commodities is concerned.

The reader may object that this description of the market is oversimplified. The producer does try to judge the demand in advance, and under monopoly conditions even obtains a certain degree of control over it. Nevertheless, the regulatory function of the market has been, and still is, predominant enough to have a profound influence on the character formation of the urban middle class and, through the latter's social and cultural influence, on the whole population. The market concept of value, the emphasis on exchange value rather than on use value, has led to a similar concept of value with regard to people and particularly to oneself. The character orientation which is rooted in the experience of oneself as a commodity and of one's value as exchange value I call the marketing orientation.

In our time the marketing orientation has been growing rapidly, together with the development of a new market that is a phenomenon of the last decades—the "personality market." Clerks and salesmen, business executives and doctors, lawyers and artists all appear on this market. It is true that their legal status and economic positions are different: some are independent, charging for their services; others are employed, receiving salaries. But all are dependent for their material success on a personal acceptance by those who need their services or who employ them.

The principle of evaluation is the same on both the personality and the commodity market: on the one, personalities are offered for sale; on the other, commodities. Value in both cases is their exchange value, for which use value is a necessary but not a sufficient condition. It is true, our economic system could not function if people were not skilled in the particular work they have to perform and were gifted only with a pleasant personality. Even the best bedside manner and the most beautifully equipped office on Park Avenue would not make a New York doctor successful if he did not have a minimum of medical knowledge and skill. Even the most winning personality would not prevent a secretary from losing her job unless she could type reasonably fast. However, if we ask what the respective weight of skill and personality as a condition for success is, we find that only in exceptional cases is success predominantly the result of skill and of certain other human qualities like honesty, decency, and integrity. Although the proportion between skill and human qualities on the one hand and "personality" on the other hand as prerequisites for success varies, the "personality factor" always plays a decisive role. Success depends largely on how well a person sells himself on the market, how well he gets his personality across, how nice a "package" he is; whether he is "cheerful," "sound," "aggressive," "reliable," "ambitious;" furthermore what his family background is, what clubs he belongs to, and whether he knows the right people. The type of personality required depends to some degree on the special field in which a person works. A stockbroker, a salesman, a secretary, a railroad executive, a college professor, or a hotel manager must each offer different kinds of personality that, regardless of their differences, must fulfill one condition: to be in demand.

The fact that in order to have success it is not sufficient to have the skill and equipment for performing a given task but that one must be able to "put across" one's personality in competition with many others shapes the attitude toward oneself. If it were enough for the purpose of making a living to rely on what one knows and what one can do, one's self-esteem would be in proportion to one's capacities, that is, to one's use value; but since success depends largely on how one sells one's personality, one experiences oneself as a commodity or rather simultaneously as the seller *and* the commodity to be sold. A person is not concerned with his life and happiness, but with becoming salable. This feeling might be compared to that of a commodity, of handbags on a counter, for instance, could they feel and think. Each handbag would try to make itself as "attractive" as possible in order to attract customers and to look as expensive as possible in order to obtain a higher price than its rivals. The handbag sold for the highest price would feel elated, since that would mean it was the most "valuable" one; the one which was not sold would feel sad and convinced of its own worthlessness. This fate might befall a bag which, though excellent in appearance and usefulness, had the bad luck to be out of date because of a change in fashion.

Like the handbag, one has to be in fashion on the personality market, and in order to be in fashion one has to know what kind of personality is most in demand. This knowledge is transmitted in a general way throughout the whole process of education, from kindergarten to college, and implemented by the family. The knowledge acquired at this early stage is not sufficient, however; it emphasizes only certain general qualities like adaptability, ambition, and sensitivity to the changing expectations of other people. The more specific picture of the models for success one gets elsewhere. The pictorial magazines, newspapers, and newsreels show the pictures and life stories of the successful in many variations. Pictorial advertising has a similar function. The successful executive who is pictured in a tailor's advertisement is the image of how one should look and be, if one is to draw down the "big money" on the contemporary personality market.

The most important means of transmitting the desired personality pattern to the average man is the motion picture. The young girl tries to emulate the facial expression, coiffure, gestures of a high-priced star as the most promising way to success. The young man tries to look and be like the model he sees on the screen. While the average citizen has little contact with the life of the most successful people, his relationship with the motion-picture stars is different. It is true that he has no real contact with them either, but he can see them on the screen again and again, can write them and receive their autographed pictures. In contrast to the time when the actor was socially despised but was nevertheless the transmitter of the works of great poets to his audience, our motion-picture stars have no great works or ideas to transmit, but their function is to serve as the link an average person has with the world of the "great." Even if he can not hope to become as successful as they are, he can try to emulate them; they are his saints and because of their success they embody the norms for living.

Since modern man experiences himself both as the seller and as the commodity to be sold on the market, his self-esteem depends on conditions beyond his control. If he is "successful," he is valuable; if he is not, he is worthless. The degree of insecurity which results from this orientation can hardly be overestimated. If one feels that one's own value is not constituted primarily by the human qualities one possesses, but by one's success on a competitive market with ever-changing conditions, one's self-esteem is bound to be shaky and in constant need of confirmation by others. Hence one is driven to strive relentlessly for success, and any setback is a severe threat to one's self-esteem; helplessness, insecurity, and inferiority feelings are the result. If the vicissitudes of the market are the judges of one's value, the sense of dignity and pride is destroyed.

But the problem is not only that of self-evaluation and self-esteem but of one's experience of oneself as an independent entity, of one's *identity with oneself*. As we shall see later, the mature and productive individual derives his feeling of identity from the experience of himself as the agent who is one with his powers; this feeling of self can be briefly expressed as meaning "*I am what I do.*" In the marketing orientation man encounters his own powers as commodities alienated from him. He is not one with them but they are masked from him because what matters is not his self-realization in the process of using them but his success in the process of selling them. Both his powers and what they create become estranged, something different from himself, something for others to judge and to use; thus his feeling of identity becomes as shaky as his self-esteem; it is constituted by the sum total of roles one can play: "*I am as you desire me.*"

Ibsen has expressed this state of selfhood in Peer Gynt: Peer Gynt tries to discover his self and he finds that he is like an onion—one layer after the other can be peeled off and there is no core to be found. Since man cannot live doubting his identity, he must, in the marketing orientation, find the conviction of identity not in reference to himself and his powers but in the opinion of others about him. His prestige, status, success, the fact that he is known to others as being a certain person are a substitute for the genuine feeling of identity. This situation makes him utterly dependent on the way others look at him and forces him to keep up the role in which he once had become successful. If I and my powers are separated from each other then, indeed, is my self constituted by the price I fetch.

The way one experiences others is not different from the way one experiences oneself. Others are experienced as commodities like oneself; they too do not present *themselves* but their salable part. The difference between people is reduced to a merely quantitative difference of being *more or less* successful, attractive, hence valuable. This process is not different from what happens to commodities on the market. A painting and a pair of shoes can both be expressed in, and reduced to, their exchange value, their price; so many pairs of shoes are "equal" to one painting. In the same way the difference between people is reduced to a common element, their price on the market. Their individuality, that which is peculiar and unique in them, is valueless and, in fact, a ballast. The meaning which the word *peculiar* has assumed is quite expressive of this attitude. Instead of denoting the greatest achievement of man— that of having developed his individuality—it has become almost synonymous with *queer*. The word *equality* has also changed its meaning. The idea that all men are created equal implied that all men have the same fundamental right to be considered as ends in themselves and not as means. Today, equality has become equivalent to *interchangeability,* and is the very negation of individuality. Equality, instead of being the condition for the development of each man's peculiarity, means the extinction of individuality, the "self-lessness" characteristic of the marketing orientation. Equality was conjunctive with difference, but it has become synonymous with "in-difference" and, indeed, indifference is what characterizes modern man's relationship to himself and to others.

These conditions necessarily color all human relationships. When the individual self is neglected, the relationships between people must of necessity become superficial, because not they themselves but interchangeable commodities are related. People are not able and cannot afford to be concerned with that which is unique and "peculiar" in each other. However, the market creates a kind of comradeship of its own. Everybody is involved in the same battle of competition, shares the same striving for success; all meet under the same conditions of the market (or at least believe they do). Everyone knows how the others feel because each is in the same boat: alone, afraid to fail, eager to please; no quarter is given or expected in this battle.

The superficial character of human relationships leads many to hope that they can find depth and intensity of feeling in individual love. But love for one person and love for one's neighbor are indivisible; in any given culture, love relationships are only a more intense expression of the relatedness to man prevalent in that culture. Hence it is an illusion to expect that the loneliness of man rooted in the marketing orientation can be cured by individual love.

Thinking as well as feeling is determined by the marketing orientation. Thinking assumes the function of grasping things quickly so as to be able to manipulate them successfully. Furthered by widespread and efficient education, this leads to a high degree of intelligence, but not of reason. For manipulative purposes, all that is necessary to know is the surface features of things, the superficial. The truth, to be uncovered by penetrating to the essence of phenomena, becomes an obsolete concept—truth not only in the prescientific sense of "absolute" truth, dogmatically maintained without reference to empirical data, but also in the sense of truth attained by man's reason applied to his observations and open to revision. Most intelligence tests are attuned to this kind of thinking; they measure not so much the capacity for reason and understanding as the capacity for quick mental adaptation to a given situation; "mental adjustment tests" would be the adequate name for them. For this kind of thinking the application of the categories of comparison, and of quantitative measurement—rather than a thorough analysis of a given phenomenon and its quality—is essential. All problems are equally "interesting" and there is little sense of the respective differences in their importance.

Knowledge itself becomes a commodity. Here, too, man is alienated from his own power; thinking and knowing are experienced as a tool to produce results. Knowledge of man himself, psychology, which in the great tradition of Western thought was held to be the condition for virtue, for right living, for happiness, has degenerated into an instrument to be used for better manipulation of others and oneself, in market research, in political propaganda, in advertising, and so on.

Evidently this type of thinking has a profound effect on our educational system. From grade school to graduate school, the aim of learning is to gather as much information as possible that is mainly useful for the purposes of the market. Students are supposed to learn so many things that they have hardly time and energy left to *think*. Not the interest in the subjects taught or in knowledge and insight as such, but the enhanced exchange value knowledge gives is the main incentive for wanting more and better education. We find today a tremendous enthusiasm for knowledge and education, but at the same time a skeptical or contemptuous attitude toward the allegedly impractical and useless thinking which is concerned "only" with the truth and which has no exchange value on the market.

Although I have presented the marketing orientation as one of the non-productive orientations, it is in many ways so different that it belongs in a category of its own. The receptive, exploitative, and hoarding orientations have one thing in common: each is one form of human relatedness which, if dominant in a person, is specific of him and characterizes him. . . . The marketing orientation, however, does not develop something which is potentially in the person (unless we make the absurd assertion that "nothing" is also part of the human equipment); its very nature is that no specific and permanent kind of relatedness is developed, but that the very changeability of attitudes is the only permanent quality of such orientation. In this orientation, those qualities are developed which can best be sold. Not one particular attitude is predominant, but the emptiness which can be filled most quickly with the desired quality. This quality, however, ceases to be one in the proper sense of the word; it is only a role, the pretense of a quality, to be readily exchanged if another one is more desirable. Thus, for instance, respectability is sometimes desirable. The salesmen in certain branches of business ought to impress the public with those qualities of reliability, soberness, and respectability which were genuine in many a businessman of the nineteenth century. Now one looks for a man who instills confidence because he *looks* as if he had these qualities; what this man sells on the personality market is his ability to look the part; what kind of person is behind that role does not matter and is nobody's concern. He himself is not interested in his honesty, but in what it gets for him on the market. The premise of the marketing orientation is emptiness, the lack of any specific quality which could not be subject to change, since any persistent trait of character might conflict some day with the requirements of the market. Some roles would not fit in with the peculiarities of the person; therefore we must do away with them—not with the roles but with the peculiarities. The marketing personality must be free, free of all individuality.

Conspicuous Consumption   69
Thorstein Veblen

During the earlier stages of economic development, consumption of goods without stint, especially consumption of the better grades of goods—ideally all consumption in excess of the subsistence minimum—pertains normally to the leisure class. This restriction tends to disappear, at least formally, after the later peaceable stage has been reached, with private ownership of goods and an industrial system based on wage labour or on the petty household economy. But during the earlier quasi-peaceable stage, when so many of the traditions through which the institution of a leisure class has affected the economic life of later times were taking form and consistency, this principle has had the force of a conventional law. It has served as the norm to which consumption has tended to conform, and any appreciable departure from it is to be regarded as an aberrant form, sure to be eliminated sooner or later in the further course of development.

The quasi-peaceable gentleman of leisure, then, not only consumes of the staff of life beyond the minimum required for subsistence and physical efficiency, but his consumption also undergoes a specialisation as regards the quality of the goods consumed. He consumes freely and of the best, in food, drink, narcotics, shelter, services, ornaments, apparel, weapons and accoutrements, amusements, amulets, and idols or divinities. In the process of gradual amelioration which takes place in the articles of his consumption, the motive principle and the proximate aim of innovation is no doubt the higher efficiency of the improved and more elaborate products for personal comfort and well-being. But that does not remain the sole purpose of their consumption. The canon of reputability is at hand and seizes upon such innovations as are, according to its standard, fit to survive. Since the consumption of these more excellent goods is an evidence of wealth, it becomes honorific; and conversely, the failure to consume in due quantity and quality becomes a mark of inferiority and demerit.

This growth of punctilious discrimination as to qualitative excellence in eating, drinking, etc., presently affects not only the manner of life, but also

From Ch. IV, "Conspicuous Consumption," in *The Theory of the Leisure Class*, by Thorstein Veblen, New York, Macmillan, 1889.

the training and intellectual activity of the gentleman of leisure. He is no longer simply the successful, aggressive male—the man of strength, resource, and intrepidity. In order to avoid stultification he must also cultivate his tastes, for it now becomes incumbent on him to discriminate with some nicety between the noble and the ignoble in consumable goods. He becomes a connoisseur in creditable viands of various degrees of merit, in manly beverages and trinkets, in seemly apparel and architecture, in weapons, games, dancers, and the narcotics. This cultivation of the æsthetic faculty requires time and application, and the demands made upon the gentleman in this direction therefore tend to change his life of leisure into a more or less arduous application to the business of learning how to live a life of ostensible leisure in a becoming way. Closely related to the requirement that the gentleman must consume freely and of the right kind of goods, there is the requirement that he must know how to consume them in a seemly manner. His life of leisure must be conducted in due form. Hence arise good manners in the way pointed out in an earlier chapter. High-bred manners and ways of living are items of conformity to the norm of conspicuous leisure and conspicuous consumption.

Conspicuous consumption of valuable goods is a means of reputability to the gentleman of leisure. As wealth accumulates on his hands, his own unaided effort will not avail to sufficiently put his opulence in evidence by this method. The aid of friends and competitors is therefore brought in by resorting to the giving of valuable presents and expensive feasts and entertainments. Presents and feasts had probably another origin than that of naïve ostentation, but they acquired their utility for this purpose very early, and they have retained that character to the present; so that their utility in this respect has now long been the substantial ground on which these usages rest. Costly entertainments, such as the potlatch or the ball, are peculiarly adapted to serve this end. The competitor with whom the entertainer wishes to institute a comparison is, by this method, made to serve as a means to the end. He consumes vicariously for his host at the same time that he is a witness to the consumption of that excess of good things which his host is unable to dispose of single-handed, and he is also made to witness his host's facility in etiquette.

In the giving of costly entertainments other motives, of a more genial kind, are of course also present. The custom of festive gatherings probably originated in motives of conviviality and religion; these motives are also present in the later development, but they do not continue to be the sole motives. The latter-day leisure-class festivities and entertainments may continue in some slight degree to serve the religious need and in a higher degree the needs of recreation and conviviality, but they also serve an invidious purpose; and they serve it none the less effectually for having a colourable noninvidious ground in these more avowable motives. But the economic effect of these social amenities is not therefore lessened, either in the vicarious consumption of goods or in the exhibition of difficult and costly achievements in etiquette.

As wealth accumulates, the leisure class develops further in function and structure, and there arises a differentiation within the class. There is a more or less elaborate system of rank and grades. This differentiation is furthered by the inheritance of wealth and the consequent inheritance of gentility. With the inheritance of gentility goes the inheritance of obligatory leisure; and gentility of a sufficient potency to entail a life of leisure may be inherited without the complement of wealth required to maintain a dignified leisure. Gentle blood may be transmitted without goods enough to afford a reputably free consumption at one's ease. Hence results a class of impecunious gentlemen of leisure, incidentally referred to already. These half-caste gentlemen of leisure fall into a system of hierarchical gradations. Those who stand near the higher and highest grades of the wealthy leisure class, in point of birth, or in point of wealth, or both, outrank the remoter-born and the pecuniarily weaker. These lower grades, especially the impecunious, or marginal, gentlemen of leisure, affiliate themselves by a system of dependence or fealty to the great ones; by so doing they gain an increment of repute, or of the means with which to lead a life of leisure, from their patron. They become his courtiers or retainers, servants; and being fed and countenanced by their patron they are indices of his rank and vicarious consumers of his superfluous wealth. Many of these affiliated gentlemen of leisure are at the same time lesser men of substance in their own right; so that some of them are scarcely at all, others only partially, to be rated as vicarious consumers. So many of them, however, as make up the retainers and hangers-on of the patron may be classed as vicarious consumers without qualification. Many of these again, and also many of the other aristocracy of less degree, have in turn attached to their persons a more or less comprehensive group of vicarious consumers in the persons of their wives and children, their servants, retainers, etc.

Throughout this graduated scheme of vicarious leisure and vicarious consumption the rule holds that these offices must be performed in some such manner, or under some such circumstance or insignia, as shall point plainly to the master to whom this leisure or consumption pertains, and to whom therefore the resulting increment of good repute of right inures. The consumption and leisure executed by these persons for their master or patron represents an investment on his part with a view to an increase of good fame. As regards feasts and largesses this is obvious enough, and the imputation of repute to the host or patron here takes place immediately, on the ground of common notoriety. Where leisure and consumption is performed vicariously by henchmen and retainers, imputation of the resulting repute to the patron is effected by their residing near his person so that it may be plain to all men from what source they draw. As the group whose good esteem is to be secured in this way grows larger, more patent means are required to indicate the imputation of merit for the leisure performed, and to this end uniforms, badges, and liveries come into vogue. The wearing of uniforms or liveries implies a considerable degree of dependence, and may even be said to be a mark of servitude, real or ostensible. The wearers of uniforms and liveries may be roughly divided into two classes—the free and the servile, or the noble and the ignoble. The services performed by them are likewise divisible into noble and ignoble. Of course the distinction is not observed with strict consistency in practice; the less debasing of the base services and the less honorific of the noble functions are not infrequently merged in the same person. But the general distinction is not on that account to be overlooked. What may add some perplexity is the fact that this fundamental distinction between noble and ignoble, which rests on the nature of the ostensible service performed, is traversed by a secondary distinction into honorific and humiliating, resting on the rank of the person for whom the service is performed or whose livery is worn. So, those offices which are by right the proper employment of the leisure class are noble; such are government, fighting, hunting, the care of arms and accoutrements, and the like—in short, those which may be classed as ostensibly predatory employments. On the other hand, those employments which properly fall to the industrious class are ignoble; such as handicraft or other productive labour, menial services, and the like. But a base service performed for a person of very high degree may become a very honorific office; as for instance the office of a Maid of Honour or of a Lady in Waiting to the Queen, or the King's Master of the Horse or his Keeper of the Hounds. The two offices last named suggest a principle of some general bearing. Whenever, as in these cases, the menial service in question has to do directly with the primary leisure employments of fighting and hunting, it easily acquires a reflected honorific character. In this way great honour may come to attach to an employment which in its own nature belongs to the baser sort.

In the later development of peaceable industry, the usage of employing an idle corps of uniformed men-at-arms gradually lapses. Vicarious consumption by dependents bearing the insignia of their patron or master narrows down to a corps of liveried menials. In a heightened degree, therefore, the livery comes to be a badge of servitude, or rather of servility. Something of a honorific character always attached to the livery of the armed retainer, but this honorific character disappears when the livery becomes the exclusive badge of the menial. The livery becomes obnoxious to nearly all who are required to wear it. We are yet so little removed from a state of effective slavery as still to be fully sensitive to the sting of any imputation of servility. This antipathy asserts itself even in the case of the liveries or uniforms which some corporations prescribe as the distinctive dress of their employees. In this country the aversion even goes the length of discrediting—in a mild and uncertain way—those government employments, military and civil, which require the wearing of a livery or uniform.

With the disappearance of servitude, the number of vicarious consumers attached to any one gentleman tends, on the whole, to decrease. The like is of course true, and perhaps in a still higher degree, of the number of dependents who perform vicarious leisure for him. In a general way, though not wholly nor consistently, these two groups coincide. The dependent who was first delegated for these duties was the wife, or the chief wife; and, as would be expected, in the later development of the institution, when the number of persons by whom these duties are customarily performed gradually narrows, the wife remains the last. In the higher grades of society a large volume of both these kinds of service is required; and here the wife is of course still assisted in the work by a more or less numerous corps of menials. But as we descend the social scale, the point is presently reached where the duties of vicarious leisure and consumption devolve upon the wife alone. In the communities of the Western culture, this point is at present found among the lower middle class.

And here occurs a curious inversion. It is a fact of common observation that in this lower middle class there is no pretence of leisure on the part of the head of the household. Through force of circumstances it has fallen into disuse. But the middle-class wife still carries on the business of vicarious leisure, for the good name of the household and its master. In descending the social scale in any modern industrial community, the primary fact—the conspicuous leisure of the master of the household—disappears at a relatively high point. The head of the middle-class household has been reduced by economic circumstances to turn his hand to gaining a livelihood by occupations which often partake largely of the character of industry, as in the case of the ordinary business man of to-day. But the derivative fact—the vicarious leisure and consumption rendered by the wife, and the auxiliary vicarious performance of leisure by menials—remains in vogue as a conventionality which the demands of reputability will not suffer to be slighted. It is by no means an uncommon spectacle to find a man applying himself to work with the utmost assiduity, in order that his wife may in due form render for him that degree of vicarious leisure which the common sense of the time demands.

The leisure rendered by the wife in such cases is, of course, not a simple manifestation of idleness or indolence. It almost invariably occurs disguised under some form of work or household duties or social amenities, which prove on analysis to serve little or no ulterior end beyond showing that she does not and need not occupy herself with anything that is gainful or that is of substantial use. As has already been noticed under the head of manners, the greater part of the customary round of domestic cares to which the middle-class housewife gives her time and effort is of this character. Not that the results of her attention to household matters, of a decorative and mundificatory character, are not pleasing to the sense of men trained in middle-class proprieties; but the taste to which these effects of household adornment and tidiness appeal is a taste which has been formed under the selective guidance of a canon of propriety that demands just these evidences of wasted effort. The effects are pleasing to us chiefly because we have been taught to find them pleasing. There goes into these domestic duties much solicitude for a proper combination of form and colour, and for other ends that are to be classed as æsthetic in the proper sense of the term; and it is not denied that effects having some substantial æsthetic value are sometimes attained. Pretty much all that is here insisted on is that, as regards these amenities of life, the housewife's efforts are under the guidance of traditions that have been shaped by the law of conspicuously wasteful expenditure of time and substance. If beauty or comfort is achieved—and it is a more or less fortuitous circumstance if they are—they must be achieved by means and methods that commend themselves to the great economic law of wasted effort. The more reputable, "presentable" portion of middle-class household paraphernalia are, on the one hand, items of conspicuous consumption, and on the other hand, apparatus for putting in evidence the vicarious leisure rendered by the housewife.

The requirement of vicarious consumption at the hands of the wife continues in force even at a lower point in the pecuniary scale than the requirement of vicarious leisure. At a point below which little if any pretence of wasted effort, in ceremonial cleanness and the like, is observable, and where there is assuredly no conscious attempt at ostensible leisure, decency still requires the wife to consume some goods conspicuously for the reputability of the household and its head. So that, as the latter-day outcome of this evolution of an archaic institution, the wife, who was at the outset the drudge and chattel of the man, both in fact and in theory—the producer of goods for him to consume—has become the ceremonial consumer of goods which he produces. But she still quite unmistakably remains his chattel in theory; for the habitual rendering of vicarious leisure and consumption is the abiding mark of the unfree servant.

This vicarious consumption practised by the household of the middle and lower classes can not be counted as a direct expression of the leisure-class scheme of life, since the household of this pecuniary grade does not belong within the leisure class. It is rather that the leisure-class scheme of life here comes to an expression at the second remove. The leisure class stands at the head of the social structure in point of reputability; and its manner of life and its standards of worth therefore afford the norm of reputability for the community. The observance of these standards, in some degree of approximation, becomes incumbent upon all classes lower in the scale. In modern civilized communities the lines of demarcation between social classes have grown vague and transient, and wherever this happens the norm of reputability imposed by the upper class extends its coercive influence with but slight hindrance down through the social structure to the lowest strata. The result is that the members of each stratum accept as their ideal of decency the scheme of life in vogue in the next higher stratum, and bend their energies to live up to that ideal. On pain of forfeiting their good name and their self-respect in case of failure, they must conform to the accepted code, at least in appearance.

The basis on which good repute in any highly organised industrial community ultimately rests is pecuniary strength; and the means of showing pecuniary strength, and so of gaining or retaining a good name, are leisure and a conspicuous consumption of goods. Accordingly, both of these methods are in vogue as far down the scale as it remains possible; and in the lower strata in which the two methods are employed, both offices are in great part delegated to the wife and children of the household. Lower still, where any degree of leisure, even ostensible, has become impracticable for the wife, the conspicuous consumption of goods remains and is carried on by the wife and children. The man of the household also can do something in this direction, and, indeed, he commonly does; but with a still lower descent into the levels of indigence—along the margin of the slums—the man, and presently also the children, virtually cease to consume valuable goods for appearances, and the woman remains virtually the sole exponent of the household's pecuniary decency. No class of society, not even the most abjectly poor, foregoes all customary conspicuous consumption. The last items of this category of consumption are not given up except under stress of the direst necessity. Very much of squalor and discomfort will be endured before the last trinket or the last pretence of pecuniary decency is put away. There is no class and no country that has yielded so abjectly before the pressure of a physical want as to deny themselves all gratification of this higher or spiritual need.

From the foregoing survey of the growth of conspicuous leisure and consumption, it appears that the utility of both alike for the purposes of reputability lies in the element of waste that is common to both. In the one case it is a waste of time and effort, in the other it is a waste of goods. Both are methods of demonstrating the possession of wealth, and the two are conventionally accepted as equivalents. The choice between them is a question of advertising expediency simply, except so far as it may be affected by other standards of propriety, springing from a different source.

Success in America   70
C. Wright Mills

"Success" in America has been a widespread fact, an engaging image, a driving motive, and a way of life. In the middle of the twentieth century, it has become less widespread as fact, more confused as image, often dubious as motive, and soured as a way of life.

No other domestic change is so pivotal for the tang and feel of society in America, or more ambiguous for the inner life of the individual, and none

Ch. 12, "Success," with footnotes omitted: From *White Collar: The American Middle Classes*, by C. Wright Mills, Copyright 1951 by Oxford University Press, Inc. Reprinted by permission.

has been so intricately involved in the transformation of the old into the new middle classes. Other strata have certainly been affected, but the middle classes have been most grievously modified by the newer meanings of success and the increased chances of failure.

To understand the meaning of this shift we must understand the major patterns of American success and the ideologies characteristic of each of them; the changing role of the educational system as an occupational elevator; and the long-run forces, as well as the effects of the slump-war-boom cycle, which lift or lower the rate of upward movement.

1. PATTERNS AND IDEOLOGIES

During booms, success for the American individual has seemed as sure as social progress, and just as surely to rest on and to exemplify personal virtue. The American gospel of success has been a kind of individual specification of the middle-class gospel of progress: in the big, self-made men, rising after the Civil War, progress seemed to pervade the whole society. The ambitious springs of success were unambiguous, its money target clear and visible, and its paths, if rugged, well marked out; there was a surefootedness about the way middle-class men went about their lives.

The idea of the successful individual was linked with the liberal ideology of expanding capitalism. Liberal sociology, assuming a gradation of ranks in which everyone is rewarded according to his ability and effort, has paid less attention to the fate of groups or classes than to the solitary individual, naked of all save personal merit. The entrepreneur, making his way across the open market, most clearly displayed success in these terms.

The way up, according to the classic style of liberalism, was to establish a small enterprise and to expand it by competition with other enterprises. The worker became a foreman and then an industrialist; the clerk became a bookkeeper or a drummer and then a merchant on his own. The farmer's son took up land in his own right and, long before his old age, came into profits and independence. The competition and effort involved in these ways up formed the cradle of a self-reliant personality and the guarantee of economic and political democracy itself.

Success was bound up with the expansible possession rather than the forward-looking job. It was with reference to property that young men were spoken of as having great or small "expectations." Yet in this image success rested less on inheritances than on new beginnings from the bottom; for, it was thought, "business long ago ceased to be a matter of inheritance, and became the property of brains and persistence."

According to the old entrepreneur's ideology, success is always linked with the sober personal virtues of will power and thrift, habits of order, neatness, and the constitutional inability to say Yes to the easy road. These virtues are at once a condition and a sign of success. Without them, success is not possible; with them, all is possible; and, as is clear from the legends of their lives, all successful men have practiced these virtues with great, driving will, for "the temple of Fortune is accessible only by a steep, rugged and difficult path, up which you must drag yourself."

The man bent on success will be upright, exactly punctual, and high-minded; he will soberly refrain from liquor, tobacco, gambling, and loose women. "Laughter, when it is too hearty, weakens the power of mind; avoid it." He will never be in a hurry, will always carefully finish up "each separate undertaking," and so "keep everything under control." He will know "that Method makes Time," and will "promptly improve small opportunities" by diligent attention to detail. He will gain an ease and confidence of endeavor, for self-reliance in all things will insure a moral presence of mind. Also, "a man's self-respect, and the respect of his wife and children for him and themselves, will increase continually as his savings augment."

To honesty, he will add "a great degree of caution and prudence;" then honesty, besides being rewarded in the hereafter, will here and now, be "the surest way to worldly thrift and prosperity." He will come to understand that "religion and business . . . are both right and may essentially serve each other;" that "religion is a mighty ally of economy . . . Vices cost more than Virtues . . . Many a young smoker burns up in advance a fifty-thousand-dollar business;" and more broadly, that religion fortifies the "integrity which is a man's best 'reserve stock.' "

This inspirational ideology does not often concern itself with the imper-sonal structure of opportunity, the limits the economy sets to the practice of personal virtues; and when it does, personal virtues still win through: "The men who are made by circumstances are unmade by trifling misfortunes; while they who conquer circumstances snap their fingers at luck." Yet in relating the detailed means of success, this literature also reveals a good deal about its social conditions. It seems to have been directed to rural and small-town boys. If city boys have better education, country boys have greater "physical and moral pre-eminence." In providing instruction in "polish," it indicates in detail how the rural "bumpkin" must conduct himself in country town and larger city to avoid being laughed at by city slickers. The aspiring boy is cautioned never to be "boisterous" nor have "free and easy manners . . . The manners of a gentleman are a sure passport to success." The city, in this literature, is imagined as a goal, but more importantly, there is a Jeffer-sonian warning about the evils of the city and the practical admonition that "Businessmen . . . are not accidental outcroppings from the great army of smooth-haired nice young clerks who would rather starve in the city than be independent in the country."

Occupationally, the legendary road runs from clerk and then bookkeeper in the country retail store, then to drummer or traveling salesman, and finally, to business for oneself, usually as a merchant. "He who seeks for the merchant of the future will find him in the clerk of today," but the intermediate step is very important and much desired. To the clerk, the drummer is a source of advice about promising locations and opportunities for new stores; the drummer can inspect opportunities for himself and learn about a wide variety of commodity "lines." He also learns to judge others quickly and shrewdly "so that in making a statement he could follow in his hearer's mind its effects, and be prepared to stop or to go on at the right moment." In fact: "All that goes towards making a man a good merchant is needed on the road by a traveling salesman."

The legendary fork in the road is often "a business career" versus farm life or life in a factory. But whatever its occupational content, it is identified with a moral choice: "Keeping on the right side" versus "being lost." He who fails, who remains a clerk, is "lost," "destroyed," "ruined." That end can be met by going either too slow or too fast, and the "easy success" of a few prominent men should not "dazzle other men to destruction."

The entrepreneurial pattern of success and its inspirational ideology rested upon an economy of many small proprietorships. Under a centralized enterprise system, the pattern of success becomes a pattern of the climb within and between prearranged hierarchies. Whatever the level of opportunity may be, the way up does not now typically include the acquisition of independent property. Only those who already have property can now achieve success based upon it.

The shift from a liberal capitalism of small properties to a corporate system of monopoly capitalism is the basis for the shift in the path and in the content of success. In the older pattern, the white-collar job was merely one step on the grand road to independent entrepreneurship; in the new pattern, the white-collar way involves promotions within a bureaucratic hierarchy. When only one-fifth of the population are free enterprisers (and not that many securely so), independent entrepreneurship cannot very well be the major end of individual economic life. The inspirational literature of entrepreneurial success has been an assurance for the individual and an apology for the system. Now it is more apologetic, less assuring.

For some three-fourths of the urban middle class, the salaried employees, the occupational climb replaces heroic tactics in the open competitive market. Although salaried employees may compete with one another, their field of competition is so hedged in by bureaucratic regulation that their competition is likely to be seen as grubbing and backbiting. The main chance now becomes a series of small calculations, stretched over the working lifetime of the individual: a bureaucracy is no testing field for heroes.

The success literature has shifted with the success pattern. It is still focused upon personal virtues, but they are not the sober virtues once imputed to successful entrepreneurs. Now the stress is on agility rather than ability, on "getting along" in a context of associates, superiors, and rules, rather than "getting ahead" across an open market; on whom you know rather than what you know; on techniques of self-display and the generalized knack of handling people, rather than on moral integrity, substantive accomplishments, and solidity of person; on loyalty to, or even identity with, one's own firm, rather than entrepreneurial virtuosity. The best bet is the style of the efficient executive, rather than the drive of the entrepreneur.

"Circumstances, personality, temperament, accident," as well as hard work and patience, now appear as key factors governing success or failure. One should strive for "experience and responsibility within one's chosen field," with "little or no thought of money." Special skills and "executive ability," preferably native, are the ways up from routine work. But the most important single factor is "personality," which ". . . commands attention . . . by charm . . . force of character, or . . . demeanor. . . Accomplishment without . . . personality is unfortunate. . . Personality . . . without industry is . . . undesirable."

To be courteous "will help you to get ahead . . . you will have much more fun . . . will be much less fatigued at night . . . will be more popular, have more friends." So, "Train yourself to smile. . . Express physical and mental alertness. . . Radiate self-confidence. . . Smile often and sincerely." "Everything you say, everything you do, creates impressions upon other people . . . from the cradle to the grave, you've got to get along with other people. Use sound sales principles and you'll do better in 'selling' your merchandise, your ideas, and yourself."

The prime meaning of opportunity in a society of employees is to serve the big firm beyond the line of a job's duty and hence to bring oneself to the attention of the higher-ups who control upward movement. This entails dependability and enthusiasm in handling the little job in a big way. "Character . . . includes . . . innate loyalty in little things and enthusiastic interest in the job at hand. . . In a word, thoroughly dependable and generally with an optimistic, helpful attitude."

"Getting ahead" becomes "a continual selling job. . . Whether you are seeking a new position or are aiming at the job just ahead. In either case you must sell yourself and keep on selling. . . You have a product and that product is yourself." The skillful personal maneuver and the politic approach in inter-organizational contacts, the planful impressing of the business superior become a kind of Machiavellism for the little man, a turning of oneself into an instrument by which to use others for the end of success. "Become genuinely interested in other people. . . Smile. . . Be a good listener. . . Talk in terms of the other man's interest. . . Make the other person feel important —and do it sincerely. . . I am talking," says Dale Carnegie, "about a new way of life."

The heraldry of American success has been the greenback; even when inspirational writers are most inspirational, the big money is always there. Both entrepreneurial and white-collar patterns involve the remaking of personality for pecuniary ends, but in the entrepreneurial pattern, money-success involved the acquisition of virtues good in themselves: the money is always to be used for good works, for virtue and good works justify riches. In the white-collar pattern, there is no such moral sanctifying of the means of success; one is merely prodded to become an instrument of success, to acquire tactics not virtues; money success is assumed to be an obviously good thing for which no sacrifice is too great.

The entrepreneurial and white-collar ways of success, although emerging in historical sequence, are not clear-cut phases through which American aspiration and endeavor have passed. They now co-exist, and each has vary-ing relevance in different economic areas and phases of the economic cycle. Each has also come up against its own kinds of difficulty, which limit its use as a prod to striving. In a society of employees in large-scale enterprises, only a limited number can attempt to follow the entrepreneurial pattern; in a society that has turned itself into a great salesroom, the salesman's ways of success are likely to be severely competitive, and, at the same time, ra-tionalized out of existence; in a society in which the educational level of the lower ranks is constantly rising and jobs are continually rationalized, the white-collar route to the top is likely to come up against competition it never knew in more educationally restricted situations.

2. THE EDUCATIONAL ELEVATOR

The American belief in the value of universal education has been a salient feature of democratic ideology; in fact, since the Jacksonian era, education for all has often been virtually identified with the operation of a truly democratic society. Moreover, the hope for more education has slowly been realized. Eighty years ago a little over half, but today over four-fifths of the children of appropriate age are enrolled in public elementary and secondary schools.

This massive rise in enrollment has strengthened the feeling of status equality, especially in those smaller cities where all the children, regardless of social or occupational rank, are likely to attend the same high school. It has aided immensely in Americanizing the immigrant. And it has spread and generally strengthened old middle-class ideologies, for teachers represent and reinforce middle-class attitudes and values, manners and skills. Yet, in spite of this reinforcing of old middle-class mores, mass education has also been one of the major social mechanisms of the rise of the new middle-class occupations, for these occupations require those skills that have been pro-vided by the educational system.

In performing these functions, especially the last, American education has shifted toward a more explicit vocational emphasis, functioning as a link in occupational mobility between generations. High schools, as well as col-leges and universities, have been reshaped for the personnel needs of business and government. In their desire for serviceable practicality, the schools have adapted themselves to changing demands, and the public has seemed glad to have its children trained for the available jobs.

The most fundamental question to ask of any educational system is what kind of a product do its administrators expect to turn out? And for what kind of society? In the nineteenth century, the answer was "the good citizen" in a "democratic republic." In the middle of the twentieth century, it is "the successful man" in a "society of specialists with secure jobs."

In the world of small entrepreneurs, little or no educational preparation was needed for success, much less to get along: one was stubborn, or courageous, had common sense and worked hard. Education may have been viewed as a main road to social equality and political freedom, and as a help in meeting opportunity so that ability and talent might be appropriately rewarded. But education was not the big avenue of economic advancement for the masses of the populace.

In the new society, the meaning of education has shifted from status and political spheres to economic and occupational areas. In the white-collar life and its patterns of success, the educational segment of the individual's career becomes a key to his entire occupational fate.

Formal requirements for entry into different jobs and expectations of ascent tend to become fixed by educational levels. On the higher levels, college is the cradle of the professions and semi-professions, as well as a necessary status-mark for higher positions. As the virtues and talents of the entrepreneur are replaced by the skills and prestige of the educated expert, formal education becomes central to social and economic success. Sons who are better educated than their fathers are more likely to occupy higher occupational positions: in one sample of urban males, studied by Richard Centers, some 46 per cent of the sons who were better educated than their fathers reached higher positions, whereas only 16 per cent of those whose education was poorer did. The educational link was specifically important in the U.S. Army during World War II: 64 per cent of the officers, but only 11 per cent of the enlisted men, had been to college.

The aim of college men today, especially in elite colleges, is a forward-looking job in a large corporation. Such a job involves training not only in vocational skills, but also in social mannerisms. Harold Taylor, president of Sarah Lawrence, writes: "The ideal graduate in the present employment market of industrial executives is a fraternity man with a declared disinterest in political or social affairs, gentile, white, a member of the football team, a student with a record of A in each course, a man popular with everyone and well known on the campus, with many memberships in social clubs—a man who can be imagined in twenty years as a subject for a Calvert advertisement. The large successful universities have confirmed this stereotype by the plans they make for the campus social life of the students and by the value system implicit in its organization. . . Even the liberal arts colleges seem bent upon becoming training schools for conservative industrial executives."

71   Success in Another Culture
Ruth Benedict

The Zuñi are a ceremonious people, a people who value sobriety and in-offensiveness above all other virtues. Their interest is centred upon their rich and complex ceremonial life. Their cults of the masked gods, of healing, of the sun, of the sacred fetishes, of war, of the dead, are formal and established bodies of ritual with priestly officials and calendric observances. No field of activity competes with ritual for foremost place in their attention. Probably most grown men among the western Pueblos give to it the greater part of their waking life. It requires the memorizing of an amount of word-perfect ritual that our less trained minds find staggering, and the performance of neatly dovetailed ceremonies that are charted by the calendar and complexly interlock all the different cults and the governing body in endless formal procedure.

The ceremonial life not only demands their time; it preoccupies their attention. Not only those who are responsible for the ritual and those who take part in it, but all the people of the pueblo, women and families who "have nothing," that is, that have no ritual possessions, centre their daily conversation about it. While it is in progress, they stand all day as spectators. If a priest is ill, or if no rain comes during his retreat, village gossip runs over and over his ceremonial missteps and the implications of his failure. Did the priest of the masked gods give offense to some supernatural being? Did he break his retreat by going home to his wife before the days were up? These are the subjects of talk in the village for a fortnight. If an imper-sonator wears a new feather on his mask, it eclipses all talk of sheep or gardens or marriage or divorce.

This preoccupation with detail is logical enough. Zuñi religious practices are believed to be supernaturally powerful in their own right. At every step of the way, if the procedure is correct, the costume of the masked god tradi-tional to the last detail, the offerings unimpeachable, the words of the hours-long prayers letter-perfect, the effect will follow according to man's desires. One has only, in the phrase they have always on their tongues, to "know how." According to all the tenets of their religion, it is a major matter if one of the eagle feathers of a mask has been taken from the shoulder of the bird instead of from the breast. Every detail has magical efficacy.

· · ·

From Ch. IV, "The Pueblos of New Mexico," with deletions in *Patterns of Culture*, by Ruth Benedict, Boston, Houghton Mifflin Co., 1961. Reprinted by permission of Houghton Mifflin Co. This book was first published in 1934.

No other aspect of existence seriously competes in Zuñi interest with the dances and the religious observances. Domestic affairs like marriage and divorce are casually and individually arranged. Zuñi is a strongly socialized culture and not much interested in those things that are matters for the individual to attend to. Marriage is arranged almost without courtship. Traditionally girls had few opportunities for speaking to a boy alone, but in the evening when all the girls carried the water-jars on their heads to the spring for water, a boy might waylay one and ask for a drink. If she liked him she gave it to him. He might ask her also to make him a throwing stick for the rabbit hunt, and give her afterwards the rabbits he had killed. Boys and girls were supposed to have no other meetings, and certainly there are many Zuñi women today who were married with no more preliminary sex experience than this.

When the boy decides to ask her father for the girl, he goes to her house. As in every Zuñi visit, he first tastes the food that is set before him, and the father says to him as he must say to every visitor, "Perhaps you came for something." The boy answers, "Yes, I came thinking of your daughter." The father calls his daughter, saying, "I cannot speak for her. Let her say." If she is willing, the mother goes into the next room and makes up the pallet and they retire together. Next day she washes his hair. After four days she dresses in her best clothes and carries a large basket of fine corn flour to his mother's house as a present. There are no further formalities and little social interest is aroused in the affair.

If they are not happy together, and think of separating, especially if they have no children that have lived, the wife will make a point of going to serve at the ceremonial feasts. When she has a tête-à-tête with some eligible man they will arrange a meeting. In Zuñi it is never thought to be difficult for a woman to acquire a new husband. There are fewer women than men, and it is more dignified for a man to live with a wife than to remain in his mother's house. Men are perennially willing. When the woman is satisfied that she will not be left husbandless, she gathers together her husband's possessions and places them on the doorsill, in olden times on the roof by the hatchway. There are not many: his extra pair of moccasins, his dance skirt and sash, if he has them, his box of precious feathers for prayer-sticks, his paint-pots for prayer-sticks and for refurbishing masks. All his more important ceremonial possessions he has never brought from his mother's house. When he comes home in the evening he sees the little bundle, picks it up and cries, and returns with it to his mother's house. He and his family weep and are regarded as unfortunate. But the rearrangement of living-quarters is the subject of only fleeting gossip. There is rarely an interplay of deep feeling. Husbands and wives abide by the rules, and these rules hardly provide for violent emotions, either of jealousy or of revenge, or of an attachment that refuses to accept dismissal.

In spite of the casual nature of marriage and divorce, a very large proportion of Zuñi marriages endure through the greater part of a lifetime. Bickering is not liked, and most marriages are peaceful. The permanence of Zuñi marriages is the more striking because marriage, instead of being the social form behind which all the forces of tradition are massed, as in our culture, cuts directly across the most strongly institutionalized social bond in Zuñi.

This is the matrilineal family, which is ceremonially united in its ownership and care of the sacred fetishes. To the women of the household, the grandmother and her sisters, her daughters and their daughters, belong the house and the corn that is stored in it. No matter what may happen to marriages, the women of the household remain with the house for life. They present a solid front. They care for and feed the sacred objects that belong to them. They keep their secrets together. The husbands are outsiders, and it is their brothers, married now into the houses of other clans, who are united with the household in all affairs of moment. It is they who return for all the retreats when the sacred objects of the house are set out before the altar. It is they, not the women, who learn the word-perfect ritual of their sacred bundle and perpetuate it. A man goes always, for all important occasions, to his mother's house, which, when she dies, becomes his sister's house, and if his marriage breaks up, he returns to the same stronghold.

This blood-relationship group, rooted in the ownership of the house, united in the care of sacred objects, is the important group in Zuñi. It has permanence and important common concerns. But it is not the economically functioning group. Each married son, each married brother, spends his labour upon the corn which will fill his wife's storeroom. Only when his mother's or sister's house lacks male labour does he care for the cornfield of his blood-relationship group. The economic group is the household that lives together, the old grandmother and her husband, her daughters and their husbands. These husbands count in the economic group, though in the ceremonial group they are outsiders.

For women there is no conflict. They have no allegiance of any kind to their husband's groups. But for all men there is double allegiance. They are husbands in one group and brothers in another. Certainly in the more important families, in those which care for permanent fetishes, a man's allegiance as brother has more social weight than his allegiance as husband. In all families a man's position derives, not, as with us, from his position as breadwinner, but from his rôle in relation to the sacred objects of the household. The husband, with no such relationship to the ceremonial possessions of his wife's house to trade upon, only gradually attains to position in the household as his children grow to maturity. It is as their father, not as provider or as their mother's husband, that he finally attains some authority in the household where he may have lived for twenty years.

Economic affairs are always as comparatively unimportant in Zuñi as they are in determining the family alignments. Like all the Pueblos, and perhaps in greater degree than the rest, Zuñi is rich. It has gardens and peach orchards and sheep and silver and turquoise. These are important to a man when they make it possible for him to have a mask made for himself, or to pay for the learning of ritual, or to entertain the tribal masked gods at the Shalako. For this last he must build a new house for the gods to bless at housewarming. All that year he must feed the cult members who build for him, he must provide the great beams for the rafters, he must entertain the whole tribe at the final ceremony. There are endless responsibilities he must assume. For this purpose he will plant heavily the year before and increase his herd. He will receive help from his clan group, all of which he must return in kind. Riches used in this way are of course indispensable to a man of prestige, but neither he nor anyone else is concerned with the reckoning of possessions, but with the ceremonial rôle which he has taken. A "valuable" family, in native parlance, is always a family which owns permanent fetishes, and a man of importance is one who has undertaken many ceremonial rôles.

All the traditional arrangements tend to make wealth play as small a part as possible in the performance of ritual prerogatives. Ceremonial objects, even though they are recognized personal property and attained by the expenditure of money and effort, are free to the use of anyone who can employ them. There are many sacred things too dangerous to be handled except by those who have qualified, but the tabus are not property tabus. Hunting fetishes are owned in the hunters' society, but anyone who is going hunting may take them for his use. He will have to assume the usual responsibilities for using holy things; he will have to plant prayer-sticks and be continent and benevolent for four days. But he pays nothing, and those who possess the fetishes as private property have no monopoly of their supernatural powers. Similarly a man who has no mask borrows one freely and is not thought of as a beggar or a suppliant.

Besides this unusual discontinuity between vested interests and the ownership of ceremonial objects in Zuñi, other more common arrangements make wealth of comparative unimportance. Membership in a clan with numerous ceremonial prerogatives outweighs wealth, and a poor man may be sought repeatedly for ritual offices because he is of the required lineage. Most ceremonial participation, in addition, is the responsibility of a group of people. An individual acts in assuming ritual posts as he does in all other affairs of life, as a member of a group. He may be a comparatively poor man, but the household or the kiva acting through him provides the ceremonial necessaries. The group gains always from this participation because of the great blessing that accrues to it, and the property owned by a self-respecting individual is not the count on which he is admitted to or denied ceremonial rôles.

. . .

The ideal man of the Pueblos is another order of being. Personal authority is perhaps the most vigorously disparaged trait in Zuñi. "A man who thirsts for power or knowledge, who wishes to be as they scornfully phrase it 'a leader of his people,' receives nothing but censure and will very likely be persecuted for sorcery," and he often has been. Native authority of manner is a liability in Zuñi, and witchcraft is the ready charge against a person who possesses it. He is hung by the thumbs until he "confesses." It is all Zuñi can do with a man of strong personality. The ideal man in Zuñi is a person of dignity and affability who has never tried to lead, and who has never called forth comment from his neighbours. Any conflict, even though all right is on his side, is held against him. Even in contests of skill like their foot-races, if a man wins habitually he is debarred from running. They are interested in a game that a number can play with even chances, and an outstanding runner spoils the game: they will have none of him.

A good man has, in Dr. Bunzel's words, "a pleasing address, a yielding disposition, and a generous heart." The highest praise, describing an impeccable townsman, runs: "He is a nice polite man. No one ever hears anything from him. He never gets into trouble. He's Badger clan and Muhekwe kiva, and he always dances in the summer dances." He should "talk lots," as they say—that is, he should always set people at their ease—and he should without fail co-operate easily with others either in the field or in ritual, never betraying a suspicion of arrogance or a strong emotion.

He avoids office. He may have it thrust upon him, but he does not seek it. When the kiva offices must be filled, the hatchway of the kiva is fastened and all the men are imprisoned until someone's excuses have been battered down. The folktales always relate of good men their unwillingness to take office—though they always take it. A man must avoid the appearance of leadership. When the chosen person has been prevailed upon and has been initiated in the office, he has not been given authority in our sense. His post carries with it no sanction for important action. The council of Zuñi is made up of the highest priests, and priests have no jurisdiction in cases of conflict or violence. They are holy men and must not have a quarrel put before them. Only the war chiefs have some measure of executive authority, not in war so much as in peace-time policing powers. They make proclamation of a coming rabbit hunt, or coming dances, they summon priests and co-operate with the medicine societies. The crime that they traditionally have to deal with is witchcraft. Another crime, that of betraying to the uninitiated boys the secret of the kachinas, is punished by the masked gods themselves, summoned by the head of the kachina cult. There are no other crimes. Theft rarely occurs and is a private matter. Adultery is no crime and the strain that arises from such an act is easily taken care of under their marriage arrangements. Homicide, in the one case that is remembered, was settled quickly by payments between the two families.

The priests of the high council, therefore, are not disturbed. They administer the main features of the ceremonial calendar. The successful prosecution of their plans could be blocked at every turn by an unco-operative minor priest. He would only have to sulk, refusing, for instance, to set up his altar or to furnish his kachina priest mask. The priestly council could only wait and defer the ceremonial. But everyone co-operates, and no show of authority is called for.

This same lack of personal exercise of authority is as characteristic of domestic situations as it is of religious. The matrilineal and matrilocal household of course makes necessary a different allocation of authority from that with which we are familiar. But matrilineal societies do not usually dispense with a male person of authority in the household even though the father does not qualify. The mother's brother as the male head of the matrilineal household is arbiter and responsible head. But Zuñi does not recognize any authority as vested in the mother's brother, and certainly not in the father. Neither of them disciplines the children of his household. Babies are much fondled by the men folk. They carry them when they are ailing and hold them in their laps evenings. But they do not discipline them. The virtue of co-operation holds domestic life true to form just as it holds religious life, and no situations arise that need to be drastically handled. What would they be? Marriage is in other cultures the almost universal occasion where some authority is exercised. But among the Pueblos it is arranged with little formality. Marriage elsewhere in the world involves property rights and economic exchanges, and on all such occasions the elders have prerogatives. But in Zuñi marriage there are no stakes in which the elders are interested. The slight emphasis upon possessions among the Pueblos makes a casual affair not only of the elsewhere difficult situation of marriage but of a dozen others, all those which according to other cultural forms involve investment of group property for the young man. Zuñi simply eliminates the occasions.

.   .   .

The lack of opportunities for the exercise of authority, both in religious and in domestic situations, is knit up with another fundamental trait: the insistence upon sinking the individual in the group. In Zuñi, responsibility and power are always distributed and the group is made the functioning unit. The accepted way to approach the supernatural is in group ritual. The accepted way to secure family subsistence is by household partnership. Neither in religion nor in economics is the individual autonomous. In religion a man who is anxious about his harvest does not offer prayer for the rain that will save it; he dances in the summer rain dances. A man does not pray for the recovery of his son who is ill; he brings the doctors' order of Big Fire Society to cure him. Those individual prayers that are allowed, at the personal planting of prayer-sticks, at the head-washings of ceremonial cleanliness, at the calling of the medicine men or a ceremonial father, have validity only because they are necessary parts of a larger whole, the group ritual to which they belong. They could no more be separated from it and still have power than one word could be taken from the long magic formulas and retain by itself the efficacy of the perfect prayer.

. . .

Just as in religion the acts and motivations of the individual are singularly without personal reference, so too in economic life. The economic unit is, as we have seen, a very unstable group of men folk. The core of the household, the permanent group, is a relationship group of women, but the women are not the ones who function importantly in the great economic enterprises such as agriculture or herding, or even work in turquoise. And the men who are necessary in the fundamental occupations are a shifting group loosely held together. The husbands of the daughters of the household will return to their maternal households upon a domestic storm and will henceforth have no responsibility for feeding or housing their children whom they leave behind. There are, besides, in the household the miscellaneous male blood relatives of the female relationship group: the unmarried, the widowed, the divorced, and those who are awaiting the passing of temporary unpleasantness in their wives' households. Yet this miscellaneous group, whatever its momentary composition, pools its work in filling the common corn storeroom, and this corn remains the collective property of the women of the household. Even if some newly cultivated fields belong as private property to any of these men, all the men jointly farm them for the common storeroom just as they do ancestral fields.

The custom is the same in regard to houses. The men build them, and jointly, and they belong to the women. A man, leaving his wife in the fall, may be leaving behind him the house he has spent his year building and a full cornroom, the result of his season's farming. But there is no thought of his having any individual claim upon either; and he is not thought of as defrauded. He pooled his work in his household's, and the results are a group supply; if he is no longer a member of that group, that is his affair. Sheep are today a considerable source of income, and are owned by men individually. But they are co-operatively herded by groups of male kindred, and new economic motivations are very slow in making their appearance.

Just as according to the Zuñi ideal a man sinks his activities in those of the group and claims no personal authority, so also he is never violent. Their Apollonian commitment to the mean in the Greek sense is never clearer than in their cultural handling of the emotions. Whether it is anger or love or jealousy or grief, moderation is the first virtue. The fundamental tabu upon their holy men during their periods of office is against any suspicion of anger. Controversies, whether they are ceremonial or economic or domestic, are carried out with an unparalleled lack of vehemence.

THE COST OF SUCCESS

Jobs 72

Paul Goodman

1

It's hard to grow up when there isn't enough man's work. There is "nearly full employment" (with highly significant exceptions), but there get to be fewer jobs that are necessary or unquestionably useful; that require energy and draw on some of one's best capacities; and that can be done keeping one's honor and dignity. In explaining the widespread troubles of adolescents and young men, this simple objective factor is not much mentioned. Let us here insist on it.

By "man's work" I mean a very simple idea, so simple that it is clearer to ingenuous boys than to most adults. To produce necessary food and shelter is man's work. During most of economic history most men have done this drudging work, secure that it was justified and worthy of a man to do it, though often feeling that the social conditions under which they did it were *not* worthy of a man, thinking, "It's better to die than to live so hard"—but they worked on. When the environment is forbidding, as in the Swiss Alps or the Aran Islands, we regard such work with poetic awe. In emergencies it is heroic, as when the bakers of Paris maintained the supply of bread during the French Revolution, or the milkman did not miss a day's delivery when the bombs recently tore up London.

At present there is little such subsistence work. In *Communitas* my brother and I guess that one-tenth of our economy is devoted to it; it is more likely one-twentieth. Production of food is actively discouraged. Farmers are not wanted and the young men go elsewhere. (The farm population is now less than 15 per cent of the total population.) Building, on the contrary, is immensely needed. New York City needs 65,000 new units a year, and is getting, net, 16,000. One would think that ambitious boys would flock to

From Ch. 1, "Jobs," in *Growing Up Absurd*, with deletions, New York, Vintage Books, 1960. © Copyright 1960 by Paul Goodman. Reprinted from *Growing Up Absurd*, by Paul Goodman, by permission of Random House, Inc.

this work. But here we find that building, too, is discouraged. In a great city, for the last twenty years hundreds of thousands have been ill housed, yet we do not see science, industry, and labor enthusiastically enlisted in finding the quick solution to a definite problem. The promoters are interested in long-term investments, the real estate men in speculation, the city planners in votes and graft. The building craftsmen cannily see to it that their own numbers remain few, their methods antiquated, and their rewards high. None of these people is much interested in providing shelter, and nobody is at all interested in providing new manly jobs.

Once we turn away from the absolutely necessary subsistence jobs, however, we find that an enormous proportion of our production is not even unquestionably useful. Everybody knows and also feels this, and there has recently been a flood of books about our surfeit of honey, our insolent chariots, the follies of exurban ranch houses, our hucksters and our synthetic demand. Many acute things are said about this useless production and advertising, but not much about the workmen producing it and their frame of mind; and nothing at all, so far as I have noticed, about the plight of a young fellow looking for a manly occupation. The eloquent critics of the American way of life have themselves been so seduced by it that they think only in terms of selling commodities and point out that the goods are valueless; but they fail to see that people are being wasted and their skills insulted. (To give an analogy, in the many gleeful onslaughts on the Popular Culture that have appeared in recent years, there has been little thought of the plight of the honest artist cut off from his audience and sometimes, in public arts such as theater and architecture, from his medium.)

What is strange about it? American society has tried so hard and so ably to defend the practice and theory of production for profit and not primarily for use that now it has succeeded in making its jobs and products profitable and useless.

2

Consider a likely useful job. A youth who is alert and willing but not "verbally intelligent"—perhaps he has quit high school at the eleventh grade (the median), as soon as he legally could—chooses for auto mechanic. That's a good job, familiar to him, he often watched them as a kid. It's careful and dirty at the same time. In a small garage it's sociable; one can talk to the customers (girls). You please people in trouble by fixing their cars, and a man is proud to see rolling out on its own the car that limped in behind the tow truck. The pay is as good as the next fellow's, who is respected.

So our young man takes this first-rate job. But what when he then learns that the cars have a built-in obsolescence, that the manufacturers do not want them to be repaired or repairable? They have lobbied a law that requires them to provide spare parts for only five years (it used to be ten). Repairing the new cars is often a matter of cosmetics, not mechanics; and the repairs are pointlessly expensive—a tail fin might cost $150. The insurance rates therefore double and treble on old and new cars both. Gone are the days of keeping the jalopies in good shape, the artist-work of a proud mechanic. But everybody is paying for foolishness, for in fact the new models are only trivially superior; the whole thing is a sell.

It is hard for the young man now to maintain his feelings of justification, sociability, serviceability. It is not surprising if he quickly becomes cynical and time-serving, interested in a fast buck. And so, on the notorious *Reader's Digest* test, the investigators (coming in with a disconnected coil wire) found that 63 per cent of mechanics charged for repairs they didn't make, and lucky if they didn't also take out the new fuel pump and replace it with a used one (65 per cent of radio repair shops, but *only* 49 per cent of watch repairmen "lied, overcharged, or gave false diagnoses").

There is an hypothesis that an important predisposition to juvenile delinquency is the combination of low verbal intelligence with high manual intelligence, delinquency giving a way of self-expression where other avenues are blocked by lack of schooling. A lad so endowed might well apply himself to the useful trade of mechanic.

3

Most manual jobs do not lend themselves so readily to knowing the facts and fraudulently taking advantage oneself. In factory jobs the workman is likely to be ignorant of what goes on, since he performs a small operation on a big machine that he does not understand. Even so, there is evidence that he has the same disbelief in the enterprise as a whole, with a resulting attitude of profound indifference.

Semiskilled factory operatives are the largest category of workmen. (I am leafing through the U.S. Department of Labor's *Occupational Outlook Handbook,* 1957.) Big companies have tried the devices of applied anthropology to enhance the loyalty of these men to the firm, but apparently the effort is hopeless, for it is found that a thumping majority of the men don't care about the job or the firm; they couldn't care less and you can't make them care more. But this is *not* because of wages, hours, or working conditions, or management. On the contrary, tests that show the men's indifference to the company show also their (unaware) admiration for the way the company has designed and manages the plant; it is their very model of style, efficiency, and correct behavior. (Robert Dubin, for the U.S. Public Health Service.) Maybe if the men understood more, they would admire less. The union and the grievance committee take care of wages, hours, and conditions; these are the things the workmen themselves fought for and won. (Something was missing in that victory, and we have inherited the failure as well as the success.) The conclusion must be that workmen are indifferent to the job because of its intrinsic nature: it does not enlist worth-while capacities, it is not "interesting"; it is not his, he is not "in" on it; the product is not really useful. And indeed, research directly on the subject, by Frederick Herzberg on Motivation to Work, shows that it is defects in the intrinsic aspects of the job that make workmen "unhappy." A survey of the literature (in Herzberg's *Job Attitudes*) shows that Interest is second in importance only to Security, whereas Wages, Conditions, Socializing, Hours, Ease, and Benefits are far less important. But foremen, significantly enough, think that the most important thing to the workman is his wages. The investigators do not seem to inquire about the usefulness of the job—as if a primary purpose of *working* at a job were not that it is good *for* something! My guess is that a large factor in "Security" is the resigned reaction to not being able to take into account whether the work of one's hands is useful for anything; for in a normal life situation, if what we do is useful, we feel secure about being needed. The other largest factor in "Security" is, I think, the sense of being needed for one's unique contribution, and this is measured in these tests by the primary importance the workers assign to being "in" on things and to "work done being appreciated."

Limited as they are, what a remarkable insight such studies give us, that men want to do valuable work and work that is somehow theirs! But they are thwarted.

Is not this the "waste of our human resources"?

The case is that by the "sole-prerogative" clause in union contracts the employer has the sole right to determine what is to be produced, how it is to be produced, what plants are to be built and where, what kinds of machinery are to be installed, when workers are to be hired and laid off, and how production operations are to be rationalized. (Frank Marquart.) There is *none* of this that is inevitable in running a machine economy; but *if* these are the circumstances, it is not surprising that the factory operatives' actual code has absolutely nothing to do with useful service or increasing production, but is notoriously devoted to "interpersonal relations;" (1) don't turn out too much work; (2) don't turn out too little work; (3) don't squeal on a fellow worker; (4) don't act like a big-shot. This is how to belong.

·   ·   ·

5

Next, what happens to the verbally bright who have no zeal for a serviceable profession and who have no particular scientific or artistic bent? For the most part they make up the tribes of salesmanship, entertainment, business management, promotion, and advertising. Here of course there is no question of utility or honor to begin with, so an ingenuous boy will not look here for a manly career. Nevertheless, though we can pass by the sufferings of these well-paid callings, much publicized by their own writers, they are important to our theme because of the model they present to the growing boy.

Consider the men and women in TV advertisements, demonstrating the product and singing the jingle. They are clowns and mannequins, in grimace, speech, and action. And again, what I want to call attention to in this advertising is not the economic problem of synthetic demand, and not the cultural problem of Popular Culture, but the human problem that these are human beings working as clowns; that the writers and designers of it are human beings thinking like idiots; and the broadcasters and underwriters know and abet what goes on—

> Juicily glubbily
> *Blubber* is dubbily
> delicious and nutritious
> —eat it, Kitty, it's good.

Alternately, they are liars, confidence men, smooth talkers, obsequious, insolent, etc., etc.

The popular-cultural content of the advertisements is somewhat neutralized by *Mad* magazine, the bible of the twelve-year-olds who can read. But far more influential and hard to counteract is the *fact* that the workmen and the patrons of this enterprise are human beings. (Highly approved, too.) They are not good models for a boy looking for a manly job that is useful and necessary, requiring human energy and capacity, and that can be done with honor and dignity. They are a good sign that not many such jobs will be available.

The popular estimation is rather different. Consider the following: "As one possible aid, I suggested to the Senate subcommittee that they alert celebrities and leaders in the fields of sports, movies, theater and television to the help they can offer by getting close to these [delinquent] kids. By giving them positive 'heroes' they know and can talk to, instead of the misguided image of trouble-making buddies, they could aid greatly in guiding these normal aspirations for fame and status into wholesome progressive channels." (Jackie Robinson, who was formerly on the Connecticut Parole Board.) Or again: when a mass cross-section of Oklahoma high school juniors and seniors was asked which living person they would like to be, the boys named Pat Boone, Ricky Nelson, and President Eisenhower; the girls chose Debbie Reynolds, Elizabeth Taylor, and Natalie Wood.

The rigged Quiz shows, which created a scandal in 1959, were a remarkably pure distillate of our American cookery. We start with the brute facts that (a) in our abundant expanding economy it is necessary to give money away to increase spending, production, and profits; and (b) that this money must not be used for useful public goods in taxes, but must be plowed back as "business expenses," even though there is a shameful shortage of schools, housing, etc. Yet when the TV people at first tried simply to give the money away for nothing (for having heard of George Washington), there was a great Calvinistic outcry that this was demoralizing (we may gamble on the horses only to improve the breed). So they hit on the notion of a real contest with prizes. But then, of course, they could not resist making the show itself profitable, and competitive in the (also rigged) ratings with other shows, so the experts in the entertainment-commodity manufactured phony contests. And to cap the climax of fraudulence, the hero of the phony contests proceeded to persuade himself, so he says, that his behavior was educational!

The behavior of the networks was correspondingly typical. These business organizations claim the loyalty of their employees, but at the first breath of trouble they were ruthless and disloyal to their employees. (Even McCarthy was loyal to his gang.) They want to maximize profits and yet be absolutely safe from any risk. Consider their claim that they knew nothing about the fraud. But if they watched the shows that they were broadcasting, they could not *possibly*, as professionals, not have known the facts, for there were obvious type-casting, acting, plot, etc. If they are not professionals, they are incompetent. But if they don't watch what they broadcast, then they are utterly irresponsible and on what grounds do they have the franchises to the channels? We may offer them the choice: that they are liars or incompetent or irresponsible.

The later direction of the investigation seems to me more important, the inquiry into the bribed disk-jockeying; for this deals directly with our crucial economic problem of synthesized demand, made taste, debauching the public and preventing the emergence and formation of natural taste. In such circumstances there cannot possibly be an American culture; we are doomed to nausea and barbarism. And *then* these baboons have the effrontery to declare that they give the people what the people demand and that they are not responsible for the level of the movies, the music, the plays, the books!

Finally, in leafing through the *Occupational Outlook Handbook,* we notice that the armed forces employ a large number. Here our young man can become involved in a world-wide demented enterprise, with personnel and activities corresponding.

6

Thus, on the simple criteria of unquestioned utility, employing human capacities, and honor, there are not enough worthy jobs in our economy for average boys and adolescents to grow up toward. There are of course thousands of jobs that are worthy and self-justifying, and thousands that can be made so by stubborn integrity, especially if one can work as an independent. Extraordinary intelligence or special talent, also, can often carve out a place for itself—conversely, their usual corruption and waste are all the more sickening. But by and large our economic society is *not* geared for the cultivation of its young or the attainment of important goals that they can work toward.

This is evident from the usual kind of vocational guidance, which consists of measuring the boy and finding some place in the economy where he can be fitted; chopping him down to make him fit; or neglecting him if they can't find his slot. Personnel directors do not much try to scrutinize the economy in order to find some activity that is a real opportunity for the boy, and then to create an opportunity if they can't find one. To do this would be an horrendous task; I am not sure it could be done if we wanted to do it. But the question is whether anything less makes sense if we mean to speak seriously about the troubles of the young men.

Surely by now, however, many readers are objecting that this entire argument is pointless because people in *fact* don't think of their jobs in this way at all. *Nobody* asks if a job is useful or honorable (within the limits of business ethics). A man gets a job that pays well, or well enough, that has prestige, and good conditions, or at least tolerable conditions. I agree with these objections as to the fact. (I hope we are wrong.) But *the question is what it means to grow up into such a fact as: "During my productive years I will spend eight hours a day doing what is no good."*

7

Yet, economically and vocationally, a very large population of the young people are in a plight more drastic than anything so far mentioned. In our society as it is, there are not enough worthy jobs. But if our society, being as it is, were run more efficiently and soberly, for a majority there would soon not be any jobs at all. There is at present nearly full employment and there may be for some years, yet a vast number of young people are rationally unemployable, useless. This paradox is essential to explain their present temper.

Our society, which is not geared to the cultivation of its young, *is* geared to a profitable expanding production, a so-called high standard of living of mediocre value, and the maintenance of nearly full employment. Politically, the chief of these is full employment. In a crisis, when profitable production is temporarily curtailed, government spending increases and jobs are manufactured. In "normalcy"—a condition of slow boom—the easy credit, installment buying, and artificially induced demand for useless goods create jobs for all and good profits for some.

Now, back in the Thirties, when the New Deal attempted by hook or crook to put people back to work and give them money to revive the shattered economy, there was an outcry of moral indignation from the conservatives that many of the jobs were "boondoggling," useless made-work. It was insisted, and rightly, that such work was demoralizing to the workers themselves. It is a question of a word, but a candid critic might certainly say that many of the jobs in our present "normal" production are useless made-work. The tail fins and built-in obsolescence might be called boondoggling. The $64,000 Question and the busy hum of Madison Avenue might certainly be called boondoggling. Certain tax-dodge Foundations are boondoggling. What of business lunches and expense accounts? fringe benefits? the comic categories of occupation in the building trades? the extra stagehands and musicians of the theater crafts? These jolly devices to put money back to work no doubt have a demoralizing effect on somebody or other (certainly on me, they make me green with envy), but where is the moral indignation from Top Management?

Suppose we would cut out the boondoggling and gear our society to a more sensible abundance, with efficient production of quality goods, distribution in a natural market, counterinflation and sober credit. At once the work week would be cut to, say, twenty hours instead of forty. (Important People have already mentioned the figure thirty.) Or alternately, half the labor force would be unemployed. Suppose too—and how can we not suppose it?—that the automatic machines are used generally, rather than just to get rid of badly organized unskilled labor. The unemployment will be still more drastic.

To give the most striking example: in steel, the annual increase in productivity is 4 per cent, the plants work at 50 per cent of capacity, and the companies can break even and stop producing at *less than 30 per cent* of capacity. These are the conditions that forced the steel strike, as desperate self-protection. (Estes Kefauver, quoting Gardiner Means and Fred Gardner.)

Everybody knows this, nobody wants to talk about it much, for we don't know how to cope with it. The effect is that we are living a kind of lie. Long ago, labor leaders used to fight for the shorter work week, but now they don't, because they're pretty sure they don't want it. Indeed, when hours are reduced, the tendency is to get a second, part-time, job and raise the standard of living, *because* the job is meaningless and one must have something; but the standard of living is pretty meaningless, too. Nor is this strange atmosphere a new thing. For at least a generation the maximum sensible use of our productivity could have thrown a vast population out of work, or relieved everybody of a lot of useless work, depending on how you take it. (Consider with how little cutback of useful civilian production the economy produced the war goods and maintained an Army, economically unemployed.) The plain truth is that at present very many of us are useless, not needed, rationally unemployable. It is in this paradoxical atmosphere that young persons grow up. It looks busy and expansive, but it is rationally at a stalemate.

The Age of Automation Begins

David Rodnick

The age of automation has not arrived like a flood sweeping everything before it, but rather like a quiet brook starting with droplets and covering only a small area. Because it has grown very slowly over the past 70 to 80 years, its impression has been felt only in this decade. Its total effect, however, may not be sensed for another thirty to thirty-five years, and our social adjustment to it may not take place for possibly fifty years beyond that.

Automation involves the mechanization of work processes; previous industrialization required that the machines duplicate the work of the human being faster and more efficiently. Automation goes further. It promises to free man from routine tasks and to spare him for the work that no machine can do: the ability to think and to solve problems creatively. What man can do routinely, the automatic machine can do better. Any task requiring repetition can be performed by automated machines with greater speed, more efficiency, and less error. The possibilities that automation opens up for benefiting mankind are endless, and its uses can make possible the worldwide eradication of abject poverty, illiteracy, and traditionalism. Unfortunately, as the world is presently constituted, automation may be a mixed blessing that brings more problems than benefits. But seen against the perspective of the future, automation could well be the answer to all of man's prayers and dreams.

Because automation is very expensive to install and because its possibilities have been only partially explored, its absorption into the fabric of American industry will be relatively slow, with only a few plants automating at a time. For years to come, most industries will still operate with semiautomatic machines, much as artisan handicrafts existed side by side with mass-production industries until a few decades ago in the United States and as they still do in France, Germany, and Great Britain. In most service industries and many consumer goods industries, automation will be slow in displacing workers, although machines may be introduced into larger industries within the next few decades, displacing even skilled employees.

Through the slowness in adopting automation, American society, as well as Western European, Japanese, and Soviet, has gained some time in which to think about the implications of automation and to adjust the population to its inevitability. Automation represents the new age of tomorrow. When it has

From Ch. 24, "The Age of Automation Begins," with deletions, in *An Introduction to Man and His Development* by David Rodnick, New York, Appleton-Century-Crofts, 1966. Reprinted by permission of Appleton-Century-Crofts.

been incorporated in most production processes and in most services, even in mass transportation, education, and entertainment, one will be able to say that Tertiary civilization has arrived (although it too may be replaced by a new civilization—perhaps one where creativity is universally organized).

Automation is a more efficient industrial system than the old system, for it preserves unusual human skills indefinitely. Under the past industrialization of Secondary civilization, the skills and experiences of the highly trained technician, engineer, or scientist died with them. Under automation the skills can be taped and transferred to machines to perform indefinitely in the future what these men had done in the past. Until new skills arrive on the scene, past skills can be produced endlessly on an extremely high level without the moods and the ups and downs of ordinary daily production by people. Highly qualified human skills can thus be preserved for posterity, as they are being saved today on film or on tape. Under automation, even the technical skills of the unusual craftsman or engineer can be used in industries all over the world, much as hi-fi records can display the talents of the performer even in the most isolated hamlet.

Although automation will initially be used in mass-production industries, the introduction of tape-controlled, multipurpose machine tools will permit small shops, where there is a production of ten to twenty items, to switch quickly from one product to another by utilizing different tapes. One automated machine tool in use in 1965 can interchange thirty-one different cutting tools and can handle hundreds of operations in proper sequence without any human hand regulating any part of the work performed.

It is fortunate for us that automation is being introduced into American industries and offices at a fairly slow rate; otherwise the adjustment problems would be much greater than our American society or government could handle at the present time. No one knows yet what to do with the individuals who are displaced by automation, for even retraining requires that some idea be held as to what to train unskilled and uneducated workers for. No attempts have been made to visualize those employment possibilities that may be open to them now or in 1975 or 1980. Even the schools continue in their traditional ways, educating young people for a society similar to that of the immediate past. Our colleges tend to duplicate one another in the proliferation of courses that have little to do with the society of the United States or of the world as it may exist during the next ten to twenty years (which is a very short time in the life of a twenty-year-old, who would only be forty in twenty years, with still another forty years of life expectancy ahead of him).

Technological progress in productivity, or the output per work hour, as a result of recent automation and improved machine tools, now permits the discharge of more than 2 million workers per year, but with output still increasing.[1] During the next ten years, at least another 1.8 million young people

[1] Ackley, Gardner, "Automation: Threat and Promise," *New York Times Magazine*, March 22, 1964.

will be leaving schools annually to enter the labor market. During the 1950's, when the number of jobs displaced by automation was far less than it will be-in the 1960's or 1970's, less than 1.3 million young people had to be absorbed into the labor market.

During the past fifteen years, automation has slowly been eroding the number of jobs in industry held by the unskilled and semiskilled; and it is now reaching out for the work done by the skilled workers. In 1950 almost 50 percent of the labor force was still employed in the production of goods, but by 1964 the number of industrial workers had fallen to less than 40 percent of the country's wage earners. Today, in the United States the number of individuals employed in services or as white-collar workers exceeds the number working in various industries. In 1947, 26,470,000 individuals worked in production and 26 million in services. In 1962 production workers had declined to 25 million, and service employees had increased to 35,670,000. If the present trends continue, there will be more than 50 million in the services in 1975, as compared to a little less than 25 million in production. But by 1975, there will be at least 85 million in the labor force.

In 1947 the automobile industry needed 649,000 production workers to turn out 4.8 million cars. In 1962 it turned out almost 7 million autos with 37,000 fewer workers. In 1951 the steel industry required 540,000 men to produce 96.8 million tons of steel. In 1962 it produced the same quantity of steel with 79,000 fewer men. As a result of mechanization, rather than automation, in the mining regions, employment dipped from 344,000 to 174,000 in ten years. In the hard coal, or anthracite, mines, employment dropped from 70,000 to a little over 12,000 during the past fourteen years; yet productivity per miner doubled.[2]

In the beginning of the industrial era, most labor in the United States was unskilled. Today less than 5 percent of all employment is unskilled. In the meanwhile, professional and technical positions increased by more than 50 percent in the past twelve years and will jump another 40 percent during the remaining 1960's. More steel, more cars, more appliances, more of everything, are being produced with fewer workers. Our problem is no longer scarcities but surpluses that continue to accumulate. Even the automobile manufacturers must come out with glamor models every six months to increase the sales of their products, which are now inching up to the goal of 10 million cars each year. Every year almost 5 million cars have to be junked, and a mounting problem for large American cities is what to do with the cars that are abandoned on public streets since there is little demand for the metal even in steel mills. To keep production going, industry is faced with the need to make its objects obsolete in a few years so that no surpluses will develop.

In agriculture a cornpicker, which costs a little over $4,000, can cut 100 tons of ears from their stalks in one day, work that required the labor of twenty men in the days before the machine. A beetpicker, which costs a little

2 Bill Francois, "The Fear of Tomorrow," *The Progressive*, March, 1962, p. 16.

over $5,000, can dig up two rows of beets at a time, shake off the dirt, cut off the tops, and drop the rest onto a conveyor belt that loads them onto a truck, replacing fifty agricultural laborers in this operation.[3] Soon all the fruit and vegetables will be plucked or picked by mechanized steel fingers and hands, and then hundreds of thousands of migrant laborers will be displaced.

The number of white-collar workers has increased enormously in the past twenty-five years as banking, financing, insurance, record-keeping, and credit have become bigger than ever before. Installment debts alone increased from $15 billion in 1947 to over $45 billion by 1962. Although the numbers have been increasing absolutely, however, the rate of increase has been dropping relatively. For example, almost half of the white-collar workers are composed of clerks and related workers, of whom two out of every three are women. Between 1940 and 1950 the number of women clerks, bookkeepers, secretaries, and related workers increased by more than 80 percent. During the 1950's the increase was only 57 percent. By the early 1960's the rate of increase had dropped to a little over 10 percent. As another example, the average annual increase of clerical workers from 1950 to 1957 was 280,000; from 1957 to 1960 it had dropped to 150,000; but by the end of 1962 there had been only 25,000 more women employed than in 1961. This gap will become narrower during the next few years.

At present, the spread between demand and supply of white-collar workers is being filled by electronic processing systems, or clerical automation. Despite the ever-rising amounts of paper work, the new data processing systems have enabled the businessman to do more work with relatively fewer employees. By 1962 almost 90 percent of the banks, insurance companies, public utility firms, and large credit houses had installed electronic processing equipment. In businesses employing between 100 to 1,000 employees, some 80 percent by the end of 1962 had installed automatic clerical and bookkeeping machines.

The rising costs of white-collar workers have made many businesses believe that the machines are now cheaper, despite their high initial cost, than the clerks, bookkeepers, and other related employees. Automation has affected the production worker considerably, but its influence on the white-collar worker has been minimal so far. The latter will not be affected by its innovations for at least another ten years; but when it does come, it will hurt him as much as it has the industrial wage earner. Neither the white-collar worker nor the industrial worker can be retrained successfully, for the techniques of automation have gone much further than the understanding of its effects upon the working population or of the jobs that could possibly be opened up to take care of the displaced worker. Despite an increase in population, the trend is toward the displacement of jobs in the traditional industries. The railroads, for example, employed two-thirds fewer in 1960 than in 1920, although new employment was created in the trucking industry and in the

[3] As quoted in *The New York Times*, October 5, 1961.

construction of highways. As productivity increases in those industries that can be automated, the number of employees will become even fewer. The petroleum industries are good illustrations of this particular trend. The Standard Oil Company of New Jersey, for example, employed 160,000 in 1950 and 140,000 in 1960; but its total revenue increased from a little over $5 billion in 1951 to almost $9 billion in 1960. Wages and salaries rose from $677 million to more than $940 million, and the cash dividends paid to stockholders went from $250 million to $500 million.[4]

As automation becomes more developed, it will affect services and trades as much as clerical and industrial fields. There will be an increased trend toward automated self-service retail establishments, self-repairs, and sales such as insurance, travel, and banking. As time goes on, appliances and cars will be repaired by removing whole units and replacing them. This trend will mean a definite attempt to simplify parts and engineering designs. Most cars, machines, and appliances at the present time have far too many parts that can go out of repair.

Construction can also be automated by having printed electrical circuits; mass-produced walls, floors, kitchens, bathrooms, and recreation rooms; and built-in electronic devices that heat, cool, clean, and light the inside rooms automatically. At the present time, the average housewife in suburbia puts in a long week cleaning, cooking, and baby-sitting. The first two can easily be taken care of by new electronic devices that require little human control. The social question for educators, parents, and legislators to answer is what will women do with their spare time in a more automated future?

The few rivulets of job displacement may become a roaring torrent within the next fifteen to twenty years. Between 1962 and 1964, for example, more than 10,000 "back office" clerks were fired from their jobs in brokerage houses. In 1963 The Chase Manhattan Bank cut down the number of its staff positions by more than 300 by using computers to take over many of middle management's decision-making functions.

The role of the computer in making decisions was illustrated by its use in planning a warehouse for the Union Carbide Company in 1963. Instead of asking its trained executives what the size of the building should be and what chemicals it should stock, the computer was asked to give its decisions through a process called simulation, whereby the various alternatives given to the computer are cross-checked in great detail at great speed. In a matter of minutes the computer calculated the movement of chemicals out of different sized warehouses, each time with different rates, shipping methods, and inventory levels. The computer next considered hundreds of ways to stock the various chemicals, and then from all these computations selected the one that was most efficient and economical. Union Carbide built its warehouse as suggested by the computer; and after completion within a matter of months,

[4] As indicated in the Annual Report for 1961.

costs were cut, sales increased, and labor saved.[5] At one time, such decisions were the prerogatives of top management, working with large staffs and having less information to base their judgments on than the computer does at the present time.

The computer does not make these decisions by itself. It must be fed the information that it needs by highly trained, specialized individuals, who collect the data and store it in the "memory" of the computer. Because the electrons can travel at the speed of light, they can tap their memory cells faster than man and do in a short period of time tasks that could not be done at all without them. Problems that would have taken thousands of years to solve by ordinary mathematical computations can be done today in a matter of minutes with the aid of electronic computers.

The electron was first discovered in 1896; but the technology that has been developed to utilize its power stems from DeForest's invention of the triode tube in 1907, which permitted the amplifying of the weak electronic impulses in both wireless and long distance telephony. For a long period of time, electronics was used primarily in communications.

The computer uses mathematical principles that have been known for almost 200 years. The problem of using the electron to take advantage of known mathematical principles, however, was not solved until after World War II. In the Bell Telephone Laboratories, the invention of the transistor with its small size and almost indestructible forms made possible the development of huge computers with extraordinary memories. (Lest the computer be overrated as a mechanical device, it needs to be pointed out that the normal human brain has the energy equivalent of some 5 billion transistors; so far most brains have been operated below capacity by their owners.) Although computers began growing to a gigantic shape, recent trends have indicated that the computers of the future may be made in miniature sizes.

The computer, or the "electronic brain," cannot think or engage in creative thought. It can only operate in simple ways. The operator of the computer must break down a problem into its simplest binary forms; this is called programming. The questions asked must be in simple yes or no forms, and they must be presented in simple formulas that the computer can understand, which is to say that a computer can only operate in terms of the information that has been presented to it. It is the information presented to the computer that enables it to act or to control other machines.

The electronic computer operates in terms of closed and open circuits; and when this is combined with a self-regulating mechanism, which is called feedback, automation is the result. The feedback again is as old as the mathematical principles used by computers. Watt's invention of the governor to regulate the amount of steam entering the cylinder head is the first modern use of feedback; the governor is self-regulating and is based upon the amount

[5] Thomas O'Toole, "White Collar Automation," *The Reporter*, December 5, 1963, p. 24.

of steam the engine is generating. A closed circuit is also a self-regulating device. The ordinary thermostat in a room is a good example of the closed circuit. As the heat rises, the mercury in the thermometer goes up, thus triggering a metal point that shuts off the furnace.

The automated machine, using the computer as its memory and motivator, can control other machines in addition to regulating itself. It can do what it is programmed to do efficiently, quickly, and without any human error. It does not get tired, moody, or bored. As a series of machines, it does what it is made to do or told to do. It begins to imitate the human brain in its memory of electron transistors and its ability to control more than one machine at a time. Because electrons work much faster than the human brain, it can tap its stored amount of information in a fraction of a second; and through its punched tapes it can make decisions or carry on certain action. (The punched tape is a modification of the punched card, which is an eighteenth century French invention. Its principle was used in the mechanical player piano of the early twentieth century.)

The automatic elevator, which has displaced thousands of operators all over the country, is a good example of how a data processing device, similar to a computer, works. It registers in its memory which buttons have been pressed on which floors; it knows where it is; and it decides whether to go up or down and where to stop. It has all sorts of safety devices built into it; for example, it cannot start if any door is open and if there is any danger, it stops and buzzes an alarm (for like the computer upon which it is patterned, it operates through open and closed electronic circuits).

The knowledge that has been built up for one industry can be transferred to another industry, much as the early mechanical principles were applied to a series of machines having similar functions. For example, the punch card machines, which were reinvented for the Bureau of the Census in 1890, were adapted to insurance and other business needs around World War I. The theories worked out for firing weapons during World War II became the basis for automating oil and chemical plants. A good deal of the spurt in automation came from the computers developed for the government in tracking missiles, in creating new weapons systems, in designing rockets and supersonic planes, and in generally solving the problems raised by a complex government that subsidizes most of the scientific and applied technological research being done in the United States today. Without the research done on computers during World War II, modern-day automation would not have progressed very far. And without the billions of dollars spent on research for weapons that may never be used by a government that spends almost half of the tax dollars on preparing for a war that may never be fought, contemporary automation could not be as advanced as it is. Preparations for war since World War II have saved industry billions of dollars in research on computers, which industry itself might never have spent, and have pushed the American economy much closer to becoming an automated industrial society than would have been the case if these defense funds had not been appropriated. Even today many of the computers used in the United States are owned by the Federal Government. In 1961 there were 9,000 Federal employees running electronic computers, and it has been estimated that there will be around 16,000 working with computers in 1966.[6]

Computers in the government, in insurance companies, in banks, and in industries have taken over a great deal of clerical, accounting, and auditing functions. They write checks, issue bills, and credit sums received to individual accounts. They operate machines through transfer devices, and they can do tasks in a short period of time which cannot be duplicated by human beings. In state highway departments, computers now study rights-of-way for new highways, add up the estimated property values, and pick out the land that combines low cost with ease of construction and directness of route. Computers tell commercial bakeries how many rolls or loaves of bread they should leave at various supermarkets at certain times of the year. They determine the most economical use of garbage trucks in large cities. They may even be used in the near future to operate diagnostic machines that will determine the various illnesses of patients.

Computers are today divided into four categories: (1) *Information,* which store data; (2) *Detroit Automation,* which link machines of production as an integral line through automatic transfer devices; (3) *Process Control Systems,* which utilize a computer to integrate a control system for continuous operation of oil, chemical, or even atomic plants; and (4) *Numerical Control,* which employ punched tape and automatic control devices to direct the operation of a series of machines.

The importance of automation in the above categories is not the mechanical aspects of connecting machines together but the supplying of information and control systems. Automation is not the machine, but the combination of principles under which self-correcting systems operate. It is an upgrading rather than a downgrading of talents. In its theory it opens up widespread application in all fields of human endeavor. Any routine decision, day-to-day task, or continuous operation can be done far better by automated machines that have captured the skills of the most diverse middle managers, technicians, and highly trained craftsmen. Automation thus offers to mankind a vista of a civilization in which only a few will be trained for production, while the larger number of individuals will be able to devote themselves to the accumulation of knowledge and the development of creativity.[7] No other civilization has been able to promise as much as the Tertiary, once it replaces Secondary civilization in man's thoughts, goals, and values.

[6] On the other hand, one of the reasons for the decentralization of industry in the Soviet Union is that it would take about one million computers to furnish the Centralized Planning Board with all the information it would need to make efficient decisions.

[7] Creativity is here used to indicate the problem-solving innovator rather than in the conventional use of this term, which refers to those with artistic aptitudes.

An example of Detroit Automation is the assembly line 1,545 feet long which since 1951 has been turning out six-cylinder engine blocks for the Ford Motor Company. Rough castings, which are produced in an automated foundry, are fed into this line. From then on, 42 automatic machines, linked together by transfer devices, automatically move the blocks through 530 precision cutting operations and borings. Formerly it took nine hours to fabricate a rough casting into a finished engine block; in the Ford plant in Cleveland it takes a little over fourteen minutes.[8] The expensive installation of machines of this type prevents their introduction in large numbers, for there must be a large savings in manpower before they can be considered a worthwhile investment. General Motors has been automating a little faster than Ford in recent years, but even it is a long way from completely automated factories. Automation as an industrial system may not take over until at least the end of the twentieth century.

The automated factory is not the beginning but the end result of automation. Automation is only a by-product of a new point of view toward production which implies a radical redesigning of machines, factories, and ways of production as well as ways of doing business. Automation requires the complete rethinking of both production and business so that more efficient methods of solving complex problems will result. For example, instead of creating large wings that flap as birds' did, man learned to fly by taking advantage of the different air speeds both over and under a wing. Instead of creating a mechanical appliance that walked like a man, early man created a round wheel that rolled over comparatively smooth surfaces. Automation in its turn will necessitate rethinking about manufacturers, manufacturing, and services.

Automation makes its greatest contribution when it permits man to carry on new tasks that were previously unattainable. Many companies have discovered that automation helps them produce a better product with less waste and that its savings are more in increasing the efficiency of production than of labor. Automation can help mankind do tasks that could never have been done at all, and it can assist in doing them efficiently and well.

At present, automation is in its infancy because it has not developed a language that computers can use without translation by programmers. The future automated machine will need no programmers as intermediaries. The truly automated machine may be invented within the next ten to twenty years and will permit a man to dictate into a machine that will then type out his letters in clean, even type. The automatic typewriter of the future will use an automated type of English with more logical spellings, and perhaps it might even correct the errors made by the one using it.

Within the next twenty years, attorneys may be connected with a central repository, which could contain all the laws, rulings, regulations, procedures,

[8] Congressional testimony by John Diebold, as quoted in *Automation: Implications for the Future*, Morris Philipson, ed., (New York, Vintage Books, 1962), p. 30.

and commentaries on legal subjects. By using his hookup to this central repository, the attorney could get information on any query he made to the central computer. The huge central repository will be able to give its answers in a matter of seconds, and the amount of research time for lawyers will be cut down enormously.[9] Scholars may have hookups to central repositories in their fields, which could supply them in a matter of seconds with the information, footnotes, and bibliography that would previously have required months if not years of research. Physicians practicing in county seats may get diagnoses of their patients' illnesses in a matter of seconds, as well as suggestions for treatment. Such computers could change the structure of the world's health needs immeasurably.

The electronic computers of today are still in their infancy. They can be compared to the machines in the first stages of the Industrial Revolution. Someday these machines may be equal to huge superbrains in the information that they will be able to store, and within the next century computers might also be able to think electronically.

At the same time, the industrial trend is toward both greater centralization and greater decentralization. The centralization will occur as large centers find themselves in a better situation to make intelligent overall decisions for national policies than do the local centers. The decentralization will take place when small urban centers become more self-sufficient than they are today through miniature computer systems hooked up to large centralized ones.

It may be possible to make goods and supply services in decentralized areas much more efficiently than in huge centers that may become too unwieldy to manage. In a society of surpluses, even the concept of international or interregional trade will make little sense when each area can supply its own needs, including its own synthetic foods and raw materials. Trade might lie in the realm of intellectual ideas and systems rather than in goods. It is quite possible that in the centuries ahead, countries (or what will then pass as countries) may prefer to exchange creativity rather than goods that after all can only duplicate what each could easily make in its own workshops.

It is not at all unlikely that within the next two to three decades daily censuses of knowledge of national decision-making purposes may take place by having every inventory computer in industry, government, business, banking, and services connected to a large analyzer in central cities. The central analyzer would then tabulate information on every transaction and every item made; on the energy used in each home, factory, and business; on the products of every farm; on the oil pumped; on the ores mined; and on the sales made and wages paid all over the United States. Instead of managerial decisions being arrived at without adequate information, the huge analyzers could perhaps be connected with other computers to make the routine decisions that

[9] David Bergamini, "Government by Computers," *The Reporter*, August 17, 1961.

are made today by the various agencies in the Federal Government. The important decisions could be made after all alternative possibilities has been analyzed and the best choice had been presented. A common input language could easily take the place of the intensive calculations required to prepare the instructions for the coded magnetic tape. This task may be simplified in the coming decades, thus making the computers even more efficient by doing away with the intermediaries of present-day programmers.

At present, there is a trend for district or regional plants and offices to make the decisions that cannot be made in the central headquarters because of their separation from the scene of day-to-day facts and operations. In the next few decades, centrally located computers could easily receive information quickly and accurately on every phase of a corporation's activities. This will enable the top executives to make decisions with the aid of computers, which can then be used for administrative guidance by the various regional plants. Within a few decades after that, even the top management decisions may be made by a new type of electronic computer that will be able to draw upon greater experiences, insights, and judgments than are possible to the average top manager today. The element of human error in far-reaching managerial decisions may well be a thing of the past.

It is also quite possible that the future top manager will require a far different training and education than he has today. He may not need to become knowledgeable about the techniques of production. His position may be that of a creative planner for the future; he may be responsible for co-ordinating the information fed him by the information-gathering computers and the data of the decision-making computers and drawing them into administrative guidelines for the future. Instead of having to devote much time to obtaining an overall picture of the company's production, sales, possibilities, and future trends, he will be able to get this information quickly in intellectually digestible forms, thus giving him more time to be the creative leader rather than the administrative head.

Automation and the use of computers in decision making may lead to an increase in creative top management, and at the same time to a decrease in the functions of routinized decision-making middle management. Supervision over production or even management of warehouses may be taken over by highly developed information-receiving computers. Any task that can be done day after day with little variation can be done more efficiently by computer, because judgment in this case may be much closer to the data than most decisions that are made on a routine daily basis. A good deal of middle management may possess traditionalist ways of thinking that have been learned from predecessors and are continued because others in the same position have made the same decisions, rather than because the decisions made are the most efficient or the best solutions.

The decisions in future management will be made by a new type of manager with an entirely different educational background, who will be trained to see more of the alternatives than present-day executives see. The decisions will be made with the assistance of computers that utilize the most complete variety of experiences and of past and present judgments. A great many corporations both in the United States and in Europe are even today turning over many of their middle management functions to computers because computers use the accumulated knowledge of middle management in much greater variety and intensity than would be possible for one or two individuals working in isolation. Automation requires a new point of view in looking upon both business and production. (Production should be viewed as an integrated system rather than as a series of individual steps.)

In the future, top management will have to become much more creative than it is today, for automation carries dangers as well as advantages. Its chief danger is that it may cause industrial decisions to become stabilized and fixed and thus lead to a form of managerial fossilization. Automation can lead to a society of leisure where thinking is left only to a few, and these few may get into the habit of making noncreative decisions for fear of disturbing the escapist reactions of the many. It can lead to a society where individuals are guaranteed a minimum standard of living just for existing, and it can lead to an oligarchic society where the few may make all the decisions for the many. In a self-satisfied society filled with material surpluses of all kinds, life can be pleasant and unexciting, and can fall into the traditional tyranny of a few over the many. An automated society puts the main burden of getting the society to function on a very tiny percentage of the population, who become its leaders, innovators, and creative thinkers. For an automated society to be successful in the future, the values of our contemporary Secondary civilization must be superseded by new values that emphasize participation, equality, and extremely high standards of civic behavior, standards made even higher by continuous competition among most individuals to be creative and socially responsible.

The problems brought by automation will affect most of the advanced countries of the world, including the Soviet Union and the United States. Automation can increase the standard of living innumerable times; it can open up new fields of endeavor; it can challenge the industrial society to produce with much higher standards; and it can revolutionize the entire world of knowledge and greatly increase the theoretical understanding of the social and physical worlds. It will conserve human energy to do the things that could not be done when individuals had to spend all their waking time working to keep themselves alive. Automation means new sights, visions, and aspirations. An automated society with high levels of scientific understanding cannot permit billions of human beings to vegetate in other parts of the world. There are too many talents to be uncovered, too many discoveries to be made, and too many insights to be disclosed. An automated society will be highly mechanized, using human labors for the creative tasks and the willing electron for the dull and routine.

On the other hand, an automated society operating within our present concepts and values will mean high unemployment and a large number of uneducated and untrained human beings. An automated society that displaces labor without turning laborers into useful and creative individuals can lead only to its chaotic breakdown, for products must be consumed and services must be used. Individuals cannot live on relief checks without losing confidence in themselves; they must be able to give something of themselves in return for the security that they expect to receive from an automated society.

We cannot have a nation made up only of passive consumers, for then the promise of a creative future will be difficult to attain. We cannot have a society in which individuals are pensioned off at the age of twenty and given a gold pass to all the ball games, all the bowling alleys, and all the cars-and-boats-for-hire agencies, without producing a mass society composed of individuals who do not carry their intellectual and moral weight. Man's great promise in the past was that he alone was able to symbolize, to think, to make of himself whatever he set out to be. Slowly and with much difficulty he has tried to keep the goal of being a creative human ever before him. Until now, only a few persons have worked toward this aspiration; and in doing so they have immeasurably benefited the rest of the population. Today and in the future, these few must be augmented by the many, otherwise the road will be thorny and beset by many obstacles of apathy, traditionalism, and authoritarianism. Men should be freed from their arduous labors so that they can become more creative, not to become vegetative and to while away the days until death comes for them. Over the past two million years men have raised their sights from mere animal levels of satisfying their hunger and sex impulses to the development of values that emphasize new goals that will provide more satisfaction to later generations.

Slowly and somewhat uncertainly, mankind is moving toward Tertiary civilization. In Primary civilization, only a few benefited directly from the creative talents of man; in our Secondary civilization the vast majority have had their elemental needs satisfied, although differences in opportunity still exist. In Tertiary civilization, men's dreams of equality with the wealthy, with the well-born, with the psychologically secure, will have a much better chance of attainment. Mankind has slowly moved from the levels of the hunter, of the peasant, of the industrial worker, and now in the next stage to the standards of the prosperous middle classes.

74   The Great Emptiness

R. M. MacIver

"In the sweat of thy face shalt thou eat bread." From this primal decree millions of human beings are now liberated. More and more men have more and more leisure. The working day grows shorter, the week end longer. More and more women are released at an earlier age from the heavier tasks of the rearing of children, in the small family of today, where kindergarten and school and clinic and restaurant come to their aid. More and more people are freed for other things, released from the exhaustion of their energies in the mere satisfaction of elementary wants. No longer is the pattern so simple as that of Longfellow's blacksmith, who "something attempted, something done, has earned a night's repose."

Released from what? When necessity no longer drives, when people own long hours in which to do what they want, what do they want to do? Where necessity is heavy upon men, they yearn for the joys of leisure. Now many have enough leisure. What are the joys they find?

The shorter working day is also a different working day. Nearly all men work for others, not for themselves—not the way a man works who has his own little plot of earth and must give himself up to its cultivation. For many, work has become a routine—not too onerous, not too rewarding, and by no means engrossing—a daily routine until the bell rings and sets them free again. For what?

It is a marvelous liberation for those who learn to use it; and there are many ways. It is the great emptiness for those who don't.

People of a placid disposition do not know the great emptiness. When the day's work is done, they betake themselves to their quiet interests, their hobbies, their gardens or their amateur workbenches or their stamp collecting or their games or their social affairs or their church activities or whatever it be. When they need more sting in life, they have a mild "fling," taking a little "moral holiday." Some find indulgence enough in the vicarious pleasure of snidely malicious gossip. Their habits are early formed and they keep a modicum of contentment.

But the number of the placid is growing less. The conditions of our civilization do not encourage that mood. For one thing, the old-time acceptance of authority, as God-given or nature-based, is much less common. Religion is for very many an ancient tale, "a tale of little meaning, though the words are

Ch. 6, "The Great Emptiness," in *The Pursuit of Happiness* by R. M. MacIver, New York, Simon and Schuster, 1955. Reprinted by permission of R. M. MacIver.

strong," reduced to ritual or the moral precepts of the Sunday pulpit. There is little allegiance to the doctrine that every man has his allotted place. How could there be when competition has become a law of life? There is incessant movement and disturbance and upheaval. And with the new leisure there come new excitations, new stimuli to unrest.

So the new leisure has brought its seeming opposite, restlessness. And because these cannot be reconciled the great emptiness comes.

Faced with the great emptiness, unprepared to meet it, most people resort to one or another way of escape, according to their kind. Those who are less conscious of their need succeed in concealing it from themselves. They find their satisfaction in the great new world of means without ends. Those who are more conscious of it cannot conceal it; they only distract themselves from the thought of it. Their common recourse is excitation, and they seek it in diverse ways.

The first kind are go-getters. When they are efficient or unscrupulous or both, they rise in the world. They amass things. They make some money. They win some place and power. Not *for* anything, not to do anything with it. Their values are relative, which means they are no values at all. They make money to make more money. They win some power that enables them to seek more power. They are practical men. They keep right on being practical, until their unlived lives are at an end. If they stopped being practical, the great emptiness would engulf them. They are like planes that must keep on flying because they have no landing gear. The engines go fast and faster, but they are going nowhere. They make good progress to nothingness.

They take pride in their progress. They are outdistancing other men. They are always caculating the distance they have gained. It shows what can be done when you have the know-how. They feel superior and that sustains them. They stay assured in the world of means. What matters is the winning.

> "But what good came of it at last?"
> Quoth little Peterkin.
> "Why that I cannot tell," said he,
> "But 'twas a famous victory."

Victory for the sake of the winning, means for the sake of the acquiring, that is success. So the circle spins forever, means without end, world without end. Amen.

The second kind have it worse. They are the more sensitive kind, often the more gifted. They want their lives to have some meaning, some fulfillment. They want the feel of living for some worthwhile end. But often there is something wrong with the seeking. They too suffer from the intrusive ego. Their seeking lacks adequate sincerity. The need of success is greater for them than the need of the thing that is sought. If, for example, they pursue some art, the art itself counts less than the renown of the artist. They would be great artists, great writers, opera singers, pathfinders. They aim high, but the mark is higher than their reach. When they miss it they grow disillusioned. They are thrust back on their unsatisfied egos, and the great emptiness lies before them.

They try to escape, but they run from themselves. They try to forget, but their only recourse is an excitation of the senses. This stimulant needs to be incessantly repeated. The little spell of liberation, the false glow, the hour of oblivion, leaves them the more desolate and adds new tensions to the returning emptiness. Then there is leisure no more, no relaxedness, no return to the things they once loved, no lingering ease of quiet discourse with friends, no natural savor of living, no perception of the unfolding wonder of things. But instead they pass from excitation to a hollow release, from release to tension, from tension to new excitation. Nothing is itself any more. And no more at the end of the day do they sink peacefully into the marvelous process of slowly gathering sleep.

Once they were so eager to make life feel real; now they shun its reality and are driven to pursue phantoms, the will-o'-the-wisp of sense-spurred distraction, the unseeing ghosts of once clear-eyed joys, the phantom Aphrodite.

But it is not only the more cultivated, the more sophisticated, and the well-to-do with their more ample opportunities, who feel the great emptiness. In other ways it besets large numbers who, finding little satisfaction in the daily work, seek compensation in the leisure they now possess. There are many besides, people who win early pensions or otherwise can get along without toil through legacies or rents or other sources of unearned income, women who have no family cares—the new, unopulent leisure class.

They have no training for leisure. They have, most of them, no strong interests or devotions. The habits of their work time convey no meaning to the time of liberation. Most of them live in cities, in drab and narrow confines within which they revolve in casual little circles. They see nothing ahead but the coming of old age. They want to regain the feel of life. Time is theirs, but they cannot redeem it.

So they too betake themselves, in their various ways, to some form of excitation. Having no recourse in themselves, they must get out of themselves. They take the easy ways out because they see no alternative. They have never learned to climb the paths leading to the pleasures that wait in the realm of ideas, in the growing revelation of the nature of things, in the treasuries of the arts, and in the rich lore of the libraries. They must seek instead the quick transport, the dream, the adventure, in the tavern or where the gamblers meet.

They would cover the emptiness they cannot fill. They make a goal of what is a diversion. The healthy being craves an occasional wildness, a jolt from normality, a sharpening of the edge of appetite, his own little festival of the Saturnalia, a brief excursion from his way of life. But for these others the diversion becomes the way of life and diverts no more. For them the filled glass is not the cheerful accompaniment of pleasant reunions but a deceitful medicine for the ennui of living. For them the gambling venture is no mere holiday flutter but a never-satisfied urge that forever defeats itself.

In 1946, in straitened England, the then equivalent of half a billion dollars was placed in bets on the horses and the dogs. Besides which, vast sums changed hands on the results of football games. For hundreds of thousands of people the major news in the daily papers, day after day and month after month, was the lists of the winners and the betting odds. England was not, is not, alone in this respect. It is only that the figures happen to be more accessible.

A former addict explained in the London *Spectator* why men do it. The gambler, he said, "gambles because it provides an emotional tension which his mind demands. He is suffering from a deficiency disease, and the only antidote he knows is gambling." He is trying to escape the great emptiness. An English worker of the semi-skilled category once said to me: "A fellow has to do something, and what is there? Maybe I have a shilling or two in my pocket. Maybe I could buy an extra shirt. It's no go. So I put them on the dogs."

By these resorts people do not escape the great emptiness. What they get is a sequence of brief delusions of escape. In time the only thing they can escape to is what they themselves know for a delusion. The resort is only a drug to make them forget the disease. As with all such drugs, the dose must be continually renewed, and it becomes harder and harder to return to the pre-addict stage. They come to look on the great emptiness as something inherent in the very nature of things. That is all life is. Now they know the drug is a delusion, but they do not know that it has bred a deeper delusion.

There are other avenues of escape that, while they may still be delusive, have the merit of not being recognized as such. Which means that the escape is actually made. In every large city, and notably in those areas where people go to spend their retirement, where the climate is mild and sunny, all kinds of special cults flourish and new ones are frequently born. To these places repair the hucksters of the supernatural and find a ready market for their wares. There are to be found the prophets of mystical union, robed and turbaned preachers of the Light of Asia, interpreters of the Rosy Cross, exponents of the heavenly trance, new healers of the soul, tuners-in of the Infinite operators in spiritual magics. Considerable numbers flock to them, some to seek a new sensation and then pass on, but some to stay and become disciples or devotees.

These last are the credulous ones, the unsophisticate, the suggestible. They search no more. The emptiness is filled. They have undergone a kind of hypnosis. They live in the nebula of their mystical dream. They meet reality no more. But at least, in a manner, they have found their peace.

Back in the days when unremitting toil was the lot of all but the very few and leisure still a hopeless yearning, hard and painful as life was, it still felt real. People were in *rapport* with the small bit of reality allotted to them, the sense of the earth, the tang of the changing seasons, the consciousness of the eternal on-going of birth and death. Now, when so many have leisure, they become detached from themselves, not merely from the earth. From all the widened horizons of our greater world a thousand voices call us to come near, to understand, and to enjoy, but our ears are not trained to hear them. The leisure is ours but not the skill to use it. So leisure becomes a void, and from the ensuing restlessness men take their refuge in delusive excitations or fictitious visions, returning to their own earth no more.

75   Personal Disorganization
Reece McGee

ANOMIE

A second form of social disorganization is *anomie*. In anomie, each individual is his own subgroup, so to speak, and the ties between the individuals are so tenuous as to be insignificant. The anomic individual is isolated and shares few meanings and values with other individuals.

The term "anomie" was used by the French sociologist Durkheim to refer to a mental state of normlessness, of being without values to structure one's behavior. (One attends college because he holds some value which makes such an expenditure of time and money worth it to him. The reasons why "it is worth the effort," of course, are various. One may be learning an occupation, hunting for a husband, doing all kinds of things, but for *some* reason college is worth it; one has the value which structures one's behavior.) The anomic person does not have such values to direct his behavior. His mental state or attitude is one of hopelessness, and he has a sense of meaninglessness and futility in life, the frame of mind suggested by Housman's famous lines about finding himself "a stranger and afraid in a world [he] never made." This is anomie.

The anomic individual is thus in a situation in which the norms that usually regulate behavior (not only the "you shalls" and the "you shall nots," but also the norms that prescribe when to wear shoes and when to wear sandals, and like choices), and thereby describe the expectations made upon one *for* his behavior, are entirely absent or have become ineffective. Under such circumstances the behavior of other people is unpredictable to the individual involved; since he is unaware of a general pattern of expectation, he cannot predict how others will behave nor direct his own behavior since he lacks expectations for it with which to guide himself. Thus the anomic individual lives in a world without direction or purpose or sense of any concern of others for his actions, and he may sink into a state of apathy and despair. A common complaint of the anomic personality is "No one cares; it doesn't matter what I do because no one cares about me."

A necessary consequence of anomie is isolation from others (whether physical or mental): estrangement from group membership with its reinforcing functions of support and solidarity, and its norm-providing behavioral expectations. Primarily, the anomic personality does not know how to behave or what to do with himself because no one cares how he behaves or expects him to behave in any particular way. He has no group to expect certain behavior from him and, therefore, does not know what to do. Secondly, the anomic personality is unable, largely for lack of social reinforcement and support, to regulate and organize his own behavior for himself. It is possible for individuals to live in isolation and still have organized lives if they have sufficiently internalized the meanings and values they once learned from others so as to go on regulating their own behavior.[1] But some persons are unable to do this, are not sufficiently strong in character to continue to regulate their own behaviors according to an internalized set of principles learned in the past. Most people need the reinforcement of social groups to keep behaving in a consistent way. An excellent if imaginary example of the individual who *can* regulate his own behavior without the immediate support of the social group is the stereotypical Englishman who dresses for dinner in the jungle. This hypothetical man does not need the support of a group to direct his actions because he has internalized the norms of how people "ought" to behave.

Thus anomie is a situation where the social controls, the regulatory principles, normally provided by group membership are absent. When they are absent and the individual is unable to meet circumstances through his own resources of character or moral strength, he has become anomic. Anomie may also result from the adherence of the individual simultaneously to two or more contradictory, incompatible, or conflicting values about the same behavior, with the consequence that he becomes frustrated or anxious and unable to predict the behavior of others or direct his own behavior consistently. Such a conflict of *values* should not be confused with the *group* conflicts Rose describes.

. . .

ANOMIC ISOLATION: THE WORLD OF FURNISHED ROOMS

A situation of anomic isolation (or an environment almost guaranteed to produce it) is what Zorbaugh calls "The World of Furnished Rooms."[3] The World of Furnished Rooms is an area of cheap rooming houses and apart-

[1] These are the people that Riesman calls the "inner directed"; see David Riesman, *et al, The Lonely Crowd* (New Haven: Yale University Press, 1950).

[3] Harvey W. Zorbaugh, *The Gold Coast and the Slum* (Chicago: University of Chicago Press, 1929).

ments and apartment hotels on the edges of the downtown within the boundaries of "Zone II" of the American city. The sociological adjectives describing it are "blight" and "substandard." (The terms refer to an area of incongruous functions and substandard housing and other facilities.) In some great metropolitan areas, especially those old enough to have had considerable experience in rebuilding their oldest sections, this rooming-house district consists largely of dwellings constructed especially for rooming-house purposes. In most cities, however, particularly those not old enough to have torn down and rebuilt Zone II, the World of Furnished Rooms consists at least partly of buildings that were originally constructed for other purposes: private homes, often once-palatial mansions: the great ornate Victorian homes of the lumber, cattle, oil and railroad barons of the last century. New York's famous brownstones, for example, are dwellings of this kind: large deteriorated houses consisting of a number of huge rooms which have been partitioned into rabbit-warrens of one- or two-room apartments.[4] In some places the original appointments of the houses are visible; the woodwork and even the tapestries and carpets with which the buildings were originally furnished may still be present. When they are, they often show startling contrasts to the squalor of their present state: entrance halls of Italian marble, sweeping colonnades and staircases, brocade hangings, mildewed and moth-holed, or twenty-foot windows with leaded panes, and black sheet-metal mailboxes clustered like swarming bees upon the wall.

The population of this jaded area accounts in part for its architectural characteristics. On the average, its inhabitants are young (64 per cent of individuals sampled in one study were under 39);[5] they are single (only about one-third were married); they are dominantly male (63 per cent). The population is also socially isolated: of the people studied by Dr. Cohen, even though two-thirds were single, over half had no steady companion of the opposite sex and a quarter of them neither wrote nor received any personal letters in the space of a calendar year. They are indeed an isolated group. They are also an extremely mobile group. The particular sample of rooming houses that she studied had a turnover of one hundred per cent in the space of 120 days; in that short time its population was numerically replaced. Between a third and a half of the residents were unemployed. There was much mobility on the part of the rooming-house keepers as well. (Typically the people who keep rooming houses, collect the rent, sweep the hall—if it gets swept—are not the owners. The keepers are hired custodians. Cohen found that 50 per cent of rooming-house keepers studied had held their jobs less than six months.) Finally, there is little contact between the roomers and the

---

[4] The university student will likely recognize the existence of a miniature "World of Furnished Rooms" in some quarter bordering his university and catering to the housing of students. Most American universities support such districts on a small scale.

[5] This and the following figures are from Lillian Cohen, "Los Angeles Rooming-House Kaleidoscope," *American Sociological Review*, 16:3, June 1951, pp. 316–326.

keepers. It is not uncommon for a keeper not to know his tenants' names, or even what they look like. The greatest single characteristic of the population of the area is *anonymity*. The people of the world of furnished rooms are persons without names, without faces, and without attachments. They come and no one knows from where; they stay and no one knows that they have stayed; they go and no one knows where they have gone.

That this characteristic anonymity of the residents of the area can sometimes reach astonishing degrees is indicated by the following personal experience of the author:

During my undergraduate days I worked for a time as a private investigator in a large midwestern city. The firm by which I was employed was given the assignment of locating a wife-deserter. We were sent a recent snapshot of the man, a complete physical description of him and his automobile, and a local address about six months old. He was a door-to-door salesman of vacuum cleaners, machines of a type not found in retail outlets. The vendor buys them at wholesale from the supplier and then sells them for whatever he can get, the difference being his profit.

We traced the man to a furnished apartment in the rooming-house area of the city. He had left this address, only two weeks before, and we ran into a blank wall. We interviewed the rooming-house keeper, a relatively recent arrival in the house herself, and all twenty-three other residents of the building. In the neighborhood we spoke to gas-station attendants, waitresses and countermen at beaneries, and all storekeepers within the surrounding blocks. The investigation produced absolutely *no* information. Of the almost one hundred persons interviewed, shown photographs, and given descriptions of the man, not one remembered him or could identify him.

One tentative identification of his car was given by a filling-station attendant. This attendant was able to recall vaguely that a man in a car of the approximate age, color, and probable make of that owned by our quarry had several times purchased gasoline from him and that he habitually carried some kind of machinery, possibly vacuum cleaners, in the rear seat of his automobile.

In the rooming house where the man we sought had lived for five weeks, more than half of the roomers were new since his departure from the address and therefore could have had no contact with him, while none of those whose tenure in the building overlapped his could recall ever having seen or spoken to him. Even the keeper had never seen the man in question, for she knew him only as "probably the man in number 14," who had arranged to rent the room by phone and always paid his rent by slipping it under her door as he passed. He had left without notice or forwarding address and with his rent four days in arrears. The local wholesaler of the vacuum cleaners had not seen him for several weeks, and, as far as we could determine, he had simply disappeared from the face of the earth.

In fact, it is not inaccurate to say that as far as there being any objective awareness of him among the residents of the area, our man had never appeared on the face of the earth at all. In terms of the impression which he made upon his neighbors, of evidence of his existence which he left behind him, of memories of contact with him retained by others, it was as if he had never really existed.

While this case may be extreme, it is not untypical of the world of furnished rooms. The rapid mobility of the inhabitants and the total anonymity of the area permit the individual to live as he pleases and to come and go as he wishes; but they also cut him off from any significant contact with other people, and make him an isolated person, with no one to care if he lives or goes to jail or dies. The frequent consequence of this state of affairs is the creation of the condition of *anomie,* of lives of quiet desperation and despair, often leading to the personal disorganizations which we will consider next: suicide, drug addiction, and alcoholism.

SUICIDE, DRUG ADDICTION, AND ALCOHOLISM

A conventional definition of suicide is "the intentional taking of one's life or the failure, when possible, to save oneself when death threatens." [6] In this country suicide is popularly regarded as the last desperate act of an individual in the depths of anguish or despair, a terminal act to end permanently the frustration of a life no longer worth living. Indeed it is this form of it in which we are interested in this case: self murder by a disorganized personality. Nevertheless, there are other forms of the act besides this anomic one, for it may be undertaken as an expression of individuality (egoistic suicide), or as an expression of strong feelings of attachment to and solidarity with a social group (altruistic suicide). These distinctions were originally drawn by Emile Durkheim, who also made note of wide cultural and other differentials in suicide rates.

Durkheim discusses the act of suicide as an expression of the relationship between the individual and the social group. In the case of the egoistic suicide, the individual has internalized and personalized certain values to the point where they are more important to him than any negative value placed on suicide, and his act, thus, *is* an expression of himself. An example of an egoistic suicide would be a student who kills himself because he has failed to gain entrance to medical school and prefers death to the necessary readjustment of hopes and expectations his failure entails. In the case of the altruistic suicide, the individual expresses his high degree of solidarity and identification with a group by suicidally leaving it. An excellent example of altruistic suicide was the Japanese *kamikaze* pilot of World War II. An anomic suicide, on the other hand, results from an estrangement from group values and support, or an inability to integrate those values without the presences and assistances of others. The individual who kills himself because his life seems utterly meaningless and to contain an excess of loneliness and despair is an anomic suicide. Durkheim describes it in this way: "[Anomic suicide]

[6] Ruth S. Cavan, *Suicide* (Chicago: University of Chicago Press, 1928), p. 3.

results from man's activities lacking regulation and his consequent sufferings." [7] Durkheim's general thesis is that the suicide rates in given social groups vary inversely with the degree of social and psychological integration of those groups—the strength of the ties that bind men to their societies. The weaker these social bonds within a group, the higher the suicide rate among its numbers. [8]

Gibbs and Martin have recently conducted empirical tests of this proposition (using measures of "status-integration," or role-conflict, as the operational expression of "solidarity"), and conclude that suicide rates *can* be predicted from such measures of social solidarity, thus supporting the theory with quantitative evidence. [9] The point of the Gibbs-Martin investigation is that certain occupational categories, such as bartenders, traveling salesmen, and movie stars, by the nature of the functions demanded of individuals filling such roles, disorient their incumbents to the role-behaviors other of their statuses demand of them, or estrange them from these role-behaviors. It is expected, for example, that a married man will stay home at night, cleave to his spouse, spend some time pottering around the house, and in general behave like a married man. But the bartender is out until all hours (often drinking) every night. The traveling salesman is home only occasionally, and the movie star may be gone on location for months at a time during which time he is expected by the nature of his occupation to make love to other people besides his spouse. In these ways stresses are introduced into the normal lives of individuals which make it more difficult for them to fill the obligations of whatever statuses they occupy. Under Durkheim's theory, people in such situations might be expected to have somewhat higher suicide rates than others, and it appears from the work of Gibbs and Martin that this expectation is realized.

DRUG ADDICTION

Like suicide, drug addiction is fundamentally social in nature, and probably, like suicide, different causes can be discovered for it. The behavior has been little studied by sociologists, however, and still awaits its Durkheim to put it into theoretical perspective. We do know that the use of drugs for narcotic, religious, and medicinal purposes is thousands of years old, and is subject to considerable cultural determination. It seems probable that the American

[7] Emile Durkheim, *Suicide,* translated by John Spalding and George Simpson (Glencoe, Illinois: The Free Press, 1951), p. 258.

[8] The ubiquity of this generalization is indicated by the fact that studies of suicide tend to show that almost any factor which weakens social relations between persons, even place of residence in a city, may affect suicide rates. Cf. Calvin Schmid, "Suicides in Seattle, 1914–1925," *University of Washington Publications in the Social Sciences,* 5:1, October, 1928.

[9] Jack P. Gibbs and Walter T. Martin, "Status Integration and Suicide," *American Sociological Review,* 23:2, April 1958, pp. 140–147.

attitude to them and their use has been powerfully influenced by two events: the fairly extensive smoking of opium in the nineteenth-century criminal underworld, and the Harrison Act of 1914 which made the use of drugs without a physician's prescription illegal, and the user by definition a criminal, thus identifying him with the underworld. That this was not always the attitude is indicated by the fact that drugs were sold extensively in "drug stores" during the nineteenth century, and were present in a large variety of patent medicines. Their use in these ways was subject to little or no public censure. People took opium in somewhat the same way in which they now take aspirins, antibiotics, or tranquilizers, although its use was probably not as extensive as is the use of these in the modern world.

The factors which motivate individuals to become drug addicts are not clearly understood. It may be that Durkheim's categories (egoistic, altruistic, anomic) might apply, for the process of becoming a drug addict, as distinguished from *motivation* for doing so, is known to be fundamentally social, and is in many cases, especially among juveniles, entered upon to demonstrate or to participate in group solidarity. The social nature of addiction is indicated by the reasons for it given by drug addicts themselves (see the

Reasons Given by 1,068 Drug Addicts for Their Addiction*

	Percent
Influence of other addicts	61.5
Self medication for relief of pain	27.2
Previous use in medical treatment	3.7
Relief of emotional distress	3.1
Curiosity	2.9
Other	1.6
Total	100.0

* Bingham Dai, *Opium Addiction in Chicago* (Shanghai: The Commercial Press, 1937). Printed with the permission of the author.

table). While self-explanation must be taken cautiously, the fact that 61 per cent of the addicts studied *reported* their addictions as due to the influence of others is in itself significant. Note, too, the very small proportion claiming that their addiction began in the course of medical treatment, a popular explanation about the way in which people become addicts. If the table is even reasonably reliable, an overwhelming proportion (nearly 95 per cent) of addicts expose themselves to addiction voluntarily and perhaps knowingly: the self-admitted reasons given by the addicts—aside from "previous use in medical treatment" and "other," a total of 5.3 per cent—all acknowledge that their addiction is essentially voluntary.

While we do not have specific knowledge of the motivating factors for entrance into addiction, we do have some excellent descriptions of the process. Howard S. Becker's "Becoming a Marihuana User" is one of these. (We must note, of course, that marijuana is *not* a narcotic drug, is *not* habit forming, and does not create withdrawal symptoms or ineradicable cravings in its user. Its use is primarily recreational, but the process by which the individual *learns to use* marijuana is very similar to that in which narcotic addicts learn their behaviors.[10])

The novice does not usually "get high" the first time he uses marijuana, perhaps because he does not know how to use it "properly." Marijuana cannot be smoked like tobacco in order to produce a narcotic effect. When it is smoked like a tobacco cigarette, no particular sensation ensues. For a marijuana cigarette to produce narcotic effect the smoke must be deeply inhaled to the farthest recesses of the lungs, along with quantities of air. This procedure is very important in the process of becoming a marijuana user, for if the product is smoked improperly and no reaction ensues, the experimenter is unlikely to continue his use of it. The first step in the sequence of becoming a marijuana user, therefore, must be learning the proper smoking techniques. The learning, obviously, can take place only in the company of other marijuana users who act as teachers.

Even after learning the techniques of smoking the drug, the new user may not be aware of its effects; he may not recognize his symptoms and reactions as those of "being high" from the marijuana. Thus in order for a person to "be high" from the smoking of marijuana three elements in the process must be present: (1) the presence of marijuana properly smoked; (2) the presence of the symptoms of the use of marijuana; and (3) recognition of the symptoms as a consequence of the possession and proper smoking of the product. It often takes a user some time to learn to recognize all of the symptoms which may accompany his use of the drug. Some of these, for example, are a feeling of cold in the extremities of the body, extreme hunger, "rubbery" limbs, mild euphoria, heightened sensitivity to external stimuli, some kind of diminution of time sense or of the awareness of time, dizziness, and tingling. Since many of these seem to be in no way related to the use of the drug or to the experience of "being high" on alcohol, the user frequently has to be taught what to look for and expect.

The final step in becoming a user of marijuana is the identification of these effects as enjoyable or pleasurable sensations, and as reactions to be sought. Marijuana-induced sensations are not automatically pleasant, as may be seen from the preceding list. They may, in fact, be unpleasant, or ambiguous, or even frightening to the new user. A taste for them, like so many tastes, must be acquired socially. Many people have not liked, upon first meeting, the tastes of onions, oysters, grapefruit, or dry martinis. In exactly the same way that one learns that onions and martinis are tasty and produce enjoyable sensations, the user of marijuana learns from other users that the effects produced by the drug are desirable. He also learns how to regulate

[10] The following discussion follows Howard S. Becker, "Becoming a Marihuana User," *American Journal of Sociology*, lix:3, November 1953, copyright 1953, The University of Chicago Press. Used with the permission of the author and the publisher.

his intake in order to avoid the gross reactions. When he has completed this learning, he may be said to be a "user" of marijuana.

The entire process is social throughout: (1) it is entered into in all probability for social reasons (few people become habitual marijuana users as a result of curiosity alone; most do so to impress friends, to indicate solidarity with a peer group, or for like reasons); (2) the techniques of marijuana smoking can be learned only from other marijuana users; (3) the user must learn, from other users, to identify the effects of the drug on his own sensations and behavior; and (4) he must learn to accept the definitions of other users of these as pleasurable and desirable.

The process of becoming a dope or narcotic addict seems to be similar to the process of becoming a marijuana user, except that in the case of the narcotic addict the pleasurable effects produced by the use of the narcotic, if any, are not his only goal. Most commonly, a person becomes addicted when the avoidance of withdrawal symptoms becomes an important stimulus for the further use of drugs. For it is possible to take narcotic drugs without experiencing addiction, so long as the withdrawal effects, which are physiological, are not identified as consequences of the failure to take further drugs. When the user identifies the withdrawal symptoms as due to a lack of drugs and takes more drugs in order to avoid them, he has become a drug addict. There are many cases on record of persons who have taken large doses of narcotic drugs without incurring addiction because they did not associate the discomfort of withdrawal symptoms with the absence of narcotics. Further, the narcotic user seldom experiences uplift or buoyancy (being "high") with drugs unless he is taught to expect it. Note, in this regard, that it is possible for individuals to become addicted to almost anything. There were newspaper reports in 1959 of an outbreak of *water* addiction in London. Addiction is apparently a psychiatric process, not a physiological one.

There is evidence to indicate that some dope addicts may be disorganized personalities, seeking escape or relief from their problems in the euphoria of narcotics. The evidence on marijuana and the reasons given by dope addicts for their addiction call this possibility into question. What *is* certain is that dope addicts are disorganized (by definition) in their persistence in socially unacceptable behaviors, and that their addiction can certainly *create* social problems, especially with regard to economic and marital matters. Since most addicts have no legal source of supply for their addiction, the only narcotics available to them are illegal ones and the cost of them is exorbitant. A five-pound sack of pure high-grade heroin, worth half a million dollars on the American underworld market, is worth only about twenty dollars in any drug store. A "thirty-pound monkey"—a big habit—may cost its owner twenty to forty dollars a day to feed. Addiction, thus, may be greatly disruptive to the lives of addicts; it does not create "criminality," however. Dope addicts seldom commit crimes of violence, although they may turn to robbery or prostitution to gain the money with which to support their habit. Contrary to the popular lore which tends to depict the "dope fiend" as a maniacal savage, heroin and morphine, being depressants, actually *repress* the aggressive tendencies of persons addicted to them.

The major point to consider is that the user, often *knowing the consequences,* and knowing his behavior condemned, *chooses* to become an outcast from the larger society in return for rewards sought by others like him. The social controls sufficient for most members of his society are not sufficient for him, and values which others obtain in other ways, or do not cherish, attract him sufficiently to stimulate his addiction. This is the theoretical problem of dope addiction. It is a problem as yet unsolved.

ALCOHOLISM

Like drug addiction, drinking and its occasional consequent alcoholism can be understood only as social phenomena. There are wide variations with regard to preferred beverages, quantities to be consumed, the circumstances surrounding the consumption, the attitudes of drinkers toward their drinks and drinking, and the attitudes of others toward the drinker. All drinking patterns are learned, and, like any other learning, require considerable reinforcement to become habitual. There are no universal patterns—even within a national culture. College students do not drink like soldiers, and Madison Avenue ad men do not drink like slum housewives, nor railroad section hands like physicians. Thus although drinking as a human social activity is millennia old, and is performed for an infinite variety of purposes— social, business, celebratory, religious and secular ritual, grief, and many others —a given person's drinking habits are learned in specific social situations.

Drinking is a pervasive feature of American society. In the United States, beer is by far the most popular alcoholic beverage, being consumed, on a per capita basis, at a ratio of about twenty gallons to two of spirits and wine. About two-thirds of the adult American population drink something at least once a year, with males drinking more commonly than females. About 75 per cent of American males take at least one drink a year, while only about 50 per cent of American women do. There are, further, distinct regional differences in drinking patterns. According to one study, roughly three-quarters of the population in New England and the Middle Atlantic states admit to drinking, whereas in the South only 45 per cent of the persons queried will say so. While accuracy of reporting undoubtedly affects these figures, they probably represent real differences. Generally speaking, younger people drink more than older people, and the behavior appears to be associated with education, for greater proportions of both sexes drink as educational levels increase. According to another study, 80 per cent of male and 61 per cent of female college students drink, although there are wide institutional variations and the actual frequencies with which college students report drinking are relatively small. Only about 21 per cent of college men and 10 per cent of college women report drinking more than once weekly.[11]

Thus drinking is a widespread, variegated, and learned phenomenon, and while *drinking* and *alcoholism* are quite different things, these facts about drinking certainly suggest that alcoholism is social and learned as well. It is possible to classify drinkers into one of several categories: [12]

Drinkers can be classified in terms of the deviation from norms of drinking behavior within a culture and dependence on alcohol in the life organization of the individual. This deviation includes the amount of alcohol consumed, the purpose and the meaning of drinking as an aspect of role playing, the degree to which such drinking handicaps the individual in his interpersonal relations, and his ability to refrain from taking a drink. There are several types of drinkers: the social or controlled drinkers, the ordinary excessive drinkers, the alcoholics, and the chronic alcoholics.

A social or controlled drinker drinks for reasons of sociability, conviviality, and conventionality. He may or may not like the taste and effects produced by alcohol. Above all else, he is able to desist from the use of intoxicating beverages when he chooses to do so. He drinks in a take-it-or-leave-it manner. There are two types of social drinkers, the occasional and the regular drinker. The former drinks sporadically and may have only a few drinks a year, whereas the regular social drinker may drink three or more times a week.

The ordinary excessive drinker not only makes more frequent use of alcohol than the regular social drinker, but in addition and occasionally under stress, may consume such quantities that intoxication results. He is given to weekend binges and is the one who, at the party, can be found sneaking drinks or just having a few more than anyone else in the place. Whatever else may be said about the excessive drinker, this type, in common with social drinkers, but with greater difficulty, may be able to curtail or completely cease drinking on his own volition. Depending upon circumstances, he may continue drinking in this manner for the rest of his life, he may later reduce the frequency and quantity of his alcoholic consumption, or he may become an alcoholic.

Alcoholics are excessive drinkers who have been defined by the World Health Organization of the United Nations as those "whose dependence upon alcohol has attained such a degree that it shows a noticeable mental disturbance, or an interference with their bodily or mental health, their interpersonal relations and their smooth social and economic functioning; or who show . . . signs of such development."

Chronic alcoholics are the most seriously maladjusted of the alcoholics and are characterized by loss of control over their drinking, which thus goes beyond the relief of psychological, physical or social stresses and becomes quasi-obsessive. The chronic alcoholic characteristically has a compulsion to drink continually. Of particular importance are such other characteristics as solitary drinking, morning drinking, and physical deterioration.

[11] Robert Straus and Seldon D. Bacon, *Drinking in College* (New Haven: Yale University Press, 1953), p. 101.

[12] Marshall B. Clinard, *Sociology of Deviant Behavior* (New York: Holt, Rinehart and Winston, Inc., 1957), pp. 298–299. Copyright © 1957 by Rinehart and Company, and printed with the permission of the author and publisher.

Beyond Technology

76

Kenneth Keniston

History sometimes presents societies with genuine turning points, eras when men are collectively confronted with a real alternative, ages when crucial decisions can be made which will affect the future for many generations to come. At some such forks in the historical road, men take what later generations will judge the wrong turn, or merely stand bewildered before the alternatives which confront them. In other eras, men choose wisely and well, acting from a courage that permits them to move forward, an understanding that enables them to refuse stagnation. Usually, such eras of potential choice are evident in a widespread sense of historical loss, a feeling that existing values and institutions no longer seem adequate, a realization that men live uneasily with values that now seem empty. In such eras, disquiet and uneasiness pervade men's lives, a nameless dissatisfaction and an even more inarticulate sense of hope for change.

Such collective watersheds are often marked by some striking political event—a revolution, a new constitution, a decisive war, a new regime. But just as often, when men can respond to the changed needs of their society before their discontents grow too great, no dramatic event signals the change: only a slow transformation, a quiet change of heart, a subtle alteration of the status quo. For every turning point marked by a violent revolution, there are many others that we perceive only in retrospect as gradual yet decisive transformations. Indeed, violent revolutions are enduring only if they are accompanied by slow and quiet transformations of men's attitudes and aspirations.

In American history there have been turning points of both kinds: some visible and dramatic, like the Civil War, others slow and quiet like the gradual extension of democratic rights in the first half of the nineteenth century. One of the most crucial of these turning points occurred between the Civil War and the First World War, the era when America changed decisively from an agricultural to an industrial nation. Beneath this visible change in the economy, and making it possible, was a deeper transformation of men's aspirations, whose importance we can only now fully appreciate. During this period, for the first time, Americans became convinced that material sufficiency, economic security, a decent living, and even prosperity were within their personal reach. These values, though long embedded in Western society, had heretofore been taken seriously as personal goals only by the wealthy, the extraordinarily ambitious, or the exceptionally lucky. Despite a slowly rising standard of living in the pre-industrial era, and despite the universality of the *dream* of affluence, most men knew it was *only* a dream, and that in reality they were destined to finish their lives as they had begun them—poor. Freedom from material want had been an impractical vision, not a concrete and immediate personal goal. But three or four generations ago, our entire nation began to transform that dream into the practical aspirations of individual Americans. Instead of merely envying the prosperous, the poor began to emulate them. From believing that only a few of any generation were destined for economic security, a whole nation came to believe that prosperity was within the reach of every man who would work and save. Freedom from want, which prior generations believed obtainable only by God's grace in the next world (if then), became a goal to be achieved by human effort in this world.

For the Americans of three generations ago—for Inburn's grandparents —the goals of abundance and prosperity made enormous sense. Poverty was still a daily reality for the vast majority of Americans; and even the prosperous, try as they might, could not completely insulate themselves from the surrounding want. For those who lack it, a decent living, an adequate home, and a good education are high and noble goals to which a whole man can unhesitatingly commit himself. Like many revolutionary visions, the dream of prosperity could be transformed into concrete personal goals only when the times were ready: the growing industrialization of America made possible the fulfillment of these aspirations of affluence, and was in turn spurred on by them. Because of the wealth and energy of this nation, the ideology of plenty proved self-confirming: convinced that history, destiny, and the laws of economics were on their side, Americans proceeded to create a society that confirmed their conviction.

In the past two generations, then, we have moved closer and closer to the milennial goal of prosperity. The vast distance between today's world and the upwardly mobile, striving, competitive, and still impoverished world of Inburn's grandparents has been the theme of much of this book. This distance cannot be quantitatively measured, but it is manifest in the contrast between the poverty of Inburn's grandparents and the relative affluence of his parents today, in the gulf between the bearded patriarch of the Victorian dinner table and the shirt-sleeved father of today's suburban cookout, in the chasm that separates the shopkeeper, milkman, farmer, and immigrant of the turn of the century from his comfortably off, well educated, economically secure (and sometimes alienated) grandson today. Most Americans no longer want for material goods, adequate homes, or educations; starvation is virtually nonexistent; and our most pressing economic problems no longer concern how to produce enough, but rather how to distribute fairly the goods we already have and to live well and nobly with them. The abolition of poverty is within the reach of our society; and for most Americans, the achievement of abundance is a fact and not a distant dream.

With the age-old goal of universal prosperity within sight, we must question whether the methods—the technological values and virtues, the instrumental goals of our affluent society—that helped us approach this goal will serve to take us beyond it. For most of us, the urgency has gone out of the quest for prosperity. The second television set means less than the first, though it may cost more. To struggle to pay a mortgage on a split-level ranch house beyond one's means is somehow less challenging than to struggle to buy a decent home to begin with. The effort to earn enough for one's childrens' ice-skating lessons is somehow less relevant than the struggle to insure them an adequate education. The acquisition of goods, money, gadgets, and commodities becomes increasingly empty; the pursuit of quantity, the cult of competition and comparison, become increasingly empty. The more one possesses, the less meaningful are new possessions.

We are approaching, I believe, a new turning point in American society. Despite our growing affluence, despite the triumphant march of technology, despite the inundation of our society with innovations, something is clearly wrong. All the signs are present: our mid-century malaise, increasingly shrill cries to "rededicate" ourselves to outworn ideologies which can no longer inspire our commitment, a loss in the sense of social power, and all of the attitudes, feelings, and outlooks I have here called the "new alienation." The vision of an affluent society no longer excites us; and so too, we are losing our implicit faith in the ancillary beliefs of technology. In nations where affluence is still a distant dream, the situation is different: in Peru or Nigeria, in Thailand or Samoa, the struggle to attain some small freedom from suffocating poverty is still a compelling struggle. Nor is the achievement of affluence complete even in America: the spate of recent books on the "forgotten fifth" of the nation, on our "invisible poor" eloquently documents the distance we must still travel. Yet these same books, with their appeal for affluence for *all*, indirectly attest to the triumph of technology. Who, a century ago, would have complained that *only* 80 per cent of the people were prosperous? And who would have dared insist that *all* might be well fed, well housed, well educated, and well leisured?

Thus, paradoxically, at the very moment when affluence is within our reach, we have grown discontented, confused, and aimless. The "new alienation" is a symptom and an expression of our current crisis. The individual and social roots of our modern alienation, I have tried to suggest, are complex and interrelated; yet if there is any one crucial factor at the center of this alienation, it is the growing bankruptcy of technological values and visions. If we are to move toward a society that is less alienating, that releases rather than imprisons the energies of the dissident, that is truly worthy of dedication, devotion, idealism, and commitment, we must transcend our outworn visions of technological abundance, seeking new values beyond technology.

SOME DETERRENTS

In the next decades of this century, Americans will be called upon to choose between three fundamentally different options concerning the future course of our society: whether to attempt to turn the clock back so as to "re-create" a bygone society in which our modern alienations did not yet exist, whether to "continue" the present triumphant march of a technological process which has created these same alienations, or whether to begin to define a new vision of a society whose values transcend technology. The first two choices would lead, I believe, to regression or stagnation; only by beginning now to articulate a vision of a society in which technology is used for truly human purposes can we create a nation of individuals, a society, that *merits* the commitment of its citizens. Yet such a redefinition of purpose has not been forthcoming, and social and political thought in America continues to be dominated by those who would have us regress to the past or those who would merely have us continue our present drift. What is it that prevents our imagining a society radically better than and different from our own?

Throughout the preceding pages I have emphasized the inherent hostility of technology to Utopian and visionary thinking. The fundamental assumptions of technology and science are metrical, comparative, analytic, and reductive. Technology concerns itself with instrumental questions and dismisses Utopian visions as impractical or irrelevant. Moreover, the growing pressure for ego dictatorship increasingly subordinates and suppresses the passions and idealisms from which cogent criticisms of our society and radical propositions for its reform might spring. Convinced that all Utopian thinking is impractical and self-defeating, we therefore cling to a technological empiricism that merely perpetuates the status quo. No doubt all established orders and all great ideologies resist fundamental change; but the technological society we live in is unusually well armored against attack, especially well equipped to subvert its critics, peculiarly able to discourage thinking that does not start from technological assumptions.

But beyond this, the very speed with which technology has accomplished its original goals has caught us off guard. The triumph of technology has occurred in an extraordinarily brief span of time: only one century separates our own era from the Civil War, technology triumphant from the beginning of the industrial era. Like a victorious and powerful army whose enemy unexpectedly surrenders, we now find ourselves without clear goals, mobilized for action that is no longer needed, and scarcely aware of the extent of our victory. We have been overtaken by success, surprised by triumph, caught off guard by victory. We have only begun to realize how far we have come, let alone to think of what might lie beyond.

Paradoxically, then, we live in a society in which unprecedented rates of technological change are accompanied by a fundamental unwillingness to look beyond the technological process which spurs this change. Even those who are most concerned over the future course of our society continue to conceive that course in primarily technological terms, emphasizing quantity, comparisons, economic output, and dollars and cents. And the imagination and commitment needed to define a future qualitatively different from the technological present are deflected—even for those most concerned with our social future—by a series of specific fallacies about the social process.

The fallacy of the psychosocial vise—A characteristic conviction of many modern men and women is the sense of being trapped in a social, cultural, and historical process they have no power to control. This sense of being inescapably locked in a psychosocial vise is often most paralyzing to precisely those men and women who have the greatest understanding of the complexity of their society, and who therefore might be best able to plan intelligently for its future. And although the sense of being trapped in history is widespread, it often appears to receive particularly cogent justification by social scientists. Recent years have seen a growing understanding of the connections between individual character, social process, cultural configuration, and historical change. Just as psychoanalysis has shown that even the most aberrant behavior "makes psychological sense" and serves definable psychic ends, so sociologists argue that social patterns that seem senseless also make a kind of sociological sense, serving "latent functions" corresponding to the unstated needs of individuals. We now know that the link between how men are raised as children and how they lead their lives as adults is a close one; that small changes in one sector of society can have enormous repercussions in other areas; and that apparently small historical transformations may spread and generalize to transform an entire community.

This awareness that individual, social, cultural, and historical processes are intimately connected is often taken as the basis for social pessimism. Because social institutions have a function, it is assumed this function can never be changed; because individual behavior, even the most irrational, has adaptive value, it is thought that no other behavior could be more adaptive. The fit between individual character and social structure is seen as a perfect fit, and the "gears" which convert historical pressures to psychological responses are seen as having a fixed and invariant ratio. The result is a deterministic sense of being caught in a psychosocial vise, locked so tightly it cannot be loosened without destroying it altogether. As a consequence, we dare change nothing at all.

In practice, the fallacy of the psychosocial vise can lead either to despair or complacency. Those who despair are usually all too aware of the enormous problems of our age: they despair because they can see no way of changing anything short of changing everything. Those who are complacent take comfort from the fact that (in retrospect) everything that happens in American society in some way "makes sense," can be explained and understood in terms of individual motives and social processes. The most dangerous trends in American society can be explained away as mere "reactions to social strain" which an omniscient sociologist could well have anticipated.

The facts, however, justify neither despair nor complacency. The "fit" between individuals and society, culture and history is never a perfect fit and is not always even a good fit. In this book, for example, I have been chiefly concerned with those who do not fit, who reject what their society demands of them. Moreover I have argued that the closeness of fit between, for example, family structure and social structure does not entail a comparable closeness of fit between family demands and the psychological needs of family members. There is, then, a kind of "slippage in the gears" of psychosocial transmission. Social institutions that now serve one function can later serve another or be replaced altogether; two men with essentially the same potential can end very differently; cultural needs and values that are salient today may become subordinate tomorrow. A "functional view" of social institutions does not require the assumption that comparable functions cannot be assumed by still other and better institutions.

To be sure, all social planning must be undertaken with the greatest possible understanding of its likely consequences. And we are probably in a better position than any previous generation to assess and gauge what these consequences will be. But the obvious fact that changes in one area of society have repercussions in others need not prevent social action. On the contrary, an understanding of the complexity of society can be an aid to social planning, helping us identify those points and moments of maximum leverage where small actions can have large consequences. There is often a kind of social "multiplier effect;" there are virtuous as well as vicious circles. Far from discouraging social planning and action, an understanding of psychosocial process can help us guide and direct it more intelligently.

The fallacy of romantic regression—One of the most common reactions against technological society is to deplore it by invoking images of romanticized past as a guidepost for regressive social change. In future years, as at present, Americans will be increasingly called upon to accept or reject the ideology of romantic regression. This ideology starts from the valid observation that our post-industrial society has lost intact community, socially given identity, stable and accepted morality, certainty and a clear collective sense of direction. From this valid observation, the regressive position attempts to re-establish a simple "organic" community, longs for Jeffersonian agrarianism, seeks a "new conservatism" which will "preserve" the values of the nineteenth century, turns to Fascism with its appeal to blood feeling and the "corporate state," or is tempted by the syndicalist vision of re-attaining "genuine" self-governing communities of workers. All of these outlooks see the solution to the problems of post-industrial society as some form of restoration, re-creation, or reconstruction of the simpler, more intact world that technology has destroyed.

Given a romantic idealization of the past, programs for social action invariably have regressive aims: to *reduce* the complexity of the world, be it material or moral; to *limit* the choices and opportunities which now bewilder men; to *inhibit* freedoms to which men owe their modern anxieties; to *narrow* the alternatives which give rise to current indecision; to *constrain* those who complicate moral, social, political, and international life; to *simplify* moral dilemmas into clear-cut decisions between good and evil. In short, the romantic seeks to solve the problms of the modern world by regressing to his image of an earlier world where these problems did not exist—be it the New England village, the grit-and-gumption ethic of the nineteenth-century entrepreneur, or even the Polynesian island.

Among social scientists, this ideology often takes the form of an idealization of primitive communities or peasant life. In such static communities, the problems of social change cannot arise; in an undifferentiated society, the problems of a divided life, "not belonging," and being forced to choose do not exist; the family cannot be specialized because it has too much work to do to survive; and ideological crises rarely occur because men and women unthinkingly accept the ideology they were born to.

The image of such a primitive community is, I believe, useful in highlighting the contrasting qualities of our social order. But it is a grave mistake to take primitive society, peasant life, the New England village, medieval life, or the entrepreneurial ethos of the nineteenth century as an adequate model for the future of our own society. On the contrary, few of us would freely choose to inhabit such a world. However romantically appealing the technicolor image of the Polynesian village, the idealized portrait of the "intact" peasant community, or the zest and simplicity of the frontier, harsher realities lie behind these romanticized images: endemic disease, grinding poverty, high infant mortality, lawlessness, and often the absence of the most elementary requirements for subsistence. Nor is the low standard of living in such communities accidental: it results from attitudes to change, to social organization, and to child-rearing that make a prosperous society impossible. And even if we could put up with such material deprivations, few of us could tolerate the oppressive social demands of such communities. Americans today may "conform," but we usually do so from choice; in most primitive societies the issue of conformity cannot arise as such because there *is* no choice. Our society may demand the arduous achievement of individual identity, but peasant communities "solve" this problem simply by allowing the young no options. We may suffer from the pressures of chronic social change, but we would suffer more in a society that persisted in its traditional ways despite evidence that they were destructive. And we may lament the loss of mythic vitality in the twentieth century, but we would lament even more an age where those who challenged the collective myth were outlawed or destroyed.

Moreover, in appealing to the image of the primitive or "intact" community as a guide for social action, we forget the eagerness with which those who dwell in such communities seek to abandon them. The destruction of tribalism, of feudalism, and of "intact community" continues to correspond with the wishes of the vast majority of those who have a choice: in the emerging nations of the world men lust after affluence and technology, not after tribal embeddedness. And even in our own history, the development of political liberalism and representative government, like the growth of technological society, was a response to the felt wishes of those who sought to escape the rigors of previous societies. Those who hark back to the values of their grandparents forget the eagerness with which these same men and women sought to create a "better world" for their grandchildren. We would find even the rigidity, complacency, and intolerance of the recent Victorian era hard to live with; the total absorption of the individual in most "primitive" societies would be even more intolerable.

However instructive the comparison of our own society with "intact" communities may be, today's problems cannot be solved by regressing to that kind of society. The new problems, the new alienations of technological society, require not regression to a romanticized past but new definitions of purpose, new forms of social organization, new goals for personal development. We must not return to the past, but transcend the present.

The fallacy of unfinished business—Perhaps the most potent deterrent of all to any fresh thinking about the purposes of our lives and our society is the fallacy of unfinished business—exclusive concentration on the remaining problems of productivity, poverty, education, and inequality as defined by technological values. This fallacy is most dangerous because it affects most those who are genuinely concerned with the problems of our society, critical of its achievements, impatient with the slowness of its "progress." Politically and socially, the only articulate alternative to those who would have us regress to the past is found among those who emphasize the unfinished business of technology, the "incomplete revolutions" which must be completed. From Lyndon Baines Johnson to Paul Goodman, the main thread of "progressive" thinking about American society assumes that our task is to complete our unfinished technological business.

I do not mean to deprecate this position. It is not wrong but inadequate; the evils pointed to are real and urgent. Gross prejudice and inequality are daily realities in much of America; poverty is a grinding and destructive fact to a fifth of the nation; millions do not and cannot get the minimal education necessary for an honored place in American life; it is genuinely alarming that we have not solved the problems of chronic unemployment. Nor will it be politically easy to solve these problems; the programs so far proposed only scratch the surface.

But the adequacy of this view to the problems of our society can be questioned. The "unfinished business" of technological society is, on a historical scale, increasingly vestigial, a "mopping-up operation." Revolutionary causes lose their impact when they have been largely accomplished; men are seldom stirred to arms in a cause already victorious. What is historically most salient is that *only* a fifth of the nation remains, by today's high American standards, poor. What should astound us is that *only* 30 per cent fail today to complete twelve years of education. And even in very recent American history, an unemployment rate of *only* four to six per cent would have been an unprecedented breakthrough to prosperity. Our efforts to relieve these problems should not abate; on the contrary, these efforts are still inadequate. But our technological accomplishments mean that if real "new frontiers" are to be found, they must lie beyond technology; and that if we do not now live in a "Great Society," then expanded Medicare, poverty programs, job-retraining, and anti-dropout campaigns will not suffice to create it.

Moreover, the values and instruments of technology will no longer suffice even to finish a technological society's own unfinished business. Our pursuit of quantity leads us to focus on such numerical indices of national and social success as the gross national product, the growth rate, the percentages of Americans employed, the proportion in high school, the divorce rate, the number of cars, telephones, and washing machines. We rejoice when these indices of success show us "ahead" of the Russians, and worry when our growth rate falls below theirs. But in each area of "unfinished business" in American life, our traditional techniques are inadequate. That traditional panacea, an increase in national output, no longer affects the poor, insulated from the main streams of the economy. More money poured into existing schools does not solve the problem of dropouts, whose prior problems are human and psychological, not merely educational. New technological innovations in industry are producing more, not less, chronic unemployment among the unskilled. And no matter how much we speed up the slow movement toward greater equality for Negro Americans, full citizenship cannot be achieved by traditional legal means alone. It also requires a deeper (and non-technological) effort to overcome the bitter legacies of slavery and oppression; and it may even require that we learn to recognize, accept, and enjoy the differences between white and Negro Americans that this legacy has created. In almost every area where our "technological revolutions" are incomplete, the instruments and values of technology will not alone suffice to carry us farther. Our urban sprawl, the chaos, disorganization, blight, and congestion of our society, our new alienations—all were *created* by our exploding, unplanned technological society; the technological process alone will not solve their problems.

But most important, the fallacy of unfinished business overlooks the crucial questions for most Americans today: What lies beyond the triumph of technology? After racial equality has been achieved, what then? Abundance for all for what? Full employment for today's empty jobs? More education that instills an ever more cognitive outlook?

It is all too easy to imagine a society in which the triumph of technology is complete. It would be an overwhelmingly rich society, dominated by a rampant technology and all of its corollaries—science, research and development, advertising, "conformity," secret invidiousness, overwhelming nostalgia for childhood, the dictatorship of the ego, a continuing deflection of the Utopian spirit. It would be a prosperous, ugly, sprawling society which men had learned not to see. It would have many entertainers but few artists, many superhighways but few open spaces to go to on them. It would be a science-fiction dream of automation, pre-processing, and home-care conveniences. Skyscrapers would rise ever taller and more sheer, and "developments" would burgeon outside the blighted urban cores.

Yet the central problems of today would merely be magnified. The pace of social change would increase and, without an over-all sense of direction, Americans would huddle ever more defensively in the present. For some, the romanticized stability of the past would grow more and more attractive, and this attraction would express itself more and more forcibly in political and social reaction. Life, already divided today, would be further divided tomorrow; and the vast majority of Americans, who could create no community within their own hearts, would be altogether without a home. As the pressures toward cognition grew, private escapes into irrationality, cults, and fads would flourish. The atmosphere would become ever more hostile to speculation, to idealism, and to Utopianism; the cult of efficiency, spread into human relations and industrial management, would relegate idealism and the noble dreams of youth to the hours after work or to "entertainment." In such a society the most talented would be alienated, yet they would be unable to find a positive voice; and their alienations would be, as now, self-destructive, carping, and self-defeating. To complete our incomplete revolutions, to finish our unfinished business, is therefore not enough, nor can it be accomplished by technological means alone. For their solution, the vestigial tasks of technology require values beyond technology.

TOWARD A MORE HUMAN SOCIETY

If we are to seek values beyond technology, purposes beyond affluence, visions of the good life beyond material prosperity, where are these values, purposes, and visions to be found? Must we, as many secretly fear, await the coming of some new prophet who will create, out of nothing, a new Utopian vision for Americans? Are we condemned to a continuation of technological society until some Messiah arrives to save us?

I believe the answer is closer to home. When, a century ago, Americans began to take seriously the goals of prosperity and freedom from want, these values were not created out of nothing: they had long been part of the Western tradition. What changed was that a dream of the good life previously considered beyond the reach of the ordinary man passed into his hands and was accepted as a concrete goal that could be achieved by ordinary men and women. The turning point at which we stand today requires a similar translation of already existing dreams of human fulfillment and social diversity into the concrete goals of individuals and of our society. The values we need are deeply rooted in our own tradition: we must merely begin to take them seriously.

The ideal of full human wholeness is as old as Periclean Athens. But in the course of Western history, this goal could be taken seriously by few men and women: as in Athens, only a small number of the leisured and wealthy, supported by the vast majority of their fellow citizens, attained the freedom from want which is a prerequisite for the implementation of this ancient goal. Even in the Renaissance, when the Greek ideal of full humanity was rediscovered, the vast majority of men and women were far too preoccupied by their incessant struggle against poverty, oppression, and sickness to have time for such lofty ideals. And even today, for most citizens of most nations of the world, the vision of a more harmonious integration of self, a more complete development of talent and ability, must await the attainment of more urgent goals of attaining freedom from want and oppression. Only those who have been able to conquer poverty and tyranny have energy to cultivate their full humanity.

But for those who do not want materially and are not oppressed politically, the quest for fulfillment beyond material goods becomes possible and urgent. There is in human life a hierarchy of needs, such that the higher needs are fully felt when, and only when, the lower needs have been satisfied. Just as thirsty men do not seek food, and the starved have no strength for sex, so freedom from political oppression and material want are prerequisites for any attempt to achieve a more harmonious integration of self, a fuller development of human potentials. Today, in America, and increasingly in other technological nations, these preconditions are rapidly being met: we can now begin to imagine realistically that a whole society might commit itself to the attainment of the greatest possible fulfillment for its members.

To be sure, by the quantitative and reductionistic standards of our technological era, goals like "human wholeness," "personal integration," "the full development of human potentials" are inevitably vague and imprecise. They point to the quality of individual life, rather than to quantitatively measurable entities. Partly for this reason, our knowledge of the sources of human wholeness and fulfillment is woefully inadequate, despite a half-century's systematic study of man. But we do know more than previous generations about the causes of human malformation, distortion, and blighting. Our systematic and scientific knowledge is, no doubt, no more than a confirmation of what a few wise men have intuitively known in the past. But what was heretofore the special wisdom of the sagacious few (which they often carried to their graves) is on the way to becoming communicable public knowledge. Gradually, we are learning to pinpoint the obstacles to full human growth, specifying those especially "lethal" psychological combinations of parentage and social circumstance for children, defining more adequately the antecedents of human pathology, and even at times learning how to intervene positively to foster full human development.

Yet even today, it is far simpler to list the obstacles to full human development, to personal integration, to self-actualization, than to prescribe the precise path to these ancient goals. For just as there are from birth many distinct individuals, each with his own unique genetic and environmental potential, there must remain many paths to fulfillment. Our modern search for a single definition for "maturity" and "positive mental health" that will apply to everyone is probably doomed to failure from the start. Responsiveness, activity, excitability, and even the capacity to learn are not only shaped by the environment, but partly determined by birth. "Fulfillment" depends on individual potential and on social opportunity; human "wholeness" depends on what there is to be made whole.

But though no single definition of human fulfillment is possible, some of its results can be defined. A whole man or woman has the capacity for zest, exuberance, and passion, though this capacity may often be in abeyance. An integrated man does not cease to experience tension, anxiety, and psychic pain, but he is rarely overwhelmed by it. Though all men must at times "close" themselves to that which would be subversive to their commitments, a whole man nonetheless retains the *capacity* for openness, sensitivity, and responsiveness to the world around him: he can always be surprised because he remains open to that which is alien to himself.

Above all, human wholeness means a capacity for commitment, dedication, passionate concern, and care—a capacity for whole-heartedness and single-mindedness, for abandon without fear of self-annihilation and loss of identity. In psychological terms, this means that a whole man retains contact with his deepest passions at the same time that he remains responsive to his ethical sense. No one psychic potential destroys or subverts the others: his cognitive abilities remain in the service of his commitments, not vice versa; his ethical sense guides rather than tyrannizing over his basic passions; his deepest drives are the sources of his strength but not the dictators of his action. We recognize whole men and women because their wholeness is manifest in their lives: what they do is "of a piece."

If no unitary definition of fulfillment and integration is possible, then a society that is to support these goals must necessarily be a diverse, heterogeneous, pluralistic, and open society. And like the ideal of individual fulfillment, the goal of social diversity is one we have never seriously considered implementing. Although the ideal of political pluralism is entrenched in our liberal tradition, this ideal has most often meant the toleration of political factions, not the encouragement of the full diversity of human talents. Politically, we may tolerate lobbies and believe in political parties; but socially our goals are given by slogans like "Americanization," "the melting pot," and increasingly today "the search for excellence" defined in cognitive terms. Though we think of ourselves as a "tolerant" society, in ordinary speech we most often couple the term "tolerate" with the modifier "barely." All too often, the "tolerance" of Americans is a thin veneer over the discomfort created by all that is different, strange, and alien to them. Once, to be sure, the image of this nation as a vast melting pot suggested the noble vision that the millions of diverse immigrants who came to this shore could be welded into a single coherent nation. But today there is no menace of an America excessively fractured along ethnic, regional or class lines. The current danger is excessive homogeneity, sameness, uniformity. Already, ethnic distinctions, regional differences, even class lines have been blurred beyond recognition in a land where almost everyone lives in the same city apartments and suburban dwellings, eats the same frozen foods and watches the same television programs at the same time on the same networks. Even the current effort of some Americans who are fearful of conformity to be "different," to develop distinctive styles of consumption and life, paralleled by the attempts of advertisers and industry to promote "personalized" and "individualized" products, tends to become only another sign of the homogenization of American society.

Romantic regionalism or the idealization of ethnicity are of course not virtuous in themselves: and even if we chose, distinctions of region and ethnic background could not be naturally preserved. But there is an inherent virtue in the appreciation of genuine human differences and the encouragement of a new social diversity based not on region, ancestral origin, class, or race, but on the special accomplishments, potentials, talents, and vital commitments of each individual. Pluralism must be extended from politics to the individual, implemented as a concrete social goal. Human diversity and variety must not only be tolerated, but rejoiced in, applauded, and encouraged.

A society of whole men and women must, then, be a society which encourages diversity, enjoying the differences between men as well as the similarities among them. Social diversity has a double connection to individual fulfillment: not only is a diverse society a precondition for human wholeness, it is its consequence—the kind of society whole men and women choose to live in. Those who are inwardly torn, unsure of their psychic coherence and fearful of inner fragmentation, are naturally distrustful of all that is alien and strange. Those whose sense of inner unity is tenuous are easily threatened by others who remind them of that part of themselves they seek to suppress. Our "one-hundred-per-cent Americans" are those whose own Americanism is felt to be most tenuous; the bigoted and the prejudiced cannot live with the full gamut of their own feelings. And conversely, those who can still sense their shared humanity with others of different or opposite talents and commitments

are those who are sure of their own intactness. The goals of human fulfillment and social diversity require each other.

Both of these ideals, I have argued, are ancient ones. They are rooted
deep in our Western tradition, and they arise almost spontaneously in those
whose material and physical wants have been satisfied. But it remains for us
to implement these visions. These are values beyond technology, credal ideals
of our civilization which we can now begin to take seriously. Probably for the
first time in human history, we can move toward a fullness of life beyond a
full larder, human fulfillment beyond material satiation, social diversity beyond consensus.